Frigates of the Napoleonic Wars

Frigates of the Napoleonic Wars

Robert Gardiner

CHATHAM PUBLISHING

LONDON

Frontispiece
The head of a very fine model of a British 38-gun frigate of
about 1800. Model No 23 in the Henry Huddleston Rogers
Collection at the US Naval Academy Museum in Annapolis,
it was long catalogued as the *Shannon*, the famous victor over
USS *Chesapeake* in 1813. Although its supposed provenance
included ownership by the Broke family, recent research by
Major Grant Walker of the Museum has cast doubt on its past.
Discrepancies between the model and what is known about
Shannon have always raised questions about the identification,
but a recent remeasurement makes the model significantly
longer and narrower than a $\frac{1}{48}$th scale replica should be. Nor
does the hull shape correspond. Nevertheless, in general
terms as a model of a British 18pdr-armed frigate it is
convincing in many details, including the masts and rigging.
United States Naval Academy Museum, Annapolis.

First published in Great Britain in 2000 by
Chatham Publishing,
61 Frith Street, London W1V 5TA

Chatham Publishing is an imprint of Gerald
Duckworth & Co Ltd

British Library Cataloguing in Publication Data
A catalogue record for this book is available from the
British Library

ISBN 1 86176 135 X

Designed and typeset by Tony Hart, Isle of Wight

Printed and bound in Great Britain
by Bookcraft (Bath) Ltd

Contents

Foreword and Acknowledgements   7

PART I: DESIGN HISTORY

Chapter 1: The Return to Moderate Dimensions, 1801-1804   9

Chapter 2: The Barham Interlude, 1805-1806   14

Chapter 3: War of Attrition, 1806-1812   21

Chapter 4: The American Emergency, 1812-1815   33

Chapter 5: Super Frigates   40

Chapter 6: Preparing for Peace, 1812-1815   58

PART II: THE SHIPS

Chapter 7: Construction   68

Chapter 8: Design   87

Chapter 9: Wartime Modifications   98

Chapter 10: Armament   114

Chapter 11: Performance   131

Chapter 12: Frigates in Action   152

Notes   191

Bibliography and Sources   200

Glossary of Technical Terms and Abbreviations   203

Index   205

In memory of
David Lyon,
a fierce critic but a steadfast friend

Foreword and Acknowledgements

THIS BOOK has undergone a long and convoluted gestation. It was conceived simply as the second part of *The Heavy Frigate*, published in 1994. This had been devoted to the big 18pdr-armed ships ordered up to the conclusion of the French Revolutionary War and Earl Spencer's term at the Admiralty; the second was intended to complete the coverage down to 1832 and the end of the 18pdr frigate. However, changes at the original publishers spelled the end of the series for which it had been devised.

The book was then recast for Chatham's new 'ShipShape' series, which was rather different and required a book which could stand on its own without reference to a previous volume. As a result it was decided to concentrate on the Napoleonic Wars – in its proper sense, from the Peace of Amiens to the Hundred Days – which is where most readers' interests lie. Having converted the thematic core of the book from a ship type to a period, it was impossible to deal with the War of 1812 without also including the 24pdr frigates and cut-down battleships that feature so prominently in that conflict. This is a large subject which probably warrants a book of its own, but certainly added to the length of this one, although the post-1815 coverage was cut back by way of compensation. I have also been forced to backtrack into the 1790s, beyond the book's strict chronological parameters, because to understand what was done in 1812 it is necessary to appreciate the Navy's earlier experience – but of course as the largest examples of their type these super frigates are irresistibly interesting.

In the original two-volume scheme for the book I had intended that the general chapters would cover different topics in each part. This concept has also required modification, so for the sake of completeness there is a degree of minor duplication with the earlier book.

Delays to its publication meant extra time for deeper research, although the broader coverage also demanded it: whether cause or effect, the result was a longer and (from an author's point of view) more satisfactory book. This coincided with the publishers' decision that the 'ShipShape' series was too constricting for all technical monographs, so released from this Procrustean bed *Frigates of the Napoleonic Wars* was allowed to find its natural extent. In an ideal world I would have written in more depth about many of the captured foreign frigates, but the book already makes more than passing reference to many of them by way of comparison with British practice, and despite all its tergiversations I feel that the book now fully justifies its title.

ACKNOWLEDGEMENTS

While working on this book I was able to draw on the specific expertise of many people who gave advice and shared information without reservation. Among those whose contribution improved the book were: Jean Boudriot, France's greatest expert on sailing warships, who was able to fill out details of the early career of Jean-Louis Barrallier; Don Canney, who gave me some background on constructional aspects of US warships; Dr Roger Knight, who shared his considerable understanding of the timber supply problem; the late Richard Saxby, with whom I enjoyed a fruitful correspondence on frigates and the Brest blockade (I should also thank Dr Roger Morriss, his posthumous editor, for details of the future publication of his work); Ivor H Smart, whose research into timber price inflation and the demise of Tanner's shipyard provided an interesting sidelight; Norman Swales, who supplied useful data about *Leander* (not to mention a reconstructed sheer plan); and last but by no means least, Tom Wareham, whose work on frigate captains was a salutary reminder that however good the ships, the men were better.

I owe a broader debt to John Harland, who introduced me to the potential of the Internet as a source of information on the most arcane topics, and posted queries on my behalf before I had my own direct access. By more traditional means, he also shared his incomparable understanding of historical seamanship.

In its final stages the book was significantly refined by the scrutiny of a number of more-or-less willing readers. Chief amongst these was David Lyon, whose variety of unexpected knowledge exceeded any web site; not only did he point to a number of areas that required expansion or correction, but he also suggested where to go for the information. For the all-important but uncongenial chore of checking the ship specification tables, I have to thank Rif Winfield, whose reverence for data is, mercifully, far greater than my own. If errors of fact or interpretation survive, they are entirely my own doing.

A book like this would be almost pointless without illustration, the most important being the original draughts. Reproducing these in any numbers would have been virtually impossible without special agreement with the National Maritime Museum, and I am grateful to Lucy Pringle for a sympathetic hearing. The final choice of draughts was made at the Brass Foundry, the Woolwich outstation where Meredith Sampson's very helpful team made the research a distinct pleasure. Processing the resulting large and complicated order was less easy, and David Taylor deserves a hearty pat on the back for fielding the author's pedantic requirements (and occasional testy complaints) with persistence and good humour.

Another organisation which proved very co-operative was the HMS Trincomalee Trust, initially in the figure of Mike Tapper, one of the Trustees, and then Keith Johnson, the senior technical officer, who answered a number of pertinent questions and supplied a batch of photographs from the archives. My old friend Roderick Stewart provided a similar service for Britain's other preserved frigate, the *Unicorn*. From further afield, another fellow-traveller, Major Grant Walker of the US Naval Academy Museum, helped with photographs of the Annapolis models, including details of their history, and passed a knowledgeable eye over the relevant captions. Richard Lawrence lent me a transparency of a highly significant Condy painting which I believe represents the elusive *Leander*, and Tony Hart pointed me towards an atmospheric painting of the shipyard that used to be outside his windows. In a similar vein, one final vote of thanks is due to Mark Myers, not only a great maritime artist but an authority on the representation of ships, who helped to track down a couple of particularly good images of frigates at sea and supplied some technical details for the captions.

Without all these people the book would have been poorer.

Robert Gardiner
London, February 2000

The Return to Moderate Dimensions, 1801-1804

THE 1790s had been a decade of significant advances in the quality of British warships in general, and frigates in particular. They had always been well built, and in terms of robust construction and an attention to seakeeping, were very well contrived for the needs of a service like the Royal Navy, whose strategy required ships that were able to stay at sea for long periods. However, as the dominant seapower Britain's greatest need was sheer numbers of ships, and this had traditionally manifested itself in a desire to keep down the size of each rate to the smallest (and cheapest) viable design. Although cost-efficient, this British policy left the larger ships of the French and Spanish navies with some tactical advantages – in the case of frigates, it was felt that their greater length made them faster on their chosen point of sailing.

What happened in the 1790s was that the Admiralty Boards, and especially that led by Earl Spencer, became convinced of the need to improve British warship design, and were prepared to find the money to match the size of enemy ships. Spencer's Admiralty also adopted a policy of building to multiple designs based on a common specification – usually one based on a French hull-form and one by each of the two

Surveyors. Furthermore, instead of then standardising on one, the next order would be for a different, and invariably larger, vessel. In this way the size of British frigates escalated quickly, and by 1800 they were equal in size to the generality of European frigates, but more strongly constructed and more heavily armed. Needless to say, it was an expensive policy.[1]

The new government under Addington that took power in February 1801 was committed to retrenchment and reform, and chose Lord St Vincent to uphold these principles at the Admiralty as First Lord. Renowned for the strict discipline he had imposed on the fleets under his command, the austere old admiral was convinced that the civil branch of the Navy would be improved by similar measures. In Sir Thomas Troubridge and John Markham he had two Naval Lords of like mind: indeed, St Vincent's language was parliamentary compared with some of their outbursts – Troubridge was notorious in the Dockyards for his view that 'all the master shipwrights should be hanged, every one of them, without exception'. A vigorous crusade against corruption and inefficiency was launched, whose results are still controversial.[2]

At the very least the Admiralty's adversarial manner

The design draught used for all the British-built ships of the *Tribune* class 36s. All followed the annotated minor changes (indicated in ticked lines) to the forecastle ports, the bridle and aftermost main-deck gunports, and the angles of some of the chainplates. The most visible difference between this group and the original *Perseverance* class design was the bridle port, but adding this also entailed rearranging all the main-deck ports by reducing the space between them. In turn this meant a different pattern of chainplates and this seems to have remained a way of distinguishing between the two groups for all of their careers. The *Tribune*s later had a sixth gunport cut in the quarterdeck barricade, which was done by dividing the mizzen chains. *National Maritime Museum Dr2126*

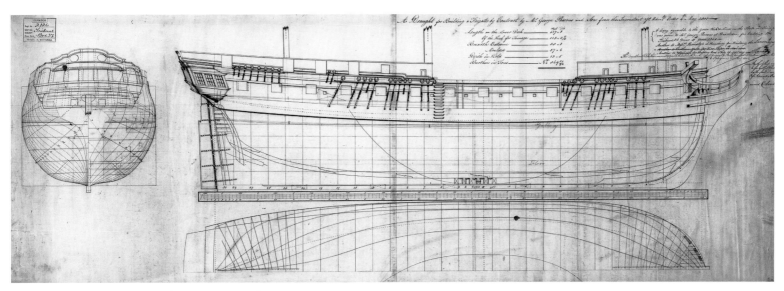

during this period reduced co-operation with the Navy Board to the coldest formality; more importantly in the long run, it soured relations with both the timber suppliers and the merchant shipbuilders, so when the time came for mobilisation the Admiralty could not put in hand the necessary new construction. The year the new administration took office was difficult, because although there was hope of peace in some quarters, the country was threatened with invasion and Napoleon had coerced the Baltic powers into reviving the Armed Neutrality that had been such a menace in the American War. Some construction had to go on, but with the government's policy of economy in mind there was a retreat from the 'big ship' policy of the previous administration. As it happened this was exactly in line with St Vincent's personal views, which were technologically conservative: as long as ships were well-found and good steady gun platforms he was confident that better trained personnel would count more than size or sailing qualities.[3]

In 1797 St Vincent had given Lord Spencer, then First Lord, the benefit of his ideas on the size of ships, listing the *Ville de Paris*, *Victory* and *Carnatic* as ideal First, Second and Third Rates. 'Frigates,' he claimed, 'are grown preposterous; I never wish to see one larger than the *Inconstant*.'[4] Not surprisingly, these were the prototypes his Admiralty chose to follow. Although none of the surviving evidence suggests that the *Inconstant* or her sisters of the *Perseverance* class were exceptional sailers – indeed the *Phoebe* class of 1794 was a lengthened version specifically designed to be faster – yet they were of enduring popularity. The early ships spent many of their later years as troopships but they enjoyed long cruising lives and were thought worthy of expensive refits right down to the end of the Napoleonic War. The new *Tribune* class were virtually carbon copies of the 1778 design, with some detail alteration in the topsides – most noticeably the built-up forecastle barricade and a bridle port under the cathead. They were probably little different under sail from the original ships, but comparatively seemed poorer because the norm for frigate performance had advanced in the interim.

One curiosity of the Admiralty's policy at this time is the ordering of a very large 38 to the lines of the *Révolutionnaire*, a French prize of very sharp hull form and excessive dimensions. On the Cork station she was known as 'the Irish racehorse' and had a reputation for extreme performance, once claiming a run of 129 miles in 9½ hours, or an average of 13½ knots,[5] but a less economical method of carrying a main battery of twenty-eight 18pdrs would be difficult to imagine. The ship is so much at odds with the rest of the Board's policy that one suspects a single strong-willed advocate – possibly Markham who was an admirer of French design practice.[6] The ship was allocated to Sheerness Dockyard, which (as explained in *The Heavy Frigate* with reference to the *Cassandra*) was tantamount to giving it the lowest possible priority. Indeed, the ship had to be transferred to Woolwich before any work could be done on her, and she was not launched (as the *Forte*) until 1814.

The Royal Yards built most of the *Tribune* class, but the first two were built by Parsons and Brindley, almost the only merchant builders still enjoying Admiralty favour. In both cases it was something of a reward for having launched their previous ships, *Resistance* and *Tartar*, on time, but Brindley also claimed special treatment because during the war years he had consistently turned away mercantile contracts in order to concentrate on naval work – the kind of priorities likely to endear him to St Vincent. Such was the mutual mistrust between Admiralty and the main shipbuilders that not a single major warship was ordered from the River (Thames) yards by St Vincent's Board. As a result it tended to look to what were called the 'out ports' for capacity, even after the coming of the short-lived peace in March 1802 relieved the cost pressure.

TABLE 1/1: *Tribune* (repeat *Perseverance*) class 36-gun Fifth Rates

Specification

Armament	Upper deck	Quarterdeck	Forecastle	Guns	Men
DESIGN	26 x 18pdrs	2 x 9pdrs, 8 x 32pdr carr	2 x 9pdrs, 2 x 32pdr carr	36	264
CHANGES BY AO:					
18 Sep 1806 (*Meleager*)		12 x 32pdr carr	As design		
12 Oct 1807 (*Iphigenia*)		12 x 32pdr carr	As design		
8 Nov 1809 (*Orlando*)		12 x 32pdr carr	As design		
13 Feb 1808 (*Salsette*)		12 x 32pdr carr	As design		
10 Mar 1808 (*Salsette*)		12 x 32pdr carr	4 x 9pdrs, no carr		
17 Mar 1807 (*Pitt*, later *Doris*)		18 x 32pdr carr	As design		

As *Perseverance* class [1780] designed by Sir Edward Hunt

	Lower deck feet-inches	Keel feet-inches	Breadth extreme feet-inches	Depth in hold feet-inches	Burthen Tons
DESIGN	137-0	113-2½	38-0	13-5	869 50/94
AS COMPLETED					
Tribune	137-1½	113-1½	38-9	13-5	884
Shannon, ex-*Pallas*	137-1½	113-4⅜	38-2¾	13-5¼	881 28/94
Meleager	137-0	113-1½	38-1½	13-5	874 58/94
Iphigenia	137-0	113-1¼	38-2	13-5	876 33/94
Lowestoffe	Never completed				
Orlando	137-0	113-1¼	38-2	13-5	876 33/94
Teak-built					
Salsette, ex-*Pitt*	137-0	112-11	38-9	13-7	902
Doris, ex-*Pitt*	137-0	113-2½	38-0	13-5	870

Notes: Despite the above armament orders, *Shannon*, *Meleager*, *Iphigenia* and *Orlando* were fitted with the design armament.

TABLE 1/2: *Tribune* (repeat *Perseverance*) class 36-gun Fifth Rates

Building data

Name	Ordered	Builder	Laid down	Launched	Sailed	Fitted at	Fate
Tribune	6 May 1801	Parsons, Burseldon	Jul 1801	5 Jul 1803	20 Aug 1803	Portsmouth	Wrecked 29 Nov 1839
Shannon, ex-*Pallas*	8 Jul 1801	Brindley, Frindsbury	Aug 1801	2 Sep 1803	12 Oct 1803	Chatham	Grounded 11 Dec 1807
Meleager	9 Jul 1801	Chatham Dyd	Jun 1804	25 Nov 1806	12 Jan 1807	Chatham	Wrecked 30 Jul 1808
Iphigenia	9 Jul 1801	Chatham Dyd	Feb 1806	26 Apr 1808	24 Jun 1808	Chatham	Broken up May 1851
Lowestoffe	9 Jul 1801	Woolwich Dyd					Cancelled 26 Jul 1805
Orlando Teak-built	3 May 1808	Chatham Dyd	Mar 1809	20 Jun 1811	20 Jul 1811	Chatham	Sold 1824
Salsette, ex-*Pitt*	12 May 1802	Bombay Dyd	19 Jul 1803	17 Jan 1805	?	Bombay	Broken up 1874
Doris, ex-*Pitt*	5 Jun 1803	Bombay Dyd	25 Apr 1806	24 Mar 1807	?	Bombay	Sold 1829

Notes: Tribune was cut down to a 24-gun corvette in 1833; she was wrecked near Tarragona. *Pallas* was renamed in Nov 1802; she was stranded near La Hogue and the wreck was burnt by the *Merlin*, 17 Dec 1803. *Meleager* was lost on Bare Bush Key, Jamaica. *Iphigenia* surrendered on 28 Aug 1810 during the Grand Port fiasco, but was recaptured on 3 Dec that year; she was lent to the Marine Society as a training ship in 1833. *Orlando* became a hospital hulk at Trincomalee in 1819.

There was much confusion between the Admiralty and the local commander, Sir Edward Pellew, over the naming of the two Bombay frigates, which continues to confound modern historians. The original intention was that the first should be called *Salsette*, but Pellew put her into service as the *Pitt*, before the arrival of the Admiralty's order of 6 Apr 1805 to name the new ship *Salsette*. The Admiralty misconstrued his references to the *Pitt* to mean one of the ex-HEIC ships he had purchased for the Navy at about the same time, and the Admiralty's instruction was taken by Pellew to mean the second vessel. It was only on 19 Feb 1807 that the Admiralty clarified its intentions by specifying that the first be renamed *Salsette* and the one laid down on 25 Apr 1806 be called *Pitt*; but to further complicate the matter, it then transpired that there had never been a formal order for the second ship, so on 18 Jul 1807 *Pitt* was ordered to be purchased complete, leading some historians to describe the ship as ex-HEIC or even as an ex-Indiaman. When this was finally sorted out, the Admiralty renamed the *Pitt* the *Doris* on 26 Aug 1807 [PRO Adm 106/2092]. *Salsette* became a lazaretto at Pembroke in 1831, then a receiving ship at Woolwich in 1835. *Doris*, in a poor state structurally, was sold at Valparaiso.

Left: With its built-up forecastle barricades at first glance this model looks like it should represent one of the *Tribune* group of the revived *Perseverance* class. However, it lacks the tell-tale bridle port of the later ships, and the arrangement of forecastle ports for both carronades and timberheads differs from the draughts. In these respects it resembles the model, No 52, in the Henry Huddleston Rogers Collection at the US Naval Academy, which is prominently marked *Perseverance*, although a note from the modelmaker dated 'Sheerness, Oct 25 1820' found inside the hull during restoration says it is the *Inconstant* (of the *Perseverance* class). The obvious conclusion is that both models are meant to portray the earlier group, but as they appeared during the wars of 1793-1815 when such barricades became the norm. The models differ in that the Annapolis vessel has the later form of integrated gangways (possible in the *Inconstant* since she survived until 1817), while the Greenwich model has the earlier separate gangways and breastworks to quarterdeck and forecastle. Models of this degree of accuracy imply that the modellers had access to copies of draughts, and it may well be that both these models were produced from a mix of plans from each group, or a basic sheer draught elaborated by observation of the actual ships. *National Maritime Museum B802*

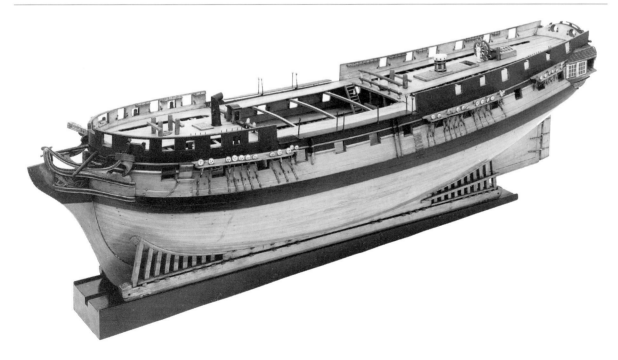

The Navy Board was instructed in June 1802 to contract with Graham of Harwich for a 36 of the *Phoebe* class. However, on second thoughts St Vincent decided that Graham was asking a war rate and, realising that the first peace contract would set a precedent, had it cancelled.[7] Apart from the pliable Brindley, nobody else received a frigate contract during the peace except Tanner of Dartmouth, for two *Apollo* class 36s. An extreme example of the Admiralty's desire for new suppliers, Tanner had never built anything of this size

This sheer draught of the *Salsette* as taken off at Portsmouth and dated 30 March 1808 is perhaps rather flattering in that it seems very close to the design, whereas the Bombay builders were eventually reprimanded for not following the intended draught with sufficient accuracy. The only obviously different feature is the profile of the quarterdeck carronade ports, which are rebated into the rough-tree rail with a slight radius in the corners; according to the *Salsette*'s captain these port sills varied in height off the deck and did not present the smooth line shown here. The indicated enlargement of the long gun ports to take carronades (the second on the forecastle, and the first and fifth on the quarterdeck) are noted as 'alterations as fitted'; most of the rest of the class had a similar arrangement by this date.
National Maritime Museum Dr2179

before and as if to underline the folly of making contracts merely on the grounds of lowest tender he was declared bankrupt before either could be completed – at vast additional cost to the Navy.[8]

St Vincent was rather more successful in securing a more distant shipbuilding source by persuading the Honourable East India Company to build ships at their yard at Bombay. Although the government was to pay for the ships, the Company was pressurised by hints from the First Lord that the Navy's timber shortage might make a parliamentary case for restricting the sizes of East India Company ships. In the event a 74 and a frigate of the *Tribune* class were ordered, and after considerable confusion over her name the frigate became the *Salsette*; a sister eventually called the *Doris* followed later. Like other warships built at Bombay they were built of teak, and in general historians have approved of this development. However, while the quality of the timber was unarguable, they may not have been as well constructed as is usually assumed. The captain of the *Salsette* complained of his ship's heavy and clumsy fastening, and after careful measurement discovered that the topsides were not identical – port heights from the gunwale varied up to 4in, and likewise the channels, catheads and quarter pieces were different port and starboard; the differences were not even consistent on each side but resulted in a zigzag appearance in the upperworks. Eventually it was discovered that the ship did not follow the draught at all closely in the underwater form, and the Bombay builders were reprimanded and instructed to conform precisely to the draught in future.[9]

War was again declared in May 1803 and an Admiralty with its mind firmly on the long term benefits of administrative reform had to face in the short term a demoralised Navy Board, a militant Dockyard work force, and antagonistic contractors. Tightening the provisions of timber purchases had produced a shortage of oak in the Dockyards and the Board was

convinced that placing contracts in the Thames merchant yards would only drive up the price of timber further. Brindley offered another 38, if it could be to the *Leda* design (he was already building one, so there would be some economies in reusing existing moulds), but the remaining 38s were ordered to the larger *Lively* design. Three builders in the out ports were found willing to deal with the Navy, and a fourth vessel was laid down at Woolwich Dockyard.

The only other frigates ordered before the Board stepped down in May 1804 saw the extraordinary revival of a 12pdr 32-gun design of 1756. Under attack in Parliament for its lack of preparedness, the Admiralty needed to demonstrate a significant increase in shipbuilding activity if it were to survive politically. Debates largely revolved around quantity rather than quality, but orders for ships were restricted by the Admiralty's reluctance to use contract builders, and the low stocks of traditional timber in the Dockyards. However, the *Circe* class were intended to utilise stocks of relatively small scantling fir available in the Dockyards and because they were of modest dimensions they could be built in fair numbers, and rapidly. In the case of the first two, they were also designed to demonstrate the advantages of 'shoaling', or organising shipwright gangs by ability in order to speed up construction time. They were certainly built quickly but it is unlikely that the succeeding Admiralty of Lord Melville was impressed by its legacy of eight puny and short-lived cruisers.[10]

Samuel Bentham, the Inspector General of Naval Works, attempted to exploit this low regard for the class by making them experimental vehicles for his ideas on improved ship construction. He wanted four out of the eight to be built to standard methods, with the others by way of comparison incorporating:

1. Reduced siding and numbers of frame timbers, saving about one-third of the usual amount.

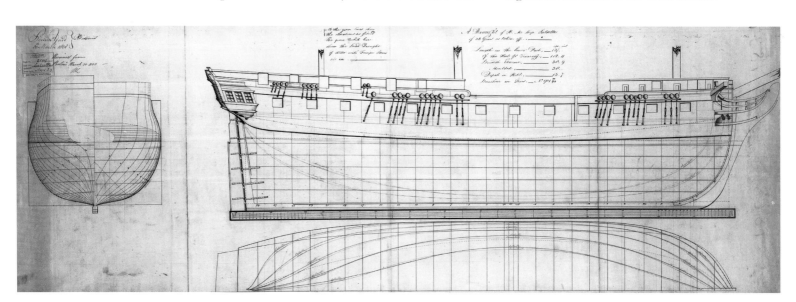

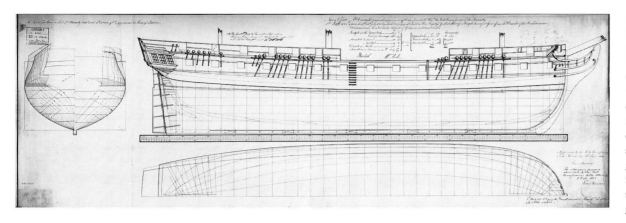

A copy of the master sheer plan for the *Forte* (the original is in poor condition but virtually identical) 'sent to Sheerness 11 Oct 1802'. In the body plan, the filling out of the French-style extreme tumblehome is shown in red, as ordered by the Admiralty on 8 October 1802. The draught also shows later alterations to the gunports on the quarterdeck and forecastle, those inside the shrouds being altered to long guns by order of 21 October 1806, although the change was never implemented. Other modifications instructed around this time but not visible on this draught include making the gangways flush and a more modern style rudder without stepped hances. The ship makes an interesting comparison with the later *Seringapatam* (see p62) since both were based on French frigates that were sister-ships (or at least near sisters).
National Maritime Museum E0845

2. Increased exterior planking, especially at the bilge, but interior planking diminished by a commensurate amount.

3. Plank to be fastened with treenails only (manufactured by his new treenail machinery), saving the cost of copper alloy bolts and spikes.

4. No sheer to the decks, 'thereby affording a tie [girder], tending to prevent the ship from hogging'.

5. Increased number of deck beams but of reduced scantling and without carlings and ledges.

6. Wood and iron knees replaced with his method of fastening with coaks and athwartship diagonal trusses to prevent racking.

7. Rigid bulkheads that resist rather than yield to racking stresses.[11]

The Admiralty was favourable but the Navy Board, who had always resented Bentham's independence, fought a masterly rearguard action and Bentham was persuaded that the ships, being needed quickly, were too far advanced to be changed without delay – not, however, so far advanced as to prevent one of them being cancelled in October 1804, two months after Bentham had raised the issue. Eventually, he was allowed to apply his ideas to one ship, the Deptford-built *Minerva*, but her construction was certainly extended by the process.[12]

Melville's short-lived administration ordered no frigates and in the four years from 1801 to early 1805 there was virtually nothing entirely new in frigate design. With the singular exception of the *Forte*, St Vincent either revived older, smaller ships or ordered a trickle of existing designs, without any apparent logic in the pattern. His peacetime administrative concern was with reform and his wartime obsession was close blockade. For this latter purpose, as he told Lord Spencer in characteristically forthright manner, 'frigates are not worth a pin off Brest; the enemy outnumbers and drives them off at will.'[13]

In this circumstance it did not matter how big they were, but he could recall numerous occasions in his career when the country's interests were jeopardised by having too few. Quantity would always be more significant than quality to a man with his strategic vision.

TABLE 1/3: *Forte* class 38-gun Fifth Rate

Specification

Armament	Upper deck	Quarterdeck	Forecastle	Guns	Men
DESIGN	28 x 18pdrs	2 x 18pdrs, 10 x 32pdr carr	2 x 18pdrs, 4 x 32pdr carr	38	284
CHANGES BY AO: 22 Sep 1806		12 x 32pdr carr	2 x 9pdrs, 2 x 32pdr carr		

Lines of the *Révolutionnaire* [French, captured 1794]

	Lower deck feet-inches	Keel feet-inches	Breadth extreme feet-inches	Depth in hold feet-inches	Burthen Tons
DESIGN	157-2	131-9⅞	40-5½	12-5	1147⁶⁸⁄₉₄
AS COMPLETED *Forte*	157-5⅝	132-1½	40-6½	12-5	1155¹¹⁄₉₄

TABLE 1/4: *Forte* class 38-gun Fifth Rate

Building data

Name	Ordered	Builder	Laid down	Launched	Sailed	Fitted at	Fate
Forte	9 Jul 1801 15 Sep 1809	Sheerness Dyd Woolwich Dyd	Not started Mar 1811	21 May 1814	Fitted for Ord	Sheerness	Transferred to: BU Oct 1844

Note: Not fitted for sea until Oct 1820.

CHAPTER TWO

The Barham Interlude, 1805-1806

THE SHORT period in which Lord Barham was First Lord (2 May 1805 to 10 February 1806) is principally remembered for the dispositions which led to the Battle of Trafalgar, for which he is often given the strategic credit. John Barrow, the Second Secretary, claimed that Barham left the running of the Admiralty to other Board members,[1] but such behaviour is inherently unlikely from the man who as Comptroller claimed to have conducted 'the whole business of the Navy Board during the last war'.[2] It is beyond argument that the policy of the new Admiralty changed dramatically, and many of the new policies bear the unmistakable stamp of Barham's opinions, so frequently and freely expressed in all his writings.

The overriding concern of the moment was the apparently imminent threat of invasion, but amidst the hectic preparations for defence the Admiralty found time to address one of Barham's most serious criticisms of earlier administrations – the lack of a long-term policy on shipbuilding. Just before he took office he gave his considered opinion that to maintain numbers it was necessary to lay down six new battleships and ten frigates per annum in merchant yards, leaving the Royal Dockyards for repairs, refits and the construction of the largest Rates.[3] As far as frigates were concerned, such numbers had not been achieved since 1795, but despite the pressing need for anti-invasion craft like gunboats, the new administration met the First Lord's avowed target (actually, for frigates it was exceeded in 1805 when eleven were ordered).

The Board also turned its attention to the Dockyards, introducing a new systematic method of reporting on resources using (a typical Barham bureaucratic touch) a newly devised form.[4] The Navy Board was instructed to obtain from the yards regular details of all slips, their current usage, the largest ships that could be built on them, and the numbers of workers that could be committed to construction without interfering with other duties; they were also to report as soon as any slip became vacant, proposing a replacement class; finally, they were told to survey the yards with a view to laying out more slips. As a result, the Admiralty cancelled some ships, and filled the building-ways with the largest vessels they could take, including three 120-gun ships – the ultimate expression of long-term planning. In this way the Admiralty began a process of maximising the capacity of the Dockyards that was to bear fruit in the following years.

Barham's time as Comptroller had been characterised by his grip on every aspect of Navy Board business, including ship design. During the American War he may have been responsible for reintroducing the 'French influence' himself, or merely instrumental through the medium of like-minded disciples;[5] certainly his time at the Admiralty in the 1790s was marked by French-inspired hull forms, an interest which did not manifest itself again until his administration came into office in 1805. It was also quick to establish a level of control over detail traditionally the preserve of the Navy Board, and again this seems to

The sheer draught used for the ships of the Repeat Amphion *class was a modification of that for* Medusa. *It notes the confusing changes to quarterdeck ports occasioned by the carronades-to-guns-to-carronades orders of the 1805-6 period. All the class were allowed an extra 7ins on the false keel by AO of 18 December 1804, and the more modern form of rudder was also substituted for the traditional hanced version in* Proserpine *and* Nereus. *National Maritime Museum Dr2270*

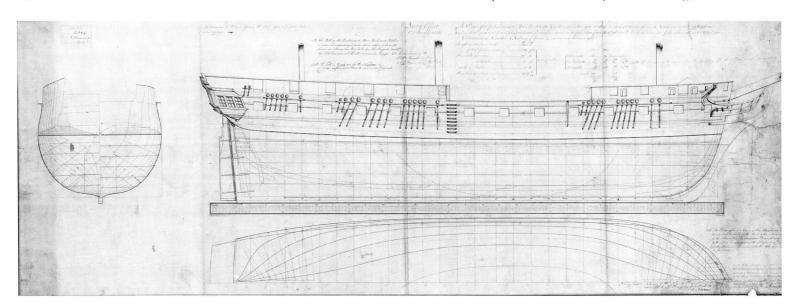

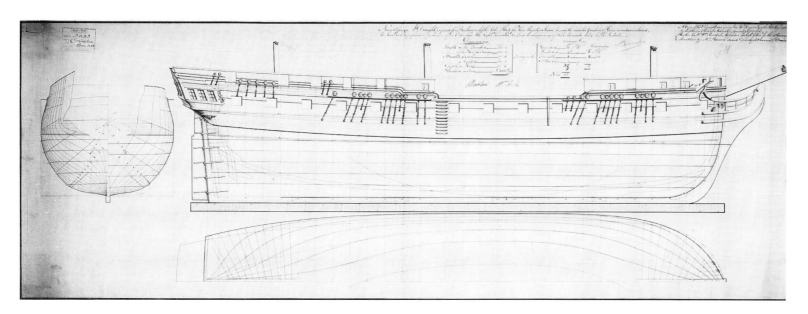

The design draught for the *Cornelia* (dated 20 June 1805) incorporated the changes applied retrospectively to the earlier ships of the *Narcissus* class, notably the berthed up forecastle and the revised head and bridle port arrangements. The draught shows some of the confusion about intended armament typical of the time: the calibre of the long guns on the upperworks is omitted (they would have been 6pdrs in earlier 18pdr 32s but the chase guns were late increased to 9pdrs for all 18pdr frigates).
National Maritime Museum E0725

indicate Barham's influence (it would have been impossible without his experience of the junior board's operations). The frigates the new Admiralty decided to build were a case in point.

Assuming Barham himself was the driving force, it was almost a decade since he had been directly involved, so was obviously out of touch with progress in frigate design. When the Navy Board sent their proposed designs for the recently ordered frigates, the Admiralty requested sight of other draughts of 32- and 38-gun ships 'of approved characters in the service . . . for the consideration of their Lordships'.[6] This gave the Navy Board something of a problem since, as a note in the file put it, there were now so many of character. They decided to send only the most highly

TABLE 2/1: Repeat *Amphion* class 32-gun Fifth Rates

Specification

Armament	Upper deck	Quarterdeck	Forecastle	Guns	Men
DESIGN	26 x 18pdrs	2 x 9pdrs, 8 x 24pdr carr	2 x 9pdrs, 2 x 24pdr carr	32	254
CHANGES BY AO: Proposed 24 Jun 1806*		6 x 9pdrs, 4 x 24pdr carr	2 x 9pdrs, 2 x 24pdr carr		

Designed by Sir William Rule

	Lower deck feet-inches	Keel feet-inches	Breadth extreme feet-inches	Depth in hold feet-inches	Burthen Tons
DESIGN	144-0	121-7½	37-6	12-6	909^{71}/$_{94}$
AS COMPLETED					
Proserpine	144-3	122-0¾	37-8¼	12-6	922^{17}/$_{94}$
Nereus	144-1	121-8¼	37-8	12-5½	917^{76}/$_{94}$

* Configuration for non-recoil carronades, with long guns in wake of shrouds; never implemented. Both were fitted as establishment, with 2 x 9pdr (8ft 6in) for chase, and 2 x 9pdr (7ft 6in).

TABLE 2/2: Repeat *Amphion* class 32-gun Fifth Rates

Building data

Name	Ordered	Builder	Laid down	Launched	Sailed	Fitted at	Fate
Proserpine	10 Jun 1805	Steemson, Hull	Sep 1805	6 Aug 1807	27 Nov 1807	Chatham	Taken off Toulon by two French frigates, 28 Feb 1809
Nereus	4 Oct 1805	Temple, South Shields	Nov 1805	4 Mar 1809	17 Jul 1809	Chatham	BU Feb 1817

Notes:
Three earlier ships of the class, *Amphion*, *Aeolus* and *Medusa*, were launched 1798-1801.

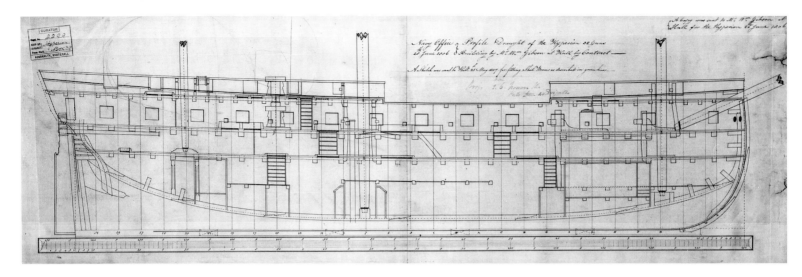

TABLE 2/3: Repeat *Narcissus* class 32-gun Fifth Rates

Specification

Armament	Upper deck	Quarterdeck	Forecastle	Guns	Men
DESIGN	26 x 18pdrs	2 x 6pdrs, 8 x 24pdr carr	2 x 6pdrs, 2 x 24pdr carr	32	254
CHANGES BY AO: 14 Feb 1806 (*Doris*) and 24 Jun 1806 (*Cornelia*)*		4 x 6pdrs, 6 x 24pdr carr	2 x 6pdrs, 2 x 24pdr carr		

Designed by Sir John Henslow

	Lower deck feet-inches	Keel feet-inches	Breadth extreme feet-inches	Depth in hold feet-inches	Burthen Tons
DESIGN	142-0	118-5	37-6	12-6	885⁹⁰⁄₉₄
AS COMPLETED *Cornelia Syren Doris*	142-5¾	118-11⅛	37-10⅞	12-6	908⁶¹⁄₉₄

* Configuration for non-recoil carronades, with long guns in wake of shrouds; never implemented. *Cornelia* was fitted as establishment, with 2 x 9pdr (8ft 6in) for chase, and 2 x 9pdr (7ft 6in) instead of 6pdrs.

The profile draught for the *Hyperion* (dated 25 June 1806) shows how confined the ship was between decks, with barely 5ft of headroom on the lower deck, proving that officers who complained about not being able to stand up in the wardroom were not exaggerating. Nor was there much depth of hold, the forward magazine taking up much of the fore platform, instead of fitting under it as was usual in British-designed frigates.
National Maritime Museum Dr2299

regarded, and eventually draughts of the *Lively* (38), *Narcissus* and *Tartar* (32s) were forwarded.

The Admiralty then asked for draughts of the *Inconstant* class (five of which St Vincent's administration had ordered), and the French *Belle Poule*, a 12pdr ship captured in 1780. Barham had never been impressed by the false economy of small but inadequate ships, and when his review of Dockyard resources revealed two *Inconstant*s allocated to slips that could build larger frigates, he had both cancelled.[7] However, the request for the *Belle Poule* draught was more significant, since it was the first manifestation of this renewed interest in French hull forms. Alongside 38s and 32s built to the Navy Board's 'approved' designs, the Admiralty ordered frigates based on the lines of the *Belle Poule* (captured 1780), *Magicienne* (captured 1781), *Topaze* (taken at Toulon in 1793), and a

TABLE 2/4: Repeat *Narcissus* class 32-gun Fifth Rates

Building data

Name	Ordered	Builder	Laid down	Launched	Sailed	Fitted at	Fate
Cornelia	10 Jun 1805	Temple, South Shields	Jun 1806	27 Jun 1808	28 Nov 1808	Chatham	BU Jun 1814
Syren	16 Jul 1805	Record, Appledore	1805				Builder failed; cancelled Jun 1806
Doris	6 Jan 1806	Record, Appledore	?never				Builder failed; cancelled Jun 1806

Notes:
Two earlier ships of the class, *Narcissus* and *Tartar*, were launched in 1801. *Syren* was in frame when cancelled, but no work had been done on *Doris*.

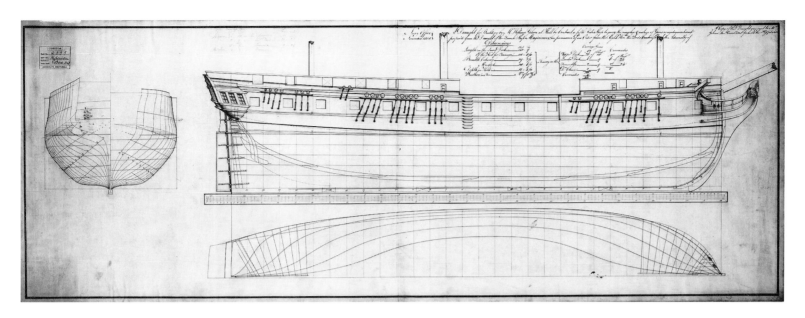

The hull form of the *Hyperion* was a very close copy of the *Magicienne*, captured as far back as 1781 but still a highly regarded 12pdr frigate in the Royal Navy when *Hyperion* was ordered. Designed by J-M-B Coulomb in 1778, *Magicienne* had been a large frigate for her times, but by 1805 she was of decidedly modest proportions for a ship intended to carry an 18pdr main battery. In the new design the original gunport arrangement was retained on the upper deck, except that the foremost port was omitted and replaced with a genuine bridle port right up in the eyes of the ship. The draught shows the half long gun/half carronade armament proposed for the upperworks in June 1806, but a pencil annotation gives the predominantly carronade allocation that was the final design proposal.
National Maritime Museum Dr2335

host of smaller craft to the lines of the *Amazon* (captured as far back as 1745, but previously employed as a model during the American Revolutionary War). It is notable that in each case the prototype was decided on the initiative of the Admiralty, and that the chosen vessels were at least a generation old. Circumstantial evidence suggests that Barham was their sponsor and that he chose designs with which he was very familiar from his younger days as Comptroller.

However, in the interim there had been a growing awareness of the disadvantages of French design practice, and the Admiralty, if not Barham himself, had to come to terms with the newly critical spirit. Common complaints about older French ships were their

TABLE 2/5: *Hyperion* class 32-gun Fifth Rate

Specification

Armament	Upper deck	Quarterdeck	Forecastle	Guns	Men
DESIGN	26 x 18pdrs	2 x 9pdrs, 10 x 24pdr carr	4 x 9pdrs, 2 x 24pdr carr	32	254
CHANGES BY AO: 24 Jun 1806*		6 x 9pdrs, 6 x 24pdr carr	4 x 9pdrs, 2 x 24pdr carr		

Lines of the *Magicienne* [French prize 1781]

	Lower deck feet-inches	Keel feet-inches	Breadth extreme feet-inches	Depth in hold feet-inches	Burthen Tons
DESIGN	143-9	118-8⅛	39-2½	12-4½	970³⁹⁄₉₄
AS COMPLETED *Hyperion*	143-9	118-7⅝	39-4½	12-4	978

*Configuration for non-recoil carronades, with long guns in wake of shrouds; never implemented. *Hyperion* was fitted with only four long guns on the upperworks: 2 x 9pdr (8ft 6in) for chase, and 2 x 9pdr (7ft 6in).

TABLE 2/6: *Hyperion* class 32-gun Fifth Rate

Building data

Name	Ordered	Builder	Laid down	Launched	Sailed	Fitted at	Fate
Hyperion	13 Jun 1805	Gibson, Hull	Feb 1806	3 Nov 1807	23 Apr 1808	Chatham	1825 to Coast Blockade; Jun 1833 BU

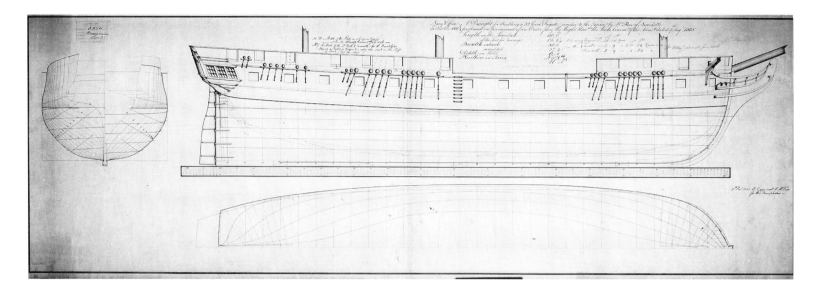

TABLE 2/7: *Bucephalus* class 32-gun Fifth Rate

Specification

Armament	Upper deck	Quarterdeck	Forecastle	Guns	Men
DESIGN	26 x 18pdrs	2 x 9pdrs, 10 x 24pdr carr	2 x 9pdrs, 2 x 24pdr carr	32	254
CHANGES BY AO: 24 Jun 1806*		8 x 9pdrs, 4 x 24pdr carr	4 x 9pdrs, 2 x 24pdr carr		

Modified by Sir William Rule from the lines of the *Topaze* [French prize 1793]

	Lower deck feet-inches	Keel feet-inches	Breadth extreme feet-inches	Depth in hold feet-inches	Burthen Tons
DESIGN	150-0	126-6⅛	38-0	12-1	971⁶⁶⁄₉₄
AS COMPLETED *Bucephalus*	150-0	126-5⅝	38-1	12-0	976

*Configuration for non-recoil carronades, with long guns in wake of shrouds; never implemented. *Bucephalus* was fitted as establishment, with 2 x 9pdr (8ft 6in) for chase, and 2 x 9pdr (7ft 6in).

The design draught for the *Bucephalus*, dated 31 October 1805. Noted as being 'similar to the *Topaze*' (a 12pdr-armed French frigate taken at Toulon in 1793), the British design is actually over 5ft longer with one less main-deck gunport per side (ignoring the bridle port right forward) and reduced tumblehome. There was, therefore, a considerable recasting of the original hull form; although the underwater body fore and aft was retained, the additional length was obtained by a parallel section amidships. As with most of the designs of this period, the upperworks show the effects of the decisions first to adopt long guns in the wake of the shrouds and then revert to a mainly carronade armament on the quarterdeck and forecastle. The changes on the draught are dated 5 July 1806 and 14 May 1807.
National Maritime Museum E0724

excessive tumblehome, which reduced stability and narrowed the spread of the shrouds, and the low free-board of main-deck ports. To counter this, the new 36 was built after the *Belle Poule* 'under the line of floatation, with *Nymphe* topsides [which were more wall-sided], taking care that the ports be as much above the surface of the water as the *Belle Poule*'s were'.[8] Similarly, for the draughts of the 32s based on the *Magicienne* and *Topaze*, if it proved necessary to allow for the additional weight of the more robust British style of construction, the Surveyors were to add length amidships; apart from reducing the tumblehome, the Surveyors were enjoined to make no other alterations.[9]

This new realism about French design shortcomings must represent something of a victory for the Surveyors, but such modifications could do little to offset

TABLE 2/8: *Bucephalus* class 32-gun Fifth Rate

Building data

Name	Ordered	Builder	Laid down	Launched	Sailed	Fitted at	Fate
Bucephalus	19 Jun 1805	Rowe, Newcastle	Aug 1806	3 Nov 1808	17 Jun 1809	Chatham	1814 troopship; 1822 receiving ship at Portsmouth; 1834 BU

the basic inadequacy of French-derived ships for Royal Navy service. The 36-gun ship became the *Pyramus*, a very small ship for her rate, and although she shared the speed of her model, the *Belle Poule*, she was leewardly in all but the smoothest conditions, pitched heavily, and sailed poorly close-hauled in stronger winds. The two 32s, paradoxically, were larger, the *Magicienne*-based 32, the *Hyperion*, being a noticeably better sailer than the *Bucephalus*, derived from the *Topaze*. However, even the *Hyperion* was leewardly, a lively sea-boat, and dangerous lying-to in heavy weather (the captain said that 'being a very low ship, particularly abaft, I have always thought it proper to keep steerage way on her in the worst weather'[10]).

All suffered from insufficient stowage and carried their gunports barely 6ft from the waterline when stored for Channel Service, although *Hyperion*'s 5ft 11in was improved by 3ins after iron water tanks were fitted at the end of the war. The cramped nature of their hulls made them barely equal to the requirements of long range cruising, and actually increased the stresses of an already demanding service. As an indication of the irritations involved, it is worth quoting one of *Hyperion*'s officers: 'She was wretchedly low between decks. In the gunroom the officers could not sit at table without two inches of the legs of chairs being cut off, and in my cabin I had to go under the hatchway to put on my coat.'[11]

The most useful contribution of the Barham Admiralty to the frigate situation was to step up the number of orders. Against the three experimental ships, it also laid down five more 32s (two *Amphions* and three *Narcissus* class), and four 38s. These ships were better bargains, particularly the three big frigates of the *Lively* class. However, the pro-French prejudice was again manifest when the Admiralty insisted that one 38 be built to the *Leda* draught, despite the Navy Board's apparent preference for the *Lively* design. The second and third *Ledas* (*Pomone* and *Shannon*) had just gone to sea, and their captains were to complain of poor stowage (as well as the lightweight Brindley system of construction), but in all fairness it may have been too recent for reports to have reached the Admiralty.

One reason for the prevalence of small frigates ordered at this time was the desire of the Admiralty to increase the number of shipbuilders capable of tendering for major warships. For anything larger than a brig the Navy Board had looked no further than the Thames and the southeast from East Anglia to the Solent for its regular suppliers, but it had been forced by criticism from the preceding St Vincent Board to cast a wider net. St Vincent believed that the traditional naval shipbuilders operated a virtual cartel so only competition from new sources would bring prices down. Barham approached the issue from another direction, being convinced that the continuing struggle with France would require Britain to use all its strategic resources, including shipbuilding, on an unprecedented scale. Every shipbuilding region would need to be used and within each area the potential of every shipbuilder would need to be maximised.

TABLE 2/9: *Pyramus* class 36-gun Fifth Rate

Specification

Armament	Upper deck	Quarterdeck	Forecastle	Guns	Men
DESIGN	26 x 18pdrs	8 x 9pdrs	2 x 9pdrs	36	264
CHANGES BY AO: 2 May 1806*		2 x 9pdrs, 10 x 32pdr carr	2 x 9pdrs, 2 x 32pdr carr		

Lines of the *Belle Poule* with topside of *Nymphe* [French prize 1780]

	Lower deck feet-inches	Keel feet-inches	Breadth extreme feet-inches	Depth in hold feet-inches	Burthen Tons
DESIGN	140-0	115-11⅝	38-2	11-11	898⁵⁰⁄₉₄
AS COMPLETED *Pyramus*	141-1	117-2⅝	38-5	12-0	920

* There was a short-lived proposal of 12 Mar 1806 to arm the quarterdeck with 8 x 9pdrs and 4 x 32pdr carr and the forecastle with 2 x 9pdrs and 2 x 32pdr carr.

TABLE 2/10: *Pyramus* class 36-gun Fifth Rate

Building data

Name	Ordered	Builder	Laid down	Launched	Sailed	Fitted at	Fate
Pyramus	28 Aug 1805	Greensword & Kidwell, Itchenor Portsmouth Dyd	Apr 1806 Firm failed; transferred to: Nov 1808	May 1808 22 Jan 1810	4 May 1810	Portsmouth	1832 receiving ship at Halifax; 1879 sold

Notes: When the builder failed the order was transferred to the nearest Royal Dockyard.

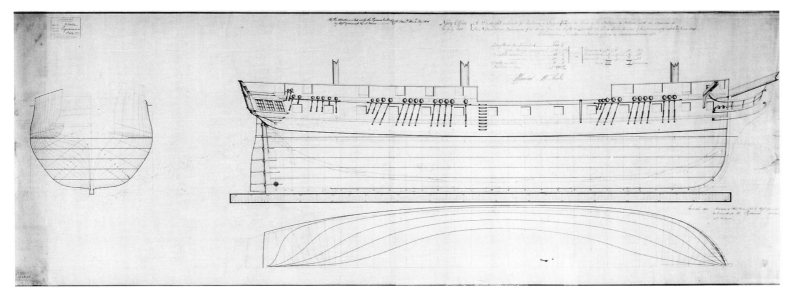

The design draught of the *Pyramus*, dated 24 July 1805. She was very small for a 36-gun 18pdr frigate, and the combination of a shallow French underwater form (*Belle Poule*) with a low French topside (*Nymphe*) made for a cramped ship. The alteration to the gunports on the upperworks is dated 2 May 1806.
National Maritime Museum E0723

As a result of this policy most frigate orders went to merchant builders outside the traditional area who had never constructed such a large warship before, although some had limited experience with Navy small craft. A form of 'apprenticeship' for the builders developed, whereby the satisfactory completion of, say, a gunboat would lead to an order for a brig sloop, and following that perhaps a frigate. Rowe, for example, had built gunbrigs and brig sloops shortly before the order for *Bucephalus*; and Temple had built sloops and two Sixth Rates prior to the contract for *Cornelia* and *Nereus*. Frigates were usually at the extreme of their capacity, and the choice of relatively small designs may have been a way of minimising the risk; but it may also have represented the largest hull that some builders could safely launch. The policy was unpopular with the Navy Board, which argued that builders at great distances from any Royal Dockyard could not be inspected properly during construction, and that the navigation of the hull after launch to a Dockyard for fitting out not only imposed delays but also exposed the incomplete ship to an increased risk of weather or enemy action. The Board was also uneasy about the financial wisdom of contracting with relatively small or untried yards: for undercapitalised businesses, manufacturing on a fixed price basis in times of high inflation was risky in the extreme.

However laudable Barham's aims in the context of the war, in the short term the Navy Board was proved right. Most of these frigates took far longer than average to build, and significantly longer to fit for sea. A high proportion were never completed at all by their original builders and were either cancelled or transferred elsewhere, causing delay and additional cost. Those that were completed did not always meet required standards: for, example, the workmanship of the Temple yard in South Shields was so poor that the *Nereus* had to be docked for a full investigation, the cost being carried by the unfortunate builder. Even if the Navy Board's exacting standards were satisfied and the yard remained solvent until delivery, there was no guarantee of profit: in January 1810 Rowe of Newcastle petitioned for some relief from the loss he incurred in building the *Bucephalus* and the brigs *Woodlark* and *Shearwater*.[12]

Virtually none of the merchant builders awarded frigate contracts in this period became regular suppliers of major warships (although Steemson of Hull went on to build one 74), so the policy might be regarded as a failure. The obvious desire of the Barham administration to improve ship design was also laudable, but equally unsuccessful since its methods were half a generation out of date. The adoption of French hull forms was now perceived as inappropriate by many, and was certainly not necessary, since the best home-grown designs were technically a match for the standard French frigates; once the massive operational superiority of the Royal Navy was brought into the equation, then there was no pressing need for enlargement or greater speed – particularly not if such 'improvements' were purchased at the expense of the fighting qualities and seakeeping essential to British dominion of the seas.

War of Attrition, 1806-1812

CHAPTER THREE

OR THE British the total victory of Trafalgar appeared to remove the immediate threat of French invasion, but the years following 1805 were to see a radical shift in the strategy of the war. Unable to defeat the British at sea by conventional means, and therefore unable to organise the knockout blow of invasion, Napoleon turned to economic warfare in an attempt to destroy the trading wealth that underpinned the British war effort.

What came to be called the Continental System was a rigorous attempt to close the ports of Europe to British shipping and so to establish French economic domination throughout occupied Europe. The policy was first mentioned on 10 October 1806, but was formalised under the Berlin Decree of 21 November 1806. Earlier, in May, the British had declared the whole coast of Europe under blockade and the French response was to prohibit the purchase of British goods or goods carried in British ships, and to announce a counter-blockade of the British Isles. The effectiveness of the French action depended on control of as many ports as possible and it was only after the Treaties of Tilsit with Russia and Prussia in July 1807 that most of Europe could be even nominally subject to the prohibition. There was further diplomatic and legalistic posturing on both sides but in essence the economic war would be won by the side that could best enforce its view.

In point of fact, Europe needed British manufactured goods – Napoleon's army is said to have marched in British boots – but Britain needed to exploit every chink in the armour of the Continental System to reach its markets. The country's substantial Baltic trade, for example, could be carried on with naval support, but this meant a huge increase in the Navy's commitments. Furthermore, the concept of blockade as understood in the international law of the time required an actual presence for enforcement. This translated into a need for ever more ships – and with the surviving enemy battle squadrons firmly blockaded in their bases, those ships would be largely frigates, sloops and small craft.

There was one further long term concern for the British government. As Napoleon came to control the resources of so much of Europe, it seemed possible that the French navy would be rebuilt, and on a hitherto unseen scale. Voicing this apprehension to the House of Lords in August 1807, Lord Selkirk spoke for many when he pointed out:

France is now in possession of the finest forests in Europe, and of countries capable of affording ample supplies of every naval store: she may command the services of all the seamen which the continent can afford, from Memel to Cadiz, and from Cadiz to Constantinople. We may look too to the certain prospect, that the whole energy of the French government will now be directed to this object: we know in fact that during all the pressure of their continental wars, the most active exertions in ship building have never been discontinued in their naval arsenals: they have now no other object to divide their attention [Austria, Prussia and Russia had been forced to make

The appearance of the late-war *Euryalus* class ships is represented by this sheer draught for the *Magicienne* dated 27 December 1810. By this stage of the conflict the quarterdeck had seven ports a side for carronades, an extra port being opened abreast the main mast, as in other British frigate classes of the time. With the three forecastle ports, this gave the class two pairs of ports more on the upperworks than were required by their established armament; some captains probably contrived to arm the spare ports unofficially, especially after 1808 when shifting carronades on trucks became popular.
National Maritime Museum Dr2168

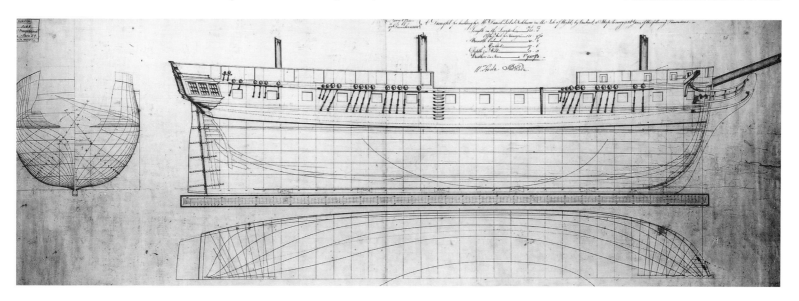

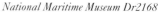

peace]; and we may be well assured that all the ability of the ruler of France will now be turned to naval affairs. The same genius, which has created such an astonishing change in the discipline and tactics of the French army, will now be unremittingly employed in the improvement of their navy.[1]

Regarded with hindsight, the acute shortage of trained

French seamen meant that the threat was probably exaggerated, but the Admiralty dare not ignore it. As a result of such pressures, the numbers of ships, rather than their individual quality, returned to the top of the official agenda.

This change of priorities at the Admiralty coincided with the appointment of Henry Peake as Second Surveyor when Henslow retired in June 1806. The new man was more highly regarded by many of the senior officers, like St Vincent and Markham, who had been so critical of the old Surveyor. However, unlike most sea officers, Peake believed that much of the preceding effort aimed at improving hull forms was misdirected. He argued that ships of similar dimensions, designed for the same weight of metal and equivalent stability, were bound to have very similar forms.[2] This is not to say that he had no new ideas – he was, for example, a strong advocate of a flatter sheer line, intended to give the midships gunports more freeboard – but he regarded appropriate size as the key to a good design.

The inevitable product of an Admiralty concern for numbers, and the Surveyor's reluctance to experiment, was a revival of the old idea of a standard design, formally abandoned with the last Establishment sixty years earlier. The battleship designs, known as the 'Surveyors of the Navy' classes, were the result of co-operation between the Surveyors,[3] but for frigates no new class was deemed necessary. To all intents and purposes the 36-gun *Euryalus* class was the standard frigate of the period: the all-round excellence of these ships was proven, while their modest dimensions suited the Admiralty's renewed concern for numbers. Of twenty-one 36s ordered between 1806 and the outbreak of the War of 1812, only *Orlando* did not belong to this class – and she was an administrative anomaly, brought about by an ill-considered order to Woolwich Dockyard to build another frigate like the one just launched (*Iphigenia*, of the *Inconstant* class revived by St Vincent's Board).

In October 1806 a programme of six *Euryalus* class 36s was ordered from the merchant yards by the recently appointed Grenville Admiralty. The new administration attempted to lay down strict terms and conditions, including placing contracts for 74s only with builders who would simultaneously agree to construct a frigate and a sloop. The Navy Board, who had also been enjoined to accept the lowest tenders, remonstrated, pointing out that few of the merchant builders had the resources to undertake multiple contracts, and underlining the dangers of judging applications solely on price. Ultimately the Navy Board's experience and discretion was allowed free rein, and none of the contracts was tied to the building of a 74: indeed, most of these frigates were built either by builders with no experience of larger vessels, or in places where such construction was impractical.[4] Even so, the Navy Board had difficulty in placing all the con-

TABLE 3/1: Repeat *Apollo* (*Euryalus*) class 36-gun Fifth Rates

Specification

Armament	Upper deck	Quarterdeck	Forecastle	Guns	Men
DESIGN	26 x 18pdrs	12 x 32pdr carr	2 x 9pdrs 2 x 32pdr carr	36	274
CHANGES BY AO:					
13 Mar 1807 (*Malacca*)		18 x 32pdr carr	As design		
6 Sep 1810 (*Malacca*)		As design			

Designed by Sir William Rule

	Lower deck feet-inches	Keel feet-inches	Breadth extreme feet-inches	Depth in hold feet-inches	Burthen Tons
DESIGN	145-0	121-9⅜	38-2	13-3	943⁵³⁄₉₄
AS COMPLETED					
Dartmouth	145-0½	121-9⅛	38-4	13-3	952
Creole	144-11	121-5⅝	38-3⅞	13-3	948⁸¹⁄₉₄
Semiramis	145-0⅝	121-10	38-2	13-3	944⁰⁄₉₄
Owen Glendower	145-3	121-11⅜	38-3½	13-3	951³⁄₉₄
Hotspur	145-0	121-9	38-4	13-3½	951⁵⁶⁄₉₄
Curaçoa	145-2	121-11	38-4	13-4	953
Saldanha	144-8	121-4⅝	38-4¾	13-2½	951
Havannah	145-0½	121-9¾	38-3¼	13-3¾	949
Theban	144-10	121-5⅝	38-5	13-4	953⁴⁹⁄₉₄
Manilla	145-0	121-8½	38-3	13-3	947²⁰⁄₉₄
Malacca, ex-*Penang*	151-11	124-4⅝	38-8	13-2	989
Orpheus	145-0	121-8¾	38-3	13-4	947²⁸⁄₉₄
Leda	145-0	121-8½	38-3	13-3	947²⁰⁄₉₄
Astraea	145-4	122-1¼	38-4¼	13-4	956
Belvidera	145-0¾	121-9¼	38-2½	13-3	945⁵⁴⁄₉₄
Galatea	145-0	121-8¾	38-3	13-3	947³⁰⁄₉₄
Maidstone	145-0	121-8¾	38-3	13-3½	947³⁰⁄₉₄
Stag	145-0	121-8¾	38-3	13-3½	947³⁰⁄₉₄
Magicienne	145-2	121-8⅜	38-3½	13-3	949⁴⁄₉₄
Pallas	145-5	122-2⅝	38-3	13-3	951
Barrosa	145-0	121-8¾	38-3	13-3½	947³⁰⁄₉₄
Tartar	145-2	121-10¼	38-3¼	13-3	949²⁷⁄₉₄
Brilliant	145-6½	122-3¼	38-3½	13-3	953⁵¹⁄₉₄
Blonde	Became a 38		See Table 6/3		

Notes: The first three of the class, *Apollo*, *Blanche* and *Euryalus*, were launched in 1799-1803. After the early loss of the *Apollo* and *Blanche*, the class was usually referred to as the *Euryalus* class.

TABLE 3/2: Repeat *Apollo* (*Euryalus*) class 36-gun Fifth Rates

Building data

Name	Ordered	Builder	Laid down	Launched	Sailed	Fitted at	Fate
Dartmouth	12 Apr 1803	Tanner, Dartmouth	Jul 1804				Firm failed Feb 1807; completed by:
	2 Jun 1809	Cook, Dartmouth		28 Aug 1813	Fitted for Ord	Plymouth	Hulked Jul 1831; BU Nov 1854 at Deptford
Creole	12 Apr 1803	Tanner, Dartmouth	Never				Cancelled 2 Jun 1809; order reinstated:
	23 Dec 1810	Plymouth Dyd	Sep 1811	1 May 1813	20 Oct 1813	Plymouth	BU Aug 1833 at Deptford
Semiramis	25 Mar 1806	Deptford Dyd	Apr 1807	25 Jul 1808	6 Sep 1808	Deptford	*Raséed* to 24 guns 1827; BU Nov 1844
Owen Glendower	1 Oct 1806	Steemson, Hull	Jan 1807	19 Nov 1808	22 Mar 1809	Chatham	Convict ship at Gibraltar 1842; sold 1884
Hotspur	1 Oct 1806	Parsons, Warsash	Aug 1807	13 Oct 1810	9 Feb 1811	Portsmouth	BU Jan 1821
Curaçoa	1 Oct 1806	Kidwell, Ichenor	Jan 1808	23 Sep 1809	23 Jan 1810	Portsmouth	*Raséed* to 24 guns Jun 1831; BU Mar 1849
Saldanha	1 Oct 1806	Temple, South Shields	Mar 1807	8 Dec 1809	6 Jul 1810	Chatham	Wrecked off Lough Swilly 4 Dec 1811
Havannah	1 Oct 1806	Wilson, Liverpool	Mar 1808	26 Mar 1811	29 Jul 1811	Plymouth	*Raséed* to 19 guns 1845; hulked Mar 1860
Theban	1 Oct 1806	Parsons, Warsash	Jun 1808	22 Dec 1809	25 Apr 1810	Portsmouth	BU May 1817
Manilla	29 Dec 1806	Woolwich Dyd	Oct 1807	11 Sep 1809	18 Oct 1809	Woolwich	Wrecked on the Haak Sand 28 Jan 1812
Malacca ex-*Penang*	19 Dec 1806	Prince of Wales Island (Penang)	Feb 1808	? Jun 1809	28 Oct 1810	Woolwich	BU Mar 1816
Orpheus	2 Mar 1808	Deptford Dyd	Aug 1808	12 Aug 1809	21 Sep 1809	Deptford	BU Aug 1819
Leda	23 Mar 1808	Woolwich Dyd	Oct 1808	9 Nov 1809	8 Dec 1809	Woolwich	Sold for BU 30 Apr 1817
Astraea	26 Sep 1808	Guillaume, Northam	Dec 1808	? May 1810	24 Sep 1810	Portsmouth	Hulked at Falmouth Aug 1823; BU Apr 1851
Belvidera	28 Sep 1808	Deptford Dyd	Dec 1808	23 Dec 1809	16 Feb 1810	Deptford	Hulked at Portsmouth Oct 1846; sold 1906
Galatea	12 May 1809	Deptford Dyd	Aug 1809	31 Aug 1810	18 Oct 1810	Deptford	Hulked at Jamaica Aug 1836; BU 1849
Maidstone	8 Jan 1810	Deptford Dyd	Sep 1810	18 Oct 1811	13 Dec 1811	Deptford	Hulked at Portsmouth 1832; BU Jun 1867
Stag	17 Aug 1810	Deptford Dyd	Jan 1811	25 Jul 1812	26 Sep 1812	Deptford	BU Sep 1821
Magicienne	14 Dec 1810	List, Fishbourne	Apr 1811	8 Aug 1812	24 Oct 1812	Portsmouth	*Raséed* to 24 guns Nov 1831; BU Mar 1845
Pallas	14 Dec 1810	Guillaume, Northam	May 1811				Firm failed; transferred to:
	1 Dec 1811	Portsmouth Dyd	Apr 1814	13 Apr 1816	Fitted for Ord	Portsmouth	Hulked at Portsmouth 1836; sold Jan 1862
Barrosa	4 Apr 1811	Deptford Dyd	Oct 1811	21 Oct 1812	10 Dec 1812	Deptford	Hulked at Portsmouth 1823; sold May 1841
Tartar	6 Jan 1812	Deptford Dyd	Oct 1812	6 Apr 1814	Fitted for Ord	Sheerness	Hulked at Chatham Mar 1830; BU Sep 1859
Brilliant	11 Dec 1812	Deptford Dyd	Nov 1813	28 Dec 1814	Fitted for Ord	Chatham	*Raséed* to 22 guns 1846; hulked as TS 1859
Blonde	11 Dec 1812	Deptford Dyd					Reordered as a 38; see Table 6/3

Notes: The launch report for *Owen Glendower* is dated 21 Nov 1808 and this is often quoted in secondary sources, but the report makes it clear that the ship was actually launched on the 19th.

Dates for *Malacca* are not listed in Navy Board records; the Order date is the first Admiralty instruction to the Navy Board to supply stores for the ship; the date in the Launched column is from Navy Board correspondence, but there is an annotation in the Progress Books 'Acct of her being launched is first noticed 6 Nov 1809'. See text for details.

Havannah survived as a TS for the Ragged School at Cardiff until sold in 1905.

Brilliant was a TS at Dundee and, from 1875, Inverness; renamed *Briton* on 8 Nov 1889, she survived until sold on 12 May 1908.

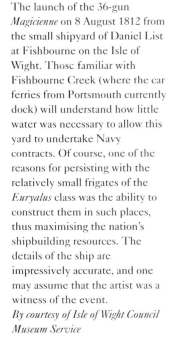

The launch of the 36-gun
Magicienne on 8 August 1812 from
the small shipyard of Daniel List
at Fishbourne on the Isle of
Wight. Those familiar with
Fishbourne Creek (where the car
ferries from Portsmouth currently
dock) will understand how little
water was necessary to allow this
yard to undertake Navy
contracts. Of course, one of the
reasons for persisting with the
relatively small frigates of the
Euryalus class was the ability to
construct them in such places,
thus maximising the nation's
shipbuilding resources. The
details of the ship are
impressively accurate, and one
may assume that the artist was a
witness of the event.
*By courtesy of Isle of Wight Council
Museum Service*

tracts satisfactorily, and two were still outstanding as late as September 1807.[5]

A huge programme of contract-built 74s was initiated in 1806 and continued by the following Admiralty of Lord Mulgrave, eventually producing the infamous 'Forty Thieves' of the 'Surveyors of the Navy' class. In these circumstances there was little money for the frigate fleet, but the Admiralty may have felt that its numbers were being sufficiently increased by capture: nine ex-French 18pdr ships were taken into service in 1806, and eight Danish frigates of like force were captured at Copenhagen in 1807.

However, this priority was to change following British intervention in the Peninsula in the summer of 1808. Supporting even a small army overseas required a substantial logistic effort, and the supply lines to Spain were vulnerable to attack from French Biscay ports; the French fleet might be tightly blockaded, but cruisers and privateers were impossible to bottle up completely. There was also the additional burden of the campaign in the Baltic and the increasingly venomous Danish attack on trade using gunboats and small craft. As a result, the Admiralty considered paying off up to twenty ships of the line and transferring their crews to frigates and smaller vessels.[6] The Navy Board was actually instructed in September to give priority to frigates over battleships in dockyard repairs and to bring forward as many as possible in the shortest realistic time-frame.

They were also asked if it might be possible to contract for some large frigates to be launched within 6-8 months, but the Navy Board proposed building six or eight frigates in the Dockyards, arguing that to place the contracts with merchant builders would drive up the price of timber beyond even the rate currently inflated by the demands of the large programme of 74s

building in merchant yards. Therefore, they had to be Dockyard-built, the Navy Board estimating that the 6-8 months deadline could be met, and the number was set by the availability of Dockyard slips.[7]

After first ascertaining that it was cheaper to build in a Royal Dockyard – the Navy Board calculated the saving to be £1000, or about 5 per cent, per ship – the Admiralty grasped the opportunity and a substantial programme of eight big frigates was put in hand immediately. These were the first 38-gun ships ordered since 1805 and they were to be built 'with all possible expedition'. Once again, existing classes were specified, the 38s being divided equally between the *Lively* and *Leda* draughts. But the Admiralty was not satisfied: it asked the Navy Board to find space for two more, although in the event only a small slip at Deptford was available. The width of the basin gates restricted this slip to building 36s, so the Deptford ship was ordered to be constructed to the *Euryalus* draught.[8] By coincidence, on the same day as the original Admiralty order to build the 38s, Guillaume offered to build a 36 on terms that had been rejected for the 1806 programme, but such were changed conditions that the tender was immediately accepted by the Admiralty, to make up the ten ships originally desired.

One late addition to this programme was the 36-gun *Malacca*, which might be called the frigate the Admiralty forgot. There are no precise dates for her construction in any of the usual central records like the Progress Books, and further investigation reveals a curious story intimately linked with the fortunes of the East India Company's station at Prince of Wales Island, modern Penang. St Vincent's initiative (covered in Chapter 1) had set in motion the building of ships in India, and his successor, Lord Melville, although of a different political persuasion, was equally enthusiastic,

and even proposed extending the programme beyond Bombay. He was keen to exploit the apparently inexhaustible timber supplies of Burma, the superb teak of Moulmein being the principal target.

Melville was well versed in Indian affairs, but deferred to the opinion of his nephew Philip Dundas, who had recently returned from India. Because Rangoon and the forested area of Pegu were subject to a 'capricious' ruler, Dundas advocated Prince of Wales Island further south, already in the East India Company's hands. The island was also claimed to be suitable for the establishment of a new naval base and dockyard much needed by the East Indies squadron operating against the Dutch colonies in the area. Since it was to be a joint venture, in 1804 the Comptroller of the Navy, Sir Andrew Hamond, met the senior officials of the Company to discuss the details of setting up a small dockyard, but there was no mention of ship-building 'as the venture seemed so uncertain'. As a result of these decisions, what had been little more than a stop-over for the Company's ships was raised to the status of a Presidency, and the man appointed as the new Governor was Philip Dundas.

It was Dundas's understanding that a prime reason for the establishment of the facilities was to build a frigate and a 74, which had figured so prominently in his early correspondence with Melville, and he began the task of setting up facilities and assembling timber without specific instructions. As a result, in November 1806 the Admiralty was startled to receive a request for the European stores for a frigate – principally the copper sheathing and ironwork – required to proceed with construction.[9] Both the Company and the Navy Board confirmed that there was no contract, but it was decided to continue and on 19 December the latter was instructed to send the required stores and a draught for a 36-gun ship of the *Euryalus* class. However, at Prince of Wales Island itself work progressed very slowly: local timber was inadequate and most needed costly importation, which forced the Governor to purchase transports and tenders to support his efforts; finance, only available in the form of Navy Bills, was also a problem. Communications, via the East India Company, were slow and infrequent, and with another change in the Board of Admiralty and the death of Hamond at the Navy Board, the Penang frigate slipped from view.

A later report into the financial mismanagement of the project notes that actual construction did not begin until February 1808, that the ship was ready for launching in June 1809, and that she was completed in January 1810.[10] In the meantime, since they had received no orders to turn the ship over to the Navy, the Company had sought, and received, Admiralty permission to fit the ship as an Indiaman and send her home in freight. As a result she was not taken over by the Navy until 11 August 1810, when she was promptly sent into dock at Woolwich for inspection and fitting

out as a warship. Although it is often assumed that the ship was built of teak, her construction was actually a mixture of timbers, some of entirely unknown characteristics; nor was she a close interpretation of the *Euryalus* draught, and was a poorer performer under sail as a consequence. The Navy's view of the ship is manifest in her very short service life.

TABLE 3/3: Repeat *Leda* class 38-gun Fifth Rates

Specification

Armament	Upper deck	Quarterdeck	Forecastle	Guns	Men
DESIGN	28 x 18pdrs	2 x 9pdrs, 12 x 32pdr carr	2 x 9pdrs, 2 x 32pdr carr	38	284
CHANGES BY AO: 18 Dec 1804 (*Pomone*)*		8 x 9pdrs, 6 x 32pdr carr	2 x 9pdrs, 2 x 32pdr carr		

'Similar to the *Hébé*' [French prize, 1782]

	Lower deck feet-inches	Keel feet-inches	Breadth extreme feet-inches	Depth in hold feet-inches	Burthen Tons
DESIGN	150-1½	125-4⅞	39-11	12-9	1062⁷⁹⁄₉₄
AS COMPLETED					
Pomone	150-2½	125-11⅝	40-2	12-9½	1076
Shannon	150-2	125-6½	39-11⅜	12-11	1065⁶²⁄₉₄
Leonidas	150-1½	125-5⅞	40-3¼	12-9	1067
Briton	149-11	125-3¾	40-3	12-8½	1079⁸¹⁄₉₄
Lacedaemonian	150-1½	125-4⅞	39-11	12-9	1073
Tenedos	150-0	125-1⅜	40-4	12-9½	1082⁵⁸⁄₉₄
Lively, ex-*Scamander*	150-1	125-1¼	40-3½	12-10	1080²²⁄₉₄
Surprise	150-4	125-8⅞	40-0½	12-9	1072³³⁄₉₄
Diamond	150-0½	125-1¾	40-2½	12-9	1076¹⁸⁄₉₄
Amphitrite	150-1¾	125-5	39-11¼	12-9	1064
Trincomalee	150-4½	125-7¼	39-11¼	12-9	1066
Arethusa	150-11	126-11	40-1	12-9	1084⁶⁰⁄₉₄
Thetis	150-9	126-7⅛	40-2	12-9	1086³²⁄₉₄
Blanche	150-1¼	125-1⅛	40-2	12-10	1073⁴⁸⁄₉₄
Fisgard	150-1½	125-4¼	40-0½	12-9	1069⁵⁄₉₄

Notes: The prototype of the class, *Leda*, was launched in 1800. The Bombay-built ships were constructed of teak. The above were the only vessels completed to the original design, but post-war a further twenty-five were ordered to modified draughts with Seppings's circular stern and 'small-timber' system of construction: *Venus*, *Melampus*, *Amazon*, *Minerva*, *Nereus*, *Latona*, *Diana*, *Hamadryad*, *Aeolus*, *Thisbe*, *Hebe*, *Cerberus*, *Circe*, *Clyde*, *Thames*, *Fox*, *Unicorn*, *Daedalus*, *Proserpine*, *Mermaid*, *Mercury*, *Penelope*, *Thalia*, *Medusa*, *Pegasus* (the last two were cancelled in 1832); orders for a further three, *Jason*, *Nemesis* and *Statira*, were transferred to the *Druid* (Modified *Seringapatam*) class.

* Never implemented; the same armament was briefly proposed for *Leonidas* and *Statira* in Mar 1806, but they and subsequent ships were ordered to revert to the design armament. The first two ships both went to sea with non-standard armament on the upperworks: *Pomone* carried 2 x 9pdrs (7ft 6in models) and 16 x 32pdr carr; *Shannon* had 2 x 9pdrs (8ft 6in chase guns), 6 x 9pdrs (7ft 6in) and 10 x 32pdr carr. *Briton*, *Lacedaemonian*, *Tenedos* and later ships completed with only 2 x 9pdrs and 16 x 32pdr carr.

TABLE 3/4: Repeat *Leda* class 38-gun Fifth Rates

Building data

Name	Ordered	Builder	Laid down	Launched	Sailed	Fitted at	Fate
Pomone	25 Nov 1802	Brindley, Frindsbury	Dec 1803	17 Jan 1805	29 Mar 1805	Chatham	Wrecked on the Needles 14 Oct 1811
Shannon	24 Oct 1803	Brindley, Frindsbury	Aug 1804	5 May 1806	3 Aug 1806	Chatham	Hulk 1831; renamed *St Lawrence* 11 Mar 1844; BU Nov 1859
Leonidas	19 Jul 1805	Pelham, Frindsbury	Nov 1805	4 Sep 1807	10 Dec 1807	Chatham	Powder hulk 1872; sold 23 Nov 1894
Briton	28 Sep 1808	Chatham Dyd	Feb 1810	11 Apr 1812	22 Jun 1812	Chatham	Hulk 1841; target and then BU Sep 1860
Lacedaemonian	28 Sep 1808	Portsmouth Dyd	May 1810	21 Dec 1812	23 Feb 1813	Portsmouth	BU Nov 1822
Tenedos	28 Sep 1808	Chatham Dyd	May 1810	11 Apr 1812	16 Jun 1812	Chatham	Convict hulk 1843; BU Mar 1875
Lively, ex-*Scamander*	28 Sep 1808	Chatham Dyd	Jul 1810	14 Jul 1813	Fitted for Ord	Chatham	Hulk 1831; sold for BU 28 Apr 1862
Surprise	10 Apr 1809	Milford Dyd	Jan 1810	25 Jul 1812	11 Dec 1812	Plymouth	Convict hulk 1822; sold Oct 1837
Diamond	30 Jun 1812	Chatham Dyd	Aug 1813	16 Jan 1816	Fitted for Ord	Chatham	Accidental fire 18 Feb 1827; wreck BU
Amphitrite	21 Oct 1812	Bombay Dyd	Aug 1814	14 Apr 1816	?	Bombay	*Rasée* 26-gun corvette 1846; BU Jan 1875
Trincomalee	30 Oct 1812	Bombay Dyd	May 1816	12 Oct 1817	30 May 1818	Bombay	In Ord May 1819-Sep 1847; corvette 1845; being restored, Hartlepool 1999
Arethusa	18 Dec 1812	Pembroke Dyd	Feb 1815	29 Jul 1817	Fitted for Ord	Plymouth	Hulk 1836; renamed *Bacchus* 12 Mar 1844; BU Aug 1883
Thetis	22 Nov 1814	Pembroke Dyd	Dec 1814	1 Feb 1817	Fitted for Ord	Plymouth	Wrecked off Brazil 5 Dec 1830
Blanche	29 May 1815	Chatham Dyd	Feb 1816	26 May 1819	Fitted for Ord	Chatham	Hulk 1833; BU Oct 1865
Fisgard	24 Aug 1815	Pembroke Dyd	Feb 1817	8 Jul 1819	Fitted for Ord	Plymouth	Hulk 1847; BU Oct 1879

Notes: Amphitrite went to the Coastguard in 1857 and was lent to War Office contractors from Jul 1862 for work on the Plymouth forts.

Trincomalee was hulked in 1861 as a TS at Sunderland, and in 1897 was sold to the Wheatley Cobb organisation as a TS called *Foudroyant*, first at Falmouth then at Portsmouth; she has been at Harlepool since 1987.

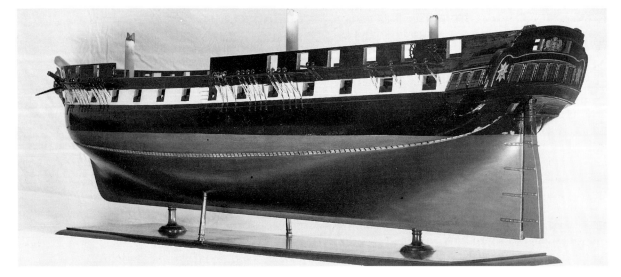

A large ¹⁄₃₂nd scale model of the *Lacedaemonian* built post-war by a modelmaker from Portsmouth Dockyard called David Harvey; he is known to have later worked in the Navy offices at Somerset House from 1839 to 1862. The paint and decorative scheme of this model post-dates 1815, but the detailing is accurate (although why the first two gunports in the quarterdeck barricade have not been cut through is a mystery). The thin strip of planking omitted serves to emphasise the fine lines of this class.
National Maritime Museum 3805

In 1809 Admiral Drury, the Commander-in-Chief on the East Indies station, pointed out the shortcomings of Prince of Wales Island as a shipbuilding centre: the poor local timber; the distance good teak had to be imported (available no nearer than Rangoon); and the high cost of labour, which was two or three times greater than in India. His advice to abandon shipbuilding there was accepted, and in the post-war years his predictions of the costs became apparent when a final account for the *Malacca* was presented by the Company, making the ship more than twice as expensive as a sister built in Britain. *Malacca* was the ultimate 'King's bad bargain'.

By the time the *Malacca* was taken over the build-quality of frigates was an important issue. One result of the post-1805 realisation that the war would be lengthy was a determination not to shorten the lives of ships unnecessarily by over-rapid construction. An Admiralty order of 16 June 1806 specified that even merchant-built frigates were to stand to season, but such was the want of large cruisers in the autumn of 1808 that the order was cancelled. This turned out to be a temporary *volte face*, battleships being again accorded priority in November, although this was reversed once more in the following May.[11] In practice, in the years before 1812, frigates were usually accorded some time to season, a process aided by the high proportion of frigates built in the dockyards at this time. A limited programme of two 36s and two 38s to be built in merchant yards in eighteen months was ordered by the Yorke administration in December 1810, but this was the only officially inspired merchant frigate building between 1806 and 1812.

The post-Barham Admiralty Boards were either short-lived or relatively inexperienced and contained no Naval Lords bent on design innovation. As a result there was a general willingness to persevere with existing 'standard' classes. But if this period saw the introduction of no new frigate designs, there were constant, if relatively minor, developments in armament, fittings and, above all, structure. Carronade carriages were subject to almost continuous alteration, and the Gover 6½ft 33cwt lightweight 24pdr was gradually introduced after 1803 (this could not be safely fired double-shotted, so was not much employed on frigates, although the *Undaunted* and *Unité* carried them for a time). The *Nisus* and *Menelaus* introduced a modified deck layout, with the quarterdeck ladderway moved abaft the capstan, and the interior bulkheads of the cabin omitted; moveable carlings and three rows of gratings a side filled up the waist, and the breastworks of the forecastle and quarterdeck were removed.[12] Most importantly, there was a continuous struggle to conserve timber and improve fastenings without loss of strength.

This is dealt with at greater length in Chapter 7, but to sum up the period 1806-12, it is significant that by 1811 the Admiralty felt that the war at sea was suffi-

ciently under control 'to take advantage of the present circumstances' to undertake the most sweeping revision of shipbuilding regulations for half a century.[13] The Yorke administration was also confident enough to do away with part of its 'strategic reserve' of laid-up ships, a small sacrifice since most would have needed major work before they were again seaworthy.[14] Although the navy was at full stretch and victory might be some way off, there was a general feeling that the war was going in the right direction. This comforting assumption was dealt a serious blow by the United States' declaration of war in June 1812.

TABLE 3/5: Repeat *Lively* class 38-gun Fifth Rates

Specification

Armament	Upper deck	Quarterdeck	Forecastle	Guns	Men
DESIGN	28 x 18pdrs	2 x 9pdrs, 12 x 32pdr carr	2 x 9pdrs, 2 x 32pdr carr	38	284
CHANGES BY AO:					
24 Jun 1806 (*Horatio* and *Spartan*)*		6 x 9pdrs, 8 x 32pdr carr	2 x 9pdrs, 2 x 32pdr carr		300
4 Jul 1807 (*Horatio*)		2 x 32pdr carr on carriages added			
26 Sep 1808 (*Crescent*)		14 x 32pdr carr	As design		
8 Nov 1809 *Menelaus* and *Macedonian*); all later ships the same		14 x 32pdr carr	As design		
21 Jun 1813 (*Crescent*)		4 more 32pdr carr, on non-recoil principle			

Designed by Sir William Rule

	Lower deck feet-inches	Keel feet-inches	Breadth extreme feet-inches	Depth in hold feet-inches	Burthen Tons
DESIGN	154-0	129-8	39-5	13-6	1071^{51}/$_{94}$
AS COMPLETED					
Hussar	154-0	129-8	39-6¼	13-6	1077^{31}/$_{94}$
Undaunted	154-9	130-3¾	39-7	13-6	1086^{5}/$_{94}$
Apollo	154-3½	129-9⅜	39-8	13-6	1085^{77}/$_{94}$
Resistance	154-1½	129-8	39-7	13-6	1081
Statira	154-0	129-10¾	39-7½	13-5½	1080
Horatio	154-3	129-11¼	39-8½	13-7	1089^{71}/$_{94}$
Spartan	154-2	129-6¼	39-8	13-6	1084
Menelaus	154-1	129-6¼	39-6½	13-6	1077^{15}/$_{94}$
Nisus	154-0	129-6	39-6	13-6	1074^{44}/$_{94}$
Macedonian	154-6	130-2⅝	39-6	13-6	1080^{64}/$_{94}$
Crescent	154-5⅜	130-1	39-7	13-6	1084^{9}/$_{94}$
Bacchante	154-0½	129-7¼	39-6¼	13-6¼	1076^{6}/$_{94}$
Nymphe, ex-*Nereide*	154-2	129-10½	39-8	13-6	1087
Sirius	155-0½	129-7⅝	39-9	13-7	1089^{50}/$_{94}$
Laurel	154-4	129-11¾	39-8	13-6	1088

Notes: The prototype of the class, *Lively*, was launched in 1804.

* Configuration for non-recoil carronades, with long guns in wake of shrouds; never implemented, but *Resistance* was completed with a modified version – 2 x 9pdrs (7ft 6in for chase), 4 x 9pdrs (7ft) and twelve 32pdr carr.

TABLE 3/6: Repeat *Lively* class 38-gun Fifth Rates

Building data

Name	Ordered	Builder	Laid down	Launched	Sailed	Fitted at	Fate
Hussar	7 Nov 1803	Adams, Bucklers Hard	Mar 1806	23 Apr 1807	27 Jun 1807	Portsmouth	Hulked Sep 1833; burnt as target ship 1861
Undaunted	7 Nov 1803	Graham, Harwich		Builder failed; transferred to:			
	6 Jan 1806	Woolwich Dyd	Apr 1806	17 Oct 1807	2 Dec 1807	Woolwich	Target ship 1856; BU Dec 1860
Apollo	7 Nov 1803	Parsons, Burseldon	Apr 1804	27 Jun 1805	26 Sep 1805	Portsmouth	Troopship 1838; BU Sep 1856
Resistance	9 Nov 1803	Ross, Rochester	Mar 1804	10 Aug 1805	19 Oct 1805	Chatham	Troopship 1842; BU Apr 1858
Statira	4 Jun 1805	Guillaume, Northam	Dec 1805	7 Jul 1807	26 Aug 1807	Portsmouth	Wrecked off Cuba 27 Feb 1815
Horatio	15 Jun 1805	Parsons, Burseldon	Jul 1805	23 Apr 1807	4 Aug 1807	Portsmouth	Screw frigate Jun 1850; sold for BU 1865
Spartan	24 Aug 1805	Ross, Rochester	Oct 1805	16 Aug 1806	6 Oct 1806	Chatham	BU Apr 1822
Menelaus	28 Sep 1808	Plymouth Dyd	Nov 1808	17 Apr 1810	21 Jun 1810	Plymouth	Hulked 1836; sold 10 May 1897
Nisus	28 Sep 1808	Plymouth Dyd	Dec 1808	3 Apr 1810	15 Jun 1810	Plymouth	BU Sep 1822
Macedonian	28 Sep 1808	Woolwich Dyd	May 1809	2 Jun 1810	6 Jul 1810	Woolwich	Taken by USS *United States* 25 Oct 1812
Crescent	28 Sep 1808	Woolwich Dyd	Sep 1809	11 Dec 1810	7 Feb 1811	Woolwich	Hulked at Rio de Janiero 1840; sold 1854
Bacchante	12 Aug 1809	Deptford Dyd	Jul 1810	16 Nov 1811	25 Jan 1810	Deptford	Hulked Feb 1837; BU Feb 1858
Nymphe, ex-*Nereide*	14 Dec 1810	Parsons, Warsash	Jan 1811	13 Apr 1812	22 Jun 1812	Portsmouth	Hulked Mar 1836; BU Mar 1875
Sirius	14 Dec 1810	Tyson, Burseldon	Sep 1811	11 Sep 1813	Fitted for Ord	Portsmouth	Hulked 1860; target 1860; BU Sep 1862
Laurel	21 Mar 1812	Parsons, Warsash	Jun 1812	31 May 1813	13 Sep 1813	Portsmouth	Hulked 1864; BU Nov 1885

Notes: Apollo was earmarked for conversion to a royal yacht in 1822, but the plan was abandoned; she was a storeship from 1853 until BU.

Menelaus served as a Customs hulk from May 1854 until sold.

Nymphe was renamed in 1811; after service with the River Police from 1861 she became a Roman Catholic chapel in 1863; she was again renamed, *Handy*, in 1871.

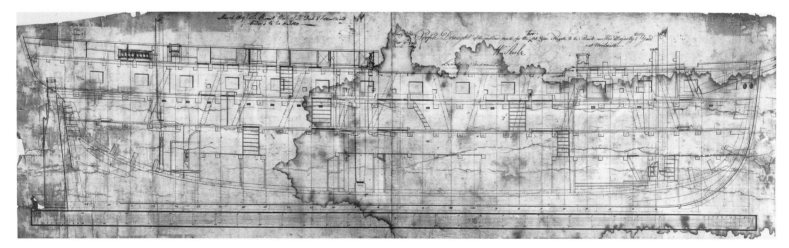

The battered and water-stained profile draught for the Woolwich-built *Lively* class ships, originally dated 17 December 1799. Annotated under the date March 1809 is an order to omit the breastworks at the break of the quarterdeck and forecastle. The gangways were flush by this date and abandoning the breastworks was another step in the process of integrating the forecastle and quarterdeck into a single deck; from 1810 the waist was narrowed by the additions of light gratings inboard of the gangways. Also left out in later ships were the top riders - the prominent angled strengthening pieces shown in ticked lines running from the lower deck to the gunwale.
National Maritime Museum Dr1976b

TABLE 3/7: Captured 18pdr ships 1803-1815

Service data

Name, origin	Built	Captured	Fate
Armed with 26 x 18pdrs on upper deck, rated 36 guns in RN			
Harfruen, ex-Dan	Copenhagen 1789	7 Sep 1807	Never cruised; sold 29 Sep 1814
Freya, ex-Dan	Copenhagen 1793	7 Sep 1807	Troopship 1811; sold 11 Jan 1816
Iris, ex-Dan	Copenhagen 1795	7 Sep 1807	Sold 31 Jul 1816
Nyaden, ex-Dan	Copenhagen 1795	7 Sep 1807	BU May 1812
Venus, ex-Dan	Copenhagen 1805	7 Sep 1807	Sold 9 Aug 1815
Nymphen, ex-Dan	Copenhagen 1807	7 Sep 1807	Sold 11 Jan 1816
Furieuse, ex-Fr	Cherbourg 1797	6 Jul 1809	BU Oct 1816
Laurel, ex-Fr *Fidèle*	Flushing 1809	Sep 1809	Captured incomplete; finished 1811; wrecked 31 Jan 1812
Essex, ex US	Salem 1799	28 Mar 1814	Never cruised; hulk 1824; sold 1837
Armed with 28 x 18pdrs on upper deck, rated 38 guns in RN			
Clorinde, ex-Fr	Basse Indre 1800	30 Nov 1803	Sold 6 Mar 1817
Surveillante, ex-Fr	Nantes 1802	30 Nov 1803	BU Aug 1814
Virtue, ex-Fr *Vertu*	Lorient 1794	30 Nov 1803	Not fitted for RN service; BU Dec 1810
Fama, ex-Sp	Cartagena 1795	5 Oct 1804	Not fitted for RN service; sold Apr 1812
Iphigenia, ex-Sp *Medea*	Ferrol 1797	5 Oct 1804	Renamed *Imperieuse* Dec 1805; hulk May 1818; sold 10 Sep 1838
Hamadryad, ex-Sp *Santa Matilde*	Havana 1778	23 Oct 1804*	Sold 9 Aug 1815
Amphitrite, ex-Sp *Anfitrite*	Havana 1797	19 Nov 1804*	Renamed *Blanche* Dec 1805; wrecked 4 Mar 1807
Milan, ex-Fr *Ville de Milan*	Lorient 1803	23 Feb 1805	BU Dec 1815
Didon, ex-Fr	St Malo 1799	10 Aug 1805	BU Aug 1811
Volontaire, ex-Fr	Bordeaux 1796	4 Mar 1806	BU Feb 1816
Belle Poule, ex-Fr	Nantes 1802	13 Mar 1806	Troopship 1814; hulk 1815; sold 4 Apr 1816
Guerriere, ex-Fr	Cherbourg 1799	19 Jul 1806	Taken and burnt by USS *Constitution* 19 Aug 1812
Rhin, ex-Fr	Toulon 1802	28 Jul 1806	Hulk 1838; sold 26 May 1884
Immortalité, ex-Fr *Infatigable*	Le Havre 1799	24 Sep 1806	Not fitted for RN service; BU Jan 1811
Armide, ex-Fr	Rochefort 1804	25 Sep 1806	BU Nov 1815
Alceste, ex-Fr *Minerve*	Rochefort 1805	25 Sep 1806	Troopship 1814; wrecked 18 Feb 1817
Gloire, ex-Fr	Nantes 1803	25 Sep 1806	BU Sep 1812
Président, ex-Fr	Lorient 1804	28 Sep 1806	Renamed *Piedmontaise* 1815; BU Dec 1815
Rota, ex-Dan	Copenhagen 1802	7 Sep 1807	Sold 11 Jan 1816
Perlen, ex-Dan	Copenhagen 1804	7 Sep 1807	Hulk Mar 1813; sold Jul 1846
Piedmontaise, ex-Fr *Piémontaise*	St Malo 1804	8 Mar 1808	BU Jan 1813
Brune, ex-Fr *Thétis*	Brest 1788	10 Nov 1808	Troopship 1810; hulk 1816; sold 1838
Alcmene, ex-Fr *Topaze*	Nantes 1804	22 Jan 1809	Temporarily named *Jewel* until May 1809; BU Feb 1816
Niemen, ex-Fr	Bordeaux? 1808	6 Apr 1809	BU Sep 1815
Bourbonnaise, ex-Fr *Caroline*	Antwerp 1806	21 Sep 1809	Never fitted for sea; BU Apr 1817
Nereide, ex-Fr *Vénus*	Le Havre 1806	18 Sep 1810	Never fitted for sea; BU May 1816
Pomone, ex-Fr *Astrée*	Genoa 1808	4 Dec 1810	*Astree* until Oct 1811; BU Jun 1816
Junon, ex-Fr *Bellone*	St Malo 1803	4 Dec 1810	BU Feb 1817
Daedalus, ex-Fr-Ven *Corona*	Venice 1809	13 Mar 1811	Wrecked off Ceylon 2 Jul 1813

Name, origin	Built	Captured	Fate

Armed with 28 x 18pdrs on upper deck, rated 38 guns in RN

Name, origin	Built	Captured	Fate
Java, ex-Fr *Renommée*	Nantes 1805	20 May 1811	Captured and burnt by USS *Constitution* 29 Dec 1812
Madagascar, ex-Fr *Néreïde*	St Malo 1809	26 May 1811	BU 1819
Ambuscade, ex-Fr *Pomone*	Genoa 1804	29 Nov 1811	BU Nov 1812
Chesapeake, ex-US	Norfolk 1799	1 June 1813	Sold 18 Aug 1819
Weser, ex-Fr	Amsterdam 1812	21 Oct 1813	Troopship 1814; sold 17 Sep 1817
Trave, ex-Fr	Amsterdam 1810	23 Oct 1813	Troopship 1814; sold 7 Jun 1821
Seine, ex-Fr *Cérès*	Brest 1810	6 Jan 1814	BU May 1823
Gloire, ex-Fr *Iphigénie*	Cherbourg 1810	20 Jan 1814	Named *Palma* to Dec 1814; sold 10 Sep 1817
Modeste, ex-Fr *Terpsichore*	Antwerp 1812	3 Feb 1814	Never fitted for sea; BU Aug 1816
Immortalité, ex-Fr *Alcmène*	Cherbourg 1811	16 Feb 1814	Temporarily named *Dunira* 1814; sold Jan 1837
Aurora, ex-Fr *Clorinde*	Paimboeuf 1808	20 Feb 1814	Hulk 1832; BU May 1851
Sultane, ex-Fr	Nantes 1813	26 Mar 1814	BU 1819
Topaze, ex-Fr *Étoile*	Nantes 1814	26 Mar 1814	Hulk Feb 1823; target 1850; BU 1851
Melpomene, ex-Fr	Toulon 1810	30 Apr 1815	Never fitted for sea; sold 7 Jun 1821

Notes: It was originally intended to rename the Danish prizes, but this was abandoned to maintain the political fiction that the ships were being held in trust until Denmark was no longer under the yoke of Napoleon. Their proposed names were: *Harfruen* (*Boreas*), *Freya* (*Hypollitus*), *Iris* (*Alaric*), *Nyaden* (*Hephaestion*), *Venus* (*Levant*), *Nymphen* (*Determinee*), *Rota* (*Sensible*), and *Perlen* (*Theban*).

* Most sources cite 25 Nov for both captures, but the dates quoted are those in Nelson's official dispatches (*Dispatches and Letters of Lord Nelson*, Nicholas ed, Vol VI, pp291-2).

Besides those listed, the following French prizes were temporarily in British hands: *Creole*, 40 guns (taken 1 Jul 1803 at San Domingo, but foundered on passage to England on 2 Jan 1804 before she could be formally registered and measured); and *Junon*, 40 guns (taken 10 Feb 1809, but recaptured 13 Dec 1809), supposedly measuring 1102 tons.

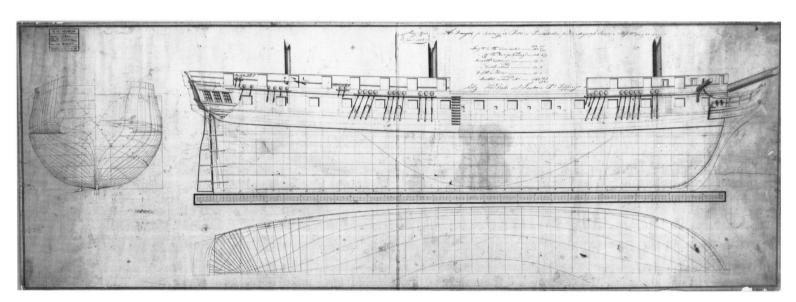

The appearance of the *Leda* class by the end of the war is well represented by this sheer draught dated 22 June 1813 for the *Surprise*. The main visual difference from earlier ships is the eighth carronade port opened abreast the main mast, which was permitted by the rearrangement of the waist and gangways and the abolition of the breastwork. Preliminary workings for the modified post-war class are pencilled on the draught, including the circular stern (which seems to have involved increasing the rake of the sternpost) and a higher head with reduced cutwater. The draught is signed by all three Surveyors - Peake, Tucker and Seppings - and must have been one of the first signed by Seppings, who had just taken up the post of Third Surveyor.
National Maritime Museum Dr7241

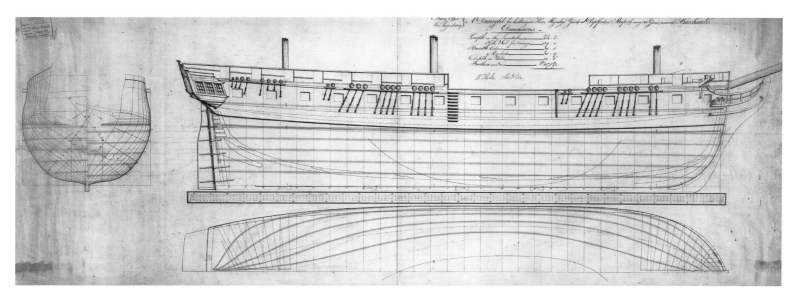

TABLE 3/8: Captured 18pdr ships 1803-1815

Specifications

Name	Length Lower deck ft-ins	Length Keel ft-ins	Breadth extreme ft-ins	Depth in hold ft-ins	Burthen Tons	Armament Quarterdeck	Armament Forecastle

Armed with 26 x 18pdrs on upper deck, rated 36 guns in RN

Name	Lower deck	Keel	Breadth	Depth	Burthen	Quarterdeck	Forecastle
Harfruen	148-7	124-5½	39-4½	11-3	1028	Never armed in RN	
Freya	148-9	124-0	39-4½	10-9	1022	12 x 32 carr	2 x 9, 2 x 32 carr
Iris	148-6	125-0¾	39-5	11-1	1033	12 x 32 carr	2 x 9, 2 x 32 carr
Nyaden	140-7	118-7⅝	38-2½	10-6	827	12 x 32 carr	2 x 9, 2 x 32 carr
Venus	143-4¾	120-10½	38-3¼	10-8¾	943	12 x 32 carr	2 x 9, 2 x 32 carr
Nymphen	140-4	117-10⅛	38-0½	10-3	907	12 x 32 carr	2 x 9, 2 x 32 carr
Furieuse	157-2½	133-2	39-1¼	12-6	1083	12 x 32 carr	2 x 9, 2 x 32 carr
Laurel	152-1	127-1	40-5	12-4	1104	14 x 32 carr	2 x 9, 2 x 32 carr
Essex	138-7	117-2⅞	37-3½	11-9	867	6 x 32 carr	2 x 9

Armed with 28 x 18pdrs on upper deck, rated 38 guns in RN

Name	Lower deck	Keel	Breadth	Depth	Burthen	Quarterdeck	Forecastle
Clorinde	158-6	133-2	40-10	12-2	1181	16 x 32 carr	2 x 12, 2 x 32 carr
Surveillante	151-6	126-11¼	40-3	12-8	1094	12 x 32 carr	2 x 9, 2 x 32 carr
Virtue	151-0	127-11⅝	39-8½	11-10	1073	Never armed in RN	
Fama	145-2¼	119-5¾	39-3	11-9	979	2 x 9, 8 x 32 carr	2 x 9, 2 32 carr
Iphigenia	147-2	122-4¼	40-1	12-0	1046	12 x 32 carr	2 x 9, 2 x 32 carr
Hamadryad	145-0	120-2½	38-10½	11-10½	966	2 x 9, 10 x 32 carr	2 x 9, 2 x 32 carr
Amphitrite	150-1	122-3⅝	39-11	12-6	1036	8 x 9, 4 x 32 carr	2 x 9, 2 x 32 carr
Milan	153-1	128-4⅞	40-1	12-8	1079	12 x 32 carr	2 x 12
Didon	153-5	127-3⅞	40-2½	12-9	1095	6 x 9, 6 x 32 carr	2 x 9, 2 x 32 carr
Volontaire	151-9	127-1 ⅜	40-0½	12-5	1084	8 x 9, 6 x 32 carr	2 x 9, 2 x 32 carr
Belle Poule	151-6	127-7 ⅝	39-11	13-4	1077	14 x 32 carr	2 x 9, 2 x 32 carr
Guerriere	155-9	129-11½	39-9	12-10	1092	14 x 32 carr	2 x 9, 2 x 32 carr
Rhin	151-0	127-2½	39-11¾	13-0	1081	14 x 32 carr	2 x 9, 2 x 32 carr
Immortalité	156-6	130-0⅝	40-7	12-0	1157	14 x 32 carr	2 x 9, 2 x 32 carr
Armide	152-11½	128-1	40-3	12-3½	1104	14 x 32 carr	2 x 9, 2 x 32 carr
Alceste	152-5	128-8⅝	40-0½	12-8	1097	14 x 32 carr	2 x 9, 2 x 32 carr
Gloire	158-0	131-8⅝	40-7½	12-10	1156	14 x 32 carr	2 x 9, 2 x 32 carr
President	158-0	132-4¾	40-6¾	12-2	1147	14 x 32 carr	2 x 9, 2 x 32 carr
Rota	153-6	128-11½	40-1	10-10	1102	14 x 32 carr	2 x 9, 2 x 32 carr

This sheer draught of the *Bacchante*, 38 guns, dated 31 August 1809 represents the appearance of the later ships of the *Lively* class. The main visual difference from earlier ships is the opening of an additional carronade port abreast the main mast, which probably meant extending the quarterdeck forward slightly. However, the new form of hance-less rudder is also noteworthy. By almost any criteria, the ships of this class were the finest British-designed frigates of the French wars. *National Maritime Museum Dr1858*

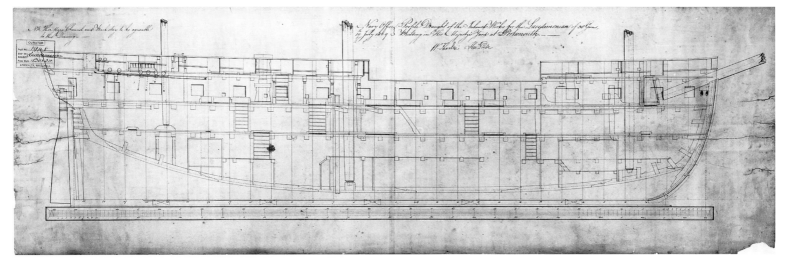

The main difference between the proportions of the *Leda* and the *Lively* classes can be seen in the depth of hold. Dated 19 July 1809, this profile of *Lacedaemonian* reveals how the French-derived *Leda*s had insufficient room beneath the fore platform for the forward magazine (abaft the fore mast), which was consequently sited in a 'hanging' position. This in turn displaced the sailroom from its usual location in British frigates to take up much of the centreline space forward of the main hatch on the midships orlop platform - although not drawn on the profile, it covered the second to fifth beams from forward. There were no major internal rearrangements of this class during the war (compare the design profile reproduced on p76 of *The Heavy Frigate*), but there were detailed improvements to the fitting out of all storerooms from 1808 onwards, as outlined in Chapter 8 below.
National Maritime Museum Dr1948

Name	Length Lower deck ft-ins	Length Keel ft-ins	Breadth extreme ft-ins	Depth in hold ft-ins	Burthen Tons	Armament Quarterdeck	Forecastle
Armed with 28 x 18pdrs on upper deck, rated 38 guns in RN (contd)							
Perlen	156-0	133-0	41-3	12-2	1203	14 x 32 carr	2 x 9, 2 x 32 carr
Piedmontaise	157-5	128-10	39-11	12-8	1092	14 x 32 carr	2 x 9, 2 x 32 carr
Brune	153-9½	126-8½	40-2⅝	12-8	1090	14 x 32 carr	2 x 9, 2 x 32 carr
Alcmene	156-1	129-5¼	40-6½	13-0	1131	14 x 32 carr	2 x 9, 2 x 32 carr
Niemen	154-2½	129-1¾	39-10¾	12-5⅞	1093	14 x 32 carr	2 x 9, 2 x 32 carr
Bourbonnaise	151-6	127-4⅞	39-10⅝	12-2	1078	Never armed in RN	
Nereide	157-0	132-2⅛	40-8½	12-2½	1165	Never armed in RN	
Pomone	152-0	127-6	40-2	12-9	1093	14 x 32 carr	2 x 9, 2 x 32 carr
Junon	154-0	129-5¼	40-3	12-5	1116	14 x 32 carr	2 x 9, 2 x 32 carr
Daedalus	152-9	126-11¼	40-3	12-0½	1094	14 x 24 carr	2 x 6, 2 x 24 carr
Java	152-5½	126-5½	39-11⅜	12-9	1073	14 x 32 carr	2 x 9, 2 x 32 carr
Madagascar	154-6¼	128-11	40-3¾	12-9	1114	14 x 32 carr	2 x 9, 2 x 32 carr
Ambuscade	152-10½	126-7	40-1¾	12-10½	1085	14 x 32 carr	2 x 9, 2 x 32 carr
Chesapeake	151-0	127-5	40-11	13-9	1135	14 x 32 carr	2 x 9, 2 x 32 carr
Weser	152-6	127-2	39-11¾	12-6	1081	4 x 32 carr	1 x 12
Trave	151-5	127-1	39-10¾	12-5½	1076	4 x 32 carr	1 x 12
Seine	152-0	126-11½	39-10½	12-8	1074	14 x 32 carr	2 x 9, 2 x 32 carr
Gloire	154-5	126-10¼	39-9	12-7½	1066	14 x 32 carr	2 x 9, 2 x 32 carr
Modeste	152-2	127-7½	39-10⅞	12-4	1081	14 x 32 carr	2 x 9, 2 x 32 carr
Immortalité	152-8	127-11⅜	39-10	12-7½	1080	14 x 32 carr	2 x 9, 2 x 32 carr
Sultane	151-6	127-0¼	39-9	12-6	1068	14 x 32 carr	2 x 9, 2 x 32 carr
Topaze	151-5⅛	126-8⅛	39-8	12-5½	1060	14 x 32 carr	2 x 9, 2 x 32 carr
Aurora	152-1	127-0⅛	40-0½	12-7½	1083	14 x 32 carr	2 x 9, 2 x 32 carr
Melpomene	152-10½	127-0⅞	40-1¼	12-6¼	1087	Never armed in RN	

The dimensions of the Danish prizes are as given on the draughts. As originally surveyed, some of the figures were a little different: *Freya* 1019 tons, *Iris* 1020 tons, *Nyaden* 908 tons, and *Perlen* 1182 tons.

Freya was fitted with the same number of Gover 24pdrs and 24pdr carr in lieu of the 18pdrs and 32pdrs listed above, in Sep 1809.

Venus, despite scantlings for 18pdrs, was originally armed with long 12pdrs on the upper deck, but in Feb 1814 these were replaced by 32pdr carr.

Essex as a troopship was established with 22 x 32pdr carr, 2 x 9pdr on the upper deck and the superstructure armament as given above.

Surveillante exchanged her main-deck 18pdrs for Gover short 24pdrs from *Narcissus* in Mar 1812.

Hamadryad was reduced to 26 x 18pdrs, 12 x 32pdr carr on the QD and 2 x 32pdr carr and 2 x 9pdrs on the FC by AO of 8 Mar 1810.

Daedalus was originally intended to carry 28 long 12pdrs, but was given Gover short 24pdrs in Oct 1812.

Weser and *Trave* as troopships were established with 12 x 32pdr carr, 1 x 12pdr on the upper deck and the superstructure armament as given above.

Modeste and *Immortalité* were never fitted for RN service, but the above was the proposed rating.

The American Emergency, 1812-1815

FOR TWO decades Britain had sustained a war – and at times single-handed – against most of the developed world. Adding the tiny navy and militia army of the USA to the ranks of her enemies should not have made much difference, except that the British government felt that it was already stretching the country's resources to the limit. The Royal Navy, in both its administrative and fighting branches, was called upon to make an even greater effort. Initially, the conflict was quite rightly resented as an irritating distraction from the principal aim of defeating Napoleon, but in the event the war was to administer a series of shocks to a service that had come to regard victory as the natural order of things.

Much nonsense has been written about this short, unnecessary and strategically indecisive war: indeed it generated a quite disproportionate cloud of rhetoric and chauvinism from its very outbreak.[1] It naturally plays a large and honoured part in the historical mythology of the US Navy, but in British naval history it is usually portrayed as little more than the exception that proves the rule. However, in purely naval terms it had a greater impact on the thinking of those in authority than any event since the invasion scare of 1804-5.

There were many in the top echelons of the Royal Navy in 1812 with personal experience of the War of American Independence, and so the strategies available to both sides would be familiar. It was evident that on land the Americans would attempt to invade Canada, while at sea since the US Navy had no ships of the line it would have to concentrate on commerce warfare. The British were reluctant to divert regular troops from Wellington's increasingly promising campaign in the Peninsula, so inevitably sought to apply a rigorous coastal blockade, with the dual aims of bottling up US warships and stifling American trade at source. A totally effective blockade of such a long and indented coastline as the eastern seaboard was impos-

The convincingly detailed engraving of USS *President* by the well-known French marine artist J-J Baugean, from his *Collection de toute les espèces de bâtiments* published in various editions from 1814 onwards. Because of American conflicts with the Barbary states the big spar-deckers would have been frequent visitors to ports frequented by Baugean, so this portrait may have been done from life. It certainly shows the ship's earlier appearance, with a complete tier of ports along the spar deck. Despite being the largest frigates afloat for nearly two decades, they received surprisingly little attention abroad and scant regard at home – until the War of 1812 changed their status forever.

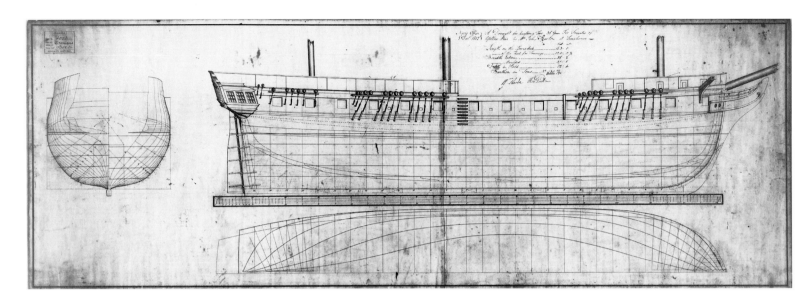

The sheer draught, dated 5 December 1812, for *Granicus* and *Hebrus*, the two *Scamander* class 36s built of yellow pine. At first glance they are virtually identical in layout, details and proportion to the *Apollo/Euryalus* class, and it is difficult to see how 2ft was lopped off the gundeck length of their prototype; in fact, it was done by reducing the space between each gunport by about 2in, and closing up all the fittings to retain their relative positions. The square tuck stern, and a higher, more utilitarian, head with hawse holes between the cheek pieces, are the main distinguishing features of the fir 36s compared with their hardwood model.
National Maritime Museum Dr2073

The profile draught for the *Scamander* class (dated November 1812) also closely resembles the interior arrangements of the *Apollo/Euryalus* class (this is reproduced in *The Heavy Frigate*, p105). In the hold the depth beneath the orlop platform was reduced by a few inches, and this may have occasioned the biggest change: moving the main powder room aft and replacing it with a between-decks 'hanging' magazine, as was usual in the smaller 32-gun frigates.
National Maritime Museum Dr1771

sible, but the main ports and estuaries could be cordoned off. Later small amphibious forces would be added to the British squadrons to allow harassing raids, designed to divert American land forces from the Canadian front, but a desired by-product was the reduction of popular support for the war. The punitive attacks were largely confined to the south, which was regarded as the centre of hawkish support for the war; the blockade strategy applied to the north, on the other hand, was designed to destroy trade already damaged by President Madison's self-imposed embargo, to make an unpopular conflict even less acceptable, and ultimately to encourage the breakaway tendencies of those states. If the Revolutionary War was any precedent then in these circumstances many otherwise idle merchantmen would turn privateers, forcing a greater proportion of the Royal Navy into convoy escort and trade protection duties.

This strategy clearly required the maximum number of cruisers, and as quickly as possible. The Admiralty's first reaction was to increase the number of frigates: a conference with the Comptroller of the Navy Board resulted in a proposal from the Surveyors to build fir frigates, which in earlier crises had 'answered extremely well'. However, the merchant yards had been traditionally reluctant to build warships in softwood, so the Navy Board proposed supplying red pine timber from

Dockyard stores. This ingenious solution offered the additional benefit of saving on scarce and more valuable oak, and was readily accepted by both Admiralty and the merchant yards.[2]

Initially six vessels were requested, and the Navy Board proposed 36-gun ships, now regarded as the baseline frigate rate. The draught was described as an *Euryalus* to the Admiralty, but in fact what was produced was an austerity version, of slightly reduced length and depth. The ends were modified with the usual square tuck stern and a more upright stem, but most main deck space was saved by reducing the overall length of the gun battery by about 3ft. The ship's profile showed a somewhat flatter sheer, and the reduced depth was probably a response to the frequent criticism of over-stiffness in earlier fir ships. However, this latter gave them an advantage of about 1ft mean draught less than the *Euryalus* while the flatter decks carried their midships gunports even higher. The only disadvantage was a reduction in stowage capacity under hatches to 14-16 weeks, as opposed to 24 for their hardwood cousins. The hull form was very similar, and they were fast, handy and weatherly, but were best when stored deep. They eventually came to be known as the *Scamander* class, but not before participating in some of the most confusing renaming and reordering in the history of the Royal Navy.

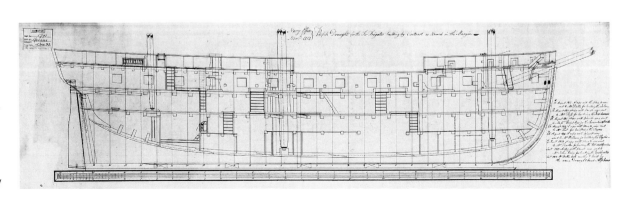

This order actually anticipated the declaration of war by the United States in June, but with President Madison's government becoming increasingly belligerent about the main issues of the rights of neutral shipping and the impressment of seamen from US ships, such an outcome had been predictable for some time.[3] At first the Admiralty's reaction was measured, with the limited programme of 'quick and cheap' fir ships not disturbing the more strategic programme of traditional hardwood ships–another *Leda* class 38 was ordered from Chatham in June, and two more to be constructed of teak at Bombay in October, with a fourth from Pembroke in December; two more 36s were also ordered from Deptford at the end of the year. This was a continuation of the policy developed since Barham's day of maximising Dockyard resources, by cutting frames before laying down new ships so that slipways were empty for the least possible time. There was no expectation that these ships would make a contribution to the immediate crisis, so none was hurried, and only one had been launched by the end of 1814.

In the second half of 1812 a series of victories by American frigates–*Constitution* over the *Guerriere* in August, the *United States* over the *Macedonian* in October, and the *Constitution* again over the *Java* in December–outraged a British public brought up on a diet of almost uninterrupted naval victories against apparently any odds. That the American ships were about 40 per cent larger and carried 50 per cent more firepower was ignored in the journalistic clamour, and public and parliamentary pressure forced the Admiralty to review its North American strategy. The answer was a wider and closer blockade combined with

TABLE 4/1: *Scamander* class 36-gun Fifth Rates

Specification

Armament	Upper deck	Quarterdeck	Forecastle	Guns	Men
DESIGN	26 x 18pdrs	12 x 32pdr carr	2 x 9pdrs, 2 x 32pdr carr	36	274

Designed by Sir William Rule and Henry Peake

	Lower deck feet-inches	Keel feet-inches	Breadth extreme feet-inches	Depth in hold feet-inches	Burthen Tons
DESIGN	143-0	120-0⅝	38-2	12-4	930²³⁄₉₄
AS COMPLETED					
Scamander, ex-*Lively*	143-0½	119-11½	38-5	12-4	941
Eridanus, ex-*Liffey*	143-3	120-0¼	38-5¾	12-4	945
Ister, ex-*Blonde*	143-6	120-1¼	38-5⅝	12-4	945
Orontes, ex-*Brilliant*	142-10½	119-9½	38-4¾	12-4	939
Tagus, ex-*Severn*	143-8	120-7¼	38-5½	12-4	948⁷⁵⁄₉₄
Tigris, ex-*Forth*	143-0	119-11⅞	38-3	12-4	934
Euphrates, ex-*Greyhound*	143-3½	120-2¼	38-5	12-4	943
Granicus	143-0½	119-11½	38-5	12-4	942
Hebrus	143-0	120-1⅛	38-4½	11-11¾	939
Alpheus	143-1¾	120-2⅝	38-6½	12-4	949

Notes: The last three of the class were built of yellow pine, the rest of red pine.

TABLE 4/2: *Scamander* class 36-gun Fifth Rates

Building data

Name	Ordered	Builder	Laid down	Launched	Sailed	Fitted at	Fate
Scamander, ex-*Lively*	4 May 1812	Brindley, Frindsbury	Aug 1812	13 Jul 1813	26 May 1814	Chatham	Sold for BU 22 Jul 1819
Eridanus, ex-*Liffey*	4 May 1812	Ross, Rochester	Aug 1812	1 May 1813	13 Jul 1813	Chatham	Sold 29 Jan 1818
Ister, ex-*Blonde*	4 May 1812	Wallis, Blackwall	Aug 1812	14 Jul 1813	11 Nov 1813	Woolwich	Sold for BU 8 Mar 1819
Orontes, ex-*Brilliant*	4 May 1812	Brindley, Frindsbury	Aug 1812	29 Jun 1813	13 Dec 1813	Chatham	BU Apr 1817
Tagus, ex-*Severn*	4 May 1812	List, Fishbourne	Aug 1812	14 Jul 1813	9 Nov 1813	Portsmouth	Sold for BU 19 Apr 1822
Tigris, ex-*Forth*	4 May 1812	Pelham, Frindsbury	Sep 1812	26 Jun 1813	24 Dec 1813	Chatham	Sold for BU 26 Jun 1818
Euphrates, ex-*Greyhound*	12 Oct 1812	King, Upnor	Jan 1813	8 Nov 1813	24 Sep 1814	Chatham	Sold 29 Jan 1818
Granicus	16 Nov 1812	Barton, Limehouse	Jan 1813	25 Oct 1813	31 Jan 1814	Deptford	Sold 3 Apr 1817
Hebrus	16 Nov 1812	Barton, Limehouse	Jan 1813	13 Sep 1813	18 Dec 1813	Deptford	Sold 3 Apr 1817
Alpheus	7 Dec 1812	Barton, Limehouse	Jan 1813	6 Apr 1814	1 Jul 1814	Woolwich	Sold 10 Sep 1817

Notes: Scamander was initially fitted at Chatham but as completed manifested many defects; she was sent to Sheerness on 24 Dec 1813 and it took five months to make good the shortcomings.

Euphrates was fitted for short-term Ordinary after launch.

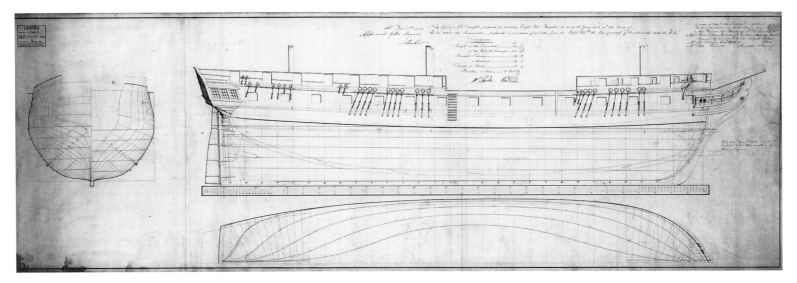

The fir-built *Cydnus* group were virtually indistinguishable from the later ships of the hardwood *Leda* class, although the softwood ships had a square tuck stern. This design sheer is dated 30 November 1812 and was approved by the Board of Admiralty the following day. The only alteration indicated on the draught is post-war: a warrant sent to Portsmouth on 7 August 1815 to increase the angle of the cathead to at least 45 degrees, raise the head, and modify the profile of the cutwater. A pencil note seems to associate this change with *Cydnus*, *Eurotas* and possibly one other.
National Maritime Museum Dr1904a

more rigorous convoying, both of which required more ships as a matter of priority, so softwood construction was again essential.

As it happened, the Navy Board had received a stream of offers from merchant yards following the May round of tendering, and the six fir ships on order had already escalated to seven when an approach by King of Upnor in October resulted in a further contract. On 6 November the Admiralty decided on a major expansion of what might be called the 'war emergency' programme, and asked the Navy Board how many could be built with available timber, allowing the usual contingency reserve for repairs, and so forth. The answer was ten: eight of red pine and two of yellow.[4] This latter was reserved for two more 36s to the existing design, but the red pine was allocated to the construction of eight 38s to a draught modified from the *Leda* class. Peake modified this design only slightly, working on the draught of one of the most recent of the class, at that time called *Scamander* (the *Leda* herself had been lost in 1808), so for a while the fir group of 38s were called the 'modified *Scamander* class' in official correspondence. A Navy Board audit of Dockyard resources in early December found that Deptford and Woolwich could spare enough timber for three more frigates, so the Admiralty ordered two more 38s of red pine and another 36 of yellow pine.

This large programme would provide the numbers

necessary for the overall strategy, but by December 1812 it was clear that simply reinforcing the North America station was not the complete answer. The single-ship defeats forced the Admiralty to consider the quality as well as the quantity of its naval assets, and once it had accepted that action was necessary it moved with speed and vigour – indeed, in retrospect it looks like an over-reaction. It was now admitted that the existing 18pdr designs would never beat one of the big US 24pdr frigates in single combat – a consummation devoutly to be wished, if the pride of the Navy and the nation was to be restored – so more powerful frigates became a high priority. These are considered in more detail in the following chapter, but since they were part of the ongoing softwood programme, they require some mention here. The only acceptable 24pdr design already in existence was the *Endymion*, built as far back as 1797 but highly regarded as a prime sailer. When the Navy Board proposed employing pitch pine for further softwood frigates, the Admiralty ordered two ships, to be rated 40s, to a modified version of the *Endymion* draught on 26 December.

These ships were to be built by the Wigram & Green yard at Blackwall, by far the largest merchant builder on the Thames, who were already contracted for five of the 38s.[5] Knowing the Admiralty's desperation to get the 24pdr ships to sea, in January 1813 Wigrams offered to convert three of the contracts for

The softwood versions of the *Leda* class followed the oak ships in their internal details. This profile, dated January 1813, was probably traced from the *Leda* master, and as a result had to be modified to take in the alterations in the quarterdeck arrangements adopted since 1810 – especially the moving of the ladderway to before the wheel (although a note says the captain of the *Tiber* had the old layout restored, 10 October 1815).
National Maritime Museum Dr1904

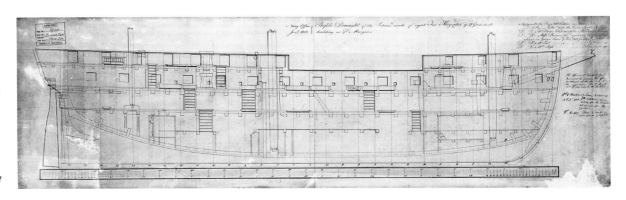

38s to 40s and promised to have three 40s and two 38s afloat by August (indeed, three ships would be launched by June); alternatively, they could build one more 40 plus five 38s. Liking to have their cake and eat it too, the Admiralty ordered the extra 40 but also had two of the 38s converted to 40s.[6] If this were not complicated enough, the Admiralty then decided to rename much of the softwood programme, applying a consistent theme of classical river names to the 36s and 38s. These developments are best summarised as follows:

On 7 July 1812 the first six 36s were registered by the traditional frigate names of *Severn*, *Liffey*, *Forth*, *Blonde*, *Lively* and *Brilliant*; the *Greyhound* was added on 12 October.

On 3 December 1812 the eight 38s were registered as *Cydnus*, *Eurotas*, *Niger*, *Tagus*, *Eridanus*, *Maeander*, *Pactolus* and *Tiber*, the two extra 36s as *Hebrus* and *Granicus*.

On 7 December 1812 the additional 38s were named *Araxes* and *Tanais*, and the 36 *Alphaeus*. The *Greyhound* was renamed *Euphrates*.

On 11 December 1812 the 36s *Blonde* and *Brilliant* were renamed *Ister* and *Orontes* (the original names then being transferred to two hardwood 36s building at Deptford, one of which was eventually completed as a 38 to make the picture even more confusing); *Lively* exchanged names with the hardwood 38 *Scamander* (the ship whose modified draught was used for the softwood versions of the *Leda*; the new 36s were henceforth referred to as the *Scamander* class, and the 38s as the *Cydnus* class).

On 26 December 1812 the two new 40s were named *Liverpool* and *Glasgow*.

On 7 January 1813 contracts for two 38s were convert-

ed to 40s and another 40 was ordered: the 38s *Tagus* and *Eridanus* took the names of the more homely rivers *Severn* and *Liffey* when they became 40s, the classical names being assigned to the 36s that originally bore the native river names; the extra 40 was called *Forth*, the name *Tigris* going to the 36.

TABLE 4/3: Modified *Leda* class 38-gun Fifth Rates

Specification

Armament	Upper deck	Quarterdeck	Forecastle	Guns	Men
DESIGN	28 x 18pdrs	14 x 32pdr carr	2 x 9pdrs, 2 x 32pdr carr	38	300

CHANGES BY AO:
30 Jun 1813   28 x 24pdrs
(*Cydnus* and *Eurotas*)

Modified by Henry Peake

	Lower deck feet-inches	Keel feet-inches	Breadth extreme feet-inches	Depth in hold feet-inches	Burthen Tons
DESIGN	150-1½	125-4⅞	39-11	12-9	1062⁷⁹⁄₉₄
AS COMPLETED					
Cydnus	150-1½	125-2⅜	40-3	12-9	1078⁸²⁄₉₄
Eurotas	150-8¼	125-2½	40-3¼	12-9	1080⁸⁄₉₄
Niger	150-0¾	125-3¾	40-0	12-9	1066⁴⁹⁄₉₄
Maeander	150-1½	125-5	40-01	12-9	1067³⁵⁄₉₄
Pactolus	150-2¾	125-6⅛	39-11½	12-9½	1065⁸⁸⁄₉₄
Tiber	150-1	125-4¾	40-2	12-9	1076¹⁰⁄₉₄
Araxes	150-6¼	125-8½	40-0	12-9½	1069⁸¹⁄₉₄
Tanais	150-8	126-0¼	40-2¾	12-10	1084⁷⁹⁄₉₄

Notes:
The 24pdrs were short guns of Blomefield (*Cydnus*) and Congreve (*Eurotas*) patterns.

TABLE 4/4: Modified *Leda* class 38-gun Fifth Rates

Building data

Name	Ordered	Builder	Laid down	Launched	Sailed	Fitted at	Fate
Cydnus	16 Nov 1812	Wigram, Blackwall	Dec 1812	17 Apr 1813	10 Jun 1813	Woolwich	BU Feb 1816 at Portsmouth
Eurotas	16 Nov 1812	Wigram, Blackwall	Dec 1812	17 Apr 1813	16 Jun 1813	Woolwich	BU Aug 1817
Niger	16 Nov 1812	Wigram, Blackwall	Dec 1812	29 May 1813	22 Jul 1813	Woolwich	BU 1820 at Halifax
Maeander	16 Nov 1812	Picher, Northfleet	Jan 1813	13 Aug 1813	21 Sep 1814	Woolwich	BU Feb 1817
Pactolus	16 Nov 1812	Barnard, Deptford	Jan 1813	14 Aug 1813	30 Oct 1813	Deptford	Sold 29 Jan 1818
Tiber	16 Nov 1812	List, Fishbourne	Feb 1813	10 Nov 1813	29 Sep 1814	Portsmouth	Sold Jan 1820
Araxes	7 Dec 1812	Picher, Northfleet	Jan 1813	13 Sep 1813	18 Sep 1814	Woolwich	Sold 10 Sep 1817
Tanais	7 Dec 1812	Ross, Rochester	Feb 1813	27 Oct 1813	22 Sep 1814	Chatham	Sold 1819

Notes: Built of red pine. Four vessels were fitted temporarily for Ordinary after launch: *Maeander* Dec 1813 – Jul 1814; *Tiber* 23 Nov 1813 – Jul 1814; *Araxes* 9 Dec 1813 – Apr 1814; *Tanais* Nov 1813 – 22 Sep 1814.

At this point there were twenty fir 36s and 38s under construction, plus five 40s, so the sheer scale of the programme was likely to cause problems. Even as the contracts were let the Navy Board was instructed to ensure that they were brought forward for fitting and manning in succession and not all at once.[7] At the same time, however, the Admiralty was calling for all dispatch in their construction, so there was a potential contradiction in their instructions. By May 1813 it was necessary to clarify the priorities, top of which were the 24pdr ships; the need for 18pdr ships was not deemed so urgent, although the 38s were built more quickly than the 36s which had been ordered earlier. However, even with the launch dates staggered, it proved far easier to build the hulls than to fit them out. Five of the 38s and one 36 were temporarily sent into Ordinary, and many of the others took months rather than the usual weeks to complete (see Table 4/2).

Besides providing more frigates, the Admiralty had to find ways of making its ships more effective in combat. The quickest form of improvement was to increase the complement of frigates, which had been cut to what many captains regarded as dangerously low numbers by order of 24 June 1806: 284 for 38s and 274 for 36s, although special application allowed many 38s a total of 300. On 26 January 1813 this was revised as follows, the larger ships being specified by name:

38s – 320 (including 5 extra Marines)
18pdr 36s – 284
18pdr 32s – 270

The 24pdr 40-gun ships, including those building, were increased from 340 to 350 men.

While this was to be welcomed in general terms, it highlighted what was probably the Royal Navy's greatest problem throughout the Napoleonic War, namely the desperate shortage of manpower. Generally speaking, the Navy had more ships than it could send to sea, and for most classes there were usually seaworthy examples laid up in Ordinary. Nevertheless, the fleet expanded inexorably, and finding both the numbers and the skills necessary to crew the ships became increasingly difficult. This resulted in establishments cut to the bone for each rate, and even then complements were rarely up to strength. Furthermore, there was the related and even more important matter of the dilution of skill: the Navy accepted more and more men with little or no experience of the sea, poor physique, or no real motivation to serve the British flag (foreigners, criminals or the politically disaffected). In many warships, and particularly the smaller rates with few officers, the proportion of skilled seamen was eroded to the point where training the new drafts became a major burden. Seamanship was given priority, since the safety of the ship depended on it, but gunnery and fighting skills were often ignored or simply forgotten under the routine operational pressures.

Thus, while it made sense to increase the complements of frigates, the question of where suitable men were to be found was not addressed; in late 1813 a number of the new fir ships went straight into Ordinary, albeit temporarily, because crews could not be found for them.[8]

The Admiralty also sought to improve the fighting capacities of existing ships. From January 1813 there was a renewed interest in lightweight 24pdrs, which by replacing their main deck 18pdrs might give standard frigates some chance against the big American spar-deckers. The Gover pattern gun had seen limited service since the 1790s, but was not regarded as sufficiently powerful for a main battery, since it could not fire double-shotted with safety. However, new designs by Congreve and Blomefield were rapidly tested and were given sea trials before the end of the year in the frigates *Eurotas* and *Cydnus* (see Chapter 10 for further details). Gunnery itself was given higher priority, a number of instructions going out to commanding officers reinforcing the standing orders 'to exercise their Crews at the Great Guns and in the use of small arms as frequently as the importance of this part of their Duty requires . . .'.[9] Not that the Admiralty believed any amount of practice would allow an 18pdr frigate to defeat one of the American spar-deckers, and until the new 24pdr-armed ships could arrive on station British frigates were prohibited from single-combat with them.[10] This was greeted with dismay at the time, and has often been misrepresented since: it did not prevent *any* single-ship action, but specifically applied to 'the larger Class of American Ships'; and even these might be attacked by any force 'with a reasonable hope of success'. Defensive, it certainly was, but not defeatist as so often claimed.

The size and speed of the 1812-13 softwood programme is an impressive indicator of the organisational powers of the Royal Navy's administration, and the capacity of Britain's industrialised shipbuilding, even after two decades of war. In all, thirty-three new frigates were built in 1813 and a further thirteen repaired ships added to the fleet. It was known that the fir frigates would not last long, but the rapid end of the European war in the spring of 1814 cast instant doubts on the wisdom of the investment. As an anti-American measure, it was easy for critics to point to the need for better ships (and larger, better trained crews) rather than for more hulls, but the Navy's frigate force was ageing and had the war gone on even a couple more years the softwood ships would have been an invaluable stop-gap.

However, the North American timber used proved of even shorter lifespan than the Baltic timbers used in earlier fir programmes (calculated at eight years), and by 1816 Parliament was asking questions about the money spent on these ships. The costs of *Cydnus* (which had already been broken up) and *Eurotas* (which was about to be), were calculated as follows:[11]

	Cydnus	*Eurotas*
	£	£
Hull (fir supplied @ £12 per load) and copper	29,708	29,666
Masts and yards	1618	1559
Rigging and stores	9775	9727
Total	41,101	40,952

This made them about 10 per cent more expensive than the previous round of contract-built hardwood ships, which could expect a life of eight years before Dockyard attention and at least twice that with some further expenditure. By contrast the red pine ships lasted an average of four and a half years and the yellow pine ships one year less before being sold or broken up. It is scarcely surprising that post-war the Admiralty refused to consider fir as a shipbuilding timber.

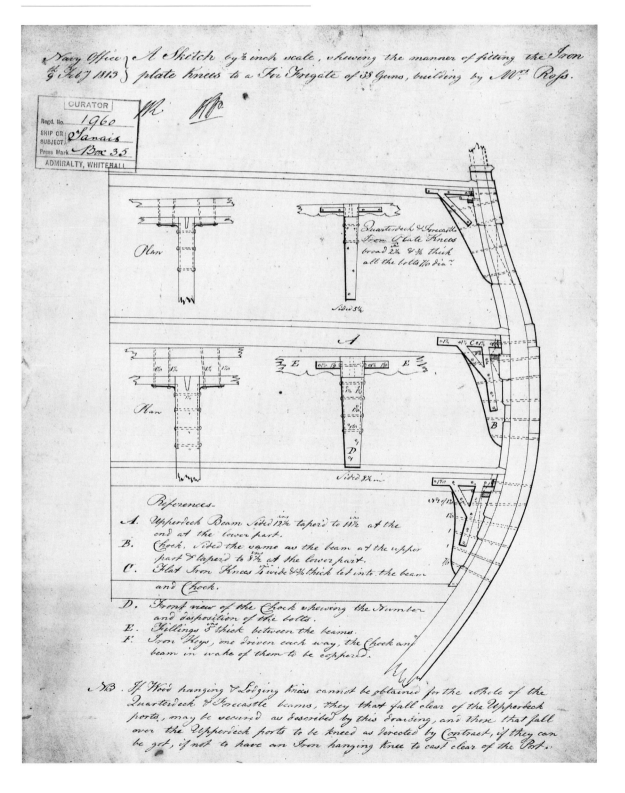

By 1812 the shortage of grown knees had driven the Navy Board to adopt a number of alternative fastening schemes, of which the most widely used was a combination of wooden chocks and Roberts's plate knees. The details of the system as applied to the fir-built 38 *Tanais* are shown in this drawing of 9 February 1813. There was great pressure to complete these ships as quickly as possible, so the builders were allowed some flexibility in the interpretation of the contract specification if the supply situation demanded it. A note at the bottom of this drawing, for example, concedes: 'If wood hanging & lodging knees cannot be obtained for the whole of the quarterdeck & forecastle beams, they that fall clear of the upperdeck ports, may be secured as described by this drawing, and those that fall over the upperdeck ports to be kneed as directed by contract, if they can be got, if not to have an iron hanging knee cast clear of the port.'
National Maritime Museum Dr1960

CHAPTER FIVE

Super Frigates

The draught of 6 September 1794 produced in response to an Admiralty Order for the cutting down of the *Indefatigable*. The ticked line shows her original profile as a 64-gun ship; the main difference between her new configuration and a purpose-built frigate is the poop platform occasioned by retaining the captain's original accommodation on the quarterdeck rather than moving it down to the upper deck. The draught may not represent the ship as finally fitted out: a note confirms the order to shorten the poop to the mizzen as successfully requested by Pellew, but his correspondence with the Admiralty twice mentions fourteen quarterdeck ports (as opposed to twelve shown on the draught), and he was eventually allowed two additional 12pdrs for the 'spare' quarterdeck ports. By the time she captured *Virginie* she was reported to carry eighteen 42pdr carronades and two long 12s on the upperworks, so must have had a total of twenty ports, which probably meant seven a side on the quarterdeck.
National Maritime Museum: Dr6199

THE VICTORIES of the big American spar-decked frigates provoked the Admiralty into considering more powerful classes than the 18pdr-armed 38 that had been the standard heavy frigate since its introduction in 1778. However, in 1812 the Royal Navy was not entirely devoid of larger frigates, nor was a 24pdr main battery a novel idea. Apart from a few French and Dutch prizes, a handful of more powerful ships had been built or converted during the 1790s, but none since. Therefore, the Admiralty's first reaction to the American emergency was to cast its collective mind back to that period, so it is necessary to examine these earlier developments in order to explain the precedents the administration was drawing upon.

THE RASÉE 44-GUN SHIPS

At the beginning of the French War in 1793, there were persistent rumours about heavily armed 'frigates' cut down from battleships and called in French *rasées*. As a stiffener to groups of conventional frigates, they were a potent threat, particularly at a time when the French were expected to follow a strategy of squadronal attacks on trade. They shared many of the characteristics of twentieth-century surface raiders, not least being the willingness of their enemies to exaggerate both their capabilities and their achievements: there were many apparent sightings, but not one was ever brought to battle, so their qualities remained mysterious. The reality was less fearsome. There were only five of them – *Flibustier*, *Brave*, *Brutus*, *Hydre* and *Scévola* – all converted from old, small 74s, possibly as a cure for the problems of decrepitude and poor stability rather than as an attempt at a potent new commerce raider. Cutting them down simply reversed the stabili-

ty problem, making them too stiff and inclined to roll their masts out, so they actually saw little sea-time. *Scévola* foundered during the Irish expedition in 1796, and the rest had been taken out of service by 1797.

They were powerfully armed, probably with twenty-eight 24pdrs on the main deck, eighteen 12pdrs and four brass 36pdr *obusiers* (the early French version of a carronade) and a complement of 500 men, so they were a potential menace, and for a while some of the frigate squadrons in home waters had a two-decker attached for protection from such brutes.[1] The danger was perfectly illustrated in June 1794 when Sir James Saumarez's Channel Island squadron was attacked by four French frigates, including the *rasées Brutus* and *Scévola*. Only Saumarez's brilliant fighting retreat into Guernsey saved his ships, and the following month the Admiralty decided that the Royal Navy must have similar *rasées*.

Another factor in the decision was the capture of the frigate *Pomone* in the previous April by Sir John Borlase Warren's squadron. Although a conventional frigate in layout, *Pomone* was very large by the standards of the day and armed on the main deck with twenty-six 24pdrs. Uncharacteristically for an officer trying to 'sell' his prize to the Navy, Warren underestimated the size of the ship – by 150 tons – but was probably right in describing her as 'supposed to be the finest frigate they had.'[2] At that time there were three other 24pdr frigates in the French navy, the *Résistance* and *Vengeance* of about the same size, and the even larger *Forte*, all of which would eventually fall into British hands by courtesy of nominally inferior frigates.

However, this could not have been anticipated by the Admiralty who proceeded as a stop-gap measure to instruct the Navy Board to select four of the best-sail-

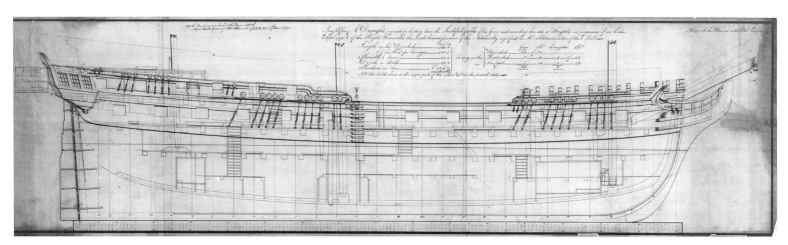

ing 64-gun ships, in good repair, to be cut down to frigates.[3] The initial choice fell on *Anson*, *Magnanime*, *Indefatigable* and *Director*, but the last had just been lent to the Customs for use as a lazaretto in Stangate Creek and in the absence of another readily available hull, the programme was reduced to three ships. They were not all identical, the first two being to one Williams' design, with the other two from Slade draughts of different classes. Nevertheless, the Navy Board used the same basic cutting-down draught, in effect removing the old quarterdeck and forecastle, while transforming the upper deck into a frigate-style long quarterdeck with gangways, but because the great cabin was at this level the quarterdeck required a poop or roundhouse. The masts and spars were reduced to those of a 50-gun ship, and the original proposal was to retain the twenty-six lower deck 24pdrs, while adding twelve 12pdrs to the upperworks to rate as a 38-gun ship. With reduced loading, the ships would draw about 1ft 6in less, giving them a midship gunport freeboard of 6ft 4in, which although not outstanding was quite respectable for a frigate, and much more acceptable than the original figure, which was less than 5ft.

The ships were converted at Chatham (*Anson*), Plymouth (*Magnanime*) and Portsmouth (*Indefatigable*) taking about five months. *Magnanime* seems to have been in a poorer structural state than the other two, costing around twice as much.[4] During the course of the work, there were second thoughts about their armament, since the carronade revolution was in full swing, so on 12 August the first two had four 42pdrs added to their quarterdecks and two more on the forecastle; *Indefatigable*, a little behind in the conversion work, followed suit in December, and thereafter they were rated as 44-gun ships.

Anson, under Philip Durham's command, was the first to sea, being allocated to Borlase Warren's highly active – and very successful – frigate squadron based at Falmouth.[5] At various times the squadron included many of the great frigate captains – Sidney Smith, Sir Richard Strachan, Richard Goodwin Keats and Sir Edward Pellew – and, since the two were closely linked, some of the finest frigates in the Navy, with Warren now flying his broad pendant in the recommissioned *Pomone*. As a result of his exploits in the *Arethusa*, Pellew had been appointed to *Indefatigable*,

but had not yet taken up his command when *Anson* arrived at Falmouth 'after a boisterous passage' in January 1795. A consummate seaman, Pellew was keenly interested in the probable qualities of his new ship, and made 'particular enquiry' of Durham about *Anson*'s 'behaviour at sea, and of her capacity in carrying her masts and sails.' Having discovered that the ship rolled heavily, and that all her officers were convinced that she was under-masted, Pellew wrote to the Admiralty to ask that *Indefatigable* retain the full spar plan of a 64-gun ship.[6]

Even from Falmouth Pellew was attempting to influence the details of *Indefatigable*'s fitting out. In the previous December, worried about potential windage, he had requested the removal of the poop or, failing that, a shortened version. An earlier *rasée* design, the cut-down 44s *Adventure* and *Sapphire* of 1756-8, had no poop, the cabin being fitted on the upper deck with sloop-like

TABLE 5/1: *Rasée* 64-gun ships, 38-gun then 44-gun Fifth Rates

Specification

Armament	Upper deck	Quarterdeck	Forecastle	Guns	Men
DESIGN	26 x 24pdrs	8 x 12pdrs	4 x 12pdrs	38	
ADDITIONS BY AO:					
12 Aug 1794 (*M & A*)		4 x 42pdr carr	2 x 42pdr carr	44	310
5 Dec 1794 (*Ind*)		4 x 42pdr carr	2 x 42pdr carr	44	310
17 Feb 1795 (*Ind* only)		extra 2 x 12pdrs			

Designed by Sir John Williams (*Magnanime* and *Anson*) and Sir Thomas Slade (*Indefatigable*)

	Lower deck feet-inches	Keel feet-inches	Breadth extreme feet-inches	Depth in hold feet-inches	Burthen Tons
DESIGN (*M & A*)	159-6	131-0	44-4	19-0	1369
DESIGN (*Ind*)	160-0	131-8	44-4	18-0	1376
AS CUT DOWN					
Magnanime	159-6	131-0	44-4	12-3	1370
Anson	159-6	130-11⅛	44-5¼	12-3	1375
Indefatigable	160-1½	131-10½	44-5	12-3	1384

Notes: Magnanime was reduced to 26 x 32pdr carr, 6 x 32pdr carr and 4 x 32pdr carr in Aug 1807 to act as a guardship for the Clyde.

TABLE 5/2: *Rasée* 64-gun ships, 38-gun then 44-gun Fifth Rates

Building data

Name	Launched	Converted at	Started	Completed	Sailed	Fitted at	Fate
Magnanime	14 Oct 1780	Plymouth Dyd	30 Jun 1794	8 Nov 1794	2 Feb 1795	Plymouth	BU Jul 1813
Anson	4 Jan 1781	Chatham Dyd	28 Jul 1794	8 Oct 1794	6 Dec 1794	Chatham	Wrecked in Mounts Bay 29 Dec 1807
Indefatigable	Jul 1784	Portsmouth Dyd	11 Sep 1794	29 Nov 1794	16 Feb 1795	Portsmouth	BU Aug 1816

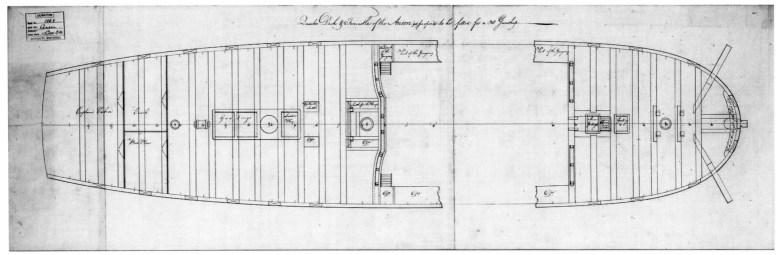

The upperworks of the 1794
*rasée*s followed the conventional
frigate layout of the time, with
separate quarterdeck and
forecastle, the small fixed parts of
the gangways forming a landing
for the ladders leading up from
the waist, and the rest of the
gangways being moveable. Note
that the captain's accommodation
was erected on the quarterdeck
aft of the mizzen. This plan
refers to the *Anson*, the first of
the *rasée*s to complete.
National Maritime Museum Dr1868

quarter badges instead of galleries. However, these ships had taken two years to convert, and the Navy Board was in no mood to waste time and money on a more elaborate reconstruction than was absolutely necessary, undertaking only to shorten the poop so as to clear the mizzen. Pellew also failed in his bid to transfer from *Arethusa* to *Indefatigable* fourteen 32pdr carronades, 'they having been given me by their Lordships' indulgence in that ship'. The Admiralty also felt that it was too soon to jump to conclusions about the masting of the ships and Pellew was again refused.[7]

He was convinced, however, that 'the cut-down 64-gun ships are likely to be very uneasy so as to endanger their masts from excessive rolling', and since he could not have an enlarged rig, he suggested a number of ways of at least ameliorating the problem. He wanted to fill all fourteen of the quarterdeck ports with the ship's original 18pdrs; the deck was built to take that weight and the ports were still fitted for the guns, which were themselves still at Portsmouth. He also requested reduced ballast, and that carried as high in the hold as possible, suggesting a trim of 19ft aft and 17ft forward, giving a full extra foot of freeboard to the midships port. The Navy Board was not disposed to hold up the ship for one Post Captain's notions, so apart from reducing the ballast (which could be done without cost or delay), the other 'improvements' were denied. Perhaps as a sop, he was allowed an extra pair of 12pdrs for the spare quarterdeck ports.[8]

However, Pellew was rapidly proved right by events. The second of the type to sail, *Magnanime*, was sent to Rear-Admiral Kingsmill's Irish squadron which, operating in the rough waters of the western approaches, was second in priority only to the Biscay squadrons when it came to the allocation of big frigates. To Kingsmill's disgust, his powerful new frigate was disabled aloft during her first operational cruise, barely two weeks after her arrival on station. Pellew's case was further reinforced by the continued poor performance of *Anson* under her existing spar plan. Durham's correspondence during the early months of 1795 contains

some embarrassing instances of his ship's misbehaviour: on 18 February, for example, he reported that 'from labouring so very hard in a sea', she had carried away her main topmast and its yard, sprung the fore topmast and the fore and main crosstrees, and carried away some of her chain and futtock plates.[9] Even *Indefatigable* reported a damaged main mast in the short voyage down Channel to join Warren at Falmouth.

This was enough evidence for the Admiralty and in March it was decided to re-rig the *rasée*s with the masts and spars of a 64, except shortened at the heels of the lower masts so that the drop of the courses would be appropriate for their cut-down upperworks. The ships were on important duties, so they could not be easily spared, and the masts were ordered to be made in advance to keep the refit time down to days rather than weeks. *Indefatigable* was ordered in first on 27 March, but discovering that the spars would not be ready for a fortnight, Pellew stayed at sea in the interim; he finally reported the ship refitted and ready for sea on 25 April. The other two had to wait longer, but both were refitted by the end of the year.[10]

Unfortunately, there is evidence that even the enlarged spar-plan never entirely solved the problem. *Anson* certainly retained a reputation as a poor heavy-weather ship, and continued all too frequently to roll her spars out. Durham's first experience with the enlarged rig during the December 1795 expedition to Quiberon was mortifying: the ship split a number of sails, regularly missed stays, and was not weatherly enough to make the port he was ordered to, crowning the indignity by going aground off Noirmoutier.[11] In the October 1798 running battle with Bompart's squadron off Ireland, *Anson*'s self-inflicted damage was more serious than anything attributable to the enemy.

These characteristics restricted the suitable employment for the ship, making the close-blockade duties so often assigned to the big frigates decidedly dangerous, and in the case of the *Anson* ultimately fatal. In 1807 she was stationed off the notorious Black Rocks, the advanced position for the blockade of Brest.

Her rendezvous in case of necessity, was Falmouth, where she had frequently taken refuge in tempestuous weather. Her commander had often regretted that she was appointed to such a station, being a bad sea boat... She rolled very deep, and was by no means calculated for such a station. She was, however, as Captain Lydiard had frequently expressed, a famous fine weather man of war; and her weight of metal, in his mind, still kept her equal to an enemy of her original class [*ie* a 64].[12]

In sheltering from a gale in December 1807 she parted her cables and was wrecked.

In the absence of any surviving Sailing Quality reports for these ships, it is impossible to analyse their characteristics in detail, but they clearly suffered the same problem as their French counterparts, namely that they were too stiff, making them heavy and rapid rollers. This is why Pellew's suggested remedies involved extra weight above the centre of gravity and less below, in an attempt to reduce the excessive metacentric height. What evidence there is suggests that they were not particularly fast or weatherly, the best quoted speed being 12½ knots before the wind in the case of *Indefatigable*.[13] That Pellew did not complain is possibly a reflection of his superb seamanship, rather than any outstanding qualities in the ship, but in 1798 he successfully applied to have the main and mizzen masts moved aft. However, it has to be said that like many an improvised design they did not perform perfectly, but they were available when they were needed. Their importance, especially in the first few years of their new careers, can be gauged by how much action they saw – usually in home waters and providing a heavier punch in the cruiser squadrons than the standard 18pdr ships could offer. Their finest hour – and certainly their best known exploit – was *Indefatigable* hounding to destruction the 74-gun *Droits de l'Homme* in a January gale in 1797: although Pellew was an outstanding officer, he was not foolhardy, and it is difficult to see him pressing the action if he had not commanded such a powerful ship.

SUPER FRIGATES OF THE 1790S

The *rasées* of 1794 were a rapid and interim response to the perceived threat of French 24pdr frigates, but the Admiralty also planned a longer-term solution. In January 1795 the Navy Board were informed of the new construction requirements for the year, which included one '40-gun ship' to be built within fifteen months, and another inside eighteen, the first indication of an Admiralty interest in a new type of frigate. Six frigates were to be built of fir and, with a further seven oak ships, became a firm programme in April, along with seven 74s, and all were to be large for their class; an eighth oak frigate was added in August as a result of an offer from a merchant builder, and at that point the draughts were specified.[14] The principle behind the programme was to contrast hull forms derived from French prizes with similar sized ships by the Surveyors, and three of the vessels were to be larger than standard 38s. There were to be two 24pdr-armed 40s, one to the lines of the *Pomone* and the other by Henslow's draught, while as a contrasting approach Rule undertook a large 18pdr design with thirty guns on the main deck instead of the usual twenty-eight. These ships became the *Endymion*, *Cambrian* and *Acasta* respectively, and all entered service during the first half of 1797.

There was a belated addition to this group, in the form a French-derived equivalent of *Acasta*. However, this ship was not to be based on a prize, but was the original work of a French designer, Jean-Louis Barrallier. A dockyard official at Toulon, he had been a leading figure in the royalist *coup* that had turned the

TABLE 5/3: *Endymion* class 40-gun Fifth Rate

Specification

Armament	Upper deck	Quarterdeck	Forecastle	Guns	Men
DESIGN	26 x 24pdrs	14 x 32pdr carr	2 x 9pdrs, 4 x 32pdr carr	40	320
CHANGES BY AO:					
10 Oct 1800		32pdr carr for all QD&FC gunports			
Nov 1803	26 x 18pdrs				
17 May 1813	26 x 24pdrs	16 x 32pdr carr	As design		

Lines of the *Pomone* [French prize, 1794]

	Lower deck feet-inches	Keel feet-inches	Breadth extreme feet-inches	Depth in hold feet-inches	Burthen Tons
DESIGN	159-2⅜	132-4¼	41-11⅜	12-4	1238⁶⁷⁄₉₄
AS COMPLETED					
Endymion	159-3⅜	132-3	42-7⅜	12-4	1277

TABLE 5/4: *Endymion* class 40-gun Fifth Rate

Building data

Name	Ordered	Builder	Laid down	Launched	Sailed	Fitted at	Fate
Endymion	30 Apr 1795	Randall, Rotherhithe	Nov 1795	29 Mar 1797	12 Jun 1797	Deptford	Hulk 1860; BU Aug 1868

port over to Lord Hood in 1793, and had taken refuge in Britain when it fell again to the republicans. Although not actually a naval architect by profession, French technical training was highly regarded (and possibly overvalued) by the Admiralty, and Barrallier was appointed 'Second Assistant to the Surveyors'. One of Barrallier's draughts for a 74-gun ship was approved without Navy Board opposition in September 1795, but

a proposed design for a frigate requested by the Admiralty in April 1796 was apparently ignored. It was not until February 1797 that the Admiralty adopted one of his frigates – and then possibly only for reasons of administrative harmony.[15]

Admiralty favour towards an outsider, and a junior one at that, provoked professional jealousy within the Navy Board, and Barrallier himself was not easy to get

The draught of the captured French *Pomone* as taken off at Portsmouth, 11 July 1794. As the first 24pdr-armed frigate captured by the Royal Navy, she was an influential vessel, being used as the model for the highly successful British-built *Endymion*. Her French origins are a little mysterious, being a one-off designed not by one of the French navy's corps of naval constructors but an aristocratic amateur and retired naval officer, Baron Bombelle. Despite her extraordinary size and only twenty-six main-deck gunports, she seems to have been designed for 12pdrs, and

later 18pdrs, according to French official records. However, she was definitely armed with 24pdrs when taken, and continued to carry that calibre when refitted for British service. The refit included the removal of the small poop, and the installation of more serviceable storerooms on the orlop platforms, but she proved too lightly built to stand up to the near-continuous cruises of a Royal Navy frigate squadron. She was reduced to an 18pdr 38 in 1799 and broken up in 1802. *National Maritime Museum Dr6235*

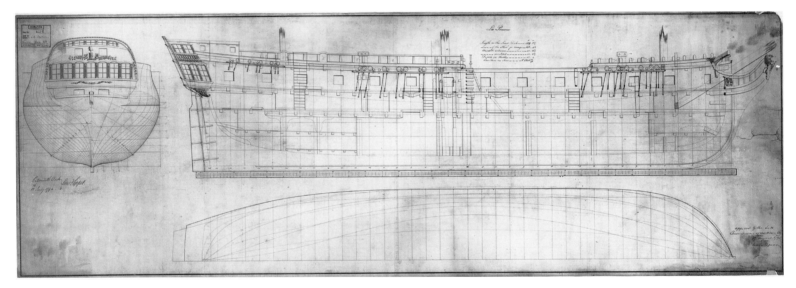

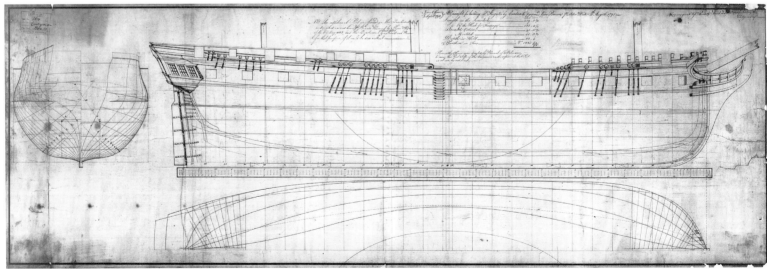

The design sheer draught of the *Endymion*, dated 2 September 1795. The hull form follows the *Pomone* closely, and circumstantial evidence suggests that the principal scantlings also imitated those in the French ship. However, the *Endymion* was fastened according to British practice, with hanging and lodging knees, rather than a thickened clamp. As can be seen, all aspects of external

appearance, including head, quarter galleries and solid barricades, also conform to British notions of elegance. Annotations on the draught refer to an extra quarterdeck port ordered in May 1813, and the raising of the main-deck ports when repaired in February 1820. *National Maritime Museum Dr1814*

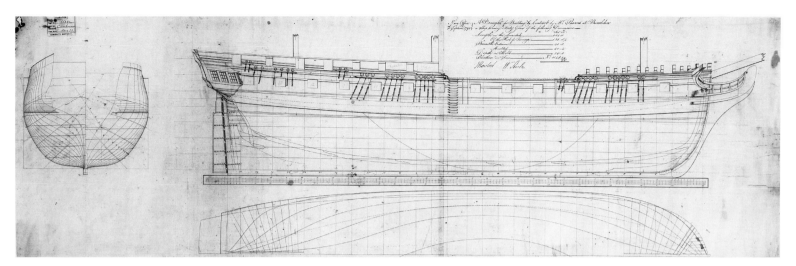

along with. He never bothered to master English – according to William Dillon, as late as 1813 he could barely make himself understood in the language of his adopted country – and, in any case, Barrallier's highly theoretical ideas were all Greek to his pragmatic colleagues. Judging by his dealings with Dillon, he was dogmatic and impatient of criticism, although Dillon also points out the prejudice against his ideas prevalent in the Dockyard. Furthermore, special arrangements had to be made to give the Frenchman a place over the heads of career shipwrights, including the administrative fiction that he had been brought up a Protestant, in order to evade legislation restricting the government employment of Catholics. At the end of 1796 the Admiralty hit on an ingenious way of soothing these antagonisms without losing the services of the *émigré*: he was sent to oversee the construction of ships as far from London as possible.

The Admiralty was keen to open up new shipbuilding resources, and when Jacobs of Milford in Pembrokeshire offered to build a 74, a frigate and a sloop, the Navy Board considered these within his capacity. The Admiralty gave instructions to proceed to contract for all three vessels, of which Barrallier was to be the overseer. It may be that the Admiralty wished to sweeten his banishment, or that they were genuinely 'desirous to have tried' his design principles – as they told the Navy Board – but they certainly allowed the Frenchman to build each to his own design, with what amounted to *carte blanche* as regards dimensions.

However, he was probably given some outline brief. In the case of the frigate, the Navy Board seems to have proposed a repeat *Acasta* before they were told that Barrallier's own draught would be used. As a result his design looks like a typically French interpretation of the same requirements – a main battery of thirty 18pdrs carried in a longer and more lightly built hull. In the event, the Navy Board were too optimistic about Jacobs' capabilities, and when his business failed with the ships unfinished, they had to be completed at the Government's expense, which from 1801 involved

renting land belonging to a Mr Greville at £250 per annum. In time this lead to the establishment of the Pembroke Dockyard, but changing the site and other delays meant that the frigate did not enter service until 1806, as the *Lavinia*.[16]

These very big frigates did not give an entirely satisfactory return on the substantial investment in their construction, although they were highly desirable commands. For the 18pdr ships, one extra main deck gun per broadside was not much of an improvement over a standard 38 at the cost of 10 per cent more tonnage. In the case of *Acasta*, building and fitting costs were about 13 per cent higher than those of a contemporary 38, and she was no longer than the *Lively* class 38s so the

The first British attempt to design a 24pdr frigate from scratch produced the *Cambrian*, whose lines were draughted by Henslow (the sheer shown here is dated 8 September 1795). In both midship section and general proportions, the ship was virtually scaled up from Henslow's earlier frigate designs. Although well built, *Cambrian* was too small for the original weight of metal and was better when reduced to 18pdrs. The addition of a bridle port is sketched under the cathead.
National Maritime Museum Dr1828a

TABLE 5/5: *Cambrian* class 40-gun Fifth Rate

Specification

Armament	Upper deck	Quarterdeck	Forecastle	Guns	Men
DESIGN	28 x 24pdrs	8 x 9pdrs	4 x 9pdrs	40	320
CHANGES BY AO:					
9 May 1797 added		6 x 32pdr carr	2 x 32pdr carr		
12 Apr 1799	lighter 24pdrs	6 x 9pdrs replaced by 32pdr carr			
1805	28 x 18pdrs				
13 May 1807	28 x 18pdrs	2 x 9pdrs, 12 x 32pdr carr	2 x 9pdrs, 2 x 32pdr carr		

Designed by Sir John Henslow

	Lower deck feet-inches	Keel feet-inches	Breadth extreme feet-inches	Depth in hold feet-inches	Burthen Tons
DESIGN	154-0	128-5¼	41-0	14-0	1148 ³⁹⁄₉₄
AS COMPLETED					
Cambrian	154-0	128-3½	41-3	14-0	1160

Notes: The main armament was soon found to stress the ship's hull and was first reduced to lighter 9ft 24pdrs, with some long 9s replaced by carronades; and then at an unspecified time in 1805 while on the Halifax station the ship was re-armed with 18pdrs, a mixture of five 9ft guns and the rest of the standard 8ft pattern.

TABLE 5/6: *Cambrian* class 40-gun Fifth Rate

Building data

Name	Ordered	Builder	Laid down	Launched	Sailed	Fitted at	Fate
Cambrian	30 Apr 1795	Parsons, Bursledon	Sep 1795	13 Feb 1797	16 Jun 1797	Portsmouth	Wrecked off Grabusa 31 Jan 1828

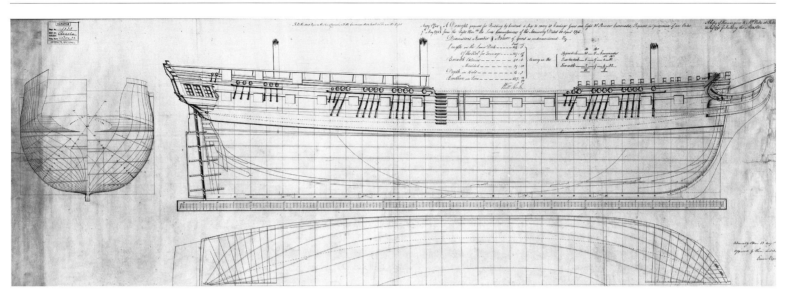

One of a pair of very large 18pdr frigate designs of the mid-1790s, *Acasta* was rated as a 40-gun ship. These 18pdr 40s were distinguished by fifteen gunports a side on the main deck; nevertheless, this sheer draught of 7 May 1795 shows modifications to the headrails and catheads to work in an extra (bridle) port right forward (very much a concern of the time). *National Maritime Museum Dr1835*

TABLE 5/7: *Acasta* class 40-gun Fifth Rate

Specification

Armament	Upper deck	Quarterdeck	Forecastle	Guns	Men
DESIGN	30 x 18pdrs	8 x 9pdrs, 4 x 32pdr carr	2 x 9pdrs, 4 x 32pdr carr	40	320

Designed by Sir William Rule

	Lower deck feet-inches	Keel feet-inches	Breadth extreme feet-inches	Depth in hold feet-inches	Burthen Tons
DESIGN AS COMPLETED	154-0	129-0¼	40-6	14-3	1127²²⁄₉₄
Acasta	154-0	128-11	40-9½	14-3	1143

Notes: The original 8ft 18pdrs were replaced by 9ft guns by AO 3 May 1797.

additional port tended to crowd her quarters; nor was she outstanding under sail. *Lavinia* did not generate quite the same level of criticism as Barrallier's other ships,[17] and she was big enough to carry fifteen ports with comfort; but as a result of a long, shallow hull, she was not very weatherly, rather unhandy, and so lightly built she strained her topsides and decks.

The 24pdr frigates were generally rather better performers under sail, but were even more vulnerable to structural problems. The 50½cwt 24pdr was a huge step up from the standard 38cwt 18pdr, and placed commensurate stresses on the ship's fabric. Being lightly built in the usual French manner, it is not surprising that *Pomone* stood in need of a Great Repair after five years of very strenuous British service. Unfortunately, this could not be provided immediately, and the ship was reduced to 18pdr guns and the masting of a 38-gun frigate in 1799; but she was not thought worth repairing during the Peace of Amiens and was taken to pieces in 1802. However, even the *Cambrian*, built to traditionally hefty British scantlings, could not carry her 24pdrs for long, first exchanging them for shorter 48cwt guns and finally 18pdrs; of course, she did carry two more guns on a deck 5ft shorter than *Pomone*, so the problem could have been anticipated. A similar reduction also applied to *Endymion*, a larger hull form of French design and scantlings but fastened to British standards; but in this case the move seems to have been designed to save unnecessary wear and tear at a time when there was no real requirement for a 24pdr-armed frigate.[18]

Of all the 'super frigates' of the 1790s, *Endymion* was the star. She was very fast, handled well, was an excellent sea-boat, and could if required carry 24pdrs without serious damage to the hull. Indeed, she was so highly regarded that she was still the benchmark for sailing qualities as late as the Experimental Squadrons of the 1830s. The only more powerful frigates to have seen Royal Navy service were the 1400-ton sister-ships *Forte* and *L'Egyptienne*; the former had been lost too soon for the lines to be taken off, but the latter, captured at the fall of Alexandria in 1801, caused a stir when first brought to England. In April 1802 the offi-

TABLE 5/8: *Acasta* class 40-gun Fifth Rate

Building data

Name	Ordered	Builder	Laid down	Launched	Sailed	Fitted at	Fate
Acasta	30 Apr 1795	Randall, Rotherhithe	Sep 1795	13 Mar 1797	24 Jun 1797	Deptford	BU Jan 1821

Notes: Coppered by the builder, 15-28 Mar 1797.

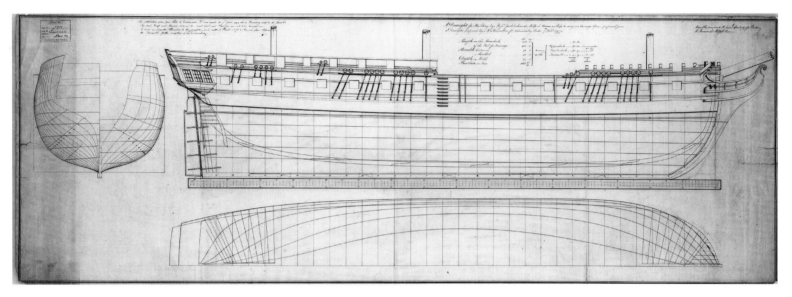

The largest British 18pdr frigate of the French Wars was the *Lavinia*, rated as a 44. She was designed by the Toulonese émigré J-L Barrallier, and, unsurprisingly, was as big as any similarly armed ship in the French navy – she was generally very similar in dimensions to the largest of Forfait's designs, like *Clorinde*, although slightly deeper in the hold in deference to British requirements for capacity. This sheer and body plan 'from a draught proposed by Mr Barrallier' is noted as a response to an Admiralty Order of 7 February 1797. A later note of 7 June 1799 instructs all the quarterdeck ports except the foremost to be converted for carronades, with a further two carronade positions on the forecastle; however, in December she seems to have been fitted with an all-carronade armament on the quarterdeck.
National Maritime Museum Dr1711

cers of Woolwich Dockyard, who had surveyed the ship, were asked for an estimate for building a ship 'exactly similar to the *Egyptienne*, with the additions of orlop deck if thought necessary, with proper store-rooms, etc . . .'. The answer was £32,277 (plus £1561 to fit the ship with British-style arrangements), about 12½ per cent more than *Cambrian* and about 26 per cent more than a standard 38 like *Naiad*. Not surprisingly, the economy-minded St Vincent administration went no further with the project. This was just as well since, according to Captain Thomas Hamilton, she was 'very insufficiently fastened and over-masted forward'. In service she proved hard on both her spars and her hull, and in November 1806 St Vincent was to inform Markham at the Admiralty: '*L'Egyptienne* has been

TABLE 5/9: *Lavinia* class 44-gun Fifth Rate

Specification

Armament	Upper deck	Quarterdeck	Forecastle	Guns	Men
DESIGN	30 x 18pdrs	10 x 9pdrs, 4 x 32pdr carr	4 x 9pdrs, 2 x 32pdr carr	44	340 (294)
CHANGES BY AO:					
14 Dec 1799		14 x 32pdr carr			
15 Jan 1805			2 x 9pdrs, 4 x 32pdr carr		
May 1806*		As design	As design		
18 Jul 1806		2 x 9pdrs replaced by 2 x 32pdr carr			
13 Nov 1809+		4 x 9pdrs replaced by 4 x 32pdr carr			

Designed by Jean-Louis Barrallier

	Lower deck feet-inches	Keel feet-inches	Breadth extreme feet-inches	Depth in hold feet-inches	Burthen Tons
DESIGN	158-0	132-8	40-8	14-0	1166⁹²⁄₉₄
AS COMPLETED					
Lavinia	158-1	132-9½	40-8¾	14-0	1172

Notes: * A report from Plymouth officers [Adm 106/1938, 3 May 1806] gives this as the armament to be actually fitted; the subsequent changes make no sense if this were not the case.

+ This order specifies two of the four long 9pdrs on the forecastle and two on the quarterdeck to be replaced by carronades, making the final armament 6 x 9pdrs and 8 x 32pdr carr on the quarterdeck and 2 x 9pdrs and 4 x 32pdr carr on the forecastle.

TABLE 5/10: *Lavinia* class 44-gun Fifth Rate

Building data

Name	Ordered	Builder	Laid down	Launched	Sailed	Fitted at	Fate
Lavinia	15 Feb 1797	Jacobs, Milford	May 1798	Builder failed 6 Mar 1806	11 Jul 1806	Plymouth	Completed by 'Government' Hulk 1836; sunk in collision 1868; wreck sold 31 Mar 1870

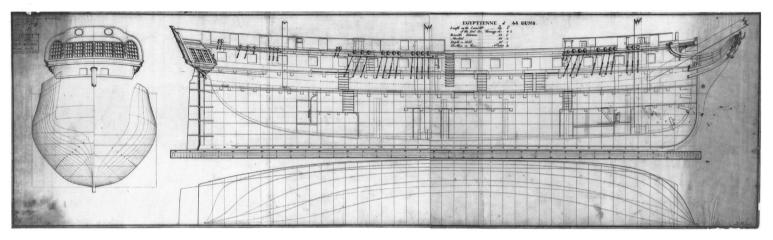

When at the end of 1812 the Admiralty began to seek a specific counter to the enormous US spar-deckers, they might well have considered the *Egyptienne*. This French prize was the largest frigate in the Royal Navy (she was only about 3ft shorter than the American ships) and could carry thirty 24pdrs on the upper deck. Unfortunately, she was very lightly built like all French ships and during her short British service had earned herself an ignominious reputation for structural weakness and a high proportion of time spent in Dockyard hands. She had been laid up since 1807, and it is unlikely that anyone who remembered the ship would have proposed her to the Admiralty as a possible model.
National Maritime Museum Dr6787

equally expensive during the time Captain Fleeming commanded her, and she has performed very little service; nearly half the time she has been in commission has been passed in port.'[19] As a result, her weak construction confined her to harbour duties from 1807.

Thus in 1812 when the Admiralty cast round for an answer to the big American frigates, the *Endymion* was the only possible starting point. The ship herself was not immediately available, since she was undergoing a year-long refit, officially described as 'Between a Middling and Large Repair', but when completed in May 1813 she was restored to her 24pdr armament and dispatched to America. In the meantime, as the one existing satisfactory prototype of her class, she became the model for the first of the new 40-gun frigates.

THE WAR OF 1812

As in 1794, the Admiralty had three ways to obtain more powerful frigates – to cut down line of battle ships, repeat an existing design, or produce an entirely new draught – and as in the previous crisis, all three were adopted.

Reviving the *rasée* concept was an obvious short-term response, and around the turn of 1812-13 the Admiralty received a number of such proposals. In January Admiral Sir Henry Stanhope sent Melville a reasoned argument for such ships, and at much the same time, Rear-Admiral Sir John Borlase Warren, Commander-in-Chief on the North America station, requested 'six or seven good sailing old ships of the line, such as *Canada*, *Captain*, *Bellona*, *Monarch*, cut

down and reduced as razies . . .'.[20] Having had *Indefatigable* and *Anson* in his squadron in 1795, Warren's interest was predictable, but the Admiralty had the satisfaction of telling him they had foreseen his request and already had the matter in hand. In fact they were acting with great vigour on a suggestion of November 1812 from Captain John Hayes.

His memo sets out a specification for 'A Sixty-Four Gun Ship to be altered for the purposes of reducing the establishment and expense, disguising her force, improving her sailing, and making her an effective and valuable cruising ship.'[21] This he intended to do by cutting away the superstructure, leaving only a round-house cabin for the captain and enough of a forecastle to cover the cooking coppers; the flush upper deck would carry twenty-six 32pdr carronades, with hammock stanchions above the gunwale to make an even line with the break fore and aft – not, strangely, to disguise the ship's force by giving her a flush profile, but to make the ship 'look handsome as the officers of the Navy Board perfectly understand.' One novel idea was to carry a single 6pdr chase gun fore and aft mounted on an elevating carriage 'in the same way as the launches' carronade fitted for firing into the tops of the enemy.' This may not have been as original as it sounds, since Philip Broke had his 9pdr chase guns so fitted in the *Shannon*, although his ideas were by no means as well known in the Navy at this time as they were to become after his victory over *Chesapeake*. In action, Broke detailed them to specific tasks, like shooting away the wheel or the headsails, but they could also be employed in clearing the tops of sharp-

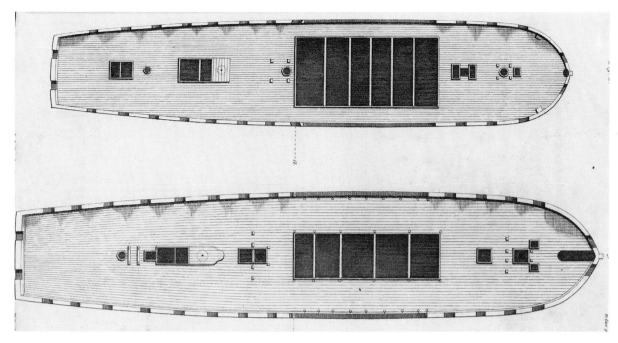

William James's comparison of a standard British 38 and an American 44, based on the deck plans of a *Lively* class ship like the *Macedonian* and the captured USS *President*. James was concerned not just to demonstrate graphically the difference in size, but also to point out the advantages of the spar-decked layout over traditional narrow gangways. As an illustration in an intentionally polemical work, it is not entirely objective, however. The American ship is shown with breeching ringbolts in the waist, implying the ability to mount guns all along the gangways: this had been true, but *President* did not carry guns in the waist, and indeed did not even have waist barricades by 1815. Equally misleading is the layout of the British ship, which represents the early members of the class and not *Macedonian*, which had the gangways widened by the light grating deck suggested by Captain Beaver. No guns were ever mounted on it, but it did make it potentially easier to fight and manoeuvre the ship simultaneously. Nevertheless, the drawing does underline why the Royal Navy needed a new class of ship to take on these huge spar-deckers.
Plate 2 from James's book A Full and Correct Account of the Chief Naval Occurrences of the late war . . . published in 1817

shooters.[22] Hayes also advocated retaining the main armament and the full rig (indeed, he wanted to increase the drop of the course to fill the height lost in cutting down), nor to land any ballast. This he calculated would save enough weight to raise the gunports sufficiently.

The speed and economy of the measure appealed to the Admiralty, and the Navy Board was instructed to investigate and report on costs and timescale, ensuring that the work caused the minimum disruption to other activities in the dockyards. However, by this time 64-gun ships, with a main battery of twenty-six 24pdrs, were simply too weak, and in any case the Navy Board pointed out that there were no 64s in Ordinary that would make economical conversions, so the Admiralty directed the junior board to find suitable small 74s instead, ensuring that the work involved was equal to the repairing of four frigates. By the end of the year they had settled on a first choice of *Thunderer*, *Monarch*, *Resolution* and *Culloden*.[23]

The differences between the *rasée* 64s and the cut-down 74s is clear from this draught of the *Saturn* as fitted at Plymouth, dated 1 January 1814. In the earlier ships everything above the lower gundeck was cut away, leaving only a light frigate-style quarterdeck and forecastle with an open waist; but two decades later the *rasée* concept was essentially a structural two-decker with minimal upperworks – a short poop and topgallant forecastle. Since they were old ships, they were given a limited amount of Seppings's diagonal strengthening; but, interestingly, the riders fore and aft were disposed in the opposite direction to his preferred orientation. According to modern naval architects, this was actually more efficient, since the riders acted more effectively in compression than tension. In fact, *Saturn*'s active life was ten years longer than her sisters, and the hull actually survived until 1868.
National Maritime Museum Dr1748

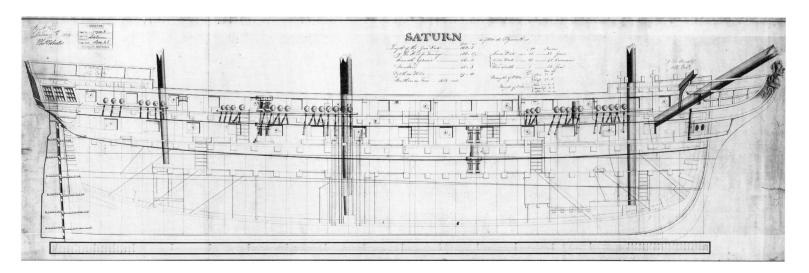

SATURN

While there were parallels with 1794, there were also significant differences. Two decades earlier, the war had barely begun, so the ships chosen to be cut down had to be in good condition, whereas by 1813 the end was in sight and there was less concern for the longevity of any conversion. As a result, the *raséed* 64s had a relatively long life, and although *Magnanime*'s last ten years were spent in Ordinary, *Indefatigable* was still so highly regarded that Warren specifically asked for the ship in 1812. Not so the cut-down 74s: they were expected to survive a few years at most, and none had an active post-war career. The concern, therefore, was to find good-sailing ships, rather than hulls in prime condition, and at first it was proposed to double the selected ships to strengthen them, rather than subject them to time-consuming repairs.[24] Despite some twenty 74s nominally available, as well as low requirements for structural condition, it proved surprisingly difficult to find suitable ships: of the initial selection *Thunderer*, *Culloden*, *Monarch* and *Resolution*, in that order, were rejected as fit for nothing except breaking up. The only substitutes that could be found were *Majestic*, *Goliath* and *Saturn*, all rescued from the ignominy of conversion to prison ships.[25] By April 1813, however, there was discussion of up to ten ships, and having thoroughly trawled the creeks and backwaters of the Ordinary, the Navy Board could only suggest conversion of the next ten small 74s due to pay off during the year.[26] The Admiralty decided not to proceed beyond three immediately, but further Small Class 74s were *raséed* after the war.

The conversion itself was also rather different from the 1794 *rasées*, which were given an open waist and frigate-like topsides. The 74s, on the other hand, were nothing like conventional frigates, and were referred to officially as 'intermediate between heavy frigates and line of battleships'. Following Hayes's brief, they retained the hull sides of what had been the upper gundeck to full height and scantlings, along with his 'flying forecastle' (what would later be termed a topgallant forecastle) and a long poop with rails. The hatchways were narrowed as much as possible, and the booms and boats carried on crutches just off the deck. The main battery of twenty-eight 32pdrs was retained, while the continuous upper deck was powerfully armed with the same number of 42pdr carronades, mounted on Congreve's novel principle whereby the gun recoiled on trucks fixed on an axle passing through the loop (it was supposed to speed up the rate of fire by suppressing the recoil—see Chapter 10 for more details). The armament was completed by a 12pdr bow-chaser on the elevating carriage (although this had become two by the time the ships went to sea) and a complement of 495 men. Although *Saturn* required some repair work, the cutting-down involved no more than about three months in dock for any of them, and *Majestic* was at sea by May 1813.

Captain Hayes, who considered himself the only begetter of the project, was given command of the first to commission, and was mightily pleased with the result. Perhaps with the problems of the 1794 ships in mind, the Admiralty was anxious to find out how the ship performed, and Hayes was ordered to report as soon as possible. He obliged with a brief paean of praise from off Cork, and a fuller report after some experience on the Boston blockade.[27] The ship was, in his opinion, 'superior to any battleship and not inferior

TABLE 5/11: *Rasée* 74-gun ships, 58-gun Fourth Rates

Specification

Armament	Lower deck	Upper deck	Forecastle	Guns	Men
DESIGN	28 x 32pdrs	28 x 42pdr carr	2 x 12pdrs	58	495

CHANGES BY AO:
(*Saturn*) 1 Mar 1814 added   1 x 5½in howitzer, 1 x 9pdr field piece

Designed by William Bately (*Majestic*) and Sir Thomas Slade (*Goliath* and *Saturn*)

	Lower deck feet-inches	Keel feet-inches	Breadth extreme feet-inches	Depth in hold feet-inches	Burthen Tons
DESIGN (*Maj*)	170-0	140-5	46-7	20-6	1632
DESIGN (*G & S*)	168-0	138-0	46-9	19-9	1604
AS CUT DOWN					
Majestic	170-6	141-0	46-9½	20-6	1642
Goliath	168-0	138-0	46-9	19-9	1604
Saturn	168-2	138-1¼	46-11	19-10	1616

Notes: Originally intended to carry only one 12pdr (on an elevating carriage), but they all went to sea with two.

TABLE 5/12: *Rasée* 74-gun ships, 58-gun Fourth Rates

Building data

Name	Launched	Converted at	Started	Completed	Sailed	Fitted at	Fate
Majestic	11 Feb 1785	Chatham Dyd	19 Jan 1813	2 Apr 1813	17 May 1813	Chatham	BU Apr 1816 after stranding
Goliath	19 Oct 1781	Chatham Dyd	6 Mar 1813	29 May 1813	12 Jul 1813	Chatham	BU Jun 1815
Saturn	22 Nov 1786	Plymouth Dyd	2 Apr 1813	28 Jul 1813	27 Dec 1813	Plymouth	Harbour service 1825; BU Feb 1868

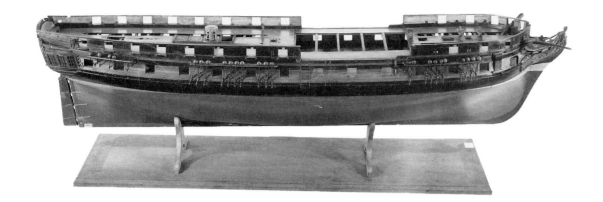

to any frigate I have served in'; she was stiff, sailed and handled well, and carried her midships ports 6ft 4in from the waterline. Furthermore, she turned out to be a very fine heavy-weather ship, working off a lee shore by carrying a press of sail for two days while the accompanying frigate remained embayed. While the frigate rolled her quarterdeck ports in the water, Hayes claimed 'it was not even necessary to make a single chair fast in my cabin.'

The 1815 Sailing Quality report is even more fulsome, containing a concentration of superlatives almost unknown in these unemotive documents. One might suspect gross exaggeration if the officer concerned was not 'Magnificent' Hayes, whose consummate seamanship was the subject of awed admiration throughout the fleet.[28] When fitting out the 1794 *rasées* the Navy Board had overridden the suggestions of Pellew, another skilful seaman, but this time the Admiralty insisted that Hayes determine the stowage and rig of 'his' ship. Hayes himself had reconsidered, since the project was no longer a cut-down 64, and as a result, the ship carried only 150 tons of ballast, 170 tons less than as a 74, while retaining much of the topside weight, making for a far easier ship, although she proved stiff enough to carry sail even in heavy weather.

Hayes made something of a career for himself after the war as an amateur ship designer, being allowed by the Admiralty to build in succession a cutter (*Arrow*, 1823), a sloop (*Champion*, 1823), and a frigate (*Inconstant*, 1836) by way of comparison with the work of the Navy's official naval architects. The last was particularly well thought-of, and Hayes clearly had a practical grasp of what made a good sailing warship. Nevertheless, he was sensitive to the charge that his praise of the *rasée* was 'partial' and he took pains to pass on a personal letter from Captain Epworth of the frigate *Nymphe*, *Majestic*'s frequently weathered and forereached squadron-mate.

I am quite delighted with your Razée, she astonishes me with her movements under every sort of sail, & her sailing surpasses every thing I have yet met with, she appears so stiff under sail, and so buoyant and easy . . .

More significantly, he added

her appearance [is] so deceptious [*sic*] that any one would go down to her for a frigate, having much of the appearance of one of the American frigates; I hope more of the small 74 gun Ships will be equipped in the

This model bears the name *Pomona* on the stern and at 1/48th scale is very close to the dimensions of the *Pomone* captured in 1794. However, even when fitted for British service this ship never carried sixteen guns on the quarterdeck, and the model is probably meant to represent the *Endymion* (built to the lines of the *Pomone*) as she appeared after 1813 when she mounted sixteen carronades on that deck: in fact, the *Endymion* draught mentions the order of May 1813 to open up the extra port abreast the main mast and extend the quarterdeck planking forward by one beam, precisely as shown in the model. Therefore, this may be a modification of an existing *Pomone* model to celebrate *Endymion*'s new-found celebrity after her successful engagement with USS *President*.
National Maritime Museum 7651

The sheer draught for the modified *Endymion* design, the *Forth* class, produced in response to an order of 7 January 1813. The principal alteration was the addition of a main-deck gunport, but the redesign also flattened out the 'hanging' of the deck – one of Peake's trademarks – which gave a little more freeboard to the midships gunports. The only alteration mentioned on the draught is a post-war raising of the catheads of the *Glasgow* (22 March 1816) to match those of the *Forth* and *Severn*.
National Maritime Museum Dr1422

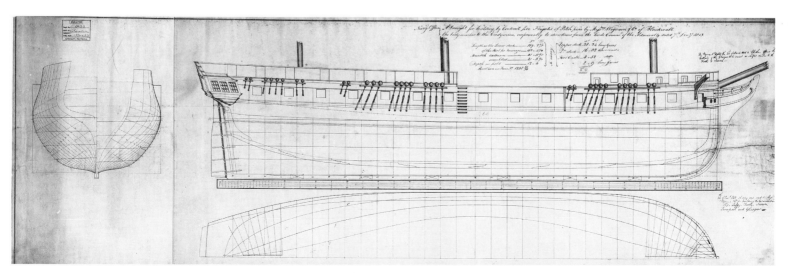

same way, these seas requiring no other ships, it would be a great saving.[29]

Judging by the draught, it is difficult to see much resemblance with an American frigate, although the *rasées* were said to carry a black-painted waist-cloth to disguise their gangway ports. Epworth concluded on a punning note, 'I hope we may see Rodgers and his Squadron, to give him a specimen of what a British Nymphe, Majestically supported can do . . .' Of course in 1815 it was a British Endymion Majestically supported that captured Commodore Rodgers' flagship, *President* (then commanded by Decatur), and it is noteworthy that on the stormy first part of the day *Majestic* led the chase, whereas in the following lighter airs *Endymion* walked away from the *rasée*.

Hayes himself was careful to point out that the set-up of his vessel would be no guide for 'a ship built with a different formed bottom', although he equally contended that 'if either of the other Razees should fail in any point, it can only be occasioned by not having

stowed & trimmed her as her form requires.' This was sound advice because the remaining pair were to a different draught, and neither became quite so highly regarded, neither being able to achieve six feet of gunport freeboard, for instance. In truth, the principal advantage of the *rasées* was their power to carry sail, which made them excellent heavy-weather ships, but – *Majestic* perhaps excepted – they would not want to fight in very high seas given their relatively low gunports. Furthermore, they were so powerful that the only likely scenario in which a *rasée* might bring an American spar-decker to battle would be in chase, when it would be more than likely that the *rasée* would have to use her lee battery – if the heel of the ship would allow it. In lighter conditions American frigates had proved themselves adept at 'ghosting', and would almost certainly escape. Thus it would only be a happy combination of conditions that would deliver one into the hands of a *rasée* – wind strong enough to overtake, but seas not high enough to prevent the use of the gundeck ports.

Pending the success of the cutting-down programme, the Admiralty decided to extend fir frigate construction to a larger class, and on Boxing Day 1812 ordered two Fifth Rates to the lines of the *Endymion* from pitch pine with scantlings suitable for 24pdrs. Although an excellent ship, *Endymion* had only twenty-six ports on the main deck compared to thirty for the American '44's, but she was the only satisfactory design immediately available. However, being based on a French design, she did not carry guns right forward, so it was possible to contrive fourteen ports a side in the revised draught. Building in pine produced a significantly lighter hull, which could make such ships very stiff, but as in this case it could be turned to advantage by carrying heavier weights. The gundeck of the new class was somewhat crowded as a result, but they suffered no stability problems: indeed, the introduction of iron water tanks served to increase stability (see Chapter 9 for the implications) and the first few ships needed restowing to reduce a propensity to heavy rolling. As a consequence of their lighter hulls and lower stowage of water, they tended to be sailed at shallower draughts compared with *Endymion*, and at

TABLE 5/13: Modified *Endymion* class 40-gun Fifth Rates

Specification

Armament	Upper deck	Quarterdeck	Forecastle	Guns	Men
DESIGN	28 x 24pdrs	16 x 32pdr carr	2 x 9pdrs, 4 x 32pdr carr	40	340

Lines of the *Pomone*. Built of pitch pine

	Lower deck feet-inches	Keel feet-inches	Breadth extreme feet-inches	Depth in hold feet-inches	Burthen Tons
DESIGN	159-2⅜	132-4½	41-11⅜	12-4	1238⁶⁷⁄₉₄
AS COMPLETED					
Severn	159-2⅝	132-2	42-3	12-4	1254⁸⁷⁄₉₄
Forth	159-3⅛	132-0¼	42-2½	12-4	1251⁶⁄₉₄
Liffey	159-1½	131-8¼	42-5	12-4	1260²³⁄₉₄
Liverpool	159-2	132-1¼	42-1½	12-4	1246⁸⁶⁄₉₄
Glasgow	159-2½	132-1⅛	42-4	12-4	1259¹⁷⁄₉₄

TABLE 5/14: Modified *Endymion* class 40-gun Fifth Rates

Building data

Name	Ordered	Builder	Laid down	Launched	Sailed	Fitted at	Fate
Severn	7 Jan 1813	Wigram, Blackwall	Jan 1813	14 Jun 1813	11 Mar 1814	Deptford	Sold 20 Jul 1825
Forth	7 Jan 1813	Wigram, Blackwall	Feb 1813	14 Jun 1813	7 Sep 1813	Deptford	BU Oct 1819
Liffey	7 Jan 1813	Wigram, Blackwall	Feb 1813	25 Sep 1813	10 Jun 1814	Deptford	BU Jul 1827
Liverpool	26 Dec 1812	Wigram, Blackwall	May 1813	21 Feb 1814	20 Jun 1814	Deptford	Sold 16 Apr 1822 at Bombay
Glasgow	26 Dec 1812	Wigram, Blackwall	May 1813	21 Feb 1814	26 Aug 1814	Woolwich	BU Jan 1829

Notes: Severn, Forth and *Liffey* were originally ordered as the 38s *Tagus, Tigris* and *Eridanus* respectively; they were reordered and renamed on 7 January 1813.

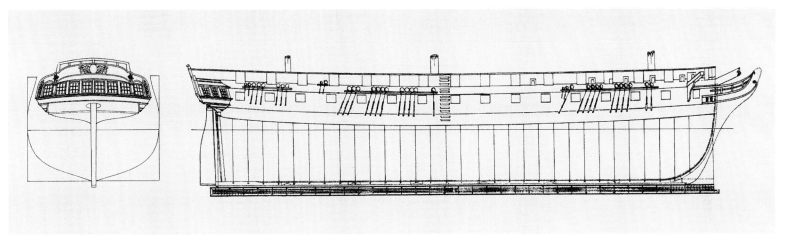

first they were complained of as somewhat leewardly, but this was cured by an addition to the false keel.[30] Once fine-tuned, they were generally good under sail, if not quite as outstanding as *Endymion* herself. Five ships of this class were on order by the middle of January 1813, all to be built by Sir Robert Wigram's yard, with three contracted to be launched by June.

The 40-gun ships were at best an interim reaction, but as further evidence of the success of the American spar-decked frigates came in, there was an increasing desire in the Admiralty to produce an equivalent. The ex-74s were more than a match for the American ships, but there were no more instantly available, and in any case if the Navy was to regain the overwhelming public confidence it had enjoyed before 1812, it needed to win a single-ship victory with something like a similar ship – and as of spring 1813, it had failed to win *any* such encounter. From the technical point of view, it was also important to investigate the properties, and possible advantages of such ships. Therefore, on 21 April the Navy Board was instructed to produce a design for 'a 50-gun ship of the frigate class with a spar deck' of about 1500 tons, one draught by the Surveyors and one by Barrallier. Assuming that there was no prior discussion of the requirement, the speed with which the draughts were delivered – three days – is a precise indicator of how little time it took to design even a radically new warship type in those days.[31]

Designed to carry thirty 24pdrs on the lower deck and twenty-eight 42pdr carronades plus two long 24s on the full spar deck, the two ships were similar in size, although, typically, the Frenchman's ship was longer. They were also about the same size as their American opponents, but whereas the American ships, built in the 1790s, were traditional in their appearance with some sheer and tumblehome, the British ships with their wall sides and flat sheerline, looked forward to a more austere, aesthetically brutal age in naval architecture. Christened *Leander* and *Newcastle*, both ships were built by the already heavily committed Wigram yard, and necessarily of softwood to get them into service as quickly as possible – indeed, they were given

priority over the 40-gun *Liverpool* and *Glasgow*. By this stage, all the fir 24pdr ships were being built in this one Blackwall yard, which by July 1813 was making such remarkable progress that the Admiralty became concerned for the quality of the work; but the Navy Board was able to reassure them that the ships were visited regularly, sometimes twice a week and often by one of the Surveyors themselves.[32]

Both ships were launched on the same day, 10 November, and sent down-river to Woolwich for fitting out. Command was earmarked for two senior captains, Sir George Collier and Lord George Stuart, and until they could arrive temporary captains were assigned to stand by the ships while preparing for sea. The *Newcastle* fell to the lot of William Dillon, so there is a

The original sheer and body plan for the *Leander* has disappeared from the Admiralty collection, although their existence was recorded some thirty years ago. This reconstruction by Norman Swales was derived from the profile and deck plans, with the midship section and details based on the *Java*, designed by the Surveyors at almost the same time. An odd but characteristic feature of *Leander* is that the spar-deck ports, instead of being staggered, sit almost directly over those on the upper deck.

TABLE 5/15: *Leander* class 50-gun Fourth Rate

Specification

Armament	Upper deck	Spar deck	Guns	Men
DESIGN	30 x 24pdrs	2 x 24pdrs, 28 x 42pdr carr	50	480
CHANGES BY AO:				
5 Jul 1813		2 x 24pdrs, 24 x 42pdr carr		450
6 Jan 1814 added		2 x 24pdrs		
1 Mar 1814 added		1 x 5½in howitzer, 1 x 9pdr field piece		

Designed by the Surveyors of the Navy. Built of pitch pine

	Lower deck feet-inches	Keel feet-inches	Breadth extreme feet-inches	Depth in hold feet-inches	Burthen Tons
DESIGN	?	?	?	?	1556 ^{10}/94
AS COMPLETED					
Leander	174-0	145-3⅝	44-10½	14-4	1556 ^{38}/94

Notes: The Navy Board's first thoughts for armament were as shown under 'Design', but the ship actually carried 4 x 24pdrs and 24 x 42pdr carr on the spar deck during her first commission.

TABLE 5/16: *Leander* class 50-gun Fourth Rate

Building data

Name	Ordered	Builder	Laid down	Launched	Sailed	Fitted at	Fate
Leander	6 May 1813	Wigram, Blackwall	Jun 1813	10 Nov 1813	18 Feb 1814	Woolwich	BU Mar 1830

This oil painting attributed to Nicholas Condy the Younger (1818-1851) portrays a British 'double-banked' frigate. Since this arrangement was abandoned in the 1820s, there are not many ships the painting could represent, and the most likely candidate is *Leander* – allowing for perspective, the painting shows that ship's unusual positioning of the spar-deck ports almost immediately above those on the main deck. If the attribution is correct, Condy is unlikely to have done the painting from life, since *Leander* was broken up in 1830 and spent much of her post-war career with a poop built on the quarterdeck. *By courtesy of Richard Lawrence*

description of the ship in his well-known *Narrative* (although its editor omitted most of an interesting argument between Dillon and Barrallier, the ship's designer).[33] Dillon was impressed by this 'splendid ship', but he was also an informed critic. She was built to light scantlings and French construction style, which 'is not so strong as ours', and Dillon claims he won a bet with Barrallier that in the first gale *Newcastle* met, her labouring would cause the sides to fall out and the decks to flatten 3ins in the crowns. More importantly, he disagreed with Barrallier about her proportions. On being told that the ship had too little draught for her size, the designer replied that he had 'made up for that by her length'. This was a common French misconception, countered Dillon: 'Experience had taught the English sailor that good depth under water, always ensured a weatherly quality . . .' and during the recent war 'on almost all occasions when we had to chase against the wind, we had been successful.' In

this, Dillon was expressing the accumulated wisdom of a navy that had spent two decades pursuing a generally reluctant enemy: the number of nominally faster ships captured in just the circumstances outlined demonstrates the basic value of his proposition.

Dillon implies that he was put to much trouble during *Newcastle*'s fitting-out, but there was only one serious difficulty, which is why the designer was summoned in the first place. The ship proved so sharp she could not stow her full allocation of water, even though she was fitted with the new-fangled iron tanks. With typical overstatement, Dillon trumpeted this 'sad annoyance to the Builder', insisting that Barrallier was 'evidently much embarrassed' – but the shortfall was only 10 out of 260 tons.

In point of fact, these teething troubles were minor and no more than any new ship would experience. When they went to sea, both *Newcastle* and *Leander* proved very fast, both exceeding 13 knots, but they

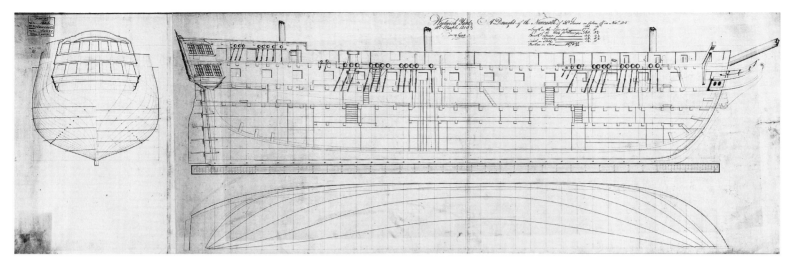

After the war the big double-banked frigates were refitted as foreign station flagships, in effect taking over the role from the old two-decked 50-gun ships. For this purpose they were given a poop to cover the admiral's accommodation built on the quarterdeck, and *Newcastle* is shown here in that configuration in a draught dated Woolwich 11 March 1816 but 'as taken off in November 1815'. Unusually, the ports on the spar deck are irregular, there being no ports abreast the main mast and only twelve large enough for carronades on each broadside, although there are also three that could accommodate long guns. Pencil marks on the draught suggest the opening of ports just forward of the main mast and behind the main backstay stool; the ship would have needed at least one more to cope with the known 1818 armament of twenty-six 42pdr carronades and two long 24's on the spar deck. As built *Newcastle* and *Leander* had a unique masting establishment, almost the size of a 74's, but to reduce the strain on the hull in peacetime the *Newcastle*'s rig was cut down; the lower masts were retained but the bowsprit was shortened by 4ft and the upper spars replaced by those of a 64-gun ship. At the same time both water and ballast were reduced, but the ship still suffered from an excessive reserve of stability producing very uneasy motions. This was eventually solved by moving 20 tons of ballast from the hold to the orlop, and stowing a large proportion of shot between decks.
National Maritime Museum Dr1446

were also leewardly (as Dillon had predicted) and initially over-stiff. Like the *rasées*, they were better in heavier conditions, although *Newcastle* was prone to heavy pitching in a head sea, but unlike the cut-down battleships, they carried their battery at least 8ft from the waterline at any state of lading.

After the war they were given poop decks, 'whereby they will be rendered substitutes for 50-gun ships with two decks'; and of course they became flagships on stations where it was necessary to keep an eye on the Americans.[34] *Leander*, probably as a result of injudicious stowage, later made herself an unenviable reputation for heavy and violent motions, but this was resolved during her 1820 commission through the joint efforts of Rear-Admiral Sir Henry Blackwood and his flag captain Sir Charles Richardson. From the Cape on his way to take command of the East Indies station Blackwood wrote an enthusiastic letter to Byam Martin, the Comptroller, boasting of an improvement that astonished those in the crew who remembered her earlier behaviour: 'there never was an easier ship, both as to rolling and pitching in all sorts of weather, a faster sailer, or in my opinion, a more perfect man of war, in

TABLE 5/17: *Newcastle* class 50-gun Fourth Rate

Specification

Armament	Upper deck	Spar deck	Guns	Men
DESIGN	30 x 24pdrs	2 x 24pdrs, 28 x 42pdr carr	50	480
CHANGES BY AO:				
5 Jul 1813		2 x 24pdrs, 24 x 42pdr carr		450
12 Feb 1814		2 x 42pdr carr to be replaced by 2 x 24pdrs		
1 Mar 1814 added		1 x 5½in howitzer, 1 x 9pdr field piece		
7 Apr 1814		To retain the 2 x 42pdr carr as well		

Designed by J-L Barrallier. Built of pitch pine

	Lower deck feet-inches	Keel feet-inches	Breadth extreme feet-inches	Depth in hold feet-inches	Burthen Tons
DESIGN	176-0	149-3	44-0	15-2	1536⁹⁰⁄₉₄
AS COMPLETED					
Newcastle	177-0	150-2¾	44-4½	14-11	1573

Notes: By her 1818 commission the ship was armed with 2 x 24pdrs and 26 x 42pdr carr on the spar deck.

TABLE 5/18: *Newcastle* class 50-gun Fourth Rate

Building data

Name	Ordered	Builder	Laid down	Launched	Sailed	Fitted at	Fate
Newcastle	6 May 1813	Wigram, Blackwall	Jun 1813	10 Nov 1813	23 Mar 1814	Woolwich	Hulk Jun 1824; sold Jun 1850

TABLE 5/19: Captured and purchased 24pdr ships 1793-1815

Service data

Name, origin	Built	Captured	Fate
Armed with 26 x 24pdrs on upper deck, rated 44 guns in RN			
Pomone, ex-Fr	Rochefort 1785	23 Apr 1794	BU Dec 1802
Armed with 28 x 24pdrs on upper deck, rated 44 guns in RN			
Amphitrite, ex-Du *Amfitrite*	Amsterdam 1797	30 Aug 1799	Renamed *Imperieuse* 1801; BU Apr 1805
Egyptienne, ex-Fr	Toulon 1799	2 Sep 1801	Hulk 1806; sold for BU 30 Apr 1817
Armed with 30 x 24pdrs on upper deck, rated 50/44/60 guns in RN			
Cornwallis, ex-HEIC *Marquis Cornwallis*	Bombay 1800	(Purchased) 13 Aug 1806	Renamed *Akbar* Feb 1811; hulk 1824; sold 1862
Forte, ex-Fr	Lorient 1795	28 Feb 1799	Wrecked off Jeddah 29 Jan 1801
President, ex-US	New York 1800	15 Jan 1815	Never cruised in RN; BU Jun 1818

Notes: Cornwallis was a teak-built cruiser purchased from the Bombay Marine; she was rated a 50-gun Fourth Rate in 1813 but enjoyed only a short career as a frigate.

There was also the ex-Dutch *Mars*, a *rasée* 44 cut down from a 68-gun ship of 1784; taken in the Texel on 30 Aug 1799, she was renamed *Vlieter* in the RN, but only served as a floating battery, from Jul 1801 until hulked in 1809, and was BU in Apr 1817.

point of quarters, means of working the ship even in action, or fighting all her guns . . .'. She had made Madeira in five days from Spithead, and on the long run down to the Cape had spent days with a beam wind doing 12 knots – and sometimes 13 knots for hours at a time – under reefed (sometimes double-reefed) topsails, topgallants, courses, jib and spanker. The heel was almost imperceptible, and the lee guns could have been fought at any time. 'I do not therefore hesitate to say that Sir Robert Wigram's child has been defamed', concluded Blackwood, and went on to advocate building a sister of teak in Bombay.

He was not entirely uncritical of the design, however: a couple of inches off the height of the abnormally high main and lower decks transferred to the orlop would benefit stowage, while the spar-deck barricades were also too high. More importantly, he felt that three of the gangway guns on either broadside were wasted – in action they would probably fire only the opening round before they got in the way, given how little space there was between the side and the boats, however judiciously they were stowed. Perhaps significantly, the post-war 'spar-decked' frigates were all completed with this more conventional frigate waist.[35]

Once the need for very big frigates had been accepted, the Admiralty had brought the considerable industrial strength of Britain lavishly to bear on the problem. By the middle of 1813 the *rasées* were joining the fleet,

The sheer and profile draught of the ex-Bombay Marine *Akbar*, dated Woolwich Yard 9 December 1813. The boxy mid-section is reminiscent of a merchant ship (and indeed the Navy Board proposed turning her into a storeship), but the profile reveals the layout of a genuine 'double-banked' frigate. Although designed for the East India Company's navy, the ship was an advanced concept: flat-sheered, with a genuine spar deck pierced by fewer openings even than the American 44s and capable of bearing a full battery of carronades. What is not apparent is the relatively shallow hull. An interesting post-war draught (No 1268) compares her mid-section with the *President*, the latter having a far deeper hold. The listed dimensions are misleading because the 'depth in hold' for the American ship was measured from the platform beam and not from the lower deck beam as for *Akbar*. In practice, the gundeck ports of the American ship were nearly 7ft further from the keel; or looked at another way, because *President*'s platform beam was level with *Akbar*'s lower deck, the American ship's depth was greater by the height of one whole deck.
National Maritime Museum Dr1384

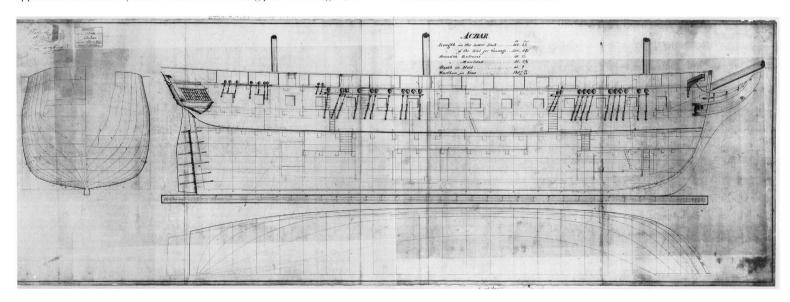

TABLE 5/20: Captured and purchased 24pdr ships 1793-1815

Specifications

Name	Length		Breadth extreme feet-inches	Depth in hold feet-inches	Burthen Tons	Armament	
	Lower deck feet-inches	Keel feet-inches				Quarterdeck	Forecastle
Armed with 26 x 24pdrs on upper deck, rated 44 guns in RN							
Pomone	159-2⅜	132-4¼	41-11⅜	12-4	$1238\frac{67}{94}$	14 x 32 carr	2 x 9, 4 x 32 carr
Armed with 28 x 24pdrs on upper deck, rated 44 guns in RN							
Amphitrite	150-9½	123-7⅝	42-5	12-9	$1183\frac{19}{94}$	10 x 24 carr	2 x 9, 4 x 24 carr
Egyptienne	169-8	141-4¾	43-8	15-1	$1434\frac{4}{94}$	2 x 9, 12 x 32 carr	2 x 9, 4 x 32 carr
Armed with 30 x 24pdrs on upper deck, rated 50/44/60 guns in RN							
Cornwallis	166-4½	142-6¼	43-4½	15-3	1388	26 x 42 carr on spar deck	
Forte	170-0		43-6		1401	16 x 32 carr	2 x 12, 4 x 32 carr
President	173-3	146-4¾	44-4	13-11	$1533\frac{7}{94}$	Never armed in RN	

Notes: Pomone had 2 x 9pdrs on the forecastle replaced by 12pdrs in Mar 1797, but was reduced to 18pdrs on the upper deck and the masts and yards of a 38-gun ship in Jun 1799.

Imperieuse ex-*Amphitrite* was hardly larger than a standard 38, and was rearmed with 28 x 18pdrs on the upper deck in Jan 1804.

Forte and *Egyptienne* were sisters, although the former had more gunports armed; in fact, it was originally planned to fit the latter with 30 x 24pdrs on the upper deck.

followed by the first of the 24pdr-armed 40s towards the end of the year, and the two 50-gun ships by the spring of 1814. In all this effort to provide spar-decked frigates, however, the Admiralty had overlooked the fact that there was already one on the Navy List. Launched as *Cornwallis* but renamed *Akbar* in February 1811, this large teak-built ship was purchased in the East Indies in August 1806 by Admiral Pellew. She had been built in Bombay in 1800 and is often described as an ex-East Indiaman, which considering her characteristics has a certain justice; but she was actually built for the Bombay Marine as a cruiser – although 'frigate' is probably too generous a description. She had made at least one round-trip to Britain with a convoy of Indiamen, and it seems that the design rationale was essentially that of a powerful long-range escort: she stowed as much water as a First Rate and her sailing qualities were barely superior to one of the Honourable Company's big China traders, but like those merchant ships she had two flush gundecks.

In naval service she did not see Britain again until July 1812, when she was surveyed and it was decided at the end of the year that she would make a good storeship. However, in early 1813 any vessel that could carry thirty 24pdrs on the lower deck needed more serious consideration, and in March the Admiralty, overriding the opinion of the Navy Board, instructed Woolwich Dockyard to report on her potential for conversion to a frigate. This was quickly agreed, and with modifications to false keel, gripe and rudder to improve her dismal sailing qualities, she was established with the full battery of main-deck 24pdrs and a spar-deck armament of twenty-six 42pdr carronades and a light 24pdr for the forecastle, being registered as a Fourth Rate of 50 guns on 9 July. In this state she sedately set sail to harass the King's enemies.[36]

She soon enhanced her reputation for spectacularly poor sailing qualities, combining lack of speed with leewardliness, and a tendency to roll her masts out. In November 1814 Captain Bullen requested longer masts in an attempt to give her more speed, but on examining the draughts of the ship the Surveyors came to the conclusion that she would never make a satisfactory frigate and reverted to their original suggestion of converting her to a store- or troopship. However, they were told crisply that it was not expedient to alter the masts, and that 'the service would not admit of her being paid off'. *Akbar* saw out the war as a cruising ship, and immediately post-war when the Admiralty was keen to have big frigates on the American stations to keep an eye on the US Navy, she was chosen as flagship and dispatched to Bermuda. In January 1816 the unfortunate Rear-Admiral Griffiths, whose flag she carried, wrote a blistering condemnation of the ship. He said it was 'impossible to describe her labouring', all three topmasts having gone by the board on the voyage out; indeed, she was 'understood to have been seldom at sea without losing her masts'. She required a radical reappraisal of her ballast, stowage and masting, which could not be carried out without recourse to a Dockyard. The ship came home in December 1816 to be laid up in Ordinary, but to prove that there was nothing wrong with the hull, as long as it was not in motion, the hulk survived to the 1860s.[37]

CHAPTER SIX

Preparing for Peace, 1812-1815

The best tribute to the long-term planning of the Admiralty is the survival to this day of two frigates from the leisurely post-war building programmes. A striking example of the longevity of teak, the Bombay-built *Trincomalee* is currently undergoing a first-class restoration at Hartlepool. The shape of the stern is the legacy of a Victorian conversion to a corvette, but otherwise the ship will be completed to the appearance of a *Leda* class 38-gun frigate of about 1815.
HMS Trincomalee Trust 190/8

ON TAKING office in March 1812 the new Admiralty administration of Lord Melville began a wide-ranging survey of the current state of the Navy, with a view to establishing what size and composition of the fleet could be sustained in the coming years. This emphasis on long-term planning had not been possible earlier in the war, and while the date of its probable conclusion could not be predicted in the middle of 1812, only a few months later Napoleon's disastrous retreat from Moscow put victory clearly in sight, even if still on the horizon. From the beginning of 1813, a distinct dichotomy in Admiralty policy begins to manifest itself with regard to *materiel* aspects of the Navy, distinguishing between short-term measures necessary to win the war and longer-term plans designed to preserve the country's hard-won naval supremacy. Thus what began as an exercise to discover the most efficient way of disposing the Navy's resources to win the war, became the basis of preparations for peace. The frigate force was to be affected by this process in three ways: its size, the quality of its construction, and the design of its ships.

FORCE LEVELS

The Admiralty audit began with a Navy Board survey of the material state of the whole fleet, detailing the age of each ship, the amount of dockyard attention last received, and estimating the probable length of service left in the hull with the normal level of refitting.[1] This was intended to establish the average lifespan of the various classes – in the case of frigates eight years – before major dockyard time was required; an essential statistic before any planning of force levels could be attempted.

The Navy Board was then set the more difficult task of estimating changes in the size of the fleet over the next three years, assuming the same proportion of repairs as had been undertaken in the previous three years. The principal question was whether any further expansion of the Navy was feasible, or indeed whether it was possible even to maintain current strength. The Admiralty was in a hurry for this information, but had to send the junior board a sharp reminder before it responded in November.[2] Having calculated the number of ships likely to be lost or come to the end of their natural lives and set them against those under construction or repairable, the Navy Board concluded that it would be possible to maintain the present level of 106 line of battle ships and (including the few remaining 50-gun ships) 120 frigates. For the latter, its assumptions were:

Ships	1813	1814	1815
To be paid off	38	17	17
Lost	4	4	4
Total	42	21	21

The large numbers to be paid off in the first year reflected a spate of frigate building and repairs during 1806-8, and in 1813 these would be replaced by new building: six in the Royal Dockyards, one at Milford (government-run but not yet a full Dockyard), eleven in merchant yards (plus one whose completion was dubious), and the ten of fir recently ordered; thirteen would be refitted in the Dockyards, and one experimentally repaired by Blackburn's at Turnchapel.[3] For each of the following years the figures would be: seven built and thirteen repaired in Royal Dockyards, and one built at Bombay.

There was some disagreement over the figures, Admiralty calculations making the frigate force 140-strong including Sixth Rates, and they also believed that if the four planned rasées were included in the thirteen to be repaired in the Dockyards during 1813, then the additional contracts placed since the report was compiled would result in four or five more in total. These extra frigates, it felt, might be postponed until 1814, but it emphasised that the 24pdr ships were to be completed with 'all convenient dispatch'. The Navy Board retorted that there was not much point in delaying these ships because they were built of mature fir and would not benefit from standing to season, so it would be better to launch them to clear the slips for further construction; if they were not required immediately, they might be laid up in Ordinary. The final figures for 1813 were to reach forty-seven: six new-built by Dockyards (including Salisbury, 50), twenty-seven in merchant yards, one at Milford; eleven repaired in the King's yards, and two at Blackburn's.[4]

From the middle of 1813 the Navy Board began to ask the Admiralty whether each ship about to be launched was to be fitted for sea. The remaining ships at Wigram's, for example, were ordered in August 'to be fitted so as to be able to be brought forward at short notice.'[5] There was already a contrasting attitude to ships building of fir and those of traditional hardwoods. The former were to be completed quickly for the immediate needs of the war, whereas long service was expected of the latter, indicated by the refusal to omit or shorten the leisurely process of seasoning. As the progress of the European land war became ever more favourable, it became clear that the oak ships were seen as a post-war reserve. This became conscious pol-

icy from March 1814, when all new hardwood ships were ordered to be fitted for Ordinary when launched. On the other hand, two months after a plan for the wholesale reduction of the fleet had been embarked upon in April, the last of the fir frigates like Tanais and Euphrates were prepared for commissioning.[6]

By this time two decades of maritime warfare with France was effectively over – the Hundred Days notwithstanding – and although the war with America dragged on until the end of the year, it was to be fought with a combination of old ships and the rapidly run-up fir frigates. The lives of these ships would necessarily be short and post-war many were kept in commission the few years until they were entirely worn out.[7] Old hardwood ships were also kept in service to spare the hull-life of new vessels, a special case being the old teak frigates, which were to remain on the East Indies station. Eventually they were ordered to be broken up in India and the crews employed to bring home the new Bombay-built vessels.[8]

DURABILITY

This policy of laying up new ships as a strategic reserve was one manifestation of a broad quest to extend the lives of British warships. This was of the utmost significance for the maintenance of naval supremacy, since if the frequency of repairs or replacement could be reduced then a larger fleet could be maintained for the same resources. Like so many of the Navy's post-war concerns, this pursuit of durability was rooted in wartime experience. Structural innovations and the timber shortages which drove them are covered in detail in Chapter 7, but suffice to say that untried mixes of timbers, lack of proper seasoning, and experimental methods of fastening left the Navy with a legacy of weak ships with a propensity to rot.

Dry rot was perceived as a growing problem from at least 1811, and the state of the new Queen Charlotte was the cause célèbre. Numerous studies were commissioned, experts consulted, and experiments conducted, and to the Admiralty's credit they approached the problem from every conceivable angle, investigating methods of felling, storing and seasoning timber, the characteristics of different species, improved techniques of construction, better ventilation, and even special treatments like injecting coal tar between frames.[9] Even the Admiralty's eagerness to have the captured Chesapeake surveyed was to find out if her timber was as liable to dry rot as the purchased American timber used in some British ships.[10]

As part of its initial survey of the state of the Navy in 1812, the Melville administration had instructed the Navy Board to consider and report on methods of better maintaining the fleet.[11] The principal concern was to extend the longevity of its ships, but also to extend the periods between time-consuming refits. For its

The quarterdeck of the frigate *Unicorn* is still protected by its original wooden roof. The division between the ship and the roof is marked by the dark-painted moulding running above the glazed-in gunports. A combination of standing to season during construction and the covering of completed hulls with weather-proof timber cladding ensured the long life of the post-war strategic reserve. Many of these ships, like *Unicorn*, were never commissioned but nevertheless served as an effective deterrent for half a century.
By courtesy of Roderick Stewart

part, the Admiralty had sought to lighten the dockyard workload by instructing all commanders to expose their squadrons as little as possible to heavy weather. However, since this was not accompanied by any alteration to the close blockade strategy, it was akin to telling captains to minimise the damage to their ships in battle. Nevertheless, the Admiralty expressed surprise in 1813 that these orders had no effect whatever in reducing the time spent refitting the fleet.[12]

At the end of the war it was proposed that cruising frigates and sloops on home service should carry reduced armaments. All 18pdr-armed frigates were to carry an upper deck battery of twenty-two guns, with nothing on the upperworks.[13] A detailed calculation of the weights involved was attached: as reduced, the armament for all classes would total 48 tons 13cwt 2qrs 0lbs, compared with the full figures of 83-17-2-0 for 38s, 76-12-3-0 for 36s, and 72-8-0-14 for 32s. This strongly suggests that the measure was intended to minimise the stresses on their hulls, with a view to extending their service lives, although the reduced complements would also be a significant contribution towards manning the maximum number of ships in an all-volunteer peacetime navy.

Wear and tear was one problem, but even this might be ameliorated if individual ships were better built in the first place. Seasoning and timber treatment was the central issue, but there was no easy, or quick answer: although the Navy Board had been investigating suit-able methods since before Melville took office, it still had no firm recommendations.[14] The question became intimately bound up with the new structural techniques, and during the course of defending his methods Seppings made numerous criticisms of wartime expediencies. He argued that the use of hardwood elements in a 'fir' ship was wasteful, because it was the short life of the softwood that sent the ship to the breakers, the hardwood then being lost. Softwood ships should be all fir, but when taken to pieces their ironwork should be returned to the Dockyards for reuse. While he opposed mixing timbers of different life-expectancies in new ships, he was not against employing fir to repair oak ships where the remaining life of the oak might be considered the same as new fir. Seppings may also have inspired the policy of keeping fir ships in commission while laying up new oak vessels; and he certainly advocated not sending new ships to tropical climates, preferring Bombay-built teak ships instead. Durability was one advantage he claimed for his structural improvements, and along with a number of his other proposals these became the post-war norm.[15]

One recurrent idea was the covering of building slips, that had been frequently advocated and was to be taken up once again by Samuel Bentham after he inspected examples in Sweden in 1807. It offered the advantages not only of speeding up construction, since building could proceed in all weathers, but also of keeping rainwater out of the ends of exposed timbers (thought to be a major source of rot).[16] The first in Britain was proposed for Portsmouth in November 1812, and a number had been completed by the end of all hostilities in Europe.[17]

The principle was also extended to individual ships laid up in Ordinary. The Admiralty had always felt that better maintenance of the reserve fleet would ultimately reduce the need for new construction, and at the end of the war the number of ships decommissioning made it a pressing matter. It began as a typical post-war retrenchment, the Navy Board being instructed to find a cheaper method of fitting ships for Ordinary – the current estimate was £598 per 74-gun ship. The proposals included replacing the canvas awning with a timber roof over the waist,[18] and in the case of frigates this was to become a full-length roof over the weather decks, an original example of which still protects the frigate *Unicorn* at Dundee.

As the war finally came to a close the Navy Board submitted its considered view on the subject of seasoning and durability.[19] It set out best practice for timber storage, promised to give up wartime shortcuts (like boiling plank to speed up seasoning), detailed all the attention being given to airing ships – and keeping out wet – during construction, and listed various trials of ideas on the subject put up by specialists. The Board also advocated further controlled experiments with techniques like barking trees before felling, and cutting timber in winter. Finally, it proposed extending the slip-covering programme, and concluded by expressing its confidence that the new structural techniques would not only add strength, but also prevent premature decay.

Although the prime concern of these measures was the battlefleet, the same degree of care was extended to the cruiser force. Frigates were all built in the Dockyards, of the best materials and at a slow pace that allowed proper seasoning. There were to be no compromises permitted. In 1816 the Navy Board reported a looming shortfall in the establishment of 160 frigates: there were only 102 available for service, and those repairing, building or ordered amounted to 25 more. This total included 23 of the 1812-13 emergency programmes, built of various kinds of north American fir 'of doubtful durability' (one frigate had already been broken up, and was the subject of a Parliamentary question); furthermore, there was only enough oak in the Dockyards for the ten frigates ordered but not so far started. Arguing from the six softwood ships of 1795-6 and the *Circe* class of 1804 that Baltic fir was superior to north American, averaging eight years' durability, the Navy Board proposed building twelve frigates of this timber. This was summarily dismissed by the Admiralty, which laid down a policy that future ships would be built with hardwoods only.[20]

Many of the resulting ships never saw active service, but were preserved in Ordinary as a strategic reserve. It is a tribute to its effectiveness that two frigates survive from this post-war policy: the *Trincomalee* at Hartlepool and the *Unicorn* at Dundee. Both are late members of the large and successful *Leda* class, but they are interesting contrasts, both in structure and current state. Launched in 1817, the *Trincomalee* was built of teak at Bombay, and, with the exception of the modified corvette stern fitted in 1847, is being restored to her original appearance, including a full rig. The *Unicorn*, on the other hand, was oak-built at Chatham – the home of Seppings's structural innovations – and displays the full panoply of round stern and diagonally braced hull; never commissioned, she also has a superb example of the full-length roof built over ships in Ordinary, and wisely this is being retained by her restorers.

NEW FRIGATE CLASSES

Design obsolescence was a slower process in the age of wood and canvas, but warships still conformed to the seemingly inexorable tendency in every class to grow

Sheer and profile draught of the French *Président* as taken off at Plymouth and dated 21 January 1811. Although the ship was captured in 1806, much of the decorative works remains French, but the fittings and tabulated mast and spar dimensions are British. Like many of Forfait's ships, she was sensitive to small changes in stowage and rig. In September 1810 the fore mast was moved forward (as shown on the draught) in response to complaints from the captain about the ship's handling. However, *Président* clearly enjoyed a good reputation for her sailing qualities, becoming the starting point for the *Seringapatam* class of 38s in 1813. *National Maritime Museum Dr1442a*

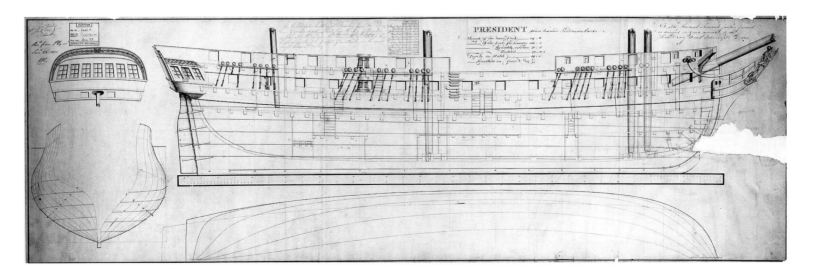

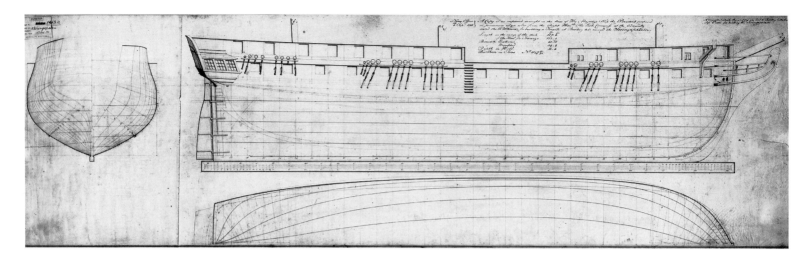

The sheer draught for the original *Seringapatam* design, dated 6 September 1813. Compared with its French prototype, the *Président*, the new class differed principally in the flatter decks (and therefore a nearly straight sheer), as well as reduced tumblehome and a more upright sternpost.
National Maritime Museum Dr1413a

in size and power over time. However, the mere introduction of a significantly more powerful type need not mean the instant demise of its predecessor. For example, the advent of the 18pdr frigate about 1780 did not spell the end of the 12pdr ship in any navy while there were only a few of the former afloat; but by 1800 with most heavy cruisers carrying 18pdr batteries, building 12pdr ships no longer made much sense. Thus some rates came to be outclassed by potential opponents, and were replaced by larger, and inevitably more expensive, types.

All navies have always faced versions of this conflict between quality and quantity, and it bears most acutely on the largest navies with the most invested in the *status quo*, and where wide commitments usually require large numbers of ships. A modern example was the acute problem for the US Navy of the 1970s which was faced with replacing large numbers of war-built destroyers with ships which some criticised as too weak but others argued were still too expensive. The balance of this 'hi-low mix' was controversial, and most of the attention was directed at the low end of the spectrum, which covered the largest number of ships.

It was much the same for the Royal Navy in 1815. The success of the American spar-decked frigates meant that Britain's enemies would build similar ships, so a costly 24pdr class would be needed to meet them. However, no navy would be able to afford more than a handful of such ships, and the vast majority of the Royal Navy's cruiser requirements, variously calculated at between 120 and 160 ships, would continue to be 18pdr-armed. The question then became one of deciding on the smallest effective design. Figures for relative costs already existed, a survey of 1812 having estimated the average annual expense for every rate in the Navy from 120 to 18 guns.[21] This calculation included all running costs, fitting and victualling, wear and tear, and wage bills for both Channel and Foreign Service, assuming provisions for 5 and 6 months and stores for 8 and 12 months respectively. For 18pdr frigates, the costs were:

Class	Home	Abroad	Home	Abroad
	Fitting & victualling		Total	
	£	£	£	£
38 guns	18,221	19,286	22,457	24,656
36 guns	14,810	16,638	20,520	22,539
32 guns	12,152	13,672	19,015	20,880

Thus a 38-gun ship was about 9 per cent more expensive to run than a 36, or 18 per cent more than a large 32. In rough terms, the same budget would keep at sea 100 of the largest class, 110 of the medium or 120 of the smallest.

Making a judgement on value for money was more difficult, and it is not clear how the Admiralty came to such decisions. In firepower terms, the weight of shot in a 38's broadside was 11 per cent greater than a 36's, and 39 per cent greater than a 32's (the latter having only 24pdr carronades compared with the 32pdrs of the bigger classes). It could be argued, therefore, that the 38 was the most cost-effective frigate of the 18pdr classes, although in practice it is more likely that the Admiralty took a more empirical view. The 32 was already out of favour, too much having been attempted on a limited displacement even for a wartime expediency. The 36 was better balanced, and in terms of numbers was close to being the standard British frigate, but at 950 tons it was probably too small by the second decade of the nineteenth century. With the exception of the emergency fir-built ships, the last 36s were all constructed at Deptford, where the width of the locks constrained the size of ships that could be built within the basin. It is no coincidence that after the basin entrance at Deptford was widened in August 1814,[22] no more 36s were ordered. This suggests that the decision to make the 38 the baseline frigate had already been taken.[23]

For ten years or more the 38s had been built to two draughts, the smaller 150ft *Leda* and the larger 154ft *Lively*. For many classes there were two competitive designs, because there were two Surveyors and each seems to have been an active sponsor of his own work. For this reason it was uncommon for a design to continue being built after the death of the designer – at least, without direct Admiralty intervention. Sir William Rule died in the spring of 1813 and no more *Lively*s were ordered, whereas *Leda*s continued to be built in numbers. At the time these decisions were being reached, the successes of the American navy had subjected Admiralty policy to a storm of criticism in both Parliament and the country. Even if Rule had lived longer, therefore, it is unlikely that the Admiralty could have countenanced more sisters for the unfortunate *Macedonian*, whereas building more *Shannon*s was beyond reproach.

The other element in the equation was the personality of Rule's successor Henry Peake. From the time he became Second Surveyor in 1806 he had shown limited ambition with regard to original hull forms, and most of the designs of the period were joint ventures, officially credited to 'the Surveyors': indeed, the largest vessels Peake seems to have draughted *ab initio* were the controversial 'coffin brigs' of the *Cherokee* class. He was unlikely to advocate a design of his own over one which had received the blessing of Admiralties stretching back to Earl Spencer's in the 1790s, so the decision to continue with the *Leda*s was probably unopposed. They were good all-round ships, very well liked, and still adequate for most cruiser services in the post-war world. There had been question marks over their structural strength, and hull capacity, but these could be addressed by Seppings' iron-strap diagonal system of construction, itself creating more space in the hold, and the introduction of iron water tanks, which greatly improved stowage.

However, a replacement for the larger *Lively* class was also required, and as it usually did when it had little confidence in its senior Surveyor, the Admiralty determined the prototype.[24] The chosen ship was the *Président*, a French prize that was 4ft longer, a foot broader but somewhat shallower than the *Lively*. However, it was to be 'an improved draught on the lines of the *Président*' that was ordered on 25 August 1813, and the surveyors complied with a proposed plan on the 4th of the following month. This was approved and the first of the class was ordered to be built of teak at Bombay as *Seringapatam*.[25]

This was the first frigate design produced since

Peake became Senior Surveyor, and conformed to his very conservative notions of his duties. He believed that the pursuit of improved performance through minor changes in hull form was fruitless, and confined his design activities to minor practical alterations, like raising the 'hanging' of decks (flattening the sheer) to increase the freeboard of midships ports. This form of tinkering with existing approved designs had not produced entirely satisfactory results in any of the 'Surveyors of the Navy' standard designs, and the same was to prove true of the *Seringapatam*s.

The class was first modified before the prototype had any significant sea-time. Compared with the *Leda*s, the new design had 9ins less height between decks, but the same amount extra in the hold, so from the second ship they were to have the berth deck lowered by 9ins.[26] The modified dimensions apparently added 18ins to the gundeck length at the same time, but this is only the product of the revised method of

TABLE 6/1: *Seringapatam* class 38/46-gun Fifth Rates

Specification

Armament	Upper deck	Quarterdeck	Forecastle	Guns	Men
DESIGN	28 x 18pdrs	14 x 32pdr carr	2 x 9pdrs 2 x 32pdr carr	38/46	315

Improved lines of the ex-French *Président* (later *Piedmontaise*)

	Lower deck feet-inches	Keel feet-inches	Breadth extreme feet-inches	Depth in hold feet-inches	Burthen Tons
ORIGINAL DESIGN	157-6	132-1	40-5	13-6	1148
AS COMPLETED					
Seringapatam	157-6	132-0½	40-6	13-6	1152
MODIFIED DESIGN	159-0	133-9⅜	40-5	12-9	1162
SECOND GROUP	159-0	133-2¼	41-5	13-6	1215

Notes: Post-war the following ships were ordered to the original draught: *Madagascar, Manilla, Druid, Tigris, Nemesis, Statira,* and *Jason* (the last three orders having originally been placed as Modified *Leda*s); but yards were instructed to adopt the modified design (which included a circular stern) during building in 1820-21. Only *Madagascar, Druid* and *Nemesis* were completed to this modified plan.

Additional ships originally ordered to the modified draught were: *Africaine, Leda, Hotspur, Eurotas, Tiber, Pique* and *Severn*; the first four were completed to the Modified design, but the others were later converted to the more substantially altered Second Group design, which all subsequent orders followed. Twelve ships were cancelled in 1831-2 and the only ships of the Second Group to complete were: *Andromeda, Seahorse, Stag, Forth* and *Maeander*.

TABLE 6/2: *Seringapatam* class 38/46-gun Fifth Rates

Building data

Name	Ordered	Builder	Laid down	Launched	Sailed	Fitted at	Fate
Seringapatam	6 Sep 1813	Bombay Dyd	Nov 1817	5 Sep 1819	30 Dec 1819	Bombay	Hulk 1847; BU Jun 1873

Notes: *Seringapatam, Madagascar* and *Andromeda* were built of teak, and the cancelled *Manilla* was intended to be.

measurement occasioned by grafting the new circular stern on to the design.[27]

Although the service of this class was entirely post-war, and therefore in strictest terms beyond the scope of this book, it is worth following the design history for the light it throws on the results of Peake's methods. As soon as she arrived in Britain, *Seringapatam* was sailed in trials against the *Active*, a frigate of a previous generation, and the results were disappointing, particularly in terms of relative speed, but also in weatherliness. The captain of the new ship, Samuel Warren, was in a good position to make an evaluation since in 1810 he had commanded the ex-French *Président*, on which the *Seringapatam* was based. His view was that despite the same hull form the new ship was deeper in the water for the same ballast, her teak-built hull being significantly heavier than the part-fir construction of the French model; but the ship also carried extra water, thanks to her iron tanks, and 150 fathoms of chain cable. She certainly sailed faster at reduced draught.

Warren also thought *Seringapatam* needed taller topmasts and topgallants, but was stable enough to land about 25 tons of ballast at the same time; the leewardliness could be countered by additions to the false keel. The internal arrangements were not perfect either, and Warren requested a number of changes, the most significant being the lowering of the magazines. As usual, the Navy Board opposed these changes, but after considerable argument was forced to agree to many of the proposals, including additional false keel and increasing the mast and spar dimensions to the establishment of the *Cambrian*; the alterations were later extended to all ships of the class.[28]

The remedial action was not entirely successful, and in 1826 the first British- (and oak-) built ship, the *Druid*, was sailed in extensive trials in the West Indies against the *Hussar*, one of the *Lively* class the new design was intended to replace. As with many later sailing trials the results were difficult to interpret, but *Druid* seemed to have the advantage close-hauled in stronger conditions. Captain Chambers had not at that point decided if

Druid was a very fast ship, but he was sure she was a fine man of war. In general, he expressed himself pleased: 'The reputation *Hussar* has gained for sailing in this country, her trim being known . . . makes the result more satisfactory.'[29] However, later captains found her less stiff than she ought to have been in fresh breezes, which would have produced difficulties with elevating or depressing the guns sufficiently in action. The other problem, common in French-derived hulls, was the small stowage of the hull, exacerbated in this class by the sharp rise of floor, which did not allow two tiers of the standard iron tanks. Trim was also sensitive, since she was easily brought down by the stern, and a draught aft of more than 18ft 4in immersed her broad quarters, causing drag. The Comptroller, Byam Martin, took the problems of the class to Seppings, who modified the design with 9ins more depth in hold, and rearranged platform beams for better stowage of the tanks.[30] Further consideration led to a foot being added to their extreme breadth, but by the time the improved ships were deemed successful the days of the 18pdr frigate were over.

Many of these problems might have been anticipated if the authorities had realised that they had a virtual prototype for the new class already under construction in the form of the *Forte*. This ship was almost a carbon copy of the *Révolutionnaire*, a French prize of 1794, which was herself a sister (or at least a near-sister) of the *Président*, used as the basis for the *Seringapatam*s; although separated by a decade both ships were designed by Forfait and exhibit almost identical hull forms. The construction of the *Forte* was given the lowest possible priority and she was not launched until 1814, more than twelve years after the original order. When this ship finally went to sea in 1820 she exhibited many of the shortcomings later experienced with the first of the *Seringapatam*s, but by then it was too late to incorporate the experience into the design of the new class.

A combination of these modified *Seringapatam*s and the *Leda*s continued to be built for fifteen years after

The sheer draught of the *Jason*, dated 27 February 1821, notes both the modified dimensions for the *Seringapatam* class and the more radically altered Second Group. An Admiralty Order of 11 October 1827 instructed the ship to be built to the Second Group dimensions, but like many of her sisters the ship was never completed at all, being finally cancelled in 1831. All the later ships of the class were designed with the circular stern, as shown here.
National Maritime Museum Dr1588

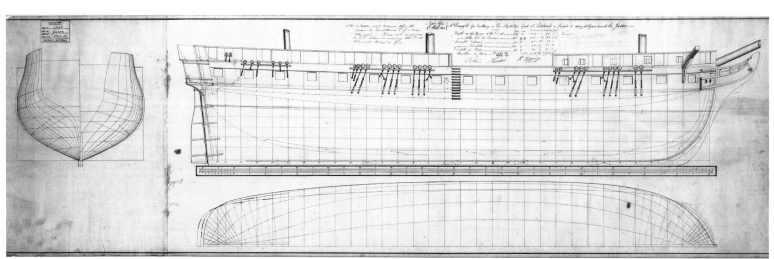

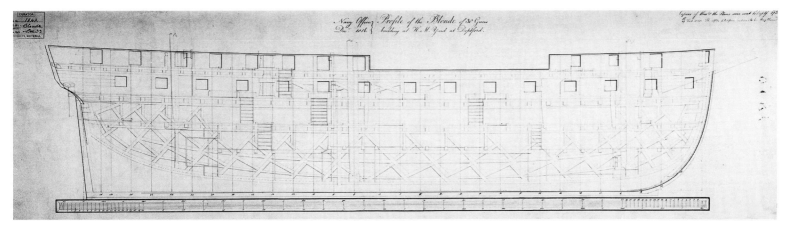

the end of the war, although structurally they were much changed by the adoption of the round stern and Seppings's other innovations like iron diagonal bracing. However, in 1831-2 the 18pdr frigate was finally abandoned, leaving some twelve of the former class and two of the latter to be cancelled.

There is no evidence during this period of any Admiralty interest in other 18pdr frigate designs, with the single exception of the *Blonde*, which resulted from an unusual initiative by the Navy Board. Ordered on 22 January 1816, this ship was originally intended to be one of the *Euryalus* class 36s, whose construction had been maintained solely because they were the largest ships that could pass through the basin gates at Deptford Dockyard. With the post-war abandonment of 36s, the Navy Board suggested converting the order to a 38 based on the lines of *Euryalus*. This may have been an exercise in economising with moulds or existing timber, but in the event the design was not simply scaled up, but added relatively more length, producing a ship midway between the two existing 38-gun designs. The *Euryalus* class had a good reputation for all-round qualities, so *Blonde* may have been an attempt to create a similar 38 to replace both designs; whatever their size, all 38s carried the same armament.

The result was a fast and weatherly ship, that performed well in the Anglo-French-Russian operations leading up to Navarino in 1827. According to her captain, she was 'so weatherly under all circumstances as to astonish everybody, English as well as French and Russians'. She was, however, somewhat crank, and an uneasy sea-boat, frequently damaging her head, and a later captain summed her up as 'a ship without any extraordinary quality, or unusual defect.'[31] Given such a mix of qualities, it is not surprising that the design was not repeated.

The other major post-war requirement was a new 24pdr class to face the American spar-deckers, and other foreign ships their successes would inevitably inspire. Goaded by the victories of USS *Constitution* and her sisters during the War of 1812, the Admiralty had felt obliged to abandon traditional restraints on size and cost for the *Leander* and *Newcastle*, but a less

extravagant design was required if peacetime ships were to be afforded in any numbers. To build the two big 50s had not been an easy decision to reach, since it implied a recognition that the Royal Navy needed ships of the same size to have a realistic chance of winning, and this had massive cost implications if applied across the whole fleet.[32] As a result, no sooner had this pair been accepted than the Admiralty approached their designers to inquire whether the same force (*ie* armament) could be carried on a smaller tonnage.

Typically, Barrallier replied that the *Newcastle* was the minimum necessary if the ship was to have the usual qualities beyond mere gun-power. Sir William Rule was terminally ill, but the other Surveyor, Henry Peake, suggested that a ship of about 1430 tons (compared with 1556 for the *Leander*) could carry the same armament. He recommended dimensions of 172ft by 43ft, making the ship narrower than *Leander* – although Peake liked to express it as proportionately greater length, which he felt would improve the ship's sailing qualities. This was worked up into a completed draught by the newly appointed triumvirate of

There is no surviving sheer plan for the *Blonde*, although as a derivative of the *Euryalus* class the lines of the ship would hold no surprises. The profile, dated December 1816, reproduced here shows a standard layout for a 38-gun frigate of the time. The hull incorporates the Seppings trussed frame, which was supposedly not applicable to frigates. The source of this statement is the well-known history of naval architecture by John Fincham, but while it may be true as a generalisation, it is clear that all the new frigate designs of around 1815 were intended to be so built. It may be that the new ships were completed with the later iron diagonal straps, but the battleship-style trussed frame was certainly employed in repairing frigates for a few years post-war. *National Maritime Museum E0728*

TABLE 6/3: *Blonde* class 38/46-gun Fifth Rate

Specification

Armament	Upper deck	Quarterdeck	Forecastle		Guns	Men
DESIGN	28 x 18pdrs	14 x 32pdr carr	2 x 9pdrs 2 x 32pdr carr		38/46	315

Enlarged lines of the *Euryalus*

	Lower deck feet-inches	Keel feet-inches	Breadth extreme feet-inches	Depth in hold feet-inches	Burthen Tons
DESIGN	155-0	143-2	39-8	13-6	1103
AS COMPLETED					
Blonde	155-1	143-2*	39-9½	13-6½	1102⁷⁵/₉₄

Notes: *This is the figure quoted in the launching report and all subsequent official lists, but by the usual tonnage calculation it should be nearer 130ft 11in.

TABLE 6/4: *Blonde* class 38/46-gun Fifth Rate

Building data

Name	Ordered	Builder	Laid down	Launched	Sailed	Fitted at	Fate
Blonde	22 Jan 1816	Deptford Dyd	Mar 1816	12 Jan 1819	13 Apr 1819	Deptford	Hulk 1850; renamed *Calypso* 1870; sold 28 Feb 1895

Notes: The ship was housed over in Mar 1817; she was in Ordinary at Greenhithe from Apr 1819 until fitted for sea at Woolwich, sailing on her first commission on 9 Sep 1824.

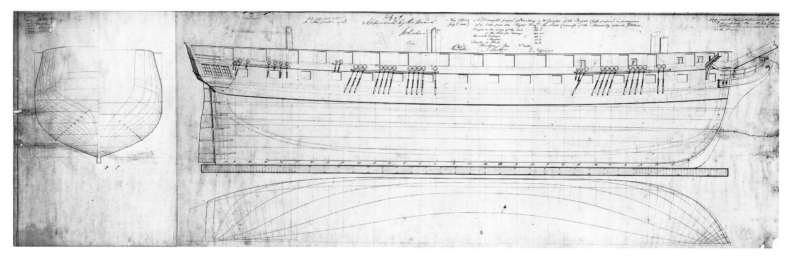

Prepared in response to the Admiralty's specification of 7 June 1813, this draught of the new '50-gun ship of the frigate class' was dated 2 July following. The *Java* was the Admiralty's considered response to the problem of providing a 24pdr frigate that was as powerful as the American spar-deckers on a displacement that would allow sufficient numbers to be built post-war to meet the similar ships the French and Russian were inspired to produce by the American victories. As originally conceived, the ship was a genuine 'double-banked' frigate, with a proposed spar-deck armament of twenty-eight 42pdr carronades and two long 24s, but by the time the ship was brought into service the waist was no longer armed. Experience had shown that the waist guns interfered with the handling of the ship in action and, forming a choke-point between the ship's side and the boom boats amidships, impeded movement fore and aft.
National Maritime Museum Dr1496a

The profile of the *Java* as built. The *Java* must have been one of the very first new designs to incorporate the Seppings trussed frame from the beginning. The scheme was generally similar to that employed in line of battle ships, although the number of main riders was actually increased. One major improvement in the structure of the *Java* over the *Leander* and *Newcastle* was that the framing was carried up to the top of the spar-deck rail, in effect incorporating it into the hull like the upper deck of a two-decker, whereas the upper battery of the earlier ships had been protected only by lightly framed berthing like that on a conventional quarterdeck. One great advantage claimed by Seppings (and generally overlooked by historians) was the economy of his system: in this drawing all the shaded elements were provided from old reused materials, which because of their short lengths could be used without any loss in strength.
National Maritime Museum Dr1504

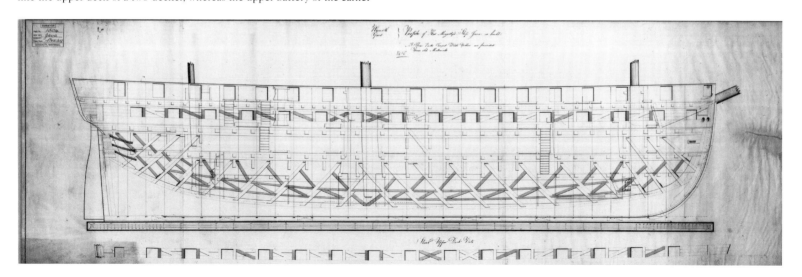

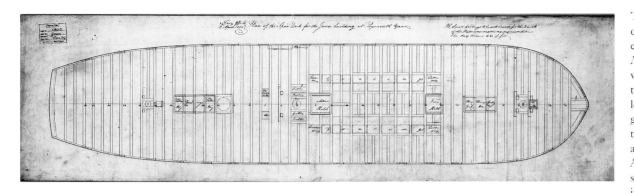

The spar deck plan for the *Java*, dated 11 April 1815. After some experience with *Leander* and *Newcastle* (see Chapter 9) the waist area was planked between the fore and main hatches, leaving only a narrow row of gratings on each side to ventilate the upper deck; the gratings had a ladderway at each end. Alterations to the draught suggest that it was originally intended to provide two parallel rows of gratings per side, but the inboard ones were planked over. *National Maritime Museum Dr1503*

Surveyors, Peake, Tucker and Seppings, and on 9 July 1813 the first ship was ordered to this design as the *Java*. This ship, to be oak-built in a Royal Dockyard, was clearly never intended for the existing conflict, and provides another example of the dichotomy in Admiralty planning between measures intended to win the war and longer-term provision for the peace.[33] With some modification – the decks were raised and a circular stern adopted – the design was used for six additional ships of the *Southampton* group ordered in 1816-17.

The existing frigate classes survived post-war, but the old gun-ratings disappeared in a major overhaul of the system. Ever since the introduction of the carronade, the actual gun-power of many classes had far exceeded its traditional rating. It was a product of custom and established usage, with no overt intention to deceive, but during the War of 1812 it was felt that the Americans had gained a distinct propaganda advantage by exploiting this dichotomy. In US warships the difference between nominal and real force was even greater than in Royal Navy practice, allowing the American media to trumpet victories over 'superior force' when exactly the opposite was the truth. Since the British had been none too careful in reporting their own triumphs for the previous twenty years, their case against the Americans was weak, but the issue became more sensitive in the post-war years because the US Navy was building radically different, and far more powerful ships, but giving them traditional ratings – a '74' with three flush decks that no more paralleled the usual European two-decker than one of the spar-decked '44's resembled a frigate. The concern was not the size or the design of them *per se* – although they gave the Admiralty pause for thought – but how they might be described in any future conflict. The British decided to set a good example and from February 1817 the new rating listed the carriage guns (long, short and carronade) actually carried. There were still a few minor anomalies, but the progress of standardisation allowed the system to work very well. The 38 thus became a 46 and remaining 36s either a 44 or a 42; a few of the bigger 18pdr ships became 48s. Of the 24pdr frigates, the 40s derived from *Endymion* were rerated 50s, the *rasées* 58s, and the 'double-banked' *Newcastle* and *Leander* went up from 50s to 60s.[34]

TABLE 6/5: *Java* class 50-gun Fourth Rate

Specification

Armament	Upper deck	Spar deck		Guns	Men
DESIGN	30 x 24pdrs	2 x 24pdrs, 28 x 42pdr carr		50	450
CHANGES BY AO: 3 Jun 1823		6 x 24pdrs, 16 x 42pdr carr		52	

Designed by the Surveyors of the Navy

	Lower deck feet-inches	Keel feet-inches	Breadth extreme feet-inches	Depth in hold feet-inches	Burthen Tons
DESIGN	172-0	145-1¼	43-4	14-3	1449³⁰⁄₉₄
AS COMPLETED *Java*	171-11½	144-9⅗	43-6	14-3	1457⁵⁶⁄₉₄

Notes: As completed the ship did not carry guns on the gangways.

TABLE 6/6: *Java* class 50-gun Fourth Rate

Building data

Name	Ordered	Builder	Laid down	Launched	Sailed	Fitted at	Fate
Java	9 Jul 1813	Plymouth Dyd	Mar 1814	16 Nov 1815	1826	Plymouth	Target ship 1861; BU Nov 1862

Notes: The ship went into Ordinary on completion and was not fitted for sea until 1826. Post-war six further vessels of the *Southampton* class were built to a design modified from the *Java* by the addition of an extra foot of breadth and three inches more depth in hold.

PART II: THE SHIPS

CHAPTER SEVEN

Construction

THROUGHOUT the wars against the French republic and empire probably the most significant, persistent and intractable worry for the Navy Board was the scarcity of suitable shipbuilding timber; for the Navy as a whole it was probably second in importance only to the growing shortage of skilled seamen. It was not, however, entirely without remedy, and both Admiralty and Navy Board adopted a variety of measures to alleviate if not overcome the problem. These included: looking for new shipbuilding resources, both within the country and overseas; searching for new sources of timber supply, and experimenting with new species, especially softwoods; introducing greater economy in the employment of timber; and finally altering the ways that ships were constructed in response to these exigencies of supply. This last is the central theme of this chapter, which culminates in the structural reforms associated with Sir Robert Seppings, but the other factors have been sketched in to demonstrate the conditions under which these innovations came to fruition. It will be seen that the famous diagonal trussed frame was not a pure engineering solution to an age-old problem, as it is so often presented, but a product of a particular set of circumstances; furthermore, it was only one (albeit the best) of a number of similar experimental schemes being tested at the same time.

NATURE OF THE PROBLEM

Ever since R G Albion published his pioneering *Forests and Seapower* in 1926, historians have been aware of the importance of naval supplies, and especially timber, to British maritime strategy. Timber shortages were a major determinant of British foreign policy, but more recent research reveals that Albion tended to both exaggerate and simplify.[1] The availability of timber fluctuated, even within quite short periods of time, and it was usually only specific types of timber – especially large-scantling pieces for frames, and 'grown' knees – that gave serious cause for concern. Moreover, in practical terms a 'shortage' could often be defined as

a scarcity of timber at a price the Navy Board thought reasonable or wished to pay.[2]

The workings of supply and demand were influenced by many factors, some within the Navy's control and some far beyond it. Of the Navy's own making, by far the most significant factor was the scale of its shipbuilding activity. While the trend in timber expenditure was generally upwards between 1803 and 1812 (rising from 40,034 to 74,346 'loads'), in some years, like 1808-9, demand was particularly high (60,886 and 64,475 loads).[3] Of course, these surges in building programmes were a response to strategic developments, which may in themselves have had a deleterious impact on timber supply; so as demand increased sharply, it was not uncommon to find supply simultaneously constricted.

For example, the Treaty of Tilsit between Napoleon and Tsar Alexander in 1807 threatened to make the Continental System truly effective and in the short-term certainly restricted British naval supplies from the Baltic. The British counter-blockade vastly expanded the theatre of war and required a commensurate expansion in the size of the Navy, prompting a huge increase in shipbuilding. An attempt to substitute American for Baltic timber was interrupted by the United States Embargo Act of 1807 and the Non-Intercourse Act of 1808, but to some extent this was gradually offset by the increasing exploitation of Canadian forests as the war progressed. Imported timber definitely grew in relative importance during this period, but, again, was subject to fluctuations: excluding thickstuff and plank, as a proportion of the total expended in the Royal Dockyards, foreign timber varied between 28 per cent in 1803, 10 per cent in 1806, 38 per cent in 1808, and 29 per cent in 1809 (the last three being years of particularly high and very similar total usage), culminating in 43 per cent of the huge emergency programme of 1812.[4]

Much of the imported timber was softwood – or at least was not oak, the preferred British shipbuilding medium – so the Navy Board faced problems of quality as well as quantity. As early as 1804, there was a renewed appreciation of the need to husband oak, and to use fir or a similar substitute wherever possible.[5] It seems to have been widely accepted that domestic forests could not provide a significant increase in the supply of oak, and by 1807 the Navy Board felt obliged to point out to the Admiralty in the context of the proposed large shipbuilding programme 'the generally received opinion of the growing scarcity of timber in the country'.[6] It is true that the shortage was most acute for specific types of timber – in February 1806, for instance, the greatest difficulty was said to be long compass timber for the upper parts of frames[7] – but they were often vital elements where traditional wooden shipbuilding could accept no substitutes. In these cases, the shipbuilders were driven to look for new techniques of construction or fastening.

The timber shortage, then, pressed with varying degrees of urgency throughout the Napoleonic Wars, but never reached a genuine climacteric. The problem was most severely felt during St Vincent's time at the Admiralty because he refused to acknowledge the workings of the market and would neither allow new contracts to be placed at the going rate nor allow the Navy Board to cancel existing agreements that price inflation had rendered onerous to the merchants. As a result of this great self-inflicted wound, stocks of timber in the Dockyards sank to a nadir of 34,562 loads in March 1803, just as the renewal of the war was making great demands on supplies. However, this situation was easily, and rapidly, remedied by a change of administration, and with it a return to a more realistic policy;

by the beginning of 1807 there were 80,660 loads in the Dockyards, although some 17 per cent of that quantity had been imported, whereas there was almost no foreign timber in store in 1803.

Concern for timber supplies occurred in regular cycles, and possibly reaching new heights with each successive 'crisis', but there was never a total, or even critical, breakdown of supply. In broadest terms this was made possible by British control of the seas and domination of the timber market, but in the context of the Dockyards it was also a tribute to the efforts of the Admiralty and Navy Board; the various strategies they employed to meet these needs claim the attention of the remainder of this chapter.

NEW SHIPBUILDING CAPACITY

Timber is both heavy and bulky so to avoid high transportation costs shipbuilding tended to be concentrated near accessible sources of suitable woodland and forest. In these circumstances, to open up shipbuilding in new areas was tantamount to exploiting new reserves of timber. The Admiralty took a number of steps in this direction,[8] but within the United Kingdom the potential was limited, not least because the timber shortage was regarded as a nationwide phenomenon.

If not at home, then extra capacity had to be sought overseas. However, it was not enough to find appropriate virgin woodland near a suitable shore; ideally, there should also be an existing industry with an indigenous skilled workforce, capable of following a specification

Fort Cornwallis on Pulo Penang, or Prince of Wales Island, in modern-day Malaysia was the Royal Navy's most remote shipbuilding yard, although activity was very short-lived. The ship in frame is presumably the *Malacca*, the only warship completed there. This print was published in 1810, by a company which also produced charts and pilots of the East Indies. *National Maritime Museum PY2727*

and a draught. It is to the Admiralty's credit that it set in train moves which eventually led to successful naval shipbuilding in Bermuda and India. The former built a number of fast advice boats and sloops based on a local model, but it was India which was to make the greatest contribution to expatriate warship building, constructing both two-deckers and frigates in limited, but significant numbers.

Using thinly veiled threats of legislation to limit the size of the largest Indiamen, St Vincent persuaded the Honourable East India Company to build warships at cost in its Bombay dockyard. The local Parsee families that provided the shipwrights already had a fund of experience building European-style ships for John Company, as well as refitting the King's warships, so it was considered no great step to constructing the latter from scratch. In May 1802 the Company's Court of Directors formally agreed to approach its Bombay directors with a view to building a 74 and a frigate annually. The Company would waive any profit on construction and would transport the necessary draughts, instructions and stores by its own ships.[9] The estimated costs, converted from rupees, were to be £38,412-10s for the 74 and £21,337-10s for the frigate.

India eventually produced a limited number of ships highly regarded for the strength and durability of their teak hulls, but the arrangement was not without difficulties. Some of these were the characteristic problems of a new venture on an entirely unprecedented scale – like the trouble involved in obtaining teak of a scantling suitable for the floor timbers of a 74. Exasperated by unaccountable delays, in October 1811 the Admiralty even threatened to build no more battleships in Bombay, but was mollified by suitable explanations. However, the Navy Board faced more regular frustrations, essentially reflecting the difficulty of controlling a manufacturing process at such distance with the long-winded communications of the time.

Perhaps symbolic of the problem was the confusion over the naming of the first two frigates (see Chapter 1),

but it gradually became clear that quality control was a more serious concern. The first survey of a teak frigate in a Royal Dockyard reported favourably on methods of construction and fastening, which generally followed traditional British practice, with hanging and lodging knees, although the bottom was largely secured with iron nails.[10] However, following criticisms from the captain (as outlined in Chapter 1), *Salsette* was given a more thorough survey in December 1812, when it was discovered that the hull form was nothing like the *Inconstant* draught to which it was supposed to have been built. The Indian builders were handed out a sharp reprimand and ordered in future not to depart from the lines of the draughts supplied.[11] There was no repetition of quite such a gross example, and in January 1814 a British Master Shipwright was appointed to oversee work at Bombay, but the Navy Board still felt it necessary to expend considerable effort, especially regarding the new diagonal construction methods, to send the Indian builders elaborate instructions and specially prepared structural models. The increasing use of iron exacerbated the difficulties because of the lack of the necessary ironworking experience in India. At first plate knees and standards were sent out, but eventually the ship structure was modified to allow the ships to sail to Britain without iron knees, which were then fitted at a Royal Dockyard.[12] Considering that they often sailed encumbered with a spare teak frame for erection in Britain, these Bombay-built ships were obviously very strong even without iron reinforcing, and they generally enjoyed far longer than average lives.

One other symptom of the absence of central management was the lack of any control over costs. When asked in January 1807 for an account of building expenses for the *Salsette*, the Navy Board did not have the information. Indeed, they could not even hazard a guess until August 1810, when they thought it amounted, less materials supplied, to £20,667; this was close to the Company's original estimate, but compared badly

The confusion over the status of the *Malacca* extends to the draught, which is described as representing 'the Honourable Company Frigate *Penang* as built at Fort Cornwallis and launched 13 Aug 1809. Prince of Wales Island, 6 March 1810'. It is annotated 'Duplicate' and 'Recd in the Navy Office 19 March 1811'. The curious ticked lines may result from the technique of copying by 'pricking through' a master draught to the paper below. Apart from increased length, the ship differs in detail from the *Euryalus* class to which she nominally belonged, most noticeably in the built-up head. Despite the various formal armament orders, the draught gives the actual 'as completed' arming of the quarterdeck as ten 32pdr carronades and two long 9s (which conforms exactly to the arrangement of ports), and four 32pdr carronades on the forecastle.
National Maritime Museum E0726

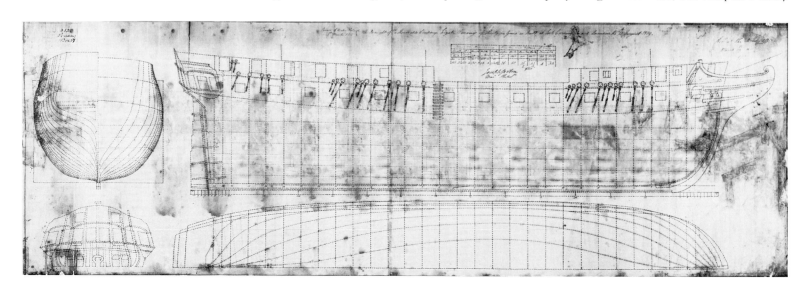

The quality of teak as a shipbuilding timber is perhaps best demonstrated by the state of the frigate *Trincomalee*'s framing. During the recent restoration work on this Bombay-built ship of 1817 it was discovered that much of the underwater hull was sound, although a few lower futtocks needed replacing, clearly seen here in the lighter coloured timbers. Since teak is now prohibitively expensive, African opepe was used instead, but it is estimated that even when restoration is complete some 50-60 per cent of the original ship timber will remain. *HMS Trincomalee Trust 232/6a*

with £17,729 for a sister ship built in a British merchant yard, and £16,187 for *Meleager* built at Chatham Dockyard. When capacity was short, the premium might be justifiable, but the real cost proved far higher. For whatever reason the issue remained unresolved, and the East India Company did not submit a full invoice until November 1820, when they claimed £27,922, but sought to add a further £27,286 for interest to cover the period November 1806 to the end of 1818.[13] The second ship was purchased complete for the even higher figure of £43,046, less £3272 for stores supplied, but the most costly of the East Indies frigates was the *Malacca*, built at the Company's station on Prince of Wales Island (modern Penang in Malaysia). This ship was reckoned to have cost £36,064 at Penang, plus £10,174 for fitting out in Bengal, and a further £2581 when the ship arrived in Britain.

While India and Bermuda were the only sources of shipbuilding outside Britain to come to fruition, they were not the only ones scouted. Some of these were unlikely, nor were they confined to British colonies: after the flight of the Portuguese court to Brazil, and the establishment of a South America squadron, in November 1809 consideration was given to the construction of a warships at Rio de Janeiro. Reports of both the timber resources, and the willingness of the Portuguese government to co-operate, proved wildly exaggerated, and the scheme was abandoned at the end of 1811.[14] British seapower could have protected facilities at Rio, but rather stranger was the proposal to build ships in Russia. Samuel Bentham, who had served in Russia before the war, believed he could persuade the naval authorities of what was then a British

ally to allow the construction of two 74s and two 36-gun frigates at a cost of about £12 per ton.[15] Quite apart from the poor reputation Russian-built vessels suffered for their short life-spans, such ships would always have been hostage to the febrile fortunes of the anti-French coalitions, so it is probably as well that Bentham failed in this venture, despite a personal visit and considerable effort on his part.

The search for additional shipbuilding capacity continued, but within British domains. In December 1808 the Navy Board began testing timber cut in Plattenburg Bay, Cape of Good Hope, and as a result in March 1811 Algernon Jones of Portsmouth Dockyard was appointed to investigate in more depth the timber resources of the Cape with a view to possible shipbuilding. Limited amounts of some exotic species were imported, but no naval shipbuilding was established in South Africa. At much the same time the Navy Board was casting cold water on a proposal from a company called Usborne Benson to build ships in Canada from north American oak. The Dockyards had been using such timber for repairs, but their experience was that it was fine when used externally, but lacked durability when closed up and excluded from the air, so the Navy Board felt that it was not 'expedient' to build with it.[16] Much of the effort to tackle the timber problem was hamstrung by this conservative, if not actively prejudiced, attitude in the Dockyards to 'non-traditional' types of wood; if ships failed, the yards were criticised, so there was a natural reluctance to take unnecessary risks. Experience, particularly with the durability of timber, took time to accumulate, but gradually supply pressures forced the Dockyards to try new species.

Part of a series of drawings, dated 11 June 1802, showing the sizes and moulded shapes of futtock timbers required for 98s, 74s and 38-gun frigates. Designed to provide patterns in the search for suitable new shipbuilding timber, the first set was sent to New South Wales in the *Glatton* in 1802, but later copies went to other far-flung areas that might have suitable woodland, including the Cape of Good Hope.
National Maritime Museum Dr509b

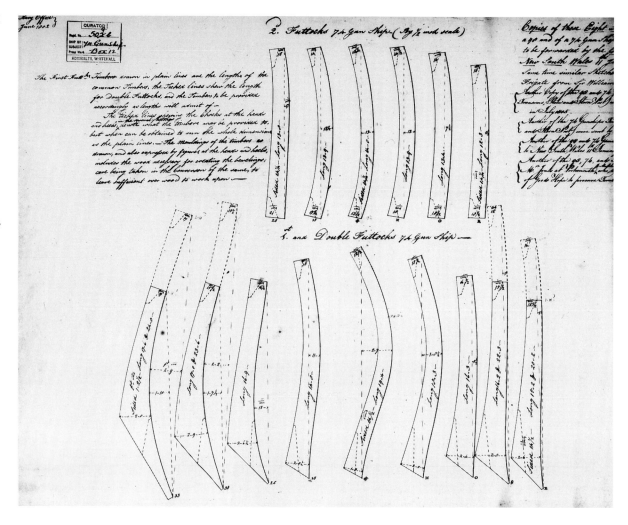

NEW SHIPBUILDING TIMBERS

Timber importation was in the hands of commercial companies and, with the exception of a few exploratory initiatives, the Navy Board did not directly determine the sources of supply, but as a major purchaser its attitude to timber of particular types and origins affected its saleability. The prime requirement was durability and resistance to rot (which was effectively the same consideration), and on those grounds English oak was first choice. Other oak was tried, but not always to the Board's satisfaction: the 'oak from Holstein' in some of *Macedonian*'s floors and first futtocks, as noted in the ship's Progress Book entry, was part of a consignment purchased in 1802, but it proved disappointing in its lack of longevity. It was much the same story with Canadian 'white oak', which was first employed for masts and spars in 1803, but was extended to the repair of hulls after about 1806.[17]

Softwoods, on the other hand, had always had their uses. Cheap, quickly-built ships up to frigate size had been constructed of fir in times of emergency – most recently seven vessels in 1795-6 – and the tactic was repeated for eight small 32s ordered in 1804. Although the generic term 'fir' was applied in these cases, later practice was to differentiate between softwood varieties, such as red, yellow and pitch pine. A close analysis of their scantlings also reveals selected use of hardwoods in areas subject to high stress or wear even in the nominally all-fir ships.[18]

As early as 1804 the Admiralty instructed the Navy Board to report on the 'propriety' of husbanding supplies of oak by ordering fir wherever possible.[19] By the end of 1806 the Navy Board was looking at the possibility of mixing timbers (previously regarded as highly dubious practice), with a view to extending the use of fir in the construction and repair of large ships to further conserve oak. It reported that fir could replace oak for the following elements:

Frame: cross chocks in midships; all topside except port timbers; upper sills on quarterdeck ports; all fillings between timbers

Orlop: middle pieces of beams, carlings and ledges (except hatchways); sailroom carlings; stanchions; wing and crown and flat of storerooms

Gundeck: middle pieces of beams; pillars; upper strake of spirketting; planking between ports; manger boards

Upper deck: all beams except hatchways; main and fore

mast partners; transom carlings and ledges (except hatchways); pillars; spirketting upper strake; planking between ports

Quarterdeck and forecastle: beams (except in wake of galley and topsail sheet and jeer bitts); spirketting upper strake; plank between ports

Roundhouse: beams and clamps

Outboard: planking from black strake upwards, except in wake of chains and channels; channels, except outer pieces; stools and [*illegible*] on quarter; portlids; rudder, except main piece

At the same time the Navy Board estimated that it would need about 41,310 loads of softwood over the next three years, and considered fir (pitch pine) from Georgia, North and South Carolina to be the best.[20] Pitch pine began to be purchased from 1805, red pine from 1808 and yellow pine from 1809, and its use grew rapidly.[21] From this date Britain's 'hearts of oak' were increasingly kept going by large-scale injections of softwood.

Concern for the performance of these timber 'mixes' can be traced in the documentation, which henceforth tends to list unusual timbers employed in building and repairing ships in central records like the Progress Books, and occasionally even on the draughts. The Dockyards were also called upon to submit regular and more detailed reports on what timbers were employed in what manner in what ships.[22] This expansion in the employment of softwoods meant that the Dockyards began to lay in large stocks, and during the American emergency of 1812, the Navy Board was pleased to point out to the Admiralty that the massive programme of fir frigates was only possible because it had so prudently accumulated so much timber of this nature.[23] Although constructed in merchant yards, these ships were all built with government timber supplied from the Dockyards and charged at the current rate of £12 per load for red pine and £10 for yellow.

Besides conventional means of supply, the Navy Board also gained useful experience of foreign timbers from the large stocks occasionally captured abroad. Not the least important benefit of the Copenhagen expedition of 1807 was the vast store of seasoned timber brought away from the Danish navy's main dockyard. At least one frigate was built at Chatham to make use of 'a great quantity of the Danish timber in store'.[24] Even the disastrous Walcheren expedition of 1809 provided frame timbers captured at Flushing and employed in the 74-gun *Chatham*; later, timber taken at the surrender of Genoa in 1814 was used in *Formidable*, ordered 1815.

By the end of the war the Dockyards were necessarily using much softwood, as well as some foreign hardwoods – Jones's mission to the Cape, for example, produced limited quantities of stinkwood that was used interchangeably with oak. While it is true that 'fir' ships included some hardwood components, it was now equally the case that 'oak' ships sheltered many softwood elements.[25] This mixed construction was blamed for the increasing incidence of rot and decay in the ships built since the renewal of the war, so the Dockyards were forced to substitute scientific investigation of the properties of timber for received wisdom. This process was to accelerate after the war, but as an example of the kind of work being done in the Dockyards one might quote a series of experiments carried out at Deptford in May 1814 to test the effects on various types of timber of steaming or boiling in a kiln (processes used to accelerate seasoning); English and Quebec oak, red pine and pitch pine were each subjected to three different methods.[26]

MORE ECONOMICAL USE OF TIMBER

While seeking to ease the supply of timber, the Navy Board was also pressed to make better use of what was available. There was an increasing emphasis on reducing waste and reusing sound materials. In October

The disposition of frame draught used for the *Lively* class 38s. Apart from the familiar changes to the gunports on the upperworks, the draught was standard for the whole class, and does not show any signs of alterations to accommodate the new scantlings establishment of 1811.
National Maritime Museum Dr6241

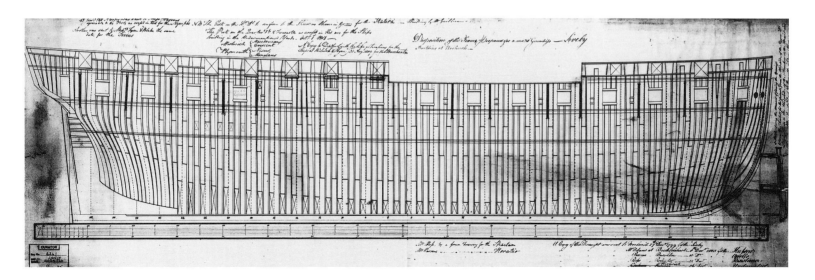

The profile draught of the *Cambrian* shows the prominent angled top riders that were features of the shipbuilding of the 1790s. While these internal stiffeners added local reinforcement, they did not contribute much to the overall strength of the hull; indeed, it was eventually decided that they were counter-productive, because as the ship 'worked' in a seaway the patches of rigidity represented by the riders tended to encourage movement in surrounding elements of the structure, tearing the ship apart. Top and breadth riders were therefore abandoned by Admiralty Order in 1806 for all ships either building or under repair.
National Maritime Museum Dr1830

1803 the economy-obsessed St Vincent Admiralty reminded the Navy Board of a store of 'fir timber, foreign and decayed timber' at Plymouth (all regarded as second quality) and wanted to know if frigates could be built with it.[27] The nominally fir-built *Thames*, 32 guns, constructed at Chatham in 1804, certainly comprised mainly old ship timbers, and her Plymouth-built sisters also incorporated reused and second-rate material in lieu of the elm and beech preferred for some features.[28] However, the attitude did not change with the administration, and the ex-Spanish frigate *Imperieuse*, which needed an expensive three-month Great Repair in 1806, was only deemed worth the effort because of the availability of 'old materials, inferior oak and fir'.[29]

As certain items, and especially knees, became rarer, more care was expended breaking up old ships – indeed, the contemporary phrase 'taken to pieces' more accurately defines the process. Dismantled ships became a recognised answer to specific shortages: for instance, in 1802 Woolwich was so short of cross chocks for the frigate *Lively* then under construction that an enquiry was sent to Sheerness to see if any were available from the recently broken-up *Nonsuch*.[30] The habit of mind persisted throughout the war, and when in anticipation of a lasting peace in May 1814 the Navy Board was asked for its opinion on the relative merits of selling or breaking up old ships, it recommended selling prizes but dismantling British-built ships for the reusable timber.[31]

Cannibalisation reached a unique pitch in the case of the *Clyde*, a fir-built 38 which by 1804 was eight years old and considered already beyond her anticipated period of service. However, she was highly regarded, and the Navy Board believed that there was enough value in her iron and wood knees, floor timbers, iron stanchions, masts, yards and 'furniture' to warrant building a similar vessel. Thus the *Clyde* was 'rebuilt' to the same draught, a process common a century earlier but probably unprecedented since; even in the early eighteenth century the rebuilt ship tended to be to a larger, better or simply newer design.[32]

While such economies were good housekeeping, to

achieve a more cost-effective use of timber required a more radical appraisal of the way it was applied to shipbuilding: in other words, it was necessary to look at ship design. In 1796 James Gambier, then serving on the Admiralty Board, designed the frigate *Triton*, an experimental ship that was built from far less curved timber than was usual. It is unsurprising, therefore, to find another Admiralty which included Gambier issuing an order that in future the futtocks of all ships were to be as near straight as possible. Wall sides certainly meant less curved timber, and this instruction of 1805 marks the beginning of a process that suppressed tumblehome, flattened the sheerline, and generally straightened the profile of all ships. Early in 1806 the Navy Board was still claiming that its greatest supply difficulty was obtaining long compass timber for the upper parts of the frame, but the new designs would gradually extinguish the requirement almost entirely. In September of the same year, a decision was taken to discontinue breadth and top riders in all ships building or repairing. This was largely because it was felt that they added weight without commensurate strength, but the timber saving was also valuable.[33]

It was perhaps inevitable that the final target for economies would be the aggregate total of timber in each ship. This was not always easy to establish, as revealed by these widely divergent estimates[34] of the loads necessary to build various classes:

Ship class	Deptford estimate		Woolwich estimate	
	Oak rough	Knees	Oak rough	Knees
44-gun	2150	100	1790	110
38-gun	2251	104	1640	90
36-gun	2083	96	1300	82
32-gun	1622	75	1100	74

Whatever the precise figure, it was widely understood that British ships were built for strength and compared with French ships of similar dimensions employed far heavier scantlings, and consequently used more tim-

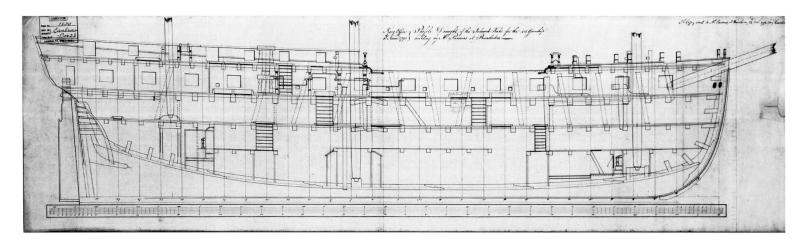

ber. In March 1811 the Admiralty decided that it was time to reconsider the whole basis on which ships of war were built. Paying lip-service to the need for strength, the Board nevertheless felt that there was scope for a reduction in scantlings to save timber and cost, and directed the Navy Board to look at the many prizes that had fallen into British hands during the war. What the Admiralty wished to achieve was a new and improved system of scantlings 'not to be deviated from on any account whatsoever'.

As the Admiralty was aware, it was advocating a return to the Establishments that dominated the first half of the eighteenth century and that were gradually abandoned after 1745. However, the Admiralty took a more sophisticated view of standardisation, knowing that a Rate-based system was unworkable in an age when ships of the same nominal gun-power varied so much in dimensions. Instead they proposed a system based on breadth, requesting scantlings lists for each breadth at fourteen 2ft intervals from 53ft 6in to 27ft 6in. The two Surveyors, seven Master Shipwrights and two Assistant Surveyors were all sent away to produce their suggestions, with the Navy Board to collate their responses. With commendable speed, the new scheme of scantlings was submitted on 1 June, and after due consideration was promulgated by Admiralty Order of 18 July.[35]

Although this Establishment of 1811 has not received much attention from historians, there can be no doubt that it was applied with vigour, the Dockyards being bombarded with orders to report on the scantlings of ships they had built since July 1811.[36] Obviously pleased with its success, the Admiralty received the new scale of scantlings with an instruction for the Navy Board to turn its attention next to standardising the methods of construction and fastening, whether or not riders were to be employed, the mode of pillaring beams, the ways of working wales, and like matters.[37] In these areas there had been considerable developments over the previous decade, but the result was that hardly two ships were identically constructed. Ironically, most of the innovations and experiments were themselves provoked by the timber shortage the new standardisation was designed to ameliorate.

New Structural Techniques

Because both the length and useable cross-section of timber was restricted by the natural size of trees, a wooden ship was necessarily composed of many relatively small pieces. As vessels grew in size the required strength became ever more dependent upon the disposition of those pieces, their scantling and, especially, the manner of their fastening. Traditionally British warships were more heavily built than their French counterparts – typically, the hull weight of a British frigate would represent about 4 per cent more of total

displacement than a similar French vessel[38] – but they were also more rigidly fastened. By the end of the eighteenth century this was widely understood, not only in the Dockyards but among sea officers, and even the mercantile community – Lloyd's insurers, whose livelihood depended upon the accurate calculation of risk, made allowance for the weaker nature of French hulls in their premiums.[39]

French framing tended to be slighter, with more room between the bends, but the main difference between the structural practice of the two nations was the way the beams were fastened to the hull sides. The British used wooden knees in both the vertical and horizontal planes (hanging and lodging knees respectively), whereas the French preference was to replace lodging knees with a form of beam shelf and a more substantial waterway timber rebated down over the beam ends. The British were convinced that their method resulted in superior strength, and there was plenty of operational experience with French prizes to support this position, usually manifest in a requirement for greater and more frequent Dockyard maintenance. Strength was a crucial 'staff requirement' for the Royal Navy's ships, reflecting its sea-control mission in general and in particular the aggressive strategy of blockade, which involved keeping the seas in all weathers and for as long as possible. Therefore any measure designed to alleviate timber shortages could not be countenanced if it threatened to compromise traditional standards of hull strength.[40] Unfortunately, one of the most pressing shortages was in wooden knees.

To form an effective bracket, a knee required equal strength in each of the arms, which were formed at right angles to one another like an inverted 'L'. These occurred naturally only in the crook of trees, where branches met the trunk; great waste was involved in obtaining them and this made wooden knees expensive, and as the timber crises accelerated, ever scarcer. There could be only two broad solutions: replace them with an effective substitute, or modify the methods of construction to eliminate them. Both approaches were tried, with varying degrees of success, before Seppings perfected a system which fused both.

The Royal Navy always travels First Class, as Jackie Fisher once remarked, and it was certainly prepared to pay for quality, but commercial necessity made the merchant shipping industry more cost-conscious. It is not surprising to find, therefore, that in the biggest merchant ships the substitution of cheap iron for expensive wooden knees was already well established in the 1790s. Under the supervision of its forward-looking Surveyor, Gabriel Snodgrass, the East India Company began fitting its ships with forged iron supports, and the advantages of these were pressed on the Admiralty in 1795 by Captain Lewis of the Indiaman *Woodcot*. The Navy was in the process of acquiring a

Among the first iron strengthening elements widely used in the Dockyards were standards, a form of inverted knee. Those illustrated were proposed for the 74-gun *Colossus*, building at Deptford, in 1801. Those on the upper deck were 5in wide, fastened with 1in bolts, while those for the lower deck were 6in with 1⅛in bolts. Standards were forged to fit the internal planking and varied in thickness from 1⅛in to 3½in for those on the upper deck, and from 1¼in to 4½in for the larger standards on the deck below. *Public Record Office Adm 106/3473, 14 April 1801.*

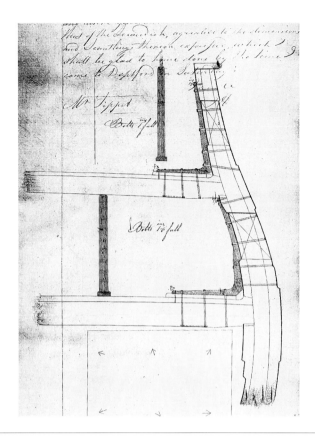

large number of Indiamen then under construction for completion as small two-deckers of 54 and 64 guns, and these introduced the Dockyards to the advantages of iron knees. With its usual caution, the Navy Board wished to treat these acquisitions as trials ships for the system, but on 30 September the Admiralty instructed them to extend the use of iron knees wherever possible.[41] In form, they seem to have been simple iron brackets, and the major disadvantage was the speed with which the motion of the ship wore down the heads and necks of the fastening bolts.[42]

The high prices demanded for wood knees affected the whole of the shipbuilding industry, and while the Royal Dockyards might be able to absorb the extra cost, a merchant yard contracted on a fixed price per ton basis would find its profit margin eroded. At times the dearth of suitable knees meant delay, which for Navy contracts might also threaten a late-delivery penalty. The incentive to solve the problem was, therefore, every bit as great for individual builders as for the Navy Board itself. One of the more successful proposals came from Josiah Brindley of Frindsbury on the Medway, who in 1803 was building the *Leda* class frigate *Pomone*. Having experienced such difficulties, he had devised (and patented) a system which did

---

Brindley's system of fastening beams without lodging knees.

Fig 1 is a plan view of the ends of four beams at the ship' side; the beams (B) may be splayed, or have additional side pieces (H) added, to make deeper tenons for the main tie pieces, or thick carlings (C) which join the beams in a continuous run. A thicker strake of planking (F) is let down on the beams along the length of the carling, and additional pieces (D) can fill the gap between the carlings and the side; these filling pieces can be made flush with the top of the beams or lower (as shown), when ledges (G) will be needed to receive the fastenings of the deck. The long bolts are indicated in ticked lines.

Fig 2 is part of a midship section, as Fig 1. The dotted piece (I) is an optional strength member.

Fig 3 is a further suggestion, an iron T-plate (B).

Fig 4 shows Brindley's iron 'square' knee (E), with rebated iron strap (C) and brace (D).

Fig 5 and 6 depict section and plan view of a method using cheek pieces (B) bolted to the sides of the beams, with dove-tailed extensions (K) beyond the beam-ends to embrace the frame timbers; optional inter-frame pieces (C) might butt up to the dove-tails, the assembly being fastened by coaks of wood or iron (D) as well as through-bolting.

Fig 7 is a plan view of the iron strap (C) in Fig 4, alternatively taken around the chock (B) or, in ticked line, around the frame timber.

Figs 8 and 9 are a tie-bolt and neck-bolt; the former can be driven through the side of the ship and bolted to the sides of the beams, and the latter driven through the tie pieces and bolted to the sides of the beams to reinforce the tenons.

The Navy Board was prepared to test the main provisions as illustrated in Figs 1 and 2, but explicitly rejected that in Fig 4; whether the other alternatives were adopted is open to doubt.

Patent Office, No 2646

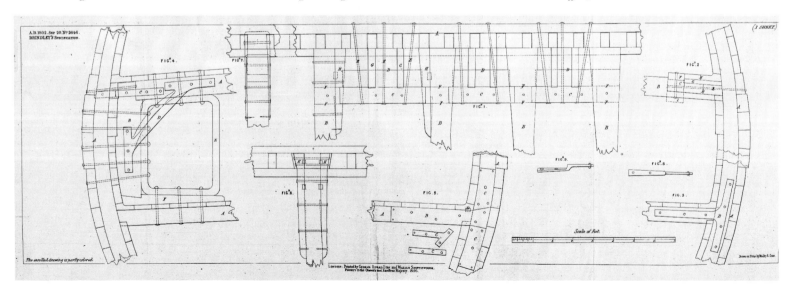

away with lodging knees altogether. Although the drawing he submitted to the Navy Board has disappeared, its accompanying description makes its main features clear.[43] Hanging knees might be retained with the system, but instead of lodging knees a carling or tie-piece united adjacent beams and was rebated into each; space between the tie-piece and the frame was filled, and the ensemble bolted through the side. There was also a thicker strake of planking let down into a rebate on the beams and fastened through them and the carling, the whole being held down by the waterway and above that the spirketting.

This interlocking system, Brindley believed, would prove stronger and more rigid than the existing method, but he also made great claims for its economy. Not only did it halve the number of knees required, but if applied nation-wide would reduce the demand for *all* knees, bringing down the price dramatically. He argued that the hugely inflated current price of knees resulted in timber merchants cutting to waste the large-scantling trees so highly desirable for futtocks just for the sake of a few knees, further escalating the overall costs of ship-timber. Moreover, his system did not require as many iron and copper bolts, and obviated the risk of decay so often occasioned by having to leave the beam ends and interior of the ship exposed while trying to obtain wood knees, since under the usual method of fastening neither the waterways nor the deck could be laid until the knees were in place. Perhaps realising that his system would be seen as a rival to the emerging use of iron, Brindley mentioned that he had seen the iron lodging knees in the *Ardent* (one of the ex-HEIC Indiamen now serving as a 64)

and calculated that his approach would have saved £1500; he also believed iron fastenings through wood, because of inherently greater friction, would be about six times as strong as those through iron.

The economic argument alone must have proved irresistible, and the Navy Board was quick to give Brindley permission to use his system for the *Pomone*, but he was cautioned that this was 'to determine upon its future introduction into practice or otherwise'. Although not mentioned in his covering letter (nor illustrated in the Patent drawing), Brindley must also have suggested a method of replacing wood hanging knees, because the same Navy Board warrant also orders the use of 'iron knees under the beams as shown in a sketch in part of their [Messrs Brindley's] said propositions, and of a weight and form that shall be determined upon between them and the Board, a drawing of which they are to produce by a large scale for approval.'[44]

The Navy Board proceeded with due caution, but Brindley was allowed to extend the same structure to his next frigate, the *Shannon*. More surprisingly, the system was adopted in a limited way in the Dockyards, even being applied to the upper deck beams of the three-decker *Ocean*, 110, which allowed her to be launched in 1805 after thirteen years on the slip, partly as a result of timber shortages. Woolwich, however, made detail modifications to Brindley's patent in the form of a 'double stop to the carlings let into the beams'; they were supported by 'double, or what are generally termed staple knees'.[45] However, the vogue for Brindley's system was short, since it simply did not measure up to its projector's claims in the matter of

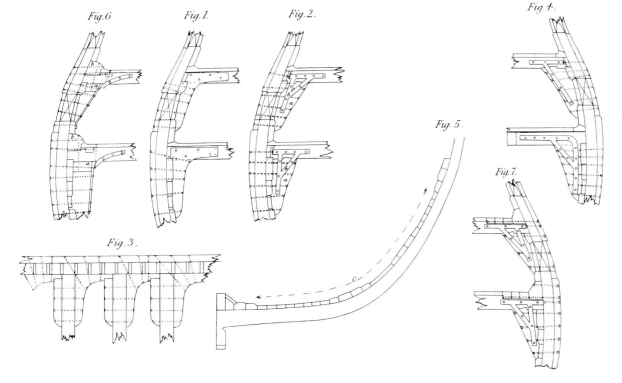

Plate 25 from Fincham's *History of Naval Architecture*, demonstrating various developments in beam fastenings in the first decade of the nineteenth century.

Fig 1 shows the traditional British use of hanging knees fixed alongside the beams, and Fig 3 a plan view of the lodging knees usually employed with them.

Fig 2 is Roberts's method of chock *under* the beam and plate knees fitted either side of the beam-end and through-bolted; the L-shaped extension of the top of the plate to form a bracket is marked 'c', but is none too clear in this section view.

Fig 4 represents what Fincham claims (without further details) are similar foreign methods developed prior to Roberts.

Fig 5 shows the deletion of the footwaling that was one element of Seppings's method, and Fig 6 the matured beam-fastening arrangement that was combined with the trussed frame; Seppings also employed chocks, but preferred fork knees, and combined these with shelf pieces (a) and thick waterways (b). These last features were inspired by French practice, including the thicker binding strakes between waterways and deck planking; with plate knees added, this system is shown in Fig 7.

Roberts plate knees became virtually the standard fastenings for frigates in the last decade of the war, this drawing dated 26 March 1811 showing the method of fixing them to be applied in the *Magicienne*, 36. The plates were 4in wide by ¾in thick and were individually forged and welded, having an L-shaped bracket to act as a lodging-knee substitute. The arms were originally longer, but by about 1807 it was found that they could be shortened without significant loss of strength. The plates were rebated into each side of the chocks and beams (the siding of the beam being tapered slightly towards the end), and through-bolted. Careful provision was made to avoid the dangers of rot, each beam-end having a score, or 'mouthing', cut in it, connecting with an opening left at the top of the chock, to allow the circulation of air. The top of the chock was jogged into the beam, and two opposed iron wedges driven in to the vertical face of the jog to tighten the whole ensemble.
National Maritime Museum Dr2169

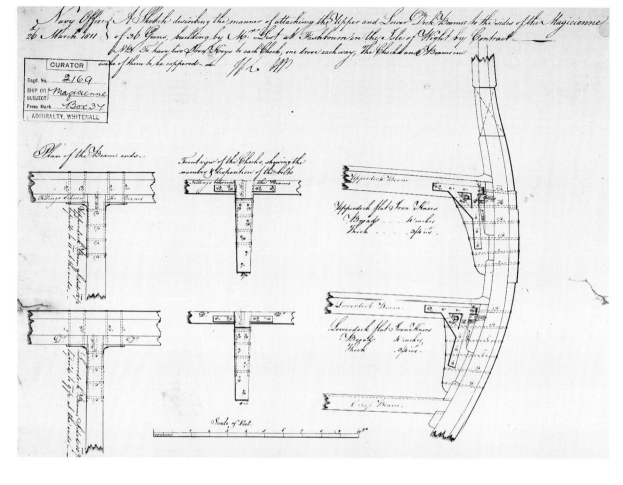

A Roberts plate knee under the main deck of the frigate *Trincomalee*. The black-painted iron wedge or 'key' can be seen in the triangle between the arms of the plate. Most of the plate knees of this ship, and indeed of the *Victory*, have survived nearly two centuries without replacement and continue to do service after the modern restoration.
HMS Trincomalee Trust 291/18

strength and rigidity. Far from 'the whole making an immense power of connection' as Brindley asserted, Captain Broke reported of the *Shannon* that 'being secured on Brindley's bolt and carling plan, without knees, her topsides are slight and *work like a basket*'.[46] In fact, *Shannon* was in such poor shape by the middle of 1813 that, being overdue for a major refit, she nearly missed her famous encounter with USS *Chesapeake*.

By January 1805, and again in May, Brindley himself was expressly forbidden to employ the system in the *Kangaroo*, the sloop he was building at Lynn. In the following October he renewed his request to use a version of it for the 74-gun *Aboukir*, but this time he proposed additional iron 'squares' under the gundeck beams, which he regarded as the equivalent of 'four knees united in one', giving sixteen times the resistance to racking stresses. He calculated the saving at £876-3s-3d per deck for a 74. The Navy Board was unimpressed, and endorsed his application with the emphatic, 'They do not approve his system for line of battle ships'; but acknowledging Brindley's plight, they added 'as knees cannot be obtained, [they] intend to fasten the ship as the *Valiant* building at Wells'.[47]

The *Valiant* was being built to a plan developed in the Dockyards which was destined to become far more significant than Brindley's in the history of the ship construction. Thomas Roberts, an Assistant to the

Master Shipwright at Woolwich, developed a form of chock which fitted under the beam (as opposed to alongside it for a conventional hanging knee) and since it was a simple triangle shape it did not require the costly crook timber of a natural knee. It was fastened by means of iron plates fixed flush to each side of the beam and chock, bolted through and forelocked. The plate also included a bracket (at right angles in the horizontal plane) that functioned instead of a lodging knee; strength was such that top and breadth riders, and standards, could be omitted.[48] Probably because it was an officially sponsored system, Roberts' iron plate knees were widely and speedily adopted, and Roberts himself was promoted to become an Assistant to the Surveyors. In September 1806 the Navy Board applied to the Admiralty for a reward for Roberts in recognition of the great value of his development, but they were told to wait until its utility was proven. A year later they renewed the request, since many more ships had been so fitted, with 'the whole of which we are perfectly satisfied.' In 1808 Roberts was duly presented with the silver medal of the Society of Arts, and an £800 pension from the king.[49] It is not entirely clear when Roberts' knees were first applied, but a published list of 1810 gives the following ships in what appears to be chronological order of application: the frigates *Lively*, 38 and *Melampus*, 36 (the 1785 ship refitted), six 32s of the *Circe* class (not the *Minerva*), the 38s *Resistance*, *Spartan* and *Undaunted*, six new-built 74s and the 120-gun *Caledonia*, the frigates *Cornelia*, *Nereus*, *Bucephalus* and *Semiramis*, the 44-gun *Dolphin* (refitted), and seven new 74s from *Ajax* to *Scarborough*.[50] *Lively* was launched at Woolwich in July 1804, so was probably the ship on which Roberts developed his system.

The list should be treated with caution, since it is unlikely that all the *Circe*s were fitted with Roberts' knees: an earlier report in the same source attributes the Brindley system to the *Thames*, and as pointed out in Chapter 1 the *Minerva* at Deptford became a trials ship for Bentham's ideas, while the official midship section draught for *Alexandria* shows a different system of chocks and knees employed at Portsmouth.[51] It is probable that journalists were no more careful about technical details then than they are nowadays: for a few years any knee-less system was credited to Brindley and after that to Roberts. In fact, a number of senior shipwrights throughout the Dockyards were working on their own ideas: the Woolwich-built *Jason* probably used Roberts' knees, and Roberts himself was seconded to Plymouth in 1804, presumably to advise on fitting his plate knees;[52] the Chatham-built *Thames* may have copied Brindley, since his yard was close by; Portsmouth definitely had its own system; but what was done at Deptford for the *Hebe* is open to doubt, although it certainly eschewed conventional knees. This class was the vehicle for many other experiments

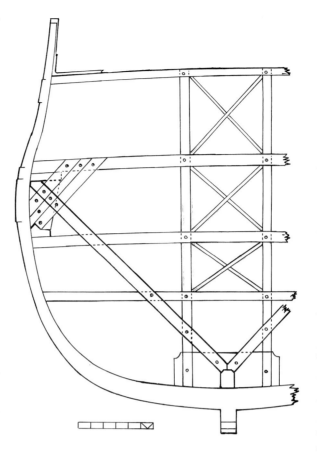

in structure, *Jason* for example having a frame scarphed together without chocks, some bends combining elm and fir.[53]

In operational terms the new knee-less systems offered the advantage of more space at the sides of the deck, which was useful in fighting the guns, but the innovation took some time to be accepted by many sea officers. For a while there was a tendency to blame every structural problem on the lack of knees: Bentham's *Minerva*, for example, complained of as being weak and very wet on deck, was thus diagnosed by her captain, whereas on inspection the Dockyard felt that poor caulking was the main problem.[54]

Bentham's system as applied to *Minerva* included some athwartship diagonal braces by way of compensating for the lack of knees, but these features were only part of a highly original approach to structure that depended for its strength on a number of ingenious details. Ignoring the radical but historical cul-de-sacs of flat decks and structural bulkheads, these included:

1. Stepped and shaped treenails, machine-made which fitted perfectly into mechanically-bored holes; they had a conical nose and were used for securing decks and the plank of the bottom.

2. Short metal screws instead of long bolts, again to secure planking.

3. Omission of carlings and ledges, replaced as deck

Bentham's scheme as applied to the 32-gun frigate *Minerva* at Deptford in 1805. The diagonal shores are similar to Snodgrass's ideas, or as Seppings pointed out, a reversed version of the old diagonal braces used since at least the seventeenth century. Bentham's unique contribution included fastening the structure with 'coques'; the continuous pillaring, with cross-bracing between; and the diagonal planking at the side as part of the knee-substitute. Bentham would probably have liked to carry this last feature right across the hull to make the kind of solid bulkheads he employed in the sloops *Dart* and *Arrow*, but it would have been impractical on the lower deck of a frigate, which required easy access fore and aft. To perform the function of a hanging knee there is a chock seated on a much enlarged waterway, while the lodging knee is replaced by a broad deck clamp or shelf piece (this last was a common practice in French and Spanish ships for at least a half-century previously).

Some of these features were applied to the 74-gun *Fame* at the same time, but she had no shores, no cross-bracing below the lower gundeck beams, and different chocks of Peake's design (see below).
Sketch after a drawing in NMM ADM/BP/38a, 22 May 1818

A proposal from R F S Blake, a shipwright at Pater (Pembroke) Dockyard, to replace the copper 'dumps' used as temporary fastenings for the plank of the bottom when it was first brought from the steam or boiling kettle. These had been left in the strakes after the permanent fastenings were driven, but Blake proposed employing a screw bolt and 'friction ring' (washer), which not only made a tighter fit between plank and frame, but could later be removed for re-use and the hole filled with a treenail. Blake estimated that the cost of the dumps was about £400 per frigate, or £550 for a line of battle ship, whereas the iron screws cost about half and could be removed to do duty for many ships. He seemed oblivious of Bentham's prior claim to such an invention. The illustrations show the screw bolt and dump; the shift of butts of the wales and diminishing strakes in a frigate; and, enlarged, where the dumps were fastened (solid heads, marked 'c').
Public Record Office Adm 1/4383, 4 June 1814.

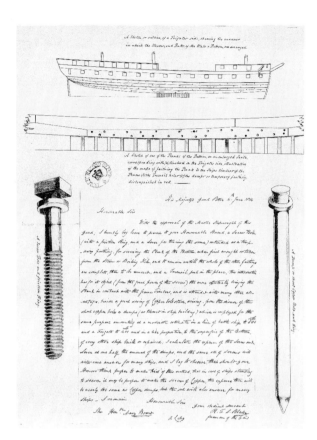

support by increasing the number of beams but reducing their width while retaining the standard depth.

4. Omission of footwalings, ceilings and all interior planking; increased external planking to compensate, but of graduated thickness.

5. Knees replaced with a French-style thicker string piece (deck clamp), but accepting that, although it secured the beams better, this approach was poorer at resisting racking stresses, it was combined with diagonal braces and solid bulkheads.

6. Abolition of crutches and breasthooks.

Bentham lost his political influence, and independence, during his abortive shipbuilding mission to Russia in 1805-7. He returned to find his position subsumed into the Navy Board, and thereafter he lost much of his motivation and energy. Nevertheless, in terms of ship construction, it is amazing how many of the innovations for which he claimed credit were to see service, often very tardily and frequently under somebody else's name. He was a pioneer of the discriminating use a wider range of timbers, advocating the selective employment of softwoods in oak ships; he worked at schemes of reduced scantlings, using smaller and therefore younger timber to save cost and waste; he invented a form of iron fastening he called 'coqueing', to connect together pieces of timber without tabling and scarphing, reducing the cost of labour and allowing

smaller timber to be used (a similar scheme of coaks was later employed by Seppings in his so-called 'small timber system').[55]

One of his developments lost for nearly a decade was a form of screw bolt which had a thread cut on the end. Instead of a conventional long bolt which was clenched over a ring, and tended to loosen as the ship worked, Bentham's bolt was fastened with a nut which could be tightened against a substantial plate. It was tested in the 74-gun *Fame* in 1805, particularly to tighten up the wood braces used instead of knees, and he had persuaded the Admiralty to adopt the measure when he was sent to Russia. Just what became of the machine for cutting threads and making bolts that he had sent to Deptford Dockyard is anyone's guess, but when in 1813 Richard Pering of Plymouth Dockyard was advocating an identical-sounding scheme, the Navy Board behaved as though the idea was entirely novel.[56]

Bentham certainly made a contribution, but given the self-serving nature of his claims, it is difficult to establish how important he was in the development of ship structure. Most of the problems he addressed were being tackled simultaneously by others in the Dockyards, and these 'official' solutions tended to find more favour with the Navy Board. Outsiders always experienced more difficulty in getting their proposals adopted, a case in point being Gabriel Snodgrass's plan for strengthening old ships first put up in February 1795. For years it was ignored and might have been consigned to oblivion had not a relative of Admiral Patton, then a Commissioner of the Transport Board, remembered it during the 1805 emergency. Desperate to get as many ships as possible to sea in order to counter the threatened invasion, the Admiralty ordered the adoption of the scheme for unserviceable ships, overriding the opposition of the Dockyards. Ships weak in frame were strengthened with transverse diagonal braces and iron knees; those with rotten hulls were doubled with an extra layer of planking from keel to gunwale. The Ordinary was plundered for suitable vessels, and twenty-two ships of the line and eleven frigates subjected to this programme were readied for sea between March and December 1805.[57]

Despite the strategic success of the scheme, its unpopularity in the Dockyards spawned a negative report which concluded that braces from the keel to the beam ends added temporary transverse strength but was certain to destroy the fabric of a weak ship, while doubling simply fastened good timber to bad. Although it was slow to acknowledge it, the Navy Board came to regard the doubling and bracing programme as a success, proving more economical and durable than expected, and not significantly impairing the sailing qualities of the ships so treated.[58] Although this was an emergency measure which was not applicable to new construction, it is important in demonstrating, firstly, that concepts like diagonal braces, iron fastenings and thicker planking were not the monopoly of Bentham – or any one projector – and, secondly, that the Dockyards and the Navy Board, while initially conservative, could accept innovation if there was good, hard, practical evidence of its efficacy.

A combination of acute timber shortages and a highly threatening strategic situation which required the refitting, repair and construction of ever-larger numbers of ships, made the years 1803-5 a time of ferment in the Dockyards. Not surprisingly, it was the period when the structural innovations of Snodgrass, Bentham, Brindley and Roberts were first given serious trial; but it also saw Robert Seppings emerge from the ranks of ordinary shipwrights to propose a series of innovations which were to prove the most important structural developments for a century or more. Although he had used some diagonal internal planking in repairing the fir frigate *Glenmore* in 1800, Seppings's first move towards the trussed frame, the hallmark of his system, came with the repair of the Large Class 74 *Kent* in May 1805 (which straightened 17in of hog in the keel). He also inserted the system in a limited way into the new *Warspite* in 1806, but this attracted less attention. Given its obvious value in repairs, Seppings's approach was probably seen as a more durable alternative to Snodgrass's methods, and in the less frenetic period after Trafalgar, it was not pursued with any vigour.[59]

Seppings was unable to make much headway with

his ideas until March 1810, and only then on the direct intervention of the Admiralty,[60] which ensured that the rebuilding of the 74-gun *Tremendous* incorporated more of Seppings's innovations besides the trusses, notably the filled-in frames, the fillings being driven in tightly by opposed wedges. He also introduced a shelf piece and forked iron knees to fasten the beam ends, as well as diagonal bracing between the ports; diagonally-laid decks were added later as well. Seppings was allowed to make a cruise in the ship and in April 1811 enthusiastically reported on the advantages of his system, which he considered fourfold, and in the following order of importance:

1. It saved English oak – about 180 trees per 74-gun ship – and since the trusses could be made with timber inferior to the internal planking it replaced, nearly one-seventh of the new English oak consumed in a line of battleship could be saved; it also allowed more use of short timbers.

2. Economy of repair and ease of discovering defects, because in the conventional system the inner lining made this difficult.

3. 'Durability, Sweetness, Dryness' and increased stowage; the fillings prevented rot to the edges of the frames, kept out the filth that usually accumulated there, and in reducing the stench of the bilges reduced the likelihood of disease; *Tremendous* also stowed 40 tons more water than previously.

Gabriel Snodgrass, the immensely experienced Surveyor of the East India Company's shipping, had been advocating changes to the Navy's methods of design and construction since at least 1771, when he gave evidence to a House of Commons committee. He was a great believer in the power of iron knees and riders, having regularly applied such remedies to old and weak Indiamen, and in this development he was eventually followed by the Navy. Some his other ideas were not taken up so readily, in particular his notion that thorough repair was a waste of resources that would be better replaced by a system of doubling and bracing. His letter to Henry Dundas of 1796 was later published in *The Naval Chronicle* in 1801, and led to a limited adoption of the system in 1805. The accompanying drawings illustrated his ideas in their entirety, which included the suppression of tumblehome and the replacement of an open waist with a flush spar deck, as his Indiamen had been designed for many years. British warships gradually adopted these features post-war, but the spar deck was more directly inspired by the American '44s' so disastrously encountered in 1812. None of the frigates repaired under the 1805 programme adopted the transverse diagonal braces shown here, being simply doubled, but the braces were not adjudged a success in the 74s to which they were applied.
The Naval Chronicle V (1801), Plate 57

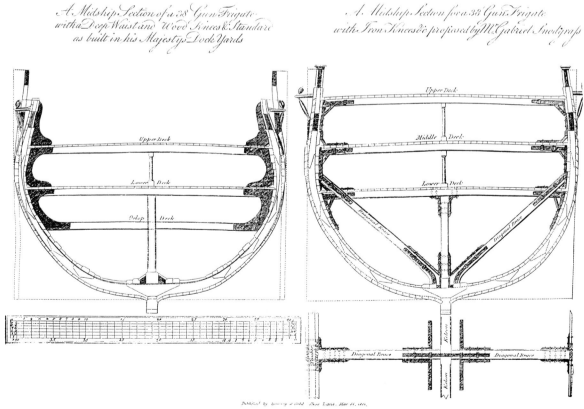

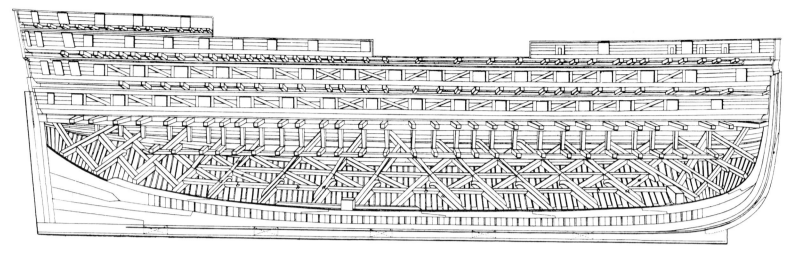

Plate 26 from Fincham's *History of Naval Architecture*, the famous illustration of Seppings's trussed frame applied to a 74-gun ship. Allowing for the addition of a circular stern, it is the same drawing published in Seppings's paper in *Philosophical Transactions* in 1814, and previously printed in *The Naval Chronicle* in 1813, but ultimately deriving from the drawing Seppings submitted in his memorandum to the Admiralty, now in PRO Adm 7/709. Although not always mentioned, the drawing specifically relates to the repaired *Tremendous*, and not to later developments of the system.

There were many proposals for improved fastening details from the Dockyards that were either rejected or were tested only briefly. Many of these were modifications of existing notions, whose originality was often disputed. This sketch shows one of Seppings's suggested alternatives to plate knees under the upper deck of a 74, a tie-bolt and reduced width chock, which appears similar to one of Brindley's proposals. The main features are a coak (A) between chock and beam; a 1½in diameter bolt that might be clenched on the beam or on the deck planking (B); and a notch (C) to drive the bolt up through the beam.
Sketch after a drawing in NMM ADM/BP/32a, 28 January 1812

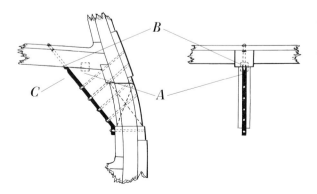

4. Safety and strength – the wedged fillings were strong and economical since they could be made from the offal of timber conversion; the fillings also protected treenail fastenings from insect destruction in hot climates.

Seppings concluded by pointing out that the ship had survived a severe gale with no sign of weakness, and suggested that further trials would soon prove the utility of his system. The Admiralty was impressed, and ordered the *Albion* to be repaired in the same manner, and Seppings later demonstrated the economy of his system by repairing the *Ramillies* with old and inferior timber.[61]

Although Seppings now enjoyed Admiralty support, it was not uncritical. Barrallier, who was often consulted by the Admiralty for an alternative opinion outside Navy Board orthodoxy, was asked for his views. He produced a long report, referring to various French authorities, which reveals that he was not an original thinker: he approved the filled frames because Groignard, an eminent French constructor, had written a complimentary paper about them in 1789; but equally he believed the trussed frame to be weaker than the ceiling it replaced, largely because Bouguer had said so in his famous treatise of 1746. Barrallier, in fact, began a whole tradition of misrepresenting the significance of

Seppings's work, in which detractors denied the originality of various aspects of his method. Fincham, for example, was one of the first in his well-known *History of Naval Architecture*, which listed various precedents for diagonal strengthening; and most recently a similar originality has been claimed for the dozen pairs of diagonal riders that Joshua Humphreys intended for the *Constitution* and her sisters. Seppings himself never claimed novelty for any part of his proposals, only for the system as a whole, and of its many advantages structural strength was but one. In the post-war years matured versions of these principles allowed far larger wooden ships to be built, and therefore historians claimed a significance for the system that Seppings himself never did, and probably did not even anticipate. Barrallier, therefore, was only the first of many critics could not see that the fully trussed frame offered a whole order of strength above the various diagonal elements that Barrallier quoted as precedents. Because he had little faith in the trusses, he criticised the power of the forked knees to resist racking stresses, preferring what he called the Peake system of reduced chock and plate knees.[62]

This underlines the fact that Seppings's evolving system was in competition with a number of alternatives, and while the Navy Board had been willing to allow a limited pluralism in styles of construction, after the introduction of the 1811 Scantlings Establishment they had been instructed to standardise structural techniques as well. It proved more difficult to achieve consensus in this regard, because just as Seppings's scheme was looking promising, there were problems with some of the chock-and-plate arrangements, particularly as applied to contract-built 74s of the Surveyors' class. The once-favoured Brindley was heavily criticised for the quality of the *Asia*, for example, and in August 1812 the Admiralty ordered a particularly close inspection of the two fir frigates he was currently building. As a result the overseer took exception to the quality of the iron in the knees, a charge indignantly refuted by Brindley, who claimed that of seventy tested in the usual way – being struck with a large hammer! – only one broke.[63]

By contrast, in the same month Seppings was summoned to explain his system to the Admiralty Board, and as a result Melville, the First Lord, thought the issue important enough to warrant a personal visit to Chatham to see for himself. In September the rebuilt *Ramillies* was undocked, and sights placed along her decks revealed hardly any movement when the ends of the hull were weighted. This was very convincing evidence, and on 29 October all ships building and repairing at Chatham were ordered to be fastened on Seppings's plan.[64] This was an important step forward, since (excepting the partial experiment with the *Warspite*) for the first time it applied the principles to new construction, which had previously been monopolised by Peake's system.

By the beginning of 1813 Sir William Rule was infirm and ill, and Peake carried most of the Surveyors' workload, so his style of fastening must be regarded as the one with official Navy Board sanction. Although it had been applied with a degree of satisfaction since

1804, there appeared to be a mounting groundswell of criticism suggesting weakness in contract-built ships like *Dublin* and *Rodney* fastened in this way. In March 1813 Seppings and Tucker (the Master Shipwright at Plymouth)[65] were sent to Portsmouth to investigate the *Rodney*, and to emphasise that the two systems were now seen as directly competitive, a week later the Master Shipwrights of Plymouth, Portsmouth and Woolwich (Tucker, Diddams and Sison) were instructed to report on Seppings's principles. Peake obviously felt that his system did not receive fair treatment in the resulting report, since he submitted a separate defence: he stopped short of accusing them of undeclared interest, although he felt the shipwrights lacked experience of his methods, and pointed out that in the *Dublin* the problem resided in the traditional hanging and lodging knees with which she was partially fastened, and that his system had been more widely applied to ships like *Invincible*, *St Domingo*, *Chatham* and *Cressy* without complaint.[66] However, Peake's position was weakened in the two months following the submission of the two reports, for in May Tucker was

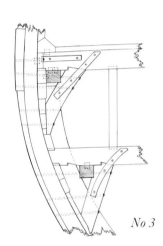
No 3

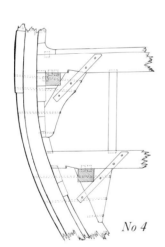
No 4

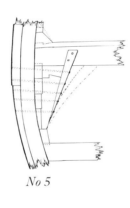
No 5

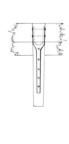

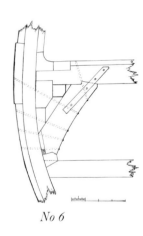
No 6

Career rivalry between the Surveyors (and the Master Shipwrights who aimed to become the next generation of Surveyors) drove much of the structural innovation in the Dockyards after 1800. The ambitious felt that to make their mark they had to put up their own individual solutions to the ever more pressing problems of timber shortages. The results were creative but chaotic, with no universally approved practice for about a decade. Roberts and Seppings were front-runners, and men like Peake produced variations that appear inspired by little more than a vain attempt to be different. The various patterns illustrated here were prepared as evidence to the House of Commons Committee on East India Shipping investigating complaints about the fastenings of recently built 74s. There are six enclosures, Nos 1 and 2 being plan and profile drawings of the longitudinal shelf pieces used by

Peake in the *Invincible*; these are copies of details on the original draughts and have not been reproduced, but the remaining four contrast methods of fastening beams, as follows:

No 3. Orlop and gundeck beams: modified system proposed by Peake, who claimed that Roberts plate knees were prone to breaking in the welds of the fore-and-aft arms, so he favoured separate L-brackets and iron straps. The chock was also different, being canted out from the side, so it did not support the beam end like the conventional triangular shape; described by Barrallier as 'reduced', this form of chock was presumably designed to save weight.

No 4. Peake's original method as applied to a number of 74s, like *Invincible*, *Rodney* and *Dublin*, whose reported weakness was the cause of the

investigation. The lack of an obvious substitute for lodging knees was addressed by the addition of the iron brackets shown in *No 3*.

No 5. Seppings's system as fitted in *Tremendous* and *Ramillies* (the only difference between the two being the thicker waterway, shown ticked, in the latter). To emphasise how economical with deck space this method was, the ticked line shows the jut of the *Invincible* chocks and the dotted/dashed line that of the *Rochfort*. The absence of a lodging-knee substitute was countered by the diagonal trussed frame.

No 6. Barrallier's version in the *Rochfort*. It also has no lodging element.

Sketches after drawings in NMM ADM/BP/34b, 13 May 1814

Plate 29 from Fincham's *History of Naval Architecture*, comparing the traditional form of British frame connected by chocked scarphs with the Seppings small-frame system, with its coaks and extra tiers of shorter futtocks. In many ways this represents the climax of Seppings's reforms and proves beyond doubt that the timber shortage was the inspiration behind his work.

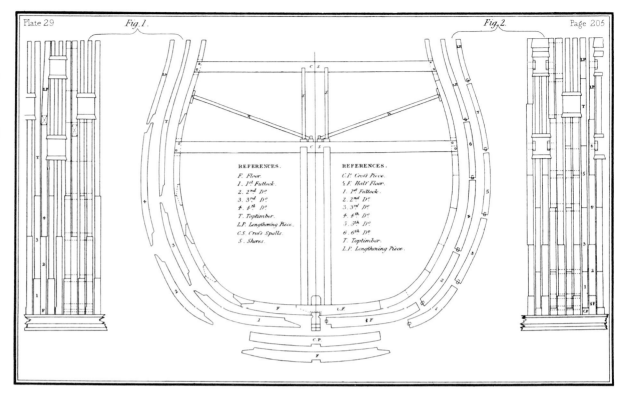

appointed Second Surveyor on Rule's death, and in an even more pointed gesture the Admiralty obtained an Order in Council to establish a third Surveyor. It was to be Robert Seppings.

This was by no means the end of the debate, and in June two entirely new fastening schemes were ordered to be investigated. In September both were judged 'not so eligible a mode of fastening as other plans now in practice', but more importantly the Surveyors promised to submit their own definitive plans shortly.[67] Since the views of the two older men and their ingenious junior were clearly divergent, this was unlikely to reflect true consensus, and in the event relations deteriorated so rapidly that no new scheme was ever submitted by Peake and Tucker. The cause of the falling-out was Seppings's proposal in November 1813 to build line of battle ships with small timber conventionally thought only fit for frigates. Already feeling professionally upstaged, Peake and Tucker combined to produce a hastily contrived alternative, but it was the contemptuous dismissal of their arguments by Seppings that destroyed all chance of a cordial working relationship. The breach was clear enough to be formally 'regretted' by the Admiralty, but nevertheless they ordered a 74, the *Thunderer*, to be built according to Seppings's plan.[68]

As with the trussed frame, the small-timber system was not especially original in its individual parts – its precursors included separate plans by Canham and Blake, both of which were rejected in 1806[69] – but it was worked out with a thoroughness and logic that made the sum far greater than the parts. Each frame

comprised more but shorter elements than the conventional disposition, bolted together horizontally, but Seppings also dispensed with chocks, employing coaks instead to butt-joint the ends of the timbers together. As we have seen, this latter innovation was claimed by Bentham, and Peake and Tucker were quick to deny any originality in the rest of Seppings's scheme: they pointed out that foreign ships were usually built with lighter scantlings, and gave precedents for designs with seven-timber frames – *Canopus*, *Implacable*, *Donegal*, and the frigates *Boadicea* and *Hydra* – and others with even more tiers of futtocks. Unfortunately, these examples were either French ships, or in the case of the frigates, French-derived, and this gave Seppings an ideal opening to expound on his structural philosophy. He was not trying to reduce hull weight to French proportions: indeed, he believed that British ships needed to be stronger ('It is one thing to lie in the harbours of Toulon and Brest, and another to be cruizing off those ports at all seasons of the year'). If anything, he thought British framing could benefit from greater moulded depth, so his scheme did not reduce the quantity of timber, but simply arranged it better, and with greater economy.

The defence of his own ideas was perfectly justified, but he was less than generous in his treatment of the opposition's. He came close to describing as a downright lie their claim to have been working on their plan since 1811, but said it was in any case based on his own work, and dismissed it as 'a bad edition' of the Canham proposal rejected in 1806. As for Tucker's assertion of a prior claim on bolted frames, Seppings said that he himself merely used them to keep the elements of the frame together, whereas Tucker's continuous chain-bolting had a different function: it was designed to prevent hogging and, as he vindictively noted, it had failed with the *Achilles*.[70]

In March 1814 Seppings's paper on the trussed frame was read to the Royal Society (to which he was himself elected later in the year), while at much the same time Peake was defending his method of fastening that appeared to have failed in ships like the *Dublin* and *Rodney*. However, the senior Surveyors, although bloodied, were not yet bowed, and there was to be one further clash in the campaign to introduce Seppings's system. In October, as a result of very favourable reports from Captain Campbell of the various innovations, including diagonal decks, in *Tremendous*, the Admiralty asked for the Navy Board's opinion on the wisdom of extending the principles to all ships. Taking advantage of Seppings's absence, Peake and Tucker produced a very negative report on the ship and suggested that such a wholesale move would be premature. Needless to say, when he found out Seppings wrote a lengthy rebuttal, and reiterated the main advantages of his system. Trying to hold the balance the Navy Board suggested applying the principles to all ships undergoing major repair, but the Admiralty had clearly made up its mind already, the First Lord minuting on 28 October, 'I think that after the experience we have had, we are justified in directing that in all ships building & which are not advanced too far according to the old system, Mr Seppings's plan should be adopted; and that it should also be adopted in all ships to be repaired, provided that the extent of the repair shall be such as to justify the alteration in the Ship's structure.'[71] At this point the battle was effectively won, although the Admiralty order to adopt the Seppings diagonal system for all future ships either building or repairing was not finally issued until 18 February 1815.[72]

However, the cavilling and criticism continued. In 1818 Seppings became embroiled in an acrimonious dispute with one J W Boswell, who claimed his patent had been infringed by the Navy's adoption of diagonal trusses. Boswell's system, incorporating some triangular bracing elements had been applied to a 200-ton merchantman called the *Economy* in 1803. The lengthy defence Seppings produced for the Admiralty gave him the opportunity to set out both the scope and the limits of his claims. It included ten schemes (with drawings) stretching back to before 1700 which had some elements of diagonal construction that prefigured his, and also referred to various critiques of his originality, including Dupin's paper to the Royal Society in 1817. Seppings refuted Boswell's claims by reference to the views of Peake, who in 1806 had approved of Boswell's scheme, whereas Seppings's own had been dismissed later by the same man as possessing 'neither sense nor science', a phrase for which Seppings never forgave Peake. This effectively proved there was little in common between Seppings's ideas and Boswell's patent, and since Sir William Rule had disagreed with Peake's assessment, the Navy had never taken up Boswell's system – undoubtedly the root cause of his complaint. Exasperated by continually defending himself against the insinuation of plagiarism, Seppings concluded by stating categorically that the only claim he had ever made was that 'no one that I am aware of, has at any time proposed the system of a diagonal trussed frame.' In this he was entirely correct: all previous diagonal methods offered nothing like the advantages of a fully trussed frame, and its historical importance is proven by the adoption of similar systems by all the world's major navies.[73]

After the war Seppings was to modify his system for frigates, replacing the timber trussed frame with diagonal iron straps. There were further detailed modifications by other hands, but it was the adoption of Seppings's basic principles that allowed the dramatic enlargement of the final generation of wooden-hulled warships. Herein lies the great value of Seppings's work in historical terms, but it is wrong to regard it as his inspiration. At no point did he suggest he could build bigger ships, and he was only concerned with strength as a subsidiary issue. In his list of advantages strength came a poor fourth, economy in timber usage heading his list. As with all the rival proposals, Seppings was driven to find better ways of constructing ships by acute timber shortages in the years after

Plate 27 from Fincham's *History of Naval Architecture*, showing the diagonal iron rider plates that Seppings developed for frigates. Following Fincham, it is often said that the wooden trussed frame system was not employed in frigates, but this is not strictly true. The iron riders were an after-thought and all the end-war frigate designs, like the *Java* and the repeat *Leda*s, originally had trussed framing schemes like those in the battleships. Even if few were actually completed with it, the wooden trussed frame was definitely used to repair frigates: there is, for example, an exquisitely coloured pair of drawings of the system as applied to the *Pyramus* in 1820 (ZAZ2845 and 2856).

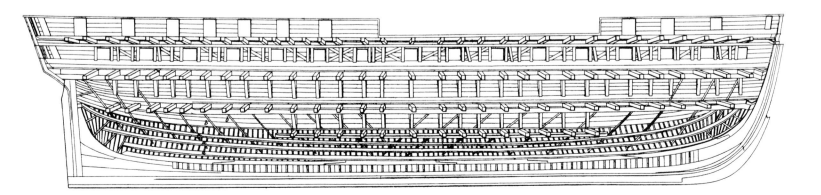

1803. Structural strength was always a vital require-ment for British warships, but the specific problem of the war years was to retain *existing* strength in ships of reduced scantlings, poorer quality timber, and uncer-tain methods of fastening. In this respect, Seppings's

system was a significant achievement, but it had to fight its way past the criticism and envy of well-placed rivals. Although it may seem so in retrospect, its suc-cess was by no means a foregone conclusion.

Details of the beam fastenings applied by Seppings in the major repair of the *Euryalus* in 1815, almost certainly including a wooden trussed frame. Although the diagonal riders are the best known aspect of Seppings's system, they were combined with many other specific features, often adapted or modified by Seppings from existing practice. The beam fastenings, for example, depended on a thick shelf

below and an enlarged waterway above the beam ends. These were probably derived from French practice, but the pieces were coaked for greater strength (plan view of shelf far left; and of waterway top). The beam chocks and iron forked knees were also an integral part of his system.
National Maritime Museum Dr2105

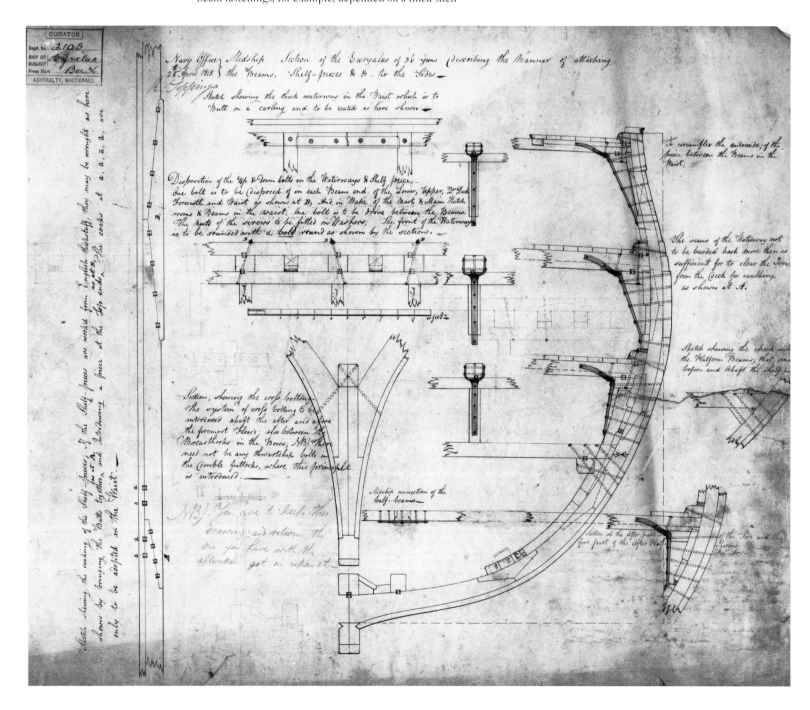

Design

T HE DECADE of the 1790s – and especially the six years of Earl Spencer's Admiralty (Dec 1794-Feb 1801) – had seen the most radical changes in the design of British frigates since their introduction in the middle of the century. Not only did they grow substantially in size, but they became progressively longer and sharper in their proportions, significantly improving their speed under sail, and by increasing the freeboard of their gunports and providing more space to work the guns, making them far better fighting ships.[1] It is not surprising that the three main classes (*Leda*s, *Lively*s and *Apollo*s) built in numbers after 1803 were all first ordered by Spencer's administration; but this recognition of their qualities was slow in coming, the succeeding Admiralties reverting to long-ingrained prejudices in favour of small ships and French hull forms. St Vincent's revived obsolescent designs of the older, shorter forms, while Barham's experimented with a number of one-off designs based on French hull forms, themselves of an older generation. Both policies were technological cul-de-sacs, and from 1806 new construction was confined to the three standard classes, until the American emergency of 1812 prompted a reconsideration.

There was little complaint from sea officers about the ships of the standard classes, which were obviously well-suited for the tasks required of a British frigate. They were strong and seaworthy enough to survive the rigours of close blockade; sufficiently capacious to stay at sea for months at a time, frequently operating far from a well-equipped dockyard; fast and weatherly enough to run down an often reluctant enemy; and when alongside, powerful enough to overcome that enemy. As a consequence, a large number of fine frigates of most belligerent nations fell into British hands, but with a handfull of noteworthy exceptions none was substantially larger, nor of noticeably better sailing qualities. Such was the general feeling of satisfaction with existing designs, that there was no motivation to adopt any as possible prototypes.

The only criticism occasionally made related to a relatively minor aspects of seakeeping, namely the fineness of their hulls forward. For example, William Skipsey of the 36-gun *Maidstone* complained about the

Hull of the restored frigate *Trincomalee* in drydock demonstrates the fine lines of the *Leda* class. Like many of the designs of the period, the hollow waterlines forward produced a tendency to pitching. Derived from J-N Sané's *Hébé* of 1782, this hull form was employed in the largest single group of French 18pdr frigates down to 1815, while the Royal Navy used it for even longer, the last of the *Leda* class being launched in 1830. Sheer numbers make it one of the most successful frigate designs of all time, although objective analysis suggests it was not absolutely perfect for British requirements.
HMS Trincomalee Trust 291/11

'lack of harping', in his view a common problem with many British designs of that generation, and almost certainly the result of the search for additional speed. Ironically, it meant that while *Maidstone* might make 9 knots on one tack with a following sea, with the sea on the bow she was reduced to 3 knots. The opinion was shared in more influential quarters, and during the discussions that led up to the 1815 revision of the stores establishment, Tucker, the junior Surveyor, told Admiral Byam Martin that he considered the majority of British ships too 'clean' forward, which gave them a tendency to plunge.[2] However, it was too small a problem to cause much concern under wartime conditions.

With the dimensions and hull forms of frigates universally approved, design attention was directed elsewhere – to other ship types, but also to ship structure. From 1806 the Surveyors were busy with the new standard battleships, as well as brigs and smaller craft, but some of the concerns of the period also influenced frigate building. Prime among these was the timber shortage and the resulting structural measures outlined in the previous chapter. One of the first orders to affect frigates was the July 1805 instruction to make all futtocks as straight as possible in future; it produced a ten-dency to reduce tumblehome and further enhance the wall-sided upperworks of British frigates.[3]

The other major change was the flattening of the sheer line, a policy associated with the new junior Surveyor, Henry Peake, appointed in June 1806. The height of the deck at stem and sternpost was unaltered, but the shallow arc running down to the midships – the 'hanging' of the deck – was straightened and so raised, giving more freeboard to the gunports in this area. Peake was a consciously conservative designer, and during the process of defining what became the 'Surveyors of the Navy' class 74s, he explained the main tenets of his philosophy. Having studied many draughts, both English and French, he had concluded that well designed ships intended for the same roles had very similar underwater forms, so there was little improvement to be gained from continually striving to modify hull lines, 'provided the principal dimensions are suitable to the required purpose of the ship, and the plane of floatation such as to ensure stability.'[4] He realised that many of the imported French forms offered a real advance in performance, not because their lines were better drawn, but because they were usually significantly bigger ships than their British

TABLE 8/1: Comparative scantlings of 18pdr frigates

	British *Horatio*, 38	French *Fidèle*, 40	Franco-Venetian *Corona*, 40	US *Constellation* class 36s
KEEL (PIECES X SIZE)	6 x 1ft 3½in sq	1ft 2in S, 1ft 3in deep [kelson]	1ft 0in S, 9½in deep [kelson]	3 x 1ft 6in S, 'as deep as may be had' [2ft]
ROOM AND SPACE	2ft 6¹³⁄₂₇in	?	2ft 3in	2ft 2in
FLOORS	13½in/13in/12in S, 11½in M	9½in S, 11in M	9in S at floorheads, 11in M	12½in S, 14½in M
LOWER FUTTOCKS	13in/12½in/12in S, 10½in M	9½in S, 11in M at orlop	8½in S, 10½in M	12in midships ('something smaller fore and aft')
SECOND FUTTOCKS	12/11½in S, 10in M	9½in S, 9½in M at lower deck	8½in S, 9in M at lower deck	11½in S, M diminishing from 14½in to 7in at gunwale
THIRD FUTTOCKS	11½in/11½in S, 9½in M	9½in S, 8in M at upper deck	8½in S, 8in M at upper deck	11½in S
FOURTH FUTTOCKS	11in/11in S, 10in M	9½in S, 8in M at upper deck	8½in S, 8in M at upper deck	11½in S, 9in M at port sill
TOPTIMBERS	11in/10in S, ?in M	9in S, 5½in M at quarterdeck	8½in S, 5½in M at gunwale	11½in S, 7in M at gunwale
PLANK OF BOTTOM	4in, 24ft lengths min	4in	4in	4in, 24ft lengths min
MAIN WALES	3ft 9½in breadth x 6in	4ft breadth x 7in	4ft 3in breadth x 7in	5ft breadth x 7in [Diagonal riders – six pairs a side]
LOWER DECK BEAMS	11in S x 10in M	9½in S x 9½in M	9½in S x 10in M	16in S x 14in M
FASTENINGS	Wood hanging and lodging knee, per beam end	Shelfpiece, and thick strake, no knees	Clamp (shelfpiece), no knees	Wood lodging and dagger knee, per beam end
UPPER DECK BEAMS	11½in S x 13in M	10½in S x 11in M	10in S x 10½in M	18in S x 15in M
FASTENINGS	Wood hanging knee and lodging knee, per beam end; iron lodging knees over riders	Wood hanging knee, two thick strakes	Wood hanging knee, clamp	Wood hanging and lodging knee, at beam end
QUARTERDECK BEAMS	8½in S x 7in M	8in S x 7½in M	8in S x 7in M	13in x 14in
FASTENINGS	Wood hanging and lodging knee, per beam end	Wood hanging knee, and shelfpiece	Clamp (shelfpiece), no knees	Wood hanging and lodging knee, at beam end
Source	NMM Adm 168/163, 19 Jul 1805	PRO Adm 106/3336, 30 Mar 1811	PRO Adm 106/3336, Nov 1811	*American State Papers*, Dec 1794

Notes: S = sided; M = moulded

equivalents. In one respect this was a potential release from the unthinking regard for French hull forms, but it also meant that Peake felt free to alter existing designs, to increase the gunport freeboard for example, in a piecemeal fashion. The results were often worse than an *ab initio* design, as witnessed by the rather mediocre 'Surveyors' class' 74s, the 'improved' *Caledonia* class 120s (which were far from improved), and the *Seringapatam* class frigates, again supposedly improved from the French *Président*. However, Peake's fir-built version of the 36-gun *Euryalus* design was a success, and he did not even attempt a serious modification of the *Leda* class for his fir 38s.

THE DECLINING KUDOS OF FRENCH NAVAL ARCHITECTURE

By 1800 the vague but widespread belief in the design superiority of French warships was in retreat: indeed, the Barham Admiralty's preference for French-derived hull-forms was its short-lived swansong. This was largely a product of greater familiarity at close quarters with the realities of French ship design occasioned by the unprecedented number of prizes that fell into British hands during these wars.

Dockyard officials had long been familiar with the weaknesses of the French constructional style, and the consequent additional time and money needed to keep them serviceable.[5] The British claim to superior strength lay in two principal areas: the first was the size of the scantlings, and the second was the greater attention paid to fastenings. Comparisons between contract specifications for British-built ships, and the occasional list of scantlings taken off prizes, prove that not only were the frame timbers of British ships more substantial, but they were also positioned more closely together (the gaps can be calculated from the 'room and space' dimension). The other factor was the securing of beams in two dimensions, with both hanging and lodging knees (or an iron equivalent), as distinct from the French habit of merely rebating the beams into a thick clamp, or shelfpiece, perhaps with the support of a hanging knee. Dockyard officials had an unshakeable

faith in the resistance of their traditional system to hogging and racking stresses, and much of the experimental effort outlined in the previous chapter was directed towards the problem of replacing scarce wood knees without sacrificing strength and resilience.

Table 8/1 compares some of the main scantling elements of a standard British 38 with selected foreign equivalents. Although built at Flushing, the *Fidèle* (later *Laurel*) was a conventional Sané design, so in all probability was framed in exactly the same manner as the run of French 18pdr frigates. Her timbers were far lighter than *Horatio*'s, and although the room and space dimension is not quoted, it is highly likely that they were also further apart. *Corona* (taken into the Royal Navy as *Daedalus*) was constructed at Venice, then under Napoleonic control, but even by French standards she was regarded as very weakly built, and as a result was originally intended to carry 32pdr carronades on the main deck in British service. The lightweight Gover 24pdrs she ultimately received were a product of the same concern for her feeble timbering. By way of contrast, the scantlings of the American '36s' were little different from their huge spar-decked 44s, so the British view of the *Chesapeake* as 'overbuilt' is understandable. One great advantage of the American framing plan in combat was the greater moulded depth of the timbers – *Constitution*'s 'Old Ironsides' nickname was well deserved – and it is significant that by 1813 Seppings believed that British ships could be improved by larger moulded dimensions in the framing.

Of the larger frigates compared in Table 8/2, the surprise is the lightness of *Endymion*'s structure. While *Cambrian*, as one would expect, is a slightly scaled-up standard British 38, *Endymion* has timbers of less siding and moulding, so may well follow the scheme of her French prototype, *Pomone*; she is, however, fastened in the British manner. It was often stressed in contemporary British sources that the American 44s had the scantlings of 74s (indeed, some mistakenly claimed that they had been laid down as such), but while this could be supported by highly selective presentation of the evidence, it was distinctly misleading. The *Constitution* was much the same size as the old British 'Common

The disposition of frame for the *Endymion* dated September 1795. The scantlings list suggests that in dimensions the frame of this ship copied her French prototype the *Pomone*; but the actual disposition of the framing seems to follow conventional British practice. The only reconsideration is a note which instructs that the port timbers be scarphed as at the after side of the second main-deck port, or that a 'cast toptimber' be introduced as at the fore side of port number twelve. *National Maritime Museum Dr1815*

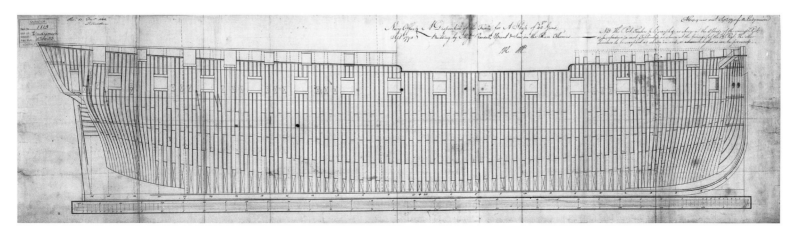

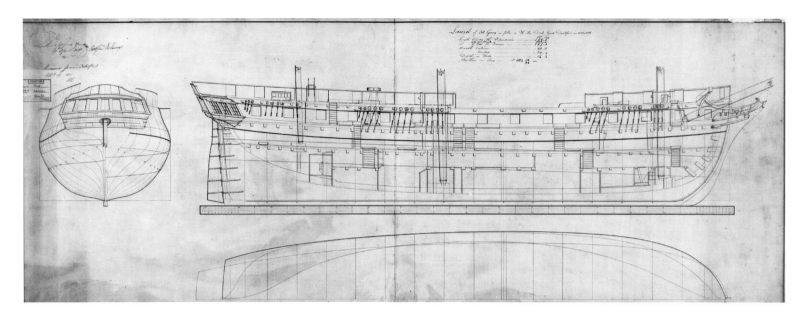

When the British captured Flushing in 1809 they discovered a frigate called *Fidèle* in the final stages of construction; the hull was towed to Deptford and fitted out as the *Laurel*, 38. The ship had been part of the Napoleonic effort to utilise the maritime resources in subject parts of the empire like the Netherlands and northern Italy, and was a standard Sané-designed frigate. Assuming that the structure also followed standard French practice, the scantlings list prepared at Deptford shows that the French navy still favoured very lightweight construction as it had done since at least the middle of the eighteenth century.
National Maritime Museum Dr7106

Class' 74 (actually longer, if somewhat narrower), so some frame elements were naturally of similar scantling – floors and lower futtocks, for example, but running up the frames to the gunwale the thickness of the sides reduced more rapidly, as one would expect in a frigate. By comparison with *Cambrian*, in fact, the American spar-deckers do not look disproportionately heavy, although the greater moulded depth of the timber is noticeable. The frames were also closer together: a mere 2in at the level of the lower futtocks, whereas *Cambrian*'s 'space' was 2½in and *Endymion*'s 3in. The *Newcastle*, designed by a Frenchman and according to anecdotal evidence regarded as lightly built, actually had thicker wales and greater moulded depth at the port sills than the American ships, although the timber was only pitch pine. There was little to chose between the ships in terms of thickness of the side just below the port sills, the total depth of external planking, moulded frame timber and spirketting coming to around 19½in, depending on the point of the chamfered planking the measurement is made; but *Newcastle*'s main disadvantage was the 5in and more between her frames, so would probably have suffered heavily if she had ever brought an American 44 to action.

Whatever their structure, all wooden ships flex, become leaky, infirm and eventually what sailors call 'crazy'. At this stage it is dangerous to keep them at sea, and they have to be sent home to refit; for Royal Navy frigates, regularly exposed to the rigours of all-weather, year-round cruising, it was a crucial limitation on their operational availability. Naturally, those more lightly built and fastened, in the French manner, suffered sooner and more seriously, and with so many French prizes in service, operational commanders began to discover the disadvantages of having such ships more frequently 'off line'. In the spring of 1798, for example, the commander-in-chief of the Channel Fleet, Lord Bridport, wrote to the First Lord request-

ing that no more French-built frigates be sent to his fleet. He argued:

The Channel frigates should be strong and in perfect condition. What occasioned my desiring English built frigates arose from the consideration of the boisterous seas they had to encounter and knowing that I have six French built frigates already with me and that I find them oftener and longer in port at a time than our own built frigates.

. . . it is supposed that French frigates sail faster than English built ones. But they are confessedly weaker, are oftener in port and not able to keep the sea on long cruises as they stow little and, having no orlop deck, they must move their cables whenever they want to get at the water that is stowed under them, which is sometimes difficult at sea.[6]

In the 1790s big frigates were in short supply and French prizes were often put into service with the minimum of repair and refit. However, from the renewal of the war in 1803 a more discriminating approach was adopted, and many prizes were not deemed fit for the Royal Navy until they were refitted to British standards. Often the survey revealed that substantial work was needed: of the frigates captured at San Domingo in November 1803 the *Clorinde*, which was barely five years old, was judged to require a four-month Middling Repair; the ten-year old *Vertu* was reckoned to need a seven-month Great Repair. Given the many pressing commitments of the Dockyards, it was difficult to justify that amount of time and resources, so *Vertu* languished as a hulk until the decision was taken in 1810 to break her up.

A number of other prize frigates failed to reach the top of the Dockyard priority list, and those that in consequence never saw active British service included the

TABLE 8/2: Comparative scantlings of 24pdr frigates

	Cambrian	*Endymion*	*Newcastle*	US *Constitution* class
KEEL (PIECES X SIZE)	6 x 1ft 3½in sq	7 x 1ft 3½in S, 1ft 2in deep	8 x 1ft 4in sq	3 x 1ft 6in S, 'as deep as may be had'
ROOM AND SPACE	2ft 6¾in	2ft 0¼in	2ft 8⅝in	2ft 2in
FLOORS	14in/13in/12in	10½in midships/10in S, 10½in M	13in S throughout, 12in M	12½in S, 15in M
LOWER FUTTOCKS	13½in/13in/12in S, 10½in M	10½in/9½in S, 9½in M	13in S, 12in M	12in midships ('something smaller fore and aft')
SCARPH TO 2ND FUTTOCK	6ft 8in	6ft 5in	7ft 0in	
SECOND FUTTOCKS	12½in/11¼in S, 10in M	9½in S, 9¼in M	12in S, 11½in M	11½in S, M diminishing from 15in to 7in at gunwale
SCARPH TO 3RD FUTTOCK	6ft 8in	6ft 5in	6ft 0in	
THIRD FUTTOCKS	11½in/11in S, 9¾in M	9½in/9½in S, 8½in M	12in S, 11in/10½in M	11½in S
SCARPH TO 4TH FUTTOCK	6ft 8in	6ft 5in	5ft 3in	
FOURTH FUTTOCKS	11in/11in S, 10½in M	9½in/9½in S, ?8½in M	12in S, 10in M	11½in S, 9in M at port sill
TOPTIMBERS	10½in (11½in sides of ports) S, 6in M	9½in (10½in sides of ports) S	11½in (12in sides of ports) S	11½in S, 7in M at gunwale
PLANK OF BOTTOM	4in, 24ft lengths min	4in, 24ft lengths min	4in, 24ft lengths min	4in, 24ft lengths min
MAIN WALES	4ft breadth x 6in	4ft breadth x 6in	3ft 10in breadth x 8in	5ft breadth x 7in
		[Breadth riders added, 11in S]		[Diagonal riders – six pairs a side]
LOWER DECK BEAMS		10in x 10in	11in x 11in	16in x 14in
FASTENINGS	Wood hanging and lodging knee, per beam end	Wood hanging and lodging knee, per beam end (iron where wood will not fit)	oak chocks, iron plate knees, one per beam end	Wood lodging and dagger knee, per beam end
UPPER DECK BEAMS		12½in x 11½in	13in x 12½in	18in x 15in
FASTENINGS	Wood hanging knees, iron lodging knees	Wood hanging knees, iron lodging knees where wood will not fit	As lower deck	Wood hanging and lodging knee, at beam end
SPAR DECK BEAMS	—	—	8½in x 12in	13in x 14in
FASTENINGS			Hanging and lodging knees, attached with circular coaks	Wood hanging and lodging knee, at beam end
Source	NMM Adm 168/124, undated	NMM Adm 168/137, undated	NMM Adm 168/175, 11 May 1813	*American State Papers*, Dec 1794

Notes: S = sided; M = moulded

Infatigable, Caroline, Vénus, Pomone (taken 1811), *Terpsichore, Alcmène,* and *Melpomène,* as well as the ex-Spanish *Fama,* the ex-Danish *Havfruen,* and the ex-American *Essex.* On being surveyed, others were found of marginal utility and were given less demanding employment, often as a troopship. The *Thétis,* reported in need of a Middling to Large Repair after her battle with the *Amethyst,* was converted to a trooper under the name of *Brune. Weser* and *Trave* were similarly converted on capture, and it was the planned employment of the ex-American *Chesapeake,* although the war ended before it could be implemented.

By the new century the older prize frigates captured in the French Revolutionary War were also beginning to show their age and the effects of hard service. A number of them, like *Sybille, Unité* and *Virginie* were given substantial repairs in 1803-5 before they could take any further part in the war;[7] others also required major attention in the following years. By the end of 1806 *Uranie* was judged so rotten, she was sold in 1807; in March 1807 *Loire* was estimated to need a massive ten-month Great Repair; and by February 1808 the *Revolutionnaire* was in need of a slightly less drastic Middling Repair. The Dockyards might be pressured into finding time for the favourite ships, but stopgap measures were applied to others – the *Virginie,* reported structurally weak in December 1807, for instance, had to make do with reduced masts and spars. These incidents were major drains on Dockyard resources, but there were many less dramatic examples: ships like *Clorinde, Fisgard* and *Sybille* were notoriously prone to leaks and made frequent calls for attention.[8]

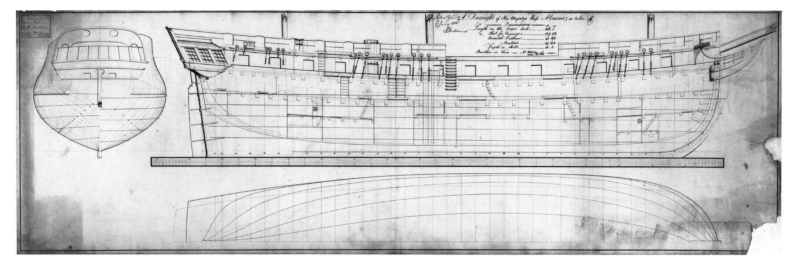

French frigate design was largely in the hands of Sané and his disciples, but there was a radical alternative tradition represented by the longer and sharper hull form of Pierre-Alexandre-Laurent Forfait which was used between 1793 and 1806 for eleven frigates starting with the *Seine* and mostly built at Le Havre and Nantes. The *Topaze* of 1804, shown here, was one of these, and was renamed *Alcmene* when captured by the British in 1809. These ships made a considerable impression on British naval officers, from the capture of *Révolutionnaire* onwards, and one became the starting point for the *Seringapatam* class. However, the burden of historical evidence suggest that they were, at best, problematical: they offered high performance in some respects, but were difficult to get the best from. Furthermore, the fine-lined form seemed to suffer even more than usual from the high-maintenance requirement of French hulls.
National Maritime Museum Dr7115

The widely held belief that French frigates cost more to maintain than British-built ships should be possible to quantify from figures for Dockyard expenditure readily available in the Progress Books. However, it is a complex issue, since it depends on numerous variables, like the age of the ship, the type of service, battle damage, and time spent overseas where there may have been unrecorded work on the ship. Furthermore, the validity of all statistics is improved by a larger sample, and, for individual subjects, by total coverage. Unfortunately, for the period under review there are surprisingly few sets of complete figures. The system seems to have collapsed under the wartime workload, and for some doubtless political reason the thinnest period coincides with St Vincent's administration of 1801-4. This makes it difficult to obtain what nowadays would be called the 'life costs' for more than a handful of ships that predate the renewal of the war.

The accompanying table is an attempt to draw conclusions based on what fragmentary evidence survives. It shows recorded Dockyard expenditure for the periods noted and the average annual figure derived from it. Since it is a reasonable assumption that the older the ship the more it cost to maintain, the launch date is included. The emphasis is on the cost of ships under

wartime conditions (since in peacetime very little, if anything, need be spent on ships, reducing the nominal average costs if included). For similar reasons, the Great Repairs carried out to many ships right at the end of the war have been separated out, since they have a substantial impact on the average.

One may be confident that the figures for the British ships are typical. For *Phoebe* and *Dryad*, the costs represent most if not all of their wartime careers. *Phoebe* was involved in a number of hard actions so might be thought to have incurred more than an average amount of repairs; on the other hand, no work is recorded on the ship in 1803-5, but even if these years are omitted, the annual average is still only £4000 (and she was not deemed in need of major attention at the end of the war, even after her battle with USS *Essex*). Partial figures for other British frigates of a similar vintage straddle these averages: *Boadicea* cost only £1874 per year over an 11-year sample and £4300 when her 1815-16 Great Repair is included; *Aigle* averaged £1739 for 12 years with no major refit; and *Naiad* averaged £2309 for 10 years and £4329 including the 1814-15 Great Repair. The interesting point is how expensive *Endymion* was to keep serviceable. To some extent this reflects her larger size, but although fastened in the British manner, she was built with lighter scantlings probably copied

	British built			French built		
	Phoebe	*Dryad*	*Endymion*	*Princess Charlotte*	*Rhin*	*Sybille*
Built	1795	1795	1797	1782	1802	1791
Expenditure	£47,615	£40,136	£91,738	£52,897	£51,313	£67,725
In period	1796-1815	1796-99, 1805-13	1798-1800, 1803-15	1803-13	1809-15	1804-14
Average pa	£3400	£3087	-	£4808	£8552	£6165
Great Repair	-	£25,538	[inc above]	£28,270	-	£30,477
In period	-	1814-15	1812-13	1814-15	[post-war]	1815-16
Average inc GR	-	£3664	£5733	£6243	-	£8183

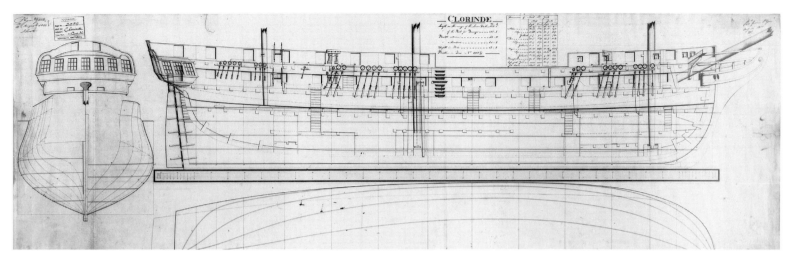

from her French model, the *Pomone*; she also needed a Middling to Large Repair before the end of the war.

Because there is less data, it is difficult to be dogmatic about whether the expenditure on the French prizes is representative. The examples, however, are significantly more costly than their British equivalents. *Sybille* was a favourite ship, but like *Princess Charlotte* needed two bouts of major work during the period covered. These were not new ships, but the surprise is the relatively new *Rhin*, the most expensive pro rata of the sample, although she did not require a Great Repair until 1817-20.

It seems likely, therefore, that the general belief in the frailty of the French structural style was not mere prejudice. Indeed, the experience of the Dockyards was consistent and could be traced back at least half a century, but this had never previously prevented British interest in the hull *forms* of French ships. However, from 1806 the Admiralty was noticeably less impressed by French design: there are examples of draughts of prizes being requested for inspection, but no orders for designs based on them.[9] Although there were still British naval officers who believed their service could learn from the French, there were fewer in positions of authority.

One unexpected source of the declining prestige of French naval architecture was Jean-Louis Barrallier, the Royal Navy's 'in-house' French constructor. This royalist *émigré*'s career was outlined in Chapter 5, but it is worth reiterating that his appointment, which flouted legislation preventing Catholics from holding public office, reflected patronage at the highest level. It also suggests just how strong was the Admiralty's eagerness to harness French design expertise to the British cause. Unfortunately, Barrallier's performance did not fulfil the great expectations of his much-vaunted French technical training. It is by no means clear that he practised naval architecture at Toulon, and it is possible that being entrusted with the single-handed design of major warships was beyond both his experience and his capacity.

Neither the 74-gun *Spencer* nor the frigate *Lavinia* were very well thought of, but his second ship of the line, the *Milford*, was the subject of a very critical report from Henry Bayntun, the ship's first captain. According to Bayntun, the ship trimmed heavily by the stern (3ft 6in was the best he could achieve, compared to the designed 1ft 9in); she also carried a slack helm, and was deficient in initial stability, commonly heeling to 12 degrees under moderate canvas even when deeply stored. The sail plan was also misconceived, the fore yards needing to be reduced so that they did not risk interlocking with those on the main, and allowing the bumpkins to be shortened – as built it was impossible to get the fore tacks on board because the cathead shroud interfered with the leech of the sail; the bumpkin had already carried away, and at a critical moment when the ship was straining to claw off a lee shore. On such small details did the safety of a ship depend.

Bayntun was later consulted on whether it was worth repeating the *Milford* design, which he thought inadvisable, at least until further trials had sorted out the ship's sailing and stowage problems. His reasons can be summarised as:

1. The excessive trim aft.

2. Iron ballast could not be increased because the hold was too confined [a typical French feature], height having been sacrificed to the orlop.

3. The ship did not carry her midships ports high enough.

4. She lacked stability.

5. She was too fine aft, and the fore and after bodies were not balanced, which made her quick in her motions [rapid and jerky pitching]; therefore, the trim was easily upset.

6. He did not approve of the upright sides, nor the great breadth and rake of the stern – wall sides were

A good example of the high maintenance costs of French-built frigates is the *Clorinde*, a five-year-old ship when captured in 1803 that required major work before she could be taken into British service. She was again repaired in 1810 when this draught was taken off. By this stage the ship was heavily anglicised in fittings and appearance, with a round bow, berthed-up forecastle, drumhead double capstans and British-style quarter galleries and below-deck arrangements; the mast and spar dimensions listed are also those of a standard 38. Note the second, emergency steering wheel forward of the great cabin; introduced in 1808, this feature is not often represented on draughts.
National Maritime Museum Dr2059

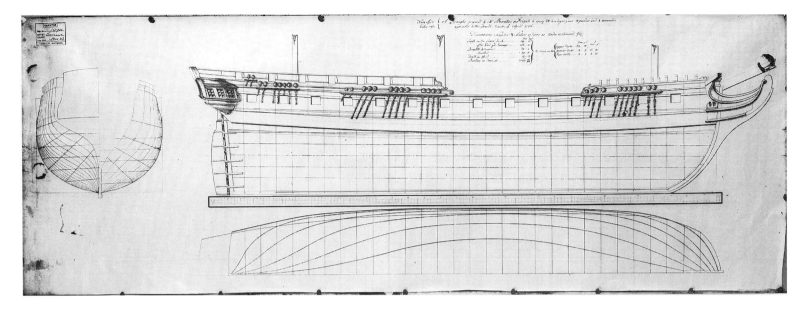

The earliest known design by Jean-Louis Barrallier is this proposed 38-gun frigate dated 5 May 1796 and noted as a response to the Admiralty Board minute of 4 April. The dimensions are: 149ft 6in x 39ft 2in x 13ft 3in, measuring 1019 tons. The hull form bears little resemblance to contemporary French designs but the proportions are close to British designs of the mid 1790s. No vessel was built to this draught and it has no bearing on the later and larger *Lavinia*, despite being so catalogued for at least a century. This was probably the draught submitted on 7 June along with Henslow's for what became *Active* and Rule's for *Amazon*, but *Leda* (from the lines of the French *Hébé*) was chosen instead of Barrallier's. However, it is likely that this draught was prepared as part of Barrallier's bid for an official post, which had succeeded on 1 June when he was appointed Second Assistant to the Surveyors.
National Maritime Museum Dr1974

cheaper to construct, he believed, but were more prone to flexing.

7. The ship did not sail well, but was very quick and certain in tacking; since reducing the head yards and raking the masts, the ship now steered well.[10]

Needless to say, the repeat *Milford* was cancelled, and the larger *Rochfort* that Barrallier was already building had to be modified; it was to be his last ship of the line.

Beyond his own very few original designs, Barrallier's chief value to the Admiralty was as a source of technical advice, providing an alternative to the 'official' Navy Board position represented by the Surveyors. Since the Frenchman was both an outsider and a relative junior, his influence was resented by the Dockyard personnel and he was inevitably drawn into the personal and professional jealousies of Admiralty-Navy Board politics. Nor was his advice highly regarded by all who sought his views. During the search for a new medium 74 in 1806, Barrallier was consulted by Captain Thomas Hamilton,[11] who found him 'so absorbed in theory that he has made many mistakes as to facts, and in practical knowledge he is certainly deficient.'

Hamilton's view could be substantiated by Barrallier's report a few years later on the new methods of construction then being tested (as outlined in the previous chapter). His was not an original mind, and had been trained to argue from precedent and reference to acknowledged authorities. He did have a command of mathematics, and could do useful calculations, like the metacentric height of his designs, for example, but the practical shortcomings of the ships he built suggest that he trusted too much to doubtful theory and not enough to empirical experience. In 1812 he produced a proposal for a new small 74 to replace the unsatisfactory *Ajax* or 'Surveyors of the Navy' class which was so abstruse that it had to be sent to Professor Inman of the School of Naval Architecture to check its calculations –

and even he declined to carry out all the time-consuming arithmetic necessary. Inman also became embroiled in a dispute with Barrallier, who had done calculations for initial stability, but not for the range of rolling Inman thought necessary.[12] It contains some interesting observations on the *Ajax* class and the *Black Prince* design then building from the reduced lines of the Danish *Christian VII* which was obviously a response to the perceived shortcomings of the *Ajax* and her sisters. Barrallier's proposed form was based on the Danish *Norge*, which he thought was 'one of the master pieces of the celebrated Chapman' (it was not: it was a native Danish design by F C H Hohlenberg). With the huge crash programme of new-building in hand by the end of the year, the Surveyors were in no hurry to consider Barrallier's design, and despite prompting from the Admiralty, did not finally report until January 1814.[13]

Nothing became of this proposal, but while the argument rumbled on the Admiralty decided it needed a radical new type of double-banked 50-gun ship to deal with the American *Constitution* class, which by the end of 1812 had proved more than a match for the standard British 18pdr frigate. In the latter half of the eighteenth century the traditional approach to a new design was to request a draught from each of the two Surveyors; following the same specification, the two designs allowed a degree of comparison and doubled the chance of one proving satisfactory. However, since 1806 the Surveyors had developed the habit of acting as a committee, so while the Admiralty ordered one of the new ships from the Surveyors, it looked to Barrallier to provide the contrast. Thus it may well have been necessity rather than the Frenchman's residual credit as a designer that gained him the commission. The resulting ship, the *Newcastle*, was a fast and powerful ship, although not as weatherly as the *Leander* produced to the same specification by the Surveyors. Before either ship went to sea, the

Admiralty invited suggestions for a less extravagant spar-decked design that could be built in numbers after the war. Barrallier, however, refused to comply, saying anything smaller than *Newcastle* could not encompass all the qualities required of a 24pdr frigate. This act of minor mutiny more or less concluded his direct dealings with the Admiralty, and his next letter in December 1815 was to announce that the restored Bourbon monarchy in France had offered him the post of *Directeur du Construction* at Toulon; this he intended to accept and was therefore resigning as Second Assistant to the Surveyors. The Admiralty congratulated him on the honour and, perhaps with intentional ambiguity, told him the Board 'entertains a due sense of his services'. Perhaps encouraged by this, Barrallier applied for a pension, but was turned down. He then asked for a grant in recognition of his service, which the Admiralty replied was 'not in their power' to concede, and Barrallier retired hurt to Toulon.[14] Whether this truly reflected the Admiralty's opinion of his worth it is hard to judge, but he did not enjoy a sparkling post-war career either, and it is difficult to suppress the notion that he was simply not a very good naval architect.[15] It was ironic that it should take the work of a French designer to undermine the status of French naval architecture; it would be doubly ironic if he were, in fact, incompetent.

THE SURVEYORS OF THE NAVY

In purely design terms, there was little development in the frigate classes between 1801 and 1812. The Admiralties of St Vincent and Barham reverted to some older and smaller forms, but three main designs (*Lively*, *Leda* and *Apollo*) continued to be built and by 1806 no others were deemed necessary. Of the other potential foreign design influences, the Danish ships taken at Copenhagen in 1807 provoked much interest, and the form of the big two-decker *Christian VII* was adopted for some ships of the line. However, the frigates did not impress, although some exhibited a highly original midship section with sharp, straight-rising floors. The most conspicuous feature – the curious, narrowed stern design of Hohlenberg's ships (supposedly the inspiration for Seppings's post-war circular stern) – was especially unpopular, and the frigates which saw any degree of British service were refitted with conventional, if confined, quarter galleries.

The persistence with three standard classes speaks volumes for the qualities of these ships, since new battleships, brigs and small craft were introduced at exactly this time. Even in 1812 the first reaction to the American war was to order more *Leda*s and an 'austerity *Apollo*' to be built in fir, but eventually the need for 24pdr-armed ships was faced.

At this point the working practices of the current Surveyors became a distinct disadvantage: the committee approach, coupled with a general reluctance to design an entirely new hull form, did not serve the Navy well at a time when radical thought was required. Although relatively good ships, the Modified *Endymion* class was a stopgap that might never have been built if it were not for the designers' instinctive recourse to an existing prototype. For the 'double-banked' frigates there was no conceivable model, and the Admiralty itself had to specify their main features, presumably based on intelligence about the ships' intended American opponents (they were very similar in dimensions). For a wholly new type of ship, the *Newcastle* and *Leander* were surprisingly impressive, backing Peake's assertion that adequate size for the task (rather than the niceties of hull form) were the key to design success. Certainly, there was little to chose between the two ships, although the Surveyors' design seems to have been more weatherly than Barrallier's. It is not clear who exactly designed the *Leander*, since Sir William Rule was very ill at the time; and because the

A Pocock watercolour depicting two of the Danish prizes taken at Copenhagen in 1807. The main subject is the conventional 74 *Justitia* but alongside is one of the newer frigates as captured, showing off the unique shape of the Hohlenberg stern. The deck narrowed radically towards the stern, and quarter galleries were omitted, but above the semi-circular taffrail were two angled 'bastions' that seem to have included chase ports which allowed oblique defensive fire. The design was very unpopular in the Royal Navy, and all the Hohlenberg frigates that were commissioned were refitted with more conventional sterns. *National Maritime Museum B5498*

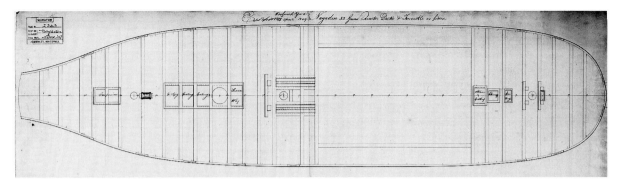

This deck plan of the ex-Danish *Nyaden* reveals the narrow 'pink stern' basis of the Hohlenberg design. By pulling in the topside, in effect progressively increasing the tumblehome towards the stern, some oblique fire could be contrived over the quarters. Naval warfare in the Baltic made great use of rowing gunboats whose favourite tactic against becalmed sailing ships was to take station off the stern and quarters where no broadside gun could bear; Hohlenberg's concept was probably intended as a counter to this.
National Maritime Museum Dr2343

A sheer draught of the *Chesapeake* taken off at Plymouth in December 1814. By this time the ship had been in British service for a year and a half, so critical comments in the survey were based on reasonable experience. The excessive overhang of the stern was prone to damage in a following sea, and despite the obviously fine lines, the ship's performance under sail was not regarded as exceptional. The survey was complimentary about the build-quality of the ship, but thought the scantlings over-size: she had originally been intended as another 44, and it is possible that the timbers collected for the original design were not reduced in siding for the smaller revised dimensions (in any case the scantlings of the 18pdr frigates were not much smaller than those for the 44s). The mast and spar dimensions were 'as now fitted' (in December 1814), and comprised a mix of standard British spars: mostly the masts of a 36 and the yards of a 38, so presumably supplied from whatever was available at Halifax.
National Maritime Museum Dr7343

sheer draught has been lost, it is not possible to compare the form with the rest of Rule's work. It can be no more than a guess, but the *Java* class was conceived as an 'economy *Leander*', so may be similar in hull form.[16] This was primarily Peake's work, and displays a hull form, reminiscent of some of the designs of Pierre Forfait, whose *Président* was to be chosen as the model for the *Seringapatam* a few months later – and like the *Seringapatam*, the *Java* design needed some modification for the follow-on class, to make them better suited to post-war conditions.

The extension of Peake's creed that allowed him to try 'improving' existing hull lines proved very fallible. For the new 38-gun class of 1813, Peake certainly took Forfait's French form as his starting point, but flattened the sheer and straightened the tumblehome; the prototype was also built of teak, for which Peake seems to have made no allowance. The resulting saga of the *Seringapatam* revealed the danger of this approach, and the design eventually required two stages of modifications before it was deemed adequate. By contrast, the unaltered *Leda* design seemed capable of absorbing, on the one hand, the greater weight of teak construction, and on the other the Seppings innovations of diagonal bracing and a round stern.

The final phase of the long wars with France and her allies added the Americans to Britain's list of enemies. Although small, the US Navy proved a tougher opponent than any so far encountered, and the unlooked-for defeats in single-ship actions led to a shake-up in many of the Royal Navy's attitudes and methods. During the war much was made of the originality of American ship

design, and especially the 'spar-deck' layout, but while this was useful in apologist propaganda, in the long run surprisingly little of American practice was adopted. The most obvious influence was the big 24pdr frigate, which once taken up enthusiastically by Britain's potential enemies and rivals like France and Russia, could not be ignored. But while the concept was undoubtedly American, the British, true to traditional concerns for quantity rather than quality, eventually settled on smaller ships as a post-war standard, and gave up the true 'double-banked' layout for frigates. Experience proved that the waist guns on the spar deck were not very effective in a long battle since they interfered with sail-handling during manoeuvres – a conclusion already arrived at in the US Navy by 1812, where the gangways were actually unarmed, whatever British accounts may have suggested.

American prizes were closely scrutinised, and in the cases of the *Chesapeake* and the sloop *Florida* were subject to commissioned sea trials, to see if there was anything to be learned from them. Far from being impressed, British officers regarded neither as a worthwhile prototype, and criticised the construction of the former and the hull design of the latter. Considering the long-standing strictures on the lightness of French hull structure, it might be thought that the British would approve of the solidity of the *Chesapeake*, but in fact they considered her overbuilt. By the time the US frigate came to be surveyed, the Royal Navy was in the throes of Seppings's revolution, which was designed to reduce scantlings (and so save timber) without sacrificing strength, even though there was also a body of

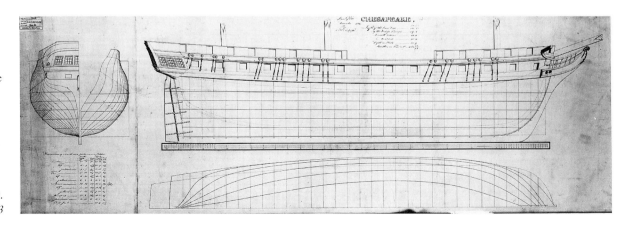

opinion that favoured framing of greater moulded depth. The American approach, with its conspicuous consumption of large-scantling timber, was fine for a small fleet with huge resources of top-quality hard-woods, but could never appeal to the economy-driven administration of the world's largest navy.

On a more detailed level, the surveys of the American prizes found nothing exceptional or note-worthy. It has recently been argued that Humphreys intended a limited system of diagonal riders for all his frigates, but if *President* ever had them, the fact is nei-ther mentioned in the survey, nor shown on the draught.[17] The ship herself was thought worthy of imi-tation, but this was a purely political decision. It had been hoped to retain the prize in service, but she would have required too much spent on her to guaran-tee a long life, so it was decided to break her up and build a replica instead. The new *President* was little more than a trophy, designed to remind the Royal Navy's rivals that dominion of the seas could not be won by a handful of individually superior ships.

This sentiment epitomises the philosophy British ship designers had followed for over a century. Seapower was a product of numbers, which could only be maintained without crippling cost to the state by restraining the size of individual ships to the minimum dimensions that could meet the 'staff requirements'. There were times when this approach prevented suffi-cient growth to keep pace with foreign developments, and British ships became so much smaller on average than their opponents that they could not properly fulfil their roles. This has always been represented as poor *design* whereas it was actually poor political decision-making, based on too rigid an application of the princi-ples of economy. In terms of pure naval architecture, the greater restraints on British Surveyors actually required them to be better ship designers than their foreign equivalents, and much of the criticism of their work, both contemporary and historical, is miscon-ceived and misdirected. It is true that British warships were often less powerful or poorer sailers, but ideally the individual inferiority was too small to make any sig-nificant operational difference. The true capabilities of British designers can be seen in the frigates of the 1790s, when dimensions were allowed to escalate to match those of probable opponents, the resulting class-es like the *Apollo*s and the *Lively*s being well-balanced designs perfectly fitted for their tasks – and able to catch and defeat any equivalent ship. The very large 24pdr spar-decked frigate was a new and very foreign concept, but the American single-ship victories of 1812 forced an Admiralty response in kind. Nevertheless, the long-term reaction was a traditionally 'minimal' ship, the *Java*, and a reversion to the strategic vision that saw the capture of the *President* as a paradigm for the fate of all individually superior ships.

The draught of the ex-American *President*, as taken off at Portsmouth, 1 December 1815. Depicting the ship as captured, this draught shows the layout of the famous spar-deckers during the War of 1812, without guns or even barricades in the waist. By convention this type of combined sheer and profile drawing represented the main elements of the internal structure, including breasthooks, top and breadth riders and the like. This is a particularly detailed example, outlining even the dagger knees and standards, but no diagonal riders of the kind fitted in the *Constitution*. When it was intended to repair the ship in 1818, all the internal works were stripped out and the survey enumerates each piece, and again there is no mention of diagonal riders. The poor state of the hull led the shipwrights to recommend breaking up the ship, but the Admiralty was so keen to retain the most important prize of the American war that the First Lord invited the Comptroller of the Navy Board to a private interview in order to impress on him the value of the *President* as a propaganda tool. As a result of this pressure the ship was surveyed again, but despite the claims made for the superiority of live oak, it was found that the only sound timber in the whole ship comprised fifty-six floors, thirty-nine first futtocks and twelve second futtocks; all the rest was defective, decayed or rotten [NMM POR/D/31, 20 May 1818]. The ship was reluctantly taken to pieces, and a replaced with a replica.
National Maritime Museum Dr1305

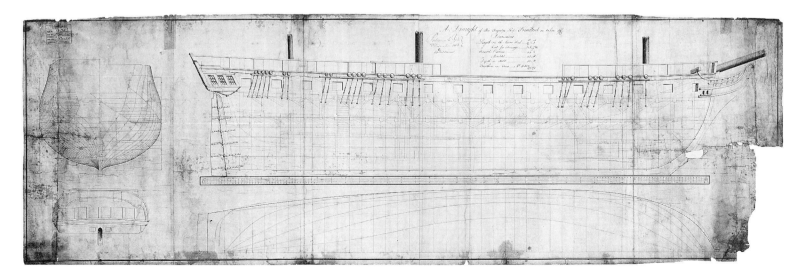

CHAPTER NINE

Wartime Modifications

TWO DECADES of almost uninterrupted warfare at sea inevitably influenced British frigates. Other chapters deal with the response to changes in strategic and economic conditions in the major areas of design, construction and armament; but there was also a myriad of more detailed modifications that sought to incorporate lessons of the fighting into the layout, internal arrangements and fittings of the ships. While no one of these in itself represents war-winning innovation, the fact that a constant stream of such developments were adopted is significant in a navy that was supposedly becoming complacent and ossified in the final years of the long conflict; if anything, the process gained momentum towards the end of the war, and many of the innovators were themselves naval officers keenly interested in improving the fighting efficiency of their service.

LAYOUT AND INTERNAL ARRANGEMENTS

The rapid growth in the size of British frigates during the 1790s was not in itself a spur to major changes in layout or internal arrangements, which had become standardised early on in the French Revolutionary War. There were orlop platforms fore and aft and over the main hold, where there were fixed compartments for magazines and filling rooms, specialist stowage space, and storerooms. Above this was an unarmed lower deck on which both the commissioned officers and the crew were berthed; actually termed the 'berth deck' in the US Navy, it was this feature that made the frigate unique, giving its complement more space per ton than any other type of warship. The upper deck housed the main battery and included the captain's accommodation aft; the growth in length of British frigates had produced more spacious gundecks, but the only significant change of the 1790s was the wide-spread adoption of a bridle port forward, which could function as a chase-port when required. Above this were the quarterdeck and forecastle, joined by gangways along the sides of the intervening waist; there was a tendency for the gangways to become more substantial and structurally integrated in this period,[1] but it was still a long way from the complete 'spar deck' of US frigates.

In the following decade, although alterations were relatively minor, individual captains continued to enjoy a degree of autonomy in the fitting of their ves-sels. The Navy Board disliked the cost and delay of customised fittings, but was sympathetic to changes that promised more efficient or effective warships, and so there were cases of individual initiatives leading to the general adoption of particular measures. A case in point was the orlop and platform arrangements of the new battleship *Warspite*, which were so admired that a committee of naval officers was set up to report on them in 1808. The layout received official sanction, and in July 'Captain Blackwood's plan' was ordered to be used as a guide in future, not only for ships of the line but also frigates and ship sloops.

Three months later the Navy Board issued a more detailed warrant, complete with drawings, which went far beyond the ground-plan of the platforms to encompass details of accommodation, rigging and armament. Some of it concerned only battleships, but frigates and sloops were included in the more general alterations. The *Warspite*'s storeroom arrangement, which made better use of available space, was adopted, but a host of apparently trivial innovations contributed at the same time to greater efficiency or to an improvement in the living conditions of the crew. Under the latter head might be counted the replacement of open bins for flour, oatmeal and pease by casks with lids to keep out vermin; paint and oil stored in leaden cisterns instead of buckets; and an ingenious new system for the live-stock 'manger', now fitted forward of the main hatch, in which the pens were divided horizontally, the top half being hung from the skid beams but the lower half mounted on trucks so it could be easily wheeled out for cleaning; there was even a new pattern of hen coop with a removable sliding base. Medical facilities were enhanced by the provision of special cots whose frames could be converted into stretchers to make it easier to get accident victims down to the sick berth.

Fighting efficiency was not forgotten, and it was this warrant that introduced the fitting of the two aftermost carronades on shifting mountings (see Chapter 10 for further detail). It also ordered the fixing of a wooden sweep or arc under each gunport to facilitate training the gun on forward or after bearings; and removed the front extensions, or horns, from gun carriages at the same time. Resistance to damage was improved by the provision of a spare steering wheel, in the case of frigates carried on the half-deck; while communications were speeded up by the installation of a row of flag lockers against the taffrail; all ladders up from the

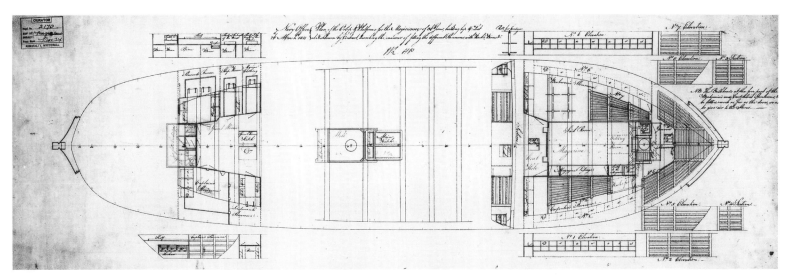

main deck were fitted on hinges and hooks, so they could be quickly removed or replaced in action.

There were also minor changes to the rigging, like the extension of the aftermost fore and main topmast crosstrees to give 3ft more spread, or the raking of the bitts according to the lead of the ropes; but a more visible modification was to the lead of the main braces, since the fixed block in the hull had been generally ignored of late, and this warrant acknowledged the new preference for taking them further aft to double blocks seized to the stern davits. Although individually trifling, all these improvements suggest a system capable of absorbing hard-won experience and deriving practical lessons from it – sliding doors the full width of the sailroom, which allowed sails to be removed from any part without disturbing any other canvas, is hardly a revolutionary advance, but on a Biscay lee shore in a full gale, when every second counted in sail changes, it might have meant the difference that saved the ship.[2]

This willingness to listen to the voice of experience was far from unique. During the fitting out of the *Nisus* in May 1810, Captain Philip Beaver requested the following modifications:

1. The waist between the gangways be filled in with two rows of gratings on moveable carlings (in effect producing a makeshift spar deck).

2. Planking over the hatch forward of the capstan and repositioning the ladderway in a new hatch just before the wheel.

3. Moving the cabin bulkhead abaft the aftermost gun.

Beaver was a painstaking officer who took his duties (and some said himself) very seriously, but his modifications were firmly based on his fighting experience. The grating deck would allow the lead of all running rigging to be kept off the upper deck, so the ship could be fought and worked simultaneously without the respective divisions getting in each other's way. He was able to point to the performance of his previous ship, *Acasta*, which had been similarly fitted at his own initiative; in an action against French fortifications at Martinique, she had fought both broadsides while tacking, and had even anchored without interrupting her firing. A further benefit on tropical stations was that the grating deck broke the power of direct sunlight and kept the upper deck cooler.

The other changes were also aimed at increased efficiency. There was only one ladderway from the half-deck, and as previously placed it was within the sweep of the capstan bars, so it was almost impossible to get directly to or from the quarterdeck when the capstan was in use without taking one's chances among stomping feet – neither safe nor dignified for any officer. Its position also interfered with the working of the head braces. Moving the ladderway aft took it beyond the radius of the capstan, and shortened the communications between the captain and the quarterdeck since the ladder was adjacent to the door of his cabin; this also brought it nearer the tiller ropes and spare wheel, which could be crucial in action. Furthermore, the move left the rest of the half-deck clear to better shelter the crew in wet weather, or to accommodate supernumeraries like troops when required.

Frigate captains were normally jealous of their prerogatives, perhaps the most visible being the large amount of space allocated to their accommodation – so big it included two guns per side of the main battery. Beaver proposed moving the main bulkhead abaft the after gun, much reducing the length of the great cabin; a bed-place and stateroom were still placed forward of this, but these were lighter, more temporary structures, and the complete gundeck was effectively ready for action at all times.[3]

Captain Hyde Parker of the *Menelaus*, fitting out at Plymouth alongside her sister-ship, so approved of these changes that he successfully requested their extension to his ship. The improvement was given

Plan of the orlop platforms for the *Magicienne*, 36 guns, dated 26 March 1811. The fittings are shown in unusual detail, including many sectional elevations of the new racking and storage bins as introduced in the 1808 reforms. These were still sufficiently novel in 1811 to require specially elaborate draughts. A note adds that the bulkheads of the boatswain's and carpenter's stores as far as the doors were to be of lattice-work to allow the circulation of air. *National Maritime Museum Dr2170*

The quarterdeck and forecastle plan for the *Amphion* class shows the original layout of the waist with only small fixed parts of the gangway at the forward end of the quarterdeck; these formed landings for the ladders up from the main deck, the rest of the gangboards being narrow and not structurally integrated. However, a note instructs that for *Proserpine* (and presumably the later *Nereus*) 'the flat of the quarterdeck and forecastle to be shifted into and to form the gangboards . . .'. *National Maritime Museum Dr2275*

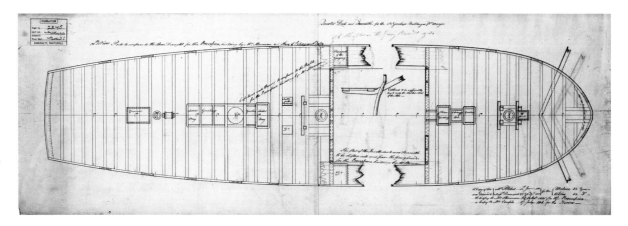

The development of the waist of British frigates over nearly two decades can be followed in this plan of the quarterdeck and forecastle layout of the *Lively* class 38s. The *Lively* herself had been designed with separate gangways (as shown on the port side), but *Hussar, Apollo, Resistance* and *Undaunted* had their gangboards integrated into the forecastle and quarterdeck by orders of 21 and 26 February 1805. The radiused corners of the quarterdeck and the breastworks at both ends of the waist were retained; the skid beams, of the same siding as the deck beams, were fastened with an iron lodging knee at each end. Subsequent ships followed this arrangement until an order of 7 March 1809 squared off the waist and deleted the breastworks for the ships building in HM Yards at Plymouth and Woolwich (*Menelaus, Nisus, Macedonian* and *Crescent*). This was associated with Captain Beaver's plan for covering most of the skid beams with light gratings, at the same time altering the positions of the ladderway and gratings on the quarterdeck. This final modification is noted under an order of 7 March 1811 as extended to the *Bacchante* (and presumably later ships). *National Maritime Museum Dr1980*

official sanction and the new layout was adopted as standard for all new frigates for the next four years, until Captain Farquarson of the *Liverpool* complained that the ladder was too near the cabin bulkhead and interfered with the wheel, thereafter on the captain's application the quarterdeck layout reverted to its pre-1810 configuration.[4]

When cut down, the *rasées* of the 1790s had followed the usual frigate arrangements as far as possible. The orlop was converted into a lower deck for berthing the crew, and although the main magazine remained forward, a small powder room was added aft. A waist with gangways was opened up, and while attempting to retain as much of the existing structure as feasible, the specification called for them to be 'generally fitted as 38-gun frigates are.'[5] However, the 1813 ships remained structural two-deckers, and in his memo on how the conversion should be undertaken, Hayes required the hatches, hatchways, boats and booms on the upper deck amidships to be narrowed as much as possible, but no less than 4ft 2ins to allow a leaguer (water cask) or iron tank to pass into the hold. The usual spare spars sat on crutches about a foot from the deck on either side of the hatch, and the launch had to be stowed (also on chocks) as far forwards as possible to allow access to about 6ft of the after hatch. With guns in the waist, space for additional boats was a potential problem and Hayes thought two 25ft cutters in quarter davits and a 25ft gig (in lieu of a barge) over the stern

would be sufficient, although a jollyboat could also be stowed inside the launch if required. During the fitting-out of the *Goliath*, Captain Frederick Maitland requested gallows to raise the boats well off the deck (the usual fitting in flush-decked ships), but was refused, presumably because of stability concerns.

There was a short topgallant forecastle and poop just above the full-height hull sides of the upper deck, but the channels had to be lowered beneath the line of the gunports (Hayes favoured carronades on the inside principle because they did not require the channels to be quite as low as those on the outside principle). Between decks he wanted the after bitts removed, the forward set shifted towards the bow, and a firehearth (facing aft) placed in the space vacated. In the hold a platform was added to stow the cables.[6]

Considering the extemporised nature of the *rasées*, they were surprisingly sophisticated in their fitting-out. Not only were they treated to the latest Seppings innovations in diagonal strengthening, but they were packed with novelties, like Congreve's carronade mountings, not all of which were favourably received. Maitland of the *Goliath* complained about Hayes's special sail plan, in which the upper masts and yards were of the same dimensions on both the fore and main; this not only rendered the ship under-canvassed but also made her instantly recognisable from any distance. Nor was he impressed by the four Taylor patent copper engine pumps fitted instead of the usual chain

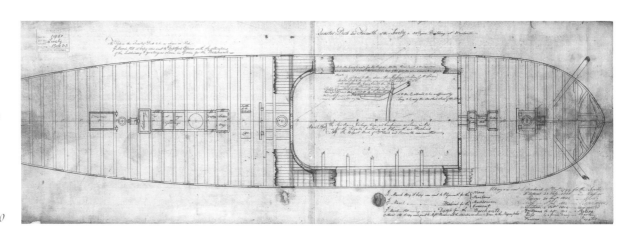

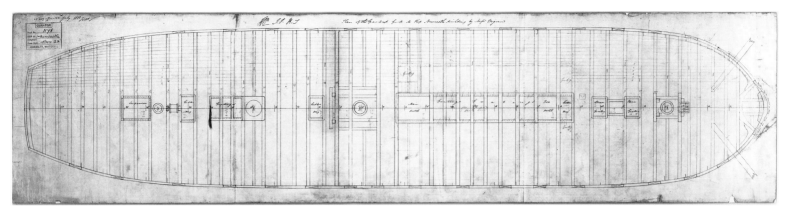

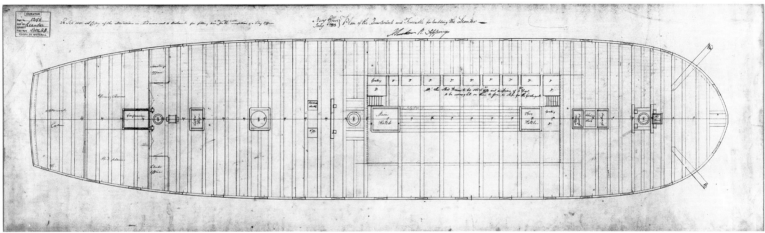

pumps; the new pumps were subject to frequent breakdown, and taking in 12ins of water per hour when she reached Bermuda, the *Goliath* was only saved by two small hand-pumps.[7] The ship probably leaked because of haste in fitting out, the one-off requirements of the *rasées* often clashing with the desire to have them at sea as quickly as possible. Their special status led to some confusion over established items like anchors, the Chatham officers being reprimanded for supplying *Majestic* with the anchors of a 64, whereas with regard to ground tackle they were intended to be treated as 74s.[8]

By comparison with the *rasées*, the new 40s needed only the rearrangement of the wardroom area to accommodate an extra cabin for the fourth lieutenant newly established in big frigates.[9]

HEALTH AND SAFETY

Previous generations of writers were wont to accuse the Navy's administrators and senior officers of scant regard for the well-being of the common seaman. However, many modern historians would take issue with John Masefield's emphasis on 'the blood and agony of thousands of barbarously maltreated men', pointing to advances in medicine and diet – particularly anti-scorbutics – and the development of exiguous but real schemes for accident compensation and pensions. The Navy fought the wars of 1793 to 1815 chron-

ically short of manpower, so in purely practical terms it would have been senseless not to take all available steps to look after those it had managed to enlist. Furthermore, it has been calculated that less than 10 per cent of all casualties resulted from enemy action: about a half was the effect of disease, and about 30 per cent from the effects of accidents in the course of duties, the remainder being made up of what the Naval Prayer calls 'the dangers of the sea'.[10]

Measures to preserve the health of seamen, therefore, were given significant priority, and even manifested themselves in alterations to the fittings of ships. The most obvious improvement was the introduction of a formal 'sick berth', initially ordered for line of battle ships in 1801 by the St Vincent administration, but extended in March 1803 to frigates. This was not the surgeon's operating theatre in battle, but a permanent small hospital for those suffering from illness or recovering from any one of the numerous accidents common on board ship. In frigates it was an area 15ft long by 11ft athwartship against the port side on the lower deck abreast the main hatch; it had a scuttle for ventilation and light. Originally it was screened by canvas, but in March 1808 this was replaced by more permanent deal boards.[11] As pointed out earlier, from 1808 it was supplied with four special cots that could double as stretchers for accident cases.

Since 1797 the habitability of the lower deck in frigates had been improved by the introduction of 'air

The spar deck was a novel concept in the Royal Navy and the plans for *Newcastle* and *Leander*, both dated July 1813, exhibit some indecision. The *Newcastle*'s plan (top) seems to suggest that the first thought was for a row of narrow hatches and gratings down the centre of the waist, giving even more space on the 'gangways' than in the American ships. However, pencil alterations delete the coamings of the centreline hatches in favour of a broader waist much closer to the US pattern. This is more clearly delineated on the *Leander* plan, the deck being planked between the small fore and main hatches, flanked by three rows of flush gratings; a note specifies that the skid beams are to be sided 9½in with a piece of 3in deal wrought on them to form a stop for the gratings. The *Leander* plan also shows the admiral's accommodation added aft in an amendment dated 22 September 1815.
National Maritime Museum Dr1178 & Dr1298

A copy of the drawing sent to all Dockyards to demonstrate the fitting of the Sick Berth for frigates, Navy Office 22 March 1803. Annotated: 'NB. This Plan is for a 36 Gun Frigate'.
Public Record Office Adm 106/3474

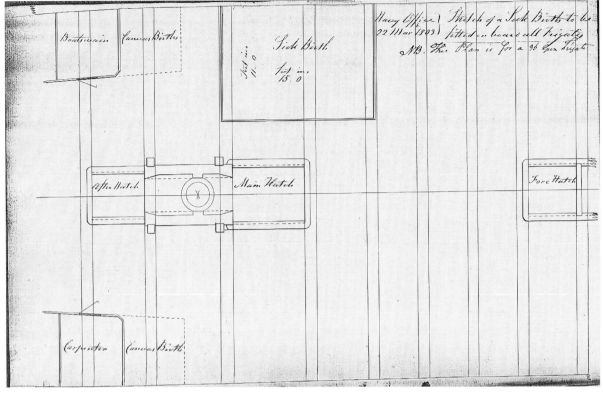

The Patent drawing for James Walker's waterproof powder barrels. Made of copper, they were reinforced with hoops forming flanges at the head and base (A-B, C-D), with a multi-layered lid. They were not so much intended for bulk powder as the storage of filled cartridges and quill priming tubes, which could be loaded at shore arsenals, obviating the dangers of filling cartridges in the magazines of ships. The powder remained perfectly dry during long periods at sea, while the barrels themselves lasted far longer than their wooden equivalents.
Patent Office No 3373

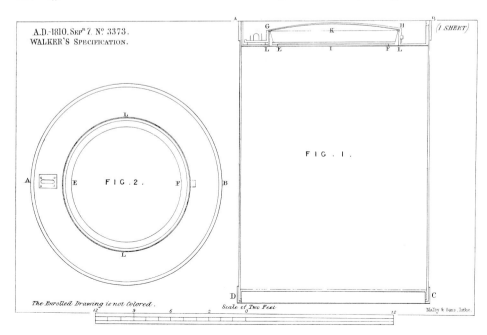

pipes' between the framing that ventilated the berthing area. In December 1804 this was implicitly declared a success by an order confirming the continuation of the practice in new construction. The efficacy of the measure was again negatively reinforced when Lionel Lukin, a prominent coachbuilder who had made himself the Navy's expert on the preservation of timber, introduced a system of airing stoves and ventilation trunking: at first this was confined to prison hulks and ships in Ordinary, but it was eventually extended to sea-going line of battle ships, although the stoves were thought unnecessary in frigates.[12]

There was little that could be done to reduce the occupational hazards of seafaring in the era of sail and the personal injuries that resulted, but there were measures that could be taken to reduce the risk of losing individual ships, which accounted for about 10 per cent of all naval deaths during the war. The most feared of all natural hazards at sea was fire, and although only ten major British warships were lost from this cause between 1793 and 1815, many more were threatened with destruction. A surprisingly common cause of fire was lightning strike, which often damaged masts and spars but might have far more dangerous implications. In much later life Vice-Admiral Lovell still vividly recalled lightning hitting the mizzen of one of his first ships: 'If the *Renown* had been one of the old 74's, whose mizen-mast stepped in the after magazine, she must have been blown up; but, fortunately, her's stepped in the gun-room.'[13] Although lightning conductors were available, for most of the war they were only supplied at the application of individual captains. However, in 1812 a new pattern was introduced, after consultation with the great chemist Sir Humphrey Davy, whose work at that time was largely concerned with the properties of electricity; it was adopted as a standard fitting, but was only to be applied to the mainmast.[14]

The security of the magazine itself was always a high priority but most of the standing arrangements had been established early in the war; improvements were minor and came in towards the end of the conflict. One such was the adoption of James Walker's patent watertight powder barrels; they were copper lined and although mainly designed to exclude damp, so preserving the effectiveness of filled charges when stored for long periods, they had the added advantage of being more flash-resistant than conventional barrels.[15] Right at the end of the war the Admiralty tested a revised plan by William Congreve (of rocket fame) for the bulk stowage of powder in magazines using lead-lined barrels. The trials in the battleship *Barham* and frigate *Hussar* were reckoned a success in September 1815 and the innovation was extended, eventually becoming the standard pattern for all ships from January 1819.[16]

In one important area of ship safety – ground tackle – the Navy has been accused of failure at this time by its tardy adoption of chain cable and Pering's round-crown anchors. Both had been available for some years and their advantages had been pressed on the Navy Board by their enthusiastic inventors; that they were eventually taken up proves their value, so at first sight there seems to be a case to answer. In fact, the issue raises interesting questions about the nature of innovation in wartime. Seen in business terms, each invention or improvement might be regarded like a commercial opportunity to be weighed in the light of risk versus reward. Any potentially high-return innovation (*ie* one likely to have a major impact on the outcome of the war) may be pursued despite high risk of failure: the best example from this war is probably the resources expended on Fulton 'torpedoes' in the attacks on Napoleon's invasion flotilla, where the gamble of untried technology was offset by the potential reward of neutralising a threat that was perceived as acute. Where the gain is only incremental, on the other hand, and achieved at the expense of disruption to already stretched lines of manufacture and supply, the innovation may be judged not cost-effective.

This latter was certainly the case with anchors, which while capable of improvement were generally satisfactory. The major shortcoming of the traditional design was a tendency to break off at the join of shank and arm, and Richard Pering's first attempt at solving the problem was not a new design but a better scheme of manufacture: the scarphs of its constituent parts were rearranged, so that vee-shaped pieces at the crown gave better support to the arms. According to Pering's own account, when he first approached the Navy Board in 1801 with his prototype anchor he was told, 'The adopting of it at present would occasion so many applications for a change of anchors for the fleet, that we think it better to defer until a peace may afford a better opportunity of determining its merits.'[17] This argument, although presented by Pering as blinkered conservatism, shows a rational concern for logistics: the disruption to the war-effort was unlikely to produce proportionate advantages.

Pering's anchor had, in any case, failed at the same point as its predecessors, but he nevertheless perse-

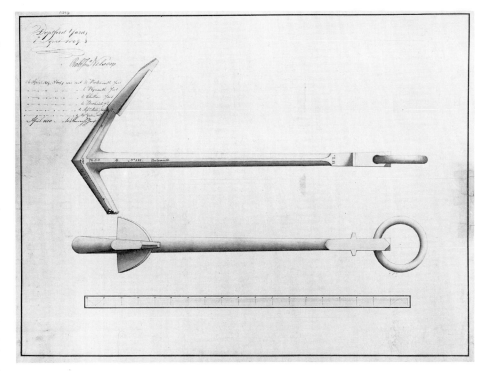

The master drawing for the new 1809 pattern anchor, dated Deptford 1 April 1809, copies being sent to all the other Dockyards and two commercial manufacturers on the 26th. The model depicted weighs 76cwt 3qrs, all others being scaled from it using a tabulated list of proportions. The drawing also shows the proofing marks: the weight in numbers on the arm and the shank near the crown (the units are hundredweights-quarters-pounds); date at the crown; individual anchor number and Dockyard; the initials probably denote the manufacturer (WL = Woolwich?) and the proof-master, as in later practice.
National Maritime Museum Dr7614

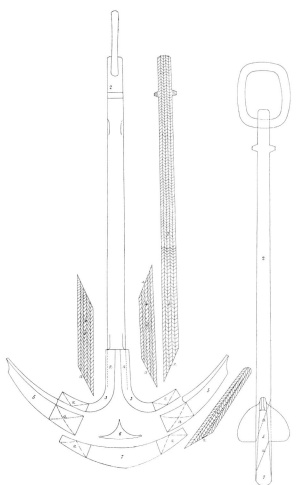

Part of the Patent specification dated 23 July 1813 for Richard Pering's anchor. It differed from standard Admiralty practice not just by the rounded crown and heart-shaped palms, but also in the mode of manufacture. This drawing is intended to demonstrate the arrangement of pieces – designed to make the arms less prone to breaking off – and also the lay of the grain in the iron bars used to forge the main pieces.
Patent Office No 3726

vered with his experiments, which eventually led to a round-crown design. A new official method of construction had been introduced in May 1809, resulting in an anchor roughly 3 per cent heavier for the same dimensions, but in the years that followed there was growing unease at what appeared to be a major upsurge in the failure of conventional Admiralty angle-crown anchors. In April 1813 a batch of Pering's design were tested in three battleships and the frigate *Menelaus*; they eventually proved superior and were formally adopted, but not until after the war.[18]

Pering was a Dockyard official, but it was a young naval officer, Lieutenant Samuel Brown, who was largely responsible for the introduction of chain anchor cable into his service. This was another case where the new material offered some apparent advantages, but also shortcomings. Chain moorings were common enough, but a working cable needed to withstand the far greater and more variable stresses of anchoring, weighing and stowage. Iron chain took up less room than an equivalent hemp cable, it needed less maintenance, and its weight made for a flatter cable catenary and so a better-holding anchor; on the other hand, the iron of the time was brittle and liable to break under sudden 'snatching' motions, and could not be cut in an emergency. It was also heavier – 100 fathoms of Brown's 1½in diameter chain weighed 100cwt compared with 48cwt for the 16in hemp of equivalent strength – and the first costs were higher: in February 1813 the Navy Board calculated the following as the comparable prices per ship:

	Iron	*Hemp*	*Extra for iron*
Common class 74	£486	£394	23%
38-gun frigate	£345	£246	40%
Sloop	£207	£144	44%

The smaller the ship, the higher the relative cost penalty, and since the smaller ships were also the most numerous, the implications for the wholesale re-equipment of the fleet were substantial. The risks were real, therefore, but the potential return was less quantifiable.[19]

Brown solved one problem in 1808 with a swivel and shackle that allowed the chain cable to be slipped easily. The character of the iron, the quality of the welds, and the design of the links remained matters of concern and it was not until 1811 that a series of trials was arranged under the auspices of Admiral Stanhope in the Thames and at the Nore. A chain cable of 150 fathoms was issued to the frigate *Crescent* in 1812, and it was severely tested for a year in the Baltic and Kattegat to Captain Quilliam's complete satisfaction, it proving particularly effective in deep water. More extensive trials at sea were carried out in HM Transport *Aid* in

the same year, and the Transport Board became an eager patron of Brown's work, much of the sea-going evidence for their value being gained from transports during the last few years of the war. However, it was probably the introduction of the stud-link by Thomas Brunton in 1813 that made chain cable genuinely practicable, and it quickly proved superior to Brown's quarter-twist links – so much so that Brown adapted them to his design, provoking a spate of ill-tempered litigation. Finally, in April 1815 sea-going trials were ordered in two line of battle ships, two frigates and two sloops. As a result chain cables of both patterns were regularly issued to sloops and small craft in addition to hempen ones from 1816 and to all larger rates from 1817, but it was to be two decades before hemp cables were entirely replaced. Traill, the first historian of chain cables, set the tone for later criticism with his sarcastic observation that 'it cannot be said that iron cables were hurriedly adopted in the Navy, or before they had been proved much superior to hempen ones'. But this was exactly the point: often it was only a cable that stood between a ship and destruction so hurried innovation was irresponsible; furthermore, the early patterns of chains were poor and time was needed for the refined designs to prove themselves.[20]

IRON WATER TANKS

It would have been strange indeed if Britain's industrial leadership had not been applied to her greatest national enterprise, the management of the Royal Navy. Iron technology was at the centre of that industrial revolution, and Chapter 7 has already revealed how the new material increasingly invaded the traditional wooden world of the sailing warship. Iron fastenings were essential to the maintenance of the traditional strength of British ships at times of timber shortages, but did not in themselves constitute radical progress until combined with the fully developed diagonal system of Sir Robert Seppings. However, in one area the superior characteristics of iron worked a major improvement not only in the quality of the ships but in the conditions of their crews. This was the introduction of iron water tanks.

The general adoption of water tanks had to await the end of the war, but the pioneering work was done somewhat earlier. Since the tanks were to form a permanent ground tier in place of moveable casks, the provision of suction pumps and improved plumbing was an essential prerequisite. British ships had been fitted with inlet valves and internal pipework for the purposes of fire-fighting and washing decks since at least the 1780s, and in 1802 at the suggestion of Captain Hamilton the valves were moved from the side of the hull to the bottom near the keel. This was improved in detail from July 1804 with the addition of a forcing pump 'on Mr Roberts' principle' that combined the virtues of a ship's pump and fire engine; a July 1806 list of ships so fitted includes most of the frigates built or refitted in the previous few years. Suction pumps and flexible leather hoses became more common in the following years, and in January 1812 an efficient forcing pump of Lieutenant Truscott's invention was ordered to be fitted to all ships in future, so the solution to the problem of how to get water in and out of fixed tanks was already in existence.[21]

The idea of tanks themselves was hardly revolutionary, since ashore the houses of the better-off were increasingly fitted with such sophistications. Samuel Bentham had installed iron tanks in his revolutionary sloops *Dart* and *Arrow* in 1796, and had received the Gold Medal of the Society of Arts in 1800 as a result.[22] However, these were large, fixed installations, eight in number holding 40 tons each; they were not transferable, and their size made the stowage of the hold somewhat inflexible.

Iron-fabricating was still a craft industry of relatively crude tolerances, and it may have been for this reason that the earliest experiments were with lead-lined tanks. These were actually small upper-deck cisterns used with the new forcing pumps to raise water from the barrels in the hold, and were quite widely employed instead of scuttle butts from September 1805. In May 1807, however, the Navy Board attempted to have these trials terminated because the medical authorities thought that the tanked water was detrimental to the health of the crews, but the Admiralty considered the evidence weak and suggested that the experiment continue.[23]

The potential of water tanks was far greater, however, and two years later the Navy Board agreed to test a new type of all-iron tank. These tanks were the work of one of the great names of the industrial revolution, Richard Trevithick, whose pioneering achievements stretched from mining to steam locomotion. He had taken out a patent in October 1808, and the following February produced a pamphlet to publicise the venture, which was quickly taken up by the Navy.[24] It was agreed that he should provide enough tanks for the ground tier of a line of battle ship, the chosen vessel being the new *Ajax* fitting out at Woolwich. Trevithick's efforts were compromised, in this as in so many of his enterprises, by a lack of capital to set up his own manufacturing facilities, and after repeated delays he failed to supply enough tanks before the ship was ordered to sea. In June 1809 the First Lieutenant, charged with fitting out the ship, refused to take the few on offer and Trevithick's complaint led the local commander to convene an ad hoc committee of two captains and two masters to evaluate the tanks. They found the larger tanks unwieldy and too high for easy stowage (they were the height of two leaguers, and interfered with two rows of casks above); the officers

also cast doubt on their ability to withstand the weight that would be placed on top of them. A smaller tank with a capacity of about two tons was regarded as more practical, and this was recommended for further trials.

The next available new ship was the frigate *Manilla*, but her captain successfully petitioned for the removal of the tanks on the grounds that having been designed for line of battle ships, they were too large. By this time the original contract was finally completed, and some eventually found their way into the *Rodney* early in 1810; the remainder went into the *Edinburgh* in April 1811.[25] The final design was a riveted box 4ft 1in square in plan, with a valve in the centre of the top panel; in order to keep the top of the ground tier flush, there were three depths to suit the rise of the floor, the smallest being a cube of 400-gallon capacity, or slightly under 2 tons.

From 1812 the tanks were fitted in ever larger numbers, but unfortunately, Trevithick did not benefit from this success. He was overstretched financially and in 1810 had been confined to a debtors' prison, from which he was only rescued – at the price of transferring

TABLE 9/1: Numbers of iron tanks fitted to frigates by February 1815

At Deptford Ship	No	At Chatham Ship	No	At Portsmouth Ship	No	At Plymouth Ship	No
IN 1812				IN 1812		IN 1812	
Barrosa	38			Java	26	Revolutionnaire	36
Daedalus	36					Surprise	28
IN 1813		IN 1813		IN 1813		IN 1813	
Amphion	36	Eridanus	22	Pique	26		
Akbar	80	Goliath	51	Laurel	8		
Cydnus	40	Majestic	40	Tagus	37		
Eurotas	38	Tigris	32	Barrosa	38		
Forth	55	Orontes	32	Fox	35		
Niger	36	Scamander	26	Nymphe	40		
Pactolus	40	Brune	38	Tiber	36		
Severn	44	Euphrates	11				
Granicus	38						
Ister	38						
Hebrus	36						
Leander	19						
IN 1814						IN 1814	
Leander	57					Nisus	40
Newcastle	59					Trave	30
Alpheus	30						
Alceste	34						
Bucephalus	40						
Liffey	44						
Liverpool	58						
Glasgow	32						

Source: ADM/BP/35a, 17 Feb 1815.

The traditional method of stowing the ballast and ground tier of water in the 36-gun frigate *Apollo*. The shaded pigs of iron ballast are a second tier, known as 'riders'. The casks are marked: 'L' = leaguer of 150 gallons; 'B' = butt of 108 gallons; 'P' = puncheon of 72 gallons; 'H' = hogshead of 54 gallons; the small casks marked 'B' are barrels of 36 gallons. Shingle was required to bed down the casks, and although its weight was calculated as part of the ballast, it had no other real function. In terms of stowage, therefore, the space between the casks was wasted.
Public Record Office Adm 106/3122, p110

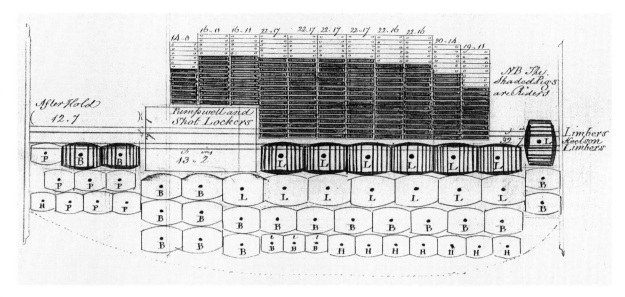

his patent rights – by another of the industrial luminaries of the period, Henry Maudslay. Described by L T C Rolt as 'without doubt the greatest mechanic of the age', Maudslay had made the parts of Marc Brunel's famous block-making machinery to unprecedented tolerances, and if anyone could manufacture a leak-proof iron tank on an industrial scale it was his newly established company, Maudslay, Sons & Field of Lambeth.[26] He later received a windfall profit from another of Trevithick's cheaply sold patents when the Navy finally adopted the iron anchor buoy for all ships in March 1813.[27]

Deptford yard began issuing the tanks, in 1810 to the *Rodney* and in 1811 to the *Edinburgh*; in the latter year Chatham fitted its first tanks to the *Warrior*. Issuing yards were extended to Portsmouth and Plymouth in 1812, when iron tanks began to be supplied to frigates – *Barrosa* at Deptford was the first – and all the fir-built emergency designs, from the 36-gun *Scamander*s to the 50-gun *Leander* and *Newcastle* were so fitted. Such rapid adoption of a costly innovation suggests general satisfaction, and indeed on 31 December 1814 the Commissioners of the Victualling Board proposed replacing casks with tanks as the ground tier of all HM ships. At his time there were 3343 tanks in service, with a further 85 in store,[28] and in April 1815 the Admiralty decided to fit all ships in Ordinary with tanks (to be filled and used as ballast), for which a further 4502 tanks would be required.

It will be apparent from the accompanying table that the number of tanks so far fitted had varied between ships of the same rate, and even those of the same design, so the Navy Board proposed a formal establishment: forty tanks for 50-gun ships; thirty-six for those of 38 and 40 guns; and thirty for 36s.[29] The fitting of tanks became standard for all ships by Admiralty Order of 4 May 1815, and the Navy Board made a start on acquiring the enormous number required by contracting for 1000 a few days later. They were to be manu-

factured by Maudslay and he was to test and certificate each before delivery to Deptford yard, which would act as a central depot, issuing them to other yards as required. A further 1000 were ordered exactly a year later, which suggests the rate at which progress was being made on the huge undertaking to convert the whole navy.[30]

The method of fitting the tanks was also standardised very quickly. Initially it seems to have been left to the discretion of individual captains (or, in practice, the Masters, who were responsible for the stowage of the hold), which accounts for the variation in numbers taken aboard similar ships. In February 1813 Captain Brisbane of the *Pembroke*, 74, sent the Admiralty his scheme of fixing a layer of planks above and below the tanks, so that the valves could work more freely and the 'trunks' (which protected the flexible hoses) would not be damaged by working the cables above. Any gaps between the tanks were filled with wood and caulked. This was swiftly adopted as official practice and reinforced by Admiralty Order.[31]

The benefits of iron tanks were numerous. Apart from generally keeping water better and longer, tanks, hoses and pumps greatly relieved the back-breaking labour of watering ship. But its contribution to the health of the crew was broader: the shingle ballast, an all too fertile source of stench and pollution, was only needed to bed down the ground tier of casks, so ships with iron tanks could give it up altogether, once again saving the crew the occasional labour of loading, unloading – or worst of all – washing the ballast.

Given the speed with which the measure was adopted, it is not surprising to find that there was also a considerable cost saving. Trevithick's promotional pamphlet argued that for a First Rate the cost of wooden casks was £2400 more than for the equivalent tanks, which would also avoid about £500 per year in cooperage; aggregating up, he estimated a regular saving to the Navy of £500,000 per annum. Even allowing for

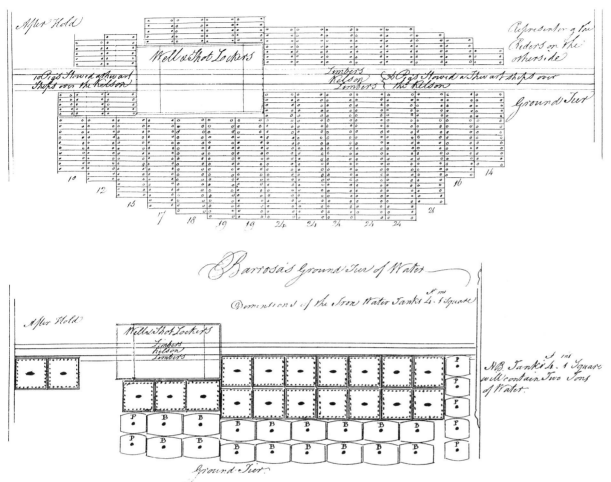

By way of contrast, *Apollo*'s sister-ship *Barrosa* was probably the first frigate fitted with the new iron water tanks. The two drawings show the iron ballast (with the rider layer shown on the other side) and the ground tier of tanks. There were 120 tons of iron pigs, but shingle was reduced to 10 tons, compared with 110 tons iron and 140 tons shingle for *Apollo*. Each tank held around 400 gallons, whereas the largest cask contained 150 gallons.
Public Record Office Adm 106/3122, p139

the traditionally wild claims of the projector, the savings must have been significant.

Ameliorating the lot of the crew was important, as was the economic advantage, but from the Navy's point of view the greatest benefit was to the qualities of the ships themselves. Because there was less wasted space between close-fitting metal boxes than between nested barrels, ships could either carry more water in total or the same amount in less space; furthermore, Trevithick calculated that because of its thinner skin a tank of the same overall dimensions as a cask contained 26 per cent more water, exclusive of the space saved between barrels. When added to the weight saved by omitting shingle ballast, this could mean, for example, that a frigate fully stored for Foreign Service might draw 6-9ins less, with consequent improvement to her sailing qualities. Furthermore, the water was also stowed lower, which usually improved the stiffness of the ship and might allow a reduction in the total weight of ballast; this was recognised as early as 1812.[32] By increasing the freeboard of the gunports and reducing the heel for any given wind condition, iron tanks also made the vessels that carried them better fighting ships. It is only fair to Trevithick to point out that all these benefits were anticipated in his patent application of 1808.

BOATS AND BOAT STOWAGE

The formal boat establishment for frigates remained unchanged during the Napoleonic Wars at one launch, a barge or pinnace, two cutters and a jollyboat (small cutter); but needless to say, there were numerous more or less official modifications for specific purposes and some experimental boats. Of the established boats, the launch was a 26ft boat for 38s, and originally a 23ft or 24ft model for 36s, but this was increased to 25ft by order of 27 August 1796 and the same boat was allocated to 18pdr 32s on 8 August 1801. The light clinker-built cutter was steadily gaining preference over both the yawl and the barge, and on 29 April 1797 the length of cutters in ships of 36 to 60 guns was increased from 24ft to 25ft. Many captains petitioned for the replacement of their barge by an extra cutter, which was generally allowed, but an order of 18 November 1798 underlined that an eight-oared cutter might be taken in lieu of the barge, but not of the pinnace. However, cutters were difficult to maintain, work which was usually done in the Dockyards at this time, so on 15 October 1800 it was laid down that carvel-built yawls should replace cutters in ships going abroad.[33]

Perhaps the greatest innovation of the period was not in the boats themselves, but in their stowage, with the widespread adoption of quarter davits. The traditional method of hoisting-out using stay tackle and yardarm was cumbersome and time-consuming, and not practical in many situations: as an example of the disadvantages, at the Battle of Lissa, the *Amphion*'s masts were so badly damaged that she could not risk sending a boat to secure her prize, the *Flore*, which subsequently escaped. Davits were first employed during the 1790s in transports, which had decks encumbered with flatboats for landing troops, so for their own boats needed a method of stowage which was convenient at sea and allowed rapid deployment when needed. Many warships already carried one of the smaller boats under fixed davits across the stern, but the advantages of a pair of hoisting davits on the quarters must have been evident to anyone who had seen the troopships in action. In an era when boat actions became ever more frequent, there would have been a considerable saving in time when hoisting out boats if half the complement need only be lowered from davits.

There is no known order relating to the introduction of boat davits. Indeed, the earliest, of 15 October 1796, is negative, prohibiting the fitting of stern davits, which were regarded as stressing the stern-frame and impeding the sailing of the parent vessel by acting as a backsail when close-hauled.[34] It does not mention quarter davits, the first reference (other than to transports) being a Navy Board response to an enquiry from the yard at Deal in September 1801 about which classes were allowed 'davits for hanging their boats over their sterns or quarters', since local naval officers were unclear about the position. The answer was that they were not to be fitted to vessels smaller than post ships,

which must mean that not only was the earlier proscription widely ignored but that quarter davits had also become popular. The Navy Board had probably acquiesced in the development without becoming entirely reconciled to the innovation. Experience was to prove that davits were not safe in small craft, so on 8 January 1805 a further order banned their fitting to vessels smaller than quarterdecked ship sloops.[35]

The davits were originally balks of timber, hinged against the side, and were really only suitable for the lighter boats, the clinker-built cutters being the usual choice. The method of fitting them was standardised on an arrangement worked out in the frigate *Dryad* and extended to the whole fleet by an order of 12 June 1811.[36] Right at the end of the wars, the objection to quarter davits in small vessels was overcome by the use of stronger but lighter iron davits; these were adopted for all flush-decked vessels.[37]

Although a ship's outfit of boats was varied, each type was called upon to perform in many roles and the experience of the war threw up services for which none was ideally suited. The perceived need for special craft inspired some officers to have boats built to their own specification – Lord Cochrane had a galley designed for the quarter davits of the *Imperieuse* that so impressed the Admiralty that they ordered the lines taken off.[38] In general, however, these freelance designs did not receive official patronage, but one that did find favour was inspired by Sir George Collier. On blockade duty in the Bay of Biscay, he felt the need for a small, highly seaworthy boat for boarding the many merchant vessels being stopped under the Orders in Council. His solution was a cross between a whaleboat

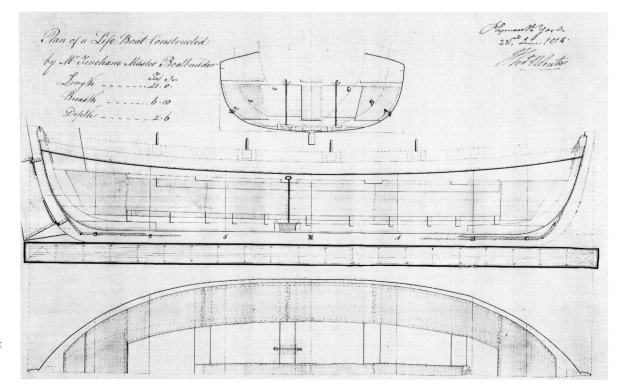

A drawing of Fincham's lifeboat, dated Plymouth Yard 22 June 1815. It is 21ft by 6ft 10in by 2ft 6in and double-ended. The shaded areas in plan and section represent the air-tight 'cases' that made the boat unsinkable.
Public Record Office Adm 106/1942

and the conventional jollyboat (which it was intended to replace), the actual design being the work of John Fincham, then the Master Boatbuilder at Plymouth Dockyard. The first was sent to Collier's frigate *Surveillante* in October 1810 and in March 1811 he enthusiastically reported from off Coruña: 'I have made some trials in dangerous seas and tempestuous weather by boarding ships when it was the opinion of every officer onboard that no other boat could have lived and she has always returned almost without receiving a spray.' Since Collier was often employed supporting Spanish guerrillas on the Cantabrian coast, it was a distinct advantage that the boat could land safely on a flat beach in heavy surf; for close support, Collier had even improvised a conversion to a mortar boat using a captured 7in howitzer on a bed of coiled rope, oakum and wet shavings. The boat's obvious superiority over the common jollyboat led to an order for a further six being placed in July 1811, and more were to follow.[39] By April 1813 three battleships had been supplied with them, as well as the frigates *Phoebe*, *Niemen*, *Medusa*, *Macedonian* and *Pyramus*.[40]

The 20ft boat was unsinkable, thanks to closed 'air trunks' (buoyancy chambers) along the sides and on the centreline, while the whaleboat form allowed it to be rowed in either direction. It would not sink if swamped, which made it safe in the heaviest seas and led to its frequent description as a 'lifeboat'. The Navy was showing an increasing interest in this concept – in July 1808 it had ordered five of the well-known Greathead patent lifeboats, intending to station one in each of the main home anchorages at Spithead, Plymouth, Leith, Yarmouth and the Downs. The Collier/Fincham design offered the possibility of a sea-going rescue boat, and in September 1813 it was proposed to build them in quantity, in the Dockyards, since they were believed too sophisticated for contract work – reflected in the price, which at £36-15s-8d per boat was about 80 per cent more than the standard jollyboat. At the beginning of 1815 the Admiralty proposed to issue one to every ship in commission in place of the jollyboat, but the Navy Board probably balked at the cost – not to mention the waste implied in storing or selling a large number of perfectly good existing jollyboats. As a result, in June 1815 Fincham produced a plan for turning conventional jollyboats into lifeboats, although he pointed out that they could not be as safe or as seaworthy as purpose-built craft.[41] However, the new Stores Establishment of 1815 (see below) authorised the replacement of the jollyboat by a lifeboat for each vessel in commission.

Returning to more warlike uses, the increasingly aggressive employment of boats in amphibious and cutting-out warfare had seen the launch officially armed with a carronade since 1796, but ingenious officers were always on the lookout for increased firepower. One such was Captain Edward Pelham Brenton,

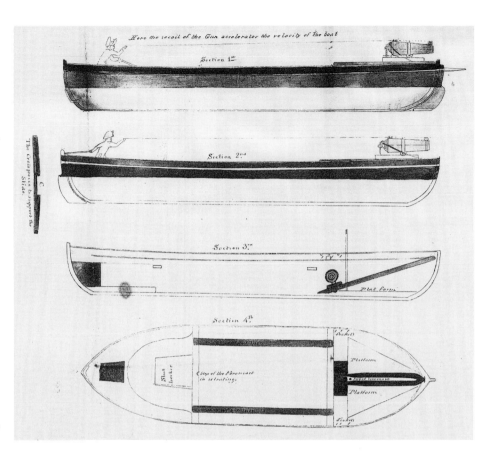

The illustration from Brenton's own memorial concerning his yawl, dated Sheerness, 26 January 1808, although the heading says the boat was invented in 1803.

Section 1st. Shows the manner of fighting the gun while retreating, the officer steering through a yoke and firing when the boat bears; he then passes forward the next cartridge from the magazine which forms his seat to the gunner on the larboard side, while a seaman on the starboard side acts as sponger and rammer.

Section 2nd. The method of fighting the boat when advancing – the boat is double-ended and the rudder can be shipped at either stem/stern.

Section 3rd. The method of securing the gun when finished with; the crosspiece support for the slide ('C') is unshipped, the gun turned athwartship, and the slide lowered into the bottom boards of the boat.

The plan view shows the general arrangement of the yawl, with magazine and shot locker aft, longitudinal thwarts in the body of the boat, and the slide forward. Brenton notes that one large lug is the best sail for the boat and then only when retreating; he did not believe anyone would try to fight the boat under sail, or indeed to sail it at all with the gun in the firing position.

Public Record Office Adm 1/5121/23

now largely remembered for his naval history of these wars and the feud it inspired with the other famous chronicler, William James. Whatever his qualities as a historian, Brenton was an intelligent and experienced officer, and in 1803 he devised a lightweight gunboat yawl to carry a 12pdr carronade forward. The boat was double-ended with rudder pintles at stem and stern, and longitudinal thwarts that the rowers sat astride, so that it could be both rowed and fought in either direction; when retreating the boat was steered from what was then the bow by means of long tiller lines to the rudder yoke, while the gun continued to fire astern.

His original intention was to provide a light gunboat that could be carried with ease in lieu of a launch by sloops and small frigates, and the first six were ordered on 5 July 1803. Brenton himself describes the early boats as 27ft by 7ft by 4ft to row ten, twelve or fourteen oars double-banked, but the Admiralty specification – 9ft for the carronade slide; eight, ten or twelve men occupying no more than 9ft amidships; and 8ft for the sternsheets implies 26ft length, and this is how they are usually classified. It took some time for their advantages to become appreciated in the fleet, but they were increasingly employed in larger rates to supplement the launch. In March 1807 a further twelve were ordered, but one strake deeper, and in March 1808 they were officially adopted instead of one cutter in a line of battle ship and instead of the launch in frigates and sloops.

Brenton himself pointed out that his yawls were vulnerable in a seaway, and could only be sailed safely when retiring – a single lug sail was best – and could never be sailed close-hauled without the gun being struck down onto the bottom boards. This lack of capacity and stability made them poor substitutes for launches, and frigate captains were quickly permitted to specify conventional launches if they preferred, although some continued to take them in lieu of a smaller boat.[42] No more were issued after March 1810, but they had obviously proved useful enough to inspire sea officers to find a more practical replacement. Applying the Navy's typical ingenuity, it was soon found possible to fit 12pdr carronades in existing barges and pinnaces, and in April 1811 the whole of the Channel Fleet was so equipped.[43]

Barges themselves fell from favour during the war,

and an order of 4 November 1811 repeated permission to substitute an eight-oared cutter on application; but by this time many captains preferred the faster-rowing gigs or the larger galleys for their personal transport. At first these were the private property of the officers concerned, but although many of the design initiatives came from private boatbuilders,[44] gigs eventually became official issue. As an indication of their new status, a standing order of March 1812 made all Navy gigs more seaworthy by the addition of a wash strake.[45]

As an indicator of the typical outfit of boats by the end of the war, the Chatham officers fitting out the *rasée Goliath* in July 1813 were ordered to provide a 30ft launch, a 28ft or 32ft pinnace (or an eight-oared cutter in lieu), a 26ft yawl, a 25ft cutter, and a 25ft gig.[46]

THE WAR OF 1812

The novelty of defeat in single-ship actions galvanised the Royal Navy into the reconsideration of many of its long-established assumptions. As a result new ship types were ordered, innovations in gunnery were given renewed impetus, and organisation and training were sharpened up. However, in the area of ship fitting there seems to have been little to learn from the Americans since no single feature was instantly adopted. Indeed, even the flush 'spar deck' that figured so prominently in British descriptions of American superiority was not introduced until 1817,[47] and even then the gangways were neither armed nor even berthed up.

In terms of detail modification to ships, there are only two measures that can be directly attributable to the War of 1812, and one of those applied only to brigs and schooners.[48] The other was extended to all frigates and sloops and was the result of an analysis of the loss of *Guerriere* and *Macedonian* by Captain John Maitland, who had considerable experience of frigate operations. Contemplating the final stages of the actions when the dismasted British frigates had been unable to bring a gun to bear, Maitland concluded that they might have benefited from small scuttles cut in the transom from which they could deploy sweeps (long oars). In his previous commands, the frigates *Boadicea* and *Glenmore*, he had used similar ports, cut on his own initiative, to sweep the ship's head around in a calm, and he felt they might be used to present an undamaged broadside when crippled aloft. He also pointed out their value for getting in a spring on the cable: they offered a far safer lead than the usual quarterdeck position where a spring was often shot away by the ship's own guns.

It was a cheap and quick alteration, and even if in practice it were to do little good, it would cause no obvious harm either. It was rapidly made standard for both new construction and any frigates and sloops undergoing a substantial repair.[49]

The 1815 Stores Committee was notable for its attention to detail: it even designed an improved poultry coop which was intended to become standard issue. This drawing represents the pattern. The key is as follows:

A. The top of the coop

B. Ground plan

C. The fore and aftside outside front

D. The fore and aftside inside front

E. Walk for the fowls

F. Grating on top

G. The doors to thwartship coops

H. Drawers

Public Record Office Adm 106/3574

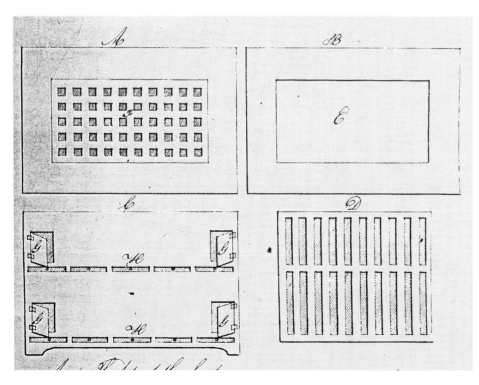

The 1814 Committee on Stores

Wartime conditions encourage experiment and innovation, much of it on local or individual initiative, resulting in many variations from the accepted standard or establishment. On the other hand, peace and the inevitable retrenchment that follows brings an opportunity to evaluate the benefits of war-inspired alterations and pressure to reimpose new standards for economy and simplicity of supply. So it was that in July 1814 the Admiralty authorised a committee 'to revise the present stores establishment', which although much modified was substantially unchanged since 1773.

The committee comprised Rear-Admiral Thomas Byam Martin, Captain James Nash, and four of the officers of the Plymouth yard–Master Shipwright Joseph Tucker, Master Attendants J Jackson and W Brown, and Builder's Assistant J Ancell. It probably began gathering evidence before it was formally constituted, and took the widest possible interpretation of its brief, since stores and equipment warrants covered stowage and so affected the internal arrangements of ships; they also encompassed pumps, boats, masts and rigging. When it reported in the middle of 1815, it proposed a far-reaching blueprint for the storing and fitting of future Royal Navy ships, in the words of the committee designed to produce economy and standardisation, 'but not at the expense of the genuine needs of the service'.[50]

A central concern of the report was the arrangements and fittings of storerooms. During the war many captains had introduced their own ideas, often 'more with a view to neatness than convenience or safety', which meant substantial waste of time and resources: all the ironwork for new bulkheads and doors had to be made from scratch, which occasioned huge expenditure of coal to fire the ship's forge. The committee proposed a standard orlop plan based on the layout of the *Kent*, but without her ornamented and expensive bulkheads. Partitions were to be plain, doing away with the 'absurd practice of glazing areas where no light penetrates'; glass was replaced with pillars to allow the free circulation of air, with sliding panels to close in cold weather (in the Navy's frigate-force alone, this measure was calculated to save £2710). Storeroom furniture was also simplified, with pigeon-holes replacing drawers wherever possible. In future there were to be no variations, and to avoid any ambiguity, the report included drawings of its recommended features.[51]

The future appearance of ships was also to be influenced by this report. While making many recommendations about the cutting, fitting and painting of hammock cloths, it proposed making stanchions with a crutch for a rail rather than the present holes for ridge ropes, resulting in a neater set of the cloths and saving on the expense of the rope. At the same time it also

Table 9/2: Sizes of hammock stanchions, 1815

	Height	Breadth	Iron thickness Below	Above
Waist	3ft 8in	2ft 2in	1¾in	1½in
Quarterdeck/Forecastle	1ft 2in	1ft 2in	1⅛in	1¹⁄₁₆in

Source: Adm 106/3574, 1815.

Table 9/3: Recommended paint allowances for a 38-gun frigate, 1807 & 1815

1807

Stored for	Service	White (lbs)	Black (lbs)	Yellow (lbs)	Red (lbs)	Oil (gallons)
6 months	Channel	50	10	30	7	6
Extra for boats, CS only		30	5	6	20	4
12 months	Foreign	240	60	140	37	30

1815

Stored for	Service	White (lbs)	Black (lbs)	Yellow (lbs)	Litharge (lbs)	Oil (gallons)
6 months	Channel	140	40	12	6	11
12 months	Foreign	440	160	42	21	40

Sources: Adm 106/2518, 20 Aug 1807; Adm 106/3574, 1815. The proportions of oil and litharge (a drying agent) were later altered slightly to: one gallon of oil for every 20lbs of yellow and white and every 10lbs of black; litharge was supplied at the rate of 1lb for every 2 gallons of oil.

decided to standardise the sizes of hammock netting stanchions, and the height of the rail from the deck – 4ft for the waist and poop, and 6ft for quarterdeck and forecastle. When adopted, this gave the sheer line of post-war British warships its characteristic straight-edge shape.

Even the paint scheme was to be changed. The committee noted that while official paint consumption appeared enormous, it was well known that every captain had to dip into his own pocket to keep his ship neat, so it recommended reducing the range of colours available. Ever since 1807 captains had been allowed to replace the traditional red interior works with yellow (actually a buff shade, as currently to be seen on the hull of the *Victory*),[52] but the new proposal was to delete red altogether and much reduce the proportion of yellow, concentrating on black and white. Apart from ironwork, the lower decks were not to be painted at all, although whitewash was allowed for the officers' cabins. The austere post-war colour scheme, therefore, was not a matter of aesthetics so much as supply – the report even recommended that ships have black hulls with white streaks, in line of battle ships two when in

TABLE 9/4: The weights and costs of
frigates' boats, 1815

Boat type and length	Weight (tons-cwt-qrs-lbs)	Building cost (£-s-d)
Launch, 26ft	3-4-0-2	84-8-1
Cutter, 25ft	0-14-2-14	34-5-11
Cutter, 18ft (jollyboat)	0-9-3-0	21-18-10½
Pinnace, 28ft	1-5-1-6	67-5-6½
Yawl, 26ft	1-3-0-0	58-7-7

Source:
Adm 106/3574, 1815. There are also costs, but not weights, for
four lengths of gigs, from 26ft to 20ft; gigs were cheaper than
cutters, by way of comparison a 25ft gig costing £26-7-4¾d.

commission, but only the upper one when in Ordinary.

Ships' boats also received the committee's attention, resulting in all launches being lengthened by 4ft (the breadth could not be altered without interfering with stowage). A new method of fitting the launch carronade was also recommended, since it took up less room. For ships under 28 guns, this longer launch would need to be replaced by a pinnace fitted for the carriage of water. The report expressed a strong preference for carvel boats, which were stronger and more easily repaired, but more than a third heavier. It, therefore, recommended that clinker boats be confined to the cutters under the quarter davits, and a jollyboat over the stern – although in the event, lifeboats on Fincham's plan were ordered to replace the latter in all ships as the opportunity arose. The report concluded with an appendix giving weights of boats, and listing the existing plethora of types – ten varieties of launch from 34ft to 19ft, nine cutters from 33ft to 14ft, four gigs between 26ft and 20ft, but only 28ft and 32ft models of pinnaces, and a solitary 26ft yawl.

There were to be many significant changes to masting and rigging (covered in Chapter 11), but the committee's impressive command of detail can be seen most clearly in its modifications to minor onboard fittings. These included removable rollers fixed in the hatch coamings to prevent cables binding on their way to the cable tier; the removal of obstructive shot racks along the coamings (fitted transversely at the end of hatches instead, with room for at least twenty rounds); running pump dales, which also impeded movement, under the deck; facing the firehearth aft so the crew were visible to the officers (although in frigates due care had to be exercised that the heat would not threaten any cables around the bitts); and a lightweight platform over the breadroom was adopted from Mediterranean Fleet practice, where it had proved very convenient for the wounded in action, since it was close to the gundecks but out of the way. There was even a new standard pattern poultry coop proposed.

The report was circulated for comments and amendments, but was generally well received. The original manuscript is annotated with the decisions on individual recommendations, the vast majority of which were accepted, and by order of 19 April 1815 all ships building or undergoing major repairs were ordered to be 'fitted on Byam Martin's plan'. The agreed details of fittings were then printed and issued to the fleet from December and the new Establishment of Stores was formally adopted in May 1816.[53] Byam Martin's obvious mastery of such technical issues must have prepared the ground for his appointment as Comptroller (head of the Navy Board) in 1816, although he had been Deputy Comptroller since January 1815.

There was a well established system whereby wartime experience was incorporated into future practice, and this process can be seen in many of the modifications covered in this chapter. In truth, naval officers had to argue their case with a sceptical bureaucracy concerned with economy and efficiency, but that was as it should be: if the Dockyards were forced to respond to every captain's whim, the result would be anarchy. In practice, a convincing argument was sympathetically received, and quickly acted upon.

Although much criticised from their own day to this for conservatism, the Navy's administrators kept a reasonably open mind about innovations, even those from outside the service. The scale of the challenge was great, as witnessed by the vast amount of surviving correspondence indexed under 'Experiments' in Admiralty and Navy Board files; the surprise is that so many apparently visionary schemes were afforded serious attention. In the midst of a long and economically demanding war, the benefit of every novelty had to be weighed against the cost of revising existing patterns, methods of manufacture, or lines of supply. Promising developments were sometimes delayed because the authorities felt the technology was immature – one may quote the example of chain cables – but they were rarely turned down flat. Frustrated inventors, with the benefit of hindsight and the certainty of the perfected product, often condemned the Navy's failure to make them rich by instantly taking up their ideas, but governments of the day did not see it as their role to fund research and development in the way that has become common in this century. Innovations or improvements needed to be instantly applicable and offer a clear benefit, and in the final analysis, it is difficult to suggest any significant technological advance that was ignored or not given a fair trial.

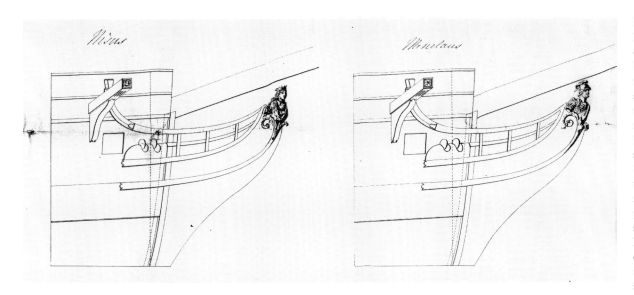

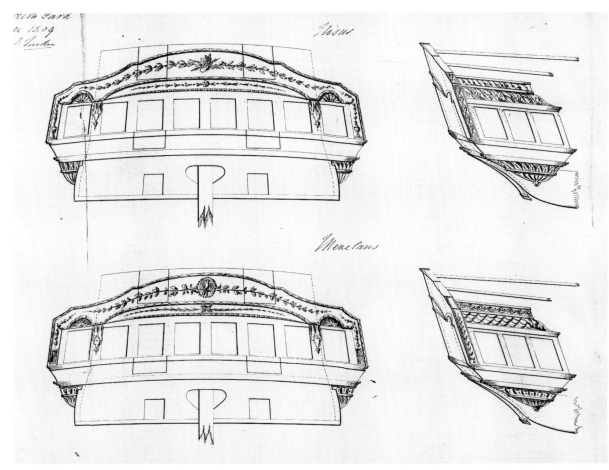

During the course of the Napoleonic Wars the decoration of British frigates tended to become less elaborate, although there was something of a reaction against the highly austere days of the mid-1790s when billets had replaced individual figures on the bows of British ships. The stylistic vocabulary of the post-1800 period was limited, but there was a distinct effort to make ships individual and the proposed decorative scheme was sent from the Dockyard to the Navy Board for approval. Some of these sketches survive, those reproduced here relating to the sister 38-gun frigates *Nisus* and *Menelaus* building alongside one-another at Plymouth. Both ships were named after kings of Greek legend, and have suitable figureheads, the warlike king of Sparta being shown in 'classical' armour.
Public Record Office Adm 1/1940, 26 July 1809

CHAPTER TEN

Armament

BRITISH FRIGATES of the Napoleonic period enjoyed three significant artillery advantages over their opponents. The first was the excellent new Blomefield pattern gun, introduced since 1787, which was well designed, mass-manufactured to the highest standards using the most advanced iron-founding technology in the world, and proved to the exacting standards Blomefield himself insisted upon.[1] The second was a powerful short-range secondary armament of large-calibre carronades, easily handled by small crews; this gave British frigates an unequalled firepower-to-tonnage ratio at the close fighting distances the Royal Navy trained for.[2] The third was the new more powerful gunpowder manufactured from cylinder charcoal, which was perfected as early as 1790 but not issued in quantity until after 1803.

LONG GUNS

When the 18pdr frigate was first introduced the type was armed with the existing 41cwt 9ft gun, but this rapidly proved too large, heavy and unhandy for the new ships, and a lighter 8ft gun of 38cwt was designed in 1782.[3] The lighter gun became the establishment for 38-gun ships, and from the 1790s for the new small 32s, but the 36s were officially still issued with the longer gun. However, by 1800 the 8ft gun was becoming standard for all 18pdr frigates, although the exigencies of wartime supply produced the occasional exception. Sometimes a captain would request the longer gun, and a few favoured the notion of a pair of longer 18s as bow-chase weapons, even when the rest of the main-deck battery comprised 8ft guns. In the case of the two 18pdr 40s, thirty guns on the upper deck made them rather crowded, so it is a little surprising to find *Acasta*'s proposed 8ft guns replaced by 9ft weapons during fitting-out.[4]

For 24pdrs there were two versions in service: a 9ft 6in weapon of 50cwt 2qrs median weight for the lower deck of 64-gun ships; and a 9ft gun of 47cwt 3qrs (usually referred to as 48cwt) for the main battery of 50s. The *rasées*, being cutdown 64s kept their 9ft 6in guns,

One of *Trincomalee*'s replicas of the Blomefield pattern 8ft 18pdr gun, the standard main armament of British frigates. In terms of metallurgy and casting standards it was probably superior to the iron guns of other major navies.
HMS Trincomalee Trust 44/2

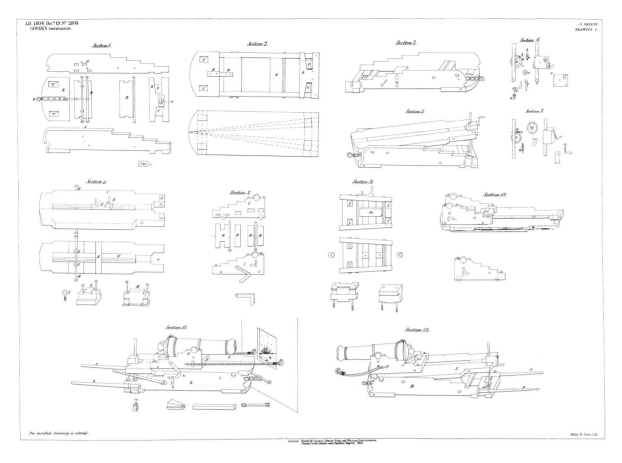

The enrolled drawing is colored.

and initially the few purpose-built 24pdr ships adopted the same gun. However, the *Cambrian*'s 24pdrs soon proved too heavy, her captain complaining in April 1799 that the guns strained her waterways and upper-works in bad weather. They were then replaced by the 9ft guns, described as 'old pattern' (pre-Blomefield), except for the two bow-chase pieces, and at the same time six 9pdrs on the quarterdeck were exchanged for the same number of 32pdr carronades.[5] Even this was not sufficient relief, and on local initiative the 9ft 24pdrs were later replaced with 18pdrs while the ship was on the Halifax station. These were a mixed bag of whatever was in store: five 9ft guns and twenty-three 8ft, only four having proper 18pdr carriages. In 1807 the Board of Ordnance had them replaced with a homogeneous battery of 8ft 18pdrs on appropriate carriages.[6]

Before 1812 there was no appreciable threat from 24pdr frigates, and most similarly armed ships in British service were reduced to 18pdrs, usually to save wear and tear on the hull. The *Endymion*, for instance, was reduced to 9ft 18pdrs in 1803, but was restored to 24pdrs in May 1813 to face the big American spar-deckers.[7] Her prototype, the *Pomone*, being lightly built in the French style, did not fare as well, and by the middle of 1799 was in need of a major refit. This could not be provided immediately, so the ship was reduced to 18pdr guns and the masts and spars of a 38; it was intended as a temporary measure, but the fabric

of the ship was in such a poor state that she was never recommissioned after the Peace of Amiens.

Prizes often received whatever was available, and in 1803 *Impérieuse*, for example, was armed with 'old pattern' 9ft 6in guns varying in weight between 49 and 52cwt.[8]

LIGHTWEIGHT LONG GUNS

The Royal Navy's attempt to replace long 18pdrs with lightweight 24pdrs is often presented as a desperate expedient prompted by the defeats of British 38s by bigger American frigates in the War of 1812. There is no doubt that these perceived humiliations galvanised the Admiralty into further action – from which was eventually developed the so-called 'medium' guns in the post-war period – but the Navy's interest in a weapon approaching the power of a long gun but with the weight closer to a carronade can be traced back into the 1790s.

The first to be tested was a private venture by John Gover, an East India Company captain who set up the Patent Gun Carriage Manufactory at Rotherhithe in 1793. With his partner James Hardum, the company's first efforts were confined to novel slide carriage designs, one of which was first investigated by the Board of Ordnance in June 1793 and then subjected to trials at Woolwich in the following October. Two 12pdr carriages were successfully tested aboard the *Queen*,

The Gover system as represented by the drawings for the 1804 modification of the original 1796 Patent, this being a better illustration since it shows the short Gover gun. The main improvements were, in any case, minor: to the screw jack, and to the rollers, which were radiused to facilitate traversing. It was clearly a complicated machine with much that could (and did) go wrong in action. Its principal advantage was its ease of working and consequent reduction in crews – five for the 24pdr compared with fifteen for a conventional carriage – and the gun supposedly traversed so easily that it could be rolled around to the side and loaded from withinboard. The inclined plane was designed to make it easier fighting to windward, counteracting the slope of the deck and reducing the recoil strain on the breeching; conversely, when fighting the lee side guns, a pawl mechanism prevented the gun running down to the port again before it could be reloaded after firing. It could also be more securely lashed against the ship's side when not in action. Furthermore, Gover also claimed superior accuracy and faster firing because the gun captain could sight directly along the line of the barrel, making fine adjustments to elevation with the jack, and firing immediately the gun came on target, without having to stand away to avoid the recoil.
Patent Office, No 2803

while Sir Sidney Smith had two of his 9pdrs in the *Diamond* fitted on Gover carriages, to his great satisfaction, in 1795. This carriage was an elaborate mounting, combining traversing action, a slide, and a bed that could be inclined using rack-and-pinion gear. By 1797 the carriage was regarded as perfected, and anticipating Board of Ordnance trials in January, the Company successfully applied for patents.[9]

More importantly in the long run, the company also developed a range of short guns, of which the 24pdr found considerable favour in the East India Company's vessels, where it offered the advantage of being worked by a small crew – five, it was claimed, instead of fifteen for the naval long gun. Light guns have a tendency to greater recoil, and the patent slide carriage was designed to cope with this problem, producing an integrated 'weapon system'. Gover sent two 18pdrs of his design for trials aboard the 74-gun *Kent* in 1799, and as a result won an endorsement from Captain Hope and Admiral Duncan that he printed for publicity and promotional purposes. Although Hope claimed he would be happy having the *Kent*'s upper deck rearmed with 32pdrs on Gover's principle, it is significant that his primary recommendation was for merchant ships or those 'where a good defence was wished to be made against an enemy by a small number of men fighting very heavy guns'.

The endorsement made the required impact and in June 1800 it was decided to test a 24pdr version designed for the main decks of frigates. When a guardedly favourable report from the Ordnance showed that with Gover's recommended 4lb charge the gun ranged out to a maximum of 2000yds, it was decided to cast twenty-six of them for a 36-gun ship in lieu of the standard 18pdrs. However, a decision on the patent carriage was left to the greater experience of the Admiralty.[10] The frigate chosen was the *Narcissus*, which was conveniently building in the royal yard at Deptford, and due to be launched in the summer of 1801. At this time the Gover gun was described as a 6ft weapon of 31 or 31½cwt, and in February the Ordnance carried out comparative trials to establish ranges compared to known data on carronades. These produced nothing like the 2000yds previously claimed.

The Admiralty could not wait for the *Narcissus*, how-ever, since it needed to test the carriages as soon as possible. At the same time as the trials of the guns, six shallow-draught merchantmen were purchased and rated as sloops but actually intended not for cruising but for less demanding employment as anti-invasion 'defence ships'. Firepower was paramount and it was intended that each would carry twelve or fourteen Govers, complete with the easily handled slide mountings appropriate for their small scratch crews.[11] Unfortunately, it was not long before it became apparent that the complicated mounting was too delicate for the usual rough usage of naval service, the first adverse report coming from the *Autumn*.[12] On the other hand, the gun could be handled by three men and a boy, a real advantage in a service perennially short of manpower.

These shortcomings had not yet come to light when the dockyard tried to fit *Narcissus*'s guns in July 1801, but it was found that the ports had not been altered for the patent carriages, which required lower sills. The gun sat 4in higher in the port, preventing even 6-degree elevation, and the Navy Board, which opposed cutting deeper ports and thus weakening the upperworks, recommended returning to the 18pdrs as designed. At first the Admiralty concurred, but with peace already under discussion the operational need for the ship was less urgent, so the delay was accepted and the ship was finally fitted with the Gover system.[13] According to the memorial presented in 1815 by Gover's partner, the maritime community was so impressed that large orders followed from both the Navy and the Honourable East India Company, but to the intense disappointment of Gover these were cancelled on the confirmation of peace.

The interest was revived on the outbreak of war in 1803, when the Gover 24pdr was earmarked for a number of purchased merchantmen, like the earlier *Autumn*. Similar shortcomings were discovered in the mountings, leading Captain Donnelly of the *Narcissus* in 1803 to obtain modified versions of the standard truck carriage for his Govers. The Carriage Department of the Ordnance was called upon to investigate, eventually concurring with Donnelly that as far as Gover carriages were concerned 'their advantages are greatly counterbalanced by their defects'.[14] Thereafter, although limited use was found for Gover guns, they were fitted on conventional carriages, and from 1806 any remaining Gover mountings were similarly replaced as the opportunity arose.

In January 1807 the Ordnance reported that besides the existing 92 Gover guns, it had in hand contracts for a further 200 to be completed by the end of the following month. At this point Blomefield produced a critique of the guns, pointing to the fact that the placement of the trunnions made them muzzle-heavy, while the chambered bore increased the risk of loading accidents in the heat of action, and because of the

TABLE 10/1: Gover gun ranges

Elevation	Recoil	1st fall	Extreme	Grazes
1°	5ft 6in	620yds	1470yds	5
2°	5ft 3in	810yds	1470yds	3
3°	5ft 6in	1097yds	1600yds	6

Source:
Report of 24 Feb 1801, Adm 1/4015. The distances are the mean of two shots at each elevation.

Table 10/2: Comparative ranges of Gover 24pdr, 18pdr of 9ft and 18pdr of 8ft

	24-pounder of 6½ft				18-pounder of 9ft						18-pounder of 8ft					
Charge	6lbs		4lbs		6lbs		4½lbs		3lbs		6lbs		4½lbs		3lbs	
Elev	1st gr	Extr	1st gr	Extr	1st gr	Extr	1st gr	Extr	1st gr	Extr	1st gr	Extr	1st gr	Extr	1st gr	Extr
PB	258	1990	247	1750	308	1825	267	1857	325	1620	275	1753	259	1883	254	1760
1°	560	2027	463	1847	797	2090	669	1853	577	1857	697	2107	675	1803	468	1763
2°	812	1900	707	1868	1076	2153	953	1853	695	1793	980	1960	877	1963	772	1700
3°	990	1930	856	1700	1221	2057	1074	1947	965	1723	1193	2160	1068	1883	916	1602
5°	1565	2230	1335	1793	1770	2330	1773	2117	1517	2100	1670	2114	1643	2017	1390	2133
10°	2420	2590	2163	2163	2217	2110	2450	2450	2207	2330	2630	2630	2483	2483	2110	2160
15°	3180	3180	2710	2710	2780	2780	3100	3100	2720	2720	3170	3170	2990	2990	2620	2620

Source: Abstracted from printed report dated 21 Nov 1810, Adm 1/4019. The original gives 'first graze' and extreme ranges in yards at each degree of elevation from point blank (PB) to 10 degrees, plus 15 degrees; it also tabulates recoil distance, and an accompanying note describes the penetration trials.

violence of the recoil the sharp-edged base ring rapidly destroyed the breeching. The Navy Board proposed the obvious remedies of moving the trunnions back, omitting the chamber, and rounding off the base ring, but also suggested giving consideration to the need for a special carriage. To prove that eighteenth-century bureaucracy could move quickly when required, within days the revisions were accepted and the gun redesigned; the existing contracts were modified to cover the new pattern, and although the completion date was put off until 17 May, by March thirty-five guns per week were being cast.[15]

Despite Blomefield's contribution, the modified gun was referred to as a 6½ft 33cwt Gover. It was largely used on the upper decks of smaller and weaker line of battle ships – with a few given all-24pdr armaments: long guns or Govers on the lower deck, Govers on the upper deck and carronades on the upperworks – and also in gunboats. Its use in frigates was not widespread,

but a few 18pdr ships are known to have applied for them: *Unité* in May 1805; the *Undaunted* in November 1807; the ex-Danish *Freya* in September 1809 (they came from the 74-gun *Goliath*); and in March 1812 the *Surveillante*, whose topsides were becoming weaker with age, exchanged her long 18s with *Narcissus*'s lighter Gover 24s. Perhaps most optimistic was the request of the captain of the *Success* to replace his long 12pdrs with Gover 24s: he was refused, but only because 12pdrs were easier to supply. However, the ex-Venetian *Corona*, originally earmarked for a main battery of either 12pdr long guns or 32pdr carronades when taken into British service as the *Daedalus*, was given twenty-eight Gover 24pdrs in December 1812.[16] Both this ship and *Undaunted* tested the frigate equivalent of the single-calibre armament, having 24pdr carronades as well; they kept two long chase guns, but for a while it was even intended to put two 24pdr guns (presumably Govers) on *Undaunted*'s forecastle.[17] With

Draught as taken off, 4 July 1795 for the ex-French *Imperieuse*; built in 1787 and captured in 1793, the ship was renamed *Unité* in 1803. After service as one of the Thames blockships manned by Trinity House, *Unité* was recommissioned as a cruising frigate, receiving some makeshift strengthening under the doubling and bracing programme of 1805. As a relatively weak ship, it is not surprising that she was fitted with Gover 24pdrs, which were actually lighter than the standard 8ft 18pdr frigate gun. In fact, most of the frigates re-armed with Govers seem to have been too small or weak for conventional weapons.
National Maritime Museum Dr1755

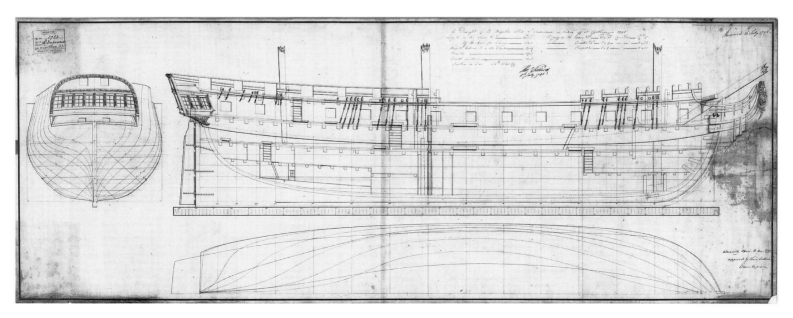

the exception of the last, which was British-built and new, the other frigates were either old, weakly built, or both, so the incentive was the reduction in weight rather than the increase in firepower.

The beginning of the end for Gover guns came with the experiments of June 1807 to establish the correct powder charge, which also proved that double-shotting was highly dangerous and impossible for the Ordnance to recommend in such a light gun. This may have been less important where the gun was the secondary armament of a battleship, assuming that its higher rate of fire might compensate over the longer period of a fleet action; but for a frigate, whose ideal tactic was an opening double-shotted broadside, such a drawback was insupportable.[18] Perhaps because so few of the short 24s were in frigates, there were no further trials until October 1810, when the gun was tested specifically against the other main-deck frigate weapons, the 8ft and 9ft 18pdrs. It was hoped to determine whether there was any advantage in the wholesale rearmament of 18pdr frigates with lightweight 24s, so the test was intended to replicate a close action at sea, with the Gover gun being fired twenty times in twenty minutes without reducing its standard 6lb charge (it was usual to reduce the charge as the gun heated up during firing). When fired double-shotted at full charge, the gun bucked so violently that it would have been unsafe between decks; at a 4lb charge recoil was acceptable, but the officers believed that the reduction in force negated any advantage of double-shotting.

The trials clearly revealed the superiority of both 18pdrs over the Gover in terms of 'first graze' distance (in practical terms, the real range) at the low angles of fire that were necessary if there was to be much chance of hitting in a sea fight. Even at quarter-charge the 18pdrs were slightly better, and were almost equal at one-sixth (see Table 10/2 for more detail). The recoil of the Gover was almost twice as violent as that of the 8ft gun and more than double that of its longer sister. In terms of penetration, while the Gover would go through the equivalent of a 74-gun ship's side at point-blank range, the 18pdrs were more effective. Trials continued at Landguard Fort, Felixstowe, and the report was considered important enough to print and distribute to the fleet.[19]

By the outbreak of the War of 1812, therefore, the Royal Navy had considerable experience of lightweight long guns, although the shortcomings of the Gover gun were also widely understood in the service. After the defeats of 1812 at the hands of American 24pdr ships, the notion of upgunning British 18pdr frigates with lightweight 24s was so obvious that it is now difficult to determine from whence exactly came the initial impetus.[20] However, the first reference to the new generation of short 24pdrs appears in a series of papers from Sir William Congreve the younger (designer of the war rocket) passed on to the Admiralty

by the Ordnance in February 1813, relating to what are specifically termed 'medium' guns. These are defined as short 24pdrs capable of double-shotting and specifically for naval use; compared with 33cwt for the Gover, Congreve's proposals ranged from 28 to 40/41cwt, with intermediate examples of 33cwt and 38cwt.

At the same time the Admiralty ordered further trials at Portsmouth aboard the Gover-armed *Venerable* and *Daedalus*, whereby twenty rounds, double-shotted were to be fired as quickly as possible with a full 6lb charge. This was too dangerous and the usual 4lb reduced charge was employed in all the trials. *Daedalus* fired her allowance in 25 minutes without harm, ranging out to around 700yds at 3° elevation. *Venerable* was not so fortunate, the breeching breaking on the tenth round, and the range (presumably with no elevation) reaching 'around two cables'. Home Popham, the ship's technically-minded captain, suggested that if the gun were cast at about 38cwt and 1ft longer it would be capable of safe double-shotting and 'would be far superior to the 18pdr'. Captain Milne, another observer of the trials, pointed out that the guns were 'so short that a great deal of the fire comes inboard and I think it would be particularly dangerous in the lower deck ports of a line of battle ship.'[21]

Although Congreve himself was not present at these test firings, it must be more than coincidence that his proposals address all the issues raised. All of the 24pdr guns outlined could be fired double-shotted, but his 30 January memo favours a 38cwt gun of 7ft 6in length (*ie* 1ft longer than the Gover) and of lengthened carronade form, to give the same protrusion from the port as a long gun with proportionately reduced weight outboard. The report of the above trials was passed on with a letter of 10 February 1813 confirming the order for the trial casting of the first two Congreve guns, which strongly suggests they were instrumental in determining not only the characteristics of Congreve's guns but also the decision to proceed. Congreve was well connected, being Equerry to the Prince Regent, and enjoyed direct access to the Admiralty, which was currently fitting carronades mounted on his principles to the 58-gun *rasées*. They were clearly interested in his gun and may have had some unofficial discussions already.

Congreve argued that the perfectly satisfactory long 32pdrs and 24pdrs weighed 193 times their shot weight and that all smaller calibres were proportionately heavier because they were cast longer than necessary just to clear the ship's side. At the same ratio as their long equivalents, 32pdrs and 24pdrs of his design could be made 48½cwt and 36cwt respectively, but adding a safety factor gave 51cwt and 38½cwt (or 40cwt for general service use). At 7ft 6in his gun gave the same 9in clearance of the ship's side as most long guns, but the muzzle was lighter, less likely to damage the top of the port in recoil, while the carronade type cup (nozzle)

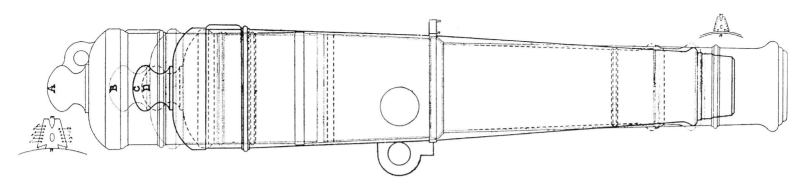

facilitated rapid loading. The gun might be cast either with trunnions or with a carronade-style loop, and the pair of guns for the trial casting were one of each.[22] The designer himself favoured the loop and a carronade-style slide mounting, because with the small size of British frigate crews also an issue in the current war, 'this increase in metal may be fought with the present establishment of our frigates, which may be perhaps not the least important point of consideration . . .'. In fact, when they came into service most were cast with trunnions and were fitted to modified versions of the standard truck carriage.

Congreve made large claims for his gun when compared with conventional weapons, including greater initial velocity, steadiness of recoil, more projection of the muzzle from the port, greater range but equal accuracy. Blomefield was unimpressed by Congreve's grasp of the principles of gun design, and at the end of February persuaded the Board of Ordnance to counterpropose a short 24pdr of more conventional form. Being as diplomatic as possible, the Board told the Admiralty that it had heard 'it is in contemplation to construct frigates of larger dimensions than those at present in the service, and capable of carrying heavier metal than the 18 pounders which are now allowed to ships of that class', and suggesting that they consider 24pdrs 'equally fortified with present designs' but of 8ft length and about 42cwt weight. The Admiralty retorted that they had no such ships in mind – although the first of the new 24pdr frigates were already under construction – but their lordships felt it would be useful to have a 24pdr that frigates could carry, although their view was that it should not exceed 40cwt.[23]

From this was born the Blomefield short 24pdr, initially a 7ft 6in gun of 'nearly 40cwt', the first thirty of which were reported ready at Woolwich in June 1813; they were earmarked for the *Cydnus*, 38. Blomefield was no stranger to short guns, and as far back as 1801 he had taken the opportunity, consequent upon the large amount of recasting made necessary by abnormally high proportion of proofing failures, to suggest shortening the 9ft 6in 24pdr, the 9ft 12pdr, and the longer 9pdrs and 6pdrs.[24] He later produced an 8ft 32pdr of the same weight as the 9ft 6in 24pdr, with a view to rearming frigates, but this development had to wait until after the war. His 24pdr gun was designed to

prove that whatever advantages of length and weight Congreve's gun possessed 'could be achieved with a more conventional, and hence more predictable form'. Nevertheless, he felt the 7ft 6in gun was not ideal for the purpose, and went on to design an 8ft gun of 43cwt as originally proposed to the Admiralty in February.[25]

In the meantime a set of Congreve guns had been sent aboard the *Eurotas*, sister of the Blomefield-armed *Cydnus*. Captain Phillimore of the former carried out a trial with his guns in the presence of many officers of the Channel Fleet, firing them eight times double-shotted at full powder allowance, and claiming if the ship were well manned he could fight both broadsides at the same time 'with ease'; he was also impressed that the ship carried their weight without straining, even in a heavy gale. His 'very favourable report' was used by the Admiralty as an argument for casting more Congreve guns, but the refusal of the Board of Ordnance to oblige provoked a bad-tempered exchange between both bodies.

To speed up the trials the Admiralty had wanted two more Congreve-armed frigates and two more with Blomefields, but the Ordnance preferred to carry out more test firings with the Congreve, which it regarded as an experimental weapon based on dubious principles. This annoyed the Admiralty, since the Ordnance had happily cast enough of the Blomefield equivalent for six frigates; in return the professional gunners regarded naval patronage of the Congreve gun as misguided. The Ordnance had good reason to be careful, but for its part the Admiralty must have remembered

A comparison of the profiles and lengths of 24pdr guns available by the end of the war. 'A' is a conventional Blomefield 9ft 6in gun. 'B' is the Gover design. 'C' is the Congreve pattern, with a carronade-type loop. 'D' is the Blomefield short 24pdr.
From Dupin, Voyage dans la Grande Bretagne

TABLE 10/3: Comparative ranges of 24pdr medium guns

Pattern	Length ft-in	Weight cwt-qr-lb	Point Blank		2½ degrees		5 degrees	
			1st graze	Extreme	1st graze	Extreme	1st graze	Extreme
Congreve	7 – 6	40-2-21	640	2075	1285	2095	1800	2400
Blomefield	7 – 6	40-0-24	410	2025	1240	2070	1750	2100
Blomefield	8 – 0	43-0-12	405	2030	1223	2030	1975	2015
Common	9 – 6	50-0-7	370	2280	1250	2300	1800	2775

Source:
Abstracted from report of trials carried out on Sutton Heath, 19-20 Nov 1813, giving ranges in yards at three different elevations. The original also includes a Blomefield 8ft 32pdr of 48cwt 3qr 7lb compared with a common 9ft 6in 32pdr of 56cwt 1qr 25lbs. PRO Adm 1/4021.

the wrong-headed opposition to the carronade thirty years earlier. Eventually a full set of comparative trials was carried out in November 1813 between Congreves, Blomefields of 7ft 6in and 8ft and the standard long 24pdr (at the same time the 8ft Blomefield 32pdr was tested against the long variant). The Congreve suffered the worst recoil, and the 8ft Blomefield was better than the 7ft 6in version, but in the matter of range it was inconclusive, and the subject of penetration was never adequately addressed.[26]

The Admiralty pressed ahead and ordered 300 Congreve 24pdrs, intending them for arming, besides frigates, the upper decks of selected 74s and, after 1815, of all First Rates. As far as the Ordnance was concerned the issue was far from settled and there were numerous trials during 1814, but Congreve went on proposing 'medium' guns of most calibres. They worked well enough in ideal conditions, Captain Aylmer of the frigate *Pactolus* reporting firing one 24pdr Congreve twenty times double-shotted at a rate of one discharge a minute, without damage to the breeching and with a breech that remained cool to the touch.

However, a sterner test was meted out to the *Eurotas*, and Captain Phillimore was to regret the widespread currency given to his earlier report. On 25 February 1814 off Brest the British frigate fought a long and sanguinary engagement with the similarly sized French 40, *Clorinde*, both ships being virtually dismasted during the action. The French ship was eventually taken the following day by another British frigate. Honours were about even with 21 killed and 39 wounded on the British side to 20 and 40 respectively for the French, but the greatly superior nominal firepower of the British ship – 601lbs to 463 – gave rise to some questions and much criticism.[27] If the Admiralty had had its way, the battle would have been a test for both types of short 24pdr, for on 2 November 1813 *Eurotas* and *Cydnus* had been ordered to exchange half their main batteries with each other. According to William James, who has a habit of getting these little details right, only six guns were exchanged, on the 25th, and when the ships met at sea in February they were returned, so that *Eurotas* fought the *Clorinde* with a homogeneous gundeck of Congreve weapons.

Having been a vocal supporter of Congreve, the Admiralty must have been embarrassed by the upsurge of criticism of the gun, and appointed a committee of naval and artillery officers to look into the matter at Plymouth. Phillimore's report of the battle, written when he had cause to think he had done well, did not mention problems with his guns,[28] but an unnamed officer of the ship later wrote:

In this action we found Congreve's experimental 24-pounders very light guns to work; but they were so lively that the allowance of powder was very soon obliged to be reduced to one-third, and subsequently one-half: about an hour and a half from the commencement of the action, one of them made a jump and actually touched the beams of the forecastle-deck; in fact, it was so hot that we were obliged to discontinue using it.[29]

The Board of Ordnance could not resist the 'I told you so', pointing out that the findings of the select committee on the battle 'furnishes a decisive practical corroboration of the correctness of their opinions, and a decisive illustration of the fallacious expectations formed by Sir William as to the benefits that would result from his construction.' Their own commentary on the Plymouth report was a thorough indictment: the claim for the gun's greater initial velocity had been disproved by experiment, and its substantial recoil required a reduced charge; at a fighting range of 1-1½ cables (240-360yds), firing double-shotted, it was unlikely that the Congreve had any penetrative advantage over a standard 18pdr, and they pointed in evidence to the *Clorinde* having seven 24pdr shot embedded in her bowsprit, yet the spar had not carried away. Furthermore, nine of *Eurotas*'s engaged guns had been rendered useless, two by breaking their bolts and seven by the action of the recoil carrying away breechings. The claim for greater range was spurious, since the gun tended to bite into its quoin on firing, giving it higher elevation; even the lightweight carronade-style muzzle was no practical advantage, since it was easily damaged by enemy fire (*Eurotas*'s carronades were frequently struck during the battle, one having its muzzle smashed by grapeshot!). As if it were not already superfluous, the report concluded with a closely argued demolition of Congreve's principles, on purely technical grounds.[30]

In the history of warfare it is rare for a weapon designed with a particular antagonist in mind to find its intended employment. The short 24pdr is no exception: not one round was ever fired at an American spardecked frigate by either the Congreve or Blomefield version. Nevertheless, the medium gun pointed the way towards a new post-war pattern of ships' armament, with even battleships carrying only a single calibre, made up of long guns, medium guns and carronades.

CARRONADES

By the late 1790s the carronade had come to dominate the upperworks of frigates. Orders of 1799 established that all ports were to be filled with carronades, except for a pair of chase guns on the forecastle and two on the quarterdeck, but in practice even the latter were sometimes replaced by carronades. The most approved mounting was the so-called 'outside principle', whereby the fighting bolt was outside the gunport, allowing the short-barrelled carronade to be run out far enough so that its muzzle flash did not endanger the shrouds.

By this stage the carronade had undergone considerable improvement, including the muzzle 'cup' extension and a screw elevating gear, while the details of the slide carriage had been fixed by a committee of naval officers under the chairmanship of Sir Peter Parker. When fitted on the 'inside principle', the mounting could be pivoted and housed next to the ship's side which was both safer in heavy weather and neater at all times, so was favoured by many frigate captains, although carronades 'in the wake of the rigging' (*ie* firing through the main and fore shrouds) were supposed to be only on the outside principle.

There were, however, many experiments, often beginning as unauthorised shipboard alterations, but later coming to public attention when seeking official approval. Most were decidedly minor, but the biggest challenge to the established principles was the search for that philosopher's stone of the ordnance world, the non-recoil mounting. If a gun did not recoil, it did not require running out; this made it faster to fire, and needed a smaller crew, since most of a conventional gun-crew provided no more than brute force for training and running out the gun. These were real advantages, and might prove a potentially valuable commercial asset to anyone who could devise a workable system.

None tried harder that Samuel Bentham, since 1796 Inspector General of Naval Works, whose brief as explained to the King included considering 'all matters relating to the building, fitting out and arming of your majesty's ships and vessels . . . '[31] He did much good work in the dockyards, but among his first achievements was the design of two radical 'sloops', the famous *Dart* and *Arrow*, as well as four smaller schooner rigged advice boats. Among the host of original features, like watertight bulkheads, these vessels included Bentham's own notions of a non-recoil carronade mounting. Both Captains Campbell of the *Dart* and Portlock of the *Arrow* reported enthusiastically on the carronade mountings, perhaps encouraged by Bentham himself, who certainly conducted an active propaganda campaign in their favour.[32]

The Admiralty was persuaded to give the issue some serious consideration, but had obviously received some information that was less favourable than Bentham's for in February 1801 it asked the Navy Board to supply any data in its possession on the disadvantages of the mounting, and in particular on whether it strained the ship employing it. The Navy Board then requested reports from any captains with experience of non-recoil mountings and ordered trials aboard the Benthamite sloops.[33] The results were encouraging enough for the Board of Ordnance to give its somewhat reluctant blessing, and the Admiralty decided to fit the mounting in the next two suitable ships. However, the

administration changed a week later, and the general run-down to the Peace of Amiens left the matter in limbo.

On the renewal of war, Bentham took up the cudgels again and in August 1803 wrote another letter on the advantages of the non-recoil mounting. This time the Admiralty responded rapidly by ordering a trial which was carried out at Woolwich that month and a report sent to the Admiralty on 5 September. This concluded that the idea was impractical (as had a previous, unspecified, report some years previously), and pointed out that even if it had been found workable, it had the disadvantage if fixed of exposing the crew during outboard loading; and if it was short enough to be traversed for loading inboard, there was the greater danger of premature firing along its own gundeck. Furthermore, the gun became dangerously overheated if fired as fast as the mounting allowed.

This was damning enough, but Bentham was so persistent that the Board of Ordnance called in all available information on the mountings in action and with Admiralty approval arranged further tests at Woolwich of a variety of Bentham's designs. As well as two senior

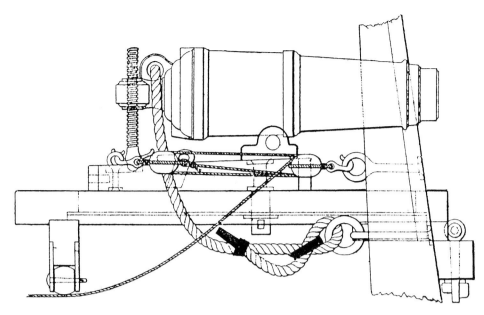

A 24pdr carronade of the developed form, with muzzle cup and screw elevating gear. Because of the publication year of its source this illustration is often dated to the immediately post-war period, but actually represents the earlier 'outside principle', the form of mounting Bentham tried so hard to supersede. It was eventually replaced from 1810, but by Cuppage's 'universal' mounting, not Bentham's ineffective non-recoil system.
From Dupin, Voyage dans la Grande Bretagne

TABLE 10/4: Carronade ranges

Charges	68pdr 5lbs 10oz	42pdr 3lbs 8oz	32pdr 2lbs 10oz	24pdr 2lbs 0oz	18pdr 1lb 8oz	12pdr 1lb 0oz
PB	450	400	330	300	270	230
1°	650	600	560	500	470	400
2°	890	860	830	780	730	690
3°	1000	980	900	870	800	740
4°	1100	1020	970	920	870	810
5°	1280	1170	1080	1050	1000	870

Source: From a report on the proper charges for carronades dated 10 Apr 1798. It gives approximate ranges in yards at the approved charges at each degree of elevation from point blank (PB) to 5 degrees.

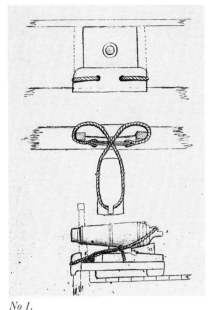

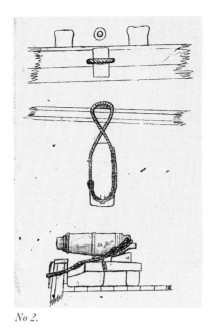

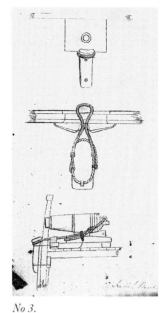

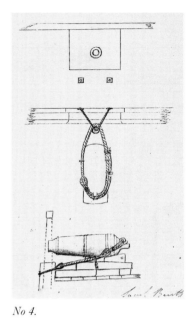

No 1.   *No 2.*   *No 3.*   *No 4.*

A series of sketches by Samuel Bentham of various non-recoil arrangements for carronades tested in December 1803.

No 1. The method used aboard the *Dart, Arrow, Netley, Milbrook,* etc [the sloops and schooners Bentham himself designed].

No 2. The mode used onboard the Deptford Lighter [the carronade is noted as a 24pdr].

No 3. The mode adapted to cases where the gunwale of the vessel is nearly flush with the deck.

No 4. The mode which was found to fail onboard the *Grasshopper* Longboat.

Public Record Office Adm 1/4516, 28 December 1803

Artillery officers, the trials were attended by Captains Smith and Sir Charles Hamilton of the Navy and Bentham himself. In most cases the breeching snapped after a couple of rounds (Bentham attempted to blame the quality of the cordage) or the securing timbers were damaged. However, one 24pdr pattern survived five rounds with a 2lb charge and a sixth double-shotted, although the 6½in breeching was considerably stretched.

Although far from impressive, this result was enough to gain the Admiralty's qualified approval for this particular pattern of mounting for ships suitable to carry it.[34] Again the administration changed, and Melville's Admiralty ordered further trials, undertaken on 9 July and 21 August of the following year. To the unbiased observer they are not much more successful than the previous experiments, although the 18pdr fired twenty times, but the 32pdr only seven. At best they were inconclusive, but probably fed up with Bentham's importunity, the Board of Ordnance refused to give an unequivocal decision until more experience of the mountings in action had been received from sea; but they did remark very pointedly that throughout the many trials of non-recoil mountings they had yet to see an entirely satisfactory design.

Yet despite this admonitory note, in July 1804 the Admiralty decided that all future carronades would be fitted on Bentham's principle, at much the same time ordering that the long guns on the quarterdecks and forecastles of battleships be replaced with carronades. In September this order was extended to frigates.[35] This sequence of orders produced confusion in the Dockyards, where it was not clear whether there were still to be two chase guns on the quarterdeck, or all carronades, and if the latter whether they were all to be non-recoil. Furthermore, it soon became clear that this change of policy had not been thought through. At

Deptford the *Melampus* was fitted for Bentham's mountings in every quarterdeck port, whereas when the Surveyor, Henslow, visited the ship it was instantly obvious to him that non-recoil mountings could not be fitted in three ports in the wake of the rigging without considerable risk. Similar problems arose elsewhere, but the Admiralty refused to bow to criticism immediately, in October deferring a decision on the future of the mounting until Bentham had finished yet more trials.[36]

In November the Board decided that existing recoil mountings could remain, but still wanted new ones converted to the non-recoil principle as the opportunity arose. Bentham was still submitting improved models in February 1805, but by May the problem of the danger to the shrouds had become too widely canvassed to be ignored any longer and one of the first actions of the new Barham Admiralty was to order the restoration of long guns in the wake of the rigging for both battleships and frigates.[37] In returning to a mixed battery on the upperworks, the Admiralty was turning the clock back to the early 1790s, and for many ships – frigates in particular – this represented a significant reduction in firepower and was not popular. Nor was it exactly what the Admiralty intended: four months later they had to issue a supplementary order explaining that it was meant to apply only to carronades on the non-recoil or inside principles and only those within the fore and main shrouds. In the meantime, a number of frigates were fitted out with a mixed battery, but most of them were expensively converted back to an all-carronade configuration, apart from chase guns, as soon as possible.

Non-recoil mountings made very few friends in the fleet and by the middle of the following year there had been sufficient adverse comment to persuade the Admiralty to stop fitting them, despite the fact that the

Dockyards had contrived some improvements.[38] The order was dated 2 July 1806, but the unhappy flirtation with the mounting was finally ended by pressure from captains to have existing mountings removed, and this was allowed by order of 30 November 1807.

Even without a modern understanding of physics, it must have been clear that to stop a gun's recoil was only possible by transferring that energy into the mounting and thence into the ship – with the damaging consequences amply demonstrated in all the trials. Bentham himself, while ingenious, was no scientist,[39] but his greatest attribute must have been persistence, since he was able to convince the Admiralty that his ideas worked in the face of so much practical evidence to the contrary. However, it should be said that an Admiralty desperately short of manpower must have wanted to believe in any system that offered the prospect of smaller crews, and this is probably at the root of Bentham's success.

GUN MOUNTINGS AND CARRIAGES

One weapon often overlooked in a formal enumeration of a ship's armament is the complement of boats, which were ever more active in the cutting-out, coastal raiding and amphibious support operations that increasing replaced ship-to-ship engagements as the French navy was driven from the seas. These had been armed since 1795, in the case of frigate's launches, with a 12pdr carronade. This had been upgraded to an 18pdr in 1803,[40] although many continued to carry a 12pdr, but there are also instances of the successful application for additional carronades to arm more boats for particular services: in August 1807, for example, *Phoebe* was supplied with two 12pdrs 'for boat use on the coast of France'. The launch was a heavy boat and could be easily outpaced under sail or oars by a barge or cutter, so the lighter boat was often preferred in suitable conditions. In the closing years of the war, for example, Hoste's *Bacchante* usually sent her 12pdr-armed barge in pursuit of Adriatic coasters and their gunboat escorts.

For launches, the practice (at Deptford at least) was to fit the slide along the whole length of the boat, so the carronade could be fired forward or aft. There was a hinged section amidships so that the carronade could be lowered on to the kelson when not in use to improve the stability of the boat. Fitting out the launch included inserting reinforcing pillars under the thwarts and adding shot racks. When pinnaces, yawls and cutters were allowed to be similarly fitted in 1811, the slide reached only from the stem to the fore part of the main thwart.[41]

Boat carronades were sometimes fitted in the tops, and from about August 1808 an idea emerged of using them to fire *at* tops from the deck, by means of a high-angle carriage. The first official attempt by the Carriage Department was rejected by the Admiralty as

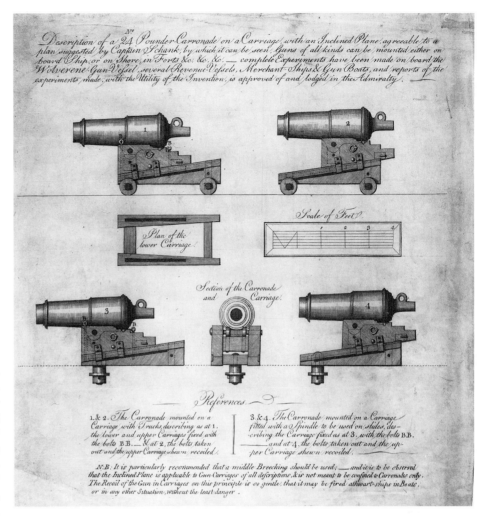

unlikely to stand up to continuous firing, but development continued. By March 1809, when experiments had been extended to include firing case shot for the purpose, there was a satisfactory carriage. In April 1809, therefore, the Admiralty issued a standing order to fit boat carronades (which could also be mounted in tops) to fire case shot at enemy tops, and to mount the two foremost poop carronades in line of battleships to do likewise.[42] At much the same time there were many experiments with high-angle shellfire from carronades which could outrange 10in brass howitzers and were light enough for gunboats. These lie outside the frigate story, but are mentioned to show that the idea of firing carronades at high elevation was part of a larger movement.

With over 12,000[43] at sea, the standard pattern carronade slide was a tempting target for inventors, and the Navy Board was pestered with proposals for improvements. Some were plainly visionary, like the futuristic design for pneumatic pistons to dampen the recoil, which was beyond the technology of the day, but there were many less radical ideas, many originating from the service itself, either from sea officers or from the Dockyards. Between them, the Navy Board and the Board of Ordnance struggled to keep an open

Among experimental mountings that did not find long-term favour was the Schank carriage on the inclined plane, designed to dampen recoil by running it uphill, which also aided the running out. Schank claimed that the recoil was so gentle that guns on this type of mounting could be fired athwartships in boats without the least danger. Originally tested in the purchased mercantile 'sloop' *Wolverine*, the mounting had limited application to frigates, but the *Loire* had her two 9pdr forecastle chase guns fitted on these mountings in June 1801. *National Maritime Museum P3837*

A sketch of the launch of *Texel* showing the fitting of a 6cwt 12pdr carronade; drawn by the 1st Lieutenant, it is dated 3 February 1804. At that time this ex-Dutch 64 was rated as a floating battery and was stationed as a guardship in Margate Roads, but her boat may have been prepared to accompany one of the many attacks on Napoleon's would-be invasion flotilla. The continuous slide is the standard mounting for boat carronades at the time, but the rig is not. The lateen spars are carried not on conventional masts but on shores, presumably to allow the gun to be moved fore and aft while under sail. In contrast to this scheme, various forms of hinged slides were later found necessary, in order to let the carronade down into the bottom boards of the boat to improve stability while under sail.
National Maritime Museum Dr7022

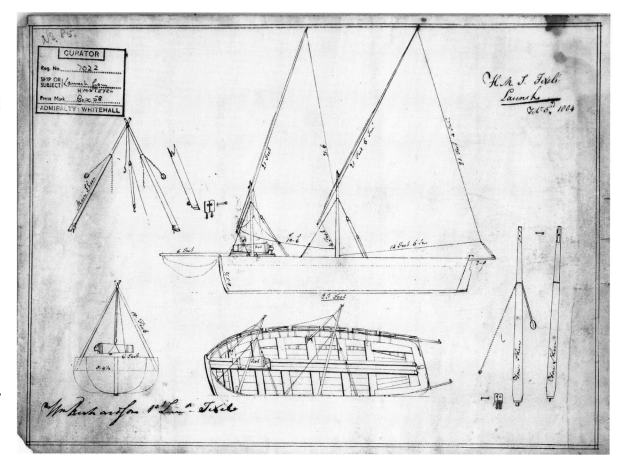

mind about promising suggestions while discouraging unauthorised modifications. It is worth noting that in 1810, long before he became the post-war hero of the gunnery revolution, Philip Broke was reprimanded for just such alterations to his carronade slides, designed to shorten the recoil and speed up the rate of fire. Yet the censure cannot be simply dismissed as the bureaucratic obsession with order, far less the reprehensible suppression of initiative; rather it was a practical desire to avoid anarchy in supply and uncertainty in action.

The plan for an improved 'shifting' carronade slide for a launch as adopted by the 1815 Committee on Stores. The key reads:

A.A. Thwarts.

B. A stout thwart to receive the bolt to secure the slide – one also to be fitted close to the transom for a similar purpose.

C. A knee to receive the slide when triced into the side – knees also are to be placed on the aftside of the after thwart.

D.E. King and eye bolts for securing the carronade and slide - similar bolts are also to be placed aft.

Public Record Office Adm 106/3574

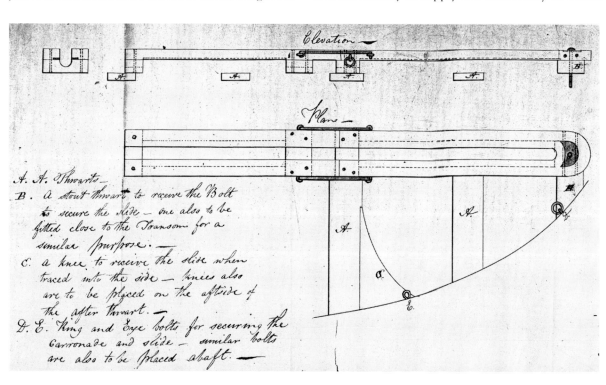

Among frequent complaints from the Ordnance about modified carriages is one pointing to the failure of the *Amelia* in a recent action off Cherbourg, in which her 'customised' carronades were held to blame.[44] In the final analysis, the honour of the service was at stake.

By contrast, when approached through proper channels, the Navy Board usually asked the Ordnance to carry out serious tests of likely innovations. Most of the practical suggestions concentrated on improvements to the elevating screw mechanism, and although of minor significance, some of these were adopted.[45] However, early in 1810 a new official design by Colonel Cuppage, Inspector of the Carriage Department, was adopted as standard; described as 'the new universal carronade slide', it was capable of fitting on both inside and outside principles and was easily housed.[46] Inventors with influence, like Sir William Congreve, were able to get more radical ideas tested and by the end of 1812 42pdr carronades on his principle were adopted for the upper decks of the new *rasée* 58s. In these mountings the slide was basically conventional, but the carronade itself had trucks fitted to an axle through the loop, so could be run up very easily; the trucks could be braked so they did not turn on firing, thus damping the recoil. Needless to say, Congreve was advocating them as suitable for all carronades, and even had a version for long guns.

Although carronades were now the chosen weapon for frigates' upperworks, they suffered the disadvantage of the slide mounting being less mobile than a truck carriage. By this stage of the war, especially in the

Mediterranean or Great Belt, many captains had experienced the galling effects of being becalmed within range of rowing gunboats, in situations where hardly a gun could be brought to bear on their tormentors. Some therefore favoured mounting the aftermost pair of carronades on trucks so they could be used through the stern-chase, or indeed any spare, ports. The Ordnance frowned on the practice, because the carriages took up more room on deck and could not control the fierce recoil as well as a fixed slide, but persistent captains often prevailed.[47] In October 1808 there

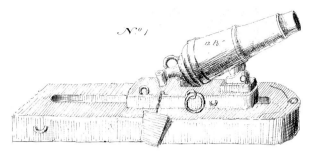
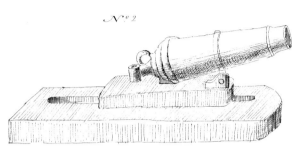

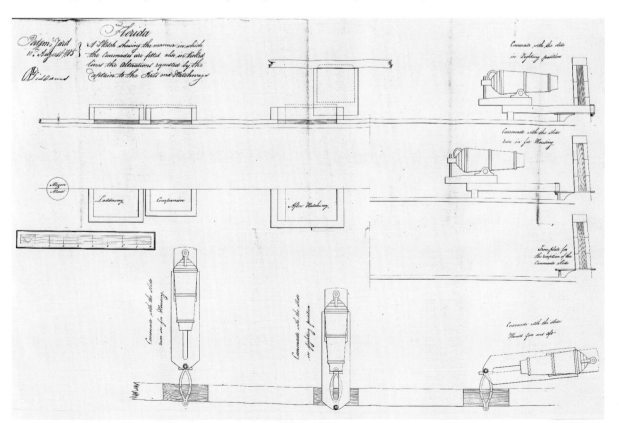

The official drawing of an 18pdr carronade on a shifting mounting as laid down by the Admiralty Order of 20 July 1808 for two of the poop carronades on ships of the line. Carronades on trucks had been issued on occasion before this, especially to frigates, so this may only have regularised an existing practice. Later that year, in October, the Order was formally extended to the two aftermost quarterdeck carronades in frigates and the design was altered to one in which the after trucks were replaced by 'castors or swivel rollers'. The following year these shifting carronades were modified for high-angle fire – principally to fire case-shot at the enemy's tops – and this may be the occasion for the pencilled note '13 Degrees Elevation' on this draught (more was required). *National Maritime Museum Dr6680*

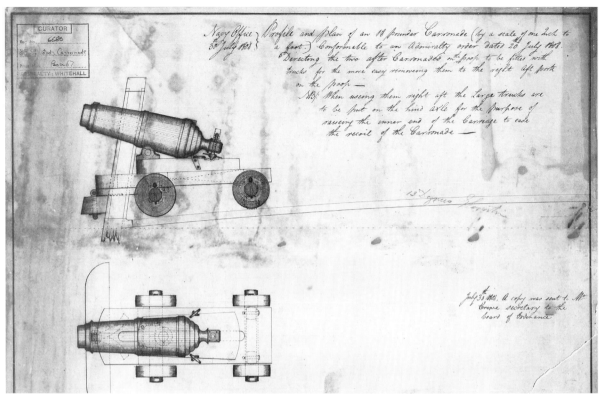

This well-known engraving from E W Cooke's volume of *Shipping and Craft* is captioned as a brig's 12pdr carronade, but the main interest is the truck carriage. As a main armament mounting this was no more standard in brigs than for any other warship type, and almost certainly represents Sir Edward Pellew's carriage for the shifting carronades.

was a general order that shifting mountings were to be supplied for the aftermost pair of carronades on the poops of line of battle ships and the quarterdecks of frigates, whereupon two competing designs emerged, each the brainchild of a famous sea officer.[48] Sir Thomas Hardy devised a version of the normal bed-and-slide mounting, but with a truck at each corner; Sir Edward Pellew, on the other hand, preferred a version of the standard truck carriage with a rear elevating screw, and both were powerful partisans of their designs.

By 1812, therefore, the plethora of modifications and non-standard mountings was adding uncomfortable pressure to the Carriage Depot's workload. The final straw was Pellew's insistence that *Impregnable*'s carronades be fitted on his principle, whereupon Cuppage, now a Major-General, proposed a committee to advise on which modifications should be adopted. A similar Ordnance-Navy committee had been convened in January 1807, but such had been the rate of change that another was required. It was a very high-powered group that met at Woolwich in March 1812: Blomefield, Douglas, Cuppage, Major-General Willington and Colonel Miller represented the Ordnance, while the Navy sent some of its best technical brains – Vice-Admiral George Martin, Rear-Admirals Sir Charles Hamilton and Byam Martin, and Captains Cockburn and Home Popham.

Although they looked at models of all existing carriage patterns, their first task was to test full-size examples of Hardy's and Pellew's shifting carriages, both of which they found difficult to traverse and too lively in recoil. Pellew's overset at the third round, but although Hardy's survived its four-round trial, it too overset when a coin replaced the elevating screw. Neither found much favour, but the simplicity of Hardy's was regarded as an advantage, while both were seen as unsuitable for small ships, taking up more room than the standard slide mounting. In the final analysis the committee was ineffective, because the Ordnance people would not make a recommendation on the in-service aspects of the carriages, which they felt was a naval matter beyond their experience.[49]

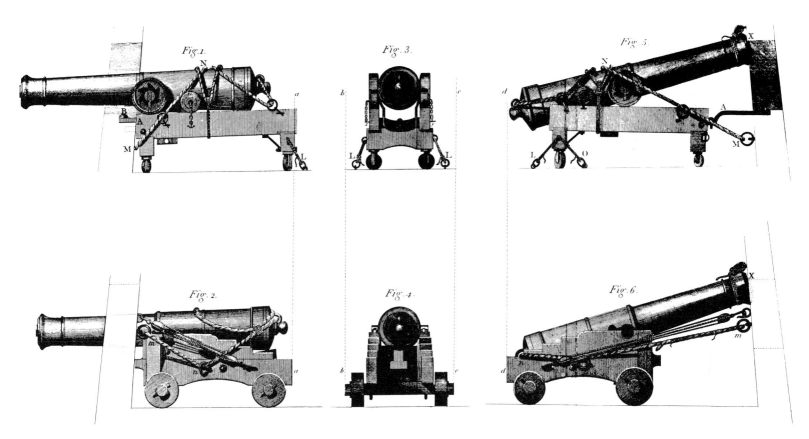

The issue rested in this unresolved state for a year, but in May 1813 a further select committee investigated the six most common carronade mountings, including taking another look at Hardy's and Pellew's. The other patterns were the 'common' 32pdr, Congreve's 32pdr 'fitted for transporting', Congreve's similar 42pdr mounting, and a 32pdr 'common transporting slide'. For Hardy's and Pellew's shifting carriages, they merely repeated the observations of 1812. Congreve's were the most radical proposals, but with the exception of reducing the iron trucks from 12in to 7in diameter, the committee left Congreve to lobby for himself by enclosing a mass of his pamphlets and printed endorsements. The Admiralty was, in any case, already testing his 42pdr mounting in *Majestic*, *Goliath* and *Saturn*, and Captain Hayes of the first named was an enthusiastic supporter.[50] The committee did point out that the cost of converting each carronade to Congreve's plan was £7-0-9d, and that existing numbers exceeded 15,000, leaving the Admiralty to consider the implications for themselves.

However, after all the deliberation the committee finally decided that the 'current common method of mounting carronades' was the best, although they suggested the following minor improvements:

A. An extra piece of wood, as proposed by Captain Jekyll, to be fixed in the rear of the present pintail, to fit in the groove of the slide to help the bed recoil in a straight line.

B. The omission of the breeching rings on the top

William Congreve was almost as prolific in the promotion of his ideas as he was in the production of the inventions in the first place. A great pamphleteer, he published a short treatise on his innovative notions of naval gun mountings in 1811. This is one of the plates from that treatise, contrasting a conventional truck carriage for a 24pdr (below) with his proposal for a traversing bed over which the gun would recoil on trucks attached to the trunnions. There is no evidence that the Admiralty took up the concept for long guns, but Congreve went on to advocate casting guns with a loop like carronades, and also illustrates a short, if conventional form of 24pdr. The Congreve recoil principle was tested on carronades, and when he was allowed to proceed with lightweight 24pdrs, these were cast with loops, although they were also close to carronades in form.
Congreve, Elementary Treatise on the Mounting of Naval Ordnance, Plate 2

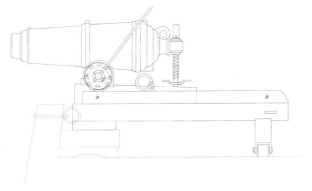

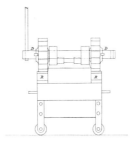

One of the drawings from Congreve's 1812 Patent, showing a side and end view of how his principle was actually employed in the Royal Navy, being applied to a modification of the standard slide carriage for carronades. This is probably the pattern fitted in the *rasée* 58s for their 42pdrs.
Patent Office, No 3565

By the end of the war the boat carronade was often mounted in a manner which combined the attributes of high-angle fire with that of a shifting carriage. The boat carronade was therefore used in ship-to-ship actions more frequently than had been the case earlier, and during the War of 1812 it was carefully enumerated among the ship's guns in incidents like Broke's famous challenge to Lawrence of the *Chesapeake*.
From Dupin, Voyage dans la Grande Bretagne

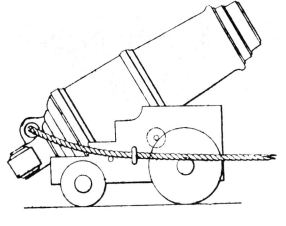

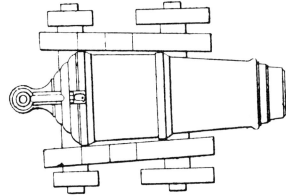

carriage, so the breeching reeved only through the cascable of the carronade.

C. The rollers under the hind block to be replaced by a solid dead block.

D. A block under the front of the slide to replace the present chock, and a loop bolt fastened in the ship's side instead.

E. The iron lever and cast iron socket in rear of the top carriage to be discontinued as a consequence of the above alterations.

These were to be the last significant changes to carronade mountings during the war.[51]

GUNPOWDER AND AMMUNITION

During the American Revolutionary War complaints about the quality of British gunpowder had been many and frequent. As a result in 1783 an artillery officer, William Congreve (the elder, and father of the rocket pioneer), was appointed to take charge of the Royal Laboratory at Woolwich, the Board of Ordnance department of gunpowder and ammunition. His investigations were far-reaching and practical experiments determined the most important elements in the production of good gunpowder. From 1785 he became increasingly convinced of the efficacy of charcoal prepared in cylinders, a process developed by Robert Watson from an invention by Dr Fordyce. When he became Inspector of Gunpowder Manufactories in

1789, Congreve was well placed to promote the new powder, which with other production improvements resulted in more powerful and longer-lasting propellants; even the regular merchants' powder was improved.

At the same time the Navy was seeing the widescale introduction of priming tubes and gunlocks, which would significantly increase rate of fire, and in July 1790 Blomefield expressed his concern at the combined effects of these innovations on the bores of guns. In action they might be subjected not only to faster firing but also with more powerful powder at the heavy charges standard in the Navy. Therefore a series of trials were carried out in August 1790, which concluded that any gun above a 9pdr could fire effectively, double-shotted at 400 yards with a powder charge one-third the shot weight. It also suggested that for perfectly dry powder the standard charge for single-shotting could be reduced from a half to a third. In pressing the need for these changes on the Admiralty, the Master-General emphasised that the advances were closely linked: since the end of the American War sea artillery had undergone the most scrupulous examination and many guns had been replaced with newer, stronger models, made necessary by the earlier failures and the potential increased power of the new gunpowder.[52]

According to the Master-General, although the new state-manufactured gunpowder was somewhat more powerful than the commercial propellant, the principal improvement was intended to be greater reliability and longer life, so it may have taken time for the superior strength of cylinder powder to become fully appreciated. In any event, there was not enough in store for a universal change in allocations and establishments, and for a few years there were three recognised standards: Red LG (cylinder), White LG and Blue LG, in descending order of strength. Unable to introduce cylinder powder in a single move, the Board of Ordnance had an ingenious idea in October 1796. Much powder was returned by decommissioning ships, whereafter it went through a sifting process and was then called 'dusted and restored'. This was generally weaker than the standard Blue LG, so until enough all-cylinder powder became available, it was proposed to mix cylinder with returned powder in a proportion to match the strength of Blue LG, producing one homogeneous, and predictable, standard.

The Admiralty agreed in principle, but first a further series of trials was carried out (see Table 10/5). This demonstrated that the 'restored' powder was now as good as merchants' Blue LG, but that pure cylinder powder at one-quarter charge was almost as good as the others at one-third charge. This must have encouraged both the Ordnance and the Admiralty to speed up production as much as possible, but even the Admiralty's formal order of 20 November 1800 introducing cylinder powder throughout the Navy was premature, and in April 1801 there was still only sufficient for line of battle ships to exchange their existing powder for the new type. Frigates, sloops and smaller craft would have to wait until after the renewal of war in 1803.

Nevertheless, a set of instructions on the use of cylinder powder was printed and distributed through the fleet, recommending a charge of one-third shot weight, or one-quarter if firing double-shotted (although the latter was to be 'restrained as much as possible', because even twenty rounds with five minutes between each produced a gun which was dangerously hot). Although the new powder was more expensive ton for ton, the potential economy of smaller charges can be gleaned from the reduced establishment. Frigates of 38 guns had been issued with 170 barrels (each of 90lbs) on Foreign Service and 156 on Channel duties, but needed only 147 and 128 respectively of the cylinder variety; for 36s the figures were 156 and 143 reduced to 138 and 120.[53] By way of comparison of strength, the gunpowder taken in the French frigate *Piémontaise* in 1808 proved in tests to possess only 85 per cent of the power of British powder.[54]

The introduction of the more powerful powder made the replacement of the remaining pre-Blomefield guns a pressing matter, especially as the Navy had experienced a recent spate of bursting guns. The examination, reproofing, and if necessary withdrawal of older guns was undertaken with 'the utmost dispatch' from March 1803, although it was not until February 1810 that the Ordnance could order the return of all 'Old Pattern' guns whenever landed. The guns and powder revolutions were, therefore, intimately linked.

There were no similarly radical changes with regard to ammunition. Round shot remained the main weapon and it continued to be allocated to frigates at the proportion of 100 per gun or carronade on Foreign and 70 on Channel Service. For other ammunition there was one establishment whatever the service: grape was 50rpg for the main armament and 5rpg for the guns on the upperworks, and for carronades the 'grape in tin cases' allocation was 4rpg; double-headed (bar shot) was allowed to long guns at 3rpg, but none for carronades; tin case was 10rpg for long guns and 4rpg for carronades.[55]

There was only one major change to this establishment, but one with a sting in the tail. At the end of 1811 the Board of Ordnance decided to discontinue the supply of double-headed shot, since it was 'not very much used'; one round per gun would be issued until stocks were exhausted. Six months later the Royal Navy went to war with a service that not only allocated as much as 25 per cent of its ammunition allowance to dismantling shot, but knew how to use it – *Guerriere*, *Macedonian* and *Java* were all disabled aloft early in the actions which led to their capture by the big American spar-decked frigates.[56]

TABLE 10/5: Comparative ranges (yards) with different gunpowder types

Single shot, at 2 degrees elevation

Charge	Cylinder 1/3rd shot weight	Cylinder 1/4 shot weight	Restored 1/3rd shot weight	'Blue LG' 1/3rd shot weight
32pdr	1402	1070	1208	1117
24pdr	1274	992	1070	1020
18pdr	1237	1037	1100	1047
12pdr	1105	1029	1031	1009

Double-shotted, at 2 degrees elevation

Charge	Cylinder 1/4 shot weight		Restored 1/3rd shot weight		'Blue LG' 1/3rd shot weight	
	1st shot	2nd shot	1st shot	2nd shot	1st shot	2nd shot
32pdr	768	916	750	900	766	926
24pdr	715	929	740	980	754	870
18pdr	650	854	766	838	721	864
12pdr	650	821	773	952	712	800

Source: Abstracted from a series of trials dated 21 Nov 1796, in Adm 1/4014.

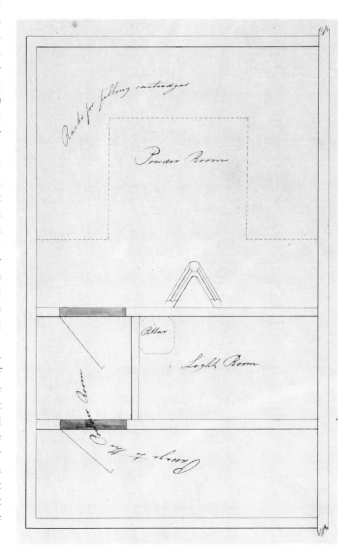

The layout of the after magazine of a 74-gun ship as fitted after 1813. The main features are the racks for filling cartridges in the powder room itself, but also apparent is the double glazing of the lantern housing from the light room.
National Maritime Museum E.0727

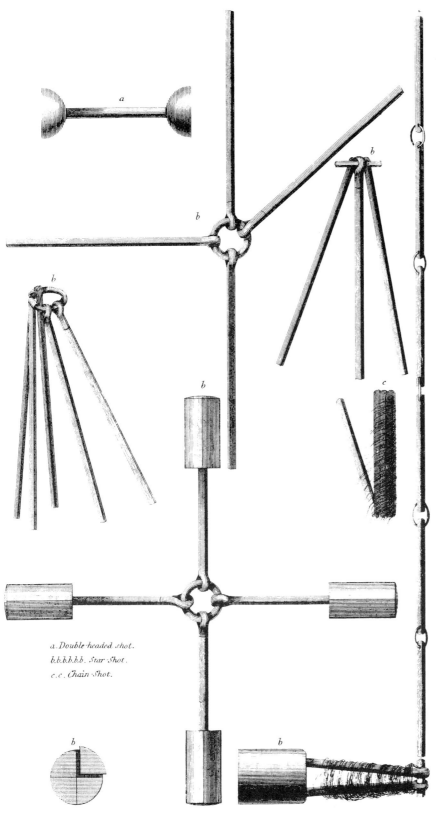

a. Double-headed shot.
b.b.b.b.b. Star Shot.
c.c. Chain Shot.

Dismantling shot supposedly taken out of the USS *Chesapeake* when captured. 'a' is the conventional bar shot; 'b' represents various forms of star shot, which are lightly lashed into a rough tubular shape, opening out on firing to form a flailing scythe of iron (a more sophisticated version has quartered cylinders on the end for greater momentum); 'c' is chain shot, which again opens out to vastly increase its radius of destruction. Such devices were very effectively deployed by the Americans during the War of 1812 to destroy the sails and running rigging of their opponents.
From William James, Naval Occurrences of the Late War, Plate 1

Performance

DURING THE course of the wars with the French republic and empire, performance under sail became an increasingly important criterion for British warships, and particularly frigates. As the battlefleets of France, Spain and the Netherlands were swept from the seas, the Royal Navy found itself facing an enemy ever more reluctant to engage except in the most favourable circumstances. The keystone of British strategy, year-round close blockade of the main bases, required the most exacting standards of structural strength and seakeeping from its ships; yet the enemy's response, in terms of sorties by individual ships or squadrons, inevitably produced a pursuit. Chasing ships with clean copper fresh from port, who had the advantage of choosing the optimum time and conditions for their escape, placed a marked stress on the seamanship of the Royal Navy's officers and the sailing qualities of its ships. Strength, seakeeping and speed were a demanding trio of requirements,

but as far as British frigates were concerned there were few complaints, and certainly no groundswell of dissatisfaction with their design as can be detected among naval officers in some earlier periods.

MASTING AND RIGGING – THE MACHINERY OF THE SHIP

Frigates were, and always had been, ship rigged, with square canvas on three masts, and fore-and-aft jibs, staysails and the mizzen driver. There had been some additions around the extremities of the spar plan in the 1790s, notably the introduction of a flying jibboom and royal masts, but after 1803 improvements were confined to details. The basic mast and spar dimensions for each rating was standardised, but in practice there were often relatively minor variations (particularly in diameter), usually produced by using what timbers were immediately available when the spars were

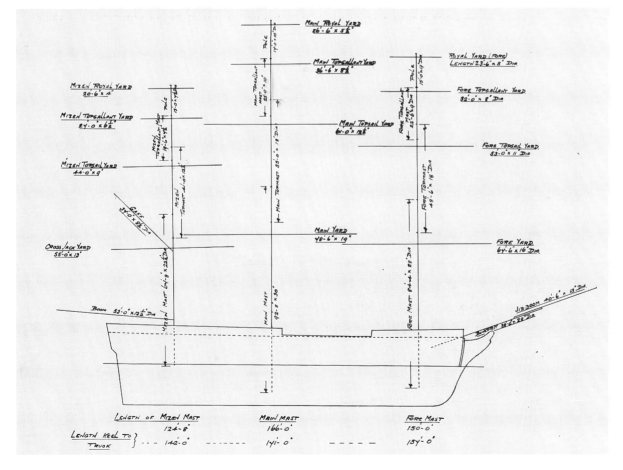

One of few surviving spar plans in the Admiralty Collection, for the *Liffey* and her sister 40-gun frigates of 1813. Compared with their prototype, *Endymion*, the mast and spar dimensions for this fir-built variant were somewhat reduced in length (although often given greater diameter), in the same way that the *Scamander* class carried shorter spars than standard hardwood 36s. The drawing is particularly useful in giving the doubling at the heads of masts and in adding the royal yards that were not regularly listed.
National Maritime Museum Dr8020

TABLE 11/1:
Mast and spar dimensions of standard British frigate classes

	38-Gun Ships		36-Gun Ships		Scamander Class		Orlando, 36	
	Length Yds-ins	Diameter Ins	Length Yds-ins	Diameter Ins	Length Yds-ins	Diameter Ins	Length Yds-ins	Diameter Ins
MASTS								
Main	30-24	29¾	30-0	29	28-12	26	30-0	27¼
Topmast	18-14	16½	18-0	16⅛	17-0	15⅛	18-0	15¾
Topgall't	9-7	9⅛	9-0	9	8-18	8½	9-24	9⅛
Fore	28-3	26	27-22	25⅝	25-0	22	27-17	25
Topmast	16-7	16½	15-30	16⅛	15-0	15⅛	15-34	15¾
Topgall't	8-3	8	7-33	7⅞	7-18	7½	7-35	7⅝
Mizzen	21-18	21	21-19*	18⅞	20-21	18¼	21-27	19½
Topmast	13-28	11½	13-18	11¼	12-27	10⅝	13-25	11⅜
Topgall't	6-32	6⅞	6-27	6¾	6-16	6½	6-28	6¾
Bowsprit	19-0	28½	18-22	27¼	17-20	25	18-18	26½
Jibboom	13 12	12	13-1	11⅝	12-10	10¾	13-12	11½
YARDS								
Main	27-26	19⅛	26-34	18⅝	24-28	17⅛	27-12	18¼
Topsail	20-9	12⅝	19-24	12¼	18-12	11¾	20-0	12½
Topgall't	12-13	7⅜	12-18	7½	11-6	6⅝	12-24	7¼
Fore	24-7	16¾	23-19	16¼	21-22	15	22-24	16½
Topmast	18-2	11½	17-20	11	16-5	10	17-32	11
Topgall't	11-0	6½	10-24	6⅜	9-30	5⅞	11-0	6¾
Mizzen croj'k	18-2	11½	17-20	11	18-12	11⅜	19-0	12
Topsail	13-26	8¼	13-12	8	12-9	6⅞	14-12	7¾
Topgall't	-	-	9-12	5¼	8-18	5½	9-12	5½
Gaff	14-0	9½	12-20	11½	[12-30	9⅛]	15-15	7⅝
Boom	[20-9	11½]	[19-24	11]	[18-12	10]		
Spritsail	18-2	11½	17-20	11	16-5	10	17-33	11
Sprit topsail	11-0	6½	10-24	6⅜	9-30	5⅞	10-18	6¼
Source	Adm 106/3336 18 Jul 1811		Adm 174/41 31 Jan 1805		NMM CHA/E/111 1 Jan 1814		Adm 106/3339 28 Jun 1815	

Notes:

38-gun ships: Based on *Laurel*, as fitted at Deptford.

36-gun ships: Based on orders for the *Dartmouth* and *Creole*. A list of 27 Apr 1815 gives the same figures, except a main mast 30-28 long and 28in diameter, and a crossjack of 19-24 length and 12¼in diam; Adm 106/3339.

Scamander **class:** Note the cut-down spar plan of this fir-built class compared with standard 36s.

Orlando: As arrived at Deptford; included to show the variation from establishment likely to be encountered in service.

Figures in brackets are calculated from the Sep 1813 rules for driver booms and gaffs.

*Mizzen steps on the lower deck.

made. Prizes were generally remasted to British standard dimensions as soon as convenient, but the draughts often record the dimensions 'as taken'.

Although there appear to be few changes to the establishments and rigging warrants, the tactical emphasis on sailing qualities led to a concern – some said an obsession – among sea officers with the fine-tuning of their ships. To some extent this was a matter of trim and stowage, but it could also be much influenced by the rake of the masts and the minutiae of rigging. Captains and their first lieutenants were allowed considerable scope in these areas, and the tactical situation encouraged experiments aimed at extracting peak performances from their ships. Furthermore, the high proportion of time spent at sea by British frigates offered many opportunities to test theories or innovations: it was not just potential enemies that were chased, but after the Orders in Council every strange sail required to be investigated.

Naval officers were not slow to promote their innovations, and the Navy Board regularly authorised alterations to test the pet theory of one captain or another, although in the name of standardisation they rarely countenanced major changes to mast and spar dimensions. Few of the more outlandish suggestions survived scrutiny, but those which experience proved to offer some real advantage were eventually added to the formal warrant. Thus the employment in the fleet of most innovations preceded the dates of standing orders listed below, often by many years.

27 Mar 1806. Bobstays no longer to be fitted to knee of head, but to bolts under the hawse holes.

18 Apr 1806. New dimensions for driver booms and gaffs.

12 Oct 1807. New rules promulgated for calculating the diameters of masts from their lengths.

24 Oct 1808. Double blocks for the main braces to be stropped to the fixed stern davits, since the 'fixed chock block in the hull is scarcely ever used'; aftermost fore and main topmast crosstrees to be given 18ins more spread; bitts to be raked according to the leads of the ropes.

28 Dec 1808. Two drivers and one main topmast staysail allowed to all rated ships on Channel Service and two of each on Foreign.

11 Jan 1812. Travelling instead of shifting backstays to be allowed to all classes of ship.

2 Sep 1813. New proportions issued for driver booms and gaffs: boom to be same length as main topsail yard and diameter as fore topsail yard; gaff to be ⁷⁄₁₀ths of the main topsail yard in length, and in diameter ⁵⁄₇ths of an inch for every yard of length.[1] These are translated in the Deptford Letter Books as follows:[2]

	Boom		Gaff	
	Length Yds-ins	Diam Ins	Length Yds-ins	Diam Ins
38 guns	20-9	11½	13-33	9⅞
36 guns	19-24	11	13-22	9⅝
32 guns	18-12	10	12-26	9

As pointed out in Chapter 9, at the end of the war there was an attempt to consolidate and synthesise the lessons of the conflict in a new establishment of stores. Byam Martin's committee also covered many aspects of masting and rigging in this report, its recommendations on these subjects being as follows:

1. Masts and yards on the fore and main be made the same dimensions.

2. Blocks in the heel of the topmast be discontinued; it is wasteful of timber, and they are in the way when the spar is stowed on the booms.

3. The jibboom heel to be left square to act as a spare mizzen topmast.

4. The dolphin striker to have jaws like a gaff, 'as employed by some captains'.

5. A reduction in the numbers of shrouds and backstays (by one pair), as well as topgallant shrouds.

6. Differences in the depths of hold meant that although lower masts were the same for ships of a particular rate, there was still variety in the drop of the courses (in the worst case, there were ten variations of 74); proposed making the *above-deck* mast length the standard dimension.

7. While considering methods of calculating mast dimensions, it noted that because of a perpetuated mistake in the establishment, the topgallants of 36-gun ships were 5ins longer than those of 38s.

8. The driver, which has too much peak, to be cut flatter.

9. Topsails are too deep and should be shortened.

10. Mizzen topsails and topgallants to be cut with more hollow at the foot to prevent rubbing the stay.

11. Abolish the middle staysail, the sprit topsail, and the mizzen topmast staysail as useless.

12. Add another fore topgallant stunsail, and increase to seven cloths the width of one of the lower ones.

13. The cut of main topmast staysail to be altered, to be longer and deeper at the foot and shorter at the head.

After further deliberation, most of these recommendations were adopted. The principal exception was the first: the Admiralty was seriously concerned about the effects of equalising the fore and main yards, and particularly on the ship's power of tacking, so it instructed the Navy Board to investigate the precedents. Byam Martin had already raised the issue in March 1813 with Joseph Tucker, Master Shipwright at Plymouth but shortly to become Surveyor, and it was Tucker's view that British ships were too fine forward to bear the enlarged fore yards necessary to equalise the canvas on both masts. When Martin proposed moving the fore mast aft, Tucker explained the inevitable consequences: it would also mean moving the magazine, reducing the hold space and therefore the capacity to stow water.[3]

It may be coincidence, but at exactly the same time the specification for fitting out the *rasée Saturn* arrived at Plymouth, and one of Captain Hayes's innovations was to equalise the sail plan of the fore and main masts above the courses. However, it was achieved by reduc-

Table 11/2: Mast and spar dimensions of large frigates

	Indefatigable Length Yds-ins	Diameter Ins	Egyptienne Length Yds-ins	Diameter Ins	Endymion Length Yds-ins	Diameter Ins	Rasée 74s Length Yds-ins	Diameter Ins
MASTS								
Main	30-24	29	33-6	32	32-0	30¼	36-0	36
Topmast	17-27	26	20-24	18¼	19-6	17¼	19-8	19¼
Topgall't	8-30	8⅞	14-12	11½	9-21	9⅝	9-22	9⅝
Fore	27-6	26⅜	29-13	30¼	29-13	27¼	31-32	30⅛
Topmast	16-2	16	18-20	18¼	17-0	17¼	19-8	19¼
Topgall't	8-1	8⅛	12-12	8½	8-18	8½	9-22	9⅝
Mizzen	26-3	18⅜	23-18	20	23-2	20	26-28*	23
Topmast	13-10	11⅛	14-11	11½	14-3	11¾	15-32	13
Topgall't	-	-	9-0	7	7-6	7¼	8-0	8
Bowsprit	18-25	28½	20-6	30	19-19	28	22-30	34⅛
Jibboom	13-8	11⅞	16-0	12¾	14-0	12	16-0	14⅛
YARDS								
Main	27-26	19¼	32-30	24	28-26	19⅞	28-4	19⅝
Topsail	20-9	12½	26-10	14½	20-24	12⅞	20-18	12¾
Topgall't	12-8	7⅜	15-0	8½	13-8	8	13-12	8½
Fore	24-5	16⅞	29-35	21½	25-6	17½	28-4	19⅝
Topmast	17-20	11⅝	24-10	14½	18-20	11⅝	20-18	12¾
Topgall't	10-18	6¼	15-0	8½	11-11	7⅛	13-12	8½
Mizzen croj'k	17-20	11⅝	24-10	14½	20-24	12⅞	20-18	12¾
Topsail	13-3	8¼	16-2	8¾	14-4	8½	15-13	9⅝
Topgall't	-	-	9-10	6	8-20	5¼	10-24	6⅝
Gaff	24-30†	13⅝†	15-6	11	13-6	11½	16-17	11½
Boom	-	-			[20-24	11⅝]	[20-18	12¾]
Spritsail	17-20	11⅝	24-10	14½	18-20	11⅝	20-18	12¾
Sprit topsail	10-18	6¼			11-11	7⅛	13-12	8½
Source	NMM POR/A/37		Adm 106/1790		Adm 174/60		Adm 106/1822; Adm 174/60	
	Dec 1794		Mar 1802		Mar 1813		1813	

Notes:

Indefatigable: The proposal is probably an old 50-gun establishment copied verbatim since it includes no modern features like a flying jibboom and quotes an anachronistic long lateen mizzen [marked †] instead of a gaff and boom.

Egyptienne: As arrived at Woolwich. It was later considered that she carried too much head sail, and a reduction in the fore masts and spars was proposed.

Endymion: Identical dimensions for 6 Jul 1808 are given in NMM CHA/E/91.

Rasée 74s: Identical dimensions exist for *Majestic*, 17 Jul and *Saturn*, 27 Apr 1813; the mizzen* steps on the orlop.

Figures in brackets are calculated from the Sep 1813 rules for driver booms and gaffs.

TABLE 11/3: Mast and spar dimensions of captured frigates

	Unité, 38		*Imperieuse*, 38		*Chesapeake*, 38		*Nyaden*, 36	
	Length *Yds-ins*	*Diameter* *Ins*	*Length* *Yds-ins*	*Diameter* *Ins*	*Length* *Yds-ins*	*Diameter* *Ins*	*Length* *Yds-ins*	*Diameter* *Ins*
MASTS								
Main	29-20	29	30-0	30	30-0	30	30-3	26
Topmast	17-4	16	18-6	16⅛	18-9	17¾	19-30	15¾
Topgall't	8-21	8½	9-0	9	9-7	9⅛	10-9	7½
Fore	26-22	24	27-22	23¾	27-22	26½	28-7	25
Topmast	15-34	16	15-30	16⅛	16-30	16¾	17-14	15¾
Topgall't	8-13	8	7-33	7⅞	8-3	8	8-3	6¾
Mizzen	21-6	19	21-19	19½	23-26	22½	22-33*	18
Topmast	13-30	11½	13-18	11¼	14-27	13¾	14-2	10
Topgall't	6-18	6¾	6-27	6¾	6-32	6⅞	7-14	6
Bowsprit	17-15	26	18-22	27¼	20-3	28¾	18-30	25¾ x 24
Jibboom	13-14	11⅝	13-1	11⅝	13-12	12	13-2	12
YARDS								
Main	26-31	17⅛	26-34	18⅝	27-26	19⅛	29-0	18
Topsail	19-24	12	19-24	12¼	20-9	12⅝	20-30	12½
Topgall't	12-24	7½	12-18	7½	12-13	7⅜	11-25	6¼
Fore	23-16	16½	23-19	16¼	24-7	16¾	26-28	16
Topmast	17-27	11½	17-20	11	18-2	11½	18-22	11
Topgall't	11-0	6⅜	10-24	6⅜	11-0	6½	10-12	6
Mizzen cro'jk	17-27	11½	17-20	11	20-9	12⅝	19-2	10½
Topsail	13-18	8½	13-12	8	13-26	8¼	14-16	8½
Topgall't	9-12	5¼	9-12	5¼	9-24	5½	-	-
Gaff	13-10	10	12-20	11½	14-6	10⅛	12-15	9
Boom	-	-	-	-	-	-	17-30	11½
Spritsail	17-27	11½	17-20	11	18-2	11½	17-33	12
Sprit topsail	11-0	6¾	10-24	6¾	11-0	6½	-	-
Source	Adm 106/3474 21 Feb 1805		Adm 174/41 2 Jul 1806		Draught 7343 Dec 1814		Adm 106/1792 3 Nov 1811	

Notes:

Unité: Spars 'as arrived'; the ship had been serving as a Trinity House blockship in the Thames.

Imperieuse: The original dimensions of 14 Jun were revised by Navy Board warrant of the above date, increasing the diameter of the lower masts to the figures shown.

Chesapeake: These dimensions are on the draught 'as taken off' in Dec 1814, which Howard Chapelle interpreted as 'as captured'. In fact, they are largely a mixture of standard British masts and spars, some from 36s but mostly from 38s, which probably means that the ship was almost entirely remasted in the year and a half between her capture and the taking off of her lines.

Nyaden: Dimensions 'as present'; they were replaced with the masts and spars of a *Euryalus* class 36.

*Mizzen steps in the hold.

---

sails, and more off the wind. Tactically, the rig was an 'own goal', because it was so distinctive, and recognisable at great distances, that the ship had no chance of surprising one of the American big frigates that were her intended quarry.[4] Perhaps for some or all of these reasons, no more was heard of the equal fore and main concept.

There was also further debate about fore-and-aft sails, and eventually it was decided to abolish the loose-footed mizzen sails in ships below 50 guns, issuing two drivers in lieu; frigates also had their drivers revised, the yards being reduced and the cut of the sail altered. The replacement of some of the staysails proved more controversial, the intention being to substitute fore and main trysails – small gaff-headed sails set on auxiliary masts, like the one that differentiated a snow from a brig. Their principal advantage was that the effort was transferred to the lower masts, rather than via the stays to the less sturdy topmasts, and since their main employment was for lying-to in bad weather, this was a major consideration. They were also set up to a rigid gaff and mast, making them far more effective going to windward than any loose-luffed staysail.

Trysails were eventually accepted, but the story of their introduction is extended and somewhat convoluted. Formal dimensions for trysail gaffs and sails were first issued in April 1797, those relating to frigates being:

	Trysail Gaff		Trysail			
	Length *Yds-ins*	*Diam* *Ins*	*No of cloths* *Head*	*Foot*	*Yards deep* *Mast*	*Leech*
38 guns	4-26	7	6½	12	10½	12½
36 guns	4-4	6⅝	6	12	10½	12½
32 guns	3-34	6½	5½	10	9½	11

However, there is no evidence that they became a common fitting, although they could be easily rigged when necessary, and it was left to the discretion of the captain. That they were not formally established is suggested by a Navy Board inquiry of November 1811 to the Admiralty as to whether they should issue trysail masts in response to the many requests from captains; it was refused, but since it seems to have applied specifically to mizzen masts, it may not apply to a main trysail.[5]

From December 1809 a fore trysail was allowed to all brigs 'upon application', so there must have been some demand for them. In December 1813, however, they were made compulsory for every 'deep waisted flush decked vessel', which in effect meant the larger brigs of 18 and 16 guns. This may well have been a response to the recent actions with American ship sloops in

---

ing the area of the main to that of the fore, and not vice-versa as proposed by Martin. Hayes's aim was to duplicate a number of masts, yards and sails to facilitate their replacement if damaged in action, but it was not appreciated by all captains of the *rasées*. Maitland of the *Goliath* complained bitterly of his ship's sailing in light conditions, but since she improved immeasurably when the wind freshened, he argued that she badly needed the lost canvas, which he calculated at 300 [sq?] yards when close-hauled with single reefed top-

The standard British ship rig of the period may be represented by this fine model of a 38-gun frigate in the US Naval Academy Museum in Annapolis. Originally catalogued as the *Shannon*, recent research has shown up too many anomalies in hull shape and dimensions to allow the identification to stand, but the model is nevertheless accurate in most general respects for a frigate of about 1800. The model carries no royal yards, nor a spritsail topmast (although this was issued, it was not always rigged); it is also rigged somewhat conservatively in details like the lead of the bobstay and of the main braces, suggesting a date nearer 1800 than 1815.
United States Naval Academy Museum, Annapolis

which British brigs had been effectively crippled by having the main gaff shot away; this gave them another large fore-and aft sail to preserve some manoeuvrability, but it was not universally popular. One of the most vociferous and well argued complaints came from Captain Farington of the brig sloop *Clio* in August 1814. In itself, his report is not significant except as background to a more general adoption of trysails.[6]

All the fir frigates of the American War 'emergency' programme were fitted with main trysails, the inspiration coming from the performance of Pellew's

Mediterranean fleet, where his battleships happily rode out severe gales under a fore, main and mizzen trysail. The Navy Board had sought his opinion and been convinced of their efficacy; in the meantime, the Admiralty had accepted the recommendation of Byam Martin's committee that the middle and mizzen top staysails be abolished, replacing them with a main trysail. However, because of the negative opinions of many officers, the Navy Board was unsure about fore trysails, so while the main was formally adopted with the other measures of the 1815 stores establishment, a trials squadron of two

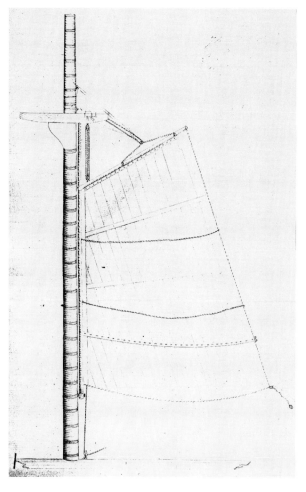

battleships, two frigates and two sloops evaluated the fore trysail. It too was eventually accepted, but not for some years after the end of the war.[7]

PERFORMANCE – THE NATURE OF THE EVIDENCE

Although captains often commented on the characteristics of their ships during the course of correspondence with the Admiralty – particularly if they had a complaint – any modern analysis of their performance depends heavily on a substantial series of formal questionnaires known as Sailing Quality reports. Some are entirely hand-written, but the vast majority comprise a standard printed form with manuscript answers, usually filled out at the end of a commission, and signed if not actually composed by the captain. The questions cover the basic aspects of the ship's performance on all points of sailing, through various conditions of wind and sea; how she handles, and whether she is stiff and weatherly; how she stows her established provisions and carries her guns; and the best trim and set-up of masts and rigging, and the resulting draught and gunport freeboard.

The earliest reports date from the 1740s, but there is evidence that the Surveyor of the time, Sir Jacob Acworth, had been encouraging the Master Shipwrights to collect exactly similar data in a less systematic fashion for some years previously; indeed, by that period the questions themselves may have already become an established convention. The forms were collected by the Master Attendant of the Dockyard where the ship lay, and it is easy to imagine that in the bustle of decommissioning a relatively lowly civilian official might have difficulty persuading a post captain to give the task his best attention, and whatever the regulations it is clear that some did not bother at all. Because the forms were filled out with varying degrees of enthusiasm and candour, generally quote peak (and therefore possibly freak) speeds, and at best represent only informed opinion, modern naval architects often deny the value of these reports as a design tool. This may be strictly true, but it misunderstands the historical context. It is no accident that the whole system was formalised at a period when British ship design was under fierce attack from politicians and sea officers, so while better reporting could be presented as an aid to better design, the principal value of this information to the Surveyors and Navy Board, when carefully selected, was to defend themselves against the criticism of sea officers, the Admiralty or Parliament.

This is not to say that the information in the reports was totally ignored in the design process, but it could only have been applied in the broadest fashion. General satisfaction with a ship or class, for example, might lead to that draught becoming the starting point for a new design, but only rarely were minor modifications made to existing draughts as a result of reports from sea; in fact, Sir Thomas Slade, Surveyor from 1755 to 1771, was almost alone in this practice. Because of their political origins, the relative value of the Sailing Quality reports (and the diligence applied to their collection) rose and fell in inverse proportion to the status of British ship design. In the 1790s the technologically adventurous Admiralty of Earl Spencer ordered a sequence of single-ship designs without apparently waiting for reports on their predecessors, although they occasionally short-circuited the process altogether by requesting information directly from the captain in the case of an important experiment (such as Gambier's *Triton*). In these circumstances, a busy wartime Navy Board may have felt that collecting Sailing Quality reports on ships that were unlikely to be repeated was a low priority. Certainly few reports survive from these years, in marked contrast to the numbers dating from the peace period of 1802-3. This latter upsurge may be another manifestation of the reforming zeal of the St Vincent Board, keen to reimpose discipline on captains grown cavalier with their paperwork. However, it is equally likely to reflect a concerted effort to support the Board's view that British warships had become too large by assembling evidence to 'prove' that the extra cost was not repaid in superior performance: in the case of frigates, the bigger ships were clearly better, although whether the improvement was cost-effective was a political judgement.

With the renewal of war, the number of surviving reports again declines steeply and, unsurprisingly, many of these relate to prizes, the qualities of enemy ships being a perennial concern. By this stage of the war any capture was usually preceded by a chase, and British officers became increasingly interested in the fine-tuning of their ships. Since the Sailing Quality reports summarised often years of experience, and listed details of how to get the best from the vessel, they must have proved valuable to succeeding captains – indeed, some modern historians assume they were principally for the captains' benefit. However, there is no evidence that officers were regularly supplied with previous reports, and much that suggests that access to such information was rare and haphazard.

In his *Narrative* William Henry Dillon tells a very suggestive anecdote about the frigate *Aimable*, an ageing French prize that by 1797 had lost her fine reputation for sailing. A number of her officers had succumbed to the sickly climate of the West Indies, and nobody remained with experience of the ship at her best. However, at Antigua her new captain made an interesting discovery:

Our Captain was aware that the *Aimable* had lost her sailing reputation, and determined if possible to regain it by altering the stowage. The strange part of this case is that, shortly after our arrival, the Captain was examining some papers in the Store-keeper's office, and there found a written document stating that the *Aimable*'s best sailing trim was 4 inches by the stern [she was previously sailed at 18 inches], signed by her senior Lieutenant of that day, John Hampstead.

This was clearly a Sailing Quality report, and its value (and rarity) was evident in the reaction to it: 'When Capt. Lobb had found this document, he was in a perfect ecstacy of joy, and instantly turned it to account.'[8]

Any captain would have found such information useful, and since most would have been obliged to fill one out at some stage in their career, they would have been aware of how much time and effort might be saved by access to such reports when taking up a new command. In some situations captains were able to meet their predecessors to discuss the ship's qualities, and some prided themselves on being able to get the best from their ships through their own skill and sea-sense, but in the majority of cases there would have been a clear benefit from recourse to existing experience. The Admiralty was eventually led to agree, and in December 1811 the whole system was revamped, and

Akbar setting sail for Bermuda, 10 August 1815, one of a series of watercolours by Admiral Sir George Back, who as a midshipman experienced a terrifying storm in which the ship was heavily damaged and eventually dismasted. British frigates were generally good sea-boats, but *Akbar* was a spectacular exception (although she had been built for the Bombay Marine and not the Royal Navy). With a huge reserve of stability, the ship rolled rapidly and regularly lost her topmasts; her seagoing naval career was brief.
National Maritime Museum X1387

new regulations introduced ordering captains to complete a report annually. The original intention was to have them sent directly to the Admiralty, and the Navy Board had to petition to get duplicate copies sent to the Navy Office as part of the new rules.[9] This also provided for a report to be left with the ship when a captain moved on.

The system was now intended to benefit the sea officers rather than the designers and the new emphasis can be seen in the revised form introduced at the same time. The simply headed 'Observations of the Qualities of HM Ship ———' becomes 'A Report on the Sailing and other Qualities of HM Ship ———', and it is the other qualities which are given prominence, beginning with far more detailed trim and stowage information for various states of lading. If the revised order of the questions is significant, priority lies with seaworthiness, stiffness under sail, gunport freeboard, and handling, speed under sail coming nearly at the end, although now being quoted in knots and fathoms which suggests a desire to be more precise. Against this, there is a distinct emphasis on performance compared with other ships: obviously more credence was placed on the fact that x regularly forereached on y than x's claim to make 10 knots closehauled; the question of the ship's best point of sailing was also subtly changed to which point of sailing offered the most comparative advantage over other ships (although many captains missed the subtlety and continued to report their ship's fastest point – almost inevitably with the wind on the quarter, so valueless as an answer). There were also several new questions, a significant one in the light of all the structural experimenting in progress at the time relating to the strength and build-quality of the ship. And to underline the intention to have these forms submitted every year, the final question required the captain to point out, and account for, any changes in the ship's performance since the last report.

The regulations were enforced immediately, resulting in a vast number of reports dating from 1812-13, but the old form continued to be used for some years in many cases.[10] The new format contained an entry specifying the period covered, and in the first round of post-1812 reports most went back at least a few years and in at least two cases to 1802, strongly suggesting that little effort had been made in these years to collect Sailing Quality reports. One reason was undoubtedly the construction of large programmes of ships to standard designs whose qualities were already well enough known, and whose performance was regarded as perfectly satisfactory. From the historical perspective, the increase in the number and frequency of the reports must be welcome, but unfortunately the new form, worded like a multiple-choice examination paper in many respects, encouraged peremptory responses. A few captains continued to expand their answers with valuable analytical comments, but the majority confined themselves to the bare minimum wordage, while the yearly nature of the obligation led many to simply repeat what little they had written the previous year.

For all their failings, if used with care and restraint, the Sailing Quality reports do provide useful insights into the performance of ships at sea. Allowing for prejudice and freak results, and the substantial influence of trim, stowage and rig, it is remarkable how consistently ships of the same class behave. In the period under review, large classes and numerous reports serve to underline the statistical validity of this proposition.

SPEEDS

A note of caution must be entered about one important aspect of the Sailing Quality reports, namely quoted speeds. Modern hydrodynamic theory casts considerable doubt on whether wooden sailing warships could ever achieve the speeds they are regularly reported to do, but the sheer scale and consistency of such claims puzzle the engineers: indeed, one prominent naval architect was reduced to suggesting that captains simply lied. Since the casting of the log was a very public event, and the resulting calculation of the ship's progress was noted in the log-books (later deposited at the Admiralty for verification by interested parties), and the Sailing Quality report itself required countersignature by other ship's officers (usually the Master and the Carpenter), any dishonest captain was running a great risk with his own and others' careers. Falsifying a log was a serious offence, although it is unlikely that the crime could be extended to cover exaggerating speeds on a Sailing Quality report; but it is unnecessary to impugn the honesty of a whole profession, when there is a simpler and less sinister answer.

In essence, before the mechanical log the value of the 'knot' employed for navigation was lower than presently defined. Speed was measured by casting overboard a flat log-ship to act as a brake, and as the ship moved forward an attached log-line was unreeled from the taffrail. The amount of line run out in a given time, measured by a sand-glass, was scaled up to give the number of nautical miles run in an hour. The line was divided with knots at regular intervals, in the same proportion to a sea-mile as the sand-glass was to an hour – eg a ½-minute glass was 1/120th of an hour and the knots should have been spaced at 1/120th a mile apart; if the ship ran off 10 knots in that period, she was reckoned to be covering 10 nautical miles an hour.

This is clearly subject to a degree of error, but in the days of dead-reckoning it was the basis of calculations of the ship's progress and hence position; latitude could be easily established, but for most of the age of sail longitude remained elusive to anyone who could not afford a good chronometer. Ships which got ahead of their reckoning might make a landfall before they expected it, with the risk of being wrecked. As a result a conservative practice grew up of over-calculating the speed, so that a ship was more likely to be astern of her reckoned position. This was achieved by shortening the distance between the knots on the log-line below the correct length. In the Royal Navy the sand-glass used was a 28-second model, so by strict calculation the knots should have been 15.7yds, or about 47ft 4ins, apart, whereas standard practice was to use a 7-fathom, 42ft, line - hence the speeds quoted in knots and up to 6 fathoms. This exaggerates the speed significantly: 13kts is only 11½kts by modern calculation.[11]

The Admiralty was offered a more accurate instrument in February 1803, when Edward Massey came forward with what must have been a prototype of the patent mechanical log widely used by the Victorian navy. But in St Vincent's day it 'did not appear calculated for HM Naval service'.[12]

In the accompanying tables, the original quoted speeds have been left unconverted. These are the figures that would have been meaningful to officers of the time, and used in any debate about the qualities of an individual ship, so modern 'interpretation' would only add an element of ambiguity. The relative performance of contemporary vessels are unaffected, but the reader is cautioned not to compare ancient and modern without due allowance for the different value of the knot.

PERFORMANCE – AN ANALYSIS

The tables summarise the characteristics of individual ships and classes, but the evidence allows certain general conclusions to be drawn about the performance of British frigates during the wars of 1803-15.

In marked contrast to some earlier periods, the salient impression is one of almost universal satisfaction with the qualities of the ships. Such criticisms as exist are infrequent and relatively minor, merely indicating that very high expectations were occasionally disappointed. In a period when bringing a reluctant enemy to battle was the overriding tactical problem, frigates suffered none of the frustrations of the battle-fleet whose chases were often hampered by the slowest-sailing ships in squadrons of mixed ability. Some French frigates escaped when pursued, but many more did not, and most Royal Navy frigate commanders believed the odds were in their favour, allowing for their superior seamanship to make a significant contribution. As a result there was none of that ingrained sense of design inferiority that had characterised, say, the 1740s, and little pressure for radical change until the War of 1812, when an entirely new type of cruiser was required.

From an analysis of the Sailing Quality reports there seems to have been a consistent emphasis in British frigate design. The priorities in what a later age would call 'staff requirements' might be summarised as weatherliness rather than sheer speed, seakeeping (particularly the ability to work the guns in all fighting weathers), strength and capacity. In these respects there was not much to choose between the qualities of the best British frigates, and the high average standard was largely the result of so many frigates being built to three standard draughts, all of which were excellent all-round designs. Based purely on their sailing qualities, it is easy to see why these classes were constructed in such large numbers, but conversely it seems that the one-off ships based on French prototypes were a pointless experiment; likewise, the revival of older classes like the *Tribune*s was probably a false economy.

Of the standard classes, the relatively small 36-gun *Apollo* class were remarkably successful quarts in pint pots, displaying most of the qualities required of a British frigate, the only reservation being their questionable stiffness, and a tendency to pitching. The two 38-gun classes make an interesting comparison and contrast: their performance is broadly comparable, but the French-derived underwater body of the *Leda*s made them less weatherly and made the stowage of a full allocation of provisions difficult. The *Lively* class, on the other hand, made an ideal, all-weather, long-range cruiser, and in terms of their fitness for British requirements undoubtedly the best of the standard frigate classes. They were highly regarded in the fleet and as late as 1826, Captain George Harris declared, 'Considering *Hussar*'s capabilities of stowage of provisions, stores &c &c, and her qualities for sailing, I should pronounce her as fine a man of war as ever put to sea.'[13] In purely objective terms, as the evidence existed in 1813, it is difficult to understand why the decision was made to standardise on the *Leda* class (which to that point had been built only in limited numbers) and discontinue the *Lively*s. In the light of recent events, it was probably thought politically expedient to build more sisters for the *Shannon* while dropping the *Macedonian* design.

The latter was replaced by a design modified from the French *Président*, which became the *Seringapatam* class. Coming into service after the war, these proved to be a disappointment, going through three modifications of the design. The sailing qualities of the early ships were controversial, and ironically the first British-built member of the class, the *Druid*, was tested in 1826 against the *Hussar* (of the *Lively* class), which was the recognised flyer of the West Indies station. To an unprejudiced eye, the reports of the captains do not reveal any obvious advantage to the *Druid*, except that she was better to windward in strong winds. Of course, the aim of the trials was to ascertain the best trim, stowage and set-up of rigging for the new ship, so *Druid* was handicapped, despite her larger sail plan. Nevertheless, the ship's qualities were still causing trouble three years later, and the ship's apparent lack of stability led Seppings to modify the design.[14]

The *Président* was the last in a long line of French hull-forms used as prototypes for British frigates, and the problems with its progeny symbolise the bankruptcy of the strategy. In most cases 'copying' a French design was a method by which the Admiralty could circumvent what it perceived as undue conservatism among the Navy's professional designers; but for over a century the principal shortcoming of British warships was not strictly poor design so much as inadequate dimensions compared with enemy vessels, and in the final analysis this was a political issue rather than a technological one. Therefore, copying a French form was only really worthwhile if it represented a quantum leap in size relative to British ships: one might quote the examples of the *Invincible*, *Courageux* and *Canopus* among the battleships, *Endymion* among the frigates, or *Bonne Citoyenne* among the sloops; each introduced something novel in terms of scale, armament or layout to its respective class, quite independent of its underwater body.

In the field of frigate design, by the time war was renewed in 1803 none of Britain's enemies had anything radical to offer. France had largely standardised on a 40-gun design by Sané – from the same prototype as the *Leda*s, making them half-sisters – and many other designs by the likes of Rolland, J-M-B Coulomb and Segondat-Duvernet followed the overall specification, and even employed similar hull-forms; a few slightly larger ships were built by Forfait, and his followers Pestel and Gauthier, with a sharper midship section, but these were no bigger than ships of the 1790s like the *Révolutionnaire*.[15] It is very noticeable that none of the many French prizes in Royal Navy service turned in exceptional performances, and from surviving Sailing Quality reports it appears that, despite the acknowledged British skill in 'ship tuning', many ex-French frigates were not quite the equal of the best British-built performers. French ships were widely believed to be excellent sailers downwind, but

vulnerable because less weatherly than their pursuers.[16] Furthermore, close-hauled they do not seem to have sailed particularly fast: 9-9½ knots is the best to be found in surviving reports.[17] They also carried their batteries slightly lower than British frigates and tended to be more lively in a seaway, so were poorer fighting machines in consequence. On the other hand, as British frigates had become longer, they had lost their traditional superiority in handiness, any advantage in manoeuvring now largely depending on the relative skills of the crews. Although the British had removed riders from their ships and experimented with novel forms of fastenings during these years, French ships were still regarded as too lightly built; and they consistently failed to live up to British stowage requirements for long cruises. It is difficult to escape the conclusion that while British frigate design had improved immeasurably in two decades, France in 1815 had not moved on much since 1795.

Of the other opposing navies, the ships of Spain and the Netherlands were commonly regarded as poor performers under sail and neither produced a frigate design that generated much interest. The Danes were the only nation besides France whose battleships inspired emulation in the British, and the big two-decker *Christian VII* was so highly regarded that a number of ships were based on her lines. However, the frigates were not so impressive: even the *Perlen*, by the same designer and sharing many of the features of the *Christian VII*, was not considered. Surviving evidence suggests that Danish frigates, like their French counterparts, were fast but leewardly, and of too small a capacity for British requirements.

In historical terms it was the US Navy which had the greatest impact, but while the ex-American prizes were inspected closely there was no great desire to copy *Chesapeake*, *Essex*, or the sloop *Frolic* for that matter. The *President* might be regarded as an exception since an exact copy was ordered in 1818, but this was

The largest frigate taken at the fall of Copenhagen in 1807 was the *Perlen*, a 1200-ton vessel designed to carry 24pdrs on the main deck. In British service she carried twenty-eight 18pdrs, although this must have meant permanently arming the bow-chase ports. The draught is dated 4 July 1809 and already the ship's most original feature, the 'Hohlenberg stern', has been rebuilt with a more conventional set of quarter galleries. It is sometimes suggested that Seppings's post-war circular stern was inspired by Hohlenberg's ideas, but there is no direct proof in favour and much circumstantial evidence to the contrary. The Danish stern was designed to improve oblique fire like Seppings's, but its timbering was little more resistant to raking fire than the usual construct of transoms, whereas the circular stern offered virtually the same protection as the ship's side. In any event, Hohlenberg's stern was very unpopular in the Royal Navy and was rapidly removed from all the frigates that carried it. *National Maritime Museum Dr7057*

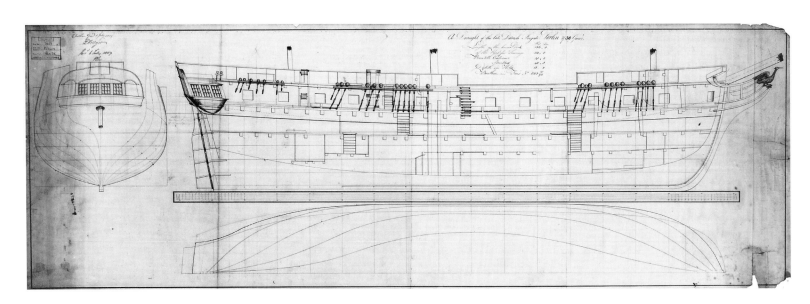

largely a political move: the old ship was in a poor state when captured in 1815 and eventually had to be broken up, but the Admiralty wished to retain the propaganda value of a *President* on the Navy List to celebrate its one great success over the American super-frigates. The influence of US ship design is far more strongly manifest in the ships built to match the concept of the big spar-deckers – initially *Leander* and *Newcastle*, which were fully their equal in performance, although being fir-built were weak and relatively short-lived; and then the more considered response of the *Southampton* class derived from the *Java* of 1813.

TABLE 11/4:
Sailing qualities of standard British frigate classes

NB Fractions of inches ignored, except ¾ which is rounded up. Any speed such as '12.4' is being quoted in knots and fathoms. More weight is given to wartime reports, since the post-war Peace Establishment reduced guns, and often fitted the economy measure of copper protectors; these slowed the erosion of the copper but allowed the growth of fouling, consequently reducing speed.

Tribune class, 36 guns, 1801

	Draught (ft-ins)		Freeboard (ft-ins) midships port	Ballast (tons)		Water	Victualled for
	fwd	aft		iron	shingle		
Tribune, 1803	16-6	19-0	7-6	95	60	90	CS
Tribune, 1819	17-3	18-8	7-9	108	0	103	CS
Iphigenia, 1815	17-10	19-2	7-8	125	40	100	CS
Iphigenia,1822	17-8	18-4	8-7	136	0	100	CS
Doris, 1816	17-6	19-0	7-0	150	40	110	FS

The original 1780 design at best showed only moderate performance under sail, and because frigates had become longer and sharper in the interim the revived class seemed relatively poorer – in 1813 the old *Inconstant* of the original group was described as 'much inferior to the frigates of the present day', and by 1822 *Iphigenia* compared with other ships was rated 'very slow indeed'. In smooth water they could manage 8-8½kts close-hauled and occasionally 12kts large, although 10-11kts was more common; they were also regarded as rather leewardly and none too stiff under their canvas. Their best qualities were a strong, dry and seaworthy hull and their handiness in tacking and wearing, being relatively short; they also stowed their provisions well and carried their gunports high.

Given the builders' cavalier attitude to the draughts supplied them, the *Salsette*, and possibly the *Doris*, can only be regarded as half-sisters. Their qualities were generally similar, however, although at the lower end of the spectrum of recorded speeds. The *Salsette* was curious in being faster directly before the wind than on any other point of sailing, which the captain thought was due to the hull being constructed too full aft and too fine forward.

Based on reports of: *Tribune* (20 Mar 1812, 15 Jul 1822, 21 Feb 1826); *Iphigenia* (1 Jan 1815, 14 Mar 1818, 10 Nov 1822); *Salsette* (12 Jul 1816); *Doris* (1 Dec 1812, 4 Mar 1816, 31 Mar 1822).

Forte class, 38 guns, 1801

	Draught (ft-ins)		Freeboard (ft-ins) midships port	Ballast (tons)		Water	Victualled for
	fwd	aft		iron	shingle		
Oct 1820	15-4	17-2	8-2	81	0	84	CS
Oct 1826	16-8	19-5	7-2	90	0	101	CS

Fast, but not outstandingly so, having achieved nearly 10kts close-hauled and 12.4 large, and preferred stronger conditions. She handled well for such a large ship, but was not very weatherly and rolled badly, especially with low sail. Her capacity was small and stowage was a problem; constructed of light scantlings in the French style, her upperworks were weak and worked a good deal.

Based on reports of 30 Sep 1824 and 30 Jul 1830

Repeat *Leda* class, 38 guns, 1802

	Draught (ft-ins)		Freeboard (ft-ins) midships port	Ballast (tons)		Water	Victualled for
	fwd	aft		iron	shingle		
Lacedaemonian, 1813	17-10	18-8	6-3	90	52	88	FS
Leonidas, 1808	15-6	18-5	7-10	90	77	96	CS
Leonidas, 1812	16-8	18-4	6-11	90	120	95	CS
Diamond, 1824	17-5	18-9	7-5	105	0	132	FS
Thetis, 1826	16-4	18-1	7-6	141	0	115	CS

Very fast, particularly going large when most recorded 13kts and *Lacedaemonian* even claimed '13½kts by repeated heaving of the log'; good but not exceptional close-hauled, 10kts being the usual figure. They stood to their canvas well and liked a stiff gale, but not heavy seas, because they were subject to deep pitching. With their French derived proportions, they were not very weatherly compared with frigates of British origin, and all captains took steps to remedy this, usually by requesting additions to the false keel and gripe – although *Surprise* shipped additional ballast until the captain decided that whatever the ship gained to windward she more than lost in forereaching.

All captains complained of poor capacity, barely 4 months' provisions going under hatches, and this needed careful stowage. In fact, they seem to have required a good shiphandler to get the most out of them. Broke of the *Shannon* noted that his ship was 'delicate in trim' and he made a habit of sailing with the bow and sternmost guns amidships, and the shot and hammocks struck below. The same care needed to be exercised in tacking and wearing, when *Shannon* was slow but sure; however, some captains were not impressed with their ships' handling. The other common criticism was of their light structure, which combined with their lively rolling and pitching in a seaway to make them work and strain constantly. This made them wet and *Leonidas*, for example, regularly needed the waterways recaulked and damaged scuppers replaced. This was a particular problem with the early ships constructed with Brindley's 'bolt-and-carling' substitute for knees, but even the Dockyard-built ships appear to have been weak, although there are no such complaints about the ships completed post-war.

One captain felt that the design was at fault in combining the fine underwater lines of a French ship with the wall-sided upperworks of British practice. Their Lordships begged to differ, and the design became the standard post-war frigate class – albeit with the far stronger diagonal structure of Sir Robert Seppings, and stowage made more efficient by the adoption of iron water tanks.

Based on reports of: *Shannon* (17 Jun 1812); *Leonidas* (5 Feb 1812, 1 Jan 1814, 1 Jan 1815, 16 Jun 1815); *Briton* (27 Apr 1830); *Lacedaemonian* (undated, but under the command of Samuel Jackson, so probably Jun 1815 when the ship returned to England); *Tenedos* (24 Aug 1815); *Lively* (31 Oct 1825, 4 Dec 1826); *Surprise* (31 Aug 1815); *Diamond* (1 Dec 1826); *Amphitrite* (6 Jan 1817, 10 Jan 1817, 18 Jan 1817); *Trincomalee* (4 Apr 1819); *Thetis* (28 Oct 1826); *Blanche* (25 Oct 1827, 1 Jan 1831).

Repeat *Lively* class, 38 guns, 1803

	Draught (ft-ins) fwd	aft	Freeboard (ft-ins) midships port	Ballast (tons) iron	shingle	Water	Victualled for
Hussar, 1808	18-2	18-7	7-4	148	40	97	CS
Hussar, 1823	16-8	18-6	8-0	127	0	124	CS
Statira, 1807	17-3	19-4	7-10	145	50	142	FS
Nymphe, 1812	17-8	19-10	7-2	130	60	140	FS

The reports on this class are remarkable for their consistency, and the almost total absence of any serious criticism. The *Lively*s were fast, weatherly and manoeuvrable – easy on the helm, and sure in stays, although like most big frigates long in wearing – good sea-boats, dry, comfortable and capacious. Capable of 13kts with the wind abaft the beam, their comparative advantage over other frigates was close-hauled when they regularly logged between 10 and 11kts. In heavy weather the superiority was even more marked, both forereaching and going to windward, and this is one of the few classes reported capable of dealing with a head sea. They stowed their provisions well – 6 months under hatches if arranged carefully, and a large tonnage of water. Given the Royal Navy's penchant for long cruises, it was a real advantage that they sailed best deep laden; in fact, the only criticism was that they did not sail so well in light conditions or when they themselves were light, but this latter problem was dealt with by taking on seawater after about three weeks at sea, a process made easier after the introduction of iron water tanks.

Based on reports of: *Hussar* (31 Aug 1813, 16 Jun 1814, 2 Nov 1826); *Undaunted* (1 Jan 1814, 1 Jan 1815, 14 Nov 1815, 2 Nov 1830); *Statira* (1 January 1815); *Horatio* (undated, but during W H Dillon's command, 1814-16); *Spartan* (5 Jul 1816, 1 & 31 Jan 1821); *Menelaus* (29 Aug 1815); *Nisus* (2 May 1814); *Crescent* (4 Sep 1815); *Bacchante* (Jul 1815); *Nymphe* (1 Jan 1815); *Laurel* (21 Dec 1814).

Repeat *Apollo* class, 36 guns, 1803

	Draught (ft-ins) fwd	aft	Freeboard (ft-ins) midships port	Ballast (tons) iron	shingle	Water	Victualled for
Manilla, 1810	17-0	18-3	7-10	80	60	110	CS
Havannah, 1812	17-8	19-0	7-4	115	135	109	FS
Galatea, 1826	17-5	18-4	7-6	95	0	115	CS

As would be expected from a class built in such large numbers, these ships were good all-round performers. They were not outstandingly fast with the wind free – only *Hotspur*, *Galatea* and *Tartar* claimed to have reached 13kts, but all were capable of 12-12½kts. Close-hauled they were relatively better, most recording 10kts, and some a touch more. They handled well, both quick and sure in stays and wearing, and were so well balanced that the 'smallest boy steers her alone' (*Semiramis*). Good in strong winds, they were easy sea-boats, although prone to deep pitching in heavy seas, and some captains made a point of removing heavy weights from their extremities; in consequence they were much affected by head seas, the captain of the *Maidstone* claiming his ship often did 9kts on one tack, but only 3kts when going about brought the sea on the bow.

However, their biggest drawback was that they were not very stiff and needed to be sailed deep: normally weatherly, they became noticeably less so as their draught reduced, some became somewhat slack in stays, and most were complained of as crank after about 6 weeks at sea. In these circumstances they had a tendency to lay over a great deal, making it difficult to fight their lee battery, which unnerved some officers – *Stag*'s captain took on extra ballast, while *Galatea*'s had the lower masts shortened by 2ft while on the Cape station. However, the initial heel was soon arrested – *Orpheus*, for example, 'carries down to a certain bearing then remains' – but the characteristic led many captains to describe their ships as 'rather crank', or at best 'tolerably stiff', as a result. Criticism of their stability became more strident for the ships which served post-war – particularly the *Dartmouth* and *Galatea* – but by this date their stowage, masting and equipment had been altered so much that it could have no relevance to the performance of the wartime ships.

There were no complaints about their capacity, and most captains contrived to stow up to 6 months' provisions under hatches.

The *Malacca*, which does not seem to have been built to the official draught, was noticeably poorer in most aspects of performance. The best her captain could find to say about her was 'a good company keeper', the classic description of the mediocre ship.

Based on reports of: *Dartmouth* (4 Dec 1826, 15 Mar 1830); *Owen Glendower* (11 May 1816, 9 Sep 1822, 11 Nov 1822, 16 Aug 1828); *Semiramis* (1 Jan 1812, 1 Jan 1814, Aug 1814, 23 Sep 1818); *Hotspur* (undated *c*1815); *Malacca* (13 Jul 1815); *Curaçoa* (1 Sep 1815); *Havannah* (1 Jan 1813, 3 Jul 1819); *Theban* (1 Dec 1812, 1 Dec 1813); *Orpheus* (2 Oct 1816); *Leda* (1 Jan 1817); *Belvidera* (29 May 1812, 12 Oct 1814); *Astraea* (5 Sep 1812); *Galatea* (4 Sep 1812, 4 Nov 1815, 6 Jan 1829); *Maidstone* (29 Aug 1815, 31 Aug 1827); *Stag* (14 Dec 1814); *Magicienne* (20 Jul 1814, undated but signed by Captain J B Purvis, who was appointed in Oct 1815); *Pallas* (14 Mar 1831); *Creole* (Nov 1814, 24 Jan 1821, 13 Feb 1824); *Tartar* (8 Oct 1821).

Repeat *Amphion* class, 32 guns, 1805

	Draught (ft-ins) fwd	aft	Freeboard (ft-ins) midships port	Ballast (tons) iron	shingle	Water	Victualled for
Proserpine, 1808	16-11	17-10	7-7	93	64	97	CS
Nereus, Jan 1815	17-3	18-6	7-7	145	50	112	CS

Nereus never seems to have registered quite the top speeds of the first three of the class – she logged 12kts large and 9.6kts close-hauled – but she shared the same basic qualities of her sisters, being very weatherly and stiff. Comparatively speaking, she was most competitive in double-reefed topsail weather on a bowline, although being very fine forward, she was sensitive to a head sea and inclined to heavy pitching; but was reckoned 'a pretty easy roller'. She handled well in all but very light conditions, and stowed her provisions without difficulty.

Based on reports of *Nereus* (1 Jan 1813, 11 Jan 1815).

Repeat *Narcissus* class, 32 guns, 1805

	Draught (ft-ins)		Freeboard (ft-ins) midships port	Ballast (tons)		Water	Victualled for
	fwd	aft		iron	shingle		
Cornelia, 1809	16-6	18-6	7-2	95	78	105	CS

There is no surviving report on *Cornelia*, but it is reasonable to assume that she shared the same moderate performance as the prototype. See *The Heavy Frigate*, p88 for details.

Bucephalus class, 32 guns, 1805

	Draught (ft-ins)		Freeboard (ft-ins) midships port	Ballast (tons)		Water	Victualled for
	fwd	aft		iron	shingle		
Aug 1816	15-8	17-0		85	0	108	?

The only surviving report dates from the ship's service as a troopship, when armed *en flute* and carrying a reduced rig. However, the almost unprecedented reduction to this role of a big frigate that was barely five years old may itself be an eloquent comment on the ship's qualities as a cruiser. The report quotes no speed above 10kts sailing large and 8.4kts close-hauled, but she was stiff, not noticeably leewardly, and there are no adverse comments on the ship's seakeeping.

Based on report of 21 Aug 1816 when a troopship.

Pyramus class, 36 guns, 1805

	Draught (ft-ins)		Freeboard (ft-ins) midships port	Ballast (tons)		Water	Victualled for
	fwd	aft		iron	shingle		
Jul 1810	17-11	17-5	6-0	135	0	79	CS
Oct 1813	16-10	17-3	6-3	124	0	90	CS
1821 (with tanks)	17-0	17-1	6-7	92	0	86	FS

The worst characteristic of this ship was her shallow hull, which meant that she stowed her provisions very poorly (only 4 months' worth could be fitted below hatches, and she did not see foreign service until fitted with iron tanks); she also carried her guns relatively low, and throughout her career she was leewardly, despite additions to her false keel and gripe. She had 21 tons of ballast landed to ameliorate heavy pitching, but she then proved rather

crank, so it was restored. Although the extra ballast made her stand better under canvas, in 1828 she was still judged 'very bad' in this respect compared with other ships. Against this, she was fast, having recorded 10kts close-hauled and 13kts large, but it was a fair-weather speed, the ship being adversely affected by a fresh blow and a big sea.

Based on reports of 13 Feb 1812, 31 Oct 1813, 30 Jun 1822, 17 Jun 1825, 15 Sep 1828.

Hyperion class, 32 guns, 1805

	Draught (ft-ins)		Freeboard (ft-ins) midships port	Ballast (tons)		Water	Victualled for
	fwd	aft		iron	shingle		
Aug 1815	16-10	18-0	5-11	90	?	100	CS
Apr 1821	16-6	18-6	6-2	138	0	110	CS
Oct 1821	17-0	18-2	5-10	109	0	122	FS

Like *Pyramus*, a relatively low hull with similar stowage difficulties and poor freeboard: one of her captains commented, 'being a very low ship, particularly abaft, I have always thought it proper to keep steerage way on her in the worst weather', but she had a sea-kindly hull and was comfortable in the heaviest gales. She was fast but leewardly, having once made 13½kts with the wind 1 point abaft the beam (although 12-12½ was her usual maximum), but was less impressive close-hauled at 9-9½kts. She was handy, and quick to answer the helm.

Based on reports of 31 Aug 1815, and 5 Apr 1821.

Scamander class, 36 guns, 1812

	Draught (ft-ins)		Freeboard (ft-ins) midships port	Ballast (tons)		Water	Victualled for
	fwd	aft		iron	shingle		
Tigris, 1814	16-8	17-7	7-9	180	0	113	CS
Tagus, 1814	17-9	18-0	7-0	150	45	106	FS
Alpheus, 1814	16-9	16-3	8-3	170	19	110	CS

Fast ships, but their relatively shallow draught made them a little leewardly, especially when reduced to only 4-6 weeks' provisions. They were good close-hauled, all having recorded around 10kts, but were regarded as better off the wind, most logging 12½kts and *Ister, Orontes* and *Tigris* 13kts. They handled well, and were quick in stays, and since an effort was made to keep down the ballast allocation, they were easy sea-boats, although some captains felt they were a little tender. The depth in hold had also been reduced compared with the oak-built *Euryalus* class in an attempt to avert the over-stiffness of earlier fir frigates, but this produced their biggest problem: the poor stowage, only 3 months being easily taken under hatches, although 4 months could be packed away with care. When stored for 6 months, they could not afford to give up any ballast, so the water stowage had to be reduced.

Based on reports of: *Scamander* (13 Nov 1818); *Eridanus* (c1815, 1 Jan 1817); *Ister* (2 Aug 1815, 31 Aug 1818); *Orontes* (21 Mar 1817); *Tagus* (1 Jan 1818); *Tigris* (1 Jan 1815, 13 Aug 1815, Jan 1818); *Euphrates* (25 Aug 1815, 1 Jan 1817, 23 Jun 1817); *Hebrus* (25 Sep 1815, 2 Nov 1816); *Alpheus* (21 Dec 1816).

Modified *Leda* class, 38 guns, 1812

| | Draught (ft-ins) | | Freeboard (ft-ins) | Ballast (tons) | | | Victualled |
	fwd	aft	midships port	iron	shingle	Water	for
Eurotas, 1813	15-5	18-1	7-6	200	0	87	CS
Araxes, 1814	16-1	17-3	8-1	160	0	96	CS
Tanais, 1816	16-3	18-3	7-5	160	40	122	FS

Like their hardwood half-sisters, they were fast but a little leewardly unless trimmed deep – as the captain of *Pactolus* summarised it, 'forereaches on oak ships, but don't weather them; weatherly with fir ships.' They mostly registered around 10kts close-hauled and nearly 13kts large (*Tanais* claimed 13-13½kts), but only if the sea was not high. They were stiffer than the *Leda*s, but some experimentation was necessary to get the ballast allocation right; nevertheless, they were generally easy sea-boats, although not at their best in heavy weather. Many sailed in company with other fir frigates of the *Scamander* class, and there does not seem to have been much between them, a lot depending on the relative trim. They did not go about quite as quickly as some captains felt a frigate should, and were certainly long in wearing, but the biggest complaint was relatively poor stowage – some captains could not get more than 3 months' provisions under hatches, and their iron tanks were absolutely essential to stow their full allowance of water.

Based on reports of: *Cydnus* (undated but *c*1815, 5 Jan 1816); *Eurotas* (undated but *c*1815); *Niger* (28 Aug 1815); *Araxes* (3 Aug 1814); *Maeander* (4 Dec 1815, 28 Oct 1816); *Pactolus* (21 Sep 1815, 6 Aug 1818); *Tanais* (29 May 1816); *Tiber* (anonymous, undated but signed J R Dacres, so from context must be *Tiber* after Jul 1814, 13 Oct 1818).

Seringapatam class, 38 guns, 1813

| | Draught (ft-ins) | | Freeboard (ft-ins) | Ballast (tons) | | | Victualled |
	fwd	aft	midships port	iron	shingle	Water	for
Seringapatam, 1821	17-2	18-6	7-9	100	0	118	CS
Seringapatam, 1822	17-4	18-0	8-2	60	0	122	FS
Druid, 1826	16-8	18-2	7-9	85	0	94	CS

Controversial ships that went through a number of modifications and may never have been entirely satisfactory. The name ship was somewhat disappointing in terms of speed, until the ballast was reduced, trim altered, and spar plan increased when she logged 10kts close-hauled and 12kts free; she also needed additional false keel before she was deemed weatherly. In other respects she was a good cruiser: an easy sea-boat, handled well, and stowed 6 months' provisions under hatches.

The oak-built *Druid* was less stiff, and her stability was to become a matter of concern, since the angle of heel would make fighting the guns difficult in action. Presumably because she could not carry sail her recorded speeds are slightly lower. However the biggest problem was the lack of stowage because of the reduced depth in hold, now down to a mere 14 weeks' under hatches. The teak *Madagascar* also required much experimentation before she was satisfactory, including shipping 30 tons more ballast and lightening the after rigging, although she still pitched heavily. All the early ships were considered best going to windward, and poor right before the wind, but in successive reports *Madagascar* logged 14kts and 13.6kts with the wind free.

Stag, first of the broadened and deepened ships, had no stability problems (she heeled 5 and 6 degrees where *Madagascar* had inclined 8½ and 9½ degrees) and stowed her provisions better, but she also carried a heavier armament of 46cwt 24pdrs. Her best recorded speeds were 8.6kts close-hauled and 11kts large, but this was very deep and the captain felt she would sail better with 90 rather than the 108 tons of ballast currently carried. She was still reckoned very weatherly, like the earlier modified ships.

Based on reports of: *Seringapatam* (30 Dec 1821, 5 Feb 1824 and 2 Dec 1829); *Druid* (letters of 15 Jul 1826, 1 & 12 Dec 1829, report of 5 Oct 1829); *Madagascar* (24 Jun 1823, 1 Dec 1831, 17 Jan 1835); *Stag* (16 Dec 1835).

Blonde class, 38 guns, 1816

| | Draught (ft-ins) | | Freeboard (ft-ins) | Ballast (tons) | | | Victualled |
	fwd	aft	midships port	iron	shingle	Water	for
Oct 1822	17-8	18-2	7-11	110	0	142	FS
Jun 1833	17-0	17-2	8-4	110	0	125	CS

'On all occasions on a wind she has considerably beaten every ship we have tried with, either by forereaching and tacking, or on a point of bearing by keeping a close luff,' reported her first captain. She was, therefore, a very weatherly ship ('her weatherly qualities considering her light draught of water are remarkable') but also fast off the wind, having logged 12½ and 13kts. At first an uneasy ship in both pitching and rolling, but somewhat ameliorated by raking her masts. She was also reckoned somewhat crank, and despite their nominal height, the lee ports were low when close-hauled in a stiff breeze. In general she was better in lighter conditions, but handled well and stowed 5 months' provisions under hatches.

Based on reports of 13 Feb 1831, Jun 1833, 1 Jan 1835 and 1 Jan 1836.

TABLE 11/5:
Sailing qualities of British large frigates

Rasée 64-gun ships, 1794

| | Draught (ft-ins) | | Freeboard (ft-ins) | Ballast (tons) | | | Victualled |
	fwd	aft	midships port	iron	shingle	Water	for
Indefatigable, 1798	18-3	19-8	7-5	104	0	84	CS
Anson, 1794	16-11	18-11	7-11	80	140	80	CS
Anson, 1799	19-7	20-4	6-10	137	180	106	CS
Magananime, 1795	16-10	19-0	7-6	120	172	121	CS

There are no formal reports on these ships as *rasées*, but it is known that they were over-stiff as converted and needed a larger spar plan. Only one report survives for the ships as 64s: this, for *Magnanime*, is damaged, but shows the ship to be generally weatherly, to wear and stay 'as well as most ships in general', and to be 'rather weatherly'; she had logged 9kts close-hauled, 11½kts with the wind free and 10½kts before the wind. By comparison, one Dimensions Book quotes speeds for the ship as a *rasée* of 10kts close-hauled and 10½kts large; the same list gives 9kts on a wind, 12kts free and 12½kts with the wind aft for the *Indefatigable*.

Based on report of 9 Jun 1782 on *Magnanime*, and speeds quoted in Adm 180/24.

Endymion class, 40 guns, 1795

	Draught (ft-ins)		Freeboard (ft-ins)	Ballast (tons)			Victualled
	fwd	aft	midships port	iron	shingle	Water	for
Jun 1797	16-0	18-8	7-2	120	26	124	CS
Jul 1813	17-10	18-11	7-1	120	0	115	CS

Since no vessel could be superior on all points of sailing and every variation of wind and water, the designation 'fastest ship in the Navy' is, strictly, meaningless; but if the accolade had to be awarded to one ship, it would certainly go to *Endymion*. Not only did this ship register the highest speed in any of the reports of the period – 14.4kts large – but was widely regarded as the benchmark for frigate performance for half a century. The above speed was recorded with the ship reduced to 18pdrs, but even with her 24pdrs restored she logged 13.6kts, and close-hauled she was capable of nearly 11kts in either condition. Furthermore, she was weatherly, very stiff but easy in her motions, and quick in tacking. She was long in wearing, especially in light winds, but apart from riding a little heavily to her anchors, this was the only criticism. She was sensitive to trim, however, sailing best when no more than 16ins by the stern, with ballast well winged up, and no unnecessary weights in her extremities.

When asked to compare their ship with others they had sailed with, the captains of the 1808-12 and 1813-15 commissions replied, with obvious satisfaction, 'not yet excelled' and 'has the advantage in all trials'. The ship remained a favourite in the fleet, and as late as 1842 was reckoned good for 13kts off the wind in a gale.

Based on reports of 8 May 1812, Sep 1815, 1 Jan 1836, 31 Dec 1842.

Cambrian class, 40 guns, 1795

	Draught (ft-ins)		Freeboard (ft-ins)	Ballast (tons)			Victualled
	fwd	aft	midships port	iron	shingle	Water	for
Feb 1802	18-0	20-0	7-5	108	125	128	CS
Oct 1820	17-5	19-5	8-4	116	0	151	FS
Dec 1823	22-7	23-3	6-1	197	0	289	FS

A fast and weatherly ship, best on a bowline when capable of 10kts close-hauled (13kts large), but only in smooth water; a seaway tended to make her more leewardly and a head sea impeded her sailing significantly. Surprisingly handy for such a big ship, she was stiff but an easy roller. Stowed her provisions well, but improved by the fitting of iron tanks.

Based on reports of 24 Apr 1802, and 6 Jul 1824.

Acasta class, 40 guns, 1795

	Draught (ft-ins)		Freeboard (ft-ins)	Ballast (tons)			Victualled
	fwd	aft	midships port	iron	shingle	Water	for
Oct 1797	17-5	19-3	8-1	120	160	134	CS
May 1811	18-1	19-10	7-6	140	60	140	FS

Not outstandingly fast, but relatively better close-hauled than large – 9kts compared to a maximum of 11½kts with the wind on the beam, and 11.4kts with the wind aft. However, she was very weatherly, a good easy sea-boat, and despite her size could wear and stay better than most frigates. She had a capacious hull, and could stow her provisions easily.

Based on report of 12 Aug 1815, and speeds in Adm 180/24.

Lavinia class, 44 guns, 1797

	Draught (ft-ins)		Freeboard (ft-ins)	Ballast (tons)			Victualled
	fwd	aft	midships port	iron	shingle	Water	for
Feb 1812	17-10	19-8	8-2	175	80	150	CS
	18-2	20-0	7-11				FS

Less controversial than Barrallier's battleship designs, the *Lavinia* was nevertheless something of a disappointment. She was initially very crank, and needed a substantial increase in iron ballast before she could put to sea. She never recorded more than 12kts large, although she was capable of nearly 10kts close-hauled, but this speed advantage was eroded by her being rather leewardly (she had a relatively shallow French-style hull). She also followed the practice of Barrallier's homeland in her light scantlings, and although well put together, her captain thought the ship 'rather slight' and weak; her tendency to heavy pitching further strained the upper works. On the plus side, she stowed nearly 6 months' provisions under hatches, handled reasonably well 'considering her immense size', and had something of an advantage over other ships in a seaway.

Based on report of 28 Feb 1812, and letters of 12 and 21 Jul 1806 in Adm 174/44.

Rasée 74-gun ships, 1813

	Draught (ft-ins)		Freeboard (ft-ins)	Ballast (tons)			Victualled
	fwd	aft	midships port	iron	shingle	Water	for
Majestic as 74	21-0	23-9	5-10	110	312	?	CS
Majestic, 1815	20-4	23-0	6-5	150	0	230	CS
Saturn, 1813	21-0	22-5	5-3	136	0	199	FS
Goliath, 1814	21-2	23-8	5-8	110	0	220	FS (6m)

Goliath and *Saturn*, which had been sisters, were very similar in performance: 9½ – 10kts close-hauled and 11-12kts large, but they needed strong winds to reach these speeds. They handled well, and were generally weatherly; they were stiff when deep, but somewhat tender when the upper tier of water was expended and more leewardly as well. They were good sea-boats, although deep pitchers, and they did not carry their lee ports as well as purpose-built frigates.

Majestic, of the slightly larger *Canada* class, was perhaps a few fathoms faster, although this might be attributed to Captain Hayes's notable skill as a ship-handler. However, Hayes's successor thought her speed could be improved by a conventional set of masts and yards. She was definitely an excellent heavy-weather ship, and carried her ports higher than her fellow *rasées*, but in conditions when any of them might have caught a big frigate, they could have faced difficulties fighting their guns – especially the lee battery.

Based on reports of: *Goliath* (Oct 1814); *Saturn* (18 Apr 1815); *Majestic* (24 Jun 1815) and letters from Hayes of 7 Jun 1813, 25 Oct 1813 and 18 Dec 1813.

Modified *Endymion* class, 40 guns, 1813

	Draught (ft-ins) fwd	aft	Freeboard (ft-ins) midships port	Ballast (tons) iron	shingle	Water	Victualled for
Glasgow, 1814	16-6	16-8	7-9	180	0	120	CS
Glasgow, 1816	16-1	17-1	8-3	192	0	79	FS
Liverpool, 1818	16-7	18-10	7-5	126	0	130	FS
Severn, 1817	15-9	17-4	8-4	141	0	126	CS

They were generally found over-stiff, heavy rollers and leewardly when they first went into service, but additions to the false keel and gripe, combined with reduced and restowed ballast cured the worst of their shortcomings. They were never very weatherly but were fast – 9.6-10.4kts close-hauled and up to 13kts large. Their handling also found few admirers at first, but once properly ballasted they steered and stayed well, although they were long in wearing like most large ships. They were better fair-weather performers than most British frigates, and could reach 12kts off the wind without being pressed. Their stowage received mixed reviews, probably because while the bread- and spirit rooms were small, the after hold was large: by the early post-war years most captains found they could stow 5 months' easily and 6 months' provisions by taking trouble.

Because the Royal Navy had so few 24pdr frigates and pursued a policy of preserving oak ships, this fir-built class saw a lot of service post-war, the *Glasgow* being especially well thought-of.

Based on reports of: *Forth* (29 Jun 1816); *Severn* (8 Jun 1823, as stationary guardship only); *Liffey* (29 Aug 1815, Oct 1821); *Glasgow* (26 Aug 1815, 1 Jul 1816, 1 Jan 1819, 27 Sep 1824, 8 Sep 1828); *Liverpool* (1 Jan 1815, 31 Mar 1819).

Leander and Newcastle, 50 guns, 1813

	Draught (ft-ins) fwd	aft	Freeboard (ft-ins) midships port	Ballast (tons) iron	shingle	Water	Victualled for
Leander, 1814	19-1	19-8	8-1	260	0	250	FS
Newcastle, 1814	18-8	19-11	8-1	250	0	246	CS
Newcastle, 1819	18-3	19-0	8-8	180	0	182	FS

Although not sister-ships, they were designed to the same specification and form an interesting comparison; the fact that there is so little to chose between them may be seen as a proof of the fatuity of concentrating design on hull forms, or simply as a demonstration that different approaches can produce similar results.

Both were outstandingly fast: *Newcastle* logged the greater speeds, by about half a knot – 13kts close-hauled under double-reefed topsails and 14kts large – but when operating together in 1814 *Leander* claimed to have had the advantage 'very much'; this may have been because she was less leewardly than *Newcastle*, although neither was particularly good in this regard by British standards. They were excellent heavy-weather ships (they could still manage 9kts in a stiff gale with a big sea), and once some fine-tuning of the ballast stowage and trim had eased their initially heavy rolling and pitching, they did not heel much to their canvas, so could fight their lee battery in any conditions. In lighter weather, they were relatively poorer in both sailing and manoeuvring, but for their size they generally handled well. With such large hulls, they had no difficulty stowing their provisions.

Base on reports of: *Leander* (31 Dec 1814, 24 Jul 1819, 31 Dec 1822, letter of 6 Mar 1820); *Newcastle* (19 Sep 1815, 4 Sep 1817, 17 Jan 1822).

Akbar, 50 guns, purchased 1806

	Draught (ft-ins) fwd	aft	Freeboard (ft-ins) midships port	Ballast (tons) iron	shingle	Water	Victualled for
Dec 1816	19-6	20-0	8-4	348	0	230	FS
Dec 1816	19-0	19-6	8-10				CS

An interesting contrast with a real frigate, not only in the prodigious capacity of the hull (as seen in the ballast and water allocations), but also in the poor performance under sail. In a strong blow the ship could manage 7kts close-hauled, perhaps 9kts before the wind, and only about 10½kts on her best point of sailing, with the wind 2 points abaft the beam. She was also leewardly and unhandy, but these shortcomings were minimal compared to her quick and violent motions in a seaway – she rolled out all her topmasts on a voyage to Bermuda in 1815, and Rear-Admiral Griffith confessed that it was 'impossible to describe her labouring'. Unfortunately, the iron water tanks made it difficult to radically reorganise the stowage of the hold, and the ship was reduced to the masts and spars of a 38-gun ship. The Navy Board, which recommended her conversion to a storeship in 1813, must have felt vindicated.

Based on report of 20 Dec 1816 and letter of 13 Jan 1816.

TABLE 11/6:
Sailing qualities of captured 18pdr frigates

Information on prize ships is sparse. Few ships have more than one report, and most none at all, indicating that in a period of general satisfaction with British frigate design, no special effort was made to analyse the characteristics of captured ships. French frigates, for which there are a representative selection of reports extant, have been treated in the design groups to which they belong, revealing broad similarities between them, but also the subtly different emphases between British and French cruisers.

Ex-American ships

	Draught (ft-ins) fwd	aft	Freeboard (ft-ins) midships port	Ballast (tons) iron	shingle	Water	Victualled for
Essex, 1815	15-6	18-6	?	100	143	130	CS
Chesapeake, 1815	19-3	21-0	8-5				FS
Chesapeake, 1815	18-6	20-9	9-6	149	80	150	CS

The only trial with *Essex* was the 4-month voyage to Britain from Chile where she was captured, but she impressed her captors as a strong and capacious ship, generally an easy sea-boat (although a heavy pitcher), which handled well. However, she was no flyer, logging no more than 8.4kts close-hauled and 11.4kts large, but she was weatherly and 'equal to the *Phoebe* in her present state'.

The report on the *Chesapeake*, which served for nearly a year as an RN cruiser, was more critical. Because the main magazine was aft, stowage of provisions was a problem, less than 4 months' fitting under hatches. She was stiff, handled well and was generally a good sea-boat, except that the excessive overhang of the stern caused the sea to strike very heavily under the counter; the captain felt the overhang would cause the ship to be damaged if taken aback. She was strongly constructed – indeed her captain thought her 'over-built' – but was very weatherly. She was better to windward than the fir-built *Niger*, but the latter ship could outrun *Chesapeake* off the wind or before it; indeed her recorded speeds are not very impressive at 9kts close-hauled and 11kts large. The report concluded with the captain's opinion that the ship was not a suitable model for copying (perhaps the real reason for commissioning the ship at the end of the war).

Based on reports of: *Essex* (17 Dec 1814); *Chesapeake* (20 Sep 1815).

Ex-Danish ships

	Draught (ft-ins) fwd	aft	Freeboard (ft-ins) midships port	Ballast (tons) iron	shingle	Water	Victualled for
Perlen, 1809	17-2	16-10	7-8	110	43	98	CS
Rota, 1809	16-8	16-8	6-3	110	10	94	CS
Rota, 1815	18-8	17-6	6-8	134	0	78	CS
Nyaden, 1809	16-10	17-0	6-0	137	10	75	CS
Venus, 1813	17-0	16-9	7-4	91	70	82	CS

Some of the two-deckers taken at Copenhagen in 1807 greatly impressed their captors (especially the *Christian VII*), but the frigates were not so highly prized. Some did not cruise at all under the British flag, while others were quickly consigned to subsidiary duties like trooping. Those that did cruise were generally found to be fast but leewardly, having shallow French-style hulls – *Iris* managed 10.6kts close-hauled and 13kts free, and *Rota* a little less. Curiously, they all either trimmed on an even keel, which was common in French ships, or by the head, which was unusual in any navy; and further experience tended to make captains increase the draught forward, because ships like *Rota* were slack in steering and staying unless so trimmed. In general, their seakeeping was good, and with the above proviso they handled well.

The biggest overall shortcoming was a difficulty in stowing British allowances of victuals and water, presumably because they were not designed for oceanic cruising. Their gunports were also rather low by British standards, although *Venus* when commissioned with main-deck 12pdrs and then 32pdr carronades in 1814-15, carried her battery better than most.

Based on reports of: *Freya* (as troopship 12 Nov 1814); *Venus* (14 Jun 1813, and 14 Feb 1815); *Iris* (17 Dec 1814); *Rota* (1 Jan 1812, and 26 Aug 1815).

The Danish *Iris*, 36 guns, as taken off in October 1809. Designed by Stibolt and launched at Copenhagen in 1796, she was generally similar to French frigates in hull form and proportions. She was particularly fine-lined forward and aft, as is graphically demonstrated in the profile by the absence of any internal works in the fore peak or abaft the after powder room. She was fast but leewardly and could never stow more than 4 months' provisions, when she carried her midships ports 6ft 0ins from the water.
National Maritime Museum Dr7101

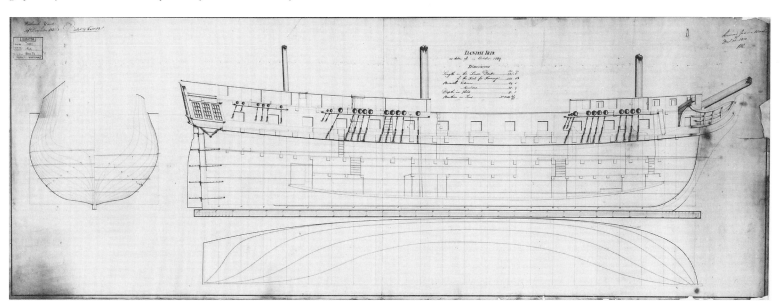

Ex-French ships

	Draught (ft-ins) fwd	aft	Freeboard (ft-ins) midships port	Ballast (tons) iron	shingle	Water	Victualled for
Milan, 1806	17-9	18-9	6-8	120	0	99	FS
Alceste, 1807	16-10	17-10	7-4	110	0	102	CS
Président, 1808	16-8	18-0	6-9	120	0	110	CS
Belle Poule, 1808	17-6	19-0	6-10	126	0	93	FS
Gloire, 1808	16-8	17-5	7-0	90	41	83	CS
Rhin, 1809	17-5	17-9	7-8	90	60	114	CS
Pomone, 1812	17-4	18-2	6-10	110	37	97	FS
Junon, 1812	17-8	18-10	6-5	90	67	69	FS
Madagascar, 1813	17-4	18-5	6-11	90	15	73	CS
Topaze, 1818	17-3	17-10	6-7	104	0	116 in tanks	FS

French frigates of this period may be broadly divided into those built to the basic Sané specification, and those of larger and sharper model designed by Forfait and his disciples.

Of those which reports survive, the following fall into the first group: *Surveillante, Voluntaire, Belle Poule, Rhin, Weser, Trave, Modeste* and *Immortalité* to Sané draughts, and *Niemen, Alceste* and *Armide* to similar designs by Rolland. As would be expected of ships built in large numbers, they were generally satisfactory. They were good, easy sea-boats, but stiff enough under canvas, although *Surveillante* was a very heavy roller until the captain winged up the iron ballast. Most logged 9-9½kts close-hauled, but ships like *Surveillante, Belle Poule, Terpsichore* and *Dunira* were said to be significantly better off the wind; the best recorded speeds were 12.6kts for *Rhin*, 13kts for *Armide* and 13½kts for *Dunira* (as captured, so in French trim). Apart from *Surveillante*'s,

no report was very enthusiastic about their abilities to windward: for example, in response to the 'weatherly or leewardly?' question, *Nieman*'s captain said 'equal', but *Armide, Alceste* (except in strong winds), and *Dunira* were thought decidedly leewardly. Their handling was generally average for big frigates, being especially long in wearing, but *Voluntaire* was 'slack in stays and long in wearing', *Armide* manoeuvred 'indifferently', and *Niemen* 'wears and stays like all French ships'; *Surveillante* carried lee helm if trimmed more than 12ins by the stern. Not all reports were on the revised form, so few were asked about the structural strength of the ships, but only *Terpsichore* was specifically found to be 'weak built'. On the other hand, none claimed to stow more than 4 months' provisions under hatches; *Rhin* could only manage this 'with difficulty' and *Belle Poule* could not fit in thirty-six bags of bread.

Reports on the second group comprise Forfait's *Clorinde, Président, Alcmene* and *Furieuse*, Pestel's *Junon*, and Gauthier's *Aurora*. Forfait's ships might be characterised as good heavy weather ships, being leewardly and slack in stays in lighter conditions. They were regarded as very stiff and carried their canvas well, but were subject to deep if easy rolling; *Président*'s counter was said to fall 'into the sea with great violence when blowing hard', but most were good sea-boats. They may have been sensitive to weights at the extremities, because *Furieuse* had two main-deck 18pdrs removed, *Alcmene* had two replaced by 32pdr carronades, while *Président* had four similarly substituted. In terms of speed, they recorded 9.4-9.6kts close-hauled and up to 13kts large; all were reckoned most superior with a quartering wind, although they also sailed well downwind. Stowage was much the same as the Sané ships; none complained of low gunport freeboard, but *Furieuse*'s ports were thought too small, allowing only 9 degrees elevation.

Pestel's *Junon* was similar in liking stronger conditions, but was considered better on a bowline, being capable of nearly 10kts and making less leeway. Her main drawback was very poor capacity, stowing only 14 weeks' provisions and 85 tons of water for Foreign Service. Gauthier's *Aurora* was also broadly comparable in speed and other qualities with the Forfait ships, being 'rather leewardly in light winds' and slack in wearing and staying; she was a heavy

Post-war draught of the ex-French *Rhin*, with pencil alterations for a circular stern, dated Plymouth Yard 1 March 1817. Typical of the numerous frigates built to a near-standard Sané design (73 out of 137 French 18pdr frigates), the ship was laid down at Toulon in 1801 and captured in July 1804 by the *Mars*, 74 when trying to evade the Rochefort blockading squadron. The sailing qualities of these ships were good, but not outstanding: *Rhin* was, after all, overtaken by a two-decker, although there were mitigating circumstances – she was probably

foul after five months at sea, the weather conditions were rough, and *Mars* was a Large Class 74, of better than average performance, with a well trained crew. Ships built at Toulon enjoyed a better reputation for durability, because of the availability of Adriatic oak, than those built on the Atlantic coast, but *Rhin* proved very costly to maintain in British service.
National Maritime Museum Dr7056

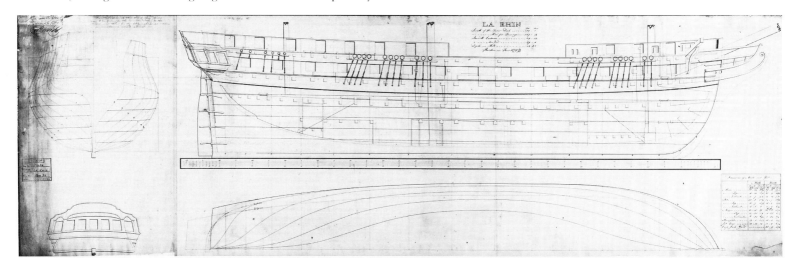

pitcher, but otherwise an easy sea-boat. There is also considerable correspondence about the leewardliness and lee helm of Pestel's *Madagascar*, which led to the mizzen being moved 3ft 6in aft and gripe added to the forefoot, although the captain continued to complain of her sailing qualities.

Based on reports of: *Clorinde* (5 Dec 1812, and 13 Jul 1816); *Surveillante* (30 Sep 1806); *Voluntaire* (27 Oct 1813); *Belle Poule* (undated but probably post-1814 as a troopship); *Rhin* (Aug 1815); *Armide* (1 Jan 1812, and undated 1815); *Alceste* (18 Sep 1815, ?as troopship); *Président* (1 Jan 1814); *Brune* (26 Feb 1812,

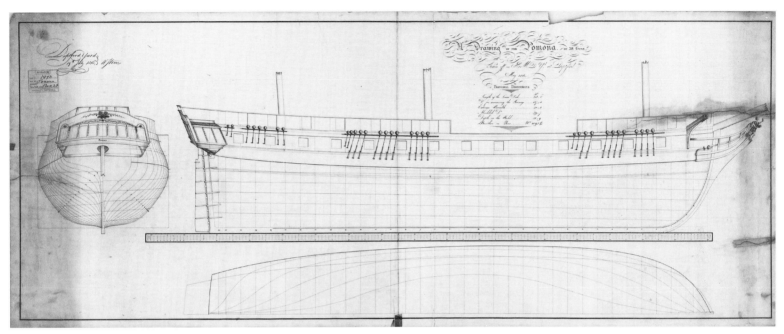

Sheer draught of the *Pomone* (called *Pomona* in the rubric), dated Deptford 19 July 1816. As the *Astrée*, this ship was one of a pair of frigates laid down at Genoa in 1803, the first to be built outside metropolitan France by the new Napoleonic Empire. With the exception of two Pestel-designed ships, all the frigates built for the navy outside France were to the most popular Sané draught, virtually *the* standard French frigate. French frigate-building was later extended to the Low Countries and the northern Adriatic, output being as follows: Genoa six (1803-12), Antwerp six (1806-12), Flushing one (captured by the British while fitting out, 1809), Rotterdam seven (1809-13), Amsterdam five (1810-13), Venice two (1811-13), and Trieste one (1813).
National Maritime Museum Dr1973

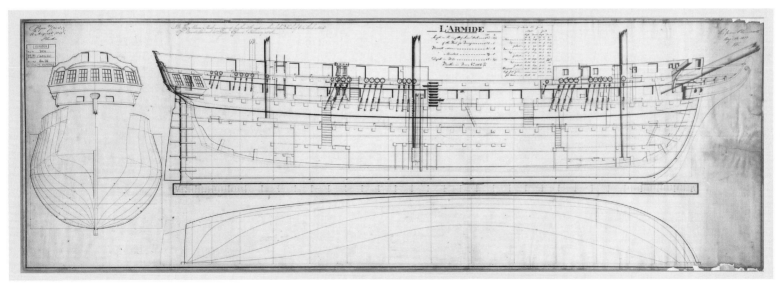

Designed by Pierre Rolland, *Armide* was the prototype of fourteen frigates built at the Atlantic ports of Rochefort, Bordeaux, Bayonne and Cherbourg between 1802 and 1813. *Armide* herself was launched at Rochefort in 1804 and was one of four frigates captured by the blockading squadron in September 1806. Slightly larger, but generally similar in form to Sané's frigates, *Armide* was also comparable in performance, although a touch inferior in terms of speed. She was reckoned decidedly leewardly, handled 'indifferently', and had never logged more than 11.2kts with the wind on the quarter and 9kts close-hauled. Like most French frigates she trimmed best on an even keel, drawing 18ft fore and aft when stored for Channel Service, in which condition midships gunport freeboard was 6ft 8in. This draught, as taken off at Plymouth, 11 August 1810, notes that the mizzen was moved aft and 6ins more false keel added in February 1813.
National Maritime Museum Dr7074

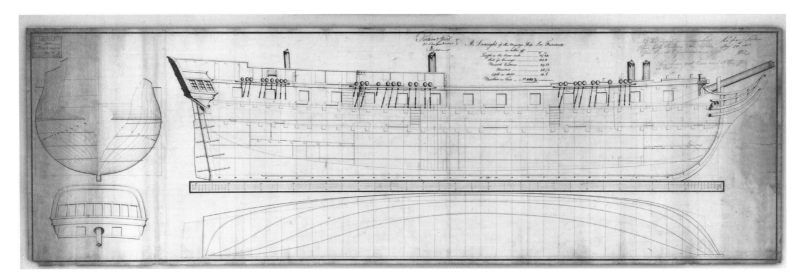

Furieuse, as taken off at Portsmouth, 21 August 1811, and not substantially altered since capture. An alternative tradition to the Sané form was that of Pierre-Alexandre-Laurent Forfait whose usual hull featured a very sharp V-shaped midsection (see *Alcmene* in Chapter 8). Forfait was responsible for a number of radical ideas, including the strange class of *frégate-bombardes* described in Chapter 12 with reference to the *Immortalité*. *Furieuse* was intended to be one

of these but was lengthened during construction, although retaining the more rounded hull form of the *bombardes*. The ship was not as fast as the usual Forfait design, but just as tricky: the fore mast required moving to improve the balance of the rig. The ship retains the small poop cabin or *dunette* found in some French frigates.
National Maritime Museum Dr7064

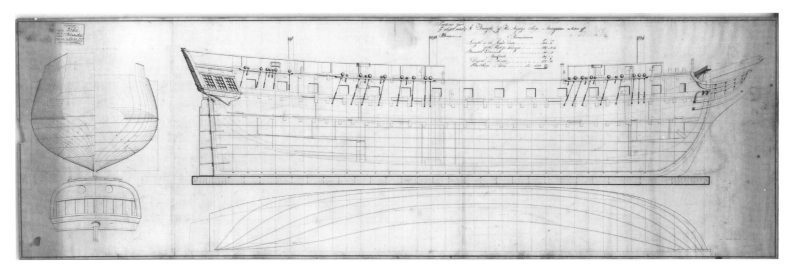

Representative of eight frigates designed by François Pestel (all constructed at St Malo, except one at Genoa), *Madagascar* was the last of the class and launched as the *Néréide* in 1809. They were smaller than Forfait's ships but exhibited a generally similar midship section, although with slight hollow in the garboards. After her capture in 1811, *Madagascar* proved a serious trial to her captain, who

complained regularly of her leewardliness and slack helm; remedies included moving the mizzen aft and adding gripe to the forefoot, but the ship was never entirely satisfactory. This draught is as taken off at Portsmouth Yard, 9 September 1813, but the ship is substantially as captured.
National Maritime Museum Dr2180

and 10 Sep 1815, both as troopship); *Alcmene* (1 Jan 1815, and 2 Dec 1815); *Niemen* (undated 1815); *Furieuse* (1 Dec 1812, and 28 Aug 1815); *Junon* (7 Aug 1816); *Madagascar* (correspondence in Adm 106/2261, 16 Sep 1813; Adm 106/2263, 11 Apr 1814); *Weser* (1 Jan 1815, and 11 Aug 1816, both as troopship); *Trave* (22 Apr 1814, and 21 Aug 1816, both as troopship); *Modeste* (as *Terpsichore* 27 Jun 1814); *Immortalité* (as *Dunira* 1 Sep 1814); *Aurora* (1 Jan 1825).

Ex-Spanish ships

	Draught (ft-ins) fwd	aft	Freeboard (ft-ins) midships port	Ballast (tons) iron	shingle	Water	Victualled for
Hamadryad, 1810	16-0	16-7	6-7	110	13	67	FS
Hamadryad, 1814	16-6	17-3	6-3	90	20	90	CS

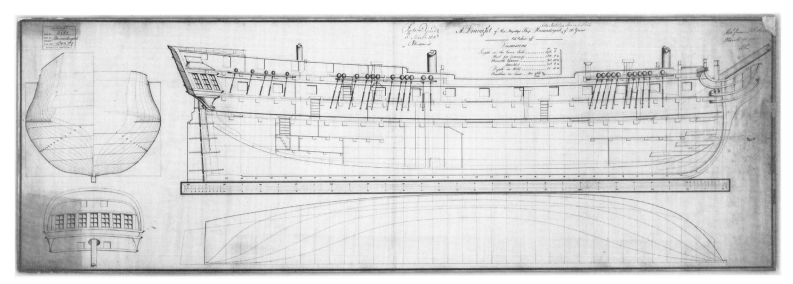

Draught of the ex-Spanish *Hamadryad*, as taken off at Portsmouth, 5 March 1810. Built in Havana in 1778, the frigate was large for her day and for some years following her capture in 1804 was rated as a 38; but she was not really big enough for the armament and in 1810 she was reduced to a 36. The hull form and proportions were very much in the French style with all the qualities, good and bad, that followed. She was reasonably fast but leewardly, very wet, and could not stow a full 6-month allocation of stores. However, unlike French ships, she was strongly built, living up to the reputation of Havana-built warships for longevity – as late as 1814 she exhibited no signs of weakness and was not broken up until after the end of the war. One curious feature – again of French inspiration – is the small cabin on the quarterdeck; these were usually removed as soon as convenient by the British and it is unusual to see it retained so long. *National Maritime Museum Dr2181*

Hamadryad is the only ex-Spanish frigate of this era for which full reports survive. In general Spanish ships did not enjoy a high reputation for their sailing qualities, and this ship was not outstanding. She logged 9.4kts close-hauled and 12.4kts large, but was reckoned very leewardly – 'most ships beat us by the wind by weathering upon us', but the ship was better going free. She handled well, and was an easy ship in a seaway, but being low she was very wet, close-hauled or large. The hull was of small capacity and could not stow 6 months' provisions, barely 4 months' going under hatches, but she was very stiff and needed no salt water in the ground tier even when most of the provisions were expended. Although very old by 1814, she was still reckoned a strong ship.

Based on reports of: *Hamadryad* (1 Jan 1814, and 22 Feb 1815). There is also a report on the *Amphitrite* (later the *Blanche*), but only covers the voyage to Britain after capture, when the frigate was towing 'a heavy vessel' and in convoy. All that can be gleaned is that the ship had no positive vices, and seemed to sail well on all points.

TABLE 11/7: Sailing qualities of captured large frigates

Pomone, 40 guns, 1794

	Draught (ft-ins)		Freeboard (ft-ins) midships port	Ballast (tons)		Water	Victualled for
	fwd	aft		iron	shingle		
Oct 1802	17-5	17-11	6-5	100	30	103	CS

A fast, stiff and weatherly ship, especially in strong conditions. Close-hauled with all sail to togallants set, she was capable of 10kts and even 6-7kts in a strong blow; off the wind she could manage 12kts in light conditions and 13kts in a gale. Captain Gower had landed 100 tons of shingle, but he felt she might give up some more because she always sailed better after about three weeks at sea had lightened her draught. Her motions were deep but easy, and she stayed and wore 'remarkably well but needs a great deal of sail set at all times'. She stowed 4 months' provisions with 123 tons of water.

Based on report of 25 Oct 1802, and speeds quoted in Adm 180/24.

Egyptienne, 44 guns, 1801

	Draught (ft-ins)		Freeboard (ft-ins) midships port	Ballast (tons)		Water	Victualled for
	fwd	aft		iron	shingle		
Mar 1807	20-0	20-0	8-0	196	0	160	CS

A remarkable vessel, sister of the *Forte* which was the largest frigate in the world when launched in 1795. She was very fast and weatherly, making 10kts close-hauled in smooth water, and between 13 and 14kts large. She handled well, except in relatively light winds, and although a deep roller was easy in her motions. Her captain felt she sailed well on all points but was particularly good on a wind, and when in trim and with clean copper was superior to most ships both fore-reaching and gathering to windward. With such a large hull, there were no difficulties with stowage.

At one time the Admiralty showed a lot of interest in the ship, but her reputation was destroyed by her weak construction and the consequent high costs of keeping her in service; otherwise she might have provided a prototype for the frigates built to match the American spar-deckers in 1812.

Based on report of 21 Mar 1807, and speeds quoted in Adm 180/24.

Frigates in Action

FRIGATES WERE the sailing navy's maids-of-all-work. Like the cruisers which were their steam-era descendants, their multifarious tasks ranged from fleet scouting to trade protection, but whereas the Victorians had cruisers designed for each of these specific roles, in earlier times the frigate was expected to fulfil most of the cruising functions within a single hull. This meant that the design requirements for a frigate were in many ways more demanding than those for a line of battle ship, which were dominated by the need to produce a good steady gun platform; structural strength was a servant of this cause, but sailing qualities were inevitably a secondary consideration. Of course, all sailing ship design was a compromise, but battleships allowed their naval architects especially small scope for ingenuity. Indeed, radical solutions were usually misconceived, as Symonds proved with his sharp V-formed hulls of the 1830s: these produced fast ships but ones whose motions were so violent they were quoted as cautionary examples in naval architectural textbooks for the rest of the century.

Frigates, on the other hand, needed speed, seakeeping, manoeuvrability, strength, firepower and capacity (for range), and all this had to be achieved within modest dimensions, in order that sufficient numbers could be built and manned. No one quality could claim obvious pre-eminence, nor could all be accorded equal priority, so the design emphases of frigates varied more than those of battleships. This gives frigate design a particular interest, but also makes it historically significant, because the ways in which sailing cruisers were optimised reflect the tasks they were expected to undertake, and the strategic priorities of the governments that funded them.

During the course of the French Revolutionary and Napoleonic Wars, the design priorities of British frigates changed subtly, and by analysing the way in which they were employed it is possible to detect alterations and extensions in their traditional roles that suggest why. Furthermore, the experience of the war was to prove that certain characteristics were more important than others, and not unnaturally these lessons tended to dominate the newer designs. This chapter

looks at the relationship between ships and roles, primarily how employment determined design, but also how the characteristics of the newer designs in turn affected what could be achieved.

I. The Roles of the Frigate

Frigates could trace their ancestry through two separate lines: to the small tenders that waited on seventeenth-century fleets for a multitude of ancillary duties; and to rather larger but still minor cruising ships designed principally to protect trade. These two strands came together in the middle of the eighteenth century in the design of the so-called 'true frigate', a vessel which was superior to its predecessors in both roles. There is a certain historical logic, therefore, in adopting the traditional dichotomy between fleet and independent operations.

A. Fleet Duties

Supporting the battlefleet was the oldest of the frigate's functions, but it was always a multi-faceted duty, and as the ships became larger and more capable, their roles also became more numerous and more demanding. The boundaries of some of these activities were not always clear, and occasionally overlapped, but what they all have in common is the operation of frigates as part of a larger, mixed force under the overall command of a senior officer.

1. Strategic reconnaissance

At the centre of the Navy's decision-making machinery was the Admiralty in London, with responsibility delegated to main-fleet commanders, but for both their sensors were individual ships across the oceans of the world. As in any modern war, intelligence was the prerequisite to action and every naval officer understood the importance of passing on information about ship movements and sightings. Where the enemy's main forces were concerned, this process could not be trusted to serendipity, so a formal system of watching the important naval bases was arranged. This was, of course, part of the process of blockade, but insufficient heavy units were available to deter every French squadron from putting to sea, so in practice they were often only being observed. At times most types of ship formed part of the intelligence network, but those specifically assigned to such duties were predominantly frigates, which were capacious enough for long-endurance all-weather cruising and sufficiently powerful to fear nothing smaller than a ship of the line, which they could in most circumstances safely outsail.

In the following analysis of the workings of strategic reconnaissance, the Trafalgar campaign of 1805 has been taken as the prime example, because it was very complex, because it offers many lessons about good and bad cruiser work, and because its detailed study

Table 12/1: Numbers of frigates in sea service, and in Ordinary or repairing

Year	12pdr ships		18pdr ships	
	SS	O/R	SS	O/R
1793	21	23	11	6
1795	49	1	36	0
1797	50	9	45	2
1799	45	13	46	4
1801	43	1	68	1
1804	22	11	57	7
1808	35	8	76	15
1810	32	3	96	8
1812	20	5	98	9
1814	11	0	103	11

The figures are drawn from the annual abstracts in James's *Naval History* and give serviceable ships in commission (first column) and those in Ordinary or under repair (second column) at the beginning of each year. Harbour service vessels and hulks are excluded.

has made the outlines familiar.[1]

In order to establish an intelligence picture, the first problem was the positioning of the ships. For the British the blockaded ports were obvious starting points, but once the enemy was at sea a degree of anticipation was required. Alternatives, however, were not infinite, because unlike modern mechanically propelled shipping which, assuming there is sufficient water, can proceed by the most direct route, sailing ships were limited by wind and tide. Furthermore, navigation was not precise, even in navies widely equipped with chronometers, and much more approximate in the merchant service. This meant that there were well-understood trade routes, often making as many landfalls as possible for safety, while certain straits and channels formed predictable pinch-points through which all ships bound for a particular destination were likely to transit (it was in one of these that Villeneuve captured the whole of a small British West India convoy in June 1805). In commerce warfare these were fertile hunting grounds for predators, but also potentially dangerous because they were likely to be well patrolled.

Similar considerations applied to fleets and squadrons. The usual way from Europe to the West Indies was via Madeira and the Canaries, so by the time Villeneuve first disappeared in April 1805 two frigates had already been dispatched in anticipation off Madeira to patrol a line southeast to northwest of the island where they were most likely to spot any approaching squadron. The cruising in pairs was common procedure, one ship to report the initial sighting and direction and the other to track the quarry. British flying squadrons being marshalled in response were

Map showing the contribution of frigates in the run-up to Trafalgar. The movements of the Franco-Spanish fleet is shown in solid black line; those of the British battlefleets in solid grey; and the operations of frigates and detached squadrons in dashed line.

Based on an original in Corbett's Campaign of Trafalgar digitally altered by Adrian Campbell-Burt

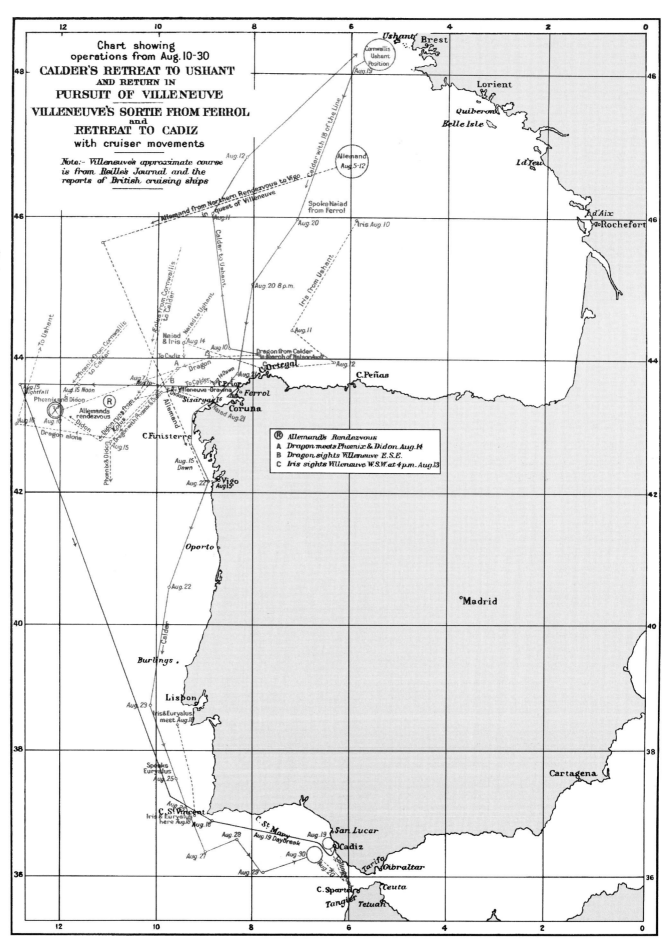

Chart showing
operations from Aug.10-30
CALDER'S RETREAT TO USHANT
AND RETURN IN
PURSUIT OF VILLENEUVE
VILLENEUVE'S SORTIE FROM FERROL
and
RETREAT TO CADIZ
with cruiser movements

Note:- Villeneuve's approximate course
is from Reille's Journal and the
reports of British cruising ships

Ⓡ Allemand's Rendezvous
A Dragon meets Phoenix & Didon Aug.14
B Dragon sights Villeneuve E.S.E.
C Iris sights Villeneuve W.S.W. at 4 p.m. Aug.13

instructed to call at Madeira, where they could expect information – even if negative – from the frigates on station.

Nelson himself, who believed Villeneuve's target was in the eastern Mediterranean, made a more elaborate disposition of his cruisers. He guessed that the French might try to slip past close in with the north African coast, so he sent three cruisers to patrol in the vicinity of an island off Tunisia, one of which was to report back; another alternative was for Villeneuve to make a landfall off the southern tip of Sardinia, so two more frigates were stationed off Toro, while Nelson's battlefleet held a central position between the two groups of cruisers. He then sent one frigate to find out if the French had slipped through the Straits of Bonifaccio between Corsica and Sardinia, another to Naples for news, and as a final resort one more to confirm that the French had not simply retired to Toulon. In all, eight ships were involved, six of which were frigates.

Later in the campaign standing cruiser lines were established, one from Cape Clear in the southwest of Ireland across the Channel approaches to Cape Finisterre, and another from Finisterre down to Cape St Vincent. In good weather a masthead lookout had an horizon of about 12 miles, and might spot a topgallant at 20, so these lines in no sense formed continuous chains – there were not enough ships for that – but were patrol sectors, ideally made up of fast-sailing frigates, that would know where to find the next in line to pass on intelligence. Between four and six were employed on the first station, and four more, under their own senior captain, on the latter. These were intended to sight marauding enemy squadrons before they got close enough to do much damage, but on a day-to-day basis were effectively disposed to defend trade and destroy individual commerce-raiders.

Apart from a calculation of the enemy's strategic goals, a commander might have recourse to ingrained navigational habits to gain some insight into the enemy's movements. When returning from the West Indies, for example, French fleets were inclined to run down the latitude of Cape Ortegal from about 500 miles out in the Atlantic. This prompted the British blockading squadrons to station a frigate far out to sea on this latitude so they would not be surprised by a superior force attacking from their rear. When so engaged, the *Loire*, one of Calder's frigates, discovered Missiessy's returning Rochefort squadron in May, and a similar understanding allowed Calder himself to intercept Villeneuve in July.

With a fleet itself in motion, detached cruisers had to have a method of re-establishing contact, and this was done through a series of pre-arranged rendezvous positions; these might be expressed in relation to a landmark, or possibly a patch of sea of given co-ordinates, but there was also a time dimension. No frigate was expected to back and fill indefinitely, and instructions were given a chronological limitation. To preserve an element of security, an admiral would number his rendezvous, and only the numbers would be used in dispatches that might fall into the hands of an enemy. The two prime requirements for suitable rendezvous points were: that they should be easy to find, which was why reference to a point of land was so helpful in reducing potential navigational error; and that it should be an area in which a waiting ship or squadron could linger, unchallenged by either bad weather or the activities of the enemy.

The orders issued by Napoleon (or his minister Decrès) to Allemand's Rochefort squadron failed on both counts. Intended to join up with Villeneuve's main Franco-Spanish fleet, Allemand was first instructed in August to wait off Finisterre in an area which was effectively the cruising ground of Sir Robert Calder's far superior fleet. Only an unlikely degree of luck saved Allemand from a fatal meeting, but he was spotted by a number of frigates, which were chased off (but not captured) by his own cruisers. His position being compromised, he felt compelled to move on to his secondary rendezvous 160 miles southwest of Ushant. This was dangerously close to the usual radius of the Brest blockading fleet's cruisers, and having seen a number of sails on the horizon, Allemand again judged it too risky to remain his allotted time. For his part, Villeneuve believed that, even if he could break out of Ferrol without being seen, he might not be able to find Allemand, given the vagueness of the chosen rendezvous. He therefore dispatched one of his smartest frigates, the *Didon*, to the second rendezvous in an attempt to bring Allemand to him, rather than vice-versa.

The attempt to make rendezvous orders cover all likely contingencies often led to elaborate 'if . . . then' propositions of a complexity that would delight a modern computer-programmer. This placed a great deal of emphasis on the strategic understanding, perception and initiative of frigate captains. The Trafalgar campaign abounds with examples of individual decision-making, for good or bad, but the cruise of the *Didon* is as good as any. The French frigate was not long at sea before she was sighted by the *Aeolus*, one of a number of frigates being sent south from Cornwallis's fleet off Brest in response to Calder's request for more cruisers to keep a tighter watch on Villeneuve. *Didon*'s captain, Milius, judged his mission more important than an engagement and turned away; after a short pursuit the *Aeolus*'s captain, Fitzroy, similarly decided his dispatches from Cornwallis to Calder, plus his information on the whereabouts of Allemand, should also take precedence. (After the war this was to prove controversial, Fitzroy being heavily criticised by the historian William James; but the Admiralty approved his priorities.) Milius, however, soon ran into another of Calder's

A fine watercolour portrait of the
Phoenix off Malta. Her capture of
the *Didon* in August 1805 played
a significant part in the Trafalgar
campaign by ensuring that
Villeneuve's dispatches never
reached Allemand's squadron.
She also deserves a major part of
the credit for contriving Sir
Richard Strachan's destruction of
Dumanoir's force that escaped
after Trafalgar. Although the
picture is dated 1819, *Phoenix* was
wrecked in 1816 so is presumably
drawn from memory; but it is
certainly a convincing
representation of the late-war
appearance of a British frigate.
National Maritime Museum 7989

reinforcements, the 36-gun *Phoenix*, which he chose not to run from. Much has been made of the fact that the British frigate was disguised as a sloop (*Phoenix* was no flyer, which may explain a disguise to tempt a faster ship to action), but with time running out Milius probably judged that if he was to make contact with Allemand he would have to fight his way past the British cruiser. He was mistaken: although *Phoenix* was a less powerful ship, and Milius fought a clever battle, he was beaten; Allemand never joined Villeneuve's fleet.

A *leitmotiv* of Corbett's masterly study of the Trafalgar campaign is the continuity of British strategic principles, which meant that naval officers possessed a deeply ingrained understanding of fundamental priorities. This allowed them a degree of confidence when acting on their own initiative, as was often required in the complex and large-scale series of operations of 1805. Villeneuve's retreat from Ferrol to Cadiz in August was tracked and reported almost entirely by frigates making chance meetings and their captains taking their own decisions. First on the scene was the *Iris*, which was soon joined by the *Naiad*, and once it was decided that Cadiz was definitely the destination of the Combined Fleet, the former sailed on to warn Collingwood's weak blockading squadron of the looming danger, while *Naiad* took the news back to the C-in-C, Cornwallis, off Brest. *Iris* then encountered the *Amazon*, a frigate sent ahead of Nelson's fleet for intel-

ligence; on hearing the news Parker of the *Amazon* proceeded first to Cork, where there were two vulnerable potential targets, a large East India convoy as well as a military expeditionary force intended for the capture of the Cape, and passing on his warning without even anchoring, pressed on to Ushant in case *Naiad* had not arrived.

Iris next ran into Henry Blackwood's famous *Euryalus*, an Irish station frigate sent to pass on the latest intelligence to Nelson. On assessing the situation, Blackwood took command and decided that the two frigates had to locate the Combined Fleet; while the faster shadowed it, the other would take the news northwards. Cape St Vincent was its one sure landfall, and here the two ships waited until they had definite intelligence of its approach. *Iris*, which had been such a conduit of information was herself then sent home with the report. Blackwood stayed in touch, although he had to work hard to avoid capture. In fact, throughout the voyage Villeneuve's own cruisers were wholly ineffectual in driving off their watchers, while on a number of occasions their poor scouting reinforced their admiral's nervousness by exaggerating the number of sails in sight.

The impressive willingness of British officers to think for themselves was obviously instilled from early in their career. When Villeneuve captured the West India convoy in June, its single schooner escort escaped, which left its commander in a quandary. A young lieutenant of less than three years standing, he was under orders to take his senior officer's dispatches home, but at the same time he realised that his sighting of the Combined Fleet was potentially vital information. He resolved his dilemma by the morally courageous decision to open the sealed dispatches, and finding they contained nothing critical, turned back to seek out Nelson.

Acting for the good of the service sometimes risked more than an individual career. In January 1805 Captain Patrick Campbell, bearing important news to his blockading squadron that Missiessy's Rochefort squadron was preparing for sea, so pressed his frigate, the *Doris*, that she was badly damaged aloft, and had to seek shelter; but in approaching the shore she then hit an uncharted rock, and was seriously holed. Some repairs were made, but a rising southwesterly gale, which would embay the blockading squadron and ensure Missiessy's escape, forced Campbell to one final effort, despite the fact that the ship was still making a lot of water. It was too much for the battered hull, the leaks re-opened, and eventually the ship had to be abandoned. For some officers at least, the strategic importance of intelligence would always outweigh the safety of any individual ship.

From the foregoing there is a strong impression that wherever Villeneuve, Allemand or Missiessy took their forces, there was usually a British cruiser in the offing to take note. It is impossible to escape the conclusion, therefore, that whatever their other qualities, the most important feature of frigates was their availability in numbers. Throughout the eighteenth (and even into the twentieth) century, this overriding requirement was to militate against the escalation in the size and cost of British cruisers. Individual incidents, however,

point to other characteristics that were valuable in frigates. They needed to be at least as powerful as their likely opponents: had the *Didon* met the 12pdr-armed *Iris* instead of the 18pdr *Phoenix*, Allemand may well have received Villeneuve's instructions. Equally, Blackwood could only keep in touch with the Combined Fleet because *Euryalus* was not out-sailed by French frigates.

2. Tactical reconnaissance

In Nelson's evocative phrase, frigates were 'the eyes of the fleet'. It was their job to find the enemy, to stay in contact, and to report to the admiral in sufficient detail to allow him to bring his fleet into action with the maximum tactical advantage. Important information included numbers and force of the enemy, formation and heading, as well as any hint of their intentions; the quality of their seamanship and gunnery was also significant. Such detail could only be gleaned by close observation over a period of time, and this is why frigates were preferred over other types for scouting. Smaller craft were too easily driven off or captured by the enemy's own outliers, while even a fast-sailing battleship sent on such a task might find itself beset by frigates and delayed long enough for an overwhelming number of enemy battleships to get into action.[2]

Frigates were the best combination of speed and gunpower, and if there were any choice British commanders seem to have preferred to use the most powerful on hand. In Howe's skirmishes with Villaret-Joyeuse's fleet before the Glorious First of June in 1794, it was the 18pdr-armed *Phaeton* and *Latona* which kept in touch with the French fleet, and they had already been chosen for the difficult task of reconnoitring Brest, for which fast and weatherly ships were essential. Similarly, in the days before Camperdown it

A dramatic illustration of the potential dangers of tactical reconnaissance: in July 1799 the frigates *Caroline* and *Triton* were sent to reconnoitre Cadiz and stumbled on the whole Combined Fleet getting underway. Undaunted, the *Caroline* carried out her task of counting the fleet (twenty-two ships under sail and seventeen at anchor), before a 74 and two frigates were sent to drive her off. On board was the sailor-artist Thomas Buttersworth, who produced this watercolour to depict the moment when the British ship suddenly tacked to throw off her pursuers; the 74 is shown tacking to follow, while the frigates stand on. With the enemy astern and to leeward, the British frigate is no longer in real danger, but the chase was kept up for an hour and a half in order mask the movements of the Combined Fleet.
National Maritime Museum A1903

was *Beaulieu*, the biggest and best of Duncan's frigates, that trailed the Dutch fleet most closely, although she herself was no prime sailer.

Tactical scouting was a dangerous activity. The 32-gun *Success*, a relatively poor performer under sail, was captured in February 1801 when tailing Ganteaume's squadron too closely. Nelson, on the other hand, felt confident enough in *Minerve*'s qualities to sail the ship right through the Spanish fleet before St Vincent; and *Sirius* was responsible for a most audacious reconnaissance in depth of the Franco-Spanish fleet in the light and misty conditions before Calder's Action. On the morning of the battle, *Sirius* nearly paid for her daring, when attempting to cut off a rich Spanish 'galleon' under tow at what was supposed to be the rear of the enemy line: the whole crew must have held their breath as the enemy van, having gone about, suddenly loomed out of the fog at half-pistol range. Luckily for *Sirius*, the leading Spanish vessels adhered to the ancient but now decaying convention that frigates were not fired on by battleships if not actively engaged.

On the other hand, the results of inadequate scouting could be grave. When Linois's squadron encountered the hugely valuable but unescorted China convoy off Pulo Auro in February 1804, Captain Bruillac in the *Belle Poule* was sent for a closer look. He got near enough to see that some ships had two tiers of gunports, but did not wait to find out if both batteries fired heavy shot. Reporting the Indiamen as ships of the line reinforced Linois's nervousness, and after a long-range cannonade he succumbed to a superb piece of bravado, retreating from a fleet of merchant ships which had formed line of battle. *Belle Poule* failed her admiral, and apart from a huge missed opportunity for damaging British commerce, 'Commodore Dance's Action' turned Linois and his navy into a laughing stock.

As this incident emphasises, in fleet scouting the qualities of the captain were as important as those of his ship. He needed to be bold, cunning and confident, but he also needed prudence, since partial intelligence was better than none, and getting too close or lingering too long risked capture. Most frigate captains were relatively junior, but since so much of their work called for individual initiative, they were an elite within the officer corps. Not that all frigate captains excelled at this kind of work: a maverick like Lord Cochrane, although brilliant in single-ship engagements, was too fond of taking on very long odds, and even Pellew in his young days was better employed in aggressive cruising than hanging on the coat-tails of a fleet. An admiral weighed a commander's strengths when allocating tasks, but the same process was applied by the Admiralty when assigning commands. Despite the pervasive workings of 'interest' in the Royal Navy of the time, the finest frigates more often than not ended up in the hands of those able to make best use of them. A good ship and a good captain was a potent weapon system, but one without the other was a waste of assets.

Generalising from his great depth of reading, Brian Tunstall, the historian of tactics, concluded that 'Failure to maintain a proper system of reconnaissance seems to have been one of the worst faults of the sailing fleet admirals.'[3] However, for the period under review his examples are all French, like Villaret-Joyeuse's assumption that the strange sails spotted during Cornwallis's Retreat in June 1795 were the main British fleet; sending any one of his numerous frigates to investigate would have disabused him of the notion. A worse – and better known – case is Brueys's complacency before the Nile. Instead of acting as pickets, his four frigates were safely anchored inside the battle-line, which was surprised in a very unready state by a squadron without any frigates at all. With prior warning of Nelson's approach it is inconceivable that Brueys would have decided that he could wait until the following morning to prepare his ships for battle.

How Nelson came to be deprived of his frigates is a story that at once underlines the importance of tactical reconnaissance while also emphasising its difficulties. In one of his most famous outbursts, Nelson claimed that if he were to die at that moment 'want of frigates' would be found stamped on his heart, and the sentiment might have applied at any time during the campaign. The frigates initially separated during the storm which dismasted the *Vanguard* in May 1798, and historians traditionally assumed that on meeting the senior frigate captain on the station, George Hope, the cruisers were ordered to Gibraltar in the belief that Nelson would have to return there to repair damages. However, a close study of their subsequent movements revealed a very active and persistent attempt by Hope to rejoin his admiral, making intelligent use of agreed rendezvous positions; he was as much in the dark about Nelson's movements as Nelson was of Bonaparte's, but it was one of Hope's frigates that found the French fleet a week before Nelson did, although none made contact with Nelson until two weeks after the battle.[4] If Nelson had retained his scouting line, he might well have intercepted the French fleet on the high seas since at one point its outlying frigates were sighted. The ensuing battle might have seen the death or capture of Bonaparte, and the history of the world would have been radically different; but in the days before electronic communications the 'fog of war' could prove impenetrable for even the most experienced frigate captain.

While there were no developments at this time comparable with the advent of radio and radar, there were incremental improvements in signalling that made reconnaissance more effective. Howe's numerical signals introduced in 1790 were a major step forward in the range of orders that could be passed from the flagship, but private ships were not issued with a complete set so that the information that might be sent back to

Frigates gathered information, but they were also required to pass it on. For this purpose they were issued with signal flags in carefully designed combinations of colours and patterns for the maximum visibility and the minimum likelihood of error in reading them. The flags themselves were also very large – those issued to frigates in the 1790s were 10ft by 12ft – as can be seen from this lively oil painting by Thomas Whitcombe of a 38-gun frigate off Torbay, a frequent refuge of the Channel Fleet. The painting is signed and dated 1810.
By courtesy of the Richard Green Galleries

the flagship was limited.[5] Groups of flags represented numbers, which stood for specific instructions tabulated in the signal book. Howe's work was codified and expanded with the first official Admiralty Signals Book issued in 1799, in which the number of potential messages was increased, especially for private ships. An important innovation was a separate Night Signals volume, which by the use of 'false fires' (flares), rockets and patterns of lights carefully screened from the enemy allowed up to seventy signals to be made. A section of 'Instructions for the Conduct of Ships Appointed to Watch the Motions of the Enemy's Fleet in the Night' was aimed directly at improving tactical reconnaissance.[6]

Despite the numbers of signals that could be made under existing systems, they were all pre-arranged and therefore fixed messages. Increasingly aggressive attempts at intelligence-gathering, largely in the service of a tighter blockade, demanded a far more sophisticated method of communication that could cover unforeseen contingencies. The answer was found in Home Popham's 'Telegraphic Code', where the number groups stood for the most frequently needed phrases, words or, if an unusual word needed spelling out, individual letters. It was developed in 1800-1 and a mature edition was published in 1803 as *Telegraphic Signals or Marine Vocabulary*, although Popham continued to improve it. The Navy was quick to adopt it and the strengths and limitations of the system are most famously demonstrated by Nelson's Trafalgar signal, where his intended 'confides' was changed to 'expects' so it could be sent with one flag-group, but 'duty' still required to be spelled out letter by letter.[7] In terms of

its value to reconnaissance, however, a better idea of its precision comes from one of *Euryalus*'s signals made two days earlier as the Combined Fleet struggled to get to sea: 'Notwithstanding (550) little (458) wind (960) many (480) of (570) enemy (249) persevere (613) to (873) get (335) outward[s;] (591) the (864) rest (1719) except (1261) on[e] (578) line (456) ready (693) yards (986) hoisted (1374)'.[8] The frigate went on to report the progress of the sortie in detailed and even longer signals, an achievement that would have been impossible with any previous signalling system. The observer was expected to provide punctuation and the tense and person of verbs (since the number stood for the word-root and all its variations), but it was infinitely superior to earlier systems which had often left the recipient grasping for the particular application of an over-generalised message.

3. In fleet engagements

Once battle was joined the traditional priority for the frigates was to stay out of the firing line. They were usually deployed on the unengaged side, their prime task being to repeat the commander's signals for those ahead and astern of the flagship who might not be able to make them out. If there were enough, each divisional flagship was also allocated a repeating ship. In earlier days, when line tactics were more rigid and signals more primitive, frigates might be summoned under the stern of the flagship and given verbal orders to pass up and down the line. This survived remarkably late and was employed by Howe at the First of June, while Duncan sent the *Circe* with orders for his advanced ships before Camperdown.

The battle of the Glorious First of June at the moment when the *Queen Charlotte* broke through the French line, as seen from the frigates. In the centre is the *Pegasus*, 28 repeating the flagship's signals, with two other frigates (probably *Southampton* and *Venus*) on either beam; the larger *Phaeton* and *Latona* are off to windward at the head of the line, and will be called into action later, but at this point none of the frigates is much more than a bystander.
National Maritime Museum A813

More fluid tactics from St Vincent onwards, with greater dependence on the initiative of individual captains, reduced the value of the manual transmission of orders, but there was a spectacular late example during Nelson's pursuit of Villeneuve to the West Indies. Nelson wanted to deliver explicit instructions to each of his captains on how to fight the enemy as soon as they caught up with them, but knowing his fleet was a long way behind, was reluctant to have any ship heave to. He entrusted the task to William Parker of the *Amazon*, described by Admiral Sir Pulteney Malcolm as 'the best frigate captain in the service'; Parker took the sets of written instructions from the flagship and raced up the line in the *Amazon*, skilfully lowering his boat on the weather bow of each ship and recovering it again from the lee quarter when the orders had been transferred. The fleet lost hardly a yard of ground.[9]

During the actual fighting frigates were usually little more than spectators, but came into their own towards the end of battles, where their undamaged condition allowed them to render assistance to crippled combatants. Dismasting was almost inevitable in a major fleet engagement, and frigates were kept busy towing damaged ships to safety. Frigates were also used to take possession of prizes, as *Lively* was at St Vincent, allowing the battleships to move on to other targets while the cruisers secured the crews of the surrendered ships.

This was no easy assignment as *Latona* discovered at the First of June: the frigate's boarding party found the crew of the 80-gun *Juste* drunk and riotous, and were hard put to transfer 150 men to the *Latona*'s hold, space being created by throwing overboard all the spare barrel stave and hoops. While the British frigates were thus employed, their French counterparts managed to spirit away a few of their own cripples, reducing the prize numbers by at least three ships.

Probably the heaviest post-battle workload was carried by the frigates of Nelson's fleet after Trafalgar. Many ships of the line were badly damaged, there were large numbers of prizes in a similar state, and when the storm came on and the allies attempted a counter-attack, the frigates were stretched to the limit recovering prize crews from ships at risk, taking out prisoners from those about to be set on fire or in danger of sinking, while attempting to preserve crippled British vessels. It is a tribute to their efforts that not a single British ship was lost, and that they were later able to burn some of the prizes which had gone ashore. Some frigates were themselves damaged in the process of towing their unwieldy charges, but all were eventually brought to the safety of Gibraltar.

Assistance to damaged ships did not always wait until the shooting stopped. At First of June *Phaeton* was sent to rescue the dismasted *Defence*, having to endure the fire of a French 74 and in the process losing two killed and five wounded; a little later *Latona* was summoned into the melee to divert attention from the disabled *Bellerophon* and was fired on by two battleships. Both frigates replied with vigour, but did not initiate the firing: indeed, such was the tradition of non-interference that *Phaeton* had to clear for action before approaching the line, and *Latona*, although cleared, had to beat to quarters before entering the fray.

It is noticeable in the battles of the 1790s that it was the big 18pdr frigates that were most active, the above pair at First of June and *Minerve* and *Lively* at St Vincent. More sophisticated tactics, like Howe's use of an Advanced Squadron combining fast-sailing two-deckers and frigates, meant that the latter were being given a more aggressive role: *Latona* certainly played her part in harassing the end of the French line on 28 May.

The Dutch went further, but, having few battleships, it was a development driven by necessity rather than tactical ingenuity, and at Camperdown their frigates were in the thick of the fighting, the *Mars* (a powerful *rasée*) even standing in the line. *Monnikendam* was particularly effective, skilfully raking the *Monarch* while the British 74 was tacking and unable to reply. Nelson at Copenhagen also had fewer ships of the line than was required to engage the whole Danish line, and a squadron of frigates led by Captain Edward Riou of the *Amazon* effectively substituted for more powerful ships. They were employed against the Trekroner battery rather than the Danish ships themselves, but survived a pounding with surprisingly little structural damage, although *Amazon* suffered heavy casualties and Riou himself was killed.

The increasing value of frigates in fleet battles as demonstrated in practice by the British and Dutch was simultaneous recognised in theory by the French, a book published by Audibert Ramatuelle in 1802 developing a number of scenarios in which frigates played a major part. He was much concerned with the problem of doubling, a tactic used both frequently and effectively by the British, and suggested a squadron of frigates en echelon at the head of the line to make it more difficult for the enemy to work round to windward. In attack, he also advocated a squadron of frigates and fast-sailing two-deckers which might double the enemy's rear.[10] Before his clash with Calder in 1805 Villeneuve issued instructions that his frigates were to act on their own initiative to seek out opportunities to 'hasten the surrender of an enemy's ship, or to cover a French ship too closely pressed . . .'.[11] In practice, as Tunstall was to remark, 'French tactics, as far as actual fighting was concerned, were completely barren,' but while the British showed less regard for written doctrine, there was a spirit of tactical innovation in the fleets of Howe, Jervis, Duncan and, above all, Nelson. Before Trafalgar, Nelson relied heavily on Henry Blackwood of the *Euryalus*, to whom he gave command of all the inshore forces including the battleships of the Advance Squadron. During the battle itself, Blackwood claimed, Nelson 'not only gave me the command of all the frigates, for the purpose of assisting disabled ships, but he also gave me a latitude seldom or ever again, that of making any use I pleased of his name in ordering any of the sternmost line of battle ships to do what struck me as best.' He was also instructed to use the frigates 'to complete the destruction of the enemy, whether at anchor or not,' without concern for saving men or ships. This delegation of a degree of authority, not only reflected Nelson's confidence in Blackwood, but also the recognition that once the firing started it would be the frigates that were best

After playing the leading role in the scouting which led to the battle of Trafalgar, Blackwood's *Euryalus* was even busier after the fighting ceased. Indeed, she became fleet flagship temporarily, when Collingwood transferred his flag from the crippled *Royal Sovereign* – shown here in an atmospheric watercolour by Pocock being towed by the frigate in the gale on the day after the engagement. Collingwood wrote his first post-battle dispatch from *Euryalus* in these conditions on 22 October. *National Maritime Museum 8501*

The last of the refugees from the Battle of the Nile, the 80-gun *Guillaume Tell* was trapped in the besieged Maltese capital of Valletta. With the French position deteriorating, she made an attempt to break out on the dark night of 30 March 1800 and having evaded the blockading ships of the line might have escaped were it not for the vigilance of Henry Blackwood, the quintessential frigate captain, of *Penelope*, 36. She was fast, but not the handiest of frigates, and Blackwood needed all of his shiphandling skill to keep *Penelope* out of the arcs of the French batteries while continually luffing under the Frenchman's stern to pour in raking broadsides. The frigate's fire brought down the two-decker's topmasts, slowing her enough for the *Lion*, 64 and eventually the *Foudroyant*, 80 to catch up and batter her into submission. After the hard-fought battle, only *Penelope* was in any condition to stay at sea, and she was therefore ordered to tow the entirely dismasted prize to the Sicilian port of Syracuse.
National Maritime Museum PY7973

placed to respond to a developing tactical situation.[12]

As frigates came to be seen as players rather than onlookers in a fleet engagement, the old conventions surrounding their immunity also broke down: indeed by the 1790s it was already a custom more honoured in the breach than the observance. At the First of June British frigates going into the melee were fired on, and French frigates even attacked the three-decker *Queen*. At the Nile the British *Goliath* and *Orion* sank the frigate *Serieuse*, which it was thought was trying to fill a gap in the French line. Nor were Spanish views very different, since once the fighting started at St Vincent, *Lively* and other British frigates were cannonaded by Spanish battleships if they so much as ventured within range. With tactics becoming less formal, it was no longer possible to anticipate how a frigate might behave in battle. Before Trafalgar, Nelson even predicted 'a Battle-Royal line-of-battle ships opposed to ships-of-the-line and frigates to frigates.'[13]

There were no major fleet engagements after Trafalgar, but the new freedom of action accorded to frigates was further developed in the smaller squadron actions which were increasingly the norm after 1805.

4. Squadron actions

With fewer ships, deployed in a greater variety of tactical situations, the squadron action was necessarily less of a set-piece than a fleet battle. Indeed, it was often a chase, in which the superior speed and weatherly qualities of the frigate could be deployed to advantage. While a frigate would always hesitate to attack a battle-

ship on her own, with the prospect of support arriving in the near future the cruiser's better manoeuvrability could be used to delay a fleeing enemy. The *Ça Ira* would never have been taken in 1795 without Fremantle's masterly harrying of the damaged 80-gun ship in the handy little *Inconstant*; and *Penelope* performed the same role in the capture of the *Guillaume Tell* off Malta. Less successfully, after the Battle of Cape St Vincent Admiral Jervis actually sent a frigate squadron to seek out the crippled *Santísima Trinidad*, and the monster 'four-decker' was harried by the little 12pdr-armed *Terpsichore* until rescued by elements of the Spanish fleet.

Diversionary attacks by frigates could make a crucial difference, and it is no exaggeration to say that Sir Richard Strachan's cruisers ensured his post-Trafalgar victory in November 1805. *Phoenix* not only decoyed Dumanoir's squadron within tactical reach, but in company with *Santa Margarita* and *Revolutionnaire* damaged and delayed the rearmost battleship, allowing the British line to catch up with the retreating French. Perhaps significantly, the 12pdr *Santa Margarita* was knocked out of the fighting by serious damage, but the 18pdr ships (which were later joined by the *Aeolus*) stood up to the punishment far better.

In comparative terms the firepower of cruisers had improved substantially during the century. Whereas most battleship rates in 1800 carried the same calibre of lower deck gun as they had done in 1700, the main battery of frigates had grown from 6pdrs through stages to 18pdrs, or even 24pdrs; they had also grown in rela-

tive size from a burthen of about 30 per cent that of a standard Third Rate to a tonnage of about 60 per cent. Frigates were now bigger and more expensive relatively, but were justified because they could also accomplish far more. British frigate captains had great confidence in the abilities of their commands to take on previously unacceptable odds, and William Parker and Thomas Capel cannot have been the only officers to plan how to attack a battleship successfully with two frigates.[14]

5. Blockade duty

For much of the British fleet the dominating experience of the 1793-1815 wars was blockade duty, nor did frigates escape their fair share. Whether the strategy was close-blockade, with the main fleet in the offing, or the kind of looser watch favoured by Howe and Bridport in the 1790s which allowed the Channel Fleet to spend more time in sheltered waters, the mainstay of the inshore squadrons were frigates. These squadrons were often stiffened with some of the more suitable two-deckers, but the brunt of the work always fell upon frigates. The blockade stations were extremely hazardous, of intricate navigation, almost always on a lee shore, and a year-round, all-weather commitment. Ships needed to be very weatherly if they were not to be wrecked; to be at least as fast and manoeuvrable as the enemy if they were to avoid capture; and to be as powerful as possible so that they could not be easily driven from their station. Continuously exposed to the

most extreme conditions and allowed the minimum time in dock, they also need to be structurally strong and well built. Such relentless requirements provided much of the impetus for the growth in the size of British frigates in the 1790s.

Although all were exacting, no two blockading stations were identical in their demands, while the strategies pursued by different admirals also imposed subtle variations on the frigates' workload. Nelson was never very interested in keeping his enemy mewed up, but always aimed to lure or decoy him into battle. During his command off Cadiz in 1797, the Inshore Squadron was moored provocatively close to the harbour, requiring frigates like the *Blanche* to be continually employed in the dangerous work of keeping Spanish gunboats at bay – even further inshore, and well within range of the batteries.[15] In the months before Trafalgar, when the Combined Fleet had taken refuge in Cadiz, Nelson employed different tactics: as he explained to his friend Ball, 'I have five Frigates, a Brig and a Schooner watching them closely, an Advanced Squadron of fast-sailing Ships between me and the Frigates, and the body of the Fleet from fifteen to eighteen leagues west of Cadiz.' He also took strenuous measures to prevent the enemy learning of any reinforcements, stationing a sloop off Cape St Vincent to direct any joining ships straight to his fleet out of sight of Cadiz.[16]

A memorandum of 7 October 1805 reveals Nelson's thinking about the ideal dispositions for the cruisers on his station and the duties he thought necessary.

This fine oil painting by Thomas Luny was commissioned by Sir Edward Thornborough in 1827 and almost certainly celebrates his exploit of reconnoitring the French Brest fleet when captain of *Latona* early in 1794. It was the first such close reconnaissance of the war and although it was to become commonplace later when backed by a blockading squadron, at the time it was regarded as a most audacious undertaking. The frigate is shown right in the mouth of the *Goulet*, probably rounding the rocks known as Les Fillettes, with the French fleet no great distance beyond in the Rade de Brest. Having been painted over thirty years after the event, the frigate reveals a few minor anachronisms, the most obvious being the quarter boats, an extremely unlikely fitting in 1794.
By courtesy of the Richard Green Galleries

The blockade of Toulon presented special difficulties because the high ground around the port made it easier to keep track of the movement of the watching British ships, which often exposed them to the risk of surprise attack. The best contrived example was the trap set for one night in February 1809, when two French frigates emerged from the darkened land to capture the unprepared *Proserpine*, brilliantly back-lit by a full moon. Other British frigates had lucky escapes, including the incident depicted here in which *Havannah* and *Curaçoa* (foreground) were chased by four large French ships; the latter split her sails and required great skill to get away. In such circumstances, it is easy to see why weatherliness and seakeeping were such high priorities in British frigate design. *National Maritime Museum PY8402*

	Frigates	Sloops
To be constantly with the fleet, 8 frigates, 2 sloops. 2 frigates and 2 sloops to go to and from Gibraltar with convoys, and to relieve the others to refit; 2 sloops to go occasionally to Lisbon with dispatches and for Purser's necessaries	10	4
To be stationed constantly off Cape St Mary's	1	
To be stationed off Cape Spartel	1	
To be stationed off the Salvages	1	
To be constantly stationed off Cape St Vincent		1
To be stationed off Cape Cautine		1
For the services of Gibraltar garrison, and to protect trade in the Straits from gunboats and privateers	2	3
To be stationed off Cape Cartagena	1	1
Most essentially necessary for service in the upper part of the Mediterranean	2	2
Malta – to convoy the trade in the eastern basin, and with the cutters and small craft to protect the island and convey the bullock vessels to Valletta	1	4
Attached to General Craig's expedition	3	
Total	22	16

At the time he had only fourteen frigates and eight sloops, and although the Admiralty had promised a further seven and three respectively, it is worth noting Nelson's constant requests for more frigates around this time.[17]

Toulon was more difficult to blockade closely, because high ground behind the port allowed observers on shore to follow the movements of a fleet in the offing, so in 1803-5 Nelson had tended to keep his fleet out of sight, hoping to draw the French out by subterfuge. This meant frigates, usually in pairs, stationed close in, but with less concern to monitor the enemy than to provoke him to action – laying salt on their tail, as Nelson expressed it.[18] This exposed them to considerable danger, since they were easily cut off; frigate captains needed to stay alert, the consequences of not doing so being demonstrated by the capture of the *Proserpine* by two French frigates in 1809.

But of all enemy bases, that most regularly and rigorously blockaded was Brest. It was also the port geographically best endowed for defence, with a narrow entrance – the *Goulet* – that hid most of the activity in the main anchorage from all but the closest reconnaissance. From the time in 1794 when Howe sent *Latona* and *Phaeton* to look into Brest, the watch on this port was largely the province of big frigates; in the days of the close blockade as applied by St Vincent and Cornwallis, they would be supported by selected two-deckers, but they often had the dreaded Black Rocks station to themselves. The duty combined repetitive tedium with the constant danger of an ironbound lee shore, and for diversion frigate captains were also

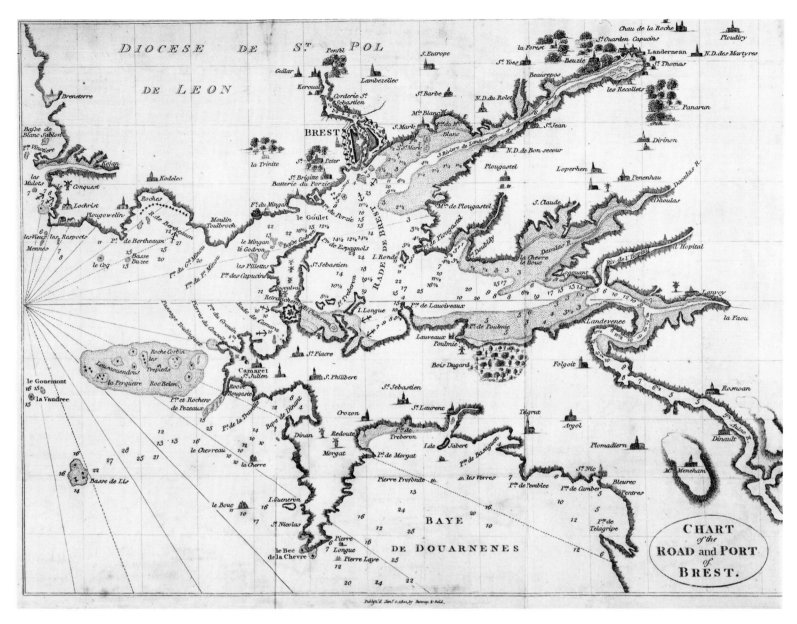

CHART of the ROAD and PORT of BREST.

expected to keep a close eye on activity in and around the port, to intercept small coastal convoys bringing supplies, and if possible to prevent the escape of French commerce-raiding squadrons, or follow and report on the sorties of larger fleets. Given these most demanding operating conditions, and the large numbers of ships involved, it is surprising that only a handful of frigates were lost while so employed: *Artois* in 1797, *Jason* and *Ethalion* in the two years following, *Hussar* in 1804, and *Blanche* in 1807. This is a tribute to the seamanship of their officers and the training of their crews, but it also reflects the strength, seaworthiness and sailing qualities of the frigates themselves.

As the war progressed and the threat of French battle squadrons diminished, many of the lesser ports were blockaded by frigates alone. Here the quarry was usually privateers or the enemy's own frigates, so the chances for a single-ship action were somewhat greater, and the duty less dull as a result. Here again,

there was price, albeit a modest one, to be paid: while blockading other parts of the French Atlantic coast *Jason* in 1801, *Shannon* in 1803, and *Laurel* in 1812 were wrecked.

6. Miscellaneous fleet duties

Despite their substantial growth in size, frigates never completely lost touch with their origins as fleet tenders, and some of the more mundane aspects of such duties occasionally fell to their lot. Although there was a well developed network of cutters and advice schooners intended to carry dispatches and orders, they were vulnerable in adverse weather conditions and some fleet commanders preferred to give up the services of a powerful frigate temporarily rather than risk the permanent loss of a vital communication. Nelson himself learnt a hard lesson when his dispatches (and the private signals) were lost in the little cutter *Swift*, captured in April 1804 by a big privateer xebec.

Despite the importance to the blockade of the waters outside Brest, the Royal Navy did not have a reliable chart of the area until Captain Thomas Hurd's survey of 1804-6 which was published in 1807. This earlier chart omits some of the smaller rocks and is thin on details of soundings. The Black Rocks, the usual station for frigates and the Inshore Squadron, were further out to the west, but Les Fillettes which appear in the *Latona* painting can be seen in the very mouth of the *Goulet*.
Plate 48, The Naval Chronicle IV (1800)

Fleets on the long deployments associated with the blockade needed fresh supplies if their crews were to remain efficient, and the shuttle of slow-sailing victuallers needed escorting. New ships joining usually brought extra stores and provisions, but – again in the interests of security – frigates themselves were sometimes sent on victualling missions.

Neither of these roles was particularly appealing to a dashing frigate captain, and the highs and lows of service with the fleet were pointedly demonstrated by a few months in the life of William Parker's *Amazon*. She was a notably smart ship and had just received a new coat of paint when in December 1804 she was ordered by Nelson to bring a consignment of live bullocks from Caligari for the fleet off Toulon. When Parker arrived with the *Amazon* looking, and presumably smelling, like a floating farmyard, Nelson, with a degree of gentle humour, inquired 'Well, Parker, of course you would not dirty the *Amazon* much for anything; have you brought a dozen and a half, or a dozen?' In fact Parker had on board sixty bullocks and thirty sheep, more than any frigate had managed to transport previously, and a delighted Nelson promised him a reward.

As it transpired, even the 'reward' had to be earned with a mission requiring skill and discretion. The Mediterranean command had been divided, a separate Cadiz station now straddling the Straits of Gibraltar. Mortifying as it was to lose the opportunity of prize money in the new war with Spain, salt was rubbed in Nelson's wounded pride by the appointment of Sir John Orde to that command. There was no love lost between the men, and Nelson suspected that Orde, the senior officer, was intercepting his dispatches and commandeering his frigates for his own ends. Nelson wanted his dispatches to get through and gave Parker verbal instructions not to be stopped if at all possible by any of Sir John's ships.

Parker did his best, but eluding a British blockading squadron even at night was not easy, and he was intercepted by a lookout frigate, the *Eurydice*. Luckily, the ship's commander was William Hoste, a protégé of Nelson who would later win his own miniature Trafalgar off Lissa in 1811, and Parker persuaded him to turn a suitably Nelsonic blind-eye. Having put the dispatches aboard the packet at Lisbon, Parker was then free to act on Nelson's hint that he was not expected back before the end of February. Taking full advantage of the opportunity, *Amazon* made a series of prizes that earned her £20,000, and despite Orde's protests about 'poaching' on his station, both Parker and Nelson (as his admiral) retained their sweet rewards.[19]

7. Coastal operations

While blockade was an active strategy, merely preventing the escape of the enemy must have seemed tactically passive to the ships involved; conversely, the strategically passive defence of Britain from invasion led to many active – indeed, highly aggressive – operations, in which frigates were to develop yet another role.

First threatened in 1797, a French invasion of the British Isles became a serious possibility with the renewal of war in 1803. Napoleon, now self-proclaimed emperor, was able to throw enormous resources into the project, not only constructing huge numbers of invasion craft in ports from the Netherlands to the French Biscay coast, but also improving many of the harbours themselves to allow the efficient embarkation and sailing of the invasion force. He did not expect this work to go on unmolested by his island enemies, and much of the effort was devoted to fortifying the ports and roadsteads with fixed batteries of guns, howitzers and mortars; he even devised a system of horse artillery that could be deployed rapidly to any threatened spot or could keep company with a coastal convoy along the shoreside roads.

With a tiny army and very few fixed defences of their own, the British knew that any invasion had to be defeated at sea. Professional naval officers had no doubts about the outcome: St Vincent's famous remark in the House of Lords that he did not dispute that the French could invade, but not by sea, was not bravado but an objective assessment of their chances. With the technology of the time, the problems of mounting a successful amphibious landing were enormous: it would have taken several tides just to get all the invasion craft out of harbour, the Channel weather was notoriously unpredictable, and the landing vessels themselves were easy targets, with poor seakeeping, no protection for the troops, and virtually no defences.

Nevertheless, British public opinion was not prepared to wait until the invasion was actually attempted, and the Navy was called upon to disrupt, hamper and delay the preparations to the best of its formidable abilities. The Royal Navy was traditionally a blue-water force, and was not well equipped for specialist inshore warfare, but was quick to adapt to the new requirements. The most significant French advantage was geographical, the coast being subject to a great range of tide, powerful currents and naturally well defended by sandbars and shallows. For these conditions the British built large numbers of shoal-draught gunboats and slightly larger gunbrigs, with relatively heavy armament. They were ideal for attacking the small craft of what came to be called the Boulogne Flotilla, but were most effective when deployed in numbers so needed some form of command and control, not least because their own officers were very junior.

The answer was to organise them in small squadrons under the command of a suitable post captain, who would provide experience, tactical expertise and, ideally, energy and initiative. Relatively young frigate captains most closely fitted the requirement and so

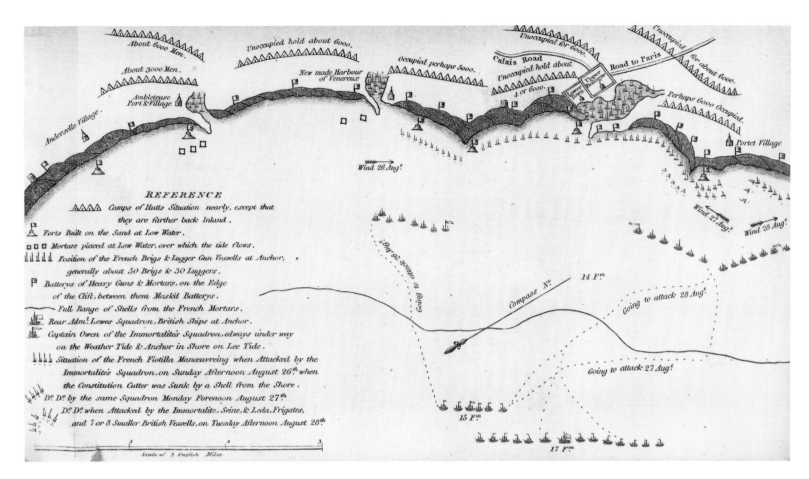

REFERENCE

ΛΛΛΛ Camps of Hutts Situation nearly, except that
         they are farther back Inland.
🏳 Forts Built on the Sand at Low Water.
□□□ Mortars placed at Low Water, over which the tide flows.
⚓⚓⚓ Position of the French Brigs & Lugger Gun Vessells at Anchor,
         generally about 50 Brigs & 30 Luggers.
P Batterys of Heavy Guns & Mortars, on the Edge
     of the Clift, between them Maskd Batterys.
——— Full Range of Shells from the French Mortars.
⚓ Rear Adml Lewes Squadron, British Ships at Anchor.
⚓ Captain Owen of the Immortalites Squadron, always under way
     on the Weather Tide & Anchor in Shore on Lee Tide.
⚓⚓⚓ Situation of the French Flotilla Manœuvreing when Attacked by the
     Immortalites Squadron, on Sunday Afternoon August 26th when
     the Constitution Cutter was Sunk by a Shell from the Shore.
⚓⚓⚓ Do Do by the same Squadron Monday Forenoon August 27th
⚓⚓⚓ Do Do when Attacked by the Immortalite, Seine, & Leda, Frigates,
     and 7 or 8 Smaller British Vessels, on Tuesday Afternoon August 28th

Scale of 3 English Miles.

frigates came to lead these mosquito squadrons off the various Channel ports. The frigate was not only flagship but also provided protection for the small craft against interference from larger French warships. There were not many sea-going men-of-war in the area, although an occasional frigate was to be found in ports like Flushing or Le Havre at the extremities of the invasion preparations. The main threat to British operations were the flat-bottomed '*prames*', powerfully armed with up to twelve 24pdrs and designed to escort the invasion fleet.

Opportunities for attack were offered to the British by the numerous coasting convoys. Because construction of the landing craft was dispersed, when completed they needed to be concentrated at their designated bases; furthermore, the vast amount of building work required raw materials to be moved in bulk and shipping was the only cost-effective method available at the time. As more and more of the invasion craft were completed, they were often moored in long lines outside their base ports, to make room for more within and also to give their crews some minimal sea-time. Targets, therefore, were many, but they were not easy to get at. Not only were the headlands and promontories bristling with gun batteries, but even if the enemy small craft could be damaged, they were simply run ashore, where more often than not they were repaired at low tide and refloated. The other method of striking

back was the more traditional tactic of shelling towns and harbours with mortar-armed bomb vessels firing explosive shells and incendiary carcasses. Both approaches were much used and between 1803 and 1806 frigates led their small squadrons in many such raids.

Probably the most effective of the frigate captains involved was Edward Owen of the *Immortalité*, 36. As a Commander, he had been given charge of a division of gunbrigs protecting the entrance to the Thames, so he was clearly familiar with the technology, but his outstanding talents in the specialist area of inshore warfare were recognised by the award of a Commodore's broad pendant when he was a post captain of only eight years seniority. His mixed squadron of small craft, gunbrigs and bombs did a lot of good if unspectacular work – they were known in the fleet as 'the fire-eaters'[20] – paid for by the frequent damage and casualties suffered by *Immortalité*.

However, the government was growing impatient at the lack of visible success and more inclined to listen to unconventional schemes, some entirely out of touch with naval realities. Owen was increasingly chosen to put these into operation, and although always prepared to register his doubts, he entered on every task with that peculiar combination of energy and prudence that makes a good special forces officer. He was involved in the abortive plan to sink stone-filled blockships in the

Based on a sketch by an officer present during the August 1804 attacks, this engraving gives some idea of the difficulties involved with attempts to destroy the Boulogne Flotilla. Apart from batteries on the cliffs, there were pile forts on the sandbanks and emplacements where mortars were placed at low water - the range is shown by the solid line, and since the cutter *Constitution* was hit by a shell and sunk on the 26th the threat was very real. The Flotilla craft usually remained inside the cover of their batteries, but they were nevertheless attacked whenever feasible, by Edward Owen's inshore squadron – 'they know well whenever they make the slightest movement the *Immortalité*'s squadron always annoys them'.
Plate 169, The Naval Chronicle XIII (1805)

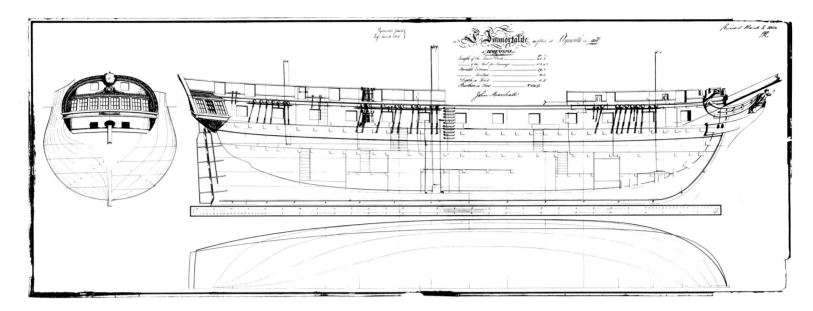

One of the frigates most heavily engaged in anti-Flotilla operations was Captain Edward Owen's *Immortalité*, 36 guns, a French prize captured in 1798. At 1010 tons she was not large by French standards, but was a distinct oddity, being one of a class of *frégate-bombardes* designed by Forfait to carry a 12in mortar and long 24pdrs. Having only twelve genuine broadside ports a side on the main deck, as a British 36 she was therefore obliged to carry guns permanently in the bow-chase ports to make up the established twenty-six 18pdrs. The biggest shortcoming of the ship was her lack of capacity, which restricted both the stores and water she could stow, and it may have been this lack of endurance that singled her out for short-range operations just across the Channel. Here she was very aggressively employed, taking some very hard knocks in the process; by early 1806 she was adjudged worn-out and beyond economic repair, so was taken to pieces.
National Maritime Museum Dr7065

entrance to Boulogne, and later played a leading part in the deployment of Fulton's 'torpedoes', primitive clockwork-fused explosive devices variously known as 'coffers' or 'catamarans' to British seamen. Discretion was another of Owen's virtues, and even among *Immortalité*'s officers the mysterious Fulton was known only as 'Mr Nobody'.[21]

Owen's association with futuristic weapons extended to rockets, and it was his practical advice that helped Congreve make a far more effective weapon out of his pyrotechnics. The first deployment of rockets had been a dismal failure, but Owen's attack on Boulogne in October 1806 was well planned and executed, 400 rockets being fired in aimed barrages. They would never constitute a precision weapon, but like the 'Scud' missiles of more recent times, they were a relatively long-range area bombardment terror weapon.

During all these attacks frigates had proved useful as headquarters ships, with enough room for the staff work of planning meetings and briefing sessions, and space to prepare the various unconventional devices often deployed. However, they were far from ideal because their deep-sea draught of around 18ft or more prevented them from giving close support in most situations, and their principal contribution to many of the raids was their large complement of boats. There was some recognition of the need for a specialist inshore support craft and John Staniforth, an influential MP, was able to foist a design of his own on the Admiralty. Three of these were built in 1804-5 as the *Combatant* class, 400-ton vessels armed with twenty carronades but drawing only 11ft when fully loaded. They were regarded by their officers as the equivalent of the French *prames*, but their seakeeping and habitability was very poor, and once the invasion threat was over it proved difficult to find them useful employment. One of the trio, the *Dauntless*, was lost as far away as Danzig (modern Gdansk) while co-operating with the Prussian

army in 1807; the other two were fitted for the defence of Gibraltar Bay in 1808, but this role was rendered unnecessary by the Spanish uprisings, when it was decided that they were unsuitable for cruising duties, the Navy Board deciding that they were 'only fit to lie as stationary ships'.[22]

Frigates were far more versatile and continued to be chosen as a flagship for small craft, even outside the Channel. In September 1805, for example, a frigate was ordered to be fitted to command the gunboats at Gibraltar.[23] Gunboat activity actually increased after Trafalgar destroyed the invasion threat once and for all, but the emphasis shifted away from the Channel to new theatres, like the Baltic after 1807 and the Peninsula from 1808. To meet these increased demands, a new kind of small gunboat designed by Commissioner Hamilton of the Transport Board was built in large numbers. It was pre-fabricated and cased 'kits' could be shipped to any part of the world by transport,[24] but its main drawback was the absence of any real accommodation. The junior officers who commanded them, therefore, were assigned to, and lived aboard, the flagship and in this respect frigates were found wanting. There was more room in small two-deckers, and as a result the largely obsolescent 50-gun ship and occasionally even a 64 were favoured for the task. At Gibraltar during the Peninsular War, instead of the frigate ordered in 1805 to command the gunboats, the Spanish 74 *San Juan Nepomuceno* captured at Trafalgar was co-opted for the task. Although little better than a hulk, she was rated as a 'sloop' (because her commanding officer was of Commander rank) and she had a total of fourteen lieutenants, each to take charge of a gunboat.[25]

8. Amphibious warfare

The expertise which was garnered in anti-invasion operations was equally applicable when the situation was reversed and the strategic situation called for amphibious landings of various scales to be made. Of course the Royal Navy already possessed an unrivalled experience of what was then called 'conjunct' operations, applied so frequently in the eighteenth-century wars that it has become characterised by some modern historians as 'the British way in warfare'; indeed, it might be argued that the Royal Navy was the pioneer of the currently fashionable concept of 'littoral' warfare.

In this form of action ships of the line, with their heavy draught, were limited in their value on a front-line which was necessarily shoal water. During the largest British landings of the Napoleonic War, at Walcheren in 1809, the battleships carried some of the troops but were explicitly ordered to be kept out of the tricky navigation of the upper Schelde.[26] Their chief function after the landings was to supply elements of their crews to man the gunboats and flat-boats that were essential to the army's progress. Frigates were the largest ships permitted to operate close inshore and in these circumstances a heavy reliance was placed on them. Prior to the operation, *Fisgard* was sent for a last-minute reconnaissance, and was charged with designating the approaches to the most suitable anchorages by stationing the small craft under her orders as sea-marks. The first wave, whose original objective was the seizure of Cadzand island to open up the Wester Schelde, was led by the highly experienced Captain Edward Owen, now flying a commodore's broad pendant in the *Clyde*, 38. The choice clearly fell on Owen because of the inshore expertise he had accumulated in anti-invasion duties, but the fact that the fir-built *Clyde* drew rather less water than her oak-built half-sisters may also have had a bearing. However, the channel was eventually forced by a squadron of ten frigates, led by Lord William Stuart in the *Lavinia*, 40.

In the ensuing operations, most of the junior admirals, as well as the overall naval commander Sir Richard Strachan, transferred their flags to cruisers, and in all twenty-three frigates were employed in the operations. As the largest ships supporting the flotillas craft, they were involved in numerous close-range battering actions for which they were hardly designed; but they were tough ships, and *Aigle* survived a direct hit by a mortar shell that exploded in the breadroom, damaging the stern frame (in fact the ship lasted until 1870 when futuristic weapons finally got the better of her–she was sunk in experiments with early self-propelled torpedoes). However, they also had some novel weapons at their disposal: Congreve rockets were well established by this date, but *Imperieuse* used some of Colonel Shrapnel's recently approved 'spherical case shot' to good effect against one battery, blowing up the magazine and silencing the guns.

Beyond continental Europe, British amphibious expertise was mainly employed in reducing the enemy's colonies. In the post-Trafalgar era in theatres like the West Indies the days of French battlefleets had long since past, and even a fugitive squadron was a rarity. This not only allowed the British freer rein to mount expeditions, but made it possible to decrease their own battleship numbers on station to a handful, throwing more of the weight of colonial warfare onto frigates. In the larger operations, like the capture of Martinique in February 1809, the organisation of the landings was often delegated to a suitable frigate captain, in this case Philip Beaver of the *Acasta*, who was regarded as something of an expert in the field. He was entirely successful and when a belated French relief force was discovered to have taken refuge in the Saintes a month later, Beaver was again given the job of landing the army that drove them out.

In these instances, while the frigates did much of the inshore work, there were a few battleships on hand in case they were needed. But there were examples of frigates achieving conquests on their own, the most spectacular being Brisbane's *coup de main* which led to the Dutch island of Curaçoa surrendering to his squadron of four frigates on New Year's Day 1807. The more theatrical versions of the story have him scribbling out the terms he demanded on the drumhead of the *Arethusa*'s capstan while the frigate's bowsprit loomed menacingly over the town walls; the demands were refused, but a concerted attack by landing parties from all four ships rapidly took the defences by storm, and resistance ceased.

On the other side of the world other Batavian colonies also fell to aggressive frigate squadrons–Amboyna, Banda Neira and Ternate in 1810–while the large-scale assault on Java the following year was principally achieved by a veritable fleet of frigates and sloops, supported by a few of the smaller two-deckers. In the Indian Ocean the whole French war-effort had depended on frigates since the departure of Admiral Linois's *Marengo* in 1806, and the British stations of the Cape and East Indies had run down the number of their own two-deckers in consequence. The commerce war was not concluded until the capture of Reunion and Mauritius in 1810, and not before the British suffered their worst defeat in a frigate action of the whole war, at Grand Port. In a hastily conceived and ill-planned attack, four frigates were lost attempting to cut out a French squadron of much the same size from a harbour of intricate channels which was almost unknown to the British commanders. Brisbane's brilliant exploit proved that Fortune favoured the brave, but Grand Port suggested she equally frowned on the foolhardy. Dash and self-confidence was possessed by most frigate captains, but in the very best these qualities were tempered by prudence and judgement.

Calculated risk-taking was the key to success in land attacks, and this was demonstrated to the greatest strategic effect in the Navy's support for Wellington's campaign in the Peninsula. From the beginnings of the

A superb example of the amphibious capabilities of a frigate squadron was the capture of the Dutch island of Curaçoa on New Year's Day 1807 by Captain Sir Charles Brisbane's force of *Arethusa*, *Latona* and *Fisgard*, 38s, and the 44-gun *Anson*. This, the final in a series of watercolours by Brisbane himself, depicts the climax of the attack with the landing parties on the beach storming the town's seaward walls. The *Anson*, with the *rasée*'s characteristic stern gallery at quarterdeck level, is far left taking possession of the corvette *Surinam*; *Latona* is ahead of her lying athwart the bow of the surrendered *Kenau Hasselaar*, 36 guns, the Dutch commodore's flagship; *Arethusa* is almost obscured by this group of ships, while *Fisgard*, at right, batters Fort Amsterdam.
National Maritime Museum PZ6996

Spanish revolt in 1808, naval forces were on hand to assist the partisan armies, and given the forbidding nature of the coastline these squadrons were predominantly frigates and smaller craft. *Lively* and *Venus* played a major part in the surrender of Vigo, as did the *Amelia* and *Statira* at Santander, and naval support for the Galician army led to the French evacuation of Coruña and Ferrol in the middle of 1809.

The Navy was also very active on the Mediterranean coast of Spain, but the ultimate expression of its amphibious expertise is to be found in its direct support of the British army in the north, once Wellington had launched his campaign in earnest. Much of the credit is due to Sir George Ralph Collier of the *Surveillante*, whose small squadron of frigates and sloops carried out a systematic programme of pin-prick raids tying down a disproportionate number of French troops in defensive positions. Although Collier continued to do much of the front-line work, in 1812 the command had passed to the more senior Sir Home Popham, an officer better known for his activities ashore than afloat, in theatres as far removed as Flanders and the Cape, South America and the Red Sea. Co-operating with the army was his speciality (and, said his critics, not co-operating with the Admiralty), but despite a controversial career he was now flying a commodore's broad pendant in the *Venerable*, 74. The stakes were raised by the embarkation of a battalion of marines, some field pieces, and arms for the Spanish guerrilla forces, so the scale of possible attacks was increased significantly, and the

resulting defensive effort exponentially. Throughout the summer of 1812 the activities of Popham and Collier so alarmed the French that Cafarelli's 'Army of the North' was kept busy fortifying every creek and coastal village when it should have been reinforcing Marmont's army further south. Wellington generally appreciated the Navy's efforts and was happy to acknowledge this contribution to his victory over Marmont at Salamanca in July 1812.[27]

Despite the effectiveness of the enlarged striking force, the presence of this line of battle ship was regarded as a major risk by both the overall commander, Lord Keith, and the Admiralty itself since the north coast of Spain was a lee shore for three-quarters of the year and lacked not only a suitable harbour of refuge in allied hands but even a safe anchorage. One of the few ports open to them was Pasajes (always called Passages in the correspondence), which it was difficult for anything bigger than a frigate to enter in bad weather. Offshore the bottom was rocky and chafed the cable, and *Surveillante* lost two anchors during her time on the coast; more worryingly, the visiting 74 *Ajax* nearly lost hers on the first day she was at anchor, and would surely have been wrecked if the weather had not remained a flat calm. Therefore, any two-decker temporarily assigned to the station had explicit orders to remain underway at all times, and this reduced their practical value to that of a distant threat.[28] So despite his successes, which had culminated in the recapture of Santander, Popham and his ship were withdrawn in the winter of 1812-13 in deference to the Admiralty's nervousness.[29]

Wellington was unimpressed by the reversion to a force of frigates and smaller craft under Collier in 1813, and complained so effectively that the Admiralty had to send out Rear-Admiral Byam Martin to explain 'what is practicable by the navy, and what is impossible on such parts of the coast as are connected with his operations . . .'.[30] Wellington's main interest in ships of the line was their large crews, for which he could envisage numerous ancillary tasks, but Byam Martin demonstrated the hazards to big ships and the consequent need to keep them standing off and on the coast, so for the army's purposes their utility was far less than the general had assumed. Battleships might appear to threaten the receding French position, but it was a largely empty ploy and there was no guarantee that the French would be intimidated. Furthermore, the captain of any ship of the line detached from the Channel Fleet would probably be senior to Collier, so the squadron would no longer be directed by detailed local knowledge painfully garnered in over six years of intense activity on the Biscay coast. Having pondered the arguments, Wellington decided he was better off as he was.

Collier continued to receive the occasional criticism from Wellington, but his responses are very revealing about the conditions under which he was operating.[31] The interdiction of communication between the many small harbours was not as complete as the army wanted, but shoal waters and bars across the mouths of many of them kept even Collier's small craft at bay: indeed, he was forced to use his frigates' boats for a close watch, involving their crews in many uncomfortable nights afloat. The sailor attempted to educate his soldier superior in the workings of wind and weather:

It is well known, my Lord, to seamen of moderate experience that in gales of wind blowing directly on a coast, where there is no anchorage but the port in possession of the enemy, the safety of the vessel's crew depends upon gaining an offing, or the consequence would be (what I fear has been the fate of several transports in this neighbourhood) certain destruction. In the heavy gales of wind in the Bay of Biscay no sail can be carried; the consequence is that the ship is not only driven at the mercy of the wind and sea, but exposed to the danger of foundering from the sea breaking into her.[32]

This was written in December 1813, and he could point to a number of fierce storms already that year.

In as far as Collier ever requested additional forces, it was principally cutters and gunboats, his frigate force (typically three to five vessels) being adequate to its tasks. With the two-deckers withdrawn the frigates took on their role as the local ship of force and the source of manpower and seamanlike expertise. Naval guns and their crews were often deployed ashore, and in March 1812 Collier had improved his ship's capability in this regard when he had *Surveillante*'s long 18pdrs replaced by Gover short 24pdrs. These were not only lighter and more easily manhandled, but with a larger ball and lower muzzle velocity were also more potent battering weapons. They were used to great effect at the siege of San Sebastian in September 1813.[33]

As Wellington advanced into France at the beginning of 1814 Collier's ships continued to give close support, his final contribution being a demonstration off St Jean de Luz which distracted the French from the land attack. He was recalled in January to take command of *Leander*, one of the pair of double-banked frigates built to meet the American spar-deckers of the *Constitution* type. At that time, with the country thirsting for revenge for the numerous American victories, it was probably the most desirable command in the Navy, and reflected the Admiralty's opinion of his achievement. Wellington continued to grouse about

Draught of the *Surveillante*, 38 guns, which was so active off the Spanish Biscay coast under Sir George Collier's command. Almost new when captured at San Domingo in 1803, she was a standard French 40 to Sané's design. Like most French frigates her lightweight construction did not stand up well to the rigours of British service and in March 1812 Collier applied to have her 18pdrs replaced with lighter Gover 24pdrs, claiming her topsides were 'weak with age'. This may have been special pleading in order to obtain weapons which would have been more useful in the land operations that were *Surveillante*'s principal employment, but the ship was soon sent to the breakers on the conclusion of the European war, suggesting that there was not much serviceable life left in the hull. This is the ship's appearance as fitted at Deptford in 1807.
National Maritime Museum Dr2031

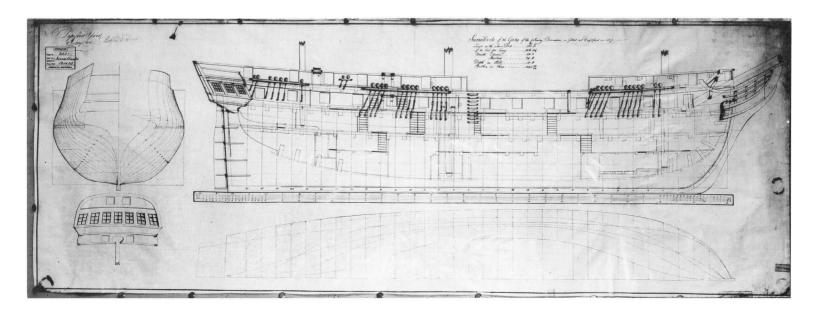

detailed aspects of the Navy's work, but he clearly appreciated its strategic value. As he told Byam Martin during his liaison mission, 'If anyone wishes to know the history of this war, I will tell them that it is our maritime superiority gives me the power of maintaining my army while the enemy are unable to do so.'[34]

9. Sea control

After ships of the line, frigates were the most powerful weapons in the armoury of the sailing navy. By their very nature battleships were usually concentrated in fleets, leaving many areas of a world-wide maritime conflict like those of 1793-1815 with little or no capital-ship presence. In these circumstances frigates were increasingly called upon to operate outside the battle-fleets, in what Julian Corbett regarded as their natural function.[35] He argued that while battlefleets seized command of the sea, it was the role of cruisers to exploit it, by controlling the 'lines of passage and communication' for the strategic benefit of the maritime power. To Corbett the real purpose of the battlefleet was to protect cruisers from the interference of the enemy, preferably by destroying his main fleet, but failing that by reducing it to inaction. His analysis was drawn from the age of sail, especially from the experience of Nelson, and from this he deduced that 'every cruiser attached to the battlefleet is one withdrawn from its true function'. The years 1793-1815 offer numerous examples of frigates pursuing this function under the, sometimes porous, aegis of the battlefleet.

The main British fleets were deployed in the Channel, the North Sea and the Mediterranean, with small squadrons in the East and West Indies. This left even important stations like Cork, responsible not only for the protection of trade in the Western Approaches but also the defence of Ireland itself, without a battle squadron. The next best thing was a force of powerful

frigates, which when concentrated could harass a would-be invasion fleet and disrupt the actual landings. In the winter of 1796-7 it was only bad weather which defeated Hoche's attempt to land in Bantry Bay, but one of the stragglers from his fleet, the 74-gun *Droits de l'Homme* was famously pursued to destruction by the *Indefatigable* and *Amazon*. The French managed to land a small force in Ireland from three frigates in August 1798, but the reinforcements under Bompart comprised one ship of the line, *Hoche*, and eight frigates. These were intercepted by a force under Sir John Warren, including three ships of the line, dispatched from Plymouth for the purpose, but although the *Hoche* was taken by Warren, six of the eight French frigates were rounded up by their British counterparts from the Irish and other stations.

From early in the war it was difficult for French battlefleets to get to sea unobserved, but small squadrons of frigates were more difficult to bottle up. At first French frigate squadrons were generally dispatched on commerce-raiding missions, but as it became increasingly risky for even small units of battleships to put to sea, frigates in groups were often used as a substitute for tasks like resupplying the dwindling number of French colonies overseas.

From 1793 the British response was to form special hunting groups in the Channel and Soundings to seek out and destroy commerce-raiders. These groups included some of the finest frigates of the day and made the name of frigate captains like Sir John Warren, Sir Edward Pellew, Sir Richard Strachan and Sidney Smith. They were immensely successful, and their prizes included some of the most powerful French frigates of the day like the *Pomone* and *Revolutionnaire*.[36] The fate of one French raiding group may serve as an example of the efficacy of these cruiser squadrons. Early in June 1796 three frigates and a

Sir George Collier's army co-operation squadron provided invaluable assistance in the Peninsular campaign, no more decisively than at the siege and capture of St Sebastian in August and September of 1813. In the foreground of this celebratory print seamen can seen manhandling guns into position and helping with entrenching and filling gabions. In the background Collier's squadron provides fire support – the frigates included *Revolutionnaire*, *Président*, *Magicienne* as well as Collier's flagship *Surveillante*. During the final assault on the citadel, the boats of the squadron carried out a highly successful diversionary attack at the rear of the castle rock.
National Maritime Museum 9946

The most improbable victory by a frigate squadron was Hoste's defeat of a Franco-Venetian flotilla of almost twice his force at Lissa in March 1811. This pair of drawings was made by an officer who was present, Lt William Innes Pocock, son of the famous marine artist. The first shows the British line of *Amphion*, *Active*, *Volage* and *Cerberus*, with the French – six frigates and four smaller craft – coming down in two lines in small-scale imitation of Nelson's attack at Trafalgar. The second drawing shows the British squadron, having worn around, with the heavily damaged French flagship *Favourite* run ashore. Three frigates surrendered (although one later escaped), while the *Favourite* was fired by her crew. Hoste's frigates dominated the northern Adriatic for years, both before and after Lissa, with only the occasional intervention of a line of battle ship.
National Maritime Museum PW0050

corvette escaped from Brest, but within days they were brought to action by two of the Irish station frigates, *Unicorn* and *Santa Margarita*, which captured the *Tribune* and *Tamise*. The most powerful French ship, the *Proserpine*, had separated before the battle but fell to another of the Irish frigates, the *Dryad*, a few days later; even the corvette, *Légère*, was taken by the frigates *Apollo* and *Doris* before she could regain port. The whole French squadron was lost in a little over two weeks.

The attack and defence of trade, even on a squadronal scale, might be regarded as conventional cruiser work, but after 1803 there were many examples of frigates operating in squadrons standing in for the battlefleet. If the enemy was unable or unwilling to send ships of the line to sea, then it was unnecessary to deploy anything stronger than frigates against them. This was particularly the case in distant colonial conflicts, the war around Mauritius in 1809-11 being almost entirely devolved onto frigates. Not only the disaster at Grand Port in August 1810, but Schomberg's action off Tamatave in May 1811, involved squadrons of frigates acting together like miniature battlefleets.

The same was true in parts of Europe. The eastern Mediterranean rarely saw a French battleship after 1805, and the British exploitation of seapower was largely in the hands of frigate squadrons. One was based on the Dalmatian island of Lissa, with the task of opposing the Franco-Venetian forces in the northern Adriatic. Venice built a number of warships up to two-

decker size on French account, and the local French naval commander, Dubourdieu, had a number of powerful frigates at his disposal. In March 1811 he took six frigates and four smaller craft to attack the British base, but was foiled by the appearance of a British squadron of three frigates and the *Volage*, 22, under the command of William Hoste of the *Amphion*. Dubourdieu divided his vastly superior force into two lines, intending to imitate the tactics of Trafalgar in miniature. However, Hoste was a protégé of Nelson (his ship went to action flying the signal 'Remember Nelson'), and in a cleverly fought battle captured two of the frigates and drove another on shore.

B. Independent Operations

Very little of the foregoing conforms to the conventional, and glamorous, image of the dashing frigate captain, operating on his own initiative, meeting the enemy in chivalrous single combat, achieving glory, fame, advancement and substantial prize money in the wake of success. True, there were many single-ship actions, sometimes against superior odds, and many officers benefited materially from their victories, but the image enshrines a misunderstanding about how these encounters came about. In contemporary accounts, like James's minutely chronicled *Naval History*, there is rarely any mention of how a frigate came to be where she was, nor any hint of her mission; the details of the action are his only concern. Modern popular books often follow the same line, leaving the reader to

This Pocock watercolour shows the frigate *Triton* lying-to, apparently assembling a convoy; the anchorage is probably St Helens Roads at the eastern end of the Isle of Wight, which was the usual rendezvous for convoys bound down Channel. Escort work was highly unpopular with the more energetic frigate captains, since it combined the constant fatigue of sheepdogging an unruly flock with little prospect of action, since most privateers (and even national commerce raiders) would avoid a well guarded convoy. In general, the larger frigates were too valuable for such duties, and even the 12pdr-armed *Triton* might consider herself unfortunate to have drawn such an assignment.
National Maritime Museum B5501

assume that single-ship encounters were little more than fortuitous, or at best the result of a frigate captain's hunting instinct, given free rein over a vast expanse of ocean. In fact, the genuinely independent cruise where the captain answered only to the Admiralty, although a scenario beloved of novelists, was in practice relatively uncommon.[37] Independent operations, therefore, as understood hereafter chiefly applies to activities outside the main fleets, but not necessarily beyond the control of their commanders; individual initiative was needed by detached frigate captains, but they were not necessarily their own boss.

When the Admiralty listed the dispositions of its ships, after the main fleets came those vessels assigned to 'Convoys and Cruisers' and 'On Particular Services'. The latter, being occasional, were not a significant element of a frigate's role, and generally meant little more than acting as transports for important individuals or valuable cargoes. As a representative sample, chosen at random, the first half of 1809 involved frigates in the following 'particular services', many associated with the British intervention in the Peninsula: *Loire* carrying specie to Cadiz and landing arms for the guerrillas in Galicia; *Amethyst* was sent to America 'for dollars'; *Africaine* was a diplomatic transport bringing home a British envoy and then taking the Duc of Orleans (later King Louis-Philippe of France) to Malta; General

Wellesley landed in Lisbon from the *Surveillante*, and General Craufurd (plus specie) from the *Niobe*; other big frigates involved with moving parts of the army to Portugal were *Arethusa, Endymion, Phoenix, Statira, Thetis,* and *Tribune.*[38]

Outside the battlefleet, 'Convoys and Cruisers' encompasses that other great frigate role, trade defence. By 1793 the Royal Navy had at least 150 years' experience of protecting the economic sinews of the country and had evolved a sophisticated system which, while never preventing all losses, always managed to restrict them to strategically sustainable proportions. Central to this defence was the ancient practice of convoy (in effect, a caravan of merchandise gathered together under armed escort), but there were more offensive tactics pursued in parallel by the 'cruisers'. At this time the term 'convoy' strictly applied to the escort and not the charges, so the Admiralty's definition combined both the passive and active aspects of trade defence.

1. Convoys

Besides those appointed by the Admiralty, convoys were also provided by local fleet commanders as part of the responsibilities of individual stations. Nevertheless, wherever the orders were issued, the close escort of convoys was not usually a job for big frigates.

In the 1790s they were in short supply and there were simply too many more important calls on their services, but even a decade later when they were the most common type of frigate (see Table 12/1), they were not often found on convoy duty. Nevertheless, there were exceptions even in the earlier period, probably the most regular being the need to provide strong protection for the Baltic trade in the period before Camperdown destroyed the threat from the Dutch fleet. Some of Admiral Duncan's most powerful frigates, including *Endymion, Acasta, Virginie* and *Clyde* accompanied the trade to and from the entrance to the Sound, but in the confined theatre of the North Sea they were never far from the main fleet. Significantly, there were no big frigates needed on this route by 1799-1800.[39]

In order to maximise its resources, the Admiralty was reluctant to countenance any 'idle' voyage, so it was common practice for any ship going out to her station, or coming home for refit, to sail with a convoy. In this manner many a big frigate found herself temporarily reinforcing the escort, but may not have been obliged to continue for the whole voyage. For example, in July 1796 the *Caroline, Alcmene* and *Druid* sailed with the West Indies convoy, but were then detached to their stations at Lisbon, Oporto and off Vigo respectively. Even when frigates formed the whole convoy escort it was often a cost-effective device for getting them to a cruising station: Duncan's frigates mentioned above often delivered their charges safely into the Sound and went on to patrol the sea between the Shetlands and Norway.

The Irish station frigates, which were refitted in Britain, usually took any available trade with them when sailing to or from their station, the Irish trade being exempted from regular convoy. In July 1796 the new *Unicorn* was ordered on completion to escort the coasting trade from the Downs, but the *Diana*, which was to have waited with them, was ordered to sea at once, so obviously operational priorities could disturb this convention. The Irish frigates occasionally found themselves on 'particular services' relating to convoys, such as *Magnanime* acting as guardship for the *Dorset*, the Irish government yacht, in August 1796; while earlier in the year *Dryad* was sent specially to bring a single ship from Milford to Spithead, but since this vessel was carrying copper for the Dockyard, it was presumably as important a cargo as a gaggle of Irish politicians.

By an Act of 1798 all foreign-going merchant ships were legally obliged to sail in convoy, with a few exceptions like the ships of the East India and Hudson's Bay companies which were well armed, or those fast enough to warrant a licence as a 'runner'. The Act also meant that the Navy had to find escorts for them, but the protection was not necessarily continuous, nor was the same level of escort afforded from assembly point to destination. Large long-distance convoys might have a close escort throughout, but they would be reinforced whenever possible in zones of particular danger. Since the oceans were vast, these were areas where the trade tended to converge, and especially in the approaches to the United Kingdom. The small but valuable convoys of East India ships were escorted to and from St Helena (and often by a small ship of the line), but the other merchant fleets were often seen safely in and out of British waters by an additional force of big frigates: in fact, a regular duty for the Irish station was to take the West Indies trade 'as far as 150 leagues to the west'. At this point, the role of cruisers in the defence of trade begins to mesh with that of convoys.

2. Cruisers

It was noted earlier that the independent cruise was by no means the most common employment for any ship, but it also seems that for heavy frigates convoy duty was a rarity – of fourteen listed under 'Convoys and Cruisers' for the middle of 1796, only *Imperieuse* was involved in convoy work (she had gone to St Helena with the *Isis*, 50, to bring home the East India trade).[40] The question that presents itself, therefore, is what was the function of cruising?

Cynics – whose ranks included some senior naval officers – saw it an little more than an opportunity for amassing prize money,[41] but the official answer as expressed in Admiralty orders was 'for the protection of trade and the annoyance of the enemy'. Taking up the first proposition, trade was protected by integrating the activities of convoys and cruisers. In the 1790s, almost all the big frigates categorised as 'cruisers' were organised into powerful squadrons commanded by specialists like Sir John Warren, Sir Edward Pellew and Sir Richard Strachan. In terms of convoy work, they functioned like a Support Group in the later stages of the Battle of the Atlantic: they joined the existing close escort when the threat required. This was easy on the outward leg, as with the usual strengthening of West India convoys by Irish frigates noted earlier. Without electronic communications, on the other hand, they could not simply be called in by returning convoys, and much depended on anticipating the regular patterns of trade.

The Admiralty's intelligence was usually good, and specific orders were sent to these squadrons in time for them to act. Taking the summer of 1796 as an example, orders in early July went to Kingsmill on the Irish station, Pellew further east, and Admiral Colpoys to look out for the Jamaica convoy; a few weeks later, with an unusual concentration of East and West India and Mediterranean convoys expected, Pellew was given explicit instructions to cruise between Latitudes 48-51 degrees, 40-80 leagues west of Scilly until he knew them to be safely past or until the end of August. The previous month Warren and Pellew had been instruct-

During the French Revolutionary War powerful frigate squadrons were based far west in Falmouth. These striking forces proved highly successful in destroying or capturing French commerce-raiders and in intercepting French trade in the Channel approaches and on the Biscay coast. The master of this kind of warfare was Sir John Borlase Warren, whose squadron brought many prizes into Falmouth, an achievement *The Naval Chronicle* thought worthy of celebration in this illustration. *Plate 34, The Naval Chronicle III (1800)*

ed to meet and strengthen the Oporto and Lisbon trade, the specific worry being a squadron of frigates known to have escaped from Brest on 7 June. Orders issued on the 11th (an impressive indication of the Admiralty's reconnaissance system) required both British commanders to 'endeavour to fall in with' this squadron. It was eventually destroyed in a series of individual actions by the Irish station frigates, which demonstrates that most single-ship engagements were not the products of chance meetings, but also emphasises that to 'take, burn or destroy' the enemy's commerce-raiders was itself a positive contribution to trade defence.

The instructions to cruising squadrons were not always specific, but they were also far from aimless patrolling. When in July 1796 Warren was ordered to cruise for one month from Ushant to the Garonne after first showing his force off St Malo 'and ranging along the coast in the neighbourhood', the Admiralty had a number of possible goals in mind. First there was the psychological value of flaunting a famous hunting group off one of France's premier privateering ports; second there was the disruption to the all-important *cabotage* (even if few coasters were actually captured); and third, there was a good chance of a number of privateers or national cruisers being snapped up. Aggressively taking the war to the enemy in this way was actually an extension of trade protection strategy, and its overall results were impressive: between 1793 and 1801 merchant ship losses amounted to only 3.44 per cent of all sailings (or 2.75 per cent if recaptures are deducted), roughly equivalent to the losses from ordinary marine risks like storm and shipwreck.[42]

In the second half of the wars, after the Peace of Amiens, the division of labour in trade defence became even more marked. The convoy system became better

organised, and offered more frequent sailings on more routes. At the same time, because the strategic situation had reduced the risk from major units of the enemy fleets, in most cases escorts could be confined to Sixth Rates and smaller, vessels large enough to cope with almost all privateers. The big frigates increasingly took on the character of hunters, actively seeking out potential commerce-raiders. These were not necesserily ships of their own kind – the numbers of French frigates taken at sea in the years after 1807 were not great – but even privateers became more difficult to find. This is a major cause of the upsurge in cutting-out expeditions, some of which were risky beyond the slim reward of a privateer; but they provided an outlet for the ambitions and natural aggression of naval officers frustrated by the lack of more conventional combat, and helped retain the moral advantage over the enemy.

After Tilsit in 1807 the war developed into an economic struggle between Napoleon's Continental System and the British concept of blockade expressed in the Orders in Council. The destruction of the enemy's trade was a traditional cruiser role, but by this time the Royal Navy had long since driven off the seas any commerce bearing the belligerents' own flags, but an elaborate pattern of licences, pseudo-neutrality and flags of convenience grew up which imposed an additional burden on cruising ships. Hereafter, virtually every sail had to be chased and probably boarded, in any season and whatever the weather. As an example, it has been shown that in 1808-9 the frigate *Amethyst* was involved in 77 chases during 266 days at sea.[43] It was very wearing on ships and crews alike since it often meant carrying a press of sail in heavy weather, and the requirement to check the suspect's papers caused boarding officers to risk their lives in small boats. Fast and seaworthy ships like the big frigates carried much of this workload, and it is not surprising that the experience led to an interest in the Navy's first unsinkable lifeboats (as outlined in Chapter 9).

3. 'The annoyance of the enemy'

Compared with a ship of the line a frigate was a relatively modest force; but a battleship was the *only* weapon of the time which was more powerful. Considered in the abstract a frigate was a highly potent, flexible and almost self-sufficient general-purpose warship. She disposed an impressive battery of relatively large calibre guns, a substantial crew trained for a variety of roles, the means to deploy them on land or in shallow water, and the incomparable mobility of the sea to use those assets to their maximum effect.

To put the firepower in context, it might be remembered that Wellington at Salamanca in 1812 had only 60 field guns in his whole army and none bigger than 12pdrs. Indeed, field artillery larger than 9pdrs was uncommon, and the 18pdr main armament of a standard 38 would provide a more powerful siege train than many armies could muster. Of course it was only rarely that a whole broadside could be brought to bear on land targets – and attacking stone fortifications with wooden ships was generally regarded as unwise – but the relative power of ship's guns explains the frequency with which field officers requested their support.

The other factor which made even a few naval guns a powerful addition to any military operation was the apparent ease with which seamen could manhandle such heavy and cumbersome items. Being experts in

the use of block and tackle and experienced in the concerted team-work required at sea, a naval crew could get artillery into seemingly impossible positions – like the summit of Diamond Rock, for example. Indeed, the crew was the frigate's most flexible asset. Apart from their seamanlike skills, at least fifty men of a Fifth Rate's complement were required by Naval Regulations to be specifically trained in musketry; to these must be added forty or so Royal Marines, who were properly drilled infantry;[44] a frigate might spare a further fifty men with at least some experience of wielding a cutlass, the result being a force well equipped for surprise assault.

To put these men ashore a frigate carried a complement of five boats, the largest of which was fitted with an 18pdr carronade in the bows for close fire support; and in the later years of the war frigates were often allowed a smaller carronade for the barge. These boats were not just the equivalent of Second World War landing craft, designed for a short dash to the shore from a mother ship: they were equipped with a sailing rig and were capable of making surprisingly long passages, sometimes being absent from their ship for days.[45] This allowed a frigate to exert control over waterways far shallower than her own draught. It became a dictum in this war that the Royal Navy's frontline was the enemy's coast: as Sir Sidney Smith put it in typically trenchant fashion, 'the frontier of Great Britain is high water mark in France. The uppermost seaweed on the beach belongs to us . . .'.[46]

In the early stages of the war frigate captains tended to use their ships against what might be considered

Unlike modern warships, which need the facilities of a shipyard to repair even moderate damage, a sailing warship was remarkably self-sufficient. Nothing short of serious underwater injury would send a wooden ship into dock, and most lesser work could be undertaken afloat, and often by the ship's own crew. Even where formal facilities were not available, the ingenuity and mechanical aptitude of the hemp-and-canvas seaman could achieve remarkable results - in this Baugean engraving a British 36-gun frigate is shown in an open roadstead replacing her main lower mast with the aid of sheerlegs. This would have been an unusual operation (mainly because it would have been difficult to find a suitable spar outside a formal Dockyard), but it does demonstrate how frigates could be kept on distant stations for months, if not years, with the minimum of shipyard attention. *J-J Baugean, Recueil de petites marines, Plate 38*

legitimate targets for seapower, namely enemy ships and shipping wherever it might be found. However, the classic cutting-out expedition often brought clashes with land defences. Throughout Europe even the smaller ports and anchorages had some batteries or fortifications – the Martello type towers of the Mediterranean, for example – but few were manned by first-class professional troops and naval officers grew adept

The process by which the Royal Navy built up confidence in its land attacks can be seen in the operation of the *Hydra*, 38 guns, in August 1806. Having chased three polaccas into the Catalan port of Bagur on the evening of the 6th, the captain reconnoitred the defences the following day and decided a cutting-out expedition was feasible. While the frigate, anchored with a spring on the cable, occupied the batteries, a force of fifty seamen and marines was sent ashore in the boats (as depicted in this near-contemporary lithograph). When the first force had stormed the substantial defences, a second landing party went in to assist in bringing out the polaccas, all of which was achieved with surprisingly small loss.

Although successful, *Hydra*'s action led Admiral Collingwood to caution his subordinate commanders against the kind of high-risk boat actions that were becoming so prevalent: 'The practice of detaching boats on a distant service out of the protection of the ship, is a cruel thing to gallant young officers, who do not like to return, even when their judgment dictates to them that they ought. They are enterprises highly injurious to the public service, because they disable the ship from performing her real duty; and they are discouraging to the men, because they shew . . . that they are schemes not directed by judgment.' (to Vice-Admiral Thornborough, 18 October 1807).

Collingwood was swimming against the tide, and as the result of such experiences, the Royal Navy came to believe that sudden assault by even small forces of seamen and marines could carry fixed fortifications of the scale found in all but the largest ports.
National Maritime Museum PW4765

at carrying such fortifications by surprise and storm. By 1809 Collingwood could boast to a colleague:

We are carrying on our operations in the Adriatic and on the coast of Italy with great éclat All our frigate Captains are great Generals, and some in the brigs are great Brigadiers. They have taken seven forts, garrisons, or castles within the two last months; and scaling towers at midnight, and storming redoubts at mid-day, are become familiar occurrences. The enemy cannot stand a galling fire from the launch's carronade, or a sharp fire of grape and musketry from the jolly boat. It is really astonishing; these youths think nothing is beyond their enterprise, and they seldom fail of success.[47]

The sheer mobility of seapower imbued even a single frigate with a disproportionate force when exerted against land targets. If one assumes an available landing force of 100 men, then to make a coast safe would entail protecting even the tiniest harbour against such a number: whether the enemy chose to do this with men or with fortifications, the result was the same massive diversion of resources from the land war.

Home Popham was to prove this on a larger scale on the north coast of Spain, but the precedent had been set in 1808 by the activities of a single frigate off

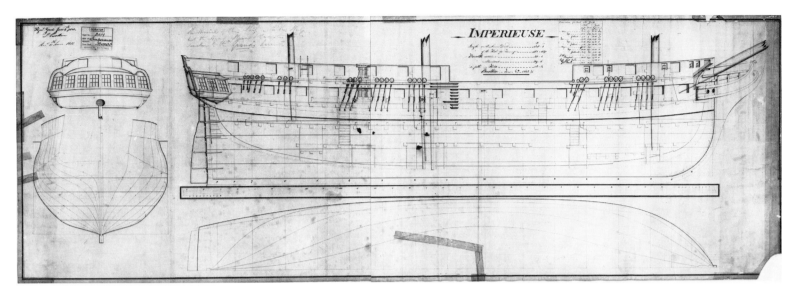

Catalonia and the south of France. Lord Cochrane's campaign in the *Imperieuse* that summer is well known, but even allowing for the highly coloured account in his autobiography, it was a textbook example of the application of seapower to a land campaign. Not only did he intervene on an almost daily basis to support the Spanish guerrillas, but he carried on his own war against the chain of French signal stations that telegraphed information about British offshore activity, thus thwarting attacks on the coasting trade. The towers were blown up, but he was careful to leave evidence suggesting that the signal books had been destroyed with them; in reality, he either copied the signals or burnt only fragments (there are original versions of these books in the National Maritime Museum to this day). The ability to read the codes indirectly enhanced the British effort against shipping, but Cochrane's activities pinned down French regiments that could have gone to Spain, and Collingwood, the Mediterranean commander-in-chief, believed that the French had been forced to withdraw 2000 men from the garrison at Figueras for coast defence duties in Languedoc.[48] Not without reason, Napoleon himself christened Cochrane *loup des mers*.

Although these attacks appear highly risky, Cochrane claims he had only one man injured in the whole campaign and in truth they were so well planned that they could not be regarded as foolhardy. There were numerous less spectacular examples of power-projection on this micro scale by frigates and small craft in theatres from the Adriatic to the East Indies, and they demonstrated what even limited naval force might achieve. Indeed, Cochrane became convinced that his tactics writ large could substitute for a continental strategy. Not only could wholly seaborne forces intervene with greater effect in Spain, but he advocated seizing the French Biscay islands as bases for a concerted campaign of coastal attacks on France itself, tying down such a high proportion of Napoleon's

troops that it would prove impossible to occupy Portugal and Spain. As a result there would be no occasion for risking a major British military force on the continent, and Wellington's laborious struggle across most of the Peninsula would have been unnecessary. Cochrane came to see small amphibious striking forces used in this way as the key to a quick, cost-effective and war-winning strategy.[49]

Perhaps few would have claimed so much for the frigate, but it is the highest tribute to its flexibility and power from one who knew best how to exploit those assets.

II. The Experience of War

For the vast majority of British naval officers, whatever their service or seniority, the overwhelming impression of the war was the reluctance of the enemy to offer battle. In so many of the naval memoirs and reminiscences published post-war, the underlying metaphor of the officer's task is that of a hunter: occasionally the foxhunter in glorious pursuit of a fleeing quarry, but more often the patient stalker of timid prey. This latter seemed particularly apposite for the frustrating monotony of blockade duty, and induced a degree of contempt for the enemy. As Philip Broke wrote to his wife after months blockading Basque Roads, ' . . . we are mousing here all day, but the vermin run into their holes and we never catch them.'[50]

Year-round close blockade was very demanding. Seamanship of the highest order was vital, but in terms of the ships employed so was seaworthiness. This comprised both seakeeping, to allow the ship to do its job in virtually all weathers, and also the sailing qualities that allowed ships to claw off a lee shore – and since the French Biscay ports were subject to onshore winds for large parts of the year, the weatherly qualities of British ships were always severely tested. A further requirement was the ability to stay on station for as long as

One of the greatest coastal raiders of all time, Lord Cochrane's famous *Imperieuse*, the scourge of the French Mediterranean seashore. A Spanish-built ship, as the *Medea* she was the flagship of Rear-Admiral Bustamente's 'treasure frigates' whose capture in January 1804 precipitated war between Spain and Britain. In British service she led an adventurous life, which included attacking grounded French ships of the line during the Basque Roads attack in April 1809, and even after Cochrane relinquished command to Henry Duncan in 1810 the ship retained her reputation as a highly effective raider on the coast of Italy.
National Maritime Museum Dr2017

For many frigate captains war service did not involve independent commands, glorious single-ship actions, or the vigorous pursuit of prize money. Instead it was a monotonous, but dangerous, round of close blockade, keeping an eye on the enemy fleet in all weathers and every season, under the confining orders of the fleet commander. None of these stations was more important or more closely guarded than Brest, and this engraving celebrates the almost insolent familiarity with which British ships treated these French waters. A British frigate is shown rounding the Parquette Rock, off the entrance to Brest Roads, with the French fleet beyond; having made a close reconnaissance, she is signalling to consorts further out.
Plate 468, The Naval Chronicle XXXVI (1816)

possible: to stow the maximum stores and provisions, and to be structurally strong enough not to require frequent dockyard attention. The study of the *Amethyst* quoted earlier found that in a period of 420 days, 266 were spent at sea, and of the remainder 140 days were taken up with repairing damage after two punishing single-ship actions.[51]

In the course of the war it became clear that British-built frigates satisfied these demands far more closely than French-built prizes. The deeper British hull-form stowed more and tended to produce better windward performance, while they were generally good seaboats. In terms of structural strength, the only modification inspired by war experience was the 1811 proposal to *reduce* the scantlings of most types, although in practice frigates were not much affected. Nevertheless, it is a strong indication that there were no doubts about the strength of British-built frigates.

Apart from reporting on the movements of heavy units, blockading frigates were charged with intercepting any smaller craft – and that after weeks, if not months, on station. As all British cruisers discovered, this usually entailed a chase. From this experience there developed an inevitable preoccupation with ships that could *catch* the enemy rather than those able to *beat* him (the latter soon became an assumed consequence of achieving the first). This was as true for battle squadrons as for cruisers and after the war it encouraged the Admiralty to indulge Sir William Symonds's notions of sharp-lined battleships, to the detriment of their attributes as gun platforms. For frigates, tradition-

ally dependent on their sailing qualities, the emphasis can be seen in the designs chosen for large-scale construction.

While logs record numerous examples of French ships out-running British frigates, it was not a common enough experience to produce any consistent criticism or complaint. There were a few well-known heavy-sailing frigates in the British fleet, but they did not belong to the most favoured classes; nor were the ex-French prizes noticeably superior. Furthermore, most of the single-ship actions resulted from the ability of a British frigate to overtake a reluctant enemy. No doubt superior seamanship and greater sea-time allowed Royal Navy officers to extract the very best that their ships were capable of, but since success was so frequent, even the theoretical difference in performance between ships of the two navies must have been negligible. In fact, if William Dillon was correct in his boast to Barrallier about the general superiority to windward of British frigates, then it explains how nominally faster ships could be caught on such a regular basis.

This concentration on the chase had its drawbacks, but it took the defeats of the War of 1812 to make them a discussion point. In preparation for writing a very influential book on naval gunnery, General Sir Howard Douglas corresponded in depth with Sir Philip Broke, whose *Shannon* won the most spectacular victory of any frigate action in the wars of 1793-1815. Douglas was intrigued by the fact that – apart from Lawrence of the *Chesapeake* – the American captains had fought their battles with circumspection and no little tactical skill, despite having far more powerful ships; the British, with the possible exception of Lambert of the *Java*, had sought nothing more sophisticated than to close at once for a point-blank gunnery duel, which could only have been suicidal against well-handled 24pdrs. Broke was forced to admit that two decades of pursuing an elusive (and, it has to be said, generally unskilful) enemy had taken its toll. Such was the inherent tactical advantage possessed by the chasing ship, that ' . . . all scientific manoeuvre has become apparently superfluous.'[52] This was a recent innovation and Broke went on to recall that towards the end of the American Revolutionary War Sir William Fairfax of the *Tartar* had been in the habit of using the ship's barge to simulate the enemy; he practised working his frigate around the target in order to get a feel for his ship's handling and to test his tactical ideas.[53]

However, as Broke had informed Douglas, 'Our modern ships of war, particularly frigates, are not perhaps so well calculated for manoeuvring as the old-fashioned ships were, being so much slower in turning, on account of their flat futtock and great length . . . '.[54] In effect, the desire for improved speed that produced the longer frigates of the 1790s, compromised their handiness, something for which earlier British frigates had been noted. By contrast French ships had always been notoriously slow going about, but as an example of the new tactical reality in the battle between *Horatio* (a *Lively* class 38) and *Junon* in February 1809, both ships proved equally long in wearing, although the British crew was a little smarter.

Douglas went on to mention the enhanced risk of damage to top-hamper if a ship carried enough sail to engage and manoeuvre simultaneously. What he did not address was the difficulty of so doing. This was one of the principal advantages of the spar deck, as advocated by Philip Beaver (see Chapter 9), in that the sail-handlers worked above the gun crews and did not interfere with their firing. This was well understood in the US Navy where the big frigates had ceased to mount guns in the waist 'gangways' for just this reason. Although a form of spar deck was introduced into the Royal Navy, during the war its benefit was minimal because by most standards British frigates were under-manned. As a result, whatever the theoretical advantages of fighting a battle of manoeuvre, British frigate crews were simply too small to allow sail-handling and serving the great guns at the same time.

A related issue was the one of crew quality. Even if they could fill their nominal complements, very few British captains enjoyed Broke's luxury of a long-serving crew. As a result, few captains believed that it was possible to train the average ship's company in *aimed* gunnery, but with regular practice they could be drilled to load and fire rapidly. Of course, to make such fire effective the range had to be short; and to get into position with the least risk of damage to masts and rigging (the usual French target) implied closing rapidly without manoeuvring. It may have looked unsophisticated, but it was actually a reasonable response to the quality constraints of an over-stretched force on the one hand, and a realistic appraisal of the threat on the other. For twenty years it provided the Royal Navy with an unprecedented string of victories, only proving inade-

Occasionally the tedium of blockade duty was interrupted by an attempted French break-out. Whether by a fleet, squadron or single ship, a French sortie was always directed to a specific end, and giving battle did not usually figure in the orders under which it operated. The result was inevitably a chase, perhaps never better depicted than in this Pocock watercolour of the *Amethyst*, 36, in pursuit of the *Thétis*, 40, on 10 November 1808. The French frigate had sailed from Lorient on a mission to reinforce the besieged island of Martinique, but was sighted off the Isle de Groix by the *Amethyst*, which signalled the fact to her consorts and set off in pursuit. This class were the largest British-built 36s in the Navy and clearly fine sailers, *Amethyst* taking about two hours to overhaul the *Thétis*; in the hard-fought battle that followed, the issue was settled by superior British gunnery and not by tactical handling, although a number of attempted French manoeuvres were countered by Captain Seymour of the *Amethyst*. *National Maritime Museum 2414*

As the war progressed single-ship actions became less battles of manoeuvre and more gunnery duels – less like fencing and more like bare-knuckle boxing. This was partly because the quality of French seamanship and training declined to the point where tactics were superfluous, but also because the ships themselves became less agile. The capture of the *Junon*, 40, in February 1809 is a case in point. Working to windward to escape the *Latona*, 38, the French frigate decided to offer battle to the *Horatio*, another 38 approaching on the opposite tack. The opening gambit saw them exchange broadsides in passing, whereupon the British frigate wore in an attempt to cut off a possible French escape to leeward. An older, and shorter, British frigate would have come about more rapidly, but the big *Horatio* gave *Junon* time to wear also and run down to leeward, although the British ship was round quickly enough to rake the Frenchman's stern in the process. In the action which followed the *Horatio* was heavily damaged aloft, by the usual French tactic of firing high, and so was unable to prevent the *Junon*, whose rigging was also in a poor state, from running out of range to leeward. She was eventually beaten by the undamaged *Latona*, which had worked her way up during the earlier fight. This French watercolour is rather inaccurate, in that the two British frigates were never engaged simultaneously, and the *Horatio* had lost her topmasts long before the *Junon* was subdued.
National Maritime Museum PAG9089

quate against the Americans, and even then not for one but for a combination of reasons – their far more powerful ships; larger crews that permitted fighting and manoeuvring at the same time; and crews of a better average standard, encouraging captains to fight a tactical battle.

After the war, new classes of frigate were introduced to address the threat of 24pdr-armed ships in the navies of America and France, but prior to this there was little suggestion that British frigates were under-armed. Indeed, the enthusiastic adoption of the carronade produced an ideal armament for a frigate, with a mix of longer range traditional cannon and very powerful short-barrelled weapons for maximum effect at close quarters. For their tonnage, British 18pdr frigates probably fired a heavier weight of shot than any opponents of the same rate,[54] and although short 24pdrs had been available since around 1800, fitting them to frigates was a low priority before 1812 – indeed, they were generally fitted where the frigate was too weak to carry the usual long 18pdrs.

It may be a crude measure of success but very few of the Royal Navy's large frigates were lost due to the direct actions of the enemy. In fact, not one was captured in the French Revolutionary War, and only a handful thereafter: *Minerve* grounded and was forced to surrender off Cherbourg in July 1803; *Blanche* was captured by *Topaze*, 40, *Département de Landes*, 22 and two sloops in the West Indies in July 1805; *Proserpine* was ambushed off Toulon by the 40-gun frigates *Pénélope* and *Pauline*, in February 1809; *Sirius* and *Iphigenia* (as well as the 12pdr *Nereide* and *Magicienne*) were lost in the Grand Port debacle in August 1810; *Africaine* was taken by *Astrée* and *Iphigénie* the following month; while *Guerriere*, *Macedonian* and *Java* were captured by American '44's in 1812. Not one of these ships was taken in equal combat, and before the War of 1812 not one by a single ship. Of the nine losses, four were destroyed during or immediately after the battle and three were recaptured, so the net loss was minuscule from a force that numbered over 100 ships by the end of the war. In the circumstances, it would be difficult to argue for additional firepower.

Such advances as were applied to the weaponry of frigates tend to emphasise their newer, more general-purpose roles. This is particularly evident in improvements to the outfit, armament and launching arrangements for the ship's boats, the 'weapons' by which the frigate's power was projected beyond the range of her long guns. The launch was regularly armed, and often a second boat as well; some frigates carried a specially designed Brenton gunboat-yawl; and captains were allowed far more freedom in their exchanges of established boats for something they found more 'suitable'. Davits on the quarters and taffrail made it easier and quicker to get most of the boats into the water, an important consideration when the operation had to be repeated frequently, as came to be the norm for many frigates by the end of the war.

The final expression of the Navy's commitment to land-attack missions can be seen in the special equipment added to the big frigates and *rasées* deployed on the North America station in 1814. The 9pdr field piece and a 5½in mortar which were designed for use ashore were the forerunner of the 'landing gun' regularly carried in Victorian times by most warship types.

In only one respect was the 'armament' of frigates weakened, and this was the 1806 reductions in the established complements. This reflected nothing more than the desperate shortage of seamen experienced by the Navy as a whole, and nowhere is this better demonstrated than in the small proportion of skilled men within those reduced numbers:

	38 guns	*36 guns*	*32 guns*
Officers	12	12	12
Petty officers	33	33	33
Able seamen	58	51	49
Ordinary seamen	56	50	49
Landmen	56	49	48
Boys, 1st class	3	3	3
Boys, 2nd class	6	6	6
Boys, 3rd class	9	9	9
Marines	48	48	42
Widows' men	3	3	3
Nominal complement	284	264	254

Even though little could be done about the skill ratio, at the time there were enough individual remonstrances from frigate captains to suggest the new numbers were seen as dangerously low by serving officers.[56] By implication, this was admitted retrospectively by the Admiralty, who reacted to the American frigate victories of 1812 by not merely restoring the original complements, but actually increasing them. However, these were still far short of French or American equivalents, and it seems that British frigates were expected to rely on the close-range fire of long guns and carronades.

It might be thought that the demands of longer periods at sea, on blockade stations or long-range cruising, would have placed an emphasis on enhanced stowage. However, the existing standards of four months endurance for Channel (*ie* home) and six on Foreign Service were theoretical maximums, and applied to the ship's stores and not victuals and water. In practice continuous sea-time was determined by other limitations, such as the life of the fresh (anti-scorbutic) supplies on board, the state of the ship' structure, or even the psychological resilience of the captain (if blockading became too strenuous, there were a number of more or less plausible excuses for seeking port). A major strategic development of the war was the establishment of a system to supply cruising ships with fresh victuals, and its importance became accepted by all senior commanders. The one significant development, albeit right at the end of the wars, was the introduction of iron water tanks. This certainly made stowage more space-efficient, but also offered advantages ranging from economy (being cheaper than casks) to improved sailing qualities. Because they kept water purer and took up less room in the hold, tanks held out the prospects of longer periods between watering as well as stowing more dry victuals in the same hull-form, both of which tended to greater real endurance.

CONCLUSIONS

With the exception of a few Barham-inspired small-ship experiments, between 1803 and 1812 frigate-building was confined to only three classes: the 36s of the *Apollo*/*Euryalus* class, and 38s to the *Leda* and *Lively* designs, each of which derived from the time of the Spencer Admiralty in the 1790s. In these years frigates had grown substantially in size, had acquired relatively longer proportions for higher speed, and once all but the chase guns on the upperworks had been replaced by carronades, attained a firepower-to-tonnage ratio far superior to that of any equivalent antagonist. Furthermore, this was achieved without significant concessions in structural strength, stowage capacity or seaworthiness. This was little short of a revolution and bequeathed to the following administrations frigate designs fully equal to the increasingly strenuous

A British 36-gun frigate hove to: it is probably a ship of the numerous *Apollo/Euryalus* class, the nearest thing to a 'war standard' frigate in the Royal Navy of the Napoleonic era. The well-known French engraver of this work, J-J Baugean, notes elsewhere that British warships, being shorter, were quicker going about than French vessels. Like all the received wisdom of seafarers, this was a generalisation that had taken decades to mature, but it was effectively out of date by the time Baugean came to make the remark. Since the 1790s British frigates had grown proportionally longer and had consciously abandoned their manoeuvring advantage in pursuit of speed.
J-J Baugean, Toutes les Espèces de Bâtiments, Plate 29

demands made on them, and fully a match for those of their enemies.

Returning to the 'staff requirements' for frigates as outlined at the beginning of this chapter – speed, seakeeping, manoeuvrability, strength, firepower and capacity – it is clear that these classes met the Admiralty's expectations closely if not perfectly. Comparing their qualities with earlier designs, the major change in priorities was the emphasis on speed.[57] This was consciously obtained at the expense of handling, but the strategic conditions made the penalty acceptable since a battle of manoeuvre became increasingly unnecessary. Seakeeping had always been an important consideration, and although subjected to the most rigorous testing of all-weather cruising during this war, it was found satisfactory (subject only to minor complaint about fine lines tending to pitching). Structural strength was more than adequate to the task, to the point where a general reduction in scantlings could be contemplated. Firepower had also increased dramatically during the 1790s, so that further developments were confined to a few specialist weapons

designed to give the frigate greater flexibility. Capacity also became less of an issue, thanks to improved logistics and the introduction of water tanks; indeed, the post-war concentration on the *Leda* class, whose French-derived hull-form did not quite meet ideal stowage requirements, was probably only made possible by the employment of tanks.

The period of the Napoleonic War, and especially after Trafalgar, was essentially one of mass construction of a few selected classes. The new designs of the period – the First Rates, the Surveyors' class 74s and the *Cherokee* class brigs – were workmanlike but far from outstanding, whereas the greatest successes were ships of the late 1790s. The *Cruizer* class brig sloops were built in larger numbers than any wooden warship in history, which is one measure of success, but the accolade for the closest match between operational requirements and design characteristics must go to the frigates of the *Apollo*, *Leda* and, above all, *Lively* classes. At a time when the frigate's roles were multiplying and expanding, they achieved everything that was asked of them.

TABLE 12/2: Disposition of frigates in selected war years

JANUARY 1794
[beginning of first full year of the war]

East Indies	REAR-ADMIRAL CORNWALLIS
18pdr frigate	38: *Minerva*
Jamaica	COMMODORE JOHN FORD
Line of battle	*Europa*, 50 (flag), one 64
12pdr frigates	32s: *Penelope, Hermione, Magicienne, Success*
	Two sloops, four schooners
Leeward Isles	VICE-ADMIRAL SIR JOHN JERVIS
Line of battle	*Boyne*, 98 (flag), two 74s, two 64s, one 50
18pdr frigate	40: *Beaulieu*
12pdr frigates	36: *Santa Margarita*; 32s: *Blanche, Alarm, Terpsichore, Iphigenia, Solebay, Blonde, Ceres, Winchelsea, Quebec*
	Three 44s *en flûte*, two Sixth Rates, four sloops, one storeship, one hospital ship, one bomb vessel, one schooner
Mediterranean	VICE-ADMIRAL LORD HOOD
Line of battle	*Victory*, 100 (flag), one 100, three 98s, twelve 74s, three 64s, one 50
18pdr frigates	38: *Aigle*; 36s: *Romulus, Leda, Inconstant*
12pdr frigates	32s: *Iris, Juno, Aimable, Lowestoffe, Mermaid, Meleager*
	Four Sixth Rates, two sloops, two storeships, one hospital ship, two fireships, one cutter
Nova Scotia	One 28
Newfoundland	
12pdr frigates	32s: *Cleopatra, Boston*
	Three sloops, two armed ships
On particular services	One 64, one 44, one 20, three sloops, one cutter
Secret orders	One 44, one survey ship, one armed tender
Convoys and cruisers	
18pdr frigate	36: *Thalia*
12pdr frigates	32s: *Concorde, Daedalus*
	Six Sixth Rates, four sloops, two armed ships, thirteen armed vessels, eight cutters
Channel Fleet	ADMIRAL LORD HOWE
Line of battle	*Queen Charlotte*, 100 (flag), two 100s, three 98s, one 80, sixteen 74s

18pdr frigates	38s: *Phaeton, Latona, Hebe*; 36: *Phoenix*
12pdr frigates	32s: *Niger, Venus, Southampton*
	One 28, four sloops, two fireships
	REAR-ADMIRAL GARDNER'S SQUADRON [returned from West Indies]
Line of battle	*Queen*, 98 (flag), one 74, two 64s, one 50
12pdr frigates	32s: *Orpheus, Heroine, Castor*
	One 44, two sloops, one bomb
	REAR-ADMIRAL MACBRIDE'S SQUADRON [for operations off Holland]
	Cumberland, 74 (flag)
18pdr frigates	36s: *Melampus, Crescent, Flora*
12pdr frigates	36: *Nymphe*; 32 *Druid*
	One 44, three Sixth Rates, six armed ships, one floating battery, three sloops, one armed vessel, one cutter
Portsmouth and Spithead	Two 98s, six 74s, four 64s, one 50, one 44
18pdr frigate	38: *Arethusa* [fitting for Channel Service]
12pdr frigates	36: *Oiseau* [fitting for Channel Service]; 32s: *Aquilon, Active* [fitting for Channel Service], *Fox* [arrived from Newfoundland], *Andromache* [to Cork with transports]
	Nine Sixth Rates, one fireship, four sloops, two storeships, one cutter, one slop ship, one receiving ship, one convict ship
Plymouth	One 80, four 74s, three 64s, one 50, two 44s
12pdr frigates	32s: *Amphion, Syren* [fitting for Foreign Service and Channel Service respectively]
	Two Sixth Rates, one sloop, one cutter, one armed vessel, one receiving ship, one convict ship, one slop ship, one survey vessel
Chatham and Nore	Three 74s, one 64, one 44
12pdr frigate [At the Nore]	32: *Astraea* [at the Nore]
[Sheerness]	Two armed vessels and a cutter Two sloops, one lugger, one receiving ship, one hospital ship, one convict ship, one prison ship

In the Thames	
18pdr frigate	38: *Artois* [Woolwich, fitting for Channel Service]
	Three sloops, one hospital ship, one storeship, one receiving ship, two yachts
In the Downs	VICE-ADMIRAL PEYTON
	Leopard, 50 (flag)
12pdr frigate	32: *Pearl*
	One 28, one sloop
At Cork	REAR-ADMIRAL KINGSMILL
Line of battle	*Swiftsure*, 74 (flag), one 64
	One receiving ship
Miscellaneous	
18pdr frigate	38: *Thetis* [gone to Leith to complete complement]
	Two sloops, three armed vessels, one yacht

JULY 1797
[between St Vincent and Camperdown; the Great Mutinies]

East Indies	REAR-ADMIRAL RAINIER
Line of battle	*Suffolk*, 74 (flag), three 74s, six 64s, four 50s
18pdr frigates	38s: *Sybille, Saldanha*; 36: *Crescent*
12pdr frigates	36: *Braave*; 32s: *Oiseau, Fox, Orpheus, Heroine*
	One 44, four Sixth Rates, four sloops, one storeship
Jamaica	VICE-ADMIRAL SIR H PARKER
Line of battle	*Queen*, 98 (flag), five 74s, one 64, one 54
18pdr frigate	38: *Tamar*
12pdr frigates	32s: *Hermione, Quebec, Ambuscade, Janus, Aquilon, Proselyte, Thames*
	Three 44s, three Sixth Rates, seven sloops, two schooners
Leeward Isles	REAR-ADMIRAL HARVEY
Line of battle	*Prince of Wales*, 98 (flag), six 74s, two 64s, one 54
18pdr frigate	38: *Arethusa*
12pdr frigates	32s: *Maidstone, Aimable, Alarm, Eurus, Mermaid*
	Two 44s, seven Sixth Rates, eleven sloops, one storeship, one hospital ship, one prison ship, one schooner, one bomb, three gunboats

Mediterranean — ADMIRAL EARL OF ST VINCENT [actually based in the Tagus]

Line of battle — *Victory*, 100 (flag), two First Rates, five 98s, fourteen 74s, one 64, one 50

18pdr frigates — 38s: *Minerve, Seahorse, Aigle*; 36s: *Thalia, Romulus, Inconstant, Emerald, Caroline*; 32s: *Pallas, Lively*

12pdr frigates — 36: *Magicienne*; 32s: *Andromache, Meleager, Southampton, Boston, Blanche, Ceres, Terpsichore, Mahonesa*
Four Sixth Rates, ten sloops, two storeships, one prison ship, hospital ship, one cutter

Nova Scotia — VICE-ADMIRAL VANDEPUT

Line of battle — *Resolution*, 74 (flag), one 64, one 50

18pdr frigate — 38: *Thetis*

12pdr frigates — 36s: *Prevoyante, Topaze*; 32: *Andromeda*
Two Sixth Rates, eight sloops, one armed ship, one prison ship

Newfoundland — VICE-ADMIRAL WALDEGRAVE
Romney, 50

18pdr frigate — 38: *Latona* (flag)

12pdr frigate — 32: *Venus*
One 28, one sloop

On particular services

18pdr frigate — One 64, one 44
38: *Imperieuse* [with sloop *Star* to Cape]
One sloop, two armed vessels, one cutter

[Channel] — 'UNDER LORD BRIDPORT'

Line of battle — *Royal George*, 100 (flag), two First Rates, four 98s, fourteen 74s

18pdr frigates — 38s: *Phaeton, Melpomene, Jason*; 36: *San Fiorenzo*; 32: *Stag*

12pdr frigates — 36: *Unité*; 32s: *Nymphe, Pique, Triton*
One fireship

[Sir Edward Pellew's squadron]

24pdr frigates — 44s: *Indefatigable, Anson*

12pdr frigate — 32: *Cleopatra*
One sloop

[Sir John Warren's squadron]

24pdr frigate — 40: *Pomone*

18pdr frigates: — 38: *Artois*; 36: *Phoebe*; 32: *Unicorn*
One sloop

[Under Sir Richard Strachan – see below]

12pdr frigates — 32s: *Daedalus, Pearl*

[Under Sir Richard King – see below]
Two sloops

[OTHER SPECIFIED SERVICES]

18pdr frigates — 38: *Clyde* [convoy to Baltic]; 32: *Alcmene* [convoy to Lisbon]
Three Sixth Rates, two sloops

[UNSPECIFIED]
One 24, two sloops, two armed sloops, three armed vessels, nine cutters, one lugger, one gunboat

[North Sea] — ADMIRAL DUNCAN'S SQUADRON

Line of battle — *Venerable*, 74 (flag), two 98s, two 80s, five 74s, ten 64s, one 56, three 50s

18pdr frigate — 40: *Beaulieu*

12pdr frigates — 32s: *Iris, Astraea*
Five 28s, fifteen sloops, seven armed vessels, one floating battery, one gunboat

[Bay of Biscay] — SIR RICHARD STRACHAN'S SQUADRON

18pdr frigates — 38s: *Diamond, Minerva*

12pdr frigate — 32: *Syren*
One 24, one sloop, three gunboats, one cutter

At Cork — VICE-ADMIRAL KINGSMILL
Polyphemus, 64 (flag)

24pdr frigate — 44: *Magnanime*

18pdr frigates — 38: *Diana*; 36s: *Doris, Dryad, Glenmore*; 32s: *Cerberus, Galatea*

12pdr frigates — 36: *Santa Margarita*; 32s: *Shannon, Greyhound*
Three sloops, one schooner, one hospital ship

Portsmouth and Spithead — ADMIRAL SIR PETER PARKER

Royal William, receiving ship (flag), one 98, one 80, two 74s, one 44, one receiving ship

24pdr frigates — 40: *Cambrian* [fitted for Channel Service]

18pdr frigates — 38: *Boadicea* [fitting for Channel Service]; 36s: *Flora, Phoenix* [both fitting for Channel Service], *Trent* [en route to Spithead]

12pdr frigates — 32s: *Tribune, Success* [both fitting for Channel Service], *Concorde* [fitting for Foreign Service]

Three Sixth Rates, four sloops, one fireship, one slop ship, one cutter, one storeship, one bomb, five prison hulks, two hospital ships, one convict ship

Plymouth — ADMIRAL SIR RICHARD KING
Cambridge, 80 (flag), one 80, one 74, three 64s, one 54, one 50, one 44 *en flûte*, two 24s, three sloops, one schooner, one hospital ship, three prison ships, one slop ship, one fire vessel

In the Downs — ADMIRAL PEYTON
Overijssel, 64 (flag)

18pdr frigates — 38s: *Apollo, Virginie*; 36: *Melampus*
One 24, four sloops, four gunboats

Chatham and Nore — VICE-ADMIRAL LUTWIDGE
Sandwich, receiving ship (flag), one 74

18pdr frigates — 38s: *Ethalion* [fitting for Channel Service], *Revolutionnaire* [en route to the Nore]

12pdr frigates — 32s: *Niger* [fitted for Channel Service], *Espion*
One sloop, one receiving ship, two hospital ships [at Sheerness], two hospital ships [at Chatham], one convict ship [at Sheerness], two prison ships [at Chatham]

Thames, etc — [Woolwich – fitting for Channel Service]
One 98, one 74, two 64s

24pdr frigate — 44: *Endymion*

18pdr frigates — 40: *Acasta*; 38s: *Naiad, Hydra*; 36: *Sirius*

[Woolwich – fitting for Foreign Service]
One 64, one 44 [fitting as storeships]

[Deptford]
One yacht, one storeship

[Jersey – Captain d'Auvergne, Prince de Bouillon]
One Sixth Rate, two cutters, two armed vessels

Miscellaneous — Two receiving ships [one off the Tower, one at Liverpool], one sloop [guardship at North Shields], one floating battery [at Hull], one convict ship [at

Falmouth], one yacht [Ireland], one survey vessel, eighty-five gunboats

To be paid off   One sloop, one fireship

MARCH 1801
[Battle of Copenhagen]

East Indies	VICE-ADMIRAL RAINIER
Line of battle	*Suffolk*, 74 (flag), two 74s, three 64s, two 50s
24pdr frigate	44: *Forte*
18pdr frigates	38s: *Sybille*, *Virginie*
12pdr frigates	32s: *Fox*, *Orpheus*, *Daedalus*
	Three sloops, one bomb vessel
Cape of Good Hope	VICE-ADMIRAL SIR RICHARD CURTIS
Line of battle	One 74, *Lancaster*, 64 (flag), three 50s
18pdr frigate	38: *Imperieuse*
12pdr frigate	36: *Braave*
	Five sloops, one armed vessel
Jamaica	REAR-ADMIRAL LORD SEYMOUR
Line of battle	*Sans Pareil*, 80 (flag), two 74s, one 64
18pdr frigates	40: *Acasta*; 38: *Seine*; 36s: *Melampus*, *Crescent*, *Apollo*; 32: *Amphion*
12pdr frigates	36s: *Decade*, *Nereide*, 32s: *Meleager*, *Lowestoffe*, *Quebec*, *Aimable*, *Juno*, *Retribution* [ex-*Hermione*], *Syren*, *Surprize* [a 9pdr Fifth Rate]
	One 44, five Sixth Rates, thirteen sloops, one schooner
Leeward Isles	REAR-ADMIRAL DUCKWORTH
	Leviathan, 74 (flag), one 64 [*en flûte*]
24pdr frigate	44: *Magnanime*
18pdr frigates	38s: *Tamar*, *Diana*
12pdr frigates	32s: *Unité*, *Venus*, *Southampton*, *Andromeda*, *Proselyte*
	One 44, three Sixth Rates, seven sloops, one storeship, one prison ship, two schooners, three gunboats, two armed ships
Mediterranean	ADMIRAL LORD KEITH
Line of battle	*Minotaur*, 74 (flag), two 80s, ten 74s
18pdr frigates	38s: *Minerve*, *Phaeton*; 36s: *Pique*, *Flora*, *Caroline*, *Penelope*, *Phoenix*
12pdr frigates	36s: *Carmen*, *Florentina*; 32s: *Santa Teresa*, *Santa Dorothea*,

	Pearl, *Mermaid*, *Success*
	Five Sixth Rates, seventeen sloops, four storeships, two bomb vessels, three cutters, one prison ship, one fireship, seven schooners and gunboats
Nova Scotia	VICE-ADMIRAL SIR WILLIAM PARKER
	America, 64 (flag), one 64
12pdr frigates	32s: *Boston*, *Cleopatra*, *Andromache*
	One Sixth Rate, two sloops, one prison ship
Newfoundland	One 24, two sloops
Convoys and cruisers	One 50, one 44
18pdr frigates	38s: *Seahorse*, *Melpomene*, *Arethusa*, *Loire*, *Active*; 36s: *San Fiorenzo*, *Trent*, *Jason*
12pdr frigates	36s: *Santa Margarita*, *Maidstone*; 32: *Greyhound*
	One 28, ten sloops, two bombs, one armed vessel, one gunboat, five cutters
[Channel]	ADMIRAL CORNWALLIS'S SQUADRON
Line of battle	*Ville de Paris*, 110 (flag), three First Rates, eleven Second Rates, two 80s, twenty 74s
24pdr frigate	44: *Indefatigable*
18pdr frigates	38s: *Clyde*, *Naiad*, *Diamond*, *Fisgard*, *Urania*, *Amelia*, *Beaulieu*, *Boadicea*, *Leda*; 36s: *Sirius*, *Doris*, *Amethyst*, *Immortalité*; 32s: *Unicorn*, *Alcmene*
12pdr frigates	32s: *Nymphe*, *Oiseau*, *Triton*, *Magicienne*, *Thames*
	One 28, five sloops, one armed brig, one cutter, one fireship
[Baltic]	ADMIRAL SIR H PARKER'S SQUADRON
Line of battle	*London*, 98 (flag), one Second Rate, fifteen 74s, nine 64s, four 50/54s
18pdr frigates	40: *Pomone*; 38s: *Amazon*, *Latona*; 36s: *Desiree*, *Blanche*
12pdr frigates	32s: *Shannon*, *Iris*, *Solebay*
	Five 24s, seventeen sloops, seven bomb vessels, three fireships, two cutters
At Cork	ADMIRAL LORD GARDNER
	Engageante, hospital ship (flag)
18pdr frigates	38s: *Revolutionnaire*, *Hussar*; 36s:

	Dryad, *Glenmore*, *Phoebe*; 32s: *Cerberus*, *Galatea*
	Three sloops
Portsmouth and Spithead	Two receiving ships, one slop ship, one convict ship, five prison ships
	[Fitting or fitted for Channel Service]
	Two 74s
24pdr frigates	44: *Anson*; 40s: *Cambrian*, *Endymion*
12pdr frigates	32s: *Castor*
	One 24, five sloops
Plymouth	One receiving ship, one hospital ship, one convict ship, one slop ship, two prison ships, one schooner
	[Fitting or fitted for Channel Service]
12pdr frigates	32s: *Ambuscade*, *Concorde*
	One 24, three sloops, one cutter
In the Downs	ADMIRAL LUTWIDGE
	Overijssel, 64 (flag)
18pdr frigate	36: *Fortunee*
	Four Sixth Rates, four sloops, one cutter, one gunboat
Chatham and Nore	Four 64s [one fitting for Channel Service, one to be paid off], 'Dutch ships'–*Amphitrite*, 44, *Ambuscade*, 32, *Galathe*,16
18pdr frigate	38: *Hydra* [fitting for Channel Service]
	One exploration ship, one fireship, one slop ship, four hospital ships, five prison ships, one survey vessel
Thames, etc	[Woolwich]
18pdr frigate	38: *Princess Charlotte* [fitting for Channel Service]
	Three sloops [fitting for Channel Service], two storeships
	[Deptford]
	One 64, three sloops [fitting for Channel Service], two advice boats [fitting for Channel Service], one slop ship
	[Elsewhere]
18pdr frigate	36: *Emerald* [at Cork en route to West Indies]
	Two floating batteries [Hull, Queenborough], three receiving ships [Liverpool, near Waterford, and off the Tower],

one convict ship [Falmouth],
one yacht [Ireland]
[Jersey – Captain d'Auvergne,
Prince de Bouillon]
Two Sixth Rates, two sloops,
two cutters

Troopships	Seven rated 32 guns, four rated 24 guns, thirty-three rated 16 guns
Gunboats	Of 50 men: fifty; 30 men: eight; 25 men: three; 19 men: fifteen

OCTOBER 1805
[Battle of Trafalgar]

East Indies	REAR-ADMIRAL PELLEW; REAR-ADMIRAL TROUBRIDGE
Line of battle	*Culloden*, 74 (Pellew's flag), *Blenheim*, 74 (Troubridge's flag), four 74s, two 64s, one 50
18pdr frigates	38s: *Phaeton*, *San Fiorenzo*; 36s: *Caroline*, *Thalia*, *Salsette*; 32: *Medusa*
12pdr frigates	32s: *Fox*, *Terpsichore*, *Concorde*, *Dedaigneuse*, *Wilhelmina*, *Greyhound* One 44, five sloops, one cutter, one receiving ship
Jamaica	REAR-ADMIRAL DACRES
Line of battle	*Hercule*, 74 (flag), one 74, one 64, one 54
18pdr frigates	38: *Diana*; 36s: *Pique*, *Fortunee*, *Surveillante*, *Princess Charlotte*; 32s: *Tartar*, *Unicorn*
12pdr frigates	36s: *Franchise*, *Magicienne*; 32s: *Mermaid*, *Seine*, *Jason* One 24, twenty-four sloops, ten schooners
Leeward Isles	REAR-ADMIRAL SIR ALEXANDER COCHRANE
Line of battle	*St George*, 98 (flag), five 74s
18pdr frigates	38s: *Africaine*, *Beaulieu*, *Leda*, *Amelia*; 36: *Ethalion*; 32s: *Galatea*, *Narcissus*
12pdr frigates	32s: *Success*, *Circe* Four Sixth Rates, thirteen sloops, seven schooners, two storeships
Mediterranean	VICE-ADMIRAL LORD NELSON
Line of battle	*Victory*, 100 (flag), two First Rates, five Second Rates, two 80s, twenty-two 74s, three 64s, one 56

18pdr frigates	40: *Acasta*; 38s: *Lively*, *Seahorse*, *Melpomene*. 36s: *Euryalus*. *Phoebe*, *Unité*; 32: *Amphion*
12pdr frigates	36s: *Renommee*; 32s: *Juno*, *Ambuscade*, *Niger* One 24, twelve sloops, two bomb vessels, two cutters, one schooner, one receiving ship
Nova Scotia	VICE-ADMIRAL MITCHELL *Leander*, 50
18pdr frigates	40: *Cambrian*; 38: *Milan*
12pdr frigate	32: *Cleopatra* Two Sixth Rates, one sloop, one schooner
Newfoundland	VICE-ADMIRAL SIR E GOWER *Isis*, 50 (flag)
12pdr frigate	32: *Pallas* Three Sixth Rates, three sloops, four schooners, one armed tender
Convoys and cruisers/ particular services	One 64, one 54, two 50s
18pdr frigates	40: *Endymion*; 38s: *Pomone*, *Diamond*; 32: *Cerberus*
12pdr frigates	36s: *Chifonne*, *Weymouth* [ex-HEIC]; 32s: *Orpheus*, *Aimable* Four Sixth Rates, ten sloops, one bomb vessel, four yachts, two storeships, four cutters, two schooners, one advice boat, one survey ship
[Channel]	ADMIRAL CORNWALLIS'S SQUADRON
Line of battle	*Ville de Paris*, 110 (flag), two First Rates, five Second Rates, three 80s, seventeen 74s, three 64s
24pdr frigates	44s: *Egyptienne*, *Indefatigable*
18pdr frigates	38s: *Revolutionnaire*, *Niobe*, *Naiad*, *Latona*; 36s: *Sirius*, *Aigle*, *Melampus*, *Crescent*, *Penelope*, *Phoenix*; 32: *Aeolus*
12pdr frigates	36s: *Decade*, *Santa Margarita*; 32: *Iris* Nine sloops, two schooners
[Downs]	ADMIRAL LORD KEITH'S SQUADRON
Line of battle	Four 74s, five 64s, three 50s
18pdr frigates	36s: *Immortalité*, *Tribune*
12pdr frigates	32s: *Venus*, *Astraea* One 44, five Sixth Rates, twenty-four sloops, three floating batteries, twelve bomb

vessels, two advice boats, three
receiving ships, one fireship,
fifteen fire vessels

At Cork	ADMIRAL LORD GARDNER *Gorgon*, 44 (? flag)
18pdr frigates	38s: *Active*, *Loire*, *Boadicea*, *Uranie*; 36s: *Amethyst*, *Flora*, *Dryad*; 32: *Alcmene*
12pdr frigates	36: *Topaze*; 32: *Druid* One 28, eight sloops, three receiving ships
Portsmouth and Spithead	ADMIRAL MONTAGU REAR-ADMIRAL SIR ISAAC COFFIN One 74, one 64, two receiving ships
18pdr frigates	38s: *Apollo*, *Amazon*; 36: *Inconstant*
12pdr frigates	36: *Mediator* [ex-HEIC]; 32: *Hebe* Two Sixth Rates, four sloops, one armed ship, two storeships, one schooner, one hospital ship, one convalescents ship, one slop ship, four prison ships
Plymouth	VICE-ADMIRAL YOUNG, REAR-ADMIRAL SUTTON Two Second Rates, one receiving ship, one 74
18pdr frigates	38s: *Hydra*, *Fisgard* Five sloops, one cutter, six prison ships, one convalescents ship, one slop ship
In the Medway	REAR-ADMIRAL ROWLEY Two 74s, one 64
18pdr frigates	38s: *Resistance*, *Arethusa*, *Virginie* Two Sixth Rates [one to Falmouth as a sheer hulk], nine sloops, two storeships, three hospital ships, two prison ships
In the Thames	REAR-ADMIRAL STANHOPE One 64
18pdr frigates	38s: *Sybille*, *Thetis*
12pdr frigate	32: *Quebec* One storeship, one schooner, one yacht, three receiving ships, three tenders, one hospital ship, one cutter
Troopships	One rated 24 guns, two rated 14 guns
Gunboats	Ninety-nine

JUNE 1809
[world-wide deployment at the height of the sea war]

East Indies   VICE-ADMIRAL PELLEW
Line of battle   *Culloden*, 74 (flag), one 74, one 64
18pdr frigates   38s: *Clorinde, Piedmontaise, Phaeton, Cornwallis* [ex-HEIC]; 36s: *Doris, Caroline* 32: *Cornelia*
12pdr frigates   36s: *Modeste, Psyche, Dover, Chiffone*; 32s: *Terpsichore, Greyhound, Fox, Sir Francis Drake, Ceylon, Dedaigneuse*
One 28, six sloops, three cutters, one receiving ship, one hospital ship

Cape of Good Hope   VICE-ADMIRAL BERTIE
One 64, *Leopard*, 50 (flag)
18pdr frigates   38: *Boadicea*; 36s: *Sirius, Iphigenia*
12pdr frigates   36: *Magicienne*; 32: *Nereide*
Six sloops, two brigs

South America   REAR-ADMIRAL DE COURCY
Line of battle   *Foudroyant*, 80 (flag), two 74s, one 64
18pdr frigates   38s: *Président, Diana*
One Sixth Rate, three sloops, three cutters

Leeward Isles   REAR-ADMIRAL SIR ALEXANDER COCHRANE
Line of battle   *Neptune*, 98 (flag), one 80, two 74s, one 64
18pdr frigates   40: *Acasta*; 38s: *Alcmene, Gloire, Blonde, Thetis, Latona*; 36s: *Ethalion, Melampus*
12pdr frigates   32s: *Circe, Castor, Jason*
Thirty-six sloops, twenty schooners and gunbrigs

Jamaica   VICE-ADMIRAL ROWLEY
Polyphemus, 64 (?flag)
18pdr frigates   38s: *Diamond, Hussar*
12pdr frigates   36s: *Helder, Franchise*; 32s: *Hebe, Daedalus*
One 44, two Sixth Rates, twenty-one sloops, seven schooners and gunbrigs, one receiving ship

North America   VICE-ADMIRAL SIR JOHN BORLASE WARREN
Swiftsure, 74 [?flag]
18pdr frigates   38s: *Horatio, Milan, Guerriere*; 36: *Penelope*; 32: *Aeolus*
12pdr frigate   32: *Cleopatra*
Two 24s, nine sloops, eleven schooners and gunbrigs, three receiving ships

Newfoundland   VICE-ADMIRAL HOLLOWAY
Antelope, 50 (flag)
18pdr frigate   38: *Sybille*
12pdr frigate   32: *Quebec*
Two Sixth Rates, three sloops, four small craft

Mediterranean   VICE-ADMIRAL LORD COLLINGWOOD
Line of battle   *Hibernia*, 110 (flag) [sic. Collingwood was about to receive a new flagship but *Ville de Paris* was finally chosen.], two First Rates, two Second Rates, two 80s, nineteen 74s, one 50
18pdr frigates   40: *Cambrian*; 38s: *Belle Poule, Apollo, Spartan, Seahorse, Leonidas, Alceste, Voluntaire, Pomone, Hydra*: 36s: *Topaze, Unité*; 32: *Amphion, Hyperion*
12pdr frigates   32s: *Thames, Ambuscade, Success*
Five Sixth Rates, twenty-five sloops, one bomb vessel, three small craft, one receiving ship

Channel Fleet   ADMIRAL LORD GAMBIER
Line of battle   *Caledonia*, 120 (flag), two Second Rates, three 80s, seven 74s
24pdr frigate   44: *Indefatigable*
18pdr frigates   38s: *Shannon, Amazon, Naiad, Amelia, Resistance, Imperieuse, Statira*; 36s: *Aigle, Seine*; 32s: *Medusa, Unicorn, Narcissus*
12pdr frigates   32s: *Pallas, Minerva*
One 22, five sloops, eight small craft

Baltic   VICE-ADMIRAL SAUMAREZ
Line of battle   *Victory*, 98 (flag), two Second Rates, eleven 74s, seven 64s
18pdr frigates   38: *Melpomene*; 36s: *Owen Glendower, Salsette, Phoebe*; 32: *Cerberus, Tartar*
12pdr frigate   32s: *Alexandria*
One 28, sixteen sloops, one bomb vessel, twelve small craft

Portugal   VICE-ADMIRAL BERKELEY
Line of battle   *Barfleur*, 98 (flag), four 74s
18pdr frigates   38: *Lively*; 36s: *Semiramis, Venus*
One 22, eight sloops, five small craft

At Cork   ADMIRAL WHITSHED
18pdr frigates   38s: *Virginie, Princess Charlotte*; 36s: *Fortunee, Dryad, Emerald*

12pdr frigates   32: *Druid*
Four sloops, two small craft

Channel Isles   REAR-ADMIRAL D'AUVERGNE, PRINCE DE BOUILLON
Two Sixth Rates, three sloops, six small craft

The Downs   VICE-ADMIRAL CAMPBELL
18pdr frigate   38: *Clyde*
Eighteen sloops, seven small craft, two victualling depots

Plymouth   VICE-ADMIRAL YOUNG
One receiving ship, seven sloops, four small craft

Portsmouth   ADMIRAL SIR ROGER CURTIS
One receiving ship, five sloops, nine small craft, one stationary ship

Sheerness   VICE-ADMIRAL WELLS
One receiving ship, three sloops, three small craft

Yarmouth   REAR-ADMIRAL DOUGLAS
One receiving ship, two sloops, three brigs

JULY 1813
[adjusting to the American war]

East Indies   VICE-ADMIRAL SAMUEL HOOD
Minden, 74 (flag), one 74
18pdr frigates   38s: *Clorinde, Hussar, Africaine, Daedalus*; 36s: *Owen Glendower, Phoenix, Malacca, Salsette*; 32: *Bucephalus*
One 22, five sloops, one hospital ship

Cape of Good Hope   REAR-ADMIRAL CHARLES TYLER
Lion, 64 (flag)
18pdr frigates   36s: *Astraea, Semiramis, Stag*
Two sloops

South America   REAR-ADMIRAL MANLY DIXON
Montagu, 74 (flag)
24pdr frigate   44: *Indefatigable*
18pdr frigates   38: *Nisus*; 36: *Inconstant*; 32: *Nereus*
12pdr frigate   32: *Aquilon*
Three Sixth Rates, three sloops, two cutters

Leeward Isles   REAR-ADMIRAL SIR FRANCIS LAFOREY
Line of battle   *Cressy*, 74 (flag), one 74, one 50
18pdr frigates   38s: *Statira, Surprize, Rhin*; 36s: *Orpheus, Pique, Venus*

12pdr frigate	32s: *Circe, Castor* Three Sixth Rates, twenty sloops, three gunbrigs, two schooners, one cutter
Jamaica	REAR-ADMIRAL BROWN *Vengeance*, 74 (flag), one 74 One 44, five Sixth Rates, six sloops, two gunbrigs, one receiving ship
North America	ADMIRAL SIR JOHN BORLASE WARREN
Line of battle	*San Domingo*, 74 (flag), nine 74s
Rasée	58: *Majestic*
18pdr frigates	38s: *Nymphe, Junon, Tenedos, Spartan, Shannon, Armide, Lacedaemonian*; 36: *Maidstone, Belvidera, Barrosa*; 32s: *Narcissus, Aeolus*
12pdr frigates	32s: *Cleopatra, Minerva* Two Sixth Rates, twenty-five sloops, three schooners, two receiving ships, one prison ship
Newfoundland	VICE-ADMIRAL SIR RICHARD GOODWIN KEATS *Bellerophon*, 74 (flag)
18pdr frigates	38s: *Sybille, Crescent*; 36: *Dryad*; 32: *Hyperion*
12pdr frigate	32: *Quebec* Two Sixth Rates, four sloops, one cutter, one prison ship
Mediterranean	VICE-ADMIRAL SIR EDWARD PELLEW
Line of battle	*Caledonia*, 120 (flag), three First Rates, four Second Rates, two 80s, eighteen 74s
18pdr frigates	38s: *Resistance, Voluntaire, Apollo, Africaine, Imperieuse, Bacchante, Undaunted*; 36s: *Unité, Aigle, Orlando, Curacoa, Havannah, Furieuse, Euryalus, Iphigenia*; 32: *Cerberus*
12pdr frigates	36: *Franchise*; 32s: *Castor, Thames* Six Sixth Rates, twenty-eight sloops, three bomb vessels, two gunbrigs, two schooners, one receiving ship, one hospital ship
Portugal	REAR-ADMIRAL GEORGE MARTIN *Stately*, 64 (flag)
18pdr frigates	38: *Pomone*; 36: *Magicienne* Four Sixth Rates, eight sloops, one gunbrig, one schooner, three mortar boats, one receiving ship

Baltic	REAR-ADMIRAL GEORGE HOPE
Line of battle	*Defiance*, 74 (flag), seven 74s, one 50
18pdr frigate	36: *Hamadryad* one 44, two Sixth Rates, fourteen sloops, three bomb vessels, thirteen gunbrigs, one schooner, one cutter
Channel Fleet	ADMIRAL LORD KEITH
Line of battle	*Queen Charlotte*, 110 (flag), two First Rates, thirteen 74s
18pdr frigates	38s: *Surveillante, Belle Poule, Briton, Revolutionnaire, Andromache*; 36s: *Iris, Pyramus, Hotspur* Six sloops, two gunbrigs, one schooner
Ireland	VICE-ADMIRAL THORNBOROUGH
18pdr frigates	38: *Leonidas*; 36: *Fortunee* Ten sloops, three gunbrigs
The Downs	REAR-ADMIRAL FOLEY *Monmouth*, 'static ship' (flag) Ten sloops, five cutters, two gunbrigs
Channel Isles	REAR-ADMIRAL HARGOOD One Sixth Rate, two sloops, one schooner, four gunbrigs
Plymouth	ADMIRAL SIR ROBERT CALDER One receiving ship, eight sloops, four small craft
Portsmouth	ADMIRAL SIR RICHARD BICKERTON One receiving ship, two 74s
18pdr frigates	38s: *Horatio, Seahorse*; 32: *Medusa* Eight sloops, three small craft, one guardship
Sheerness	REAR-ADMIRAL SIR THOMAS WILLIAMS One receiving ship, four sloops, two gunbrigs
Yarmouth	VICE-ADMIRAL R MURRAY Two receiving ships, four sloops, three small craft
Off the Texel and Schelde	ADMIRAL YOUNG
Line of battle	*Impregnable*, 98 (flag), one 80, ten 74s
18pdr frigate	36: *Desiree*
12pdr frigate	32: *Jason* Nine sloops, seven gunbrigs

Leith	VICE-ADMIRAL OTWAY One receiving ship
12pdr frigate	32: *Alexandria* One Sixth Rate, seven sloops, four gunbrigs
Convoys and particular services	Four 74s
18pdr frigates	38s: *Madagascar* [cruising with *Barham* and *Centaur* to the westwards], *Niemen* [convoy from St Helena], *Niobe* and *Rota* [convoy to Quebec]; 36s: *Theban* and *Doris* [convoy to China], *Phoebe* ['Secret Orders' – sent to the Pacific to hunt down USS *Essex*], *Galatea* [with specie to Lisbon], *Nymphen* [with specie to Lisbon]; 32: *Unicorn* [with specie to Lisbon] Three sixth Rates, ten sloops, two cutters, two schooners
Unappropriated	One Second Rate, nine 74s
Rasée	58: *Goliath*
24pdr frigates	50: *Akbar*; 40: *Endymion*
18pdr frigates	38s: *Cydnus, Eurotas, Président, Menelaus, Horatio, Niger, Laurel*; 36s: *Ethalion, Eridanus, Tribune, Creole*; 32s: *Amphion, Druid* Four Sixth Rates, ten sloops, one bomb vessel, four schooners
Troopships	Eighteen, including the ex-frigates *Melpomene, Brune, Romulus, Freya, Mermaid, Fox*
Prison ships, stationary ships, etc	Thirty-eight

Notes:
Based on the station lists in PRO Adm 8. These were compiled on a monthly basis and the time-lag in receiving information from overseas stations means that they were never entirely up-to-date and sometimes incomplete. However, since the function of this selection is merely to demonstrate the distribution and employment of frigates at selected phases in the war, they are accurate enough. All frigates are named and differentiated by armament and rate, since this had some bearing on their deployment, but apart from the flagship the remaining force on the station is given in summary only.

The lists are reproduced in the original order of station and ships, the only alteration being to separate frigates by main-deck calibre and to correct inaccuracies in their listed ratings.

Notes

Abbreviations used in the notes

Adm – Admiralty; correspondence in the PRO is prefixed 'Adm', that in the NMM by 'ADM'

AO – Admiralty Order

MM – The Mariner's Mirror, the journal of the Society for Nautical Research

NMM – National Maritime Museum, Greenwich

NRS – Navy Records Society. Individual volumes are identified by short titles, the full reference being given in the Bibliography

PRO – Public Record Office, Kew

WO – War Office

CHAPTER 1. THE RETURN TO MODERATE DIMENSIONS, 1801-1804

1 This period is covered in depth in the author's *The Heavy Frigate* (London 1994), Chapters 3-6.

2 The best recent study of its impact on the Dockyards is Roger Morriss, *The Royal Dockyards during the Revolutionary and Napoleonic Wars* (Leicester 1983).

3 St Vincent had a low opinion of the Surveyors, but he never saw the necessity to match French ships in point of size. He once wrote to Admiral John Markham, then at the Admiralty, that he believed the Surveyors 'had less science than any two men you can name in any country in Europe', yet they still believed that they could improve the lines of any prize used as the model for a British ship. He approved of Markham's efforts to get line of battle ships with 6ft of freeboard to the lower deck guns, yet cautioned against building 74s bigger than *Impétueux* or *Donegal*, nor First Rates beyond the *Ville de Paris* or *San Josef*, none of them the largest examples of their classes. Letter of 15 Sep 1806, reproduced in J S Tucker, *Memoirs of St Vincent*, p310.

4 NRS *Spencer* II, p212.

5 Reported in *The Naval Chronicle* II (1799), p535, 15 Oct 1799 in a full gale whilst in pursuit of the privateer *Bordelaise*; the nickname is quoted by Abraham Crawford, who served in the ship, in his *Reminiscences of a Naval Officer*, p11 (1999 edition).

6 See his correspondence with Commissioner Sir Thomas Hamilton in NRS *Markham*, pp310ff.

7 NRS *St Vincent* II, p190, letter of 23 Jul 1802 to Evan Nepean explaining his second thoughts; PRO Adm 106/2089, order cancelling, 12 Jul 1802.

8 Tanner's was an extreme case of what the business world calls 'overtrading'. His Dartmouth yard had expanded rapidly, to the point where in January 1805 *The Naval Chronicle* reported it employing 200 artificers, having just launched its third warship in six months. However, he was clearly under-bidding on naval contracts, and was caught out by rapidly increasing timber

price inflation on the renewal of the war. The crisis came in Feb 1807, when the fireship *Thais* was rejected on the grounds of poor workmanship, and it became clear that virtually no work had been done on the two frigates. The Navy Board was instructed to act against Tanner for breach of contract, and this drove him into bankruptcy; PRO Adm 2/311. The author is indebted to Ivor H Smart for the information on timber prices.

9 Long note appended to Sailing Quality report, PRO Adm 95/48, 12 Jul 1816; the design problem is dealt with in more detail in Chapter 7.

10 See the author's earlier book, *The First Frigates*, for details of this class. Although the orders for the last six were confirmed by the Melville Board, the preceding Admiralty had already ascertained from the Navy Board that there was fir enough for another six (the maximum number that could be built without disturbing other work in the Dockyards), and effectively ordered them a week before leaving office; PRO Adm 2/305, 1 and 7 May 1804.

11 PRO Adm 2/305, 10 Aug 1804.

12 The context of Bentham's innovations is explored in more detail in Chapter 7.

13 NRS *Spencer* III, p375.

CHAPTER 2. THE BARHAM INTERLUDE, 1805-1806

1 Sir John Barrow, Bart, *An Auto-biographical Memoir*, p277. Barham, in fact, had agreed on a form of division of labour with the rest of the Board, allowing himself time for the important issues.

2 Letter of Jul 1786 to Pitt, NRS *Barham* II, p217. The latest biography of Barham, John Talbott's *Pen and Ink Sailor*, notes the high proportion of memos and correspondence either in Barham's autograph or carrying his signature.

3 A memo on the state of the Navy, dated Apr 1803, suggesting a remedy for the present run-down state of the active fleet. NRS *Barham* III, p20.

4 PRO Adm 2/308, 24 Jul 1805.

5 Mulgrave is sometimes credited with the choice of *Courageux* as a prototype in the late 1770s: *The Naval Chronicle* VII (1802), p362. Gambier, a relative and political ally of Barham's, also showed much interest in ship design.

6 NMM ADM/Y/2, endorsement on letter of 20 Jun 1805.

7 NMM ADM/Y/3, 26 Jul 1805. *Lowestoffe* and *Iphigenia*; the latter was re-instated on 20 Jan 1806 because half the frame was prepared and Sheerness had no replacement work, but the ship was moved to a smaller slip.

8 ADM/Y/3, 25 Jul 1805.

9 NMM ADM/Y/3, 7 Aug 1805. The relevant paragraph ran: 'if any difficulty should arise in respect to carrying the additional weight occasioned by the difference in the mode of building between the English and the French the same is to be obviated by a greater length of floor and consequent length of ship, preserving the lines of the French frigates in all other respects . . .'; PRO Adm 2/308, 9 Aug 1805.

10 PRO Adm 95/44, sailing quality report of 31 Aug 1815.

11 NRS *Boteler*, pp85-6.

12 This issue is dealt with in more depth in the author's *Heavy Frigate*, Chapter 7. Although not all ordered by Barham's administration, the frigates affected by bankruptcy were *Syren*, *Doris*, *Pyramus*, *Pallas*, *Dartmouth* and *Creole*; in addition, without giving his reasons Graham of Harwich refused to proceed with the *Undaunted* in Jan 1806 and the Navy Board took action to retrieve all materials (Adm 2/309, 25 Jan 1806). The letters relating to *Nereus* and Rowe, dated 2 May 1810 and 10 Jan 1810, are abstracted in PRO Adm 12/144, cut 91.1.

CHAPTER 3. WAR OF ATTRITION, 1806-1812

1 Speech of 10 Aug 1807, reproduced in *The Naval Chronicle* XVIII (1807), p276.

2 NMM ADM/Y/5, 9 Sep 1806.

3 For the controversial story of the 'Forty Thieves' and the three-decker designs, see Brian Lavery, *The Ship of the Line* I, pp134ff.

4 PRO Adm 2/310, 20 Oct 1806. Steemson, who built the *Owen Glendower*, was later awarded a contract for a 74, but it was not part of the 1806 tendering round.

5 PRO Adm 2/313, 30 Sep 1807. The contract for *Havannah* went to Tanner, Dartmouth, shortly before the yard's bankruptcy; Guillaume of Northam then tendered for this and the unplaced *Theban*, but negotiations failed.

6 Reported in *The Naval Chronicle* XX (1808), pp229-33.

7 NMM ADM/Y/9, 15 Sep 1808; PRO Adm 2/315, 26 Sep 1808.

8 ADM/Y/9, 21 & 23 Sep 1808; PRO Adm 2/317, 26 & 29 Sep 1808.

9 A file entitled 'Copies and Extracts of Papers and Correspondence relative to the Establishment of a Naval Arsenal at Prince of Wales Island' is preserved in PRO Adm 1/3916 and forms the basis of these paragraphs. It is annotated 'East India House, 20 Nov 1806' and was presumably put together in response to the Admiralty enquiry about how the frigate came to be started.

10 PRO Adm 49/14. This is part of an investigation by the Accountant General's department into the costs of shipbuilding in India; there is a whole file devoted to the

Malacca. The clear shortcomings of Prince of Wales Island as a yard must cast serious doubts on the impartiality of Dundas's views. In a survey of 1815, some of the ship's frame was described as 'pine, or wood of that description'; NMM POR/D/31, 19 Jun 1815.

11 PRO Adm 2/315, 15 Oct 1808; NMM ADM/Y/9, 28 Nov 1808, but still insisting frigates be built 'as expeditiously as possible'; PRO Adm 2/317, 2 May 1809.

12 PRO Adm 2/320, 26 May 1810.

13 PRO Adm 2/322, 11 Mar 1811; Navy Board's reply and proposals, 18 Jul 1811. What was being requested was the laying down of a system of scantlings and fastenings that amounted to a formal Establishment.

14 See the list in *The Naval Chronicle* XXIV (1810). It included the large frigates *Vertu*, *Infatigable* and *Fama* which had never served in the Royal Navy after their capture.

CHAPTER 4. THE AMERICAN EMERGENCY, 1812-1815

1 William James, an otherwise meticulous chronicler of naval events, is a perfect example. Any thing to do with the Americans reduces him to heavy sarcasm: see his *Naval History* V, pp354-6, and throughout *Naval Occurrences*. According to Professor Andrew Lambert, James's work was an officially encouraged attempt to counter some of the wilder American claims that continued to inflame Anglo-American political relations for decades after the war: see R Gardiner (ed), *The Naval War of 1812*, p17.

2 PRO Adm 106/2257, 2 May 1812; Adm 2/325, 4 May 1812.

3 PRO Adm 2/325: order to build six frigates, 4 May 1812; draught approved 9 May. The need for more frigates had been discussed with the Comptroller on 2 May. On 9 May instructions were also sent to the commanders-in-chief of the transatlantic stations warning them of the probability of hostilities with the Americans breaking out at any time; Mahan, *The Influence of Sea Power on the War of 1812* I, p385.

4 PRO Adm 106/2259, Navy Board response of 14 Nov 1812.

5 Their naval output for 1813 was eventually one 74, three fir 38s, five fir 40s, and the huge spar-decked 60s *Newcastle* and *Leander*; P Banbury, *Shipbuilders of the Thames and Medway*, p124.

6 PRO Adm 106/2259, 6 Jan 1813; Adm 2/326, 7 Jan 1813.

7 PRO Adm 2/326, order of 7 Dec 1812.

8 Melville's letter to Lord Keith of 3 Sep 1813 states that six of the line and sixteen frigates (besides numerous smaller craft) are at that moment lying idle waiting for crews; NRS *Byam Martin* II, p368.

9 Standing orders to commanding officers on the North America station from Admiral Sir John Borlase Warren, 6 March 1813. Quoted in Dudley (ed), *The Naval War of 1812* II, p59.

10 Orders to all commanders-in-chief, 10 July 1813, in Dudley (ed), *The Naval War of 1812* II, p183.

11 NMM ADM/BP/36a, 9 Apr 1816.

CHAPTER 5. SUPER FRIGATES

1 The armament estimate is from James, *Naval History* I, p56. However, he overestimates their numbers by treating some renamings as separate ships. The latest French research gives the armament as twenty-eight 36pdrs and fourteen 18pdrs, far more powerful than the British believed; *Nomenclature des navires français, 1792-1799*, by Cdt Demerliac. These ships exerted influence in some surprising quarters, Joshua Humphreys admitting to the US Congress in a report of 23 Dec 1794 that the new frigates were similar in size and concept to the French *rasées*: see *American State Papers. Class IV Naval Affairs*, Vol I, p8.

2 PRO Adm 1/100, 24 Apr 1794.

3 PRO Adm 106/2219, 28 Jul 1794.

4 She had endured a long and arduous commission on the East Indies station at the end of the previous war, and had been laid up since. She was also the first of the trio to be taken out of active service, becoming a guardship for the Clyde in 1803; from decommissioning in Aug 1804 she lay in Ordinary until broken up in 1813. By contrast, the *Indefatigable* had never been commissioned. The total conversion costs for the three ships were: *Anson* £8428; *Indefatigable* £8764; *Magnanime* £17,066.

5 Lt Reuben Mangin, who served in the squadron summarised its achievements between 1795 to 1797 as follows: 'Twenty-five ships and vessels of war, including privateers, captured; twelve ditto destroyed; eighty-seven merchantmen taken, nineteen ditto, recaptured, and fifty-four destroyed; twenty-three neutrals detained, and part of each cargo condemned:–*total 220*.' in John Marshall, *Royal Navy Biography*, Supplement, Part I, p241.

6 PRO Adm 1/102, 23 January 1795.

7 For the 1756 ships see *First Frigates*, pp26-30; for Pellew's requests PRO Adm 106/2219, 24 Dec 1794; Adm 106/2087, 12 Feb 1795; Adm 1/102, 31 Jan 1795.

8 PRO Adm 1/102, 7 Feb 1795; WO 55/1831 & Adm 2/274, 17 Feb 1795.

9 Kingsmill to Admiralty, PRO Adm 1/612, 20 Feb and 9 Mar 1795; Durham to Admiralty, Adm 1/1717, 18 Feb 1797.

10 Pellew to Admiralty, PRO Adm 1/102, 31 Mar and 3 Apr 1795; according to Adm 180/7 *Anson* was remasted during routine maintenance, 3 Aug – 1 Sep, and *Magnanime* 14 Oct – 13 Nov 1795, both at Plymouth.

11 PRO Adm 1/1717, 14 Dec 1795.

12 *The Naval Chronicle* XIX (1808), p452.

13 PRO Adm 180/24 has some notation relating to sailing qualities and lists a few speeds.

14 PRO Adm 2/274, 6 Nov 1794, 26 & 31 Jan 1795. The Navy Board was asked to find out how many ships could be built in merchant yards, and when informed the Admiralty then set out its requirements; this programme was cancelled when the merchants could not be persuaded to accept lower prices, but a more modest version of the programme was reinstated in Apr: Adm 106/2087, 31 Jan, 30 Apr & 11 Aug 1795. See *Heavy Frigate* for complete programme.

15 It has been widely assumed by British historians that Barrallier was an *ingénieur-constructeur*, or naval architect, but he was actually trained as a civil engineer and spent his whole career in the corps responsible for the French navy's buildings as an *ingénieur des bâtiments civils* (letter to the author from Jean Boudriot, 9 Jan 2000). When and where he acquired his knowledge of ship design is a mystery, but some of his memorials to the Admiralty display considerable theoretical expertise – although, of course, the practical results leave much to be desired. Barrallier's first draught, dated 5 May 1796, is noted as a response to an Admiralty minute of 4 Apr; it shows a conventional 1019-ton 38-gun frigate, although some features are noticeably French. Eventual order, PRO Adm 2/281, 9 Feb 1797.

16 It is perhaps an indication of the heights from which Barrallier derived his favour if not his patronage that his first 74 was called *Spencer*, after the First Lord of the Admiralty at the time, while the frigate, named in 1797, was almost certainly named, not after the wife of Aeneas of classical legend, but for Earl Spencer's wife, a famous and influential political hostess.

17 Barrallier's second ship of the line, the *Milford*, was the most controversial. When asked by the Admiralty for his view on building another to the same draught, her first captain, Baynton, produced a damning critique of the *Milford*'s stability, seakeeping and sailing qualities, and adversely compared her with the ex-Danish *Christian VII*. This led to the cancellation of a sister-ship, the *Sandwich*, in 1811 in favour of the *Black Prince* class based on the lines of the Danish prize. Nevertheless, such was Barrallier's influence that he was able to get a lengthened version approved, built at Pembroke and launched in 1814. Copies of three letters from Baynton, the dates unfortunately destroyed by water damage (but about 1809-10), can be found in Adm 95/42. See Chapter 8 for further detail.

18 Captain Paget requested the substitution in August 1803 because the ship was deeply laden and in heavy weather laboured 'prodigiously', when the 'weight and working of the guns materially weakened the topsides and upperworks.' At first this was refused, but in Nov Paget tried again, and this time the Admiralty agreed to the change: PRO Adm 1/2325, 5 Aug and 15 Nov 1803. The ship was carrying 9ft 18pdrs in Oct 1808, Adm 160/154. The ship proved costly to maintain (see Chapter 8), although Collingwood thought her 'complaining very much, owing to her enormous masts'; to Lord Mulgrave, 11 Dec 1807, *Public and Private Correspondence of Vice-Admiral Lord Collingwood*, p325.

19 Letter from Woolwich officers, 16 Apr 1802, PRO Adm 106/1790; NRS *Markham*, pp337 and 62.

20 Dudley (ed), *The Naval War of 1812* I, p650.

21 The covering letter is missing, but the undated memo is in PRO Adm 1/1946, and endorsed by the Admiralty Secretary on 28 Nov 1812.

22 Peter Padfield, in *Broke and the Shannon*, refers to these as mounted on swivels, but while they may have been traversing, they cannot have been fitted on the usual swivelling yoke which allowed no recoil; this would have been a palpable impossibility for a long 9pdr given that even 32pdr carronades could not be made to work on 'non-recoil' mountings.

23 PRO Adm 106/2095, 28 Dec 1812; Adm 106/2259, 12 Jan 1813.

24 NMM ADM/BP/32c, 30 Dec 1812.

25 All three had been out of service for some time:

Goliath at Chatham since Nov 1808; *Majestic*, also at Chatham, since Jun 1810, and *Saturn* at Plymouth since Jan 1811.

26 These are listed in PRO Adm 106/2260, 1 Apr 1813; there is also an estimate of the number of 42pdr carronades likely to be needed which also suggests an Admiralty plan for ten ships.

27 Letters of 7 Jun, 25 Oct and 18 Dec 1813, copied in PRO Adm 95/47.

28 He had acquired his sobriquet by an incredible feat of seamanship that saved the 74-gun *Magnificent* from near-certain destruction on the stormy night of 16 Dec 1812; it was a variant of club-hauling that boxed the ship round on her heel, allowing her to claw off a lee shore.

29 Copy letter of 19 Sep 1813, PRO Adm 95/47.

30 Complaints began to come in around the end of 1814, mostly about the ships labouring when going free, and often requesting lower masts. *Severn* was much improved by winging up the ballast, and the same restowing was applied to *Liffey* and *Liverpool*, while all were given additional false keels to combat leewardliness. PRO Adm 106/2265, 1 Nov, 13 & 19 Dec 1814.

31 PRO Adm 106/2260, 21 & 23 Apr 1813. There were certainly conferences between the Surveyors and the Admiralty about previous new designs, and there probably were in this case, but as no minutes of such meetings survive it is impossible to give a date.

32 PRO Adm 106/2261, 20 Jul 1813.

33 NRS *Dillon*. Most of the relevant matter can only be found in the original MS in NMM Lewis Collection MS/10/58.

34 PRO Adm 106/2267, 8 Aug 1815. Originally the *Java* was to be similarly fitted, but the order of the 14th specified only the these two.

35 PRO Adm 95/49, copy of a letter of 6 Mar 1820.

36 For general background see Commander D J Hastings, *The Indian Navy*; her conversion to a frigate can be found in PRO Adm 106/2095, summaries of letters between 21 Jul 1812 and 9 Jul 1813.

37 Bullen's request of 17 Nov 1814 and the Surveyors' response are digested in PRO Adm 12/163, with more detail in Adm 106/2265; Griffiths' criticism is copied in Adm 95/48.

CHAPTER 6. PREPARING FOR PEACE, 1812-1815

1 NMM ADM/BP/32b, 1 Apr 1812. This throws some interesting light on contemporary events: the *Guerriere*, for example was reckoned to have less than a couple of months' life left in her when she was captured, while the *Shannon* was due for a major refit at the time she met the *Chesapeake*.

2 Original order, 3 Jul 1812, PRO Adm 106/2095; reminder, 7 Nov 1812 (the Navy Board's excuse was 'the importance of the subject requiring long deliberation'); response, 27 Nov, both NMM ADM/BP/32b.

3 The Navy Board usually disapproved of repairing in merchant yards because the work involved in a repair was almost impossible to predict, making it difficult to keep costs under control. However, Blackburn of Turnchapel had submitted a very detailed proposal, including a 20-page price list for every aspect of the

work, and the Navy Board had agreed to give it a trial. NMM ADM/BP/32b, 28 Oct 1812.

4 PRO Adm 2/326, 19 Jan 1813; NMM ADM/BP/32c, 24 Jul 1813. The Navy Board insisted that its figure of 120 included traditional Sixth Rates, but not the sloops recently made Post Captains' commands (and therefore *de facto* Sixth Rates).

5 PRO Adm 2/329, 6 Aug 1813. Although wanted as soon as possible, the large numbers of new fir frigates completing in such a short space of time were proving difficult to man and equip.

6 On 1 Mar 1814, the Navy Board sought direction on how to fit newly launched ships in future, PRO Adm 106/2262. The Admiralty replied with their instructions on the following day, Adm 106/2096. The scheme for the reduction of the fleet was dated 30 Apr 1814, NMM ADM/BP/33c; the fir frigates were ordered to be commissioned on 24 Jun, Adm 106/2263.

7 The Navy Board was formally ordered on 4 Sep 1816 to employ only the ships of the least probable durability during the peace; at the same time the building of any further fir frigates was disapproved, PRO Adm 106/2097.

8 PRO Adm 106/2263, 4 May 1814; Adm 106/3123, 29 Jul 1816.

9 Details are preserved in numerous reports by experts like Lukins and Murphy, and even Barrallier was consulted. The most important can be found in NMM ADM/BP/31b-35b, dated 26 Sep and 2 Oct 1811; 20 Jan, 21 May, 7 Aug and 18 Aug 1812; 29 Oct 1813; and 21 Mar 1815. The problem with the *Queen Charlotte* was the Canada oak and pitch pine used in her topsides, which was said to be in a 'high state of fermentation'; it was proposed to treat the ship with a chemical vapour that included arsenic and sulphur.

10 PRO Adm 106/2265, 26 Oct 1814.

11 The Navy Board consulted all the Dockyards in turn, their reports on masting timber coming in during Jun 1812 and on the preservation of shipbuilding timber in Nov 1812; they are to be found in PRO Adm 106/2057.

12 PRO Adm 2/326, 19 Jan 1813.

13 PRO Adm 106/2267, 25 Aug 1815. A note saying 'It is not intended to arm these ships on the quarterdecks and forecastles' has been struck through. The main battery was also changed from twenty for 38s and eighteen for 36s and 32s.

14 NMM ADM/BP/33c, 25 Oct 1813 reminding the Board that the Admiralty's order of 20 Jan 1812 remained unfulfilled.

15 His recommendations are contained in a letter of 14 Jan 1814, under cover of a letter from the Navy Board dated 15 Feb 1814 in NMM ADM/BP/34a. Some of these issues are covered by J J Packard's article 'Sir Robert Seppings and the Timber Problem', *MM* 64, but it is not very systematic in its approach and misses the wider context.

16 The Navy Board proposed covering slips in its report of 27 Nov 1812, but it had also been asked specifically by the Admiralty in a separate enquiry whether ships built under cover lasted longer, PRO Adm 106/2095, 22 Oct 1812.

17 Adm 106/2095, 5 Nov 1812. The standard work on Dockyard architecture, Jonathan Coad's *The Royal*

Dockyards 1690-1850, is not specific about the timing of their introduction, but says that Portsmouth apparently had a number of slips covered by 1814. Without quoting a specific reference, Packard in 'Seppings and the Timber Problem' credits Bentham with erecting a roof over No 2 Slip at Chatham in 1813; he also claims that Seppings had been advocating covering individual ships since at least 1806, and was ordered in 1812 to roof over the new 100-gun ship to be built at Chatham.

18 PRO Adm 106/2263, 3 May 1814. Other measures included painting exposed decks with white lead paint, and allowing warrant officers on board to occupy wardroom cabins to avoid having to build temporary structures on the upper deck.

19 PRO Adm 106/2267, 28 Jun 1815.

20 NMM ADM/BP/36b, 12 Aug 1816.

21 NMM ADM/BP/32a, 9 Jan 1812.

22 PRO Adm 106/3339, 2 Aug 1814.

23 For these last few 36s the Admiralty usually ordered 38s and had to be reminded that the 36 was the largest that could be built on the available slip at Deptford.

24 At this time Peake, and the Second Surveyor, Joseph Tucker, were at loggerheads with the new Third Surveyor, Robert Seppings concerning various structural innovations (see Chapter 7). Seppings, however, enjoyed the confidence of Melville's Board.

25 The order to Bombay included the construction of a second set of teak frames to be brought home in the *Seringapatam*, PRO Adm 106/3123, 6 Sept 1813. They were to be used for the *Tigris*, but by 1822 it was intended to fit the ship with a circular stern, so no transoms were included in the consignment, 7 & 18 Jan 1822, Adm 106/3123.

26 Initially ordered for *Madagascar* and *Manilla*, 19 Aug 1820, then all frigates of the class, 16 Jan 1822: PRO Adm 106/3123 and /2099.

27 Drawings of the circular stern and a ¾in to the foot model were sent for the two Bombay frigates by order of 18 Dec 1821, PRO Adm 106/3123. It seems that the information did not arrive in time to modify the *Madagascar*, which is not listed as having one.

28 Warren's report, PRO Adm 1/2721, 14 Jun 1821, corroborated by Captain Sir James Gordon of the *Active*, Adm 1/1293. Details of changes, Adm 106/2154, 24 Jul 1822; extended to rest of class, 17 Sept 1822.

29 Letter of 15 Jul 1826 from Carlisle Bay, Barbados, PRO Adm 95/50.

30 Copies of letters from Captain Hamilton to Byam Martin of 1 & 12 Dec 1829, and a questionnaire answered by the Master are filed in PRO Adm 95/51. An annotation says 'I have read these papers to Sir R Seppings', and a note initialled 'RS' summarises the modifications.

31 From Sailing Quality reports of 14 Feb 1831 in PRO Adm 95/51, and 1 Jan 1835 in Adm 95/54.

32 British ships had been significantly smaller than those of their principal enemies – with a few exceptions in the 1760s and 1790s – for more than a century and a half. By implication, superior organisation, better training and sounder finance had been relied upon for success, but the tiny US Navy forced the quality (at this time usually synonymous with size) of ships into the equation.

Post-war the Royal Navy, in effect, gave up the attempt to rule the seas with small ships, and thanks to the structural reforms of Sir Robert Seppings the British were able to build better and often larger ships than those of their likely enemies. The subject is dealt with in great detail by Andrew Lambert in *The Last Sailing Battlefleet*.

33 Original response to Admiralty enquiry, 3 May 1813, PRO Adm 106/2260; instruction to provide draught, 7 Jun 1813, and order for ship, 9 Jul 1813, Adm 106/2095; armament (as *Newcastle* and *Leander*) proposed and accepted, 19 and 21 Jul 1813, Adm 106/2261.

34 The new ratings for specific ships, including exceptions, can be found in James, *Naval History* VI, Abstract No 6 and the notes thereon.

CHAPTER 7. CONSTRUCTION

1 See Morriss, *Royal Dockyards*. Dr Roger Knight has also shown that Albion tended to twist his source material to inflate the potential importance of American forests. See 'New England forests and British seapower: Albion revised', *The American Neptune* XLVI (1986), pp221-9.

2 For example, 4in oak plank rose in price steadily from £7 per load in 1795, reaching a temporary peak of £8-5s for a time in the spring of 1797, but could only be obtained for £10-10s during the 'crisis' of 1802-4; it was steady at £11-8s between 1807 and Nov 1810 when it rose still further to £15; NMM ADM/BP/31a, report of 26 Nov 1811.

3 Figures from Morriss, *Royal Dockyards*, Table 12, p83. They cover only expenditure in the Royal Dockyards but probably reflect in general terms the ebb and flow of naval shipbuilding as a whole, but not the total timber market which was also affected by the demand for mercantile shipping, itself responding to trade fluctuations.

4 Figures extracted from Morriss, *Royal Dockyards*.

5 PRO Adm 106/2091, 26 Mar 1804. This was in fact a restatement of a concern that had existed since at least 1771 when a committee had reported on the perceived deterioration in the timber supply; and Charles Middleton had chaired a far more thorough enquiry which published its findings in 1792 as *The Eleventh Report of the Commissioners appointed to enquire into the state and condition of the Woods, Forests and Land Revenues of the Crown*.

6 PRO Adm 106/2241, 16 Jul 1807.

7 NMM ADM/Y/4, 5 Feb 1806.

8 See *Heavy Frigate*, Chapter 7 for some examples.

9 Order to Navy Board, 5 Jun 1803, PRO Adm 106/3123; this 'case' file conveniently summarises the significant correspondence, and is the basis of the following paragraphs.

10 *Salsette*, 25 Apr 1808. Fastening with iron was regarded as perfectly acceptable in the East because teak's oily texture was thought to possess anti-corrosive properties.

11 PRO Adm 106/3123, 31 Dec 1812.

12 Details in PRO Adm 106/3123, 20 Jul 1815.

13 PRO Adm 49/14 includes a series of financial papers relating to shipbuilding in the East Indies. As with everything relating to these ships, confusion reigns: the file gives the building dates of the second ship, original-

ly *Pitt* and later *Doris*, but refers to *Salsette*. St Vincent's original agreement is probably the root of the problem since for political reasons he wanted a below-cost estimate announced, the Comptroller being instructed to make up the difference by 'private engagement' whenever the true costs became known: see NRS *St Vincent* II, p243. By contrast, the arrangements at Bermuda were both straightforward and economical: NMM ADM/BP/32a, report of 23 Oct 1812.

14 Two long reports from F J Hawkes survive in NMM ADM/BP/31b, under cover of 8 Oct 1811. He believed that initial enthusiasm from local shipbuilders, one of whom felt capable of building a frigate in two years and a 74 in three, evaporated in the face of covert opposition from the governor. However, Hawkes also came to the conclusion that the quality of the timber was not very high, and the only suitable compass timber contained an oil that was corrosive to iron fastenings. Nor was local shipbuilding economical as the British had been led to believe – he quoted the case of a 32-gun frigate that had taken three years to build and cost the equivalent of £33,750.

15 PRO Adm 2/39, 24 Dec 1805; Bentham was in Russia from 31 Jul 1805 to 4 Dec 1807, and the plan seems to have been to build on the White Sea from a timber called 'Melesse', said to be abundant there; NMM ADM/BP/31a, letter of 13 May 1811.

16 PRO Adm 106/ 2245, 22 Dec 1808; Adm 106/2253, 30 Mar and 25 Mar 1811 respectively.

17 PRO Adm 180/10 PBs; Adm 106/2239, 21 Jul 1806. Timber was also imported from Australia under an earlier initiative of St Vincent's Board. The first consignment was brought home in the *Glatton* and in March 1805 the officers of the Woolwich yard reported favourably on most of the rather unscientifically named species (black gum, blue gum, iron bark, stringy bark, mahogany and box), except the lignum vitae, which was inferior to that from the usual sources (Adm 106/1791). Fuller details can be found in R J B Knight & Alan Frost (eds), *The Journal of Daniel Paine*, App II.

18 See *Heavy Frigate*, p35.

19 PRO Adm 106/2091, 26 Mar 1804.

20 PRO Adm 106/2240, 17 Nov 1806.

21 A full report on timber usage since 1801 is contained in NMM ADM/BP/31a, 26 Nov 1811.

22 As an example, Deptford reported on the timbers used to repair the frigates *Aeolus* and *Phaeton* and to build the 36-gun *Brilliant*, 27 Aug 1814 and 14 Jan 1815 respectively, PRO Adm 106/3339. The latter includes some exotic species, including stinkwood (from the Cape) used as a substitute for English oak, pitch pine, East Country [Baltic] plank and Prussia deals.

23 PRO Adm 106/2257, 2 May 1812.

24 PRO Adm 106/2243, 30 Apr 1808; the booty from Copenhagen dockyard filled 92 transports; its value was estimated at £305,665-7s-1d (Adm 106/2245, 5 Nov 1808).

25 Deptford built the frigates *Bacchante, Maidstone, Stag, Barrosa* and *Tartar* between Jul 1810 and Apr 1814 with a combination of English and Quebec oak, pitch pine, red pine, some other unspecified 'fir', Danzig Crown plank and East Country deals: detailed report in PRO Adm 106/3338, 26 Jul 1814.

26 PRO Adm 106/3338, 1 Jun 1814.

27 PRO Adm 106/2090, 15 Oct 1803.

28 NMM ADM/Y/1, report from Samuel Bentham, 15 Aug 1804; PRO Adm 106/1937.

29 NMM ADM/Y/4, 5 May 1806.

30 PRO Adm 106/3564, 8 Jul 1802.

31 PRO Adm 106/2263, 26 May 1814.

32 NMM ADM/Y/1, reports of 4 Sep and 1 Oct 1804; *Clyde*: AO Adm 2/306, 19 Oct 1804.

33 For *Triton* see *Heavy Frigate*; Adm 106/2091, 8 Jul 1805; NMM ADM/Y/1, 5 Feb 1806. The abolition of riders was resisted by the Surveyors, and St Vincent was to congratulate Markham on subduing the 'obstinacy' of the opposition, 'all the ships either built or repaired with them being completely ruined'; letter of 15 Sep 1806, reproduced in J S Tucker, *Memoirs of St Vincent*, p310.

34 PRO Adm 106/3322, 4 Mar 1789.

35 PRO Adm 2/322, 11 Mar 1811; Adm 106/2254, 1 Jun 1811; Adm 2/323, 18 Jul 1811. An actual scantlings list does not seem to have survived: the heavily culled BP series of original Admiralty in letters from the Navy Board does not include such a list; most of the surviving Dockyard correspondence is in the form of letter-book copies, which do not regularly reproduce enclosures, so while it is possible to date the submissions made by yards like Deptford, the actual proposals are missing.

36 See for example the sidings and moulded dimensions of timbers for *Barrosa/Tartar*, 36s and *Bacchante*, 38, from Deptford, PRO Adm 106/3338, 26 Jan 1814. These are not very detailed, so the evidence is inconclusive, but when compared with contract specifications for pre-1811 built sister-ships, the new establishment does not seem to have imposed any radical changes: the biggest difference is the reduction of the bottom planking from 4 inches to 3½ inches.

37 PRO Adm 2/323, 18 Jul 1811.

38 See author's article in *Warship Volume III*, p275 for weight breakdowns.

39 C Northcote Parkinson (ed), *Trade Winds*, Ch 1; P Crowhurst, *The Defence of British Trade 1689-1815*, p100.

40 It is significant that in the revised Sailing Quality report form introduced in Dec 1811, there is a new section specifically questioning the strength of the ship.

41 PRO Adm 106/2220, 29 Sep 1795; Adm 106/2087, 30 Sep 1795.

42 At least according to Barrallier in his later report on Seppings's system, NMM ADM/BP/31b, 4 Dec 1811.

43 PRO Adm 106/1456, letter of 4 Mar 1803. The Patent is No 2646, dated 20 Sep 1802; the single-sheet drawing contains nine figures and includes a number of alternatives, and slight variations from the scheme described to the Navy Board.

44 PRO Adm 106/1456, undated but responding to Brindley's letter of 4 Mar 1803; there is also an undated letter to Mr Wood the overseer telling him to ensure that the work is done very accurately, because the success of the system depends upon it; he is also to refer to the Board if there are any attempted deviations from what has been agreed.

45 *The Naval Chronicle* XIV (1805), p331; Adm 106/2516, 1 Jul 1805.

46 Author's italics, Adm 95/46, Sailing Quality report of 17 Jun 1812. The *Ocean* was no better: when serving as the Mediterranean flagship, Collingwood reported 'This fine new ship is built and secured in a way that will not succeed'; and later reported that he had castigated the 'ill-judged experiment' in an outspoken letter to the Navy Board, saying 'I have given my opinions in behalf of England, whose existence depends upon her Navy. Had the French devised a plan for its destruction, they could not have discovered a more effectual one.' Letters of 7 Nov 1806 and 18 Feb 1809 to J E Blackett, *Public and Private Correspondence of Vice-Admiral Lord Collingwood*, pp253 & 496.

47 PRO Adm 106/1457, letters from Brindley of 30 Jan, 28 Mar, 31 May and 8 Oct 1805, with Navy Board endorsements.

48 PRO Adm 106/2517, 10 Sep 1806.

49 PRO Adm 106/2239, 27 Sep 1806; Adm 106/2242, 20 Sep 1807; *The Naval Chronicle* XX (1808), p22.

50 *The Naval Chronicle* XXIII (1810), p112.

51 *The Naval Chronicle* XIV (see author's *First Frigates*, p117).

52 A letter of Jun 1804 asks when he will be returning to Woolwich. *Circe* and *Pallas* seem to have been fitted with iron knees on the gundeck, but the yard officers were instructed in Sep 1804 to use whatever was to hand for the knees of the quarterdeck and forecastle but under no circumstance to delay the launching of the ships, 12 Jun and 4 Sep 1804, PRO Adm 174/39.

53 R F S Blake, *Description of Various Plans for the Improvement of Naval Architecture*; Blake claimed the credit for this, and said it was widely adopted by the Surveyors.

54 NMM ADM/Y/4, 25 Mar 1806.

55 The best summary of Bentham's claims regarding his contributions to ship design and construction is contained in one of the four memorials of his services submitted after his post was finally abolished at the end of 1812, in NMM ADM/BP/33b, under cover of 24 Apr 1813. Besides the features noted in the main text, Bentham also lists among his achievements: more economical pure copper sheathing nails; bolt nails of mixed metal; standardised pintles and braces; iron water tanks, for which he received the Society of Arts' Gold Medal in 1800 (yet the idea had been recently patented by another as if newly invented – a reference to Richard Trevithick); watertight metal powder canisters; glass bullseye illuminators for lower decks; storage bins; non-recoil gun mountings; roller handspikes for training carronades; enlarged breeching rings for carronades and improved quality breeching rope. Unfortunately, the objectivity of the document must be questionable, since it is a contribution to Bentham's campaign for a substantial pension.

56 NMM ADM/BP/33c, 24 Jul 1813. Pering was Clerk of the Cheque at Plymouth and the author of a pamphlet on premature decay in warships; he also patented a number of innovations in anchor design and manufacture. Credit for the introduction of screw bolts was also claimed later by Richard Blake, in *Various Plans*; he may well have believed it was his invention since he addressed a memorial dated 4 Jun 1814 on the subject to the Navy Board, complete with full scale drawing, PRO Adm 1/4383.

57 Snodgrass's first proposal to strengthen old ships, 16 Feb 1795, Adm 106/2087; *The Naval Chronicle* XXVIII (1811), p293 for Admiral Patton's contribution; acceptance of the programme, PRO Adm 106/2091, 6 Feb 1805.

58 Reports from yards on doubling and bracing programme, NMM ADM/Y/5, 25 Jul 1806; Navy Board's reconsidered opinion, 27 Nov 1812, NMM ADM/BP/32c.

59 This account of the progress of the Seppings system is largely taken from his own manuscript, 'A brief explanation of the principles on which a new system of shipbuilding has been founded', submitted to the Admiralty and preserved as PRO Adm 7/709.

60 See Morriss, *Royal Dockyards*, p37.

61 Full report in NMM ADM/BP/31a, 15 Apr 1811. It is notable that all the ships repaired by Seppings enjoyed far longer than average lives.

62 NMM ADM/BP/31b, 4 Dec 1811; *Fincham, A History of Naval Architecture*, p198; Commander Tyrone G Martin and Commander John C Roach, 'Humphreys's Real Innovation', *Naval History* 8/2 (Mar/Apr 1994). Large claims are made for both the efficacy and the historical importance of the six pairs of diagonal riders designed by Humphreys for his big frigates. The sided and moulded dimensions of these timbers are given elsewhere, but the scantlings list which is the principle evidence is a transcription of a lost original and the wording is unclear, but it does specify that each arm is made up of three sections tabled and bolted together; how such timbers could be 'prestressed' as the authors claim, is difficult to see. There is no doubt they would have had some effect in combatting hogging, but by way of contrast Seppings used *twenty* pairs of iron diagonal straps in frigates some 20ft shorter.

Even at the time Humphreys's ideas were not a clear-cut success. The diagonals in the *United States* were removed in 1806, and it is unlikely that *President* ever had them (she certainly did not have any when captured in 1815 – Seppings's detractors would have been delighted to find yet another 'precedent' for his system); even Humphreys's son Samuel, when Chief Constructor in 1830, gave his opinion that the riders were ineffective. (Information from Don Canney, from his forthcoming book on US sailing warships)

63 PRO Adm 106/2095, 1 & 13 Aug 1812; Adm 106/2258, 12 Aug 1812; NMM CHA/K/22, 9 Dec 1812.

64 PRO Adm 106/2095, summons to attend the Admiralty 5 Aug, to adopt Seppings's system at Chatham, 29 Oct 1812; Melville's visit, Adm 7/709; *Ramillies* report, NMM CHA/K/22, 12 Sep.

65 Tucker was a man with his own notions of structural strength. One of his schemes was to continuously chain-bolt the topside frame timbers, a scheme he applied to a refit of the frigate *Amethyst* – see *Heavy Frigate*, p58 for drawing.

66 Admiralty orders to report on Peake's fastening plan, 29 & 31 Mar 1813 and 5 Apr 1813 on Seppings's plan, PRO Adm 106/2095; Report on Seppings's submitted 27 Apr, and on Peake's, 28 Apr 1813, Adm 106/2260.

67 The plans were the work of Aylen, Foreman of New Work at Portsmouth, and Hookey, Master Boatbuilder at Woolwich, report of 1 Sep in response to Admiralty Orders of 19 & 24 Jun 1813, PRO Adm 106/2261.

68 Seppings's original proposal of 5 Nov 1813, the counter-proposal by Peake and Tucker of 6 Jan 1814 and related correspondence is gathered together under cover of 15 Feb 1814 in NMM ADM/BP/34a.

69 The Canham improvements applied mainly to the floors, and was turned down because it did nothing to solve the principal shortage of long curved toptimbers, NMM ADM/Y/4, 5 Feb 1806. Blake made wider claims for his system: he cited two meetings in Mar 1806 with the Navy Board which included the submission of drawings and models of the framing pattern as applied to a 74; he implies that the scheme was applied to the *Invincible*, a ship previously delayed five years by lack of suitable timber. A drawing of his plan is printed in his book *Various Plans*.

70 Chain-bolting had been specifically prohibited by the Navy Board on 7 Sep 1810, after it had been applied at Plymouth on the *San Josef, Scipion, Bedford* and other ships. It was considered to add weight without strength; PRO Adm 106/2521.

71 All correspondence on this matter is under cover of 27 Oct 1814, including the Surveyors' report of 22 Oct and Seppings's rejoinder of the 26th.

72 PRO Adm 106/2096.

73 Details of the *Economy* can be found in *The Naval Chronicle* vols XX, pp305-310 and XXII, pp298-9. Seppings's deposition, with drawings, is in NMM BP/38a, 22 May 1818; in chronological order, his precedents are:

1. The old system of athwartship diagonal shores, given up 'some sixty years earlier' [in fact, if Seppings had known his naval history, they could have been traced back to at least the *Mary Rose* and Henry VIII's navy]. They provided only partial strength, and suffered the disadvantages of noise and strain when the hull worked, while making stowage difficult.

2. *Maida*, an old French ship of the line with diagonal footwaling recommended by M Gobert. [This system was first tried in 1705 and was widely used in the French navy until about 1750. It was well known, having been attacked by Bouguer in his influential treatise of 1746 for its ineffectiveness.]

3. Bouguer's own system of diagonal pieces between pillars in the hold.

4. Chapman's similar system of diagonal braces between pillars in the hold [more effective than Bouguer's according to Seppings], first published in 1768.

5. Proposal by a Christopher Wilson for diagonal fastenings for timber pieces first published in Oct 1795.

6. Snodgrass's proposal of 1796 [that used in the doubling and bracing programme of 1805]; in effect a reversal of the scheme in No 1, and abandoned for the same reasons.

7. Bentham's ideas employed in *Dart* and *Arrow* in 1796 [no diagonal pieces, but athwartship framing and enlarged shelfpieces anticipate elements of Boswell's scheme].

8. Boswell's system, published in the *Repertory of Arts* in 1803.

9. Bentham's concepts applied to the frigate *Minerva* in 1805: diagonal shores like Snodgrass's system, diagonal planking next to the side, cross bracing between pillars under the beams, and a shelfpiece instead of lodging knees [this last feature was common in

French and Spanish ships, and Seppings said he himself had seen it in a French ship at least thirty-six years earlier].

10. A variation on the *Minerva*'s construction used in the 74-gun *Fame* at the same time.

CHAPTER 8. DESIGN

1 These developments are covered in the author's *Heavy Frigate*, Chapter 8, so need not be reiterated here in detail.

2 PRO Adm 95/44, 29 Aug 1815; Adm 106/3574, Appendix 1.

3 PRO Adm 106/2091, 8 Jul 1805. Not all sea officers approved of the new policy of wall sides, nor of larger ships: Collingwood, for example, while he was C-in-C Mediterranean observed to the First Lord that 'the wall-sided ships, and those heavy masted, are a continual burden on the docks and arsenals; while the ships of the old establishment, as the *Terrible, Saturn, Zealous, Queen*, and such whose sides fall in, are most to be depended on in winter for service.' 11 Dec 1807, *Public and Private Correspondence of Vice-Admiral Lord Collingwood*, p325.

4 NMM ADM/Y/5, 9 Sep 1806.

5 For details see the author's 'Les frégates françaises et la royal navy', *Le Petit Perroquet* 21 (Spring 1977) and 24 (Autumn 1978). In summary, French frigates were considered more lightly built, inadequately fastened, and (because longer and shallower) particularly susceptible to hogging stresses; in consequence, they were more expensive to keep in service and generally enjoyed shorter active lives. There is overwhelming evidence that this was true for at least the period between the 1740s and 1780s, but the general principles seem to have applied even down to 1815.

6 Bridport to Spencer, 17 May & 19 Jun 1798; reference by courtesy of the late Richard Saxby. These will be printed in the forthcoming Navy Records Society volume on the Blockade of Brest 1793-1801, edited by Roger Morriss.

7 This was part of the 'doubling and bracing' programme. It is worth noting that of the five 18pdr frigates included, the two British-built ships (*Thetis* and *Thalia*) were somewhat older than the French trio, having been launched in 1782; *Sybille* was nine years younger, *Virginie* twelve, and even the oldest, *Unité*, was five years junior.

8 The generalisations are based on examples in NMM ADM/Y/- series, all from 1804-1809 period; reference was also made to specific cases noted in the Progress Books, PRO Adm 180/-.

9 A late example was the *Modeste*, PRO Adm 106/2263, 6 Jun 1814.

10 Copies of the correspondence are filed in PRO Adm 95/42: although water damage has erased the dates of his letters, Bayntun was captain of the ship from June 1809 to the autumn of 1810. On 8 July 1809 the Surveyors pointed out that the *Milford* draught needed about 200 tons more displacement amidships since when stored for Channel Service the lower deck ports had only 5ft 2in freeboard, but at that time the Admiralty decided the second ship should be built without alteration (Adm 106/2247). However, in 1811 the sister ship, to have been called *Sandwich*, was finally cancelled.

11 He was Commissioner of the Transport Board, but a frequent correspondent on technical matters with the Admiralty, and the designer of the 'Hamilton gunboat'. At this time he was promoting the virtues of the *Leviathan* class, which eventually became the basis of the *Blake* class 74s. NRS *Markham*, p329.

12 The report can be found in Adm 1/4382, 9 Sep 1812.

13 PRO Adm 106/2262, 14 Jan 1814; an Admiralty list of matters awaiting an answer, dated 25 Oct 1813, includes the order of 14 Dec 1812 to report on the design.

14 NMM ADM/BP/35c, 26 Dec 1815; resumé of Admiralty response in Adm 12/173, same date. NMM ADM/BP/36a, 4 Jan 1816.

15 At Toulon his post was administrative and he was not personally involved with ship design up to his retirement in Dec 1817. Presumably on the strength of his father's influence, his son Louis was made an honorary constructeur in Feb 1816, and entrusted with two big frigate designs in the late 1820s. See Jean Boudriot, *The French Frigate*, pp228-9.

16 Norman Swales, who is reconstructing a lines plan of the *Leander* for modelmaking purposes, found that a scaled-up *Java* midship section fits the deck plans very closely.

17 Commander Tyrone G Martin and Commander John C Roach, 'Humphreys's Real Innovation', *Naval History* 8/2 (Mar/Apr 1994). Apart from a survey afloat, nothing was done to the ship before her repair was ordered in 1818, when the docking revealed the extent of the decay in the ship. This survey provides almost conclusive proof that there were no diagonal riders in the ship because it lists all the internal works in the order in which they were removed, and does not mention anything that could be construed as a diagonal rider; NMM POR/D/31, 7 May 1818. The combined sheer and profile draught is more detailed than usual, showing every dagger knee and a few conventional diagonally placed top and breadth riders, but nothing like the system claimed for *Constitution*.

CHAPTER 9. WARTIME MODIFICATIONS

1 It was typical of the technological conservatism of the St Vincent Admiralty that it tried to reverse this trend, ordering that no ship should be fitted with fixed gangways without specific orders, 3 Dec 1803; PRO Adm 106/2534.

2 Full details can be found in PRO Adm 106/2519, warrants of 3 Sep and 24 Oct 1808; the original Admiralty Order is 7 Jul.

3 PRO Adm 174/53, 28 May 1810: copy of Beaver's letter forwarded to the officers of Plymouth Dockyard to explain the rationale of the work.

4 Admiralty Order of 14 Jun 1814, PRO Adm 106/2263; reversing order of 26 May 1810, Adm 2/320.

5 NMM ADM/POR/A/37, 7 Sep 1794.

6 NMM ADM/CHA/K/22, 30 Jan 1813.

7 PRO Adm 1/751, 24 Aug 1814.

8 *Majestic* was supplied with six 22in cables and four bower anchors, two of 66cwt, one of 59cwt and one of 58cwt, 27 Sep 1813. *Goliath* received the proper weights, her full outfit of anchors being six (measured in cwt-qrs-lbs): 67-3-0, 66-3-10, 66-1-0, 66-3-14, 16-1-0, 8-1-0, 30 Sep 1813. NMM CHA/B/19.

9 NMM CHA/K/22, 17 Feb 1813.

10 Michael Lewis, *A Social History of the Navy*, p420. His figures are for 1810 but as a broad generalisation they probably apply to the whole of the wars.

11 PRO Adm 106/2231, 14, 17 and 24 Mar 1803; a drawing of the fitting for a 36-gun frigate is dated 22 Mar, Adm 106/3474; revised order of 21 Mar 1808 digested in PRO Adm 12/133.

12 See the author's *Heavy Frigate*, p49 for their introduction; Admiralty Order of 8 Dec 1804, PRO Adm 106/2091. Lukin's own memorial of his services lists the thirty-five ships whose fitting he superintended between June 1807 and Aug 1811; not one of them is a frigate, Adm 1/4836, 28 Aug 1811.

13 Vice-Admiral W S Lovell, *Personal Narrative of Events, From 1799 to 1816*, p22.

14 PRO Adm 106/2095, 10 Nov and 11 Dec 1812.

15 NMM ADM/BP/34b, 17 Oct 1814, requests permission to adopt the barrels and includes testimonials to their value gathered during 1812-14.

16 PRO Adm 106/2096, 10 Jun, 26 Aug and 14 Sep 1815; Adm 106/2098, 9 Jan 1819.

17 Richard Pering, *A Treatise on the Anchor*, p39.

18 Adm 106/2057, 9 Mar 1811; Brian Lavery, *The Arming and Fitting of English Ships of War*, p35.

19 Weight data from John Edye, *Calculations relating to the Equipment, Displacement, etc of ships and Vessels of War*, p84 – Brunton's stud-link cables were about 10 per cent heavier again; costs in PRO Adm 106/2259, 25 Feb 1813.

20 T W Traill, *Historical Notes on Chain Cables*, pp16-35; PRO Adm 106/2259, 11 Feb 1813; Adm 106/2266, 15 Apr 1815; Lavery, *Arming and Fitting*, p49.

21 PRO Adm 2/300, 31 Dec 1802: the improvement was ordered to be adopted in all ships; Roberts' pump first ordered 17 Jul 1804 and confirmed to include frigates 15 Sep 1804, Adm 106/2525; list of ships with Roberts' pump and vertical pipes, Adm 106/2239, 14 Jul 1806. After years of development the Truscott pump was successfully tested in the *Malta*, Adm 106/2523, 20 Jan 1812. See Lavery's *Arming and Fitting*, Chapters 13 and 34 for further details.

22 NMM ADM/BP/33b, 24 Apr 1813.

23 By this date they were fitted in at least eight battleships, including the *Royal George*, and the frigates *Penelope, Amethyst* and *Santa Margarita*. Reports from their captains were forwarded to the Navy Board in response to the latter's recommendation of 29 May 1807 (PRO Adm 106/2241), along with the strong hint that Their Lordships did not see sufficient grounds to discontinue issuing the tanks. All the reports were brief, but none noted any undue sickness or health problems among the crews; *Amethyst* had the most experience to call on, having had a tank since commissioning in 1799; NMM/A/3013, 9 & 18 Jun 1807. In the event they were not withdrawn until 1822, when wooden tanks were substituted; Adm 106/2537, 9 Mar 1822.

24 Francis Trevithick, *Life of Trevithick* I, Chapter XIII. Written by his son, like most family histories this is a very partial account, although it gets the basic chronolo-

gy right. Trevithick is said to have called a committee of Navy and Victualling Board experts 'a lot of old women' to their faces, because of their concerns for health, so it is surprising that he received such a rapid and favourable response – initially ordered by the Admiralty on 10 Mar 1809 for the *Royal Oak*, but subsequently transferred to the *Ajax*; PRO Adm 106/2093.

25 The story can be followed in the correspondence from Admiral Sir Henry Stanhope dated 24 Jun, 8 Jul, 12 Jul and 7 Oct 1809, in PRO Adm 1/1406; Seymour of the *Manilla* successfully requested their removal 7 Nov 1809, Adm 12/144; the orders of 30 Jan 1810 and 9 Apr 1811 are in Adm 12/144 and /146.

26 L T C Rolt, *Isambard Kingdom Brunel*, p30.

27 After limited trials in ships going abroad, iron nun buoys were ordered for all ships by warrant of 31 Aug 1813, PRO Adm 106/2536; there were three sizes, that for Fourth and Fifth Rates being 3ft 10ins long by 2ft 1ins diameter at the bulge, Adm 106/2523, 18 Mar 1812. The patents for both buoys and tanks were registered in the name of Robert Dickinson, Trevithick's partner and source of capital, so Maudslay acquired Trevithick's share, but not exclusive rights. A highly decorated example of a nun buoy from the yacht *Royal George* of 1817 is on display in the Royal Naval Museum, Portsmouth.

28 NMM ADM/BP/35a, report of 17 Feb 1815.

29 NMM/BP/35a and PRO Adm 106/2266, 21 Apr 1815.

30 PRO Adm 106/2267, 11 May 1815; 106/3339, 26 May 1815; Adm 106/2097, 25 May 1816.

31 NMM CHA/K/22, 23 Feb 1813 for details; PRO Adm 106/2095, 12 Feb 1813 for instructions, which included the supply of the necessary 'dunnage'.

32 PRO Adm 106/2095, order of 3 Oct 1812 reducing the ballast establishment of tank-fitted ships.

33 All dates are from the Index to Standing Orders 1792-1805, PRO Adm 106/2534.

34 PRO Adm 106/2511.

35 PRO Adm 106/2534.

36 PRO Adm 106/2522. Brian Lavery reproduces a drawing of the scheme in *Arming and Fitting*, p237.

37 PRO Adm 106/2537, 18 Sep 1815.

38 PRO Adm 106/2093, 30 Jun 1809.

39 PRO Adm 106/1321, 20 Mar 1811 from Collier; Adm 106/2254, 18 Jul 1811; Adm 106/2256, 25 Feb 1812.

40 PRO Adm 106/1942, 21 Apr 1813. After an AO of 7 Aug 1813 the lifeboat was generally allowed in lieu of a jollyboat when requested.

41 PRO Adm 106/2093, 5 & 18 Jul and 24 Nov 1808; costs Adm 106/1941, 10 Feb 1812; order to issue a lifeboat in lieu of a jollyboat, Adm 106/2537, 28 Apr 1815; Adm 106/1942, 18 Sep 1813 and 11 Jun 1815 (enclosing Fincham's drawing).

42 PRO Adm 2/302, 5 July 1803; Brenton's own illustrated memorial, dated Sheerness 28 Jan 1808, is Adm 1/5121/23; Admiralty Order of 5 & 25 Mar 1807, Adm 106/2092; order of 31 Mar 1808, Adm 106/2243; frigate captains were allowed launches instead of Brenton's yawls by order of 22 Aug 1808, Adm 106/2536.

43 PRO Adm 106/2522, 1 Apr 1811.

44 For example, a Mr Glandfield received a contract to build twenty-four of his 22ft gigs designed to replace jollyboats in ship sloops and brigs; PRO Adm 106/2524, 5 Jan 1813.

45 PRO Adm 106/2536, 11 Mar 1812.

46 NMM CHA/K/23, 6 Jul 1813.

47 PRO Adm 106/2097, AO of 1 Sep 1817 that the quarterdecks and forecastles of all ships were to be joined in a continuous spar deck in future.

48 In many of the smaller actions between British brigs and American ship sloops, the brigs had been quickly rendered sitting targets by the gaff being shot away, depriving them of the main sail and with it any power of manoeuvre. As a result brigs and schooners were issued with chain slings for the gaffs: AO 6 Sep 1815, PRO Adm 106/3574.

49 The speed of decision-making was commendable: the proposal was put to the Navy Board on 16 Jan 1813, was approved and ordered by the Admiralty on the 21st and by the 28th the instructions had gone out to the Dockyards: PRO Adm 106/2095, 16 Jan 1813; NMM CHA/K/22, 28 Jan 1813.

50 The dating of the committee is difficult. One quotation in the report refers to a cross-examination of 11 Mar 1813, while Tucker could not be described as Master Shipwright after his promotion to Surveyor at the end of May 1813; yet when the Navy Board returned its comments on the completed report in Jun 1815, it described it as produced in response to the Admiralty Order of 18 Jul 1814 (PRO Adm 106/2267). The original of the report itself, complete with later annotations, appendices, plans and sketches is preserved as Adm 106/3574, but is undated.

51 Most of the drawings are reproduced in Lavery, *Arming and Fitting*, pp194 etc.

52 PRO Adm 106/2535, 13 Aug 1807.

53 The printed report, dated 14 Dec 1815, complete with drawings, can be found in NMM ADM/BP/35c, 30 Dec 1815. Adm 106/2537, 29 May 1816: 'The Establishment of Stores of 1815 to supersede all others'.

CHAPTER 10. ARMAMENT

1 Thomas Blomefield (1744-1822) was an artillery officer with considerable experience of naval warfare, having served in bomb vessels during the Seven Years War and floating batteries on the Canadian Lakes during the American Revolution. In 1780 he was appointed Inspector of Artillery and Superintendent of the Royal Brass Foundry, where he began the important reforms that marked his time at Woolwich. For further details see H A Baker, *The Crisis in Naval Ordnance*.

2 By comparison, France had no iron *obusier* proper until 1804 (and it was not introduced in numbers until after 1808); and the US Navy had to import British carronades in the 1790s for her new frigates.

3 See *Heavy Frigate*, pp95-7 for the full story.

4 PRO WO 55/1832, 3 May 1797.

5 PRO Adm 2/288, 12 Apr 1799.

6 PRO Adm 1/4018, 10 May 1807.

7 PRO Adm 160/154, gives armament as at 12 Oct 1808, but the reduction was ordered in Nov 1803; 24pdrs restored by AO 17 May 1813, WO 55/1835.

8 PRO Adm 160/154, 19 Aug 1803.

9 The first patent was No 2151, dated 8 Dec 1796. A brief history of the Gover company is provided by the abstract of a memorial from Hardum, dated 9 Oct 1813, applying for financial recognition of his services, to be found in PRO Adm 1/4022, 20 Mar 1815. It is a sad tale of how they were eventually swindled and driven into bankruptcy, with Gover dying penniless; Hardum, Gover's 'money assistant', himself lost £4000.

10 PRO Adm 1/4015. The report is dated Woolwich 9 Jun 1800 and on the 12th the Board reported that it had ordered the set for the frigate.

11 PRO WO 55/1833, 2 Feb 1801.

12 PRO Adm 1/4015. Capt Richardson of the *Autumn* complained of breakages to the ironwork, especially the 2¼in bolt that attached the slide to the ship's side. Gover, in a riposte dated 14 Sep 1801, claimed that the breeching was set up too slack so the bolt took the force of the recoil, but admitted that the 'catch pall' and brass sockets for the screw jacks needed to be made of better metal. Another purchased sloop, the *Hermes*, found she could not house the guns, because the mounting stood only 6in from the deck, which was not enough to clear the horizontal arm of the ship's iron standards; PRO Adm 106/1790, 24 Sep 1803.

13 PRO Adm 2/296, 24 Jul 1801. AO 5 Aug 1801, Adm 106/2089: since the reversion to 18pdrs was formally ordered, it has been wrongly assumed that the Gover guns were never fitted – see *Heavy Frigate*, p48, and followed by Caruana, *The History of English Sea Ordnance* II, p323; but the ship definitely had Gover guns in 1804/5 – see PRO Adm 160/154 – and in 1812 according to the Sailing Quality report.

14 PRO Adm 1/4017, 17 Aug 1805.

15 PRO Adm 1/4018, 6 Jan 1807 original report; 10 Jan 1807 Blomefield's critique; Adm 106/2240, 15 Jan 1807; 1/4018, 17 Jan to be revised as specified; 9 Mar 1807 production rate.

16 PRO WO 55/1839, 2 Jan 1812 and 15 Oct 1812.

17 PRO WO 55/1834, 11 Nov 1807, but changed on the 30th, so may have been nothing more than a clerical error.

18 The Admiralty, however, thought the principle worthy of further exploration, and ordered the casting of a short 18pdr in sufficient quantity to arm two frigates, PRO Adm 2/312, 26 Jun 1807. The result was a 6ft gun fired by a 4½lb charge, Adm 1/4019, 17 Apr 1808; it seems to have been fitted in the 32-gun *Unicorn*.

19 PRO Adm 1/4018, 5 Jun 1807; Adm 1/4019, 15 Oct 1810 comparative trials with long 18s; PRO Adm 1/4019, 31 Dec 1810.

20 For example, a letter dated 1 Dec 1812 to the *Naval Chronicle* advocates replacing 18pdrs with Govers for all heavy frigates on the America station.

21 This section is based on a series of papers in PRO Adm 1/4021: 26 Jan 1813 for full details of report; 10 Feb 1813 for Congreve's original proposals.

22 At least one modern writer believes Congreve lifted the principle from the Carron Company's 'cannonade', a hybrid gun-carronade much used in the merchant service: Caruana, *English Sea Ordnance* II, p316.

23 PRO Adm 1/4021, 26 Feb 1813, and Admiralty response 1 Mar 1813.

24 PRO Adm 1/4015, 15 May 1801.

25 PRO Adm 1/4022, quotation from report of 12 Dec 1814.

26 Phillimore's original letter of endorsement to Congreve is printed in James, *Naval History* VI, App 4. Trials report is in Adm 1/4021, 29 Nov 1813.

27 The dogmatic but usually meticulous historian William James was one of the most influential critics, dismissing suggestions that the gun was at fault by reference to Phillimore's own earlier endorsement of the Congreve gun. Phillimore was so exasperated by the criticism of his performance that he sought out James and gave him a good thrashing, a piece of rough justice that must have been cheaper, and more satisfying, than recourse to a lawyer.

28 Certainly, in defence of his own account of the battle, James said he could find no evidence of such criticism in the official correspondence to which he had access.

29 John Marshall, *Royal Navy Biography*, Supplement - Part I (London 1827). This also prints Phillimore's report to Admiral Keith.

30 The full details of the 12 Dec 1814 report can be found in the file on Congreve guns passed on to the Admiralty by the Board of Ordnance, with a covering letter of 26 Jun 1815, in PRO Adm 1/4022. Earlier the Admiralty had ordered a survey of the damage to the *Clorinde*, which, in terms of the hull, does not seem to have been extensive: penetrative hits by 24pdrs were confined to two which passed right through the lower deck, six on the upper deck (one of which passed right through), one on the forecastle, and three 'trifling' hits on the quarterdeck; NMM POR/D/30, 21 Apr 1814.

31 PRO Adm 1/3525.

32 PRO Adm 1/4015; 6/11/99. The sloops also carried two of the lightweight 32pdrs of Sadler's design, but they were cast with too little windage for the safe employment of ordinary shot, and were removed by AO of 21 May 1800, Adm 1/4015.

33 Report from three officers on trials in the *Arrow*, 12 Feb 1801, and *Dart*, 3 Mar 1801, PRO Adm 1/4015.

34 PRO Adm 1/4016, reports of 29 Aug 1803 and report of 28 Dec 1803; Admiralty response minuted on reverse.

35 PRO Adm 7/677, 16 & 26 July, 14 Aug 1804.

36 Henslow, PRO Adm 106/3472, 2 Oct 1804; deferred decision Adm 106/2091, same date.

37 PRO Adm 7/677, 24 Jun 1805.

38 Improvement to non-recoil carronade, NMM ADM/Y/3, 6 Dec 1805.

39 Captain Thomas Hamilton's view quoted in Morriss, *Royal Dockyards*, p47.

40 Original order PRO Adm 2/276, 29 Aug 1795; upgrading WO 55/1833, 10 Aug 1803.

41 PRO Adm 106/3388, 31 Jan 1811: a pay scale for fitting boat carronades which lists the various stages of the job.

42 PRO Adm 1/4019, 24 Aug 1808, 15 & 22 Mar 1809; Adm 7/677, 8 Apr 1809.

43 This is the Carriage Depot's own estimate; they also calculated that there were 1700 in store at Woolwich and about the same number in the out ports: Adm 1/4021, 21 May 1813.

44 Presumably, the abortive attack on the *Amazone*, 40 guns, on 24 Mar 1811. The Inspector of the Royal Carriage Depot described them as fitted on 'a very injurious system': PRO Adm 1/4020, 3 May 1811.

45 Since most were never widely adopted, or were of only minor significance, little space has been devoted to them, but for those interested in following up these developments, the references are listed below:

PRO Adm 1/4017

> 3 & 16 Oct 1805 Ward, and Stradley, improved elevating screws
>
> 23 Dec 1805 new type screw coin in *Immortalité*
>
> 13 Jan 1806 Brenton's design in *Amaranthe*

Adm 1/4018

> 4 Nov 1806 Mr Hookham's principle – *Voluntaire*.

46 PRO Adm 106/2521, 6 Mar 1810; seven models were made and sent to the Dockyards.

47 Riou of the *Amazon*, for example, applied for two of his 32pdrs to be so fitted, PRO Adm 2/289, 6 Jun 1799; and two extra 32pdrs on trucks were supplied to *Horatio* in 1807, Adm 2/312, 4 Jul 1807; other examples with two carronades on trucks include *Iphigenia* in 1811 and *Creole* in 1813, while *Lacedaemonian* in 1813 had an exotic additional armament of one 32pdr carronade on trucks for the main deck, two 'light' 18pdr guns for the spare quarterdeck ports and four medium 18pdrs for the forecastle: WO 55/1835.

48 The original warrant of 24 Oct 1808 specifies that the mountings have trucks at the front but 'castors or swivel rollers' at the rear, PRO Adm 106/2519.

49 PRO Adm 1/4020, 4 & 20 Mar 1812.

50 *Majestic* had fired five rounds at full charge followed by seven at reduced allowance without trouble, although the recoil was substantial; the mounting took up so little room that there was no need to train it to the ship's side, and the 42pdr could be run up easily by two men: PRO Adm 1/4021, 18 May 1813.

51 PRO Adm 1/4021, report of 21 Jun 1813.

52 Blomfield's letter of 29 July is enclosed with the full report dated 23 Aug under the cover of the Master-General's letter of 2 Sep 1790, in PRO Adm 1/4010. Some of the range data from a different source is reproduced in Caruana, *English Sea Ordnance* II, p352, but the arrangement is difficult to extract meaningful information from. He also mentions cylinder powder whereas the manuscript source specifies only White and Blue LG as the powder used.

53 A copy of the Instructions dated 29 Apr 1801 can be found in PRO Adm 7/677; the previous established proportion is in Adm 160/150, 22 May 1799.

54 Over three firings with a 3oz charge in a 7in mortar a 60lb ball was fired an average of 595ft by the British powder and 516ft by the French. *The Naval Chronicle* XXI (1809), p23.

55 Full details of these and other Ordnance stores can be gleaned from PRO Adm 160/150.

56 Ordnance to Admiralty 27 Dec 1811, Adm 1/4020; S Tucker, *Arming the Fleet*, p95.

CHAPTER 11. PERFORMANCE.

1 All from Standing Orders to the Yards, 1801-1814, PRO Adm 106/2513-2525, and the relevant indexes, Adm 106/2534-2537.

2 PRO Adm 106/3338, 30 Aug 1813.

3 PRO Adm 106/3574, full report with annotations.

4 PRO Adm 1/751, 24 Aug 1814.

5 PRO Adm 106/2255, 22 Nov 1811.

6 The exchange between Admiralty and Navy Board on the matter are in PRO Adm 106/2096 and /2264, 5 & 10 Aug 1814.

7 PRO Adm 106/2265, 21 Nov 1814; the reports from the six ships were forwarded to the Navy Board by the Admiralty on 24 Sep 1816, but although the covering note survives, the enclosures have disappeared, Adm 106/78.

8 NRS *Dillon* I, pp301-2.

9 PRO Adm 106/2255, 31 Dec 1811, agreed by AO 4 Jan 1812.

10 The old-style forms are bound as Adm 95/45, while the new ones start with Adm 95/46, despite a considerable overlap in dates.

11 The practice is detailed in Burney's 1815 edition of Falconer's *Marine Dictionary*, and elaborated at length in Nares' *Seamanship* of 1862 and Smyth's *Sailor's Word-Book* of 1867, so clearly persisted.

12 PRO Adm 12/103, 3 Feb 1803.

13 PRO Adm 95/50.

14 Report of the trials against *Hussar* in Adm 95/50, while later correspondence regarding the ship is copied and filed with SQ report in PRO Adm 95/51.

15 Jean Boudriot, *The French Frigate*, Chapters VII.

16 As Dillon pointed out to Barrallier – quoted in Chapter 5.

17 *Niemen* claimed 11kts 'with a following sea', but since that is the answer given for each wind strength and degree of sail carried, it is doubtful if the captain was paying proper attention to the questions.

CHAPTER 12. FRIGATES IN ACTION

1 This section is largely based on J S Corbett, *The Campaign of Trafalgar*.

2 Battleships were occasionally employed in this way: *Bellerophon* and the Advanced Squadron before the First of June was one example; and *Dragon* was sent by Calder to find Nelson in August 1805.

3 Brian Tunstall, *Naval Warfare in the Age of Sail*, p2.

4 M K Barrit, 'Nelson's Frigates: May to August, 1798', *MM* 58, pp281-95.

5 According to Tunstall, *Naval Warfare*, p195, frigates' signal flags were 10ft by x 12ft in size.

6 Tunstall, *Naval Warfare*, p230.

7 After a century of misunderstanding, the signal is now known to have been made as follows: telegraphic flag, then 253 (England) 269 (expects) 863 (that) 261 (every) 471 (man) 958 (will) 220 (do) 370 (his) 4 (D) 21 (U) 19 (T) 24 (Y).

8 NRS *Logs* II, p163.

9 Augustus Phillimore, *The Life of Admiral of the Fleet Sir William Parker, Bart, GCB, from 1781 to 1866*, Vol 1, p289.

10 Tunstall, *Naval Warfare*, p236-7.

11 Quoted in James, *Naval History* III, pp366-7.

12 Tunstall, *Naval Warfare*, p251.

13 Phillimore, *Life of Parker* I, p251. In the British fleet it was widely believed that in battle all enemy ships were combatants: indeed, in Sep 1807 Collingwood had to instruct all his commanding officers that in future engagements they were not to fire on enemy small craft purely engaged in life-saving – but he also insisted that no British ship give up the pursuit of an enemy in order to give them assistance. *Public and Private Correspondence of Vice-Admiral Lord Collingwood*, p312.

14 Phillimore, *Life of Parker* I, p308.

15 John C Dann (ed), *The Nagle Journal*, pp210-11.

16 Sir Nicholas Nicolas (ed), *The Dispatches and Letters of Nelson* VII, p111 & VII, p51.

17 Nicolas (ed), *The Dispatches and Letters of Nelson* VII, pp85-6, slightly precised.

18 Phillimore, *Life of Parker* I, p228.

19 Phillimore, *Life of Parker* I, pp256-76.

20 *The Naval Chronicle* XIII (1805), Plate 169.

21 Abraham Crawford, *Reminiscences of a Naval Officer* (1999 ed), p59.

22 PRO Adm 106/2244, 4 Aug 1808.

23 PRO Adm 106/2091, 10 Sep 1805.

24 PRO Adm 106/2244, 26 Jul 1808.

25 Captain William Penrose Mark-Wardlaw (ed), *At Sea with Nelson: being the life of William Mark, a purser who served under Admiral Lord Nelson*, p205.

26 *The Naval Chronicle* IV (1800), p269.

27 After the battle Wellington wrote to General Lord William Bentinck '. . . I find that Sir Home Popham, with a few hundred marines and guerrillas of the north has succeeded in preventing Caffarelli from dispatching anything to Marmont's assistance, except cavalry . . .' Quoted in Hugh Popham, *A Damn'd Cunning Fellow*, p201.

28 NRS *Barham* III, p362.

29 NRS *Keith* III, p284. Keith's letter to Melville of 5 Sep 1812 suggests that Popham was withdrawn because he was not getting on with Spanish army officers – a legacy of his activities at Buenos Aires – but Keith proposed to send him to Catalonia in the following season 'where the weather is good and the anchorage too', a reflection of his view of the dangers of operating battleships on the Cantabrian coast.

30 NRS *Byam Martin* II, p360: Melville to Lord Keith, 3 Sep 1813.

31 Correspondence in NRS *Keith* III and NRS *Byam Martin* II.

32 NRS *Keith* III, p308.

33 NRS *Keith* III, p305. When applying for the rearmament Collier told the Navy Board that the topsides of his ship were weak from age, but this may have been a ploy since structural weakness was one of the few reasons the Board would definitely accept for non-standard changes to the Establishment of ships.

34 NRS *Byam Martin* III, p409.

35 *Some Principles of Maritime Strategy*, pp110ff.

36 Lt Reuben Mangin's summary of the squadron's successes has already been quoted in Chapter 5, footnote 5.

37 Montagu Montagu recalled his service in the *Dryad* about 1799 with nostalgia: 'Assuming her to be what a man of war should be, in equipment – company – and discipline, and as most were, the command of a cruising frigate in those days might be considered the finest position under the sun, and, if with a roving 'commission' – then growing rare – one to be envied by the gods.' He went on to define it as 'A commission from the Admiralty, giving the Captain discretionary power to go where he pleased,' but qualified the statement with 'of course always under some limitation.' Reynald Ramseyer, *Montagu: Capitaine de Vaisseau*.

38 Extracted from Board Journal, for Jan-Jun 1809, PRO Adm 7/255.

39 Both the generalisations and the individual examples in this section are based on an analysis of the Registers of Convoys, in the PRO Adm 7/782ff series, cross-referred to the relevant Board Journals, Adm 7/229ff. The former give the ships and their escort in each convoy, while in the latter it is possible to find a summary of the orders under which they were operating. The analysis concentrated in most detail on the periods 1796-8 and 1808-9, but with sufficient breadth to determine that these years were not atypical.

40 Board Journal, Apr-Sep 1796, PRO Adm 7/229: there is even a hint that the duty was a punishment for Captain Lord Fitzroy, who had just been reprimanded for allowing an alarming proportion of his crew to desert.

41 A modern study, Richard Hill's *The Prizes of War*, concludes that although it was a powerful incentive, prize money rarely led a naval officer to neglect his duty.

42 C Ernest Fayle, 'Shipowning and Marine Insurance', in Northcote Parkinson (ed), *The Trade Winds*, p41.

43 T N R Wareham, 'Frigate Captains of the Royal Navy, 1793-1815', PhD thesis, University of Exeter 1999.

44 The revised Establishment of 12 Nov 1806 allowed 45 Marines to a 44-gun ship, 40 to both 38s and 36s and 35 to a 32-gun ship; PRO Adm 106/2517. These numbers were increased in 1808 to 48 Marines for 38s and 36s and 42 for 32s: for the bigger frigates these comprised 2 subalterns, 2 sergeants, 2 corporals, 1 drummer, and 41 privates: NMM CHA/E/91, 3 May 1808.

45 Although the circumstances were different and the boat crews smaller, when surveying George Vancouver was in the habit of storing his boats for three weeks or more of independent sounding ahead of his ship. G S Richie, *The Admiralty Chart*, p42.

46 Sidney Smith to Earl Spencer, 21 Jul 1795. Reference by courtesy of the late Richard Saxby.

47 To Rear-Admiral Sotherby, 30 Jun 1809; *Public and Private Correspondence of Vice-Admiral Lord Collingwood*, pp532-3.

48 Donald Thomas, *Cochrane: Britannia's Last Sea-King*, p133.

49 Thomas Cochrane, *Autobiography of a Seaman* I, p335.

50 P Padfield, *Broke and the Shannon*, p66 quoting letter of 31 Mar 1811.

51 T N R Wareham, 'Frigate Captains'.

52 Padfield, *Broke*, p11; this phrase is used almost verbatim in *Naval Gunnery* and it seems Douglas followed Broke's ideas very closely, although he also corresponded with Captain Samuel Pechell.

53 This raises the interesting question of how frigate captains learned their trade. Unlike fleet tactics, single-ship actions seem to have attracted little theoretical work in print, and there are no hints of specific doctrine; as Broke implies, it was presumably learnt from superiors. It is also worth noting in post-war seamanship manuals the prevalence of advice on chasing: one example would be A J Griffiths, *Observations on some Points of Seamanship* (Portsmouth 1828).

54 Howard Douglas, *Naval Gunnery* (1855 ed), p485.

55 A standard British 38-gun frigate fired 0.48lbs per ton; the broadside of a French 40 was 364 French *livres* (or 392lbs English measure), making 0.36lbs per ton in 1793; or 380 *livres* (409lbs English) and 0.375lbs per ton in 1808 after the adoption of the iron carronade. For comparison, a US spar-decked 44 fired 0.56lbs per ton.

56 The original order of Jun 1806 reduced crews from 300 men to 284 for 38-gun ships, and established 274 on all frigates with twenty-six 18pdrs on the main deck. However, many ships already had smaller official complements, and since it was primarily an exercise in conserving manpower, the older figures were retained. There were numerous applications for additional men, and examples of the exceptions allowed include *Clorinde*, whose original complement was 330 but reduced under the 1806 order, and revised to 300 on the captain's application in Oct 1808; and the 36-gun *Unité*, after an argument, in Oct 1808 was established with 284 (both NMM ADM/Y/9); and by AO of 26 Oct 1809 all 36s of twenty-six main-deck 18pdrs, with lower established numbers, were brought up to the standard 274. There were also examples of frigates established with higher complements from the beginning: the 38-gun *Niemen* with 300 in Aug 1808. The ex-French prizes obviously caused most controversy, but even British-built ships like the *Horatio*, 38 also had their crews increased beyond the revised minimum, in this case to 300 men (later examples from PRO Adm 106/2093).

57. Some of the more conservative officers, like Collingwood, felt that the search for speed had led to the over-masting of some ships, which strained the hulls and required more maintenance; he also believed the problem to be more pronounced in the new larger, wall-sided designs (see Chapter 8).

Bibliography and Sources

PRIMARY SOURCES

Admiralty Library, London
List of HM Royal Navy, 1 Jul 1817 (from 1 Jul 1814, corrected to 23 Oct 1831)

Public Records Office, Kew (PRO)

Adm 1   Admiralty In Letters
100-1406   From Flag Officers, 1794-1809
1717-2721   From Captains, 1795-1821
3508   From RNC Portsmouth, 1812
3525   Relating to Inspector General of Naval Works, 1798
3916   From East India House, 1806
4014-4022   From Board of Ordnance, 1786-1815
4383   Promiscuous 'B', 1814 [Blake]
4836   Promiscuous 'L', 1811 [Lukin]
5021/23   Brenton's yawls

Adm 2   Admiralty Out Letters
138   Lord's Letters, 1799
267-331   To Navy Board, 1790-1815
614-622   Secretary's Letters, 1796-1797
806   Secretary's Letters, 1799
1101   Relating to convoys, 1806

Adm 3   Admiralty Minutes
123   1799

Adm   Admiralty Miscellanea
64   Schedule of convoy lists sent to Lloyd's, 1808-1815
65   Lists of ships under specific convoys
68   Register of convoys
229-255   Board Journals, 1796-1809
677   Ordnance Establishments, 1679-1809
579   1815 Establishment of Boatswain's sea stores
580   1815 Establishment of Carpenter's sea stores
709   Seppings's description of his new system of shipbuilding
783-791   Registers of convoys, 1797-1809

Adm 8   Ships' Stations, Captains, etc
70   January 1794
74   July 1797
81   March 1801
90   October 1805
97   June 1809
100   July 1813

Adm 12   Admiralty Indexes & Digests
62-173   1794-1815

Adm 49   Accountant General's Dept
14   Costs of shipbuilding in India
94   Promiscuous papers relating to shipbuilding 1784-1797
103   Signals for ships under convoy, 1805
136   Digest and index of standing orders 1658-1765

Adm 51   Captains' Logs
2524   *Leander*, 1813-14
2589   *Newcastle*, 1813-14

Adm 83   Surveyor's Office Orders from Admiralty
1   1813-1815

Adm 87   Surveyor's Office In Letters
1   Relating to ships, 1806-1829
2   823-1837

Adm 91   Surveyor's Office Letterbooks
4   Minutes 1818-1819
5   Minutes 1820

Adm 95   Controller's Office Miscellanea
7-8   Annual accounts [estimates for building ships 1791-1807]
39-54   Sailing quality reports, 1792-1842
69-74   Draughts of water and qualities of ships, 1793-1826
80-82   Dimensions of ships as built, 1800-1827
85   Ships to be built, scantlings, etc, 1794-1807

Adm 106   Navy Board Correspondence
78   In Letters from Admiralty, Sept 1816
1321-1334   In Letters from Sea Officers 'C', 1810-1822 [Collier]
1456-1457   In Letters promiscuous 'B', 1802-6 [Brindley]
1793-2057   In Letters from Dockyard officers, 1790-1818
2086-2099   Abstract of In Letters from Admiralty, 1791-1822
2150-2151   Registers of In Letters from foreign yards, 1808-1820
2154-2156   Digests of correspondence, 1822-1823

2216-2275   Letterbook copies of Out Letters to Admiralty, 1791-1818
2399-2400   Letterbook copies of Out Letters to Sea Officers, 1812
2508-2520   Standing Orders to the Yards, 1756-1814
2534-2537   Index to Standing Orders 1792-1822
3122   Ballast plans
3123   Shipbuilding at Cochin and Bombay, 1802-1822
3319-3339   Deptford letter books, 1st series, 1779-1815
3367-3373   Deptford letter books, 2nd series, 1797-1811
3388   Deptford letter books, 2nd series, 1792-1794
3472-3474   Deptford letter books, 7th series, 1781-1805
3556-3564   Sheerness, Commissioner's letter books, 1786-1802
3574   Report of Committee on Sea Stores, 1814
3575   Secret Letters c1800-1804

Adm 160   Ordnance
150   Proportions, Tables &c, 1780-1830
154   Guns on board ships at Chatham, 1803-1812

Adm 174   Plymouth Dockyard Correspondence
25-62   Officers letters and warrants from Navy Board, 1794-1814
137-138   From Officers to Navy Board, 1813-14

Adm 180   Progress and Dimensions Books
6-11   Progress Books
19   Dimensions Book
23-24   Dimensions and qualities

WO 55   Board of Ordnance Miscellanea
1830-1835   Ships' armament lists, 1793-1826
2022   Portsmouth Ordnance Office, 1797

National Maritime Museum, Greenwich (NMM)

ADM/A   Navy Board Orders and Instructions from the Admiralty
2883-3013   1796-1807

ADM/BP   **Admiralty In Letters from Navy Board**
30-38   1810-1818

ADM/CHA **Chatham Dockyard correspondence**
/B/19   Out Letter books to Navy Board, 1813
/E/91-2, 111   In Letters from Navy Board, 1808, 1814
/K/1-23   Abstract of Navy Board orders, 1796-1813

ADM/POR **Portsmouth Dockyard correspondence**
/A/36-55   Dockyard Officers' In Letters from Navy Board, 1793-1811
/D/27-31   Officers' reports, 1796-1818

ADM/Y   **Admiralty In Letters from Navy Board relating to shipbuilding, etc**
1-9   1804-1809

Adm 168   **Contract Specifications**
124   *Cambrian*, 1797
137   *Endymion*, 1797
158   *Astraea*, 1808
159   *Ister*, 1813
163   *Horatio*, 1805
165   *Tanais*, 1812
175   *Newcastle*, 1813

Lewis Collection
MS/10/58   Ms of Dillon's narrative, Vol 5

RUSI   **Royal United Services Institution Collection**
/NM/63   List of HM Navy, 1795-1807
/NM/64   List of HM Navy, 1 Jan 1808 corrected to 31 Dec 1816
/NM/65   List of HM Navy, 1 Jan 1817 corrected to 31 Dec 1830
/NM/74   List of HM Navy, corrected to 1804
/NM/77   List of HM Navy, 1812 corrected to Jun 1825

The Patent Office, Newport

2151   Gover's improvements in carriages for cannon, 7 Jan 1797
2646   Brindley's method of constructing ships, 20 Oct 1802
2803   Gover's improvements in the construction carriages for cannon, 19 Jan 1805
3172   Trevithick & Dickinson's new method of stowing cargoes of ships, etc, 28 Apr 1809
3373   Walker's machine or vessel for the conveyance of gunpowder, 6 Nov 1810
3565   Congreve's improvements in gun and carronade carriages, 10 Jul 1812
3637   Dickinson's improvements in vessels for containing liquids, 14 Jul 1813
3726   Pering's method of making an anchor on new principles, 17 Sep 1813

SECONDARY SOURCES

Navy Records Society volumes
Dillon: Michael Lewis (ed), Vice-Admiral Sir William Dillon, *A Narrative of my Professional Adventures*, 2 vols (London 1953 & 1956).
Barham: Sir John Knox Laughton (ed), *The Letters and Papers of Charles, Lord Barham, Admiral of the Red Squadron, 1758-1813*, 3 vols (London 1907-1911)
Boteler: W G Perrin (ed), *Boteler's Dialogues* (London 1929)
Byam Martin: Admiral Sir R Vesey Hamilton (ed), *Journals and Letters of Admiral of the Fleet Sir Thomas Byam Martin, 1773-1854*, 3 vols (London 1898, 1900 & 1902)
Keith: W G Perrin (ed), *The Keith Papers: selections from the letters and papers of Admiral Viscount Keith*, Vol 1 (London 1927); Christopher Lloyd (ed), Vol 3 (London 1955)
Logs: Vice-Admiral Sir T Sturges Jackson (ed), *Logs of the Great Sea Fights*, 2 vols (London 1899 & 1900)
Markham: Sir Clements R Markham (ed), *The Correspondence of Admiral John Markham, 1801-7* (London 1904)
St Vincent: D B Smith (ed), *The Letters of Admiral of the Fleet the Earl of St Vincent whilst First Lord of the Admiralty. 1801-1804*, 2 vols (London 1922 & 1927)
Spencer: J S Corbett (ed), *The Private Papers of George, Second Earl Spencer, First Lord of the Admiralty, 1794-1801*, 4 vols (London 1913-1934)

American State Papers. Class IV Naval Affairs, Vol I (Washington, DC 1834)
Anon, *Service Afloat, or the Naval Career of Sir William Hoste* (London 1887)
H A Baker, *The Crisis in Naval Ordnance*, NMM Monograph 65 (London 1983)
M K Barrit, 'Nelson's Frigates: May to August, 1798', *The Mariner's Mirror* 58 (Aug 1972)
P Banbury, *Shipbuilders of the Thames and Medway* (Newton Abbot 1971)
Sir John Barrow, Bart, *An Auto-biographical Memoir* (London 1847)
Jean-Jérôme Baugean, *Collection des toutes les espèces de bâtiments de guerre et de bâtiments marchands qui naviguent sur l'océan et dans la Méditerranée* (Paris 1814)
——— , *Recueil de petites marines* (Paris 1817)
R F S Blake, *Description of Various Plans for the Improvement of Naval Architecture* (London 1833)
Jean Boudriot, *The History of the French Frigate* (Rotherfield 1993)
William Burney, *A New Universal Dictionary of the Marine . . .originally compiled by William Falconer* (London 1815)
Adrian Caruana, *The History of English Sea Ordnance*, Vol 2 (Rotherfield 1997)
Jonathan Coad, *The Royal Dockyards 1690-1850* (Aldershot 1989)
Thomas Cochrane, *Autobiography of a Seaman* (London 1860)
G L Newnham Collingwood (ed), *Public and*

Private Correspondence of Vice-Admiral Lord Collingwood (London 1829)
William Congreve, *An Elementary Treatise on the Mounting of Naval Ordnance* (London 1811; reprinted Ottawa 1970)
J S Corbett, *The Campaign of Trafalgar* (London 1910)
——— , *Some Principles of Maritime Strategy* (London 1911)
Abraham Crawford, *Reminiscences of a Naval Officer*, 2 vols (London 1851; new edition, 1 vol London 1999)
P Crowhurst, *The Defence of British Trade 1689-1815* (Folkestone 1977)
John C Dann, *The Nagle Journal: a diary of the life of Jacob Nagle, sailor, from the year 1775 to 1841* (New York 1988)
Cdt Alain Demerliac, *Nomenclature des navires français de 1792 à 1799* (Nice 1999)
Howard Douglas, *Naval Gunnery* (4th ed, London 1855)
W S Dudley (ed), *The Naval War of 1812*, 2 vols (Washington, DC 1985 & 1992)
Charles Dupin, *Voyages dans le Grande Bretagne, entrepris relativement aux services publics de la guerre, de la marine, et des ponts et chaussées, au commerce et a l'industrie, depuis 1816*, 4 vols (Paris 1825-26)

John Edye, *Calculations relating to the Equipment, Displacement, etc of Ships and Vessels of War* (London 1832)

John Fincham, *A History of Naval Architecture* (London 1851)

Robert Gardiner, 'Les frégates françaises et la royal navy', *Le Petit Perroquet* 21 (spring 1977) and 24 (autumn 1978).

————, 'Frigate Design in the 18th Century', 3 parts, in *Warship Volume III* (London 1979)

————, *The First Frigates* (London 1992)

————, *The Heavy Frigate, Vol I: 1778-1800* (London 1994)

————, *The Naval War of 1812* (London 1998)

Joyce Gold (ed), *The Naval Chronicle*, 40 vols (1799-1818)

A J Griffiths, *Observations on some Points of Seamanship* (Portsmouth 1828)

Commander D J Hastings, *The Indian Navy* (London 1988)

Richard Hill, *The Prizes of War: the naval prize system in the Napoleonic Wars 1793-1815* (Stroud 1998)

William James, *Naval Occurrences of the late War between Great Britain and the United States of America* (London 1817)

————, *The Naval History of Great Britain*, 6 vols (expanded edition, London 1837)

R J B Knight (ed), *Shipbuilding Timber for the British Navy: Parliamentary Papers, 1729-1792* (New York 1993)

———— & Alan Frost (eds), *The Journal of Daniel Paine, 1794-1797* (Sydney, NSW 1983)

————, 'New England forests and British seapower: Albion revised', *The American Neptune* XLVI (1986), pp221-9.

Vice-Admiral William Stanhope Lovell, *Personal Narrative of Events, From 1799 to 1816* (2nd ed London 1879)

Andrew Lambert, *The Last Sailing Battlefleet: maintaining naval mastery, 1815-1850* (London 1991)

Brian Lavery, *The Ship of the Line: the development of the battlefleet 1650-1815* (London 1983 & 1984)

————, *The Arming and Fitting of English Ships of War* (London 1987)

Michael Lewis, *A Social History of the Navy* (London 1960)

David Lyon, *The Sailing Navy List* (London 1993)

A T Mahan, *Sea Power in its relations to the War of 1812*, 2 vols (London 1905)

Captain William Penrose Mark-Wardlaw (ed), *At Sea with Nelson: being the life of William Mark, a purser who served under Admiral Lord Nelson* (London 1929)

John Marshall, *Royal Navy Biography*, Supplement - Part I (London 1827)

Commander Tyrone G Martin and Commander John C Roach, 'Humphreys's Real Innovation', *Naval History* 8/2 (Mar/Apr 1994)

Roger Morriss, *The Royal Dockyards during the Revolutionary and Napoleonic Wars* (Leicester 1983).

Lt George S Nares, *Seamanship* (2nd ed, London 1862)

Sir Nicholas Harris Nicolas (ed), *The Dispatches and Letters of Vice Admiral Lord Viscount Nelson*, 7 vols (London 1844-47)

J J Packard, 'Sir Robert Seppings and the Timber Problem', *The Mariner's Mirror* 64 (May 1978)

P Padfield, *Broke and the Shannon* (London 1968)

C Northcote Parkinson (ed), *The Trade Winds* (London 1948)

Richard Pering, *A Treatise on the Anchor* (London 1819)

Augustus Phillimore, *The Life of Admiral of the Fleet Sir William Parker, Bart, GCB, from 1781 to 1866*, 3 vols (London 1876)

Hugh Popham, *A Damn'd Cunning Fellow: the eventful life of Rear-Admiral Sir Home Popham KCB, KCH, KM, FRS 1762-1820* (Tywardreath 1991)

Reynald Ramseyer, *Montagu: Capitaine de Vaisseau* (Yens, Switzerland 1992)

G S Richie, *The Admiralty Chart* (London 1967)

L T C Rolt, *Isambard Kingdom Brunel* (London 1970)

Admiral W H Smyth, *The Sailor's Word-Book* (London 1867)

John E Talbott, *Pen and Ink Sailor: Charles Middleton and the King's Navy, 1778-1813* (London 1998)

Donald Thomas, *Cochrane: Britannia's Last Sea-King* (London 1978)

T W Traill, *Historical Notes on Chain Cables* (London 1885)

Francis Trevithick, *Life of Trevithick*, 2 vols (London 1872)

J S Tucker, *Memoirs of Admiral the Right Hon the Earl of St Vincent*, 2 vols (London 1844)

Spencer Tucker, *Arming the Fleet* (Annapolis, MD 1989)

Brian Tunstall (edited by Nicholas Tracy), *Naval Warfare in the Age of Sail* (London 1990)

T N R Wareham, 'Frigate Captains of the Royal Navy, 1793-1815', PhD thesis, University of Exeter 1999.

Bennet Woodcraft, *Alphabetical Index of Patentees of Inventions* (London 1854; reprinted New York 1969)

Glossary of Technical Terms and Abbreviations

Admiralty Formally the Lords Commissioners for executing the office of Lord Admiral, the Board of Admiralty or simply Admiralty was the senior body responsible for the administration of the Royal Navy. It was an office of central government so was politically appointed, but usually included senior naval officers as advisors, at first called Naval Lords and later Sea Lords. Its head was the First Lord of the Admiralty, a Cabinet post that was sometimes held by a seaman like St Vincent or Lord Barham in this period, but was more often a civilian. The Admiralty was charged with the military direction of the Navy, administered through a permanent secretariat, *materiel* aspects being delegated to an older, but junior body, the Navy Board (*qv*).

AO Admiralty Order (the Admiralty issued Orders whereas the Navy Board's instructions were called Warrants).

bobstay Piece of standing rigging running from the end of the bowsprit to the bow of the ship to offset the upward pull of the jibs.

Bombay Marine The English or Honourable East India Company virtually ruled British India in the eighteenth century and necessarily had its own forces. Its navy, which included ships of frigate size and smaller, was known colloquially as the Bombay Marine.

bracing *See* doubling.

breasthooks A form of horizontal knee used to strengthen the internal bow structure.

burthen Tonnage calculated by a formula based on the dimensions of the ship; it was not a displacement figure, but a very crude measurement of internal volume. In the Royal Navy the product of the calculation was divided by 94, so when given precisely the burthen figure included full tons and 94ths.

cabotage The French coasting trade. With few roads and canals France was heavily dependent on local shipping, which consequently was a major target for British attacks.

carlings Fore and aft timbers between the deck beams.

carr Carronade; a lightweight short-barrelled weapon invented by the Carron Company and introduced into naval service during the American Revolutionary War.

carvel Style of boat- or shipbuilding in which the planks fit flush edge-to-edge, and do not overlap as in clinker; it implies the pre-erection of a frame.

cascable The moulding at the breech end of a gun, including the button and any breeching ring.

cathead Timber beam projecting from the bow of a ship, used as a fixed crane in the handling of the anchors.

chase guns Guns fitted to fire forward ('bow chase') or aft ('stern chase') when in pursuit or being pursued. These tended to be medium calibre long guns – most commonly 9pdrs in frigates – with an emphasis on accuracy since there was never likely to more than a pair that could be brought to bear in such situations. Some captains liked longer versions of the quarterdeck calibre, believing this meant greater accuracy, and some had favourite guns unofficially acquired or purchased from their own resources; brass guns were sometimes favoured for this purpose.

C-in-C Commander-in-chief.

clamps Thick planks of fore-and-aft timber forming a support for the beam ends; also called beam shelves or shelf pieces.

Clerk of the Cheque A senior Dockyard clerical official, whose responsibilities were mainly financial; he answered to the Comptroller of the Navy Board.

close-hauled Sailing as near to the direction of the wind as possible, in a square rigged ship making an angle of about 70 degrees to the wind.

Comptroller The head of the Navy Board (*qv*).

crank Unstable, liable to large angles of heel, so unable to carry what would be regarded as an appropriate amount of sail for a given set of conditions. The opposite of stiff (*qv*).

CS Channel Service (*ie* in home and European waters).

cwt Hundredweight (112lbs or 50.8kg).

doubling [and bracing] The process of adding an extra layer of planking over the lower hull of weak or unstable ships. As an emergency measure it was applied in 1804-5 to a number of unseaworthy line of battle ships and frigates in a scheme promoted by Gabriel Snodgrass, Surveyor of the Honourable East India Company, which for some ships also included bracing with diagonal shores from the keel to the ends of the lower-deck beams.

floorhead The top of the floor timbers (*see* futtock); the line formed by the floorheads was used as a fairing line in naval architecture.

forelock An iron wedge driven through a slot in the end of a bolt to hold it in place.

footwaling Interior planking over the lower portions of a ship's hull.

forereach To go past, or to gain upon; it implies going faster through the water, but a leewardly (*qv*) ship might nevertheless not match a slower but more weatherly (*qv*) one over a given course to windward.

freeboard The distance between the waterline and any major opening in the hull or, if none, the weather deck.

frigate Although the term has applied to many ships types over the centuries there has been a consistent association with speed. From the late seventeenth century the word came to mean a seagoing cruising ship, too small for the line of battle, but large enough for independent action. Perhaps descending from the galley-frigates of the 1670s, these ships tended to feature an unarmed (or partially armed) lower deck, which gave their main battery sufficient freeboard to be fought in all reasonable weathers. In the 1740s French designers lowered the position and headroom of the now totally unarmed lower deck, producing a snug and weatherly above-water profile; with separate forecastle and quarterdeck above the battery, this historians came to regard as the 'true frigate' layout. It was the basic pattern for all the frigates covered in this book, although the advent of the spar deck in effect gave frigates two complete batteries.

FS Foreign Service.

futtock One of the timber elements of a ship's frame. A frame (or strictly a framed bend) comprised overlapping pairs of floor timbers, futtocks and toptimbers (*qv*).

Great Repair The largest of three generalised levels of attention applied to British warships in the Royal Dockyards, it amounted to almost a complete reconstruction, often replacing large parts of the framing. A Middling Repair was the next level, which might also include renewing some if less of the structure, while a Small Repair involved minimal replacement. There seems to have been no formal thresholds between one category and another, but all implied more work than the regular maintenance described as a Refit.

hances Steps in the profile of the upperworks or the rudder.

hogging The fine lines fore and aft in a ship mean that they have less buoyancy than the midship area, so wave action in a seaway produces a tendency for the ends to droop, which is called hogging (in extreme examples the keel becomes arched in the middle like a hog's back). The stresses caused by hogging are damaging to the structure of the hull, the movement of individual elements of the structure reducing strength, causing leaks and eventually leading to decay in the timbers. Although less common, the opposite effect is called sagging.

Indiaman Common description of any ship

trading with India, but usually those of the Honourable East India Company, which were the largest ships in the merchant marine.

kelson An internal keel fitted over the floor timbers.

knees In traditional shipbuilding the naturally grown wooden brackets that fasten pieces of the structure together at right angles, most commonly used to attach deck beams to the sides. Those supporting the beams in the vertical direction were known as hanging knees and those in the horizontal as lodging knees; in special cases hanging knees were fixed at angles, when they were known as dagger knees. The shortage of grown knees in the 1790s and later led to the adoption of various substitutes, most commonly simple chocks under the beam ends reinforced with iron plates or brackets which were also referred to as knees.

lazaretto Quarantine accommodation, often a hulk.

leewardly When sailing with the wind anywhere except directly astern, sailing ships make progress not only forward but also drift sideways, the drift increasing the closer the ship attempts to sail to the direction of the wind. A vessel which loses a lot of ground downwind is said to be leewardly as opposed to weatherly (*qv*).

load A timber trade measure, originally the amount of wood that could be carried on a single cart, which translated as about 40-50 cubic foot or one ton, the rough equivalent of one large tree.

Middling Repair *See* Great Repair.

moulded *See* scantling.

Navy Bills An instrument of credit issued by the Navy itself in payment for goods and services. Bills were payable in strict chronological order of registry, and the larger the bill the longer the period to maturity, hence the larger the discount the recipient would have to allow if he wished to sell on the bill for cash.

Navy Board Formally, the Principal Officers and Commissioners of the Navy, a body which could trace its ancestry directly to Henry VIII's days, which made it older than the Admiralty, its nominal superior. It was answerable for almost all except the operational side of naval affairs: it was responsible for the *materiel* of the Navy, from ship design and construction to the administration of the Dockyards; it was also charged with controlling the expenditure of the Navy; and via subsidiary boards to look after victualling and the sick and injured; lesser roles included the hire of transports. The Board was composed of civilian specialists and senior naval officers; they were career bureaucrats and did not change with the government, so providing an element of continuity in contrast to politically appointed Lords of the Admiralty. The Board met under the chairmanship of the Comptroller, and included the Surveyors (the Navy's chief naval architects), the Clerk of the Acts (chief clerk) and various other commissioners with

or without portfolio; there was also a commissioner in each of the Royal Dockyards, although they did not usually attend meetings.

Ord Ordinary. The establishment of ships laid up out of commission and the men who manned them, so called because they were supported out of the Ordinary Estimate voted by Parliament, as opposed to Extraordinary expenditure that covered items like new shipbuilding.

PB Point blank.

pdr Pounder (calibre of gun expressed as weight of shot fired).

qrs Quarters; a measurement of weight – a quarter of a hundredweight (*qv*).

racking stresses The tendency to change the transverse shape of the ship, principally caused by heavy rolling. In wooden ships this action is particularly detrimental to beam-end fastenings.

rasée A ship physically cut down from a superior rate. At this time it usually referred to a line of battle ship which was reduced to a frigate by removing one gundeck, but post-war it was also applied to corvettes cut down from frigates by removing the quarterdeck and forecastle.

rpg Rounds per gun.

sagging *See* hogging.

scantling The cross-sectional dimensions of timber; the 'sided' dimension was the thickness, which tended to be consistent, while the 'moulded' dimension was the depth, cut to size by reference to a mould or pattern, so usually varying according to shape.

scarph A joint formed by angling the ends of each piece to be connected.

sea-boat A ship's qualities as a sea-boat summarises how well it behaves in relation to the actions of the sea – its degree of rolling, pitching or shipping water, for example.

shelf pieces *See* clamps.

sheer The rise of the decks, wales or other longitudinal lines from midships towards the bow and stern of a ship.

sided *See* scantling.

Small Repair *See* Great Repair.

spar deck A deck over the skid beams in the (traditionally open) waist that turned the separate forecastle and quarterdeck into a single structure; by extension it was applied to the whole of this deck in so-called 'double-banked' frigates.

spirketting Interior strakes of planking above the waterway (*qv*) up to the sills of the gunports.

standards Inverted knees (*qv*), placed on a deck rather than under it for strengthening purposes.

stiff Stable; able to carry sail without undue heel. The opposite of crank (*qv*).

stunsail Phonetic spelling of studding sails, additional fair-weather canvas set outside the main square sails on temporary yards and booms.

Surveyor of the Navy A civilian member of the Navy Board responsible for technical aspects of ship construction and design. Chosen from the ranks of the Master Shipwrights of the Royal Dockyards, the Surveyors served in pairs from the middle of the eighteenth century until 1813 when a Third Surveyor was appointed.

taffrail The upper part of a ship's stern.

thickstuff Strakes of planking above and below the wales which was thicker than the norm; in the timber trade the term was also used more generally for thicker planking (of above about 4in sided dimensions).

toptimber The uppermost element of the ship's frame. *See also* futtock.

treenails Wooden pins used for fastenings in wooden shipbuilding. They could be secured by driving wedges into the ends, which were then cut flush and caulked. Unlike iron bolts and nails, they did not corrode when wet.

trim The fore and aft 'sit' of the ship in the water. If the ship draws more water aft than forward she is said to 'trim by the stern' (the usual situation for square rigged sailing ships), or 'by the bow' if the reverse is the case; 'on an even keel' refers to an equal draught fore and aft. Obtaining the optimum trim was crucial to extracting the best performance from sailing ships and the appropriate stowage of ballast, water and provisions was an art that every efficient naval officer had to master.

trunnion The short cylinders protruding horizontally from the barrel of a gun forming an axle on which it was elevated or depressed.

TS Training ship.

tumblehome The curving in of the topside above the waterline; when seen in athwartship section, the curve was concave, forming an almost flat S-shape. It was more pronounced in ships of the seventeenth and early eighteenth centuries and persisted longer in French ships than British, the latter tending towards decidedly straighter topsides from the 1790s known as a 'wall-sided' form.

wall-sided *See* tumblehome.

waterway The thickened strake of deck planking over the beam ends.

weatherly When sailing with the wind anywhere except directly astern, sailing ships make progress not only forward but also drift sideways, the drift increasing the closer the ship attempts to sail to the direction of the wind. A vessel in which the loss of ground downwind is minimal is described as weatherly, as opposed to leewardly (*qv*).

windage The small difference between the diameter of the bore of a gun and the size of the shot fired from it, often expressed as a fraction of the bore diameter.

working The movement of parts of the ship's structure in relation to one another in a seaway, leading to the loosening of joints, caulking and so forth. *See also* hogging *and* racking stresses.

Index

Page references in *italics* refer to illustrations and maps and their captions; those in **bold** refer to tables. All ships are British warships unless otherwise specified; launch or capture dates are given to identify ships of the same name or those outside the scope of this book.

Aboukir (1807) 78
Acasta 43, 45, *46*, 46-7, 99, 114, **145**, 145, 169, 175, **186-9**
Active (1799) 64, *94*, *173*, **185**, 187-8
Acworth, Sir Jacob 136
Adams, Henry (shipbuilder) **28**
Addington, Henry, Viscount Sidmouth 9
Adventure (*rasée* 1758) 41-2
Aeolus **15**, **25**, 155, 162, **188-90**
Africaine (capt 1801) 174, 183, **188-90**
Africaine (1827) **63**
Aid (transport) 104
Aigle (capt 1782) **185-6**
Aigle (1801) 92, 169, **188-90**
Aimable (capt 1782) 137, **185**, 187-8
Ajax (1809) 79, 94, 105, 170
Akbar **56**, 57, **105**, *137*, 146, **146**, 189
Alarm (1758) **185**
Albion (1802) 82
Alceste **29**, **31**, 148, **148**, 149, 189
Alcmene (1794) 175, **186-8**
Alcmene (capt 1809) **29**, 32, 148, 150, 189
Alcmène (Fr) 91
Alexandria 46
Alexandria (1806) 79, **189-90**
Allemand, Rear-Admiral Zacharie *map* 154, 155-7
Alpheus **35**, **105**, 143
Amazon (capt 1745) 17
Amazon (1821) **25**
Amazon (1799) *94*, 156, 160-1,166, 172, **187-9**
Ambuscade (1773) **185**
Ambuscade (capt 1798) **187-8**
Ambuscade (capt 1811) **30**, 32, 91, 189
Amelia (capt 1796) 125, 170, **187-9**
America (1777) **187**
Amethyst (1799) 174, 176, 180, *181*, **187-8**
Amiens, Peace of 10, 46, 115, 121, 176
amphibious and coastal operations 73, 166-72, 169, 177, 178, 179, 183
Amphion class *14*, **15**, 19, *100*, **142**, 142-3
Amphion **15**, **105**, 108, *173*, *173*, **185**, 187-90
Amphitrite (Neth) **187** *see also Imperieuse*
Amphitrite (1816) 25-6
Amphitrite (capt 1799) **56**
Amphitrite (capt 1804) **29**, **31**
Ancell, J 111
anchors 102-4, *103*, 106
  chain cables 103-4, **104**, 112
Andromache (1781) **185-7**
Andromache (capt 1799) **190**
Andromeda (1784) **186-7**
Andromeda (1829) **63**
Anson 41, **41**, 42-3, 42, 48, **144**, *170*, **186-7**
Antelope (1802) 189
Antigua 137
Apollo (1794) *173*, **186**
Apollo class (1799) 11, **23**, *34*, 87, 95, 97, 139, **142**, **142**, 183-4, *184*
Apollo (1799) *106*, *107*, **187**
Apollo (1805) 27-8, *100*, **188-190**
Appledore **16**
Aquilon (1786) **185**, 189
Araxes 37, **37**, 144, **144**

Ardent (1796) 77
Arethusa (1781) 41-2, 169, *170*, 174, **185**, **187-188**
Arethusa (1817) 25-6
Armide **29**, **31**, 148, 148, 149, 149, **190**
Arrow (1796) 51, 105, 121, *122*
Artois (1794) 165, **185-6**
Asia (1811) 82-3
Astraea (1781) **185-6**, 189
Astraea (1810) 22-23, 142, 189
Astrée (Fr) *149*, 183
Aurora **30**, 32, 148-50
Australia *72*
Austria 21
Autumn (1801) 116
Aylmer, Captain Rt Hon F W 120

Bacchante 27-8, *31*, *100*, 123, 142, **190**
Back, Admiral Sir George *137*
Baltic Sea 10, 21, 24, 38, 104, 168, 175, **186-7**, **189-90**
Bantry Bay 172
Barbary States *33*
Barfleur (1768) **189**
Barham (1811) 103, **190**
Barham, Lord 14-19, 35, 87, 95, 122, 183
Barrallier, Jean-Louis 43-4, 46, **47**, 53-4, **55**, 65, 82, *83*, 93-5, *94*, *94*, 145, 180
Barrosa 22-3, **105**, 106, *107*, **190**
Barrow, Sir John 14
Barton, John (shipbuilder) **35**
Basque Roads 179
Bateley, William **50**
Baugean, J-J *184*
Bayntun, Captain Henry 93
Beaulieu (1791) 158, **185-8**
Beaver, Captain Philip *49*, 99, *100*, 169, 181
Belle Poule (capt 1780) 16, 18-19, *19*, *20*
Belle Poule (capt 1806) **29**, **31**, 148, **148**, 149, 158, **189-90**
Bellerophon (1786) 161, **190**
Bellona (1760) 48
Belvidera 22-3, 142, **190**
Bentham, Samuel 12-13, 60, 71, 81, 84, 105, 121-2
  bolts 80
  fastening system *79*, 79-80
Berkeley, Vice-Admiral Sir George **189**
Berlin Decrees 21
Bermuda 57, 70-1, 101
Bertie, Vice-Admiral Sir Albemarle **189**
Bickerton, Admiral Sir Richard **190**
Biscay, Bay of 42, 99, 108, 166, 171, 176, 179
Black Prince (1816) 94
Blackburn, Isaac (shipbuilder) 59
Blackwall yard **35**, 36, **52**, 53, **54-5**
Blackwood, Rear-Admiral Sir Henry 55-6, 98, 156-7, 161, *161-2*
Blake, R F S *80*, 84
Blanche (1800) 163, 165, 182, **185-7**
Blanche (ex-*Amphitrite*) **29**
Blanche (1819) 25-6, 29, 163
Blenheim (1761) **188**
blockade strategy 13, 21, 24, 33-5, 42, 60, 68, 84, 87, 108, *148*, 153, 163-6, **164**, 176, 179, *180-1*
Blonde (capt 1782) **185**, 189
Blonde (1819) 22-3, 65, *65*, **65-6**, 144, **144**
Blomefield, Thomas *see under* guns
Boadicea (1797) 84, 92, 110, **186-9**
bolts 80, *80*, *82*, 141
Bombay Dockyard **11**, 12, 24-5, **25-6**, **56**, *56*, 56-7, 59-61, **63**, 63, 70

Bombay Marine 57, *137*
Bompart, Admiral J-B 42, 172
Bonne Citoyenne (capt 1796) 140
Bordeaux **29**, *149*
Boston (1762) **185-7**
Boswell, J W 85
Bouguer, Pierre 82
Boulogne 166, *167*, 168
Bourbonnaise **29**, 32
Boyne (1790) **185**
Braave (capt 1796) **185**, **187**
Brave (Fr) 40
Brazil **26**, 71
Brenton, Captain Edward Pelham *109*, 109-10
Brest **29**-30, 42-3, 155-6, *163*, 164-5, *165*, 173, 176, *180*
Bridport, Admiral Lord 90, 163, **186**
Brilliant (1814) 22-3
Brilliant (1812) *see Orontes*
Brindley, Josiah (shipbuilder) 10-11, **11**, 12, 19, **26**, **35**, 81, 141
  'bolt and carling' system *76*, 76-9, 82-3
Brisbane, Captain Sir Charles 106, 169, *170*
Briton 25-6, **190**
Broke, Captain Sir Philip 48-9, 78, 124, 179-81
Brown, Lt Samuel 104
Brown, Rear-Admiral William **190**
Brown, W 111
Brueys d'Aigalliers, Admiral F-P, comte 158
Bruillac, Captain 158
Brune **29**, 32, 91, **105**, 149, **190**
Brunel, Marc 106
Brunton, Thomas 104
Brutus (Fr) 40
Bucephalus 18, 19-20, 79, **105**, 143, **143**, 189
Bucklers Hard **28**
Bullen, Captain 57
Burlesdon **11**, **28**, 46
Burma 25, 27
Bustamente, Rear-Admiral G H *179*
Buttersworth, Thomas *157*
Byam Martin, Rear-Admiral Thomas 55, 64, 89, 111-12, 126, 133-5, *171-2*

Ça Ira (Fr) 162
Cadiz *map* 156, 156, 163, 166, 174
Calder, Admiral Sir Robert *map* 154, 155, 161, **190**
  'Calder's Action' 158
Caledonia (1808) 79, 89, **189-90**
Calypso see Blonde (1819)
Cambrian 43, *45*, **45**, 46, **46**, 47, 64, *74*, 89-90, **91**, 115, 145, **145**, **186-9**
Campbell, Captain Sir Patrick 85, 121, 157
Campbell, Vice-Admiral Sir George **189**
Camperdown, battle of 157-9, 161, 175
Canada 33-4, 38, **45**, 71-2, 115, **185-90**
Canada (1765) 48, 146
Canaries 153
Canopus (capt 1798) 84
Cape Finisterre 155
Cape of Good Hope 71, *72*, 142, 169-70, **187**, 189
Cape St Vincent *map* 156, 156, 163
  battle of 158, 160-2
Capel, Captain Thomas 163
Captain (1787) 48
Carmen (capt 1800) **187**
Carnatic (1783) 10
Caroline (1795) *157*, 175, **186-9**
Caroline (capt 1809) 91
carronades *11-12*, *14*, **15**, 17-19, *21*, *26*, 27, *31*,

40, *40*, 42, 48, 50, 53, 57, *66*, 67, *70*, 89, 100, 109-10, 114-15, 117, 120-3, *121*, **121-2**, 123, *124*, 178, 183
  mountings and carriages 98, 100, 120-5, *121-2*, *124-5*, *127*, 127-8, *128 see also* guns
Cartagena **29**
Castor (1785) **185**, **187**, **189-90**
Centaur (1797) **190**
Cerberus (1794) *173*, **186-90**
Cerberus (1827) **25**
Ceres (1781) **185-6**
Ceylon (1808) 189
Chambers, Captain Samuel 64
Champion (1823) 51
Chatham Dockyard **11**, **15**, **23**, **26**, **28**, **35**, **35**, **41**, **50**, 61, 79, 83, 101, **105**, 106, **185-7**
Chatham (1812) 73, 83
Cherbourg **29**-30, 124, *149*
Cherokee class brigs 63, 184
Chesapeake (US, capt 1813) **30**, 32, 48, 59, 78, 89, 96, 96, *130*, **134**, 140, 147, **147**, 180
Chiffonne (capt 1801) **188-9**
Christian VII (capt 1807) 94-5, 140, 147
Circe class 12-13, 61, 79
Circe (1804) **25**, 159, **189-90**
Cleopatra (1779) **185-6**
Clio (1807) 135
Clorinde **29**, **31**, 90-1, *93*, 120, 148-9, 189
Clyde (1796) **25**, 74, 169, 175, **186-7**, 189
Cochrane, Captain Lord 108, 158, 179
Cochrane, Rear-Admiral Sir Alexander **189**
Cockburn, Captain Sir George 126
Coffin, Rear-Admiral Sir Isaac **188**
Collier, Captain Sir George 53, 108-9, 170-1, *171-2*
Collingwood, Admiral Lord 156, *161*, *178*, 178-9, **189**
Colossus (1803) 76
Combatant class 168
'Commodore Dance's Action' 158
Concorde (capt 1783) **185-8**
Congreve rockets 128, 169
Congreve, Sir William 50, 100, 103, 118-20, 125-8, *127 see also under* guns
Constellation (US) 88
Constitution cutter *167*
Constitution (US) **29**, **35**, 65, 82, 89-90, **91**, 94, 171
Continental System 21, 68, 176
convoys 36, 153, 156-8, 167, 174-6, **185-8**, **190**
Copenhagen **29**, *147*
  first battle of 161
  second battle of 24, 73, 95, *95*, *147*
coppering 25, 60, 131
Cornelia **16**, 20, 79, 143
Cornwallis, Admiral Sir William 155, 164, **185**, **187-8**
Cornwallis see Akbar
Corona (Fr-Venetian) 88, *117 see also Daedalus*
Corsica 155
Coulomb, Joseph-Marie-Blaise 140
Courageux (capt 1761) 140
Craufurd, Major-General Robert 174
Creole (capt 1803) **30**
Creole 22-3, **190**
Crescent (1784) **185**, **187-8**
Crescent (1810) 27-8, *100*, 104, 142, **190**
Cressy (1810) 83, **189**
crew conditions 107
crews 10, **15**, *16*, 19, **22**, 27, 82, 101-5, 111, *111*, 160, 165-6, 179, 181-2, *183*
  impressment 35

numbers 38, *115*
see also shiphandling
Cruizer class brigs 184
Cuba **28-9**, *151*
Culloden (1783) 49-50, **188-9**
Cumberland (1774) **185**
Cuppage, Colonel *125*, 125-6
Curaçao **22-3**, 142, *164*, **190**
Curaçao Island 169, *170*
Curtis, Admiral Sir Roger **187**, **189**
Cydnus class 37
Cydnus 37, 37-9, **39**, **105**, 119-20, 144, **190**

Dacres, Rear-Admiral James **188**
Dacres, Captain James 144
Daedalus (1780) **185-7**
Daedalus (capt 1811) **25**, **29**, **32**, 89, 117, **189**
Dart (1796) 105, 121, *122*
Dartmouth **22-3**, 142
Dauntless (1804) 168
d'Auvergne, Rear-Admiral Philippe **186**, **188-9**
davits 107-8, 183
Davy, Sir Humphrey 102
de Courcy, Rear-Admiral Hon Michael **189**
Deal yard 108
Decade (capt 1798) **187-8**
Decatur, Captain Stephen (USN) 52
decks **10**, **13**, *32*, *34*, **40**, 41-2, *42*, *49*, 55, 63-4, *66-67*, *91*, 99, 111
covered *60*, 61
deck layout 27, 34, *36*, 85, 98-101, *100*
Decrès, Vice-Admiral Denis, duc 155
Dedaigneuse (capt 1801) **188-9**
Defence (1763) 160
Defiance (1783) **190**
Denmark 24, 73, 161
design influence 140
prizes 24, **29**, **31-2**, 90, 94-5, *95*, 117, 140, 147, **147**, *147*
Département de Landes (Fr) 182
Deptford Dockyard 13, **23**, 24, **28**, **35**, 36, **43**, **52**, 62, 65, **66**, 73, *74*, *76*, 79-80, **105**, 106, 116, 122-3, *149*, *171*, **186-7**
Desiree (capt 1800) **187**, **190**
Diamond (1794) **25-6**, 116, **186-9**
Diamond (1816) **25-6**, 141
Diana (1794) 175, **186-9**
Diana (1822) **25**
Diddams, N 83
Didon **29**, **31**, 155, 157
Dillon, Captain William 45, 53-5, 137, 142, 180
Director (1784) 41
Dixon, Rear-Admiral Manly **189**
Dolphin (1781) 79
Donegal (capt 1798) 84
Donnelly, Captain Ross 116
Doris (1806, cancelled) 16
Doris (1807) *see Salsette*
Dorset (1753) 175
double-banked frigates 95-6, 171
Douglas, General Sir Howard 126, 180-1
Douglas, Rear-Admiral **189**
Dover (ex-HEIC 1804) **189**
Dragon (1798) *map* 156
Droits de l' Homme (Fr) 43, 172
Druid (1783) 175, **185**, **188-90**
Druid (1825) 25, **63**, 64, 139, 144, **144**
Drury, Rear-Admiral William O'Brien 27
Dryad (1795) 92, **92**, 108, 173, 175, **186-90**
Dublin (1812) 83, *83*, 85
Dubourdieu, Admiral Bernard 173
Duckworth, Rear-Admiral Sir John **187**
Dumanoir-Le Pelley, Admiral Pierre 162
Duncan, Admiral Lord 116, 158-9, 161, 175, **186**
Duncan, Captain the Hon Henry *179*
Dundas, Henry *see* Melville, Lord
Dundas, Philip 25
Dundee *60*, 61
Dunira 30, 148 *see also Immortalité*
Dupin, Charles 85
'durability' concept 58-61, *60*, 71-2, 81, 90, *148*
Durham, Admiral Sir Philip **41**, 42

East India Company **11**, 12, 24-5, 27, *56*, 57, 70-1, 75, *83*, 116, 175
East Indiamen 25, **56**, 75-7, 116, 158
East Indies 27, 57, 156, 169, 172, **185**, **187-9**
see also Penang
Economy (GB merchantman) 85
Edinburgh (1811) 105
Egyptienne 46-8, *48*, **56**, 133, 151, **151**, 188
Emerald (1795) **186-7**, **189**
Endymion 36, 43, **43**, *44*, 46-8, *51*, **52**, 52-3, 67, 89, *89*, 90, **91**, 92, 92, 93, 95, 115, *131*, **133**, 140, 145-6, **145-6**, 174-5, **186-8**, **190**
Engageante (capt 1794) **187**
Epworth, Captain Farmery 51
Eridanus (ex-*Liffey*) **35**, *35*, **105**, 143, **190**
Espion (capt 1794) **186**
Essex (US, capt 1814). **31**, 91, 92, 140, 147, **147**, **190**
Ethalion (1797) 165, **186**
Ethalion (1802) **188-90**
Euphrates (ex-*Greyhound*) **35**, 59, **105**, 143
Europa (1783) **185**
Eurotas 37, 37-9, **39**, *63*, **105**, 119-20, 144, **144**, **190**
Eurus (capt 1796) **185**
Euryalus class *21*, 22, **22**, 24, *24*, 25, 65, *65*, **65**, *70*, 89, 183 *see also Apollo* class
Euryalus 86, *map* 156, 156, 159, 161, *161*, **188**, **190**
Eurydice (1781) 166

Fairfax, Sir William 181
Falmouth **23**, 26, 41-2, *176*, **188**
Fama (Sp) **29**, **31**, 91
Fame (1805) *79*, 80
Farington, Captain William 135
Farquarson, Captain 100
Favourite (Fr) *173*
Felixstowe 118
Ferrol *map* 156, **29**, 156
Fidèle (Fr) **88**, 89, *90 see also Laurel* (capt 1807)
Fincham, John 82, *84-5*, *108*, 109, 112
fire-fighting 102, 104-5
Fisgard (capt 1797) 91, 169, *170*, **187-8**
Fisgard (1819) **25-6**
Fishbourne **23**, *24*, 35
Fleeming, Captain Hon Charles 48
fleet strengths 9, 14, *22*, 24, 34, 38, 58-61, **59**, 61-3, 90, 96-7, **153**, 157, 164
Flibustier (Fr) 40
Flora (1780) **185-8**
Flore (Fr) 108
Florentina (capt 1800) **187**
Florida (US, capt 1814) 96, *125*
Flushing **29**, 73, 89, *149*, 167
Foley, Rear-Admiral Sir Thomas **190**
Ford, Commodore John **185**
Fordyce, Dr 128
Forfait, Pierre-Alexandre *61*, 64, *92*, 96, 140, 148, *150*
Formidable (1825) 73
Forte (1799) 40, 46, **56**, 141, **141**, 151, **187**
Forte (1814) 10, **13**, *13*, 64
Forth class *51*
Forth 37, **52**, **63**, **105**, 146
Fortunee (1800) **187-90**
Foudroyant (1798) *162*, **189**
see also Trincomalee
Fox (1780) **105**, **185**, **187-90**
Fox (1829) **25**
France
design influence 9-10, 13, *13*, 14, 16-20, *20*, **28**, 43-6, *48*, 52, 54, 63-4, 84, *86*, 87-90, *92*, 93-4, 115, 139-42, 146, *151*, 184
invasion threat 40, 80, 103, *124*, 166-8
prizes 24, **29-32**, **43**, *61*, 63-4, 75, 84, 89-91, 93, 120, **148**, 148-50, 151, **151**, 172, 180
rasées 40
shipbuilding 21, 74-5, 82, **92**, *149*
Franchise (capt 1803) **188-90**
freeboard *141*, **141-8**, **150-1**
Freya **29**, **31**, 117
Frindsbury **11**, **26**, **35**, 76

see also Brindley (shipbuilder)
Frolic (US) *125*, 140 *see also Florida*
Fulton, Robert 168
Furieuse **29**, **31**, 148, *150*, **190**

Galatea (1794) **186-8**
Galatea (1810) **22-3**, 142, **190**
Gambier, Admiral Lord 74, 136, **189**
Ganteaume, Admiral Honoré, comte 158
Gardner, Admiral Lord **185**, **187-8**
Gauthier, Jean-François 40, 148
Genoa **29**-30, 73, *149*
Gibraltar *map* 156, **23**, 158, 166, 168
Gibson (shipbuilder) 17
Glasgow 37, *51*, **52**, 53, **105**, 146, **146**
Glatton (1795) 72
Glenmore (1796) 110, **186-7**
Gloire (capt 1806) **29**, **31**, 148, **189**
Gloire (capt 1814) **30**, 32
Glorious First of June, battle of the 157, 159-62, *160*
Goliath 50, **50**, 100, **105**, 101, 110, 117, 127, 134, **145**, 145-6, 162, **190**
Gorgon (1785) **188**
Gover, John 115 *see also under* guns
Gower, Vice-Admiral Sir Erasmus **188**
Graham (shipbuilder) 11, **28**
Grand Port **11**, 169, 173, 183
Granville, Lord 22
Greyhound (1783) **186-9**
Greyhound (1812) 37 *see also Euphrates*
Griffiths, Rear-Admiral Edward 57, 146
Groignard, Antoine 82
Guerriere **29**, **31**, 35, 110, 129, 183, **189**
Guillaume, Robert (shipbuilder) **23**, 24, **28**
Guillaume Tell (Fr) *162*, *162*
gunboats *109*, 109-10, 125, 163, 166, 168, 171, **185-8**
gunnery 38, 64, 87, 99, 110, 157, 180-1, *181*
gunports 9, *11*-14, *20*-1, *26*, *30*-1, *33*, 34, *34*, 40, 42, *51*, 52, 53, *98*, 100, 116, **168**
bridle ports 9, 10, **11**, 98
freeboard 18-19, 87-9
gunpowder 114, 118, 128-9, *129*, **129**
storage 100, *102*, 102-3
guns 9-10, **10**, 22, **22**, **29**, 31, 34, *34*, 40-2, **41**, **43**, 45, **45-7**, 48-50, **50**, **52**, 53, 56-7, **57**, 60-2, **63**, 65, 67, 114-30, 141, 162-3, 171, *171*, 177, 183-4
Blomefield guns **37**, 38, 114, *114*, 116-17, 119, *119*, 119-20, 126, 128
Congreve guns **37**, 38, 118-20, *119*, **119**
Gover guns 27, *32*, 38, 89, *115*, 115-18, *116*, **117**, *119*, **119**, 171, *171*
mountings and carriages 98, 115-16, 121-8, *123-8*
see also carronades

Hamadryad (1823) **25**
Hamadryad (capt 1804) **29**, **31**, 150, 151, *151*, **190**
Hamilton, Captain Thomas (Commissioner of Transport Board) 47, 94, 104, 168
Hamilton, Rear-Admiral Sir Charles 122, 126
hammock stanchions 111, *111*
Hamond, Sir Andrew (Comptroller of Navy Board) 25
Hampstead, Lt John 137
Hardum, James 115
Hardy, Captain Sir Thomas 126-7
Harfruen **29**, **31**, 91
Hargood, Rear-Admiral Sir William **190**
Hartlepool **26**, 61
Harvey, David **28**
Harvey, Rear-Admiral Sir Henry **185**
Harwich 11, **28**
Havannah **22-3**, 142, *164*, **190**
Hayes, Captain John 48-50, 52, 100, 127, 133-4, 146
Hébé (capt 1782) *94*, **185**
Hebe (1804) 79, **188-9**

Hebe (1826) 25
Hebrus 34, **35**, **105**, 143
Helder (capt 1809) **189**
Henslow, Sir John 22, 43, *94*
Hercule (capt 1798) **188**
Hermione (1782) **185**
Heroine (1783) **185**
Hibernia (1804) **189**
Hoche (Fr) 172
Hohlenburg, F C H 94-5, *95-6*, *140*
Holloway, Vice-Admiral John **189**
Hood, Admiral Lord 44, **185**
Hood, Vice-Admiral Sir Samuel **189**
Hope, Rear-Admiral Sir George 116, 158, **190**
Horatio 27-8, 89, **89**, 142, 181, *182*, **189-90**
Hoste, Captain Sir William 123, 166, 173, *173*
Hotspur **22-3**, **63**, 142, **190**
Howe, Admiral Lord 157-9, 161, 163-4, **185**
Hudson's Bay company 175
Hull 17, 20, 23
hull forms 9-10, 22, 152, 180-1, 184, *184*
Humphreys, Joshua 82, 97
Hurd, Captain Thomas *165*
Hussar (1799) 165, **187**
Hussar (1807) **27-28**, 64, *100*, 103, 139, 142, **142**, **189**
Hydra (1797) 84, *178*, **186-9**
Hyperion 16-17, **17**, 19, 143, **143**, **189-90**

Immortalité (ex-Fr *Alcmène*) *see Dunira*
Immortalité (ex-Fr *Infatigable*) **29**, **31-2**
Immortalité (capt 1798) 148, *150*, 167-8, *167*, **168**, **187-8**
Imperieuse (1801) *see Amphitrite* (capt 1799)
Imperieuse (capt 1804) 74, 108, 115, *117*, **134**, 169, 175, 179, *179*, **186-7**, **189-90**
Implacable (capt 1805) 84
Impregnable (1810) 126, 190
Inconstant, and class (1783) 10, *11*, 16, 22, 51, 70, 141, 162, **185-6**, **188-9**
Indefatigable 40, 41, **41**, 42-3, 48, 50, **133**, **144**, 172, **186-9**
Infatigable (Fr) 91
India **11**, 24-5, 27, 59, 70
Inman, Rev Dr J 94
Invincible (capt 1747) 140
Invincible (1808) 83, *83*
Iphigenia (1780) **185**
Iphigenia (capt 1804) **29**, **31**
Iphigenia (1808) **10-11**, 22, 141, **189-90**
Iphigénie (Fr) 183
Ireland 10, 40, 42, 172-3, 175-6, **185-90**
Iris (1783) 156-7, **185-7**
Iris (capt 1807) **29**, **31**, 147, *147*, **188**, **190**
ironwork 25, 60, 65, 70, 74, 78, *83*, 85, *85*, 106, 111
see also chain cable *under* anchors, *and under* water storage
Isis (1774) 175
Ister (ex-*Blonde*) **35**, 37, **105**, 143

Jackson, J 111
Jacobs (shipbuilder) 45, 48
Jamaica **11**, **23**, 175, **185**, **187-190**
Janus (capt 1796) **185**
Jason (1794) 165, **186**
Jason (1800) **187**
Jason (1804) 79, **188-90**
Jason (canc 1831) **25**, **63**, *64*
Java (1815) **53**, 65-7, *66-7*, **67**, *85*, 96-7, **105**, 141
Java (capt 1811) **30**, **32**, 35, 129, 181, 183
Jervis, John *see* St Vincent, Admiral Earl of
Jewel see Alcmene (capt 1809)
Jones, Algernon 71, 73
Juno (1780) **185**, **187-8**
Junon (capt 1809) 30
Junon (capt 1810) **29**, **32**, 148, **148**, 150, 181, *182*, **190**
Juste (capt 1794) 160
Justitia (capt 1807) *95*

Kangaroo (1805) 78